TARGETING THE
MESSAGE

TARGETING THE
MESSAGE

A RECEIVER-CENTERED PROCESS FOR PUBLIC RELATIONS WRITING

WILLIAM THOMPSON
University of Louisville

**Targeting the Message: A Receiver-centered Process
for Public Relations Writing**

Longman, 10 Bank Street, White Plains, N.Y. 10606

Associated companies:
Longman Group Ltd., London
Longman Cheshire Pty., Melbourne
Longman Paul Pty., Auckland
Copp Clark Longman Ltd., Toronto

Associate editor: Hillary B. Henderson
Production editor: Dee Amir Josephson
Editorial assistant: Jennifer A. McCaffery
Cover design: Wanda Kossak
Text art: Tech-Graphics
Production supervisor: Edith Pullman
Compositor: University Graphics

Library of Congress Cataloging-in-Publication Data

Thompson, William, Date.
    Targeting the message : a receiver-centered process for public
relations writing / by William Thompson.
        p.   cm.
    Includes bibliographical references and index.
    ISBN 0-8013-0748-1
    1. Public relations.   2. Public relations—Authorship.
3. Publicity.   I. Title.
HM263.T468   1996   95-34685
659.2—dc20   CIP

1 2 3 4 5 6 7 8 9 10-CRS-0099989796

Contents

CHAPTER 4   **Legal Issues and Ethics: A Day-to-Day Guide
for the Professional   89**

CHAPTER 12 Looking Them in the Eye: Applying Receiver-centered Writing in Face-to-Face Media 341

APPLICATIONS WORKBOOK

Introduction:
The Transformation
of Public Relations

At the age of 39, I feel as if I'm a dinosaur in my own field. I've already lived through the summer morning in 1982 when our office typewriters were toted away and replaced by computers. I was around several years later when fax machines, computer modems and satellite services replaced couriers as the fastest way to deliver a news release.

I've seen the transformation of television, in which the four major broadcasters have been nearly overwhelmed by a plethora of cable networks, each tightly targeted to serve small sections of society. Video technology and production have become so simple and inexpensive that almost any organization can afford to produce its own electronic communications program.

In those few short years, I've seen paste-up and layout artists supplanted by desktop publishing and the new technology spawn thousands of highly specialized magazines, internal publications and advertising media. I have witnessed the emergence of computer projectors, interactive computer-video presentations and computer-generated voice transmission. I've seen customer computer database management become common at even the smallest companies.

I've been a participant in replacing the primitive intellectual foundations of traditional public relations with theories and techniques from all communication areas. As integrated marketing campaigns have become common, I've seen public relations professionals start to work with persuasion models from advertising, product-use statistics from marketing, theories from organizational communication and evaluation techniques from direct marketing.

But all the new machines and theories haven't been responsible for the most profound change in public relations. The most dramatic transformation I've witnessed is in the role of public relations in institutional management. Even where the changes have not been fully realized, there is a perception among public relations professionals that they now belong in the organization's management coalition. Increasingly, they feel that communication is not merely an adjunct to a company's profit-making goals, but an essential component of the company's survival and prosperity. It's been a radical transformation.

This book is about that transformation. *Targeting the Message* is about meeting organizational goals through public relations writing at a historical moment when new technology and a fresh strategic vision make it possible to reconceptualize what public relations writing can accomplish.

As a communication management text, *Targeting the Message* places the persuasive tasks of public relations writing in a framework of communication theory that's drawn from all communication fields. The book outlines a management-by-objective (MBO) planning process that helps us conceptualize institutional problems and the way communication can solve them. It incorporates primary and secondary research methods in MBO planning and examines traditional as well as emerging research technologies, like customer database tracking and psychographics analysis.

However, *Targeting the Message* is, first and foremost, a writing text. After years in the writing classroom, I wanted to prepare a book that helped students learn how to write, not how to talk about writing.

The book is motivated by my belief that persuasive writing is not some gift from the Muses, too mysterious for mere mortals to understand. We have more options in writing instruction than simply admiring good writing, then telling students to "do the same thing." I contend that text can be analyzed and broken into structures we can understand and integrate into our own writing.

I believe certain principles apply to all types of persuasive writing. In all persuasive writing, we must capture the interest of our target audience immediately. We must develop argument patterns that forcefully present our institution's position in the context of our reader's needs. Finally, we must move receivers to take actions that benefit them and the organization.

If you contemplate writing in those terms, communicating in different media means building layers of skills on a core of knowledge. Thus, writing radio features or speeches or advertising does not demand different sets of rules but rather involves adapting your writing to the strengths of the medium and recognizing the way receivers use each medium.

In line with this overall philosophy, the book begins with four chapters on communication principles and planning, followed by three chapters on writing basics. The book's final eight chapters are arranged in four modules. Each module contains one chapter detailing writing formats and processes for specific media and a second chapter summarizing the most current applications of communication technology and targeting techniques to help us deliver cost-effective messages to precise publics.

The book gives students numerous opportunities to learn and practice the communication skills the text discusses. The case studies and management assignments at the end of most chapters let students apply information from each chapter to specific writing assignments and related management problems. Those assignments are structured around a variety of professional situations detailed in 12 case studies found in the Applications Workbook that follows the text. Students can gain additional writing practice through the Think Pieces at the end of each chapter, which can be employed either as starters for classroom discussion or for short essays on public relations practices.

In response to requests from my own students, I've included frequent self-guided learning opportunities. Section A of the Applications Workbook includes an abridged version of *The Associated Press Stylebook* to assist students in learning the rules that govern media writing. Each section compiles important guidelines about punctuation, capitalization and other journalism style rules. The accompanying quizzes can be used to test students' knowledge of those rules, as well as help develop their editing and proofreading skills.

Section B of the workbook contains a number of individual sections explaining common writing and grammar problems, offers techniques for solving them and provides exercises for practicing those techniques. It's designed as a diagnostic and teaching tool for students who discover they have difficulties with dangling modifiers, parallel structures or other problems.

The chapters include Management Problems and Writing Assignments keyed to the case studies in Workbook Section D, which opens on p. 481. The keys refer to Workbook Section D, followed by case study and question numbers. Thus D1.2 is Workbook Section D, case study #1, question #2.

To reinforce the lasting value of this book to students as they become practitioners, I've also included Additional Reading and Ready Reference sections at the end of most chapters. The Ready Reference sections contain examples of public relations document formats, lists of media reference books, full texts of longer public relations documents and collections of writing tips.

All these learning opportunities are intended to help students explore the role of public relations writing in this emerging technology and this new mind-set. As you can perceive, *Targeting the Message* is not intended to create mere functionaries who can write public relations documents. Instead, I hope it will help develop organizational administrators who can place communication within an overall strategy for meeting an institution's goals. That's an objective that can create a powerful role and a positive influence for public relations within an organization's management structure. It's a goal toward which we should all strive.

ACKNOWLEDGMENTS

The following reviewers contributed to the development of this book.

Lori Bergen, Kansas State University

John M. Butler, University of Northern Iowa

John S. Detweiler, University of Florida

Elizabeth B. Dickey, University of South Carolina

Suzette Heiman, University of Missouri

Linda Hon, University of Florida

Debra A. Kernisky, Northern Michigan University

Genevieve G. McBride, University of Wisconsin

Lynn Masel Walters, Texas A & M University

# part ONE

Planning: Translating Receiver-centered Principles into Public Relations Action

As a public relations practitioner who practiced before he learned the theory behind what he was practicing, I came early to believe that public relations is communication that works, and likewise, communication theory is theory that works. I wanted theory to guide my tactics and explain my audience's actions. But I came to understand that a practitioner needs to depend on communication theory for more than that.

Without a strong and relevant base of theory, planning and research, a practitioner is forced back on the ways tasks have always been done. That's not such a bad alternative if you're lucky enough to be in a field where nothing ever changes and all the problems that need to be solved have been solved by your predecessors.

Unfortunately, that's not a luxury we in public relations have any longer. With new audiences, unimagined media choices, emerging technologies and demanding new organizational expectations, we've got to have practitioners with the understanding and the creativity to deal with unfamiliar situations and a new environment.

When it's not possible to get the answer from a book, it's necessary to understand the principles that underlie communication. That's what this first section of the book is about.

I outline what I call the receiver-centered model of communication, a collection of theories drawn from several communication disciplines that stress a new orientation to our audience's communication needs. We see how to find and isolate the audiences that are most likely to respond to our persuasive appeals.

Chapter 2 examines the organizational context in which public relations operates and develops a planning routine that helps guide both public relations actions and the writing that will support the goals we're trying to reach.

Chapter 3 details the research resources and techniques used to learn about audiences, how to reach them and how to determine whether our communication efforts worked in gaining action from our publics.

Chapter 4 develops an ethical and legal framework in which the practitioner must operate in an increasingly litigious and morally confusing time.

Together, these topics embrace the mandatory knowledge and tactics public relations writers need before they write. They give the practitioner the ability to react to any situation, even those that we cannot even predict today.

That's what theory is for.

## chapter 1

Communication Theory in Real Life: A Practitioner's Guide to Receiver-centered Communication

REAL-LIFE LESSONS

A few years ago, a city government official asked me to oversee the rewriting of the city's building codes, zoning ordinances, sign restrictions and the community's other legal rules concerning construction and development.

It wasn't a task with which I am normally confronted. Although I have had experience in politics and government, my usual duties involve writing news releases and feature stories, not codifying the arcane language contained in the city's ordinance manual.

But I was there and was being asked to rewrite or, more precisely, translate ordinances. It seems the mayor had been elected on the promise that he would increase the number of new businesses locating in the city. To deliver on that promise, he wanted to streamline the process of obtaining needed building permits and zoning decisions. He thought that was a way the city could foster speedier growth and create a pro-business environment.

His first step was to consolidate all the city offices that dealt with those decisions into one central location. That was easily done. The prospect of new offices and the chance to get new office furniture quickly overcame the bureaucrats' objections.

But even with the offices located in one place there remained a major problem: The ordinances themselves were written in legalese so unintelligible and convoluted that the construction supervisors, plumbers and small-business people for whom they were supposedly written couldn't understand them.

Inevitably, misinterpretations during the permit process delayed important development projects. Sometimes those mistakes even stopped construction at the building site, idling scores of workers who nonetheless drew their wages while they waited. The circumstances certainly didn't contribute to the pro-business atmosphere the mayor wanted.

However, when the mayor wanted to rewrite the ordinances so that someone other than lawyers could understand them, he ran into problems. Each of the departments had its lawyers and technical specialists who knew how to interpret the ordinances. These were people whose sense of power and self-worth derived from their being the only people who really knew what the high-flown language meant. Even though the obscure writing hurt the city's development efforts, they didn't want the procedures rewritten.

Repeatedly, the mayor asked the permit offices to submit new, more readable versions of their procedures. Repeatedly, the offices responded with reincarnations of the same incomprehensible rule books. Finally, I was called in to break the deadlock and push the reforms through.

My job then, and the philosophy that guides this book now, is simple. Human communication works only if the humans for whom the communication is intended can understand it and want to know about it. We must design the message to mesh with the needs and capacities of the audience for whom the message is intended. Writing meant to guide the actions of carpenters isn't any good if only lawyers can understand it or want to read it. Writing is useless when it does not reach the people on whom the organization relies to succeed.

As public relations practitioners, this is our lifetime work. We are specialists in using communication to talk to publics that can help meet the goals the organization wants to reach. We are specialists in energizing the actions and commitments of people both within and outside the organization to help solve problems that afflict the organization.

That's the process this chapter starts. The first step is to understand the central significance of your audience as you begin to create your messages. After that fundamental recognition of receiver-centered communication processes is achieved, I'll develop some ideas about the strategies people use when they evaluate and respond to persuasive messages. From these basic building blocks, we'll soon be able to start developing planning sequences for converting those persuasive messages into concrete improvements for your organization.

WHAT YOU'LL LEARN

- That the receiver, not the sender of a message, determines whether a communication act is completed.
- That a public's possibility of communicating in a situation depends on that public's involvement in the problem and capacity to change the situation.
- That people use different processes to make decisions, depending on how important they view the decision and whether they think they'll get emotional or rational rewards.

- That writers need to adjust their writing to excite the interest of their intended audience and move it to a behavior that will fulfill their client's objectives.

FUNDAMENTAL CHANGES IN PUBLIC RELATIONS TASKS

Public relations is entering a new phase in its history. With the expanding number of public relations professionals working in all areas of American life, in nonprofit organizations, corporations, citizen advocacy groups, and government, the field is becoming more and more competitive. Public relations—generally referred to as PR—is increasingly being asked to show its value in making businesses more competitive. Clients are more frequently demanding that practitioners prove PR's effectiveness in moving opinions and creating a more advantageous business environment.

New computer and video communication technology is rapidly changing PR routines, and the field's expanding knowledge base has made possible a more scientific approach to communication. The more frequent successes have helped us gain more frequent opportunities to be closely involved in formative institutional management decisions. PR professionals are increasingly represented in the executive councils where important institutional decisions are being made.

Public relations writing reflects the changes in the field. No longer do PR writers' jobs consist exclusively of feeding stories to the media. No longer do their qualifications and training consist solely of being able to write stories in newspaper style.

This generation of public relations professionals is watching the field become a profession, with specialized knowledge and specialized practitioners. There have been fundamental changes in the way PR writers perform their work, including a new integration of communication theory into their daily routines.

Although the field is still developing and the information is still tentative, this book will strive to establish writing strategies for the most common public relations media by evaluating publics, their communication needs and the most effective ways to reach them. It's a structural approach to writing based on receiver-centered communication.

THE PRACTITIONER'S FIRST QUESTIONS

First, let's examine three questions basic to any professional communication task:

1. Why are you communicating?
2. With whom should you communicate?
3. What will motivate the people with whom you are communicating?

One point to emphasize initially is that there is a difference between public relations writing and much of the writing you've probably done up to this point. Most of what you've written has been expository writing, defined as writing intended to convey information or explain something that is difficult to understand. Such writing is designed to pass along information to people who don't yet know it. Most academic and journalistic writing fits this model.

Public relations writing is persuasive writing. It is not intended simply to transmit information, but to give to a defined public information that demonstrates the benefits of adopting certain attitudes and behaviors. Those attitudes and behaviors coincide with the interests of the institution sponsoring the communication.

Memory Memo 1.1
Questions central to any communication task:

- Why are you communicating?
- With whom should you communicate?
- What will motivate the people with whom you are communicating?

Public relations writing today aims to meet specific objectives related to institutional goals, whereas formerly the main intent was merely to get as many mentions of the client before the public as possible. Although many uninformed people still equate public relations with publicity—working with the mass media, placing stories that highlight clients in newspapers, magazines, and on television—that role is becoming smaller all the time.

Public relations today involves a new recognition by business of a social environment. A business now has to coexist not only with other businesses that have their own competent, aggressive public relations units, but also with well-organized citizen groups fighting for clean water, civil liberties and a thousand other causes. They too are represented by PR professionals.

The current business environment has forced institutions to monitor constantly the attitudes of their important publics, communicate their own positions and adjust their management practices to cope with changing public concerns.

Consequently, public relations tasks today aren't limited to communicating the company's message to the world but now encourage the world to talk to the company. PR practitioners then use that information not only to adapt the client's message to important publics, but to adapt corporate policies so the institution can thrive in a changing environment.

Predictably, as the field has expanded and grown more management-oriented, PR writing tasks have become more numerous, more involved and more demanding. It's not uncommon for a public relations writer, during the course of a month, a week, or sometimes even a day, to create a news release for a major metropolitan newspaper, a script for a videotape to be presented to the company's board of directors and a teaching supplement for third-grade children on the company's role in the local economy. More and more, PR practitioners must be able to analyze any audience, from hometown employees to overseas business contacts, and to work in any medium, from the neighborhood newsletter to satellite video transmission. They must therefore understand emerging scientific theory and the technology of communications.

Still, in this age of high-tech communications, the fundamental question that drives a communication campaign is still: "Why are you communicating?"

PUBLIC RELATIONS MANAGEMENT:
OPINIONS INTO ACTION

If you are issuing a news release simply because your company always issues a news release in a particular situation, you are most likely wasting your efforts. If you are writing a speech for your president to deliver to a local veterans' organization because it is your company's policy that top officials speak to community groups at least three times a year, you are probably not using your time efficiently.

These examples of PR mismanagement focus on public relations activities, rather than on the goals we want to accomplish by undertaking the activities. To put it in a different light, it would be like an auto manufacturer establishing a goal of making 300,000 cars during the coming year—but having no plans about how to sell them.

Instead, PR practitioners need to adopt a management system that focuses on the results we want to get from our communication efforts. As public relations consultant Mary Ann Pires suggests in Box 1.1, those results should contribute to the goals of the organization that employs us.

The idea of coordinating PR goals with organizational goals sounds too obvious to discuss. But in the past and even today, public relations professionals have not linked their communication goals with the company's objectives, have not pointed out the positive contributions their communication efforts can make to the company's overall performance. Instead, PR people have evaluated their success by the number of news releases they've written or the number of press clippings they've collected mentioning their clients.

For business executives who evaluate their institution's other divisions in terms of their contributions to company profits, a PR practitioner's attempt to justify his or her salary by boasting of having written 20 releases in a week's time might seem rather pathetic. A more persuasive claim to make to prove his or her value to the company might be that one of those releases, about a new industrial robot, generated 10 phone calls from potential customers.

A public relations planning system can help us show the bottom-line results professional communication can obtain. Through such a system, communication can be studied, assessed and managed the same way as other administrative functions.

Although several different planning approaches have been suggested to integrate public relations goals into the overall management function, I believe a method called management by objectives (MBO) provides a rigorous institutional focus and stimulates the creativity that is the ultimate end of any public relations planning process. Public relations management by objectives is essentially what the name implies—a management system that focuses on the intended objectives of a communication event rather than on the activities undertaken to communicate.

Public relations practitioners using MBO don't ask managers to evaluate PR performance based on the number of press releases they issue or the pages of newsletter copy they write during a month. That only proves they are working hard, not necessarily that they are doing anything to help their organization be successful. Instead, practitioners using MBO establish explicitly defined objectives for their communication campaigns that are related to overall company goals. Objectives are set before they plan the efforts to reach those goals. When the campaign is over, they

BOX 1.1   Views from the Field

Mary Ann Pires
Pires is principal partner in The Pires Group, a commu-
nications consulting firm specializing in public affairs
management based in Ardsley, New York. She has ad-
vised some three dozen Fortune 500 firms since the
firm's 1985 founding.

How does public relations gather influence within an
institution's management?

By being the best source of emerging issue and trend information within the
organization. One way to do that is by working with consumer and public interest groups. It's the No. 1 early warning system. They will give you information that predates anything that ever appears in a newspaper. It foreshad-
ows any legislation by years. It is, bar none, the most anticipatory way to
operate. Fifteen years ago in Boston, a group called 9 to 5 was just getting on
its legs, and one of the first issues they seized upon was the damage done by
video display terminals. I took that issue to my employer and got hooted out
of the room. Ten years later I learned that same company had to embark on a
major effort to combat the harm being done to their employees by terminals.
That company could have gotten a 10-year jump on this issue if they had
taken it seriously. A decade later, the regulations were mandated by government and it cost much more to fix them.

So we want to talk to people who are our adversaries as well as
those publics who are our friends?

If an organization wants to influence public policy today, its position has to be
more than one of its own self-interest. It's the unnatural allies that spell success
in public policy. If you're a corporation and you show up to lobby with the
Chamber of Commerce, that's what everybody would expect. But if you show
up with support from the minority community, an elderly group or environmentalists, those groups are not perceived to be the natural allies of companies. It demonstrates you are advocating a position that has some public benefits. One of our clients, a medical testing laboratory, was interested in seeing
national quality standards [set] for testing labs. Why? Because they were already
operating at a high standard. Advocating by themselves, however, it looked like
a very self-interested agenda. Yet the issue had enormous consumer appeal.
Wouldn't you and I prefer to have our blood test evaluated by a professional
than by someone's receptionist? We took it to consumer groups and elderly

groups and we said: "We think this is in your self-interest." Well, lo and be-hold, they thought this would help their constituents, too. They helped lobby, and their participation enhanced our client's position greatly.

Can we view a primary role of public relations as building coalitions?

Yes, if you're talking long term. Right now, however, this is pretty cutting-edge for far too many organizations. In the third-party group work we do, I tell my clients that if somebody who hasn't spoken to them in the past re-turns their phone calls, then they've got their first return on their invest-ment. If a consumer or public interest advocate alerts them to an issue that's gaining steam, so they can gather their resources a bit, that's a measure of penetration, a measure of trust. If an organization carries information about your issue in their publications, that carries a priceless third-party evaluation. Too many organizations have yet to grasp that public relations exists not just to prevent things from happening or to minimize risks. Ideally, we're in the business of maximizing support.

So we slap together a coalition every time we're faced with a problem?

You can't just brew up instant coalitions like you would instant coffee. It's far better to have relationships with dozens of groups and then bring them issues as they emerge. They will be there for your company if the relation-ship has been cultivated. Of course, they won't always do what you want them to do. But I tell my clients that if they can "buy" a group it's not worth having. It's the integrity of a group that makes their allegiance worth having and adds such impact.

—Used with permission of Mary Ann Pires

evaluate their success in terms of the institutional goals they have helped the com-pany reach by their communication efforts on this one project. That integrates pub-lic relations activities with the organization's profit picture and brings practitioners into the highest management circles.

But I'm getting ahead of myself. Planning is such an important topic that we'll spend the next chapter discussing it.

TRADITIONAL COMMUNICATION MODELS: A REALITY CHECK

The second major question for all professional communicators is deciding with whom we communicate, to learn how to select audiences that have the greatest potential to respond to our communication.

Too often, PR practitioners have wasted time trying to convince people who have already made up their minds on an issue, or they have ignored groups interested in and important to their cause whose opinions were still unformed enough to be shaped by a persuasive message. If we are interested in cost-effective communication, we must know what type of person is most likely to respond to our message.

Let's start with the most basic communication model. Figure 1.1 is a simplified version of the Yale information processing model. You've probably seen it before.

sender ⟶ message ⟶ medium ⟶ receiver

FIGURE 1.1   The Yale information processing model
Although the Yale model accurately describes communication from the sender's perspective, it does not predict when a receiver will decide to listen and respond to a message.

The Yale model speculates that communication occurs when an individual, a sender, decides on a message and transmits it through a medium, which could be a newspaper, a whispered conversation, a television broadcast, a letter or hundreds of other ways. The medium delivers the message to a receiver, and communication has occurred.

Or has it? What happens when a manufacturer's public relations practitioner decides to convey a message about a stupendous technological breakthrough in computer chip technology? The practitioner writes a press release, then sends it to a newspaper editor. The editor reads the release's letterhead, remembers he has gotten a whole string of useless, irrelevant releases from that particular company before, and throws the release away.

Even though all the steps in the traditional communication model have been followed, communication hasn't occurred. It's like a solitary actor shouting from a bare stage into an empty theater: If there isn't anyone there to hear the play, the drama has never happened, the thoughts have never been transferred.

BUT IS ANYBODY LISTENING? THE RECEIVER-CENTERED COMMUNICATION MODEL

Scratch one communication model. A modification of the Yale model called the receiver-centered communication process seems to describe the communication process better. It's an informal model I developed to help guide public relations writing.

My receiver-centered communication process stems from ideas formulated by William J. McGuire, who concentrated on the aspect of communication that started after the Yale model ended. McGuire maintained that communication is controlled by the receiver. Communication, McGuire reasoned, hasn't occurred merely because the receiver receives a message; communication does not occur until the receiver decides to yield to the message.

Receiver-centered communication model

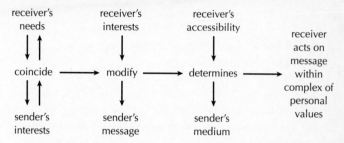

FIGURE 1.2 The receiver-centered communication model

In the receiver-centered communication model, as in McGuire's, the receiver arbitrates communication success, but my model also integrates the sender/message/medium steps of the Yale model. Figure 1.2 shows the receiver-centered communication model. A discussion of the basic questions that underlie each step follows.

Does Your Audience Have a Reason for Listening?

During the communication process, the receiver decides whether to attend to the message. Does the information the sender wants to communicate have any relevance or interest to the receiver? If it doesn't, the receiver won't pay any attention.

Does the Message Have to Be Changed to Influence Your Audience?

Memory Memo 1.2
The receiver-centered questions:

- Does your audience have a reason for listening?
- Does the message have to be changed to influence your audience?
- Do you reach your audience with the medium you've chosen?
- Does your audience react the way you predicted?

Is the message presented in a way the intended receivers can understand and recognize as being meant for them? Is the vocabulary too complex or too simple? Are the examples relevant to the receivers' prior experiences or future self-interest? If the message isn't designed to draw the right audience, the intended communication won't occur.

Do You Reach Your Audience with the Medium You've Chosen?

Has the sender chosen a medium that the desired public uses? To cite a most obvious example, if you're trying to communicate to children and you place your message in *The Wall Street Journal*, effective communication has not occurred.

Does Your Audience React the Way You Predicted?

Has the receiver acted on the message in a way that indicates he or she has understood the message as the sender intended? Even when you've followed all the preceding steps, you've still got to consider that because your audience's experiences may differ from yours, it may interpret your message differently from the way you would.

In one case, an advertising campaign intended to show a clothing company's belief in racial harmony instead sparked protests by African-American groups who felt the ads sent messages reinforcing images of black slavery. In that situation, even though the steps of the Yale communication model were followed, the persuasive communication act was not fulfilled. The lesson: Instead of being obsessed with the information we want to communicate, we should be sensitive to the information our publics want to receive.

The receiver-centered communication model forces a public relations writer to study the audience and place its needs foremost when designing the institution's message.

The simple rule: Before we write, we have to understand our audience. We must know what its members need to know and want to know to make their lives better. We need to be able to predict what motives they have for accepting new information and yielding to new ideas.

No matter how well written our release or script or backgrounder is, if the audience members don't find anything in it that affects their lives or jobs, they won't read it. If they don't read it, we might just as well not have bothered to write it. That's the bottom line.

TARGETING PEOPLE WHO CARE: THE SITUATIONAL THEORY

For receiver-centered communication to be effective, we need to find a way to predict when people are going to be interested in listening and yielding to a message.

The University of Maryland's James Grunig has developed a convincing model for predicting when people are going to take these steps. Grunig's situational theory maintains that if we can identify the people who are likely to communicate about a situation, as well as those people who probably won't, we can design a cost-effective communication plan. That's logical, because we can then devote more time and resources to the relatively smaller number of people whose support can help (or whose opposition can hinder) our institution's activities.

Grunig theorized that the potential to communicate is one of the strongest indicators that a person will develop attitudes that translate into action—buying a product, voting for a candidate, speaking in favor of an issue at a public hearing or contributing to a charity. Transforming opinions into action is the ultimate goal of all public relations activities.

The Search for Information Seekers

Grunig split communication behaviors into two categories, which he called information seeking and information processing. Information seekers are individuals eager to receive and accept a message about a particular subject. They often take the message and communicate it to others, thus increasing the original communication's impact and leading additional people to accept that viewpoint. Information seekers are the people most likely to translate information into action.

Information processors, on the other hand, exhibit what Grunig calls "passive communication behavior." They don't look for information but merely process information that presents itself to them. They are unlikely to act after receiving information or to pass their knowledge along to others.

However, a person can be an information processor in one situation and an information seeker in another situation. The important thing to remember about Grunig's situational theory is that a person's communication behavior depends on the situation.

When you slump in front of the television set watching your ninth commercial for a hamburger chain during a 60-minute show, you are probably an information processor. You are aware a commercial is on and could probably name the advertiser if someone asked you, but you are no longer actively gathering information from the commercial, and you're probably not going to share information about the commercial with members of your family.

Let's observe you in your public relations classroom, however. You are poised on the edge of your chair, eager to receive new information, anxious to share your insights with classmates during discussion. You want to find more information, knowing that, in the long term, it will be important to your professional life and, in the short term, it will be important to your hopes of graduating from college. In this situation (at least as I have fancifully described it) you are an information seeker.

This theory readily translates into public relations situations, too. An office manager, burned out in his job after 14 years, comes home and drops into the depths of his recliner. Huddled behind his newspaper, his communication efforts with his family, even in response to direct questions, are limited to proto-human grunts.

But ask him about baseball, and he suddenly becomes animated. He discusses the shortcomings of the hometown manager, recites statistics of long-dead pitchers, and, red-faced and panting, demonstrates the prowess he possessed decades ago.

Obviously, here is a near full-time information processor, until we awaken his passion for baseball. In communicating about baseball he is an information seeker, going to the stadium for games, buying baseball encyclopedias at the bookstore and trying to convince others of his views of the sport. In this one situation, he has translated information into action. On that one topic, he is a prime candidate for public relations messages.

Grunig has isolated three elements that help determine whether an individual will be an information processor or an information seeker in a particular situation. He proposes that people tend to be information seekers, and thus the best targets for our communication efforts, when they are involved in situations in which they (1) recognize the issue as a problem,

---

Memory Memo 1.3
The best targets for a communication campaign are people who

- see our issue as a problem or opportunity
- feel that the issue affects their lives
- believe they can do something to solve the issue

(2) feel the problem affects their life somehow, and (3) believe there are few barriers to prevent them from doing something to solve the problem.

Here is each component outlined in more detail:

Problem Recognition: Can You See the Dilemma?   Grunig contends that people usually must perceive something is a problem before they will become information seekers. For instance, as a city prepares to build a new airport, the new facility's prospective neighbors may see the new airport and its noise as a very large problem. City residents who don't live near the airport site are much less likely to view noise as a problem.

As you might expect, the airport's neighbors are much more likely to become information seekers, gathering information about the new facility and communicating their displeasure to others. City residents who live miles from the airport and are never assaulted by the noise of 3 a.m. flights over their houses likely will receive news about the new airport passively and be less likely to communicate their support or displeasure about the project to others. They are more likely to be information processors.

Constraint Recognition: Can You Do Something about It?   Grunig says the likelihood of people communicating about a situation is affected by whether they foresee factors limiting their behavior and their ability to change a situation. For instance, if a man watching a television program hears about an investment opportunity that promises a tremendous return, he probably will seek information about the investment only if he has enough money to invest. Otherwise, he will merely process the information, as there is very little he can do to take advantage of the situation.

Similarly, if a women's rights activist hears about a march in Washington, she'll likely be interested in learning about the march, its organizers and even bus transportation and hotel accommodations in the capital. In that situation she's an information seeker. But if the march is scheduled for a day when she knows she must make a vital presentation to her company's board of directors, she will merely record and process general information about the march and not seek other information about it. When a situation presents barriers to taking constructive action, we usually become information processors.

Level of Involvement: Is It Your Problem?   There's one last variable that helps predict whether someone will be an information seeker or processor in a particular situation: whether a receiver perceives he or she is highly involved in the issue.

For instance, a Midwestern farmer may recognize that gang violence in cities is a serious problem. But he doesn't believe he's responsible for the situation or that his small-town life is threatened by immense urban problems.

Grunig argues this lack of involvement in the issue would make the farmer less likely to seek information about gang violence and unlikely to communicate with others about the subject. However, urban high school principals with higher involvement levels might seek out information, attend conferences and speak to groups of parents and students about the problem.

With information about these three elements, Grunig maintains, public relations people can more accurately target their communication efforts to the information seekers who might be eager to receive information about a situation. Those information seekers are more likely to take action based on that information. By targeting these people who recognize a problem, who do not see barriers to solving the problem, and who feel personally involved in the situation, we have parameters to help guide us to receptive and cost-efficient audiences for our public relations messages.

PREDICTING WHEN MESSAGES BECOME ACTION: THE LEARN–FEEL–DO PERSUASION MODEL

Now that we have some guidance about audiences to whom we should direct our communication, it's time to study how people respond to messages.

Many social scientists have attempted to explain persuasion through a "hierarchy" model. There have been many hierarchy models (see Figure 1.3), but the idea behind each is basically the same: When people make decisions about whether to adopt a new idea, their decision process moves through a rigid sequence of programmed steps, called a hierarchy.

Advertising professionals formulated the AIDA model. AIDA, an acronym for "at-

FIGURE 1.3 Traditional hierarchical needs and persuasion models

These models credibly describe rational decision-making processes, but because people undertake many actions based on impulse or emotion rather than rational thought, these hierarchical models fail to predict many decision processes.

AIDA	Hierarchy of Needs	Adoption Process
action	self-actualization	adoption
↑	↑	↑
desire	esteem	resolution
↑	↑	↑
interest	social	preference
↑	↑	↑
attention	safety	evaluation
	↑	↑
	physiological	interest
		↑
		awareness

tention-interest-desire-action," is the sequence researchers thought consumers followed as they made buying decisions. AIDA assumes the first job of an advertisement is to get an audience's attention, after which you gain its interest and then stimulate a desire for the product. Finally, the audience acts to buy the product.

Another hierarchy model is Maslow's hierarchy of needs, in which people meet their needs in a definite sequence. Maslow said that until the basic needs for air and food are met, people don't spend much time thinking about or working to satisfy their need for housing. Until they have a roof over their head, they don't pay much attention to having a nice house. According to Maslow, it's only after they have a nice house that they begin to seek answers concerning their relationship to their creator and their place in the world.

Traditional Persuasion Hierarchy Models

A hierarchical model that tries to explain persuasion is called the adoption process model. It also maintains that people go through a definite series of steps as they acquire new information or new attitudes.

The adoption process model states that people first develop an awareness of an idea or product and then an interest in it. Then they go through a period of evaluation and trial, from which comes a preference, then a resolution of intention. Finally, they adopt the new idea as their own.

But all these models predict actual human behavior very inadequately. For example, Maslow believes survival, safety and social needs must be satisfied before a person will attempt to satisfy esteem needs. If that's true, why would a college student use money needed to purchase a month's worth of gasoline and groceries to buy a $300 leather jacket instead? Obviously, all his lower level needs won't be met, but he is acting, growling stomach and all, to satisfy an esteem need.

Similar difficulties arise with the adoption process model. When an 11-year-old girl declares she is for the Republican candidate in the next election, or a business executive buys a new brand of gum, it's hard to trace a hierarchical thought process that led from awareness through evaluation to these actions. The girl copies arguments her Republican parents have made. The executive buys a brand of gum because he likes the packaging. There's not much climbing through the hierarchy in these decisions. The girl is reacting based on a viewpoint held by her parents, which they perhaps developed after evaluation or perhaps adopted because their parents were Republicans. The executive acts out of a knowledge that the consequences of a bad decision are very insignificant—he can afford 35 cents to see if he would like the new brand of gum.

How Are People Persuaded? It Depends

The problem with all the hierarchical models is they often fail to describe how people respond to communication. They simply don't predict the way people react in many situations.

The persuasion process is too complicated for one simple model to explain and predict behavior in every situation. And, as we academics often find when we try to make reality fit a tidy model, life often forces us to accept a somewhat more unkempt explanation. In the case of persuasion, the best we can do is say, "It depends."

How does persuasion work? Well, it depends on the type and level of involvement of the person considering the issue or the product. It depends on the importance the person attaches to the issue. It depends on whether the people involved in making a decision are using emotional or rational considerations as they ponder their choices.

One model that's been used primarily in advertising helps us understand some of the variation in the ways people approach decision making. It stems from research on hierarchical models that shows these models have at least two basic faults.

First, people don't necessarily proceed through every level of the hierarchy before making a decision. Often, the level of involvement and consequences of making a bad decision change the number of steps they take. For example, a convenience store customer might need to be aware only of a candy bar brand to choose it. However, a candy company president's decision about whether to commit a half million dollars to manufacture and market a new candy bar would usually involve all the decision steps listed in the hierarchy.

Second, the hierarchy isn't always in bottom-to-top sequence. Although the hierarchies generally specify that a person learns about an issue, then develops and internalizes a feeling or belief about the issue, and then does something to reinforce or confirm that feeling, in some decision processes those components occur in a different sequence.

To correct some of these faults, researchers at the Foote Cone & Belding advertising agency developed what they called the "learn–feel–do" model. They postulated that people approach buying decisions about products according to the importance they attach to their decision and whether the purchasing decision is made to satisfy an emotional or a rational need. In short, there are times when people adopt an opinion about an issue or product before they assess the issue's or product's strengths and weaknesses. As we saw in the chewing gum example, sometimes they do something before they learn about a product.

However, people usually don't make decisions dictated by their emotional needs without logic slipping in to a greater or lesser degree. Conversely, logical decisions are usually colored by emotion. Reinforcing this idea of "it depends," the learn–feel–do model asserts that we should look at this decision-making process as a continuum in which people assess how important the consequences of making the wrong decision are and whether they emphasize emotional viewpoints or rational thought in making decisions.

To represent these variations, the learn–feel–do persuasion model is presented as a grid with two perpendicular axes (Figure 1.4). The vertical line represents the importance of the decision, ranging from situations in which the consequences of making the wrong decision are minor to those in which the potential consequences could be devastating. The horizontal axis represents the degree of rational thought involved in a decision process, ranging from a decision made completely emotionally to one made completely rationally.

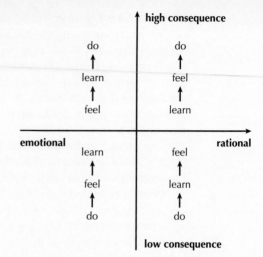

FIGURE 1.4   The learn–feel–do persuasion model. The learn–feel–do model asserts that individuals consider many factors in making a decision, or sometimes don't think about it at all. By analyzing a decision-making process in terms of the rational thought used and the consequences of the decision, practitioners can more accurately predict the decision-making sequence in a specific situation.

Different decisions entail different decision strategies for different people. In situations in which the decision is important and the rational processes dominant (such as in deciding to buy an expensive machine for a factory), people usually follow a learn–feel–do hierarchy. That is, they learn all they can about competing brands of machines, develop a conviction about the machine they have decided on, and then purchase the equipment. You'll notice this sequence follows the steps outlined in most of the traditional hierarchical models.

But what happens when someone is making a decision about what stand to take on abortion? It's a very important decision. But emotional and not rational factors often predominate in making such a decision. In those cases we often have a feeling about what we want to believe before we've developed any balanced knowledge about all the issues involved in the controversy. Thus, we'll often see people seek information to justify their initial emotional reactions to the issue, so that they can carry out their original intentions with a good conscience. They are using the feel–learn–do hierarchy of decision making.

Let's look at another quadrant in the model. The lower left corner illustrates the do–feel–learn sequence, a high-emotion, low-consequence decision in which emotions and the desire to satisfy immediate needs greatly influence the action.

An example of a do–feel–learn behavior process is when a waiter asks if you will have dessert after a satisfying meal. You've been trying to lose a little weight, but the dessert tray excites an emotional response in you, which you justify by telling your-

Memory Memo 1.4
Knowing your way through the learn–feel–do model:

- *Do* happens first in low-consequence decisions.
- *Do* happens last in high-consequence decisions.
- *Feel* happens earlier in emotional decisions.
- *Learn* happens earlier in rational decisions.

self you've already violated your diet tonight anyway. This decision summarized: You anticipate an emotional reward and minimal perceived consequences to making the wrong decision. You do (eat the cake), feel (great about the chocolate rush), and learn (from the scales, that you'll never get thin engaging in this sort of behavior).

The last quadrant is the do–learn–feel sequence in the lower right. Again, we have a low-involvement decision, but here thought is involved in the decision-making process. For example, a man attends a free lecture on plastic surgery sponsored by a hospital. He had been contemplating a facelift, but didn't want to spend the money or risk the embarrassment of going to speak personally to a plastic surgeon. The free lecture lets the man take a relatively minor, risk-free step reinforcing his desire for a facelift, lets him learn more about the process, and helps him develop a conviction about whether he wants to go through the surgery. In short, he can decide and act on a relatively unimportant issue (whether to go to a free lecture), learn about the issue, and then develop a conviction (do–learn–feel).

TRANSLATING COMMUNICATION THEORIES INTO ACTION

How do these esoteric models relate to planning real-life public relations writing tasks? Well, they give us the audience evaluation tools we need to pursue a cost-effective, receiver-centered writing process. They demonstrate that our writing must be relevant to the audience we are addressing. We need to structure our writing so it immediately and repeatedly shows how the information we are communicating can affect our readers' lives. We need to reinforce in our readers' minds how they can act on the issues we present.

The models give us insight into the motives that spur people to act as a result of a communication event. Grunig's situational theory shows us how important it is to convey information in our public relations messages that helps our publics recognize that a problem exists (problem recognition). We must demonstrate that our audience can be involved in solving the problem (level of involvement), and we need to recognize the barriers that prevent them from acting (constraint recognition) and show them that they can overcome them.

After we structure information to encourage our readers to become information seekers rather than processors, we must be aware of motivational patterns in the persuasion process. The learn–feel–do sequence can help us analyze an audience and predict its reaction to information. We should then be able to project whether our audience will respond most effectively to emotional or rational arguments and sequence our communication acts accordingly. We should be able to determine if we need to sponsor an educational campaign on an issue before asking a public to decide or take action. Or we might find the audience thinks a decision's bad consequences are so remote that they'll act before evaluating their decision. Our analysis might even lead us to restructure our institution's marketing strategy to convert a high-consequence decision, like a patient opting for a facelift, into a series of low-consequence ones that start with requesting a brochure on plastic surgery.

Using the insights into our audience gained through these models, we can design realistic, workable strategies for mounting the types of cost-effective, objective-driven communication campaigns I advocated earlier in the chapter. We can predict how certain people will conceptualize decision processes in certain situations. We can involve and motivate important publics to see the goals they share with our organization. In sum, we can start to manage communication within an organizational framework—setting realistic goals, integrating those goals into management perspectives, and designing effective processes to reach the goals. That's the ultimate purpose of this book—to explore the strategies for effective and efficient public relations communication that will further public relations in its growth as a management profession.

SUMMARY

- The public relations writer's job has expanded from publicity efforts to planning how communication can help organizations meet important goals.
- Any professional communication task is framed by the following questions: Why are you communicating? With whom should you communicate? What will motivate your audience?
- Institutions exist in a competitive environment in which consumer, civil rights, and other groups use public relations practitioners to challenge powerful organizations directly.
- Public relations practice now centers on two-way communication, in which practitioners not only communicate institutional policies to other publics, but also bring outside opinions into the organization so that it can adapt to new environments.
- A public relations management-by-objective system evaluates communication efforts according to how well they help the institution reach its overall goals.
- The receiver-centered communication model asserts that a message's receiver controls whether a communication act is completed. Thus, writers need to structure their writing and delivery methods to conform to the receiver's capabilities, desires and interests.
- Grunig's situational communication model theorizes that the potential to communicate is related to the probability of an individual's taking action. People tend to become information seekers in a situation in which they (1) recognize the situation as a problem, (2) have high involvement in the issue, and (3) see few constraints on their ability to correct the problem.
- Hierarchy persuasion models, such as the adoption process model, are inadequate in predicting human decision making because people skip steps in the hierarchy and don't always follow the same series of steps.
- The learn–feel–do persuasion model asserts that an individual's decision process varies in different situations depending on that person's perception of the decision's importance and whether he or she will use emotional or rational factors to make the decision.

In the next chapter, we'll examine how planning can help the writer develop a broad outline for the communication process and find specific creative answers to communication problems.

THINK PIECES

1. What are some differences between writing for public relations projects and writing for academic assignments?
2. Define some of the different institutional goals of a ballet company, a nursing home, an employment service, and a politician.
3. How would you evaluate an ad campaign that advertised expensive clothes on bus transit cards?
4. Think of a subject about which you are excited. Analyze your reaction to it in terms of Grunig's information seeker model.
5. Determine and analyze a behavior that might be adopted through the persuasion sequence in each of the quadrants (Figure 1.4) of the learn–feel–do persuasion model.

MANAGEMENT PROBLEMS

D2.2

D3.4

D7.1

D10.3

ADDITIONAL READING

Foote Cone & Belding. *How Advertising Works: An FCB Strategy Planning Model*. New York: Foote Cone & Belding, 1978. Cited in A. Jerome Jewler, *Creative Strategy in Advertising*, 5th ed. Belmont, Calif.: Wadsworth, 1995.

Grunig, James E., and Hunt, Todd. *Managing Public Relations*. New York: Holt, Rinehart and Winston, 1984.

Hovland, Carl I., Janis, Irving L., and Kelley, Harold H. *Communication and Persuasion*. New Haven, Conn.: Yale University Press, 1953.

Lauzen, Martha M., and Dozier, David M. "Issues Management Mediation of Linkages Between Environmental Complexity and Management of the Public Relations Function." *Journal of Public Relations Research* 6:3 (1994): 163–184.

McGuire, William J. "Persuasion, Resistance and Attitude Change," in *Handbook of Communication*, ed. Ithiel de Sola Pool et al. Chicago: Rand-McNally, 1973.

Maslow, Abraham. *Motivation and Personality*. New York: Harper & Row, 1970.

Smith, Ronald D. "Psychological Type and Public Relations: Theory, Research, and Applications." *Journal of Public Relations Research* 5:3 (1995): 177–199.

## chapter 2

Creative Communication Planning: The Persuasion Platform

REAL-LIFE LESSONS

You're placed into a large room filled with automobile parts—seat covers and tie rods, fenders and exhaust manifolds, thermostats and pistons. You're shown a picture of the car all these parts would combine to make and then told to make one just like it. What's your response? Unless you're an extraordinary human being, the enormity of the task would overwhelm you. Where should you start? What should you do with all the parts you don't recognize? If you are talented and lucky enough to assemble it, how would you know what's wrong if it doesn't start? Not many of us could ever assemble a working car under those circumstances.

However, if we can break this complex task into individual steps, there's hope. There are eight components that make up the brake assembly. By assembling each part in sequence, we can get a working mechanism. Repeat it three times for the other three wheels. There are three parts to assemble to make the air cleaner. Step by step, part by part, it's possible to assemble an entire automobile.

This is the principle that led to the assembly line. By breaking down a complex process into small, discrete steps, it's possible for non-engineers to make a car, a locomotive or a computer.

Once a task has been segmented into these small actions, each action can be further broken down and studied to see how it can be made more efficient. Would a worker be able to assemble a radiator faster if the hose that needs to be attached is picked up with the right or the left hand? Could the interior be made more efficiently if all the stitching were done before the seat was put into the car? Again, by evaluating how we do each action, we can make the process more efficient and less costly.

Communication is surely as complex as making a car. So when you're told your organization needs to communicate more effectively with your audiences, that's akin to putting you in the room filled with car parts. There are so many chances to confound the audience or to deliver the wrong message to the wrong audience. Different publics may read the same message and draw dramatically different conclusions from it. How do you determine if you communicated effectively?

Just how do you improve the odds that your communication is going to obtain the right results? The same way it's possible to build a car. By breaking down the communication task into small units, it's possible to understand and improve the communication process. Equally important, by segmenting the communication task, it's possible to find important elements in the communication that you can measure so that you can truly determine if your organization is communicating effectively. That's the essence of communication planning.

WHAT YOU KNOW

- An effective public relations message must orient the sender's communication goals within the context of the receiver's self-interest.
- Different audiences will perceive the same situation and their possible responses to it in vastly different ways.
- It is possible to predict the audiences that will most likely act in a situation and determine the messages that will persuade them to act.

WHAT YOU'LL LEARN

- Public relations communication can be segmented into specific components, which can be more easily planned and assessed for maximum effectiveness.
- Public relations activities should not be based on tradition, but on a clear sense of the problem to be overcome and the audience whose support is necessary to solve that problem.
- Being able to quantify the effects of communication gives practitioners vastly increased power in organizations.

CREATIVITY AND CONTROL: THE RATIONALE FOR PLANNING

When I make presentations on planning to executives, several audience members invariably tell me that planning sounds wonderful but that they are too busy to take the time to plan. However, when I start exploring their work processes, I discover that even though they aren't aware of it, they are planning.

Do they have at least a primitive understanding of why it's important to conduct a certain communication campaign? Yes? Then they're planning. Do they speculate on the audience they need to convince to meet that goal? Then they're planning. Do they try to decide on an issue that will be most persuasive to that audience?

Do they select a medium for delivering the message? Do they make some crude calculations about whether the expected benefits justify the mailing and printing costs and the time spent on the project? That's planning.

At some level, planning is a part of any project, and in some simple situations, the procedures I've just outlined are good enough. But there are definite advantages to formalizing the planning process. First, planning allows you to do your job better. Expanding and formalizing the thought processes you use to design a project lets you contemplate new audiences that might be important to your success and forces you to think more rigorously and expansively about what might motivate those audiences. Planning also makes you more inventive in choosing the media that will reach your target audience. Instead of locking you into formulaic ways of solving certain problems, planning can lead you to more creative messages and more innovative methods to attack your institution's communication difficulties.

In addition, formal planning results in a document that helps persuade your own supervisors of the project's importance to the institution. It also provides you with effective arguments to convince management to provide the personnel, money and time to complete and succeed in your communication efforts.

Contrary to what harried practitioners believe, planning usually doesn't add to the workload but actually allows you to gain control over it. Public relations practitioners are busy people, a problem compounded by the comprehensiveness of the practitioner's assigned role as "organizational communicator." In many organizations, management defines "communication" as everything from producing video news releases to stuffing envelopes. Although both tasks involve communicating through a medium, one obviously is a better use of a practitioner's professional capacities.

Because planning gives you a way to demonstrate the returns from communication tasks, you and your supervisors can begin to set priorities for the tasks in your workload. Tasks that are most important to the organization's success deserve your best effort and the investment of the organization's money, facilities and personnel. Those tasks that marginally improve the organization's welfare might be expendable. You'll know only if you undertake planning efforts.

Planning also helps you complete a communication task on time and with the fewest complications because it lets you better understand the sequencing and complexity of the activities involved in completing the campaign. That's vital in establishing your credibility and professional success.

THE PERSUASION PLATFORM: STEP-BY-STEP COMMUNICATION

Planning a communication campaign begins with remembering the steps that constitute every communication act. As suggested in the first chapter, effective communication focuses on satisfying the needs and desires of our audiences. With a knowledge of what motivates our publics, we can select messages that will be most persuasive to them and present it in a format to which they'll respond.

The 10-step planning system detailed in this chapter is an expansion of the receiver-centered communication model discussed in Chapter 1. I adapted the persuasion platform for public relations writing tasks from two different planning procedures, one used primarily by business administrators and the other employed by advertising professionals.

Businesses often use a form of the management-by-objective (MBO) planning process, which I discussed earlier. It's designed to help identify important organizational problems and channel management efforts to solve them. Additionally, it provides a very specific procedure to determine if the manager has reached the goal that will help the organization.

The other planning procedure is called the creative platform. It's very effective in helping advertising writers conceive and execute creative and persuasive messages and presentations.

I've combined those two planning methods into a 10-step process called the persuasion platform. Synthesizing the strong management focus of MBO with the creative platform helps the PR practitioner transform his or her creativity into a structured, disciplined document that can help solve organizational problems. The 10 steps are listed in Memory Memo 2.1.

Memory Memo 2.1
Steps in the persuasion platform:

- Isolate the institutional problem
- Determine a campaign objective
- Describe the target audience
- Predict the persuasion sequence
- Define the persuaders
- Develop the creative strategy
- Select the media
- Determine the timetable
- Calculate the budget
- Determine the evaluation process

The persuasion platform is useful for all types of communication tasks. I use it to isolate the persuaders that will motivate the audiences of news releases or speeches or to create catchy headlines and visuals for posters and brochures. It not only helps stimulate the creative process involved in PR writing, but its management orientation relates your writing tasks to your company's goals.

The first step is to address an organizational problem that can be solved through a communication campaign. Perhaps the problem is a lack of knowledge about a manufacturer's employee wellness program. Communication through a printed announcement might help correct that situation. It might be a hospital sanitation problem that training sessions with staff members could help prevent. The problem could be customer service complaints at a catalog house, which additional phone lines and operators might help solve.

The following discussion outlines the practitioner's thought process as the campaign evolves through each step. A complete persuasion platform is contained in the Ready Reference section at the end of this chapter.

Isolating the Institutional Problem

The persuasion platform first briefly describes the client's problem by examining the historical, social, economic or perceptual elements that have caused the problem. In short, we develop a reason for communication before we communicate.

Contrary to one of our society's (and the profession's) basic perceptions—that communication is good any time, with everyone and about any subject—misguided or unneeded communication is a waste of effort and organizational resources and may possibly be counterproductive to an institution's overall objectives. Let's say you work for a company whose CEO has just sold one of the company's major divisions to a competitor for millions of dollars. As your competitor integrates its new holding, it fires 4,000 of your company's former employees. Meanwhile, your company's CEO, who has major stock options in your suddenly enriched company, gets a multimillion-dollar payback, and becomes the nation's highest-paid executive. She wants you to publicize her vast riches in major business publications, newspapers and television network news programs. Should you try to dissuade her from her desire for prestige and fame?

Perhaps you should, if you don't want to stir up the resentments and protests of the former employees, who are now collecting unemployment for the same reason the CEO is on the top of the heap. There's no doubt the communication effort would help the CEO's personal standing among her peers and might contribute to her morale and performance. But do those personal benefits outweigh the potential harm the organization might suffer if it appears the company is boasting about the CEO's status?

I don't think so and I would forcefully argue against the CEO's instructions. PR practitioners should communicate only in circumstances in which a communication effort can help them solve some real organizational problem. Certainly, there are enough of those situations: the need to communicate with a certain public to reverse an attitude that is threatening fund-raising efforts, to support a sales effort for a newly introduced product, to minimize the possible damage to employee relations from an industrial accident, or to gain a sympathetic hearing on a rezoning permit from a neighborhood preservation group.

This first step, defining the institutional problem, is important for two reasons. First, detailing an institutional problem guides us toward the tasks that will yield the most dividends for the organization and keeps us focused on those efforts that will represent the best investment of our time and talents.

Second, defining the institutional problem tells you what tasks you shouldn't do. It lets you avoid tasks that are motivated more by tradition than by any real contribution they make to the organization's success. This helps a practitioner gain power within the organization by showing how his or her efforts are directly related to reaching the company's overall goals.

Determining a Campaign Objective

Once we've determined what problem an organization wants to solve, it's possible to develop an objective, a one-sentence statement that predicts a specific outcome for your communication effort. An objective must meet the five criteria in Memory Memo 2.2. An objective must be unambiguous, realistic, measurable, and must contain a deadline for the task to be completed. Most important, it

Memory Memo 2.2
A good MBO objective

- must solve an institutional problem
- must be measurable
- must be unambiguous
- must be realistic
- must contain a deadline

must help solve the institutional problem you've isolated in the plan's first step.

Let's look at some objectives. Assume you are concerned about a drop in the number of stockholders who are reinvesting their dividend checks in additional company stock. A communication campaign about the convenience and benefits of automatic reinvestment might help improve the situation.

Let's first look at a poorly written objective for this campaign:

Make extensive improvements in communication efforts to our corporate stockholders.

This objective does not have a measurable goal. How can you tell if you have made "extensive" improvements? And how can you know what an improvement in communication is? Additionally, the objective does not have a deadline for completion. Should we expect improvement by next week, or in a decade? This objective won't help you plan your communication efforts, and it gives you no method to evaluate your success.

Here's another objective that's almost as bad:

By April 1, send stockholders one letter from the company president explaining the benefits of automatic reinvestment.

Here you have a deadline for completion and a measurable goal. That's good. However, you are not measuring an objective that is important to the organization; you are merely measuring an activity for reaching the goal. What good is it to the company if you can prove you've mailed a letter? Instead, you need to relate your communication efforts to an organizational goal.

Now let's look at the same situation, but with a well-written objective statement:

By April 1, increase by 5 percent the number of current stockholders enrolled in the automatic stock reinvestment plan.

This objective contains all five of the elements necessary for guiding a cost-effective communication program. It has an objective that is important to the organization as a whole—reinvestment in company stock. It establishes an unambiguous, measurable goal. In this case, it is probably realistic to expect a 5 percent increase in program participation. Finally, there is a deadline when you will evaluate whether your communication campaign has been successful.

It's important when writing objectives to examine the situation for a component that can be measured. This is a central issue in the evaluation process because it is impossible to measure "improved communication." Fortunately, as Chuck Sengstock points out in Box 2.1, there are many secondary measures that are valid indicators of improved communication.

In a media campaign announcing a new use for an old product, you could measure the additional number of units sold, or the larger dollar volume of sales. At a catalog company suffering from poor customer relations, you might judge the effects of the communication campaign by measuring the average amount of time telephoning customers are on hold before they speak to a sales representative.

You can even measure the effects of communication on something as vague as better employee education. If research determines improved training for custodians might help prevent hospital-borne infections plaguing the operating room, you can measure the effect of that communication by having the hospital lab determine if there are fewer germs on operating room tiles after the training.

In this last scenario, notice that we did not evaluate our communication success by testing workers after the training session. Although that test might show that workers know what we wanted them to know at the end of the training period, it wouldn't necessarily tell us if they applied it in the workplace. Because our goal is to help the organization solve its problems, the MBO planning process always attempts to measure results that are as closely associated as possible with the solution to its institutional problem.

Describing the Target Audience

After you've established a definite objective for your communication efforts, the next step is to determine whose support can help solve the organizational problem you've just detailed. Put simply, you need to determine the individuals or groups who can help you meet your overall goal, as well as those who can sabotage that quest.

This is an important step, because you can't possibly afford to talk to everyone in the world about your issue. This may confound some clients who suggest that "everyone in the world is a potential buyer of my product." That's simply not true.

I'll give you an example. Let's say you work for a large supermarket. Everyone eats food, so everyone in your city is a potential customer, right? Wrong. Some people are rich enough to hire people to do their grocery shopping for them. In other households, only one family member makes the food-buying decisions for the whole family. The poorest people may not have enough money to buy food, and, for many other low-income families without adequate transportation, distance becomes the determining factor in choosing a grocery store. You must decide to whom to direct your message for the maximal impact, concentrating on some audiences and ignoring others.

Initially, we try to decide what audiences have the greatest capacity to affect our organization. Grunig, with his situational communication model, has already given us a way to evaluate different publics to decide whether we should commu-

BOX 2.1   Views from the Field

Charles A. Sengstock, Jr.
Sengstock is director of corporate public relations for Mo-torola Inc. in suburban Chicago. He coordinated changes in the company's public relations management effort that helped Motorola become one of the first three winners of the Malcolm Baldrige National Quality Award.

Isn't public relations too complex to lend itself to quality control techniques used for factory work?

When Motorola introduced the quality concept to public relations, we said this doesn't apply to us—we're creative, we're unique, we're special. The problem with public relations is that many of the tasks are nonrepetitive and many products are nonstandard. But when we began to study it, we found the large projects we did were made up of standardized, repetitive skills—a menu of skills that we did over and over. For instance, no two press confer-ences are ever the same, but there are certain common skills used in every press conference. There are skills for site selection, and there are project management, editing, writing and organizational skills. You can take one very big project and break it down into the services or tasks you have to un-dertake to complete it. Then you try to eliminate the mistakes you make and the time it takes to do each task.

But so often we're trying to foster something as nebulous as a "better relationship" with an important public. How do you mea-sure that?

It can be done. In our office, for instance, we have used telephone response time as a quality measure for our media relations program. If the media calls, someone from the office has to return the call within an hour. We've kept stats on that for over a year. When we first started out, we were counting six to eight defects a month. Every month, we try to drive the defects down, to five per month and then to four or three the following month. You're try-ing to make continuous improvement.

Are there other ways we can improve the quality of public rela-tions efforts?

Studies have found a direct relationship between shorter cycle time and higher quality. In public relations, you sometimes have five or 10 approval cycles for every project. When you cut those people out of the work cycle, you reduce the cycle time. You don't need six people proofreading a report; one will do. We always look at any project to discover those activities that aren't adding value to the final product. It's not adding value when people are waiting for a process to be completed, when a product or a service is standing still waiting for something to happen, or for something to be delivered. When you map the process, these things pop right out at you.

But don't these analysis methods limit the creativity practitioners bring to solving an institution's public relations problems?

The analytical methods are not meant to replace creative thinking. But creativity is also required in the way you combine the menu of skills to deal with the problems at hand: identifying the target audience, the media to reach that audience, and the communication keys or actions required to modify audience behavior or to convince them of your organization's position on an issue.

—Used with permission of Charles A. Sengstock, Jr.

nicate with them. As you'll recall, he said people who are most likely to communicate are also most likely to take an action. Thus, people who are most likely to take an action are those who have (1) high problem recognition, (2) a high level of involvement, and (3) low constraint recognition. By evaluating any public through these lenses, you'll be better able to determine which ones have the highest potential to respond to your communication campaign.

A caveat is necessary here. Remember that you shouldn't restrict your communication efforts to people who like your organization. Environmental activists who are constantly picketing your company, union members who exchange nasty comments about your president in the cafeteria or dissident stockholders who disrupt your annual meetings are important publics with which to communicate. They have a capacity to hurt your company just as much or even more than your most loyal employees or stockholders can help it.

Grunig's situational theory places equal importance on people who don't like your institution. Moreover, the communication potential of any public, either friendly or adversarial, can be evaluated through Grunig's three questions. Do they view the situation in your company as a problem? Do they have a high level of involvement in the situation? Do they see few obstacles to doing something (in this case, something that's most likely harmful to your organization) about the situation? If any public, friend or foe, emerges from this test with a high potential to be information seekers, you should design a communication campaign to answer their concerns and capitalize on their motivations for being involved in the issue. That often means developing a different persuasion platform that will reflect that different public's perception of the issue and develop a specific persuasive message that will motivate them.

Demographic Analysis.   After you identify the publics with whom you want to communicate, you describe them demographically, using information from your own consumer research or from commercially produced research like the Simmons Study of Media and Markets, which we'll examine in Chapter 3.

Where does your audience live? How old are they? What do they do for a living? How much money do they make? Are they men or women? Are ethnic characteristics important in determining who will be interested in your message?

This demographic information determines the people who have the capacity to act on your message. Obviously, if you're trying to sell diamond rings, you've first got to find people who have enough money to buy them. If you're trying to get people to join a national snowmobiling club, your communication efforts should target geographic areas with a lot of snow. If you're working for a record company marketing big band music, your most cost-effective audience will likely be people who were young adults in the 1930s and 1940s. That is valuable information as you try to design a cost-effective communication program.

There's one additional factor you need to consider as you determine the right audiences to which to direct your message. Remember that there is sometimes a difference between the people who use a product or service and the person who makes the decision about using the service. That may seem like a strange distinction to make. Let me explain.

Who pays for McDonald's food? Parents, of course. But is that the audience you want to target in a communication campaign?

I would argue that it isn't. Instead, you need to determine who makes the decision to go to McDonald's. Those of you with children in the house will know it's the kids who control many of the decisions about where the family will eat. You'll notice that McDonald's follows that wisdom in its many targeted campaigns aimed at various age groups ranging from 3-year-olds who've barely graduated from diapers to 17-year-olds who are almost ready to graduate from high school.

That rationale for targeting applies to adults too. For years, Federal Express touted its overnight delivery services to business executives. But Federal Express research discovered that secretaries and middle-managers, not executives, made decisions about what delivery service to use. After refocusing their advertising campaigns to appeal to those demographic groups, Federal Express found even greater success.

Psychographic Analysis.   Demographic descriptions certainly help determine the audience with whom we should be communicating, but a demographic description is hardly enough. Although demographics determine whether someone has the capacity to act, they don't necessarily tell you if a person is motivated to take an action. Motives are often revealed by the psychographic traits you discern in your target publics, descriptors that will be essential in developing the message to persuade that audience.

For example, if you are working for a company that sells fur coats, you know your audience must have a certain income level. Demographics can show you the audience that has the capacity to buy your expensive product. From that information, you know that if you placed a story in a college newspaper or a magazine that serves a low-income area about your store's exotic furs made from endangered animals, those placements wouldn't help you sell many fur coats. But even if you communicated to high-income individuals, would you be finding your target audience of fur buyers? Not necessarily.

Yes, that group would include people who could afford a fur coat. But if you live in a community that has a passionate animal rights movement, you might find yourself communicating with an equal number of people who think it's morally wrong for anyone to buy a fur. By not targeting your market tightly enough, not only have you spent money to communicate with an audience that won't help you meet your sales goal, but you've energized an audience that might otherwise have remained passive. Instead of selling furs, you might end up with a riot at your door.

Psychographics can help the professional communicator isolate those characteristics that make certain people support an idea or a product and other people revile it. In fact, discovering an individual's personal rationale for taking action is much more important in targeting an audience and constructing a message than knowing an individual's income level. If we can target a communication campaign to a tightly focused group, a campaign that emphasizes those ideas they use to make a decision, it's possible to create a very cost-effective and persuasive presentation.

In constructing an audience's psychographic description, you need to be expansive, exploratory—even speculative. As the think–feel–do persuasion model showed, emotions have a place in virtually every decision process and are the dominant factor in a large number of decisions people make. Out of those loves, hates and desires come the basic reasons why people buy products, support causes, adopt ideas.

Although there are ways to use focus group research, lifestyle surveys and media- and product-use statistics to help guide and develop your psychographic analysis (discussed in Chapter 3), every psychographic analysis begins with your own basic knowledge of the audience and its perception of your organization and your product or idea. For instance, here's a psychographic analysis for an urban college's in-state recruiting effort to students in rural areas:

These high school students can't wait to get out from under the wing of their parents. They are excited about college and their future, but at the same time they are a little insecure about leaving home. They are adventurous and want big-city life that they've never experienced in their small-town high schools. But although they want a new experience, they are a little insecure about their rural backgrounds and about their capacity to be accepted in a prestigious East Coast or West Coast university. They yearn for freedom but they'd like to be in a place where there would be at least a few people with similar backgrounds and where they could return to familiar surroundings for a weekend if city life gets too hectic.

You can begin your psychographic analysis by isolating one primary psychological factor that affects your audience's behavior. For example, does your audience consider itself practical, and thus would it support school reform laws, viewing them as a no-nonsense, self-help tool for the disadvantaged? Do people in your audience feel frustrated by their humdrum lives? If so, would they rent a fantasy hotel suite that looks like a jungle tree house, complete with loincloths for the occupants? Do they remember their own childhood as innocent, and so would they sign an anti-pornography petition to try to restore that world to their children?

With such psychographic information we can begin to see how an individual in the target audience might perceive the emotional or rational rewards of adopting an idea or buying a product or service. Such information is going to be very important in fine-tuning the audience selection process that will target your message and help you develop a persuasive message for that audience.

Predicting the Persuasion Sequence

Knowing your audience and the self-image, attitudes and ideas that are important to them leads us logically to the next step in the persuasion platform: planning the message that might move them to take an action that will help you meet your objective. The first step is to establish the probable persuasive sequence your audience members will follow as they consider their decision on your issue.

In Chapter 1, we examined the learn–feel–do persuasion model as a method for predicting how people will approach a decision. It is time to apply that model to real-life situations. After examining your audience's relationship to the issues and the ideas your audience will consider, you will be able to predict their decision-making process.

Given your audience's financial background, would the decision you're asking it to make represent a huge sacrifice? If not, it might be a low-consequence decision. If the decision you want also doesn't demand that people in your audience sacrifice their ethics or other things they value, then it's definitely a low-consequence decision and you can place the decision process in the lower half of the learn–feel–do model. If you determine it's a high-consequence decision, it goes in the upper half of the model.

Now we turn to the other dynamic in the persuasion sequence model, the emotional/rational factor. Are people in your audience making the decision based primarily on the emotional rewards they expect, or are they mainly using reason to decide what to do? If emotions are a small part of the decision process, the sequence belongs on the learn–feel–do model's right side. If emotion is the major factor, the process belongs on the left side of the model. Once you've oriented the decision factors in the persuasion model, you should be able to predict the persuasion sequence.

Deciding on the Persuaders

Knowing the persuasion sequence is important because it will help you decide what persuaders will be most effective in motivating your audience to make the decision that would help your client. For instance, if you were selling a toy train, anything you were to say about the product's quality materials, the manufacturer's 40th anniversary, the train's five-year warranty, or the store's convenient check-verification policy wouldn't convince a father who wants to buy a train for his son like the one he had as a child. What's more likely to push the father into a buying decision is seeing a soft-focused photo of a 1950s living room with a father and son playing with a toy train. Emotion, almost independent of rational thought, is the primary motive behind the father's buying decision.

Main Persuader.   In deciding on persuaders, you must first establish the primary force that will persuade your target audience to take the action you desire. You should be able to reduce it to one simple, declarative sentence that states a single motive for your primary audience.

Having determined audience descriptors and the persuasion sequence, you should have a good understanding of what aspect of your product or idea will be most persuasive. If you have determined that emotional rewards will rule the decision process, will a patriotic suggestion, such as that buying a particular car will keep jobs in the United States, be the most compelling persuader for your targeted audience? Or will perceived romantic pleasures anticipated from buying a sexy new sports car drive the audience's buying decision?

If rationality is primarily driving the decision, what aspect of the product or idea will most successfully persuade your audience? If you're working for a politician, why is her idea of letting a private firm manage prisons convincing? Is it because the firm's services will cost 15 percent less than state management? Or will voters more likely be persuaded if your client tells them that fewer private prison inmates return to crime? Whether emotional or rational reasons are important, your main task is to find the most persuasive idea for the particular audience you've described earlier in the platform. That will help you construct your document's lead sentence.

Secondary Persuaders.   After you establish the main persuader, you need to determine other elements of the idea or product that will help convince your audience to act. For instance, even though the audience will be most swayed by an emotional reason, are there rational reasons that bolster their decision-making process?

Secondary arguments can build a more persuasive case. For example, in the model train scenario, quality and warranty are secondary persuaders. Another example: Even though a taxpayer is convinced a new income tax for the library will help local children get ahead in an increasingly competitive world (primarily an emotional rationale), the fact that property taxes will be lowered and fixed-income senior citizens will not have to pay the occupational tax (both rational reasons) will help convince voters to support the tax.

Developing the Creative Strategy

Now, and only now, are you ready to distill your communication strategy from the bits of information you've discovered. The strategy statement is essentially a prediction of how the audience will receive and process the communication event to form a perception. The creative strategy statement (1) tells how the persuaders will affect the reader's mind, (2) incorporates what is known about the reader's psychographic and demographic characteristics, and (3) describes how the persuasion effect will meet the organization's objectives.

The strategy statement is often a free-form, stream-of-consciousness play of ideas and facts until a central conception of the persuasive message comes into focus. Will an emotional or rational appeal be more effective with your audience? What audience characteristics lead you to that conclusion? How can you construct the message to best emphasize those appeals to your audience? What do you want the receiver to think or feel after receiving your communication? Can you expect your audience to make a snap judgment about the issue or will people need to contemplate before they decide to accept or reject your proposal?

Here's an example of a strategy statement for a health magazine directed to young adults:

These 30-something men and women, confronted by their first wrinkles, know that their former lack of concern about their health and fitness just won't do anymore. Their carefully constructed self-image of vitality and kid-like exuberance won't accept reading a health magazine that discusses menopause, prostate cancer and other concerns of the over-50 crowd. They aren't worried so much about modifying their health habits to prevent illness as they are about preserving their attractiveness. If we demonstrate that our magazine is unconventional, youth-oriented and devoted to a health regimen that doesn't demand too many sacrifices from their party-filled lives, this young adult audience will likely integrate this magazine into their lifestyles.

Now let's examine an actual situation to see the process at work. I was hired by an organization comprised of five community choruses. The coalition had been formed to present a joint fund-raising concert on either Nov. 11 or Nov. 18. I was expected to devise a plan that would sell concert tickets.

How does one start? You can start anywhere. In this case, I started with a date. Nov. 11 is Veterans Day, and from that initial notion came a series of decisions. I recommended a concert on Nov. 11, so that we could transform the patriotic spirit of our area's residents into ticket sales. It seemed only natural to schedule the concert in an auditorium built to honor the city's World War I veterans and, just as naturally, I suggested the concert focus on patriotic music.

Those decisions led the group to direct the majority of its marketing to veterans' groups like the American Legion and the Veterans of Foreign Wars. To emphasize the event's two components—choral music and patriotism—to those groups, the concert theme was "Singing America's Praises." The logo colors and all the event's correspondence were, of course, red, white and blue. The patriotic images were intended to convince our target publics that we recognized the debt our country owed to its veterans. One good way to honor them would be to buy a ticket to the concert.

That's the general thought process that stimulated the creative strategy statement for one particular campaign. The only thing I can guarantee is that this creative strategy statement would be of little use to any other campaign. The creative strategy statement is intended to stimulate the creative act that is vital in a communication strategy. The concert example shows how the writer's imagination and creativity can be used to construct a unique communication campaign from information about audiences and their motivations.

Selecting the Medium

Once you know how you are going to present your message, you can pick the medium or media through which you'll transmit it. That decision usually involves more than deciding to write a news release. Should you use a brochure directed to a specific audience instead of communicating through newspapers or broadcast media directed to a mass audience? Would a one-on-one visit with pressure-group leaders be more effective? What about advertisements, speeches, newsletters, telephone marketing, or personal letters? There are scores of channels you could employ in your campaign. Don't abandon any possibility without thought.

Picking media is a big task and will be discussed in detail in Chapter 3 and in the application chapters. However, I want to emphasize here that a major part of planning a successful communication campaign lies in choosing a medium that reaches the precise audience that will help you solve your institutional problem. As I discussed in the psychographic section earlier in this chapter, when you're trying to sell fur coats, communicating with all people who are wealthy can actually be counterproductive to your campaign. If possible, you need to reach only those people who can afford a fur coat and who don't think it's morally objectionable to wear furs.

The targeting task often means bypassing mass media outlets and using more tightly focused media instead. It's not nearly so difficult with the proliferation of specialized magazines, newsletters and cable channels, as well as the increasing technology and selectivity possible with direct-marketing campaigns.

It's also necessary to select the type of media that best suits your message. For instance, research has found people can comprehend complex information more easily if it is in print media, but emotional appeals are usually more effective when received from broadcast media.

Developing the Timetable

Now that you've chosen and shaped the communication tools you'll use in your communication campaign, you can plan the details. The first step is to verify that the deadline date established in your objective is advantageous to your organization's goals. The timing of your communication campaign can often determine the success or failure of your efforts.

My own experience confirms this. A nonprofit arts organization for which I worked had for years sponsored a weeklong series of music performances by African-Americans in September. It was poorly attended, scarcely covered by the media, and a financial drain on the organization.

However, when I moved the music festival to February to coincide with Black History Month, it dramatically changed the event's fortunes. Because the media sought stories to highlight Black History Month, there was vastly greater media coverage, which drew more people to the concerts. The event actually showed a profit for the first time. A simple change of dates meant a significant change in the campaign's success.

Determining a timetable also helps you in other ways, as Memory Memo 2.3 specifies. After you've determined that the communication event has the correct timing—not competing with similar events, mega-events like the Super Bowl or religious holidays and scheduled for the most propitious time of the year or even hour of the day—you begin working backward from that date to build a timeline for the project.

Memory Memo 2.3
A timetable will

- help you capture the advantages of timing communication events
- help you determine if you've got enough resources to finish on time
- establish guideposts that let you check your progress

How many days or weeks before your deadline should the media be informed? How long before that must printing be done? Do sites have to be rented or stages and seating assembled? How long will that process take? Do other departments have to approve your plans or perform tasks for the campaign? How many days or weeks must you add to the process so that can be accomplished?

This routine is tremendously important. Assembling all this information lets you determine if the task is feasible with the time and staff you can devote to it. That early warning provides a cushion of safety so you can assemble any additional resources or personnel you'll need to complete the project on time. It allows you to pace your workload and provides a frequent check on whether you're on schedule to complete the project. All that information can be invaluable in helping to guarantee your capacity to reach your organization's objective.

Calculating the Budget

After determining what you want to accomplish and how you will undertake the task, the next step is to determine how to pay for the campaign and, just as important, whether the returns you anticipate from the campaign justify the expenditure. Campaign costs include expenditures for staff time, printing, mailing, advertising, travel, space rental and other expenses that occur with specific campaigns.

Although specific methods for estimating the cost-effectiveness of a communication campaign are beyond the scope of this chapter (we'll discuss some procedures in the final chapter), it's possible to justify expenses by computing how much money it costs to communicate with each prospect, or how much it costs to get a sale, ticket order or contribution. Even better is to determine how many dollars you have to spend in communication costs to get $100 in revenue.

Determining a budget is very important. A budget allows you to justify your efforts relative to the organization's goals. If you're spending $8 for a communication effort that generates $100 in revenue, you have obvious proof of how valuable you are to the organization and a legitimate claim on the organization's resources to support your efforts. Conversely, if your budget shows that you have to spend $105 to gain $100, you've received valuable justification for restructuring or even abandoning the project. Even the recommendation that you abandon a communication effort is extremely valuable as you try to use your organization's resources of money, personnel, time and talent to best effect.

Determining the Evaluation Process

The final step in the PR planning process is to determine if you've met the goals you've established. The evaluation is generally a one- or two-sentence statement that repeats the objective and deadline and indicates the procedure you'll use to measure whether you've met your goal. For instance, if you're trying to fund an endowment, it might be as simple as counting the total dollars pledged. In other situations, you might count the number of paid registrations for a conference or time how long it takes for a worker to perform a task.

Building evaluation into the process is a vital step in any planning system. Judging the success and payback of every major organizational communication process provides vital data on techniques that work or don't work. That helps guide you and your staff to the most efficient and effective tactics in subsequent campaigns.

PLANNING AND THE CURRENCY OF POWER IN THE ORGANIZATION

In many organizations, public relations is viewed as an adjunct to the institution's real purpose, to turn profits. In those organizations, the practice of public relations is viewed essentially as a social activity to gain for the company a pleasant image among its workers and the community.

But in professional organizations, public relations planning is vital for building respect and power for public relations practitioners. The planning processes force practitioners to establish definite goals for public relations activities that are directly related to the company's other bottom-line goals. When PR practitioners reach those goals, the demonstrable value that public relations had added to the organization allows practitioners to buy their way into the company's ruling coalition. That's why I call public relations planning the currency of power.

SUMMARY

- Planning, either formal or informal, is a part of any public relations communication process.
- Formal public relations planning improves the probability of a communication campaign's success by guiding practitioners to consider all elements of the communication process: selecting audiences and predicting their needs and characteristics, then selecting persuasive messages and media that will most effectively move those audiences.
- Planning helps the practitioner gain control over resources and commitment within the institution by providing a mechanism that proves the value of communication activities to the organization, establishing priorities for the PR tasks that are most beneficial, and helping practitioners finish projects on time.
- A persuasion platform is a public relations planning process that combines the business management techniques of the management-by-objective process with the advertising industry's creative platform.
- The persuasion platform's 10 steps help to define an institutional problem that communication can address, describe an audience that can help the institution solve the problem, stimulate a message that will persuade that audience, and determine the work necessary to deliver that message to the targeted audience.
- Determining an institutional problem before beginning a communication campaign focuses a practitioner's efforts on those tasks that return the greatest dividends to the institution.
- A communication campaign objective sets a measurable goal that, if met, would contribute directly to solving the institutional problem. Objectives should be reachable and stated so it can be precisely determined if they've been met within a specified period.
- Although communication can't be measured explicitly, practitioners can isolate and measure the direct or indirect results of communication by determining changes in attendance, profits, participation, time or productivity that follow a change in communication practices.
- Demographics is a statistical description of an audience that includes age, income, profession, geographic location, gender and race. Demographics generally help the practitioner identify people who have the capacity to act on a message.
- In defining a targeted audience, practitioners must define the people who have the capacity to make a decision about your issue or product. Sometimes that public differs from the one most directly affected by the issue.
- Psychographics describe an audience by isolating its probable emotional, self-image and lifestyle factors. Psychographics generally help the practitioner identify people who have a motive to act on a message.
- Although demographics often help us find a medium through which to deliver a message to a specific audience, psychographic factors are often more helpful in creating a message that will persuade the audience to take a particular action.

- An audience's demographic and psychographic descriptors can help a practitioner decide on the most persuasive reasons for that audience to act on an issue.
- The creative strategy is a play of ideas and facts that helps a writer develop a central creative conception of a public relations message. It is developed by speculating how the persuaders will support and enhance the audience's needs and self-image to make its members undertake an action that meets the institution's objective.
- A medium for a public relations message should reach the precise members of the public you need to convince and be perceived as credible by that public.
- The persuasion platform's timetable is an estimate of the time and staff commitment a project will require and establishes guideposts that assure a project will be completed on schedule.
- Calculating a budget is vital: It is a formal request for organizational resources to support your communication effort as well as an indication of whether the potential benefits from your campaign justify those expenses.
- The persuasion platform's evaluation statement restates the objective and summarizes the procedure that will be used to determine whether the communication effort has satisfied that objective.

THINK PIECES

1. Describe yourself demographically, then psychographically. Which media would be effective in reaching people with your demographic profile and your psychographic profile?
2. Analyze how different audiences might be interested in a story from today's newspaper. Which audience would be most important for the story? Why?

MANAGEMENT PROBLEMS

D1.5
D7.5
D9.3
D10.1
D10.5

WRITING ASSIGNMENTS

Persuasion Platforms
D2.7
D4.9
D9.8
D10.5

ADDITIONAL READING

Broom, Glen M., and Dozier, David M. *Using Research in Public Relations: Applications in Program Management*. Englewood Cliffs, N.J.: Prentice-Hall, 1990.

Crable, Richard E., and Vibbert, Steven L. *Public Relations as Communication Management*. Edina, Minn.: Bellwether Press, 1986.

Dozier, David M., et al. *Manager's Guide to Excellence in Public Relations and Communication Management*. Hillside, N.J.: Lawrence Erlbaum Associates, 1995.

Ferguson, S. D. "Strategic Planning for Issues Management: The Communicator as Environmental Analyst." *Canadian Journal of Communication* 18:1 (Winter 1993): 33–50.

Grunig, James E., and Hunt, Todd. *Managing Public Relations*. New York: Holt, Rinehart and Winston, 1984.

Hiebert, Ray, ed. *Precision Public Relations*. New York: Longman, 1988.

Longren, Richard E. *Communication by Objectives: A Guide to Productive and Cost-Effective Public Relations and Marketing*. Englewood Cliffs, N.J.: Prentice Hall, 1983.

Nager, Norman R., and Allen, T. Harrell. *Public Relations Management by Objectives*. Lanham, Md.: University Press of America, 1991.

Noelle-Neumann, Elizabeth. *The Spiral of Silence: Public Opinion—Our Social Skin*. Chicago: University of Chicago Press, 1984.

Petty, Richard, and Cacioppo, John. *Communication and Persuasion*. New York: Springer-Verlag, 1987.

Shafer, Peter. *Adding Value to the Public Affairs Function*. Washington, D.C.: The Public Affairs Council, 1994.

Smith, Ronald D. "Psychological Type and Public Relations: Theory, Research, and Applications." *Journal of Public Relations Research* 5:3 (1995): 177–199.

Standard Format for Persuasion Platform

my pr firm

123 Main Street / Hometown, Any State / 12345 / 505 555-1234

TITLE IDENTIFYING CLIENT AND PROJECT

Client Problem:

The client problem is a brief exploration of the difficulties the client wants to overcome. The client problem should not be concerned exclusively with "improving audience awareness" or "increasing sales," but should explore the root causes of the difficulties that keep your client from gaining its desired impact on certain discrete audience groups.

Objective:

The objective statement should be one declarative sentence that isolates a single, measurable goal that's important for the institution to reach and then states a deadline and a way to determine if that goal has been met.

Audience Characteristics:

Demographic statement: The demographic statement identifies the targeted audience by age, income, residence, profession, gender, race, marital status, and other factors that indicate the audience's capacity to make a decision. A common mistake is to develop one persuasion platform to persuade two distinct publics. Because audiences are so different, it won't work. If you want to target two audiences, design a separate persuasion platform for each audience. *Psychographic statement:* The psychographic statement uses surveys, marketing statistics, focus group interviews (and sometimes the practitioner's informed but informal psychological analysis) to explore self-image considerations that determine the audience's motive to make a decision that will help your client.

Probable Persuasion Sequence:

The probable persuasion is your best prediction of the decision sequence your targeted audience will use in responding to your persuasive message. You'll choose one of the quadrants from the learn–feel–do model after assessing whether your audience considers this a low- or high-consequence decision and whether the audience perceives that emotional or rational rewards will be most important.

43

Persuaders:

Main selling idea: The main selling idea will be a single declarative sentence derived from the persuasion sequence's prediction. If you indicate that emotion will drive behavior, your main selling idea will be an emotional persuader. If you indicate rational rewards will drive behavior, your main selling idea should provide reasoned incentives to your intended audience.

Secondary persuaders: The secondary persuaders provide the weight of evidence in the decision process. They give receivers extra reasons to act as the client desires.

Creative Strategy Statement:

The creative strategy statement is often free-form, stream-of-consciousness brainstorming that speculates on how the main selling idea will influence the psychographic motives of the intended audience to convince that audience to take the action that will satisfy the client objective. Often, it results in a headline or word play that will be important in creating your persuasion document.

Media Choices:

Choosing your media forces you to consider the wide variety of mass media as well as specialized media that will deliver your persuasive message accurately and credibly to your intended audience.

Timetable:

The timetable requires the public relations practitioner to contemplate how scheduling will affect the perception of and response to a communication event. The timetable also helps you determine if you can finish a project within the allotted time and provides useful guideposts to keep you on schedule. The information in the timetable will be more useful if presented in tabular rather than narrative form.

Evaluation Statement:

The evaluation statement repeats the measurable goal and the deadline from the client objective statement, and describes the method you will use to measure whether you've reached that objective.

Full Text of a Persuasion Platform

**PERSUASION PLATFORM FOR MORELAND CHORUS
SEASON BROCHURE**

Client Problem:

After a period of internal dissension and financial hardship, the Moreland Chorus is trying to remake its image under the guidance of a new musical director who wants to emphasize more accessible, popular music. This is a change from recent history when the chorus was known for performing difficult and very serious classical music.

Although this entails a change in the way people view the chorus, it is probably a very positive change, as two other choruses performing serious music are beginning operations. However, the Moreland Chorus's ability to target its traditional customer, the arts-conscious person, has been weakened by these two other groups, which are sponsored by mainstream professional music organizations.

Objective:

Sell 160 season tickets by the end of the Oct. 16 concert.

Audience Characteristics:

Demographics: middle- to upper-income individuals primarily in midtown and East End locations. Ages 28 to 60.

Psychographics: Our target audience really hasn't entered the city's cultural mainstream. We are trying to attract yuppies who want to buy a little sophistication to accompany the rest of their success. They want to feel they belong to something that is making a difference, that is having the impact of changing the city or the culture, because the other activities in which they are involved are having that effect. However, they want all this without much effort on their part. Even though they have settled into the security of home and hearth, they still think of themselves as "hip" and want the feeling they are on the cutting edge of life.

They position themselves against the culture of the preceding generation. Even though they think highly of themselves, they have not been admitted to the society structure of their community and associate the established arts organizations with that rejection.

Probable Persuasion Sequence:

do–feel–learn

Persuaders:

Main selling idea: The Moreland Chorus is a fun, accessible cultural experience.

Secondary persuaders:
    Tickets don't cost much.
    There are few concerts to which to commit.
    Some popular selections are on each concert program.
    Composers of our generation are featured.

Creative Strategy Statement:

I feel the fastest way to establish this new perception in our audience's eyes is to state more or less directly what it is we are opposed to. We can say we are opposed to boring music, to looking at a concert as some sort of delicate china music box that we can observe and marvel at but cannot touch or enjoy. We want to establish a concept that is very age-centered— that talks about composers of our generation and pokes fun at the self-important conceptions of the old-time organizations.

Instead, we are offering fun—music and culture that are accessible, music and culture that are presented well but that don't take themselves seriously; music and culture performed in ways that translate the excitement of being onstage—of being a part of the concert experience—to people in the audience.

Media Choices:

    three-fold brochure mailed to audience targeted by age, income and lack of affiliation with other mainstream performing arts groups
    follow-up postcard
    news release
    newspaper ad
    program stuffer for opening concert
    personal sales pitch by conductor at first concert

Timetable:

July 30:	brochure copy approved by board
Aug. 12:	brochure printing completed
Aug. 18:	addressing completed; drop in mail
Sept. 10:	follow-up postcard to people who haven't responded
Oct. 1:	news release mailed to music critics and calendar editors
Oct. 10:	newspaper ad advertising first concert
Oct. 16:	concert; distribute fliers for season ticket

Budget:

printing and production costs		*ticket revenue*
brochure:	$850	
postcard:	$600	
release:	$56	
ad:	$400	
postage:	$230	
administration:	$160	160 tickets @ $30 each =
printing and production costs		*ticket revenue*
Total cost:	*$2,296*	*Total revenue: $4,800*
Net profit:	*$2,504*	*Cost-effectiveness ratio: 1.92*

Evaluation Statement:

Count number of paid season ticket orders at end of Oct. 16 concert. Total should be 160 or more.

## chapter 3

PR Research and Targeting: Information for Decision Making

REAL-LIFE LESSONS

In one of my first projects after college, I worked for a state association of county administrators fighting a gasoline sales tax sponsored by the state highway department. The proposed tax, which was to be voted on in the fall election, would have raised $63 million of gasoline taxes, and the state highway department would have taken every cent for itself, even though counties maintained a vast majority of the state's roads.

My job was to prove that county roads in the state were underfunded, so that there would be persuasive evidence for voters that they should vote down the tax increase. I called librarians, a national association of state treasurers, economists, construction companies and national government experts. I asked them if they could tell me how my state rated on the proportion of state gas tax funding given to county road districts. No one knew, so I started trying to find out for myself. For days, I sat at my desk poring over columns and columns of tiny numbers on pages and pages of photocopies pulled from U.S. Department of Transportation statistics. I carefully poked the keys of a handheld calculator, adding up a column of expenditures to get a state total, then adding another series of numbers to figure the money that counties and towns spent on roads, and finally adding a set of numbers to obtain the money spent on state-maintained roads. Then I started dividing to get the proportion of the total each jurisdiction spent on roads and divided that number to obtain a ratio that I could use to compare one state to another so I could rank-order them.

That was one state. That was 88 calculations. Fifty states, seven days and 4,400 calculations later, I could rank-order the states in terms of the percentage of each state's gas tax revenue. Just one simple statistic.

But with those thousands of taps on my calculator, I found my state was the nation's second stingiest in sharing state gas tax money with its county road districts. With that, I had the raw data for a news release that helped my client defeat the state gasoline tax vote. Two years later, the group had a new initiative on the ballot that gave the counties and small cities over half of the revenue the new gas tax would raise. I had accomplished my task.

Fifteen years later, it's a different matter. Now, with just a few keystrokes on a computer, I can get *t*-scores, *z*-scores, regression analyses, and scores of other types of statistics crunching.

The whole concept of public relations research has changed. When I started, I determined PR effectiveness by the number of newspaper clippings I could amass during the year. I bragged about my 1,800 column inches and carried a fat scrap book with pieces of newsprint hanging from the sides.

Now, there's an emphasis on proving the worth of public relations by showing whether it helps in reaching an organization's goals. Before we plan a campaign, we now evaluate audiences to see whether they can deliver benefits to the institution. Instead of dragging out press clippings to prop up our self-image, we now demonstrate that our work contributed to better productivity, or bigger profits, or fewer labor disputes.

That's the point of research in contemporary public relations. We don't do it just to look educated or to build a perception of professionalism. We do it because it gives us a better chance of success and proves the successes we bring to our clients.

WHAT YOU KNOW

- Segmenting audiences into differentiated groups that respond to different persuaders helps guide cost-effective communication efforts.
- Determining an audience's psychographics as well as its demographics is necessary to predict messages that will motivate each audience to action.
- Choosing the right media, including non-mass media, is very important in involving publics that can take action.

WHAT YOU'LL LEARN

- There are a vast number of research resources that can guide the planning of each aspect of the persuasion platform process.
- Tracking the actual behavior of intended audiences is the most accurate gauge of a practitioner's persuasion efforts.

USING THE RESEARCH RESULTS YOU ALREADY KNOW

Although the idea of research may sound overwhelming, involving particle accelerators, electron microscopes, white lab coats and doomed white mice, research toward writing is something you've been doing all your life.

You've discovered how to construct sentences to make them the most intelligible to your readers. You've learned all sorts of general information that simplifies your communication tasks, such as that most Americans know where Chicago is, so that it isn't necessary to tell them it's in the United States, but it is necessary to tell Americans where Katmandu is. You probably know that sending a letter through the post office is a much more economical medium to reach your parents than buying a network television commercial. These are all forms of informal research that you have encountered in your previous education. Because you know this information, you're better able to design an effective message for a particular audience.

Formalize these steps and that's basically what research for writing is all about— effectively and systematically gathering information about your organization, the audience with which you want to communicate, the media through which you can communicate and the effectiveness of the message in performing the tasks you want to accomplish. Sometimes that information stems from personal experience. Often it is learned by studying the published reports of experts. Sometimes it comes from personally interviewing experts. Often it comes from undertaking independent research activities yourself. In this chapter, we'll learn how to standardize the research process that encompasses all these different methods.

CONVERTING RESEARCH INTO WRITING

In Chapter 1, we discussed how the receiver-centered communication model helps guide the writing process. As you will remember, the receiver-centered model was based on the premise that we must consider the information needs of the person receiving the message before we form the message to answer those needs.

That task calls for research. The only way we can understand what is important to our audience is to systematically observe and interpret behaviors and attitudes of the audience with which we are trying to communicate. But as Memory Memo 3.1 points out, finding out about our audience is only the first of the research efforts we have to make as a public relations practitioner.

> *Memory Memo 3.1*
> *Research for writing gathers information systematically about:*
>
> - your organization's reasons for communicating
> - the audience whose help you need to solve your problems
> - the media to reach that audience
> - how effectively you've reached your goals

In fact, research accompanies each step in the communication model (see Figure 3.1). As we've seen, we must know about the audience's information needs before we can compose a message. Equally important is to know the organizational problems that can be solved through communication. That's also a question research can help us answer.

Research can also give you information on your audience's appropriate reading level and familiarity with jargon. That information, along with knowledge of other factors, will help you design a message appropriate for your audience's capabilities.

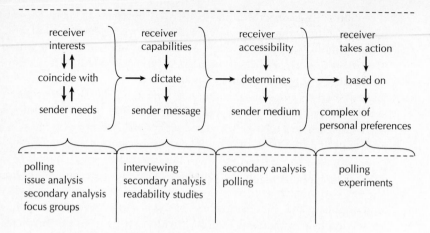

FIGURE 3.1   Research in the receiver-centered model
Research should occur at each step of the receiver-centered communication model. Here are the most common types of research undertaken during each step in the communication model.

In addition, research can tell you which is the best medium to reach your audience and then can help you evaluate the success of your campaign.

For many public relations practitioners, research provokes feelings of dread. Because many students enter public relations fields because of strong communication and language skills, they often feel insecure when they learn that research, and what they perceive as its reliance on statistics, will be an important part of their daily duties. It's true that basic statistical knowledge is needed for some forms of research, but research is much more than simply crunching numbers.

Remember that you're involved in many simple aspects of research every day. Let's say you go to the same restaurant and order french fries every day for four weeks. After four weeks you notice the fries are always overcooked on Wednesday. When you investigate, you find the regular cook's day off is Wednesday. You conclude that's the reason for the burned french fries. In effect, you've done research. Research is simply the systematic gathering of information about a problem.

COMMUNICATION AUDITS: FINDING WHAT WORKS AND WHAT YOU SHOULD WORK ON

One of the first tasks research can accomplish is to find out if you need to communicate at all. Too often, through ignorance or misinformation, practitioners neglect communication campaigns vital to their institution's security and prosperity and instead spend too much time and energy communicating about issues unimportant to the organization's success. At other times a lack of knowledge causes them to waste their energies communicating in ways that are counterproductive to the institution's mission. As James Strenski points out (see Box 3.1), public relations must show a

BOX 3.1   Views from the Field

James B. Strenski
*Strenski is chairman and chief executive of Public Commu-
nications Inc., in Tampa, Fla., and one of the founders of
WORLDCOM Group, an international partnership of public
relations firms.*

*You talk about tracking the bottom-line results of public relations.
What does that mean?*

Tracking bottom-line results starts with setting measurable objectives at the
outset of a public relations program. If it's a marketing program, objectives
could include whether we generate a specific number of inquiries over a period of time, or whether there are specific increases in sales that we can
trace to public relations exposure. If the program is related to employees,
we might measure whether we can detect increases in productivity or de-
creases in absenteeism. If it's an issues management situation, we could use
before-and-after perception surveys to measure changes in public attitude.

*It seems difficult to determine the effects of communication. How
can it be done?*

Public relations is not an exact science. It is difficult to determine the effects
of communications, but if you use benchmark studies to establish where you
started from, it's much easier to decide what changes you've made. If you
know what initial perceptions you're trying to correct, you're much more
likely to implement a communications program that a year or 18 months
later will show marked changes for the better.

*What strengths does an institution gain by incorporating a
comprehensive research program in its public relations efforts?*

Research is the foundation for any public relations program. It provides
CEOs and their staff or counsel with an objective view of where they stand
with key audiences. Carefully designed, it can also provide an early warning
system for changing audience needs and attitudes toward an organization.
That gives CEOs a chance to look to the future and plan for challenges and
competition down the road instead of simply reacting to short-term market
shifts. With that long-term view, an institution can develop realistic and relevant programs to solve its problems and respond to new opportunities in
the marketplace. Finally, public relations research gives practitioners a way
to justify new initiatives and their costs by showing the bottom-line results
in higher sales or changing attitudes.

—Used with permission of James B. Strenski

bottom-line orientation if it is to justify management's investment in communication activities.

Research can help pinpoint the communication duties that will be most important for your institution's public relations unit. Communication audits are a first step to that goal. A communication audit, in its simplest form, is similar to a financial audit undertaken by an accountant. A financial audit attempts to form an economic portrait of a company by analyzing areas of waste and impropriety as well as spotlight company products that have excellent returns. Such a profile is useful to investors and company managers as they decide how efficiently the company has been using its resources to produce goods or services.

A communication audit examines communication issues, as Memory Memo 3.2 states, by determining the opinions and attitudes important publics have toward an institution and comparing them to opinions and attitudes the institution wishes they had. In many ways, a favorable public impression of an institution can be as vitally important to its success as a flattering financial audit, as those managers who have endured consumer boycotts, employee strikes and the fallout from industrial accidents or tampering could attest. Just as financial factors affect a business's prospects for survival and profit, public opinion can help create and sustain stockholder investment, consumer satisfaction, and a favorable business and regulatory environment.

Memory Memo 3.2
A communication audit

- determines the attitudes our organization's publics hold
- compares them to the ones we would like them to hold

Communication audits are generally conducted through some form of polling or survey method, which will be discussed later in this chapter. A typical communication audit might seek to discover the public's perception of a company's commitment to environmental issues. By surveying representative individuals from the company's many important publics, a public relations practitioner can assess whether the company has been successful in communicating its attention to the environment. Just as important, the practitioner can find if the company has been more successful in publicizing its recycling efforts than in making people aware of its pollution control measures, for instance, or see if certain publics are lagging in their understanding of the company's plans. With that knowledge, it will be possible to design a targeted campaign to correct certain misconceptions about the company's environmental commitment or to reach certain audiences.

ISSUES FORECASTING: FACING ISSUES BEFORE THEY BECOME PROBLEMS

Whereas communication audits are very helpful in assessing the effectiveness of past communication efforts and in constructing relatively short-term plans for public relations communication, other methods are useful for long-term, strategic plans. If we think one of the important roles of public relations is to foresee and react to societal changes before they become problems, we must have ways of detecting those groundswells of public opinion early. That important public relations objective calls for issues forecasting, a complex and still-developing area of PR research.

As presented in popular magazines on the eve of a new century, issues forecasting seems to rely as much on wishful thinking and psychic talents as on a strong research base. Some of this informal futures research is based on little more than speculation.

For instance, one magazine predicted the 1990s would be vastly different from the 1980s because aging baby boomers would deemphasize their careers and demand more leisure time. Other predictions seem more ludicrous. An issue of *USA Weekend* ran a feature article predicting men would reassert their masculinity in the 1990s by starting to wear boxer shorts.

However, issues forecasting can also be more scientific and systematic. Although there are scores of different issues forecasting techniques and numerous ways to evaluate issues forecasting data, most PR practitioners use one of the four major types of forecasting models listed in Memory Memo 3.3. Although more forecasting techniques are being developed constantly, three of these are relatively simple and accessible for the majority of PR writers.

Memory Memo 3.3
Four PR forecasting models:

- Scanning—using media to predict future trends
- Scenario writing—writing contingency plans
- Trend extrapolation—betting on trends reversing
- Computer simulations—predicting with computer numeric models

---

Scanning: Using the Media to Help Predict New Opportunities

Scanning is probably the simplest form of issues forecasting research. Individuals review specialized journals in their field for new developments that may change the basic issues or products in the industry. Just as important, they also systematically review consumer magazines, publications dealing with politics, ethics, lifestyles and other issues, and even new developments in television programs and advertising. The individuals reviewing the media sources generally write a critique indicating what they think is new or significant about what the media are communicating. From that distillation of current media subjects, analysts draw social and economic trends that may be important in predicting future consumer desires and planning communication and marketing strategies to meet them.

Scenario Writing: Preparing to React to the Possibilities

In scenario writing, your task is to explore the ramifications of particular events or courses of action systematically. If your company were to have a major industrial accident or a product liability suit, what would be the worst possible result in terms of media coverage, worker protests, insurance claims, and public outcry? After figuring out that worst-case scenario you can begin to develop an institutional policy that would make those extreme circumstances less likely to occur, as well as plan a communication campaign to minimize the damage if any of those scenarios were to happen.

Trend Extrapolation: Using the Cycle of History to Predict Trends

Trend extrapolation is founded on the assumption that many major social and economic trends follow a regular pattern. Statisticians and social scientists have found that after a trend moves in one direction for a certain period of time, there generally is some reaction, a backlash, that tends to return the activity closer to previous levels. As you know from your own reading and experiences, business cycles, birth rates and other demographic and economic movements can sometimes be predicted by these repeating cycles. In addition to those matters that seem more purely mathematical, trend extrapolation has been used to help estimate patterns of social activities, including such seemingly unpredictable elements as levels of political activism, sexual permissiveness or even women's fashions.

Computer Simulations: Imagining the Future Through Numbers

In addition to these methods, an increasing number of issues forecasting applications are being found for computer simulations. The simulations use mathematical formulas accounting for major variables from population growth to consumer complaints to employee satisfaction indexes. By calculating the interplay among those business and environmental factors over a period of time, computer simulations help predict a probable scenario.

Analyzing and Using Issues Forecasting Data

After these trends have been isolated, their effect on the institution must be predicted before a coherent communication campaign can be established to address them. For instance, your scanning of major consumer media reveals a number of articles predicting that as male baby boomers age, their attitudes (along with their bodies) will soften and they'll be looking for more intimacy in their relationships.

If you conclude that this is a legitimate trend, you'll need to determine how it will affect your company. If your company makes blue jeans, it may be necessary to add to the product line jeans that are cut fuller for more mature, full-bodied men.

In addition to basic changes in what the company sells, it's important to adjust your company's message. To persuade an older audience, it may be necessary to change the emotional focus of your commercials and promotions to appeal to comfort instead of styling and sexuality. You may want to replace young models in your ads with older men, or replace the he-man cowboy appeals of earlier commercials with images of men enjoying time with their children or male-bonding camaraderie with their friends. This perceived change in your audience might even lead you to change the media you use to reach your customers.

You'll notice your research begins to take you into areas that aren't usually defined as being within the management scope of public relations. That's what it's supposed to do. As with all research directed toward defining topics that will be important to your institution, issues forecasting should serve as an early warning system to help address potential problem areas your client might face before they become problems. Instead of merely modifying a communication effort to address an old problem, issues forecasting sometimes compels the institution to change its products or even its fundamental philosophy.

Remember the lessons that management-by-objective planning stresses. Instead of mechanically continuing previous communication campaigns, use the knowledge gained from research to guide you in concentrating your time, money and communication skills toward those problems where your efforts will help your organization most.

SECONDARY RESEARCH: DISCOVERING WHAT OTHERS HAVE FOUND

Although there is frequently a need to do independent, original research, many public relations problems can be solved by examining marketing research, public opinion polls, government statistics, census data and other research that has already been compiled.

Government Statistics: Your Tax Dollars Researching for You

There are thousands of sources for this previously collected information, or secondary research. One of the most prolific compilers of information is the federal government. You can get a quick impression of the volume of statistics the government collects by looking at a book called *The Statistical Abstract of the United States*. It has information on population growth, industrial production, and even figures on how many people during past years were murdered by strangulation.

But the Statistical Abstract is only the beginning. Most levels of government, from city to federal, record transcripts of all hearings and public meetings. In addition, federal, state and local governments compile thousands of reports each year, on subjects as diverse as air pollution, welfare reform, technological advances, and housing statistics. The government also keeps detailed records on most court cases.

Let's examine the extent of information available from just one of those government agencies. The Census Bureau compiles many studies in addition to the familiar Census of Population. The bureau also collects statistics for censuses of retail trade, wholesale trade, housing, agriculture and transportation.

Again, the extent of the information available is impressive. In the Census of

Retail Trade, you could find how many convenience stores there are in your county, how many people they employ and what the average sales per store is. That is routine material that you might expect is available somewhere.

However, the Census Bureau also publishes very esoteric information. Using a volume called Block Statistics, for instance, it's possible to take a single city block and tell not only how many people live on that block, but what the block's average household income is, how far its residents have to commute to work, what type of job they have at the end of that trip, or even how many toilets they have in their homes.

I don't offer this information to suggest that to finish a communication task you'll often need to know the average number of toilets in a particular city block. This merely illustrates how much information the government collects on Americans. There will often be times when someone in your organization prefaces a statement by saying, "If we only knew. . . ." The important thing to remember is that there's a good chance some researcher has collected information about the subject. If you have the persistence and the skills to find it, you'll most likely be able to answer that question.

In short, there is a tremendous amount of information available to you and your organization from the federal government. Luckily, three indexes to this vast store of knowledge exist. The Congressional Index is the guide to congressional debate. The Congressional Information Service (CIS) is a way to find transcripts of congressional hearings and committee research reports. The American Statistics Index (ASI) leads you to information contained in government studies and publications. Using the ASI, it's possible to search for a very specific statistic. Arranged by subject, the ASI will refer you to the correct report or census form. Although the government has been somewhat slower than other information sources to use available computer technology to help researchers, it is now bringing compiled indexes onto microfiche and compact discs.

Most federal statistics from July 1976 to the present are accessible by using a computer disk file called the Monthly Catalog to U.S. Government Publications. The same listings in book form also catalog government publications issued before 1976.

The ASI, CIS and the Monthly Catalog of U.S. Government Publications can be found in most major college libraries or public libraries. If you have specific research questions involving census statistics that the Census Bureau hasn't collated in a way that precisely solves your problem, most Census Bureau data is also available on computer tapes so your company's programming specialists can extract particular information.

Information from local and state government sources is not so well indexed. Although some states and localities have thorough filing and retrieval systems, others do not. For this information, consult a research librarian in a local library for guidance on finding those sources.

Publication Indexes: Experts, Experts Everywhere

Magazines and journals also provide information useful in public relations tasks. You retrieve this information through publication indexes. You're probably already familiar with the one covering general interest publications, the Reader's Guide to Periodicals. For newspapers, NewsBank lists articles from nearly every U.S. daily newspaper. Major newspapers like *The Wall Street Journal, The Times of London* and the *New York Times* publish complete indexes for their own newspapers. Many other newspapers have library services available that index all newspaper articles.

In addition to these sources for consumer publications, there are indexes for specialized journals: for business magazines, the Business Periodicals Index; for the natural sciences, the Biological and Agricultural Index; for medical journals, the Index Medicus; for information from sociology and psychology journals and other related areas, the Social Sciences Index.

Databases: Better Research Through Computers

Increasingly, the data in the indexes above as well as millions of other items of information are being put into computer databases. The presence of this information in a computer does more than just switch your search from a book to a computer screen, as Memory Memo 3.4 details.

First, the computer database compiles all the sources about a particular topic so that you can examine all the articles written about the subject for years and years without having to go from one annual or semiannual volume to another to get a complete picture. More important, the database can combine research topics so you can more precisely target your search. Virtually every database allows you to search for research topics by using key words, which are words about important topics discussed in the article.

Memory Memo 3.4
Computer database advantages:

- combines research sources so you don't have to examine many separate volumes
- combines research topics so you can target your search

For instance, if you were working for a college faculty union and researching the teaching effectiveness of part-time college faculty members, you would find there are more than 1,600 articles that are categorized by the key words *teaching effectiveness* in the Education Index, 28,000 articles on *college faculty*, and about 600 articles listed using the key words *part-time faculty.* Although it would be virtually impossible to check 30,000 articles to see if any deal specifically with your precise subject, you can ask the computer to give you only education journal articles that include information on all three areas (teaching effectiveness, college faculty, part-time faculty). With those instructions, the computer goes through all those thousands of articles and weeds out all but the 16 articles that specifically discuss the teaching effectiveness of part-time faculty at colleges and universities. This sort of power tremendously simplifies the search for background information from which to compile releases and other writing.

Databases are increasingly giving researchers more power. As it is commonplace for publication articles to be typeset using computers, more and more databases no longer rely solely on key words. Instead, because every word in the article already has been typed into a computer, another computer can search every word in every article in the entire database looking for a specific word or series of words. For example, Nexis, a news service that covers major news publications, gives you the power to conduct an on-line search through an entire database for instances in which your company has been mentioned in an article or a trend has been mentioned in the mainstream press.

Some of the major database sources that might be useful to public relations practitioners are listed in the Ready Reference section at the end of this chapter.

Audience Surveys: Converting Audience Actions into Audience Profiles

You can find even more information on audiences and the media that can reach them by using marketing statistics research compiled by two companies: Simmons Market Research Bureau and Mediamark Research. These multivolume sets of statistics are organized into three basic categories. The first section deals with overall demographic information about the general population, including age, education level, income, occupation, race, gender and geographic location. The two reference directories then break the population into smaller and smaller demographic subgroups. For instance, the directories list the total number of men and women in the population, then give the number of women from 18 to 24 years old who are homemakers and have children under age 5. For each of those subgroups, the services collect the same statistics: For instance, they tell how many female homemakers between 18 and 24 live in the Northeast, or have a household income of more than $50,000, or graduated from college.

Both Simmons and Mediamark also examine which types of people can be reached through individual advertising media. With these media-use statistics, you can find out not only how many people watch the "CBS Evening News," but how many watchers there are among men who make between $25,000 and $35,000 (or women who live in the Southwest, or blacks, or clerical workers). The same statistics are given for all other regular network programming, including comedies, dramatic series and movie programs. You can find the same information for approximately 150 major magazines, 24 radio networks and more than 20 cable television networks, ranging from The Weather Channel to MTV.

The statistics also include radio listening habits, detailing, for instance, how many female homemakers who live in rural counties listen to the radio in the late morning, or how many men who did not graduate from high school listen to classical music radio stations. The statistics even extend to examining consumer attention to billboards and direct-mail advertising.

The third section of both Simmons and Mediamark examines the characteristics of people who use certain types, as well as certain brands, of products. Using the same demographic categories, each statistical service details whether more Midwesterners or more Southerners drink whole-bean caffeinated coffee and whether women who make under $15,000 a year buy more Pledge furniture polish than those who make over $50,000 a year.

Each then provides a breakdown of the media used most widely by the buyers of certain products. Thus, it's possible to know if it's more likely that a woman who buys sewing handicrafts by mail order watches "All My Children" or "60 Minutes."

The range of products and services for which it is possible to trace this information is truly staggering. The list of products for which Simmons summarizes marketing statistics includes cars, alcoholic beverages, 24-hour banking cards, foreign travel, kitchen spices, charitable giving, fast-food restaurants, and hemorrhoid remedies.

This extensive marketing data can benefit a PR practitioner in many ways, some obvious, some more obscure. For instance, it's apparent that you could use the information about media-use patterns to help choose which media outlets would reach the consumers of your company's product. By looking at the product-use statistics, you could compile a fairly accurate demographic portrait of the type of person who uses your company's services.

There are other, more intriguing uses for the statistics. In Chapter 2, we discussed the relative inefficiency of demographic information in predicting human behavior. Demographics, we said, showed a receiver's capacity to take action, whereas psychographics revealed a motive to take action.

In Chapter 2, the only psychographic descriptions we could amass were pure speculation. With the Mediamark and Simmons marketing statistics we are forming a more defensible psychographic interpretation. I'll give you an example. Let's say your company is exploring how to conduct a PR communication campaign supporting the marketing effort for a spice rack that uses a computer to dispense the product.

By looking up heavy users of seasonings and spices (Sidebar 3.1), you can learn something about people most likely to buy this product. In the pure demographic data, few bits of information seem significant. If you look for index numbers in column D that diverge sharply from the average, which is 100, you'll find very few high index numbers that indicate concentrations of people who use lots of spices. There are a few very low index numbers that indicate people who don't use spices: people who did not finish high school, single-parent and single-person households, poor people and people over 65. It basically seems that everyone uses spices. How is it possible to target a communication campaign if everyone uses a product?

You can't target if demographics are all you know. But by looking at the media-use patterns, you're much more likely to discover important information about your audience's motives for buying spices. That's logical, because people have no choice in demographic characteristics such as what age or gender or race they are, and only a limited choice about where they live, what type of job they have or whether they're married. However, they do have a lot of choices in what they read, watch or listen to. We can see the psychographic publics into which people cluster by looking at the media-use patterns for heavy spice users. Here you find large index numbers for *Money*, *Mother Earth News*, *New York Magazine*, *Omni*, *Popular Science*, *Road & Track* and *Ski* magazines.

What can you discern from those media choices? It would appear that heavy users of spices are younger and more health conscious, better educated and more politically liberal than the average person. They have enough money to invest and to engage in leisure activities, and they are eager to embrace new technology.

SIDEBAR 3.1   Mediamark Marketing Statistics

Marketing statistics such as those found in the Mediamark research can provide valuable information in defining audiences and messages for public relations tasks. Whereas the product-use statistics (see the top section of statistical material) can help you construct a demographic portrait of the audience, the media-use statistics can help users project an audience's psychographic profile. By examining high and low index numbers in column D, practitioners can discover what interests and lifestyles product users indicate about themselves. These patterns can be used to guide our communication efforts to interested publics and even dictate the form or presentation of our messages.

Here's how you read the statistics. At the top of the first page in the first column, labeled "Total U.S.," is the total number of female homemakers in the United States. The first line of column A indicates that 43,064,000 of these women buy seasoning and spices.

The fifth line of column A, a subtotal of those female homemakers, lists 7,056,000 homemakers who are college graduates and who have purchased seasonings and spices in the last six months. Column B indicates that 16.4 percent of all the women who bought spices in the past six months were college graduates.

Whereas columns A and B indicate what proportion of the total audience of spice buyers is comprised of college graduates, columns C and D tell us how likely it is that college graduates will buy spices. Column C, for instance, states that 58.9 percent of all college graduates bought spices or seasonings in the past six months. Column D translates that percentage into an index number that compares the percentage of college graduates who have purchased spices with the spice-buying behavior of all female homemakers. Looking at the top of column C, you see that 54.8 percent of all female homemakers purchased spices. That percentage is assigned the index number 100. The index number corresponding to the 58.9 percent of college graduates buying spices is thus slightly above 100—in this case, 107.

By isolating the characteristics connected with high and with low index numbers, a PR practitioner can determine audiences to target with messages, as well as audiences not cost effective to target. In this example, high index numbers in column D for heavy spice use coincide with women who are age 25–44, have attended college, have higher incomes, live in the West, have children, and are black. They tend to listen to black-oriented broadcast programming or classical and educational programs. Those same characteristics appear in the spice buyers' print media preferences, among which magazines like *Atlantic Monthly* and *Essence* have high numbers. Also notice the high numbers for upscale home magazines like *Bon Appetit, Architectural Digest* and *Gourmet*. Low index numbers coincide with low education and income, Southerners, and young people and older adults.

What are the implications of all these numbers? They tell us to concentrate our messages on younger, well-educated, prosperous mothers who take pride in elegant entertaining. Many of them may be black. The statistics indicate our payback might be much less if we send messages to very young women and older women, especially if they are poor. In addition, women in rural areas and in the Southeast United States are unpromising prospects.

By targeting our messages to those publics and shaping the message to correspond to their concerns, we have some valuable guidance toward building cost-effective communication.

16 SEASONINGS & SPICES

BASE: FEMALE HOMEMAKERS	TOTAL U.S. '000	ALL A '000	ALL B % DOWN	ALL C % ACROSS	ALL D INDEX	HEAVY MORE THAN 5 A '000	HEAVY B % DOWN	HEAVY C % ACROSS	HEAVY D INDEX	MEDIUM 3-5 A '000	MEDIUM B % DOWN	MEDIUM C % ACROSS	MEDIUM D INDEX	LIGHT LESS THAN 3 A '000	LIGHT B % DOWN	LIGHT C % ACROSS	LIGHT D INDEX
ALL FEMALE HOMEMAKERS	78526	43064	100.0	54.8	100	7808	100.0	9.9	100	14633	100.0	18.6	100	20623	100.0	26.3	100
WOMEN	78526	43064	100.0	54.8	100	7808	100.0	9.9	100	14633	100.0	18.6	100	20623	100.0	26.3	100
HOUSEHOLD HEADS	25974	12046	28.0	46.4	85	1669	21.4	6.4	65	3875	26.5	14.9	80	6502	31.5	25.0	95
HOMEMAKERS	78526	43064	100.0	54.8	100	7808	100.0	9.9	100	14633	100.0	18.6	100	20623	100.0	26.3	100
GRADUATED COLLEGE	11984	7056	16.4	58.9	107	1307	16.7	10.9	110	2556	17.5	21.3	114	3193	15.5	26.6	101
ATTENDED COLLEGE	13532	8463	19.7	62.5	114	1820	23.3	13.4	135	2870	19.6	21.2	114	3773	18.3	27.9	106
GRADUATED HIGH SCHOOL	32922	18510	43.0	56.2	103	3285	42.1	10.0	100	6737	46.0	20.5	110	8488	41.2	25.8	98
DID NOT GRADUATE HIGH SCHOOL	20088	9034	21.0	45.0	82	1395	17.9	6.9	70	2470	16.9	12.3	66	5169	25.1	25.7	98
18-24	7148	3578	8.3	50.1	91	578	7.4	8.1	81	1125	7.7	15.7	84	1875	9.1	26.2	100
25-34	18929	11670	27.1	61.7	112	2211	28.3	11.7	117	3739	25.6	19.8	106	5720	27.7	30.2	115
35-44	15611	9462	22.0	60.6	111	2269	29.1	14.5	146	3416	23.3	21.9	117	3777	18.3	24.2	92
45-54	11202	6151	14.3	54.9	100	1163	14.9	10.4	104	2456	16.8	21.9	118	2532	12.3	22.6	86
55-64	11170	6352	14.8	56.9	104	1025	13.1	9.2	92	1903	13.6	17.8	96	3333	16.2	29.8	114
65 OR OVER	14466	5851	13.6	40.4	74	562	7.2	3.9	39	1904	13.0	13.2	71	3385	16.4	23.4	89
18-34	26077	15248	35.4	58.5	107	2788	35.7	10.7	108	4864	33.2	18.7	100	7595	36.8	29.1	111
18-49	47337	27834	64.6	58.8	107	5719	73.2	12.1	122	9464	64.7	20.0	107	12651	61.3	26.7	102
25-54	45742	27283	63.4	59.6	109	5643	72.3	12.3	124	9611	65.7	21.0	113	12029	58.3	26.3	100
H/D INCOME $50,000 OR MORE	13928	8946	20.8	64.2	117	1799	23.0	12.9	130	3512	24.0	25.2	135	3636	17.6	26.1	99
$40,000 - 49,999	10122	6028	14.0	59.6	109	1300	16.6	12.8	129	2266	15.5	22.4	120	2462	11.9	24.3	93
$35,000 - 39,999	5855	3668	8.5	62.6	114	783	10.0	13.4	134	1324	9.0	22.6	121	1581	7.6	26.7	102
$25,000 - 34,999	14224	8021	18.6	56.4	103	1575	20.2	11.1	111	2650	18.1	18.6	100	3796	18.4	26.7	102
$15,000 - 24,999	15253	8243	19.1	54.0	99	1434	18.4	9.4	95	2429	16.6	15.9	85	4380	21.2	28.7	109
LESS THAN $15,000	19144	8158	18.9	42.6	78	917	11.7	4.8	48	2452	16.8	12.8	69	4788	23.2	25.0	95
CENSUS REGION: NORTH EAST	16184	8668	20.1	53.6	98	1639	21.0	10.1	102	2923	20.0	18.1	97	4106	19.9	25.4	97
NORTH CENTRAL	19695	12023	27.9	61.0	111	2080	26.6	10.6	106	4067	27.8	20.6	111	5875	28.5	29.8	114
SOUTH	27669	13666	31.7	49.4	90	2112	27.0	7.6	77	4401	30.1	15.9	85	7153	34.7	25.9	98
WEST	14978	8706	20.2	58.1	106	1976	25.3	13.2	133	3242	22.2	21.6	116	3489	16.9	23.3	89
ANY CHILD IN HOUSEHOLD	34596	20938	48.6	60.5	110	4249	54.4	12.3	124	7345	50.2	21.2	114	9343	45.3	27.0	103
UNDER 2 YEARS	6567	3675	8.5	56.0	102	812	10.4	12.4	124	1297	8.9	19.8	106	1566	7.6	23.8	91
2-5 YEARS	13153	8120	18.9	61.7	113	1659	21.2	12.6	127	2824	19.3	21.5	115	3637	17.6	27.7	105
6-11 YEARS	15995	9642	22.4	60.3	110	2123	27.2	13.3	133	3287	22.5	20.6	110	4232	20.5	26.5	101
12-17 YEARS	15115	9188	21.3	60.8	111	2024	25.9	13.4	135	3335	22.8	22.1	118	3827	18.6	25.3	96
WHITE	68467	37294	86.6	54.5	99	6669	85.4	9.7	98	12689	86.7	18.5	99	17936	87.0	26.2	100
BLACK	8737	5091	11.8	58.3	106	1032	13.2	11.8	119	1632	11.2	18.7	100	2427	11.8	27.8	106
HOME OWNED	54413	30946	71.9	56.9	104	5727	73.3	10.5	106	10880	74.4	20.0	107	14340	69.5	26.4	100
ALL FEMALE HOMEMAKERS	78526	43064	100.0	54.8	100	7808	100.0	9.9	100	14633	100.0	18.6	100	20623	100.0	26.3	100
METRO SUNDAY COMICS	12082	7575	17.6	62.7	114	1399	17.9	11.6	116	2818	19.3	23.3	125	3357	16.3	27.8	106
MODERN BRIDE	1411	849	2.0	60.2	110	*128	1.6	9.1	91	*285	1.9	20.2	108	*436	2.1	30.9	118
MODERN MATURITY	13739	7663	17.8	55.8	102	1189	15.2	8.7	87	2449	16.7	17.8	96	4025	19.5	29.3	112
MODERN PHOTOGRAPHY	829	574	1.3	69.2	126	*71	.9	8.6	86	*270	1.8	32.6	175	*233	1.1	28.1	107
MONEY	2458	1729	4.0	70.3	128	*376	4.8	15.3	154	730	5.0	29.7	159	623	3.0	25.3	97
MOTHER EARTH NEWS	1532	928	2.2	60.6	110	*306	3.9	20.0	201	*291	2.0	19.0	102	*332	1.6	21.7	83
MOTOR TREND	*505	*314	.7	-	-	*65	.8	-	-	*111	.8	-	-	*138	.7	-	-
MS.	1385	861	2.0	62.2	113	*133	1.7	9.6	97	*291	2.0	21.0	113	437	2.1	31.6	120
NATIONAL ENQUIRER	10637	5759	13.4	54.1	99	897	11.5	8.4	85	1878	12.8	17.7	95	2984	14.5	28.1	107
NATIONAL GEOGRAPHIC	13031	8015	18.6	61.5	112	1540	19.7	11.8	119	2850	19.5	21.9	117	3625	17.6	27.8	106
NATIONAL GEOGRAPHIC TRAVELER	1234	808	1.9	65.5	119	*132	1.7	10.7	108	*370	2.5	30.0	161	*307	1.5	24.9	95
NATIONAL LAMPOON	418	*251	.6	60.0	109	*54	.7	12.9	130	*114	.8	27.3	146	*83	.4	19.9	76
NATION'S BUSINESS	*407	*309	.7	-	-	*68	.9	-	-	*137	.9	-	-	*104	.5	-	-
NATURAL HISTORY	594	*347	.8	58.4	107	*41	.5	6.9	69	*104	.7	17.5	94	*202	1.0	34.0	129
NEWSWEEK	8166	5129	11.9	62.8	115	809	10.4	9.9	100	2001	13.7	24.5	131	2319	11.2	28.4	108
NEW WOMAN	2452	1498	3.5	61.1	111	*174	2.2	7.1	71	655	4.5	26.7	143	670	3.2	27.3	104
NEW YORK MAGAZINE	564	*315	.7	55.9	102	*98	1.3	17.4	175	*147	1.0	26.1	140	*70	.3	12.4	47
NEW YORK TIMES (DAILY)	1092	470	1.1	43.0	78	*91	1.2	8.3	84	*167	1.1	15.3	82	*211	1.0	19.3	74
NEW YORK TIMES MAGAZINE	1611	737	1.7	45.7	83	*129	1.7	8.0	81	*275	1.9	17.1	92	333	1.6	20.7	79
THE NEW YORKER	1185	766	1.8	64.6	118	*186	2.4	15.7	158	*301	2.1	25.4	136	279	1.4	23.5	90
OMNI	1087	782	1.8	71.9	131	*195	2.5	17.9	180	*219	1.5	20.1	108	*369	1.8	33.9	129
PREVENTION	5501	3248	7.5	59.0	108	633	8.1	11.5	116	1199	8.2	21.8	117	1416	6.9	25.7	98
PSYCHOLOGY TODAY	2340	1604	3.7	68.5	125	*233	3.0	10.0	100	541	3.7	23.1	124	830	4.0	35.5	135
PUCK	9158	5431	12.6	59.3	108	1180	15.1	12.9	130	1750	12.0	19.1	103	2501	12.1	27.3	104
READER'S DIGEST	26428	15480	35.9	58.6	107	2972	38.1	11.2	113	5365	36.7	20.3	109	7143	34.6	27.0	103
REDBOOK	10199	6486	15.1	63.6	116	1250	16.0	12.3	123	2186	14.9	21.4	115	3050	14.8	29.9	114
ROAD & TRACK	429	*322	.7	75.1	137	*71	.9	16.6	166	*57	.4	13.3	71	*194	.9	45.2	172

How does that information change your writing strategy? At the simplest level, it gives you a list of media outlets to which you can direct your message with some certainty of reaching a high proportion of logical prospects.

Moreover, it gives you some clues about the tone and texture your message should have. From the psychographic profile you've been able to construct, it would appear that a message that uses more sophisticated vocabulary would be appropriate. Your message will be best received by the media gatekeeper if you design it to fit with the interests of the gatekeeper's audience, in this case by emphasizing new technology (computer-dispensed spices) that enhances a well-educated audience's leisure activities, activities that might include healthful gourmet cooking.

There are sources for similar information on local audiences too, as highlighted by Memory Memo 3.5. The International Demographic Media Audit presents an analysis of demographics, and media and product use patterns similar to Mediamark, for local media in large- and medium-sized cities.

You can also find information that demonstrates how much money people in certain localities spend on certain types of products. Standard Rates and Data Service (SRDS), a multivolume reference manual that contains information about advertising media, presents product expenditure indexes for every U.S. county. Thus you can compare counties for their residents' spending on investments, recreational activities or furniture. Instead of being limited to a county's income levels or racial characteristics (which the SRDS includes as well), you can use the SRDS statistics to discern lifestyles. That's important information as you try to plan a message.

The CACI Study of Demographic Information for Every ZIP Code in the United States presents the same information broken down by single zip codes. With CACI, it's possible to compare the people and their buying habits in individual towns within counties or even individual neighborhoods within cities. It's a great reference source for your organization's local audiences, not only because of its detailed information but also because you don't have to undertake the research yourself.

Among other sources of secondary research on audiences are public opinion polls. Although some polls are conducted by private companies for their own use and thus aren't available to others, there are literally thousands of polls conducted every year that are available to the public.

Memory Memo 3.5
Psychographic research sources:

- Mediamark and Simmons marketing statistics summarize
  - gender, age, income and other demographic factors
  - national media preferences by demographic factors
  - media preferences by product choices
  - product choices by demographic factors
- International Demographics Media Audit summarizes
  - all Mediamark factors, but for local major market media
- SRDS summarizes
  - demographic data by residence in states and counties
  - buying patterns by residence in counties
- CACI summarizes
  - demographic data by residence in ZIP codes
  - buying patterns by residence in ZIP codes

The most important are the Roper and Gallup polls, both of which publish indexes to their surveys. A vital part of their usefulness is that those companies have been tracking the changes in public opinion on specific issues for years. Thus, you're able not only to find out how the public felt about an issue last month, but often you'll be able to discover how they felt about the same issue decades ago.

Media Lists: Finding All the Ways to Reach Your Audience

In addition to helping gather information so that you can develop a persuasive and appropriate message, secondary research assists in making a wise choice about the medium you can use to reach your audience. Before making this decision, you first need to be aware of studies evaluating the ability of different media to persuade people.

The same considerations that guide all your other public relations decisions should guide your choice of a medium to deliver your message. Again, you should not make decisions based solely on how inexpensively you can deliver a message. You should instead look at the effect of your communication. You should carefully examine the cost effectiveness of the medium in delivering a message to the specific public that you want to reach. In addition, you need to evaluate the cost effectiveness of the medium in convincing that specific audience to undertake an action or adopt an opinion that's helpful to your organization.

Many public relations campaigns rely too heavily on mass media outlets, because mass media are usually the least expensive methods to disseminate information to the greatest number of people. However, with a few exceptions, the most effective medium in motivating people to act on a message is person-to-person communication, followed by other media with personal characteristics. In fact, studies have shown that mass media are least effective in persuading people. Figure 3.2 shows the progression of media effectiveness. As messages are more personalized and are placed in media that are more specialized or targeted, they generally become more effective in persuading their receivers to adopt the message. This places a dif-

FIGURE 3.2 Effectiveness of media

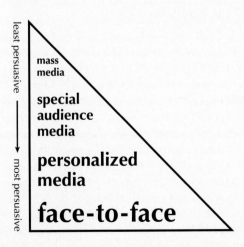

least persuasive ⟶ most persuasive

mass media

special audience media

personalized media

face-to-face

ferent imperative on practitioners, leading them to balance cost with a medium's effectiveness in moving a target audience to action.

However, it's still necessary to weigh the high cost of personal media with the possible returns. Even though a personalized letter is usually an effective communication medium, you can't send a letter to every single person in the country. You need to know ways to select a more concentrated audience that is interested in your message.

Obviously, in many situations you have a concentrated group of people who have already demonstrated an interest in your message. For instance, your company's shareholders and employees have an abiding interest in your message, and you opt for telephone calls, one-to-one communication and other forms of personal communication rather than publications to reach and influence them. This decision is reinforced by Grunig's situational theory of communication discussed in Chapter 1, which suggests you can profitably invest more money in communicating with active information seekers. Thus, union leaders, large shareholders and even small shareholders and community environmental activists, if they are vocal, might deserve a more personal form of communication with top company officials.

What about situations in which you don't know or haven't collected the names of people who might be interested in your message? To find that target audience, you need to know how to match the information you want to communicate with an audience that wants that information. Then you can use research sources to discover the medium that's most likely read by that audience.

We've already examined the Mediamark and International Demographics Media Audit, which detail the characteristics, lifestyles and habits of audiences of general interest media such as television stations, newspapers and magazines. There are also more highly targeted media that give you the capacity to reach specific audiences with specialized information needs and desires. These media might include employee newsletters, industry journals, newsletters and computer information services. We'll discuss some of the research sources to find those media in Chapter 11.

Mailing Lists: People Telling You Their Interests

There are other ways to launch an even more tightly focused and personalized campaign and profit from other organizations that have already done much of your audience research for you.

Mailing lists may seem to be a rather low-tech method, and in the past, they often have been. When the major sources of available mailing lists were those of subscribers to general-interest publications like *Time* magazine, *Reader's Digest* and the *Saturday Evening Post*, the targeting of a specific audience was rather inexact. However, with current technology, mailing lists have become a cost-efficient method of distributing your message to audiences that are very likely to be information seekers about your message. That's possible with the advent of new, tightly specialized publications and their similarly specialized subscriber lists.

The growth of specialized mail-order and direct-marketing catalogs as well as the availability of special-interest mailing lists have provided even more specifically focused collections of names. With these catalog and response-generated lists, it's possible to find a select group of people who have already demonstrated their interest in a particular subject. For example, you can buy a list of people who have purchased gourmet cooking utensils, own a yacht, have contributed to nonprofit arts organizations or have bought home security devices. Commercial mailing list companies collect the names of individuals with specialized interests and demographic characteristics. This allows PR practitioners to deliver more specialized messages to individuals who are most likely to respond, thus capitalizing on the effectiveness of personal communication. A single page from the catalog of a major mailing list company in Figure 3.3 shows just how

FIGURE 3.3   Partial listing from a mailing list catalog

SIC

Names can be supplied by SIC CODE (Standard Industrial Classification, the code number assigned by the government to most categories of businesses, professions; institutions and organizations to identify each group. Please inquire for quantities & prices by SIC.

QUANTITY		PRICE
2,950	Sisterhoods, Jewish	$45/M
2,500	Skating Rinks	$45/M
49,700	Skeet & Trap Shooters	Inquire
3,900	Ski Shops	$45/M
1,200	Ski Centers & Resorts	$85
4,900	Slaughterhouses, Meat Packers	$45/M
26,100	Slip Cover & Upholstery Shops	$45/M
2,000,000	Small Business Owners (By Individual Name)	$65/M
2,500,000	Small Businesses	$45/M
550,000	Small Town Businesses	$45/M
2,450	Snowmobile Dealers	$45/M
1,200	Soap Manufacturers	$85
350	Soccer Clubs	$85
34,287	Social Register Families	$45/M
109,171	Social Service Organizations	$45/M
91,934	Social Studies Teachers	$60/M
4,175	Social Workers	$45/M
7,114	Sociologists	$45/M
2,500	Sociology Department Heads, College	$60/M
2,767	Soft Drink Bottlers, Distributors	$45/M
9,804	Sororities, Fraternities	$45/M
5,187	Sound Systems	$45/M
831	Souvenir Shops	$85
41,766	Space Scientists	$45/M
29	Sperm Banks	$85
2,940	Sporting Goods Mfrs	$45/M
71,772	Sporting Goods & Bicycle Retailers	$45/M
10,563	Sporting Goods Wholesalers	$45/M
9,330	Sports Medicine Specialists	$45/M
2,100,000	Sportsmen, Hunters	Inquire
115	Sports Teams (Professional)	$85
11,824	Sportswear Retailers	$45/M
8,034	Sprinkler Systems (Lawn)	$45/M
2,759	Sprinkler Systems (Fire)	$45/M
100	Square Dance Callers	$85
329	Stadiums, Arenas & Athletic Fields	$85
1,537	Stamp Dealers	$85
46,483	Stamp Collectors	$45/M
2,400	Stamping Plants, Metal	$45/M
5,303	State Government Officials	$45/M
7,461	State Legislators	$45/M
4,870	Stationers	$45/M
393	Stationery Chains	$85
35,336	Stationery Stores	$45/M
13,101	Statisticians	$45/M
2,423	Steamship Ticket Offices	$45/M
5,709	Steel Service & Warehousing	$45/M
7,422	Steel & Iron Industry Executives	$45/M
629	Steel Retailers	$85
148	Steeple Jacks	$85
39,779	Stenographics & Reproductive Services	$45/M
13,713	Stereo & Hi Fi Equipment Dealers	$45/M
465	Stevedoring Contracting	$45/M
4,021	Stock Brokers, Main Offices	$45/M
8,504	Stock Brokers, Branches	$45/M
47,823	Stock Brokers, Partners, Officers, Executives, Managers of Firms	$45/M
17,000	Stock Brokers, Registered Representatives	$75/M
8,000	Stock Exchanges, Companies Listed	$45/M
925,000	Stockholders & Investors	Inquire
80,000	Stockholders & Investors, Women	Inquire
17,014	Stonemasons & Bricklayers	$45/M
19,908	Storage, Household & Commercial	$45/M

QUANTITY		PRICE
2,880	Store Front Contractors	$45/M
7,864	Storm Windows & Doors	$45/M
76,575	Structural & Construction Engineers	$45/M
17,308	Structural Steel-Erection	$45/M
1,390	Stucco Contractors	$85
	STUDENTS, HIGH SCHOOL/COLLEGE	Inquire
	SUBSCRIBERS (See Pages 20-22)	
5,202	Summer Camps	$45/M
15,903	Superintendents, Schools	$60/M
193,645	Supermarket & Grocery Stores	$45/M
3,241	Supermarket & Grocery Chains	$45/M
1,057	Supermarket & Grocery Chains with 10 or more stores	$85
1,762	Supermarket & Grocery Chains with 5 or more stores	$85
25,408	Surgeons	$45/M
1,463	Surgical & Medical Instruments	$85
13,679	Surveyors, Land	$45/M
8,564	Swimming Pool Contractors	$45/M
6,423	Swimming Pool Services	$45/M
527,000	Swimming Pool Owners (Residential)	$65/M
1,907	Swimming Pools, Public	$85
1,100	Symphony Orchestras	$85
2,917	Synagogues	$45/M

T

QUANTITY		PRICE
10,375	T-Shirt Retailers	$45/M
7,163	Tackle, Fishing Dealers	$45/M
699	Tailors	$85
400	Talent, Casting Agents	$85
19,703	Tanning Salons	$45/M
9,905	Tapes & Records Dealers	$45/M
85,433	Taverns, Bars, Cocktail Lounges	$45/M
6,193	Tax Assessors, Business	$45/M
1,293	Tax Assessors, Government	$85
7,508	Tax Law Firms	$45/M
21,881	Tax Exempt Foundations	$45/M
55,000	Tax Exempt Organizations	$45/M
44,745	Tax Preparation Services	$45/M
382,275	Tax Shelter Investors (By Type)	$65/M
6,918	Taxicab Companies	$45/M
3,748	Taxidermists	$45/M

TEACHERS

QUANTITY		PRICE
525,000	TEACHERS, COLLEGE (See College Professors)	$60/M
1,100,000	TEACHERS, ELEMENTARY SCHOOLS, BY GRADE	$60/M
880,000	TEACHERS, HIGH SCHOOLS	$60/M
14,193	Teachers, High School, Art	$60/M
31,290	Teachers, High School, Business Education	$60/M
85,424	Teachers, High School, English	$60/M
31,323	Teachers, High School, Home Economics	$60/M
44,164	Teachers, High School, Industrial Arts	$60/M
9,871	Teachers, High School, Languages	$60/M
107,089	Teachers, High School, Mathematics	$60/M
51,961	Teachers, High School, Music	$60/M
108,700	Teachers, High School, Physical Education	$60/M
29,455	Teachers, High School, Science	$60/M
42,423	Teachers, High School, Social Studies	$60/M
21,878	Teachers, High School, Special Education	$60/M
250,000	Teachers, Home Address	Inquire
100,175	Teachers, Kindergarten	$60/M
1,100	Teachers (Training) Colleges	$85
9,884	Technical, Trade, & Vocational Schools	$45/M

QUANTITY		PRICE
2,557	Technical, Scientific Libraries	$45/M
15,000,000	Teenagers (Select by Age)	Inquire
8,017	Telephone Answering Services	$45/M
5,128	Telephone Companies	$45/M
6,639	Telephone Company Executives	$45/M
1,515	Telephone Interconnect Companies	$85
12,553	Telephone & Telephone Equipment Stores	$45/M
164,982	Telex Subscribers	$50/M
19,203	Temporary Placement Agencies	$45/M

TV/RADIO

QUANTITY		PRICE
5,547	TV Cable Companies	$45/M
391	TV Cable Companies (Networks)	$85
2,600	TV Closed Circuit Systems	$45/M
1,220	TV (Public) Executives	$85
20,900	TV & Radio Dealers	$45/M
34,000	TV & Radio Executives	$45/M
10,600	TV & Radio Station & Publishing	$45/M
6,350	TV Rental	$45/M
20,000	TV Service & Repair	$45/M
1,040	TV Stations	$85
171	TV Stations, Educational	$85
212	TV Stations, Religious	$85
8,750	Tennis Clubs	$45/M
1,400	Tennis Court Contractors	$85
1,750	Tennis Equipment Retailers	$45/M
850,000	Tennis Players	Inquire
4,900	Testing Laboratories	$45/M
230	Textbook Publishers	$85
11,000	Textile Executives	$45/M
8,700	Textile Mills	$45/M
170	Theater Chains	$85
800	Theatres, Live	$85
11,000	Theaters, Movie	$45/M
900	Theatrical Agents	$45/M
320	Theology Schools & Colleges	$85
24,300	Therapists, Child	$45/M
44,200	Therapists, Hearing & Speech	$45/M
62,100	Therapists, Physical	$45/M
8,495	Thoracic Doctors	$45/M
6,260	Thrift Shops	$45/M
14,100	Tile & Terrazzo Contractors	$45/M
40,500	Tire Dealers	$45/M
3,000	Tire Wholesalers	$45/M
3,500	Tobacco Shops	$45/M
2,100	Tobacco & Sundries Wholesalers	$45/M
4,000	Tool & Die Shops	$45/M
9,000	Tool Wholesalers	$45/M
3,400	Tour Operators	$45/M
11,500	Tourist Attractions, Amusement Parks	$45/M
1,850	Towel & Linen Companies	$85
41,000	Towing, Automotive	$45/M
46,000	Toy, Hobby, Model & Craft Shops	$45/M
6,900	Toy Stores	$45/M
3,200	Toy Wholesalers	$45/M
860	Toy & Games Manufacturers	$85
7,700	Tractor Dealers	$45/M
3,700	Trade & Business Associations	$45/M
3,200	Trade & Business Publications	$45/M
17,200	Trade Show Exhibitors, Executives	$45/M

INQUIRE ABOUT OUR
LISTS ON DISKS
LOWEST PRICES ANYWHERE
SEE INSIDE BACK COVER

specifically you can target messages. Notice entries for slaughterhouses, sperm banks, square dance callers and steeple jacks.

In some cases, the detailed information you can obtain about people from mailing lists has frightening implications for personal privacy, which we'll discuss in the next chapter. It's possible, for example, to obtain mailing lists of people who have purchased sexually explicit publications and sexually oriented merchandise. Another company offers a mailing list of 28,000 people who have purchased talismans, incense, charms and other products for performing occult religious ceremonies. A third company offers to sell your name if you have "contributed to ransom POWs still believed to be held in Vietnam." For good or ill, mailing lists give you a remarkable ability to find clusters of people who are allied by their interest in some activity.

Information about most commercially available mailing lists is compiled in another volume of the Standard Rates and Data Service. Most of the lists give you the opportunity to select specific geographic areas, allowing you to specify particular states, ZIP codes, census tracts or carrier routes. Some lists even let you make selections based on the recency of a purchase by a person on the mailing list or the value of the product an individual purchased. Once you've purchased the lists, there are commercial services that merge and purge lists so you aren't paying to mail several copies of the same piece to the same person.

Mailing lists provide not only the opportunity to find certain types of people, but the assurance that you can construct much more personal and thus much more persuasive messages to those people. It's surely going to be a growth area in public relations.

A similar level of selection can be developed in telephone communication campaigns, too. In some cases mailing list companies compile phone numbers to match the addresses they have gathered. Even if the mailing list does not include a phone number, there are other companies that compare the names and addresses on the mailing list you have obtained against a list of phone numbers. That gives your telemarketing workers a calling list of likely prospects for your message.

PRIMARY RESEARCH: WHEN NO ONE HAS FOUND WHAT YOU WANT TO KNOW

Oftentimes even expert researchers find it impossible to recover the precise information they need from secondary sources. They may have a huge quantity of information that gives valuable background but that unfortunately doesn't answer the specific questions they have about their own research problem. At that point, it's necessary to make more independent efforts at research. In public relations tasks, those efforts usually involve interviewing, administering a questionnaire, designing an experiment or some combination of the three.

All primary research starts with secondary research. Unless you know what other people have written about your subject you can make two grave mistakes: You may waste your time doing research someone has already done, and you have few ways to verify the results you obtain if you don't know what other researchers have found.

Once you've examined all the existing research, however, you may discover that you need more information. As with all research, you need a plan to help direct your research. Part of that planning process is having enough knowledge about the capabilities and applications of different research methods that you'll be able to apply the most efficient system.

Interviews: Information Straight from the Source

One of the most common methods of independent PR research is interviewing. Interviewing skills are involved in gathering information from individuals and from focus groups, both important information sources for public relations tasks.

Most people think interviewing is simple. It's not. To be an effective interviewer, you must start with a strategy. You have to know what information you want to obtain during the session and then you need a plan for getting that information from your source or sources.

First, a word about what interviewing isn't. An interview isn't a conversation; it's a planned, structured communication event intended to gather information from a source. Of course, if you're a good interviewer, your source will find it's like talking to an interesting friend. Although you and your source may enjoy the experience, you always must be aware of the information you need to discover.

What does that mean in practical terms? In an interview situation you can't merely rely on your gift for gab. In fact, clever, experienced sources who want to avoid talking about a difficult subject will often ask you questions, and before long you'll be telling the source your opinions about the interview topic in a 20-minute oral exposition, the textual density of which would make Kierkegaard proud. You need to spend a lot more time listening than talking. Remember that you are trying to get information from your source.

After completing your secondary research of the topic, you should carefully consider what information you need from your interview subject. Then prepare a list of questions that will draw that information from your source. This will keep you focused and remind you of information that you set out to collect.

In compiling your questions, avoid ones about procedures and minutiae you should have found in your research. Don't waste valuable interview time asking your source how many years she's been director or where he went to school.

If you're having trouble thinking of questions or you find yourself asking mundane questions, you might use a formula that LaRue W. Gilleland at the University of Nevada–Reno originated called the GOSS formula. GOSS stands for Goal, Obstacle, Start, Solution, which Gilleland says are all part of any undertaking. Here are some general questions that arise from the GOSS formula:

Goal: What was your objective in beginning the project? What problem did you want to solve?

Obstacle: What problems did you have in implementing your plans? Who was opposed to it?

Start: How did you decide to tackle this problem? What were the first steps to undertaking the effort? What was it like in the early days as you struggled to put the project together?

Solution: What made your plan work? How did you discover the answer to your problem? What's happened since you started your efforts?

All these questions, and the variations you invent yourself, help reveal why and how humans work toward an end. That's very important information, because receiver-centered communication assumes we can't design a truly persuasive message unless we know what motivates people to take an action. Those very motivations are what we try to encourage in others with our communication efforts.

Now that we have some guidelines for formulating questions, there are some questions you shouldn't ask. For instance, avoid questions that might prompt your source to answer in the way he or she thinks you want. For example, if you asked a question like, "I really think pig knuckles dipped in peanut butter taste good—don't you agree?" you'll oftentimes prompt people who don't have such exotic eating habits to agree with your suggestion.

The same warning applies to other types of prompts. If you are emotionally involved in an issue and let anger or admiration show through in your question, you'll often encourage your interview subjects to adopt the same attitude and possibly skew their answers away from the most truthful responses.

Even though it's important to write questions before going into an interview or a focus group session, always be prepared to deviate from the order or even to take the line of questioning in an entirely new direction if you discover something you hadn't anticipated. There will be times when the topic your subject volunteers will turn out to be much more exciting than the area your limited knowledge initially led you to ask about. You need to be flexible to the opportunities presented to you.

Questionnaires: Think Before You Ask

Our society's fascination with surveys is demonstrated by the vast number of public opinion polls that are conducted. In addition to the long-standing public opinion polls like Roper and Gallup, many newspapers also sponsor polls on what local people say they believe. You need to exhaust those sources of surveys before undertaking your own.

Questionnaires are probably the most common form of formal public relations research. Often they are used because PR practitioners think their job is to change public opinions on issues, and, to do this, they must ask their target publics if their viewpoints have changed. But in an organization using management-by-objective methods, PR practitioners aren't merely looking to change opinions. Instead, the goal is to have their publics undertake some behavior that will help their organization. (Surveys don't do an adequate job of measuring changes in behavior, anyway, because they usually measure only publicly expressed opinions about a subject, instead of the privately held beliefs that more often determine behavior.)

For instance, a survey found that 70 percent of the citizens polled in one state said their state should pass a law requiring seat belt use. However, after the law was passed only 28 percent of the citizens complied with the law. This reveals that surveys often reveal only what survey subjects want other people to think about them, not what they would truly do.

Surveys can be very useful if they are conducted in such a way that they help you establish a baseline of what an audience is thinking about or feeling at a certain point in time. They can help you understand the response you might expect if your institution undertook a certain action. They can thus help you make and justify decisions and give you power to win the approval of governmental regulators, citizen groups and other bodies who count public opinion as an important component in their own decision-making process.

Doing your own polling is not such a treacherous undertaking. However, because it is possibly more dangerous to have bad results of a public opinion poll than to have no survey information at all, it's necessary to know the major difficulties that plague surveys.

Sampling Errors: When You Don't Find the Right Public.   Two major types of errors commonly occur as researchers compile and administer questionnaires: sampling errors and, for lack of a better name, nonsampling errors.

A sampling error occurs when the group of people whose opinions you have polled are not representative of the larger group you want to know about. To have an accurate survey, you must be very conscientious and careful in your efforts to gather a true and representative sample.

A random survey means just that. You need to draw a sample from the public whose opinion you want to know, and every person in that population must have an equal chance to be selected.

There are many ways to find yourself with a nonrandom sample. Most of them seem innocuous at first. Let's say you pick the first 100 names in the phone book. That would seem to be a group of people who would likely represent the entire population of your city. However, polling only those first 100 individuals gives you a much greater chance of questioning people who are related or belong to the same religious or ethnic group and who may share opinions that are not necessarily those of the population as a whole. Additionally, if you use this method you have no way of contacting people at the lower end of the economic scale, who can't afford a phone, or on the higher end, who are more likely to have unlisted numbers.

As you can understand from this one example, samples have to be chosen systematically to avoid sampling errors. For instance, if you survey worker attitudes before writing a new overtime policy, you could choose to poll only employees on the night shift, the source of most complaints. But if you do that, the new overtime policy you design may engender a new set of resentments among the daytime employees you didn't survey. In short, your polling methods haven't let you find a representative sample of the entire workforce affected by the overtime policy.

The same thing might happen if you do a telephone survey to find if a company's shop-at-home service would be profitable. If you conduct your survey only between 9 a.m. and 5 p.m., your survey results won't be very accurate. It's obvious that families in which both the husband and wife work would be prime candidates for a shop-at-home service. Yet, if you call only during the day you won't be able to capture those opinions because those people will be at their jobs.

Sampling problems can also occur if you have poll takers stand inside a shopping mall on a weekday morning and ask people their opinions as they pass. First, you have no assurance you are getting the proper balance of males and females. Depending on the part of town the shopping center is in, you may be getting predominantly upper or lower socioeconomic classes to respond. Your poll takers may not question certain types of people with whom they are uncomfortable or with whom they have had a bad experience. Any of these factors can hopelessly skew your poll results. (See Sidebar 3.2.)

SIDEBAR 3.2   Random and Nonrandom Samples

Results from surveys or experiments can't be trusted unless you're able to select a representative sample of the public whose opinions or behaviors you're trying to discover. Researchers must guarantee that each person within the population they're studying has an equal chance to be selected to be interviewed. Following is a summary of random and nonrandom samples.

Nonrandom Samples

These are distinguished by the lack of a system in selecting research subjects. As a result, it's impossible to determine if the people selected accurately reflect the viewpoints of the group you're trying to study.

Accidental Sample. The most familiar form of accidental sample is the questionnaire presented to shoppers at malls. Any results from an accidental sample are overwhelmed by problems. The difficulty of generalizing the findings beyond the subjects at a certain geographic site and the researcher's bias in choosing people to interview are only two of the problems with this type of sample.

Purposive Sample. A purposive sample is the type of sample generally used by reporters. If a sports reporter is trying to find reaction to new National Collegiate Athletic Association academic requirements for athletic recruits, he or she might call four or five football and basketball coaches in the region. However, with a small sample and without a system to overcome any conscious or unconscious biases that might affect the reporter's selection of sources, the results can't be reliably generalized to the population as a whole.

Self-selected Sample. If the survey's subjects have complete control over choosing to be involved in the sample, it's a self-selected sample. A television station's call-in poll is an example. Unfortunately, people who take the time to volunteer for polls are not necessarily representative of a population.

Random Samples

These establish a pool of all members or certain subgroups of the population and then use a systematic procedure to select individuals randomly for the sample.

Probability Sample. This is the most accurate sample. A probability sample draws every possible member of the population into a pool, then uses a mathematical sequence to select individuals who will be interviewed for the survey. Thus, personal biases can't influence the sample's selection.

Quota Sample. Quota samples are intended to assure that certain ethnic, national, religious or other subgroups are represented in the sample. If a school with a 5 percent minority population wants to know its students' opinions and wants to guarantee that 5 percent of its sample represents minority viewpoints, it could establish a quota sample. It would place all minority students into one pool of names, and all other students into another pool. Then it would use a mathematical sequence to select a representative proportion of the sample from each subgroup randomly.

Area Sample. To cut costs, researchers sometimes pick samples from certain neighborhoods or regions to represent subgroups in a population. Thus, a certain socioeconomic group might be obtained by selecting a particular census tract. Again, all the members in the census tract are put into a pool, and then the people to be interviewed are randomly selected from the pool. A similar selection procedure is used for each subgroup in the population.

Sampling errors can occur in a variety of other ways. Sex researcher Shere Hite distributed 100,000 questionnaires on women's sexual habits to women's clubs nationwide. Of the 4,500 women who volunteered responses through this mail-in survey, 70 percent of the women married over five years said they were having extramarital affairs.

When Hite's methods were analyzed, there were a number of problems. Most obviously, a poll that has only a 4.5 percent response rate doesn't inspire much confidence. It also seemed the women who responded weren't representative of the entire population of women. Although many women do belong to women's clubs, a larger proportion don't belong to any club, which meant that most women didn't even get a chance to respond to the survey.

Another factor that affected Hite's results was that respondents chose to include themselves in the survey, and it's not certain that women who choose to reveal their sexual history are representative of all women. These self-selected samples are among the most common sampling errors. Because of self-selected samples, you need to distrust local TV news call-in polls, as well as the White House's reporting of the percentage of supportive phone calls and telegrams after a presidential speech.

How can you prevent sampling error? As much as possible, pollsters need to design mechanical methods of selecting a random sample to eliminate any conscious or inadvertent bias the researchers might have. For instance, if you're doing a phone survey, you might want to employ random-sequence dialing, in which your callers dial every 100th or every 1,000th number (588-1001, 588-1101, 588-1201, 588-1301), instead of picking every 100th number from a phone book.

In addition, look for artificial barriers that may unintentionally prevent all segments of your target population from participating in your sample. Don't just poll people you can reach during the traditional workday, or within a single department or within a single level of management in your company. If you do, you might have a survey you think is finding the opinions of all the people in your city or your company but it is actually a poll of all the people who are at home to answer their phones between 9 a.m. and 5 p.m. or who are employees earning more than $50,000 a year. The time of day when you poll, the physical location you choose, even the people you choose to do your polling may influence your chances of obtaining a representative sample.

Nonsampling Errors: When You Don't Ask the Question Right.   The other major source of mistakes in questionnaires lies in the way the questions are phrased and presented. Even if your sample is correct, mistakes in formulating and administering the questions can distort the results you obtain from the polling process. These are called nonsampling errors.

For instance, if you survey one group of workers about their job satisfaction before they begin their shift and another group of workers after their shift, some portion of the differences you note may be attributable to the second group's fatigue rather than their actual job satisfaction. Only by keeping as many of these secondary factors as consistent as possible between survey groups can you avoid these types of errors.

Another source of nonsampling errors occurs because the very act of studying an individual or a public can sometimes change its behavior or responses to questions. As we noted previously, sometimes people tell their questioners what they think the pollsters want to hear rather than what they truly believe.

These nonsampling errors sometimes occur because the questions are phrased in a confusing or misleading way. That can lead to answers that aren't the true feelings of the public being surveyed. For instance, if the question uses technical jargon or abbreviations your respondents don't understand, your results won't necessarily be accurate.

One of the main reasons for nonsampling errors is the questions prompt certain answers. This is the same problem we noted in conducting interviews. To avoid question bias, you must be careful when you frame questions so that you don't suggest answers to your subjects. Sidebar 3.3 contains some recommendations to eliminate those prompts. The suggestions are equally useful in framing questions for an interview or a survey.

SIDEBAR 3.3   Question Bias: Some Suggestions

Whether your research tool is a survey, a focus group or an interview, question bias has the potential to invalidate the accuracy of your results. Here are the most common forms of question bias and some suggestions as to how to correct them.

Bias Resulting from Behavioral Expectation

This type of bias occurs when the question suggests that most people feel a certain way about an issue. The following is a behavioral expectation question:

Nearly 80 percent of workers think their job's health insurance benefits should be improved. Do you agree?

The question forces workers to contradict majority opinion if they want to disagree. To correct behavioral expectation bias, phrase the question simply and directly.

Are you satisfied with your job's health insurance benefits?

Bias from Leading Information

Questions biased by leading information provide more subtle cues about the correct answer, but the cues could still influence a subject's response. The following is a leading information question:

Some people say men who work in occupations like truck driving, janitorial work and garbage collection should be paid the same as females who are engaged in woman's work, jobs such as being a receptionist or a shopgirl, which are often the source of discretionary income to buy luxuries. Do you agree with this policy of comparable pay for men and women?

By comparing "occupations" to "jobs" and "men" to "females" and asserting that pay from "woman's work" buys only luxuries, the question may prompt research subjects to answer in a certain way. To correct bias from leading

SIDEBAR 3.3   (continued)

information, simplify the question, removing adjectives and descriptors that could encourage respondents to interpret the question inaccurately. A better version of the previous question might be:

> Some people say jobs that demand the same education, training, skill or effort should be paid the same. If this policy were in effect, a job like truck driving, which is traditionally held by a man, might draw less pay than a job traditionally held by a woman, such as being a secretary, if the secretary's job demands more education and involves more responsibility. Do you agree with this policy of comparable worth pay?

Bias Resulting from Unequal Comparison

Questions contain unequal comparison bias if subjects are given response options that could be interpreted as being dramatically different. Again, respondents are prompted to answer in a certain way. Here's an example of unequal comparison bias:

> Whose position do you support in the Frawley Forest debate?
> a. the mine owners
> b. the Federal Bureau of Mining officials
> c. the Citizens for Environmental Awareness

Although the response options are factual and not necessarily manipulative, the respondents' interpretation of the options might lead them to choose option c. If a researcher wants a more accurate answer, the options should be rewritten to eliminate the connotations subjects might attribute to each answer. The following is a better version of the previous question:

> Which position do you support in the Frawley Forest debate?
> a. Open an additional 10 percent of the Frawley State Forest for mining.
> b. Permit current mining but conduct an extensive review of its environmental and economic effects.
> c. Close existing mining operations and forbid future mining in Frawley State Forest.

Bias from Unbalanced Categories

This type of bias is caused by not giving a subject equal opportunities to respond positively or negatively to a question. Here's a question containing unbalanced category bias:

The university currently spends 4 percent of its annual budget on sports. Should this amount
   a. be increased a great deal?
   b. be increased somewhat?
   c. be increased a little?
   d. stay the same?
   e. be decreased?

With three positive options and only one negative option, respondents, especially those without strong opinions on the subject, find themselves making positive comments. This type of bias is easily remedied:

The university currently spends 4 percent of its annual budget on sports. Should this amount
   a. be increased a great deal?
   b. be increased somewhat?
   c. stay the same?
   d. be decreased somewhat?
   e. be decreased a great deal?

Experiments: Tracking How Communication Changes Behavior

Many PR practitioners have relied on questionnaires instead of integrating experiments into their work. This may be the result of a misunderstanding of what experiments are. Contrary to the perception that experiments are conducted only by scientists before bubbling test tubes, an experiment is simply the formalized testing of a proposition. An experiment tries to isolate one factor among the many that might have caused a result to see what effect that factor had on the actions of a substance, person or group.

That's something a questionnaire can't do. Questionnaires essentially measure what a person will admit to someone asking a question, which can sometimes be something very different from the truth. A striking example of such prevarication occurred during the 1990 presidential elections in Nicaragua. Well-designed public opinion polls found the ruling Sandinista government would win a landslide victory. But on election day just two days later, the government's democratic opponent won the presidential race. What happened? According to analysts, voters who feared pressure or violence from revealing their views lied to the canvassers. When it counted, in the voting booth, they powerfully voiced their true feelings.

Instead of being content to measure what people say they will do, PR experiments are designed to measure whether someone's actions have changed because of communication. Experiments are perfectly suited to testing the final part of our communication model—whether behaviors have changed. Because changing actions is the crux of the definition of persuasion, it's obvious that experiments, and not questionnaires, are more legitimate in proving the power of communication in solving management problems. (You'll find an outline of the PR experimental procedure in Sidebar 3.4.)

Experiments also fit more closely into management-by-objective planning methods. The MBO process discussed in Chapter 2 is targeted specifically at finding real-life changes in an organization produced by altering some aspect of its communication program. That is what a traditional experiment tries to measure as well.

Employing experiments in management-by-objective planning will only be ef-

---

SIDEBAR 3.4   Outline of the Experimental Procedure

Experiments are a method of systematically observing changes after something in an environment is altered. Because management by objective is based on the same principle, experiments can be integrated into many public relations efforts. As MBO implies, all PR research arises from institutional problems and should be used to solve institutional problems. These are the steps in the PR experimental process:

1. State an institutional problem.
2. Select an individual element of the problem that can be measured and is relevant to solving the problem.
3. Establish exact definitions so that your measurements are accurate and consistent.
4. Search published studies for any with similar subjects or methods.
5. Develop a hypothesis.
6. Design the experiment:
   - Select the experimental design.
   - Define and select experimental and control groups.
   - Define changes you'll make in experimental group's environment.
   - Formulate testing procedures.
7. Run the experiment and obtain the data.
8. Analyze and interpret the data to make generalizations and inferences.
9. Integrate your findings into your planning and management procedures.

fective if you use the experimental process to test issues that are important to the organization. All too often, PR practitioners become sidetracked and measure the wrong goal. For instance, let's imagine you're put in charge of recruiting workers and designing informational materials for your company's wellness program. In writing your MBO plan for the project, your objective is that 20 percent of the workers contacted will attend the organizational meeting.

That's a fine effort, but what does it have to do with your organizational goals? It might be nice to have good attendance at the meeting, but that is only a secondary goal and probably a weak predictor of whether the company's workers will take less sick leave.

A better objective would be to find if employees in the wellness program take fewer sick days after they've been enrolled in the program for six months. You might propose that you'll have a 10 percent decrease in employee sick leave because of your efforts to enroll employees in a company wellness program.

It requires little effort to design this type of experiment in a research plan, but you must be careful. Let's say you take 100 employees from an assembly line in one of your buildings and look at their attendance before and after the wellness program. If the program starts in the summer and a winter flu epidemic roaring through the factory infects 40 percent of the wellness program workers six months later, is the program a failure? Not necessarily, because a properly designed experiment might find that employees not enrolled in the wellness program were hit even harder.

Would it be better to design your objective to measure whether workers participating in the wellness program took fewer sick days than those who weren't enrolled in the program?

There are still problems. How would you know whether the people who enrolled in the wellness program were less healthy at the program's outset than the average worker? If they were less healthy at the outset, those wellness program workers might have made extraordinary progress in improving their job attendance but still compare unfavorably to the other workers at the end of six months.

Although there are several possible experimental designs (see Sidebar 3.5) you could use, for most PR tasks it's best if you use a two-group pretest-posttest experiment. This experimental design picks two groups, one of which receives a "treatment," in this case the wellness program activities. The other group (the control group) doesn't participate in the wellness program.

However, both of the groups are evaluated before the program starts. By determining the number of sick days members of each group use during a given month before the treatment begins, you can tell if there are differences between the groups. Thus, you will know if the differences you observe at the end of the experiment are the result of an initial difference between the groups.

After the pretests, one group proceeds through the wellness program. After the program is over, both groups are evaluated again to see how many sick days each has taken. If there is less absenteeism in the group that has gone through the program, you can detect that.

As mentioned earlier, an experiment's strength is in its ability to isolate the individual components of a process that contribute to a final result. Because you've

SIDEBAR 3.5 Experimental Designs Adaptable to Public Relations Tasks

Choosing the most appropriate experimental design balances cost considerations against the consequences of drawing the wrong conclusion from a poorly designed study. Here are four common experimental designs.

Pretest/Posttest

In a pretest/posttest experiment, the experimenter tests a group's performance or attitude, then changes the situation—for example, by raising wages or instituting communication programs. After the change, the experimenter tests the group again to see if its performance or behaviors have changed since the treatment. The disadvantage of a pretest/posttest design is that the experimenter cannot prove that the treatment caused the observed changes. Between the first and second test, group members might have been affected by other factors, like fatigue, experience or weather, that might be responsible for the changes.

Posttest Only

In a posttest-only experimental design, the experimenter uses a random sequence to pick members of two groups. One group will receive training, information or some other treatment. The other group (the control group) will not. After the experimental group completes the treatment process, both groups are tested to see whether the treatment has caused some observable difference between the groups. The disadvantage: The experimenter doesn't necessarily know the groups had equal skills or attitudes before the study started. Thus, any differences after the treatment may be because one group was more talented or more antagonistic before the treatment was given.

Multiple Pretest/Posttest

In a multiple pretest/posttest design, the experimenter randomly picks the members of two groups, just as in the posttest-only form. However, this design tests the performance or attitudes of each group before the treatment. This establishes the respective level of each group before the experiment. Then both groups are tested after the treatment. Any changes the experimenter observes in the two groups after the treatment can probably be attributed to the treatment. This is the best experimental design, but it is also the most expensive.

Nonequivalent Control Groups

This experimental design is similar to a posttest only, except the experimental design is used when two groups can't be randomly chosen. It's often employed when a company wants to observe the impact if an entire factory is converted to a different management system. As it's impossible to select a random control group from within the factory, the experimenter chooses to use a similar factory's workforce as a control group. An experimenter could also employ a nonequivalent control group form within a two-group pretest/posttest design.

tested both groups, you can eliminate the uncertainty over whether environmental factors caused the changes in job attendance. For instance, if the flu epidemic swept through the factory, you would be able to tell whether, in the midst of massive worker absenteeism, the employees who went through the program had better performance. You can review the steps in a two-group, pretest-posttest experiment in Memory Memo 3.6.

As with other evaluation research, experiments give you the capacity to show the power of communication in solving organizational problems and provide invaluable information about changing, reinforcing or even abandoning current communication efforts to make your total communication program more cost-effective.

However, a few warnings on experiments seem advisable. Remember that in communication research, the objects on which you are experimenting are not chemicals or cancer cells, but people. Because of that, you need to be very aware of your responsibilities as a researcher and your subjects' rights as human beings. You must be sure that as a result of your research you are not harming them either physically or emotionally. Further, you must guarantee that your research does not violate their constitutional and human rights, including the right of privacy from intrusive researchers, should your subjects so request.

Memory Memo 3.6
Steps in a two-group pretest/posttest experiment:

- Pick a control group and a treatment group.
- Test each group to determine each group's performance.
- Change the situation for treatment group.
- Test both groups to determine each group's performance.
- Figure performance differences of each group between tests.
- Compare the difference between each group's performance.
- If the treatment group's performance difference is substantially greater than the control group's, the treatment had an effect.

RECORD KEEPING AND RESEARCH: YOUR PROFESSIONAL MEMORY

One final point about research: Research is an ongoing, cumulative process, in which each step of your research for every project, and even many things you do outside your work, adds to your knowledge and your tactics in solving communication problems.

Initially, that means you need to be thinking about your communication tasks and objectives as you scan the newspaper, read professional journals, talk to colleagues and talk to people you meet in an airport or a restaurant. Clip newspaper articles and transcribe notes to yourself about your conversations or experiences that might have relevance to some future task.

You also need to record your actions and results from your communication campaigns. When were releases mailed to a certain media outlet? How many people attended a groundbreaking ceremony you promoted? What was the cost for printing the posters and conducting the sessions of an employee training program? Did your company experience a productivity increase as a result? How much?

Obviously, those mailing dates and printing bills, newspaper clippings and musings will do you no good if they are stuffed haphazardly in a box in the back of your office closet or underneath your bed at home. You must make conscientious efforts to classify your collected facts and file them in a way that allows for easy retrieval.

Although one alternative is to keep papers in file folders, it's much more efficient to put at least a copy of your own notes, memos and letters in a computer storage bank. If, instead of writing notes, you type them directly into the computer, you can file each note under several key words that will help you access the information later. When that time comes, you can ask the computer to examine all your files to find records under any of those subject names, and it will bring up only those memos related to those topics. It's the equivalent of filing the same note in three or even 10 file folders with different names on them. And, of course, you can also perform the same computer search procedures to select only those articles that mention each of two or three specific areas. We discussed those in the database research section earlier in this chapter.

With scanners, you can also store and retrieve most newspaper and magazine clippings on computers. A scanner, which is an attachment that can hook up to most computers, can visually scan a sheet of characters or pictures and convert the images to computer language. Those documents can be filed, changed, and even put directly into other documents without retyping. Other scanner systems allow you to make photocopy-type reproductions of your documents, which can be cross-indexed and retrieved by using a series of key words.

In addition, there are many computer file-management systems commercially available. Generally, they not only allow you to find a particular file by the key word or words, but they can make a word-by-word search through all your available computer files for a particular word or group of words. Scanners and computer file-management systems are much easier to control than traditional paper filing systems and allow you to improve the quality of your knowledge tremendously as you approach a project.

Learning about research is a lifelong enterprise. Every year new technology, methods and procedures supplement the knowledge we have about our audiences and their motivations. Knowing that information is a vital component of any writing process, and even amid hectic professional workdays, you need to program time, effort and expenditures for discovering information that will make you a more effective communicator.

SUMMARY

- Public relations research is a systematic method of collecting information that will help reduce uncertainty in an organization's decision-making process.
- Research accompanies every step of the receiver-centered communication process. It helps the practitioner determine with whom the institution should communicate and helps him or her shape a persuasive message, pick the medium through which to reach the target audience, and determine whether the audience took an action because of the message.

- A communication audit assesses an important public's view of a particular issue and compares it to what the organization wishes it were. That knowledge helps practitioners concentrate their communication resources on specific publics and specific issues that are important to the organization's success.

- Issues forecasting is research designed to predict issues that will be important to the institution in the future. This early-warning system permits practitioners to avert or plan for crises and positions the institution to take advantage of future changes in the business or social environment.

- Public relations most commonly uses three different types of issues forecasting: Scanning predicts important trends by assessing the way an issue is covered by mass media and specialized journals; scenario writing explores the ramifications of possible events on an institution; and trend extrapolation exploits knowledge about recurring historical and social trends to predict future events.

- Secondary research is information collected from previously compiled studies. Practitioners can find most federal government statistics by referring to the American Statistics Index or the Congressional Information Service. Various publication indexes are used to locate information in newspapers, magazines and professional journals.

- Computerized databases make secondary research much more convenient by allowing researchers to search years of publication indexes with one command. Even more important, the computer lets the researcher examine thousands of articles and glean just those articles that contain information on specific topics.

- Marketing statistics resources such as Simmons and Mediamark provide demographic information about the buyers of thousands of products and services. Both also analyze the audiences of major magazines, network television shows, and radio and cable television networks. These statistics allow practitioners to discover the media their prospective customers will most likely read or watch. It's also possible to draw audience psychographic descriptions from the media-use patterns and use that information to fashion messages that more nearly reflect the interests of a particular product's audience.

- Practitioners can determine local product-use patterns with SRDS and CACI. Standard Rates and Data Service contains general product expenditure patterns in individual counties. The CACI Sourcebook provides indexes of expenditures for every ZIP code in the United States.

- Although mass media can deliver a message to the greatest number of people for the least cost per person, person-to-person messages and other types of personal media are generally more effective in motivating people to act on a message. Because personal media is more expensive per message delivered, PR practitioners must concentrate their efforts on individuals who are the most likely prospects by using specialized media. Mailing lists are one way to select those individuals with very specific interests.

- Effective interviewing is a planned strategy of questions to obtain information from a person. One plan is the GOSS formula, which suggests all human achievements can be understood by studying a person's formulation of a goal, obstacles to overcome in achieving the goal, the circumstances that stimulated the start of the project, and the solution the person found. Structuring questions around those basic principles can elicit the personality and passion involved in an enterprise.

- Although questionnaires are the most common form of primary research in public relations, they measure only opinions, not the deeply held attitudes that are more likely to determine an individual's behaviors.

- Sampling errors occur when not all people in the population you are studying have an equal chance of offering their opinions. Sampling errors can often be prevented by instituting a system that eliminates any environmental reasons that might result in an unrepresentative sample, or any conscious or inadvertent bias the researcher might have.

- A common source of nonsampling errors is faulty question construction. If not carefully written, questions can often prompt certain answers that invalidate the results of a survey or an interview.

- Because experiments are designed to observe whether behaviors change after modifying one aspect of an environment, they are perfectly suited to evaluate a management-by-objective communication process. The experimental design that most accurately measures the effect of those modifications is the two-group, pretest-posttest design.

- Record keeping is a way of establishing baseline data concerning successful communication tactics and background information that could help in future communication planning.

THINK PIECES

1. What would a communication audit reveal about your college's administration? What information could you offer your college's leaders that could help them capitalize on the college's positive points and minimize the bad elements? Could any of these factors be improved by a communication campaign?

2. Have you noticed repeated stories in the newspaper or on TV concerning one topic? What societal changes or emerging attitudes might you be able to extrapolate from those stories?

3. What other magazines do you think people who read bicycling magazines might read? Do you believe they would read conservative political magazines? What might that mean in terms of the way you would design messages to those audiences?

4. What elements might be overrepresented or underrepresented if you tried to measure your college's student attitudes by administering a poll to your writing class? What claims can you realistically make about the results of such a survey?

MANAGEMENT PROBLEMS

D6.3

D7.5

WRITING ASSIGNMENTS

D10.13

D12.4

ADDITIONAL READING

Babbie, Earl. *The Practice of Social Science Research*, 7th ed. New York: International Thomson, 1995.

Brady, John. *The Craft of Interviewing.* New York: Vintage, 1976.

Broom, Glen M. "Co-orientational Measurement of Public Issues." *Public Relations Review* 3 (Winter 1977): 100–119.

Broom, Glen M., and Dozier, David M. *Using Research in Public Relations: Applications and Program Management.* Englewood Cliffs, N.J.: Prentice-Hall, 1990.

Futures Group, The. "Computers Play Future Scenarios." *Public Relations Journal* 51:4 (October 1995): 48.

Hauss, Deborah. "Measuring the Impact of Public Relations: Electronic Techniques Improve Campaign Evaluation." *Public Relations Journal* 49:2 (February 1993) 14–21.

Lauzen, Martha M. "Toward a Model of Environmental Scanning." *Journal of Public Relations Research* 7:3 (1995): 187–203.

Pavlik, John J. *Public Relations: What Research Tells Us.* Newbury Park, Calif.: Sage, 1987.

Rubin, Rebecca B., Rubin, Alan M., and Piele, Linda. *Communication Research: Strategies and Sources.* Belmont, Calif.: Wadsworth, 1986.

Stewart, David W., and Kamins, Michael A. *Secondary Research: Information Sources and Methods.* Thousand Oaks, Calif.: Sage, 1993.

Ward, Jean, and Hansen, Kathleen A. *Search Strategies in Mass Communication*, 2nd ed. White Plains, N.Y.: Longman, 1993.

Database Sources

With more than 5,400 publicly available databases, one of the more difficult problems has been to find the most appropriate database. To solve that problem, there is a database that lists other databases, called the Gale Directory of Databases (the print version is the Information Industry Directory). It's a good place to start many research tasks. Although the subjects of databases range from a summary of newspaper articles to one that provides English translations of Chinese patents, here are some databases that might be used by PR practitioners.

ABI/INFORM—index of 800 primary business publications

AP NEWS—full text of Associated Press coverage of general news, business and sports

ASI—database version of the American Statistics Index, which indexes statistical publications from 500 federal offices and agencies

BUSINESS WIRE—unedited text of news releases from more than 10,000 companies, PR firms, colleges and political organizations

COMPANY INTELLIGENCE—marketing and financial information on about 100,000 private and public companies in the United States

ENCYCLOPEDIA OF ASSOCIATIONS—electronic listing of 75,000 nonprofit organizations throughout the world

FEDERAL REGISTER—full text of the Federal Register, a daily update of official U.S. government agency actions

INVESTTEXT—the world's largest database of industry and business analysis with more than 1,500,000 records

NEXIS—full-text information on more than 1,000 magazines, newspapers and wire services

PR NEWSWIRE—complete text and indexing of all news releases found on this commercial release service

THE ROPER CENTER FOR PUBLIC OPINION RESEARCH—full text of U.S. public opinion polls compiled by the Roper polling organization since 1937

PTS NEWSLETTER DATABASE—provides access to newsletters

PTS U.S. FORECASTS—list of published forecasts of economic trends

STANDARDS & SPECIFICATIONS—specifications for materials, safety and testing to fulfill government and industry contracts

ULRICH'S INTERNATIONAL PERIODICALS DIRECTORY—electronic version of the massive publication directory; lists more than 190,000 serials from 200 countries

Sources of Secondary Research

There are thousands of sources for locating secondary research. Here are just a few that will probably be available in a medium-sized library. Many are available in database or microfiche form as well as on paper.

To find general information and frame your research questions:

almanacs
encyclopedias

To locate background information from general-interest publications:

Readers' Guide to Periodicals—articles from general-interest magazines
NewsBank—microfilm listing articles from hundreds of newspapers
Individual newspaper indexes—Major newspapers, such as the New York Times, the Wall Street Journal and the London Times, publish indexes to their publications. An increasing number of smaller newspapers are now offering electronic search-and-retrieval services for articles in their own publications.
Facts on File—day-by-day summary of all major news events, indexed by subject, with brief description of event
Editorials on File—editorials from major city newspapers, categorized by subject

To find magazine and journal articles on specialized subjects:

Business Periodicals Index
Index Medicus—indexes articles from hundreds of U.S. and international medical journals
Education Index
Social Sciences Index

Virtually all the specialized subject indexes are also available in computer database form.

To find experts and interview sources:

Encyclopedia of Associations—tens of thousands of organizations listed alphabetically and by subject interest, with statement of purpose, principal officers, addresses and phone numbers
Reference Book of Corporate Managements—lists of board members and main officers for most corporations
Who Owns Whom—company ownership traced to the holding companies and multinational corporations that control their actions
United States Government Manual—lists of offices in Congress, executive branch, courts and agencies, including duties, names of principal staff officers, addresses and phone numbers

To find specialized statistical information and reports:

Index to International Statistics—statistics compiled on foreign business, government and social trends

Statistical Abstract of the United States—general statistics on the United States

American Statistics Index—listing by subject of the reports compiled by U.S. government agencies, including the census office. Census reports include reports for agriculture, wholesale and retail trade, housing, local government, etc.

CIS—transcripts of congressional hearings, committee research reports, etc.

Public opinion polls:

Gallup Report and the *Harris Survey*—With the indexes to these national polling services, you can track changes in public opinion for 50 years.

Regional newspapers surveys—An increasing number of newspapers are sponsoring local or regional public opinion polls. Use newspaper indexes to find these polls.

To find local facts:

City directory—R.L. Polk and Co. publishes this directory, which provides personal information on the resident or business located at every address in the city

State directory—published by state governments or private publishers, this directory provides financial statistics and names, addresses and titles of state and local government officials and employees

Chamber of Commerce directory—provides names of principal officers and the addresses and phone numbers of most local businesses

## chapter 4

Legal Issues and Ethics: A Day-to-Day Guide for the Professional

REAL-LIFE LESSONS

In my speeches and consultation sessions, I'm often confronted with business executives and even public relations practitioners who view ethics as a business luxury. They defend their viewpoint vehemently: Nobody is ethical, so why should my company be ethical? People are ethical only when they think someone is watching, so ethics are just a show to impress other people. A company adopts an ethics philosophy once it's successful and can afford to be forgiving to those companies that aren't so ethical. In short, their point is that the dog-eat-dog competitiveness of business and the high-minded idealism of ethics don't belong together. One naturally overwhelms and destroys the other.

My usual response is to tell them the story of Manville Corp. In the early 1970s, Manville Corp. was a success, well anchored in the top half of the Fortune 500. It made floor coverings, wood and building products, and most ominously, asbestos insulation and associated products.

For over 60 years, the scientific and medical world had been worried about the health implications of asbestos fibers. By 1931, there had already been 50 medical journal articles published on the ill effects of asbestos, and the British government had forced British manufacturers to improve the exhaust ventilation and dust suppression in asbestos factories and instituted periodic medical exams for workers engaged in particularly dusty processes.

In the face of this and more than 100 additional scientific articles over the next 30 years, Johns-Manville, as the company was then known, did little to warn its own employees or the construction workers who used its products of the damaging effects of breathing asbestos fibers. Finally, in response to a 1964 study linking asbestos with lung cancer and white-lung disease, Manville put warning stickers on its products. It did little else to educate its customers about the dangers, nor did it recommend safety procedures, choosing instead to wait until the federal government mandated safety rules for asbestos products.

Finally, in the 1970s product liability suits brought by construction workers claiming they had been crippled or were dying because of Manville's asbestos products started to pile up. By 1982, when the federal government finally established the standards, there had already been 16,500 personal injury suits filed against Manville, and company lawyers predicted that 90,000 other cases might be filed. The potential bills could be twice the company's total worth. Manville filed for bankruptcy.

Through years of bitter, acrimonious negotiations and a flood of negative media coverage, Manville claimed it had no responsibility to the workers who were laboring for breath because of their work with Manville's products. In fact, Manville said it was the U.S. government's responsibility to pay the suits, some of which arose because of work in the 1930s and 1940s, because the government delayed establishing safety standards after the 1964 study.

Meanwhile, Manville was collapsing. Its stock price plunged from above $300 in 1977 to around $8 twelve years later. As a result of the bankruptcy agreement, the firm was obliged to give up 80 percent of its outstanding stock to the trust established to pay for the potential settlements. Manville and its insurance companies placed $842 million in cash and $730 million of the company's stock into the trust fund. Then, starting in 1991, Manville started paying a minimum of $75 million a year into the trust fund, and in 1992, the trust gained the right to requisition up to 20 percent of the company's annual profit in addition to the standard annual payment.

There were other, more human costs. To meet its obligations, Manville had to fire over two-thirds of its work force, putting 16,000 employees out of work. It even had to sell its headquarters building near Denver.

The total bill is an estimated $2.5 billion to $3.5 billion through the first two decades of the 21st century. The irony is that Manville quit selling asbestos products anyway.

What's the moral of the story? Ethical values do have bottom-line consequences for a firm. Manville was nearly destroyed, not by a lack of aggressive business savvy so prized by the business executives I've met, but by its failure to recognize and then live up to its moral obligations.

The laws and ethical strictures that guide the public relations profession greatly foster our institutions' ethical outlooks and serve as the necessary foundation for long-term business success. This chapter explores the laws we must follow to contribute to that prosperity and gives guidance about the ethical standards that may evolve into the laws of the future.

WHAT YOU KNOW

- An important role of public relations is to integrate an institution into its social and political environment.
- Effective public relations depends on identifying and communicating with publics that will be affected by an issue.

- Each component of an audience is best persuaded if a message highlights the self-interests that are most important in making its decision.

WHAT YOU'LL LEARN

- The practice of public relations and adherence to ethics have very similar outcomes: Both help an organization adjust to new societal environments.
- Conforming to legal standards and ethical behaviors makes the coercive actions of governmental regulations or legal judgments against an organization less likely.
- A strong commitment to ethics can make a company more competitive.

COMMUNICATION LAW AND ETHICS: WHAT IT'S NOT

An understanding of communication law and ethics is a complex, but necessary, part of a PR practitioner's knowledge. Failing to understand and adhere to the laws and standards in our society that govern communication can create massive problems for PR professionals and the institutions for which they work.

However, adhering to communication law and ethics should not be viewed merely as moving through a checklist of technical details to keep our companies and us from being hauled into court. Instead, as A. Bruce Crawley suggests in Box 4.1, an understanding of law and communication ethics helps define our role within society and, indeed, how our society perceives itself.

For public relations professionals who are dedicated to understanding how public perception creates an environment for institutional success, that is valuable information. Understanding the basic philosophy underpinning our laws and ethical standards helps us direct our institutions to goals beyond the mere minimum the law prescribes. Indeed, as Memory Memo 4.1 reminds us, it gives us the opportunity to more fully adapt our institutions to an ever-changing social and economic environment. It allows us to see what our society values and helps us create the perception and the reality that our companies are progressive and humane and recognize their roles in creating a society that is safe, harmonious and prosperous. A supportive public is, after all, the ultimate goal of public relations and can be instrumental in our organization's survival and success.

> **Memory Memo 4.1**
> ***Anchoring our organization's actions in ethical standards lets us***
> - adapt our organizations to the changing societal environment
> - create the perception and reality that our organization has met those standards
> - develop a supportive pool of public belief in our mission that lets us do our job with a minimum of coercive interference

BOX 4.1 Views from the Field

A. Bruce Crawley
Crawley is president of Crawley, Haskins & Rodgers Public Relations, a Philadelphia-based public relations firm. Prior to establishing his own firm, Crawley was senior vice president and director of public and investor relations for First Pennsylvania Bank and First Pennsylvania Corp.

Is it hard to sell the benefits of ethics to institutional managers?

As a society, we've recently come through a period—the 1980s—in which ethics were not considered very useful. When society as a whole seems to condone moral slippage, it's very difficult to communicate effectively with managers that they should "toe the line" ethically. In the disastrous aftermath of that period, however, we now recognize that somebody should have been listening to the people who were espousing ethical practices. In the savings and loan debacle, for example, the failures weren't due to economic reversal but primarily to fraud, deception and unethical behaviors among institutional managers, so a case can clearly be made that ethical behavior isn't just for your conscience. It's not just to appease some ethereal angel sitting on your shoulder. It's not necessarily spiritual. A lack of ethics also can have a disastrous impact on the bottom line. Institutional managers can understand that kind of message.

Then there's a connection between ethics and profits?

To the extent the public is not satisfied that a company is operating fairly and ethically, the company risks a backlash in the marketplace. When Exxon made the kind of responses it made to its Alaska spill, the public didn't believe the company had a real commitment to operating in a fair and ethical fashion. As a result, people stopped buying Exxon gas and started to destroy and return the company's credit cards. I don't believe Exxon reduced its marketing efforts or that it purposely closed any outlets during this period. A significant portion of the sales Exxon lost during that time can be traced directly to the fact that the public perceived that the company was not conducting itself in an ethical fashion. There is a connection between ethics and profits.

Is there some rule book for ethical behavior to guide us?

The public relations profession, like other professions, has its stated code of ethics, but we can't find all the answers there or in any other textbook or manual. There are actions that are not *illegal* today that certainly aren't morally or socially acceptable. Unfortunately, in our litigious society, management too often has been guided by whether an action is *legally* defensible. There is, however, a more effective decision-making process. Our mission is to bring the perspective of the real world, the perspective of the broader society, into our companies. That perspective is critical, because from that will come a clear sense of what is morally acceptable in the society in which we operate. If we, as practitioners, lose that perspective, if we cut ourselves off from that sense of how the public might respond to certain actions by our employers or clients, we become ineffective. It's important to sit at the table with management but it's also necessary to maintain contacts outside the corporate conference room and beyond the walls of the corporation. We also need to sit down with community activists and with the interest groups that impact the client and bring that perspective to the client. Beyond our professional society's code of ethics, we gain a sense of what is morally appropriate behavior, on a situational basis, from our publics.

I can foresee situations in which I might be ordered to undertake some unethical task. What are my options?

There are three basic options. First, you should try to convince your managers that their decision is not in the best interests of the institution. To accomplish that, you generally should be prepared to present examples from similar situations in which the results have been damaging for the corporate entity. Second, you can refuse to assist in the action on the basis of principle. I have done that on several occasions, sometimes risking the wrath of top management. It can be professionally uncomfortable, to say the least. Third, you can resign. The practitioner who builds a reputation for hiding the truth or intentionally misleading the media or the public is headed for a short career. Once we lose our credibility and gain a reputation for unethical behavior, we are virtually useless as a conduit for information about our client or employer.

—Used with permission of A. Bruce Crawley

SPEECH: IT'S NOT AS FREE AS YOU THINK

A discussion about legal issues in communication and public relations has to begin with an examination of the legal definition of speech. We've always been told our society is built upon the foundation of free speech. We see evidence of that in a cacophonous society, in which lawyers wage battles claiming free speech includes showing dirty movies, burning the flag or begging on the streets.

Many of us have an impression that in the United States, individuals, groups, institutions and corporations can say anything they want anytime they want to say it. But free speech isn't as free as many of us believe, and many of those restrictions on speech directly affect the public relations practitioner.

Political Speech: The Unrestrained Campaign Trail

It's useful to examine laws governing speech as if there were three basic types of speech, all of which have different degrees of freedom. The least restricted speech is political speech. Political speech is the communication exchanged in the conduct of our government's institutions. The testimony in the courtroom, the debate in the Senate, the discussions in a council meeting, and the insults on the campaign trail are all examples of political speech.

One of our society's founding principles is that the political system functions best when all its participants have the fewest restrictions on their ability to exchange viewpoints. That has led to the relative freedom enjoyed by political speech.

For instance, the courts afford special protections from libel and slander laws for lawmakers, judges and officials while they are carrying out their official duties. The courts even extend that protection to the media, which would normally be liable for defamation, when they are reporting on the political process.

The courts have decided that even the most disgusting, bigoted speech must be tolerated if it is central to the political process. Thus, political candidates with racist platforms cannot be denied broadcast advertising time for their campaign ads on television or radio stations that sold air time to their opponents.

Although it conflicts with our democratic self-image of one person, one vote, the courts are so supportive of free political speech that they have even been reluctant to place limits on the money that corporations or individuals can give to support political causes. Although the courts have upheld restrictions on campaign contributions to candidates for political office, no such limits have been placed on individual or corporate support for political referendum issues or for supporting other political causes.

This sometimes raucous speech that distinguishes political activity is the idealized form of free speech that Americans both complain about and proclaim as their greatest strength. However, there are other types of speech to which this same freedom doesn't apply.

Private Speech: It's Free When It Doesn't Hurt Others

The communication between individuals in their daily affairs—so-called private speech—is less free than that given to political officials. We all know one hackneyed example of the restrictions placed on private speech: When you're in a crowded theater, you can't yell "Fire!" because the resulting panic might hurt people. The police could come and arrest you. That's a restriction on private speech.

There are other legal consequences that could await you if you exercise your private free speech rights too vigorously. For instance, it's possible you could be taken to court for slander if you announce to your class that a classmate fenced stolen television sets to pay his tuition bills.

That's understandable, you say, because your language might be hurting the reputation or future of your classmate. Yet a senator could accuse another senator of the same crime in a Senate debate that's being broadcast on national television, and the besmirched senator couldn't do too much about it.

The freedoms and restrictions of private speech generally extend to the media, too. Although it clashes with the perception that many people have of the media, print and broadcast news organizations are unable to exercise full measures of free speech, because they are subject to libel laws, invasion of privacy laws, obscenity laws and restrictions on printing or airing government secrets. At times, they are prevented from revealing the names of criminal court witnesses or even from printing the names of plaintiffs. That is hardly the anarchistic freedom of speech we generally attribute to reporters.

Within those bounds, however, the media have a great deal of freedom to express themselves. For instance, within the bounds formed by libel, obscenity and other laws, media outlets, just like individuals, have no legal obligations to be objective or evenhanded in their coverage. If a newspaper consistently wants to present a certain group's or political party's orientation and neglect other viewpoints, the other party's only recourse is to complain.

With the repeal of the fairness doctrine, that same principle applies to broadcast outlets, too. In fact, the only restriction that inhibits any media is the equal time provision that requires broadcast outlets to provide approximately equal amounts of air time for candidates for the same office to present their viewpoints. But again, that applies only to political candidates and only to broadcast outlets.

Those freedoms go even further. Even if a court is virtually certain a particular message will overstep the freedoms extended to private speech, it can't merely stop someone from saying or writing it. Instead, the courts have ruled that although a person can be prosecuted or sued after they have communicated, any form of prior restraint is almost always unconstitutional.

Commercial Speech: The Constrained World in Which PR Works

Few such protections are afforded to commercial speech, the messages organizations use to inform potential customers about products or services the companies would like them to purchase and use. In fact, in comparison to political speech, it seems that virtually anyone can restrict commercial speech.

In addition to being subject to all the restrictions regulating private speech, there are more stringent requirements placed on commercial speech. Despite our noble words about free speech, commercial speech can be controlled by government, by industry trade groups, and even by the media itself. As commercial speech is the primary tool of public relations practitioners, we'll examine some of the principles that explain how commercial speech can be controlled.

Government Controls: Alphabet Agencies Lining Up to Limit Speech.   Federal and state governments control commercial speech in many ways. Through the Federal Trade Commission, the federal government enforces rules on false and deceptive advertising. The Food and Drug Administration controls marketing of food, drugs, cosmetics, medical devices, and other consumer products that might cause

health problems. The Bureau of Alcohol, Tobacco and Firearms regulates advertising of those products. The Agriculture Department controls seed, meat and insecticide advertising, and the Securities and Exchange Commission polices advertising of stocks, bonds and other securities.

These government agencies have the power to order advertisers to change their claims. For instance, in recent years we've seen skirmishes over what properties "light" products must contain to be labeled as such. The federal government even has the power, as demonstrated by laws regulating cigarette advertising on television, to ban completely advertising for certain products in certain media. States have given themselves similar powers to prevent certain professions from advertising and to regulate the content and disclaimers contained within particular types of advertisements.

In contemplating whether a government restriction on commercial speech is appropriate, judges consider the following five questions, reviewed in Memory Memo 4.2:

> *Memory Memo 4.2*
> *Government standards for controlling commercial speech:*
>
> - Does the communication concern a legal activity?
> - Is the communication misleading?
> - Are there valid reasons for controlling the message?
> - Will the regulation meet the need for control?
> - Is the regulation more restrictive than necessary?

Does the Communication Concern a Legal Activity?   Judges have ruled that the government can prohibit commercial speech that discusses criminal activity. That creates some unusual situations. We can agree that burglarizing a home is illegal, but while it's perfectly legal to discuss plans to burglarize a home because it's private speech, is it illegal to advertise tools that can be used to break into homes? The courts have ruled that it is. It's quite legal, in other words, to restrict commercial speech that might promote illegal behavior.

Is the Communication Misleading?   If the average person seeing an advertisement or other form of commercial speech is misled by its wording, illustration or tone, the government has a right to intervene and control the communication. For instance, a complaint issued against a certain brand of mouthwash questioned its suggestion that using the product would prevent colds. As a result of the investigation, a federal agency ordered the manufacturer to deny the claim specifically in the product's ads for several years.

Are the Reasons for Controlling the Communication Valid?   Agencies restricting commercial speech also must consider whether there is a valid reason for controlling the speech. In essence, agencies have to decide whether enough good will arise from the restriction to justify hindering free speech. Will restricting ads for cigarettes decrease lung cancer rates? Will limiting the amount of advertising during Saturday morning TV cartoons aid children's development? Before the government restricts commercial speech, it first must ascertain if there is some justifiable reason for doing so.

Is the Regulation Effective in Meeting the Need for Control?   If there is some justification for restricting speech, does the proposed restriction accomplish the intended purpose? As a result of the television ban on cigarette advertising, do fewer children and adults smoke? Does requiring brokerage firms to place disclaimers on their ads help prevent consumers from making poor investments?

Those questions might be answered affirmatively. However, in some cases it seems that the restrictions don't accomplish what they intended or that they are too broad. That leads to the fifth question.

Is the Regulation More Restrictive than Necessary?   In certain cases, the courts have found controls on commercial speech too restrictive. For instance, the U.S. Supreme Court ruled that state laws prohibiting pharmacies from advertising prescription drug prices prevented consumers from gaining valuable information they needed to make comparisons and reasonable decisions. Since then, courts at various levels have dismissed similar restrictions that prevented home owners from placing For Sale signs in their yards and drugstores from advertising contraceptives. In each of those cases, judges have ruled that any positive result gained by restricting the communication was outweighed by the disadvantages for sellers and consumers.

Trade Association Limits: Slowly Relaxing Standards.   Trade associations and state professional regulatory organizations, especially groups like the American Bar Association and the American Medical Association, have exercised some control over their members' commercial speech. Those organizations, their affiliates or their professional review boards have traditionally prohibited their members from advertising or have restricted the types of information members could include in any advertising.

Although the courts have not completely forbidden professional organizations from limiting the commercial speech and advertising of their members, the restrictions have been reduced. For example, the prohibition on lawyers advertising prices for routine legal services has been removed. Similar restrictions on other professionals have also been dismissed.

Media Restrictions: Where Free Speech and Commercial Speech Collide.
For all their professed allegiance to First Amendment principles, media outlets are responsible for a large proportion of the restrictions on commercial speech.

Some of those restrictions arise from individual media outlets' standards. Contrary to what many people think, newspapers, magazines, and radio and television stations don't have any obligation to accept advertising they don't want to run. They don't even have to give a reason. With the few exceptions concerning political candidate advertising in broadcast media discussed earlier, publishers and station owners have total control over who does and does not advertise in their media. Many newspapers, for instance, refuse to sell advertising to movies rated NC-17. *Reader's Digest* does not accept any cigarette advertising. Other magazines refuse to run ads for contraceptives, underwear or liquor.

Similarly, there are no laws, rules or principles that prevent media outlets from enforcing their own political or social philosophy. An environmental group, for instance, can legitimately refuse to run ads in its publications for an oil company or for a cosmetics company that uses animal testing to determine its products' safety.

Broadcasters may also restrict commercial speech. The television networks have standards offices that dictate what products can be advertised on television and even the way advertisers can advertise accepted products. This creates some ludicrous contrasts. Daytime soap operas feature hunky stars and gorgeous starlets quivering in various states of undress between various illicit sexual rendezvous, but when the commercial break starts, the networks suddenly become very prudish. Until recently, for instance, live women were not allowed to model bras in television ads, which is why former film star Jane Russell had to drag a mannequin around with her for years as she advertised Playtex bras.

Sometimes the standards offices are even more cautious. Although most stations accept beer commercials, few will accept commercials in which people actually drink beer. On one commercial that suggested a certain cologne's fragrance led to amorous activities, the network standards office insisted the commercial be reshot so both the man and woman were wearing wedding rings. This suggests that you need a clear understanding of the standards that advertising outlets enforce so you won't waste your company's resources on creating an advertisement a station won't air.

RESTRICTIONS ON COMMERCIAL SPEECH: AN OUTLINE OF EVERYDAY PR LAW

Because commercial speech is subject to so many restrictions, let's examine the major legal standards that guide our communication efforts.

Libel: Tough Tests Make It Hard to Prove

Many people think that only the media can be guilty of libel. That's not true at all. Anyone writing in any medium is subject to libel, ranging from the publisher of a major metropolitan newspaper to the editor of a neighborhood association newsletter, or even to the writer of a memo at a small company.

We first need to distinguish slander from libel. Slander and libel are the two forms of defamation. Slander is defamation that is confined to a spoken medium. Libel is defamation that is in a fixed form, whether written or representational. Thus, headlines, articles, advertisements, cartoons, photographs or even statues can be libelous. Even media that we consider spoken, like broadcast news reports and speeches, might be libelous, because they were at one point in written form and thus could be considered in a fixed form.

U.S. defamation laws have emerged from the need to balance the free flow of information vital to a democracy with the desire to protect individuals from having their personal or professional reputations destroyed by false information. The laws are generally interpreted to give speakers and writers great freedom to communicate information.

Tests for Libel.   Libel laws favor writers, as witnessed by the many routes through which a writer can avoid being found guilty of libel. However, because many of the same offenses can be pursued either through a libel or invasion of privacy suit, writers need to be careful. Invasion of privacy law leans toward protecting the interests of the person about whom something is written.

There are seven basic tests on which libel suits are judged. (See Figure 4.1, on the next page.) If the person suing for libel fails to meet any one of those seven tests, the libel suit is generally dismissed. That's a daunting task for any attorney and explains why the vast percentage of libel suits ultimately fail.

Let's examine those seven tests.

Publication.   Plaintiffs in a libel case first have to prove the potentially libelous statement was published. This is probably the easiest task, as courts have established that the publication test has been met if only three people know about the statement. If one person has written a statement about another person and a third person has seen that statement, publication has occurred. That's all that's needed. The hundreds or thousands of readers or viewers that might receive the message are superfluous because only those three people are needed to establish publication. That means that even notes exchanged between coworkers that criticize another worker could be libelous.

Identification.   Plaintiffs in a libel case have to prove that they can be identified by a substantial, respectable group of people to whom their reputations are important. This too is a relatively easy task. Obviously, if a person is identified by name in an article, script or other fixed form, the identification test has been passed.

However, judges have also interpreted the law to mean that identification has occurred if a "substantial, respectable group" for whom a person's reputation is important would likely be able to identify a person merely through a description. For instance, if a neighborhood newsletter criticized a home owner who let his dog run loose as "the insane, irresponsible, criminally deviant man on Franklin Avenue whose Great Dane is as revolting as he is," most judges would rule that the identification test had been met, even in the absence of an exact name.

Defamation.   Defamation is a much harder element to prove than publication or identification. Defamation has been defined by the U.S. Supreme Court as an "utterance tending to impugn the honesty, virtue or reputation, or publish the alleged or natural defects of a person and thereby expose him to public hatred, contempt or ridicule."

It's not enough to say something unpleasant about a person. Judges have maintained that it is not defamatory if a writer falsely states that a married woman is pregnant or mistakenly suggests someone has died. There's no disgrace in either so it's not defamation.

Although laws differ among the states, most state legislatures have defined four categories of defamation. They are:

1. Damaging a person in his or her public office, profession or occupation. Although this would seem to be the most productive area under which to bring libel suits, in practice it has become one of the most difficult to prove. For instance,

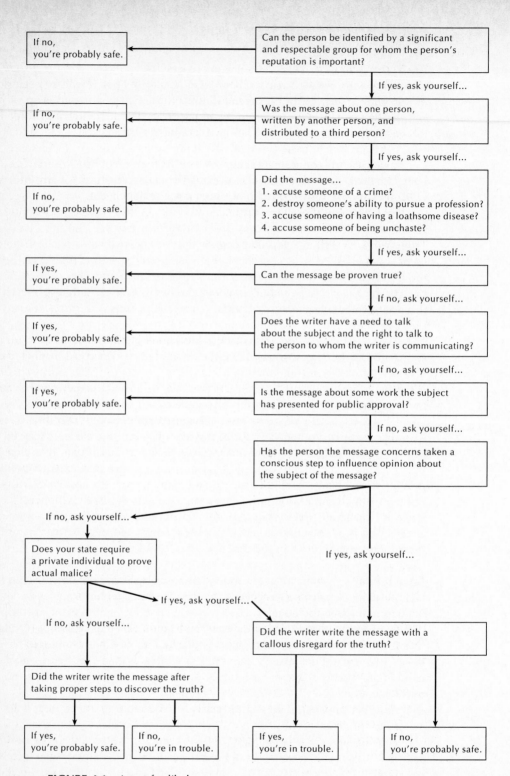

FIGURE 4.1 A test for libel

courts have ruled that communication about public officials has to be both false and motivated by malice before it can be considered defamatory. Similarly, even though it would damage a car dealer's reputation if a writer said his cars were poorly built and overpriced, it's very unlikely a judge would rule that was defamation. In reality, it's necessary to accuse someone of an act that would be considered criminal or deeply immoral before this statutory test can be met.

Two cases will help show this. Israel's former defense minister was accused by *Time* magazine of deliberately encouraging the massacre of Palestinians in a refugee camp in Lebanon. A jury found that statement was libelous. In another case, a newspaper stated that a Jewish kosher deli sold pork. As that was a grievous violation of Jewish dietary laws and destroyed the delicatessen owner's ability to carry on his business, that was also ruled defamatory.

2. Accusing a person of being unchaste. Although this definition was originally formulated only to protect a woman from being falsely accused of not being a virgin, the definition has been extended to include false accusations of promiscuity. At least one case has extended the statute's coverage to protect men from false charges of sexual impropriety.

3. Accusing someone of having a loathsome disease. This category was originally formulated to protect individuals from being shunned by false reports that they were suffering from leprosy, mental illness, and even cancer. This category had been little used until recently, when the advent of Acquired Immune Deficiency Syndrome (AIDS) made it more prominent.

4. Accusing someone of a crime. This is the most common form of libel suit because it's easiest to prove. If a writer falsely states a man has fathered a child out of wedlock by a 15-year-old girl, the man might sue for libel under the "unchaste" category, but he would more likely be successful if he sued under the "crime" standard. Because in most states any sexual relationship between an adult male and an underage female is statutory rape, the man could say he had been defamed by being falsely accused of committing a crime.

The same rationale would apply if a used car dealer were falsely accused of resetting the odometers on his dealership's cars. The dealer could sue under the "damaging in his profession" category, but because tampering with odometers is a crime in virtually every state, the case would be easier to win if the dealer could convince a jury that the writer falsely accused him of committing a crime.

Truth. In addition to publication, identification and defamation, a plaintiff in a libel case also has to prove the allegedly libelous statement was not true. If a statement is true, it's of no consequence how heinous the conduct of which a person is accused. No judge or jury will uphold a libel judgment. It doesn't matter if a writer accuses a minister of strangling furry baby kittens with bookmarks from the Bible. If the writer can prove it's true, the minister has no chance of winning a libel case.

However, we need to make a distinction here between truth and accuracy. A writer is afforded no protection from libel if he or she said a person "allegedly" stole funds from his corporation, or if a writer reports that a source "claims" a woman was engaged in promiscuous sex. "Accurately" repeating a report or transcribing an interview into a story is not an adequate libel defense unless the writer can prove he or she found evidence that the statement attributed to someone else was true, in and of itself.

Fair comment.   The fifth test for a libel case is fair comment. To win a libel case, the plaintiff also has to prove that he or she was not involved in an issue or activity upon which the writers had the right to express their opinion.

The courts have ruled that writers are free to criticize the work of people who deliberately go before the public, who seek the public's approval for their work, and whose own actions invite public interest in their lives. In concrete terms, that means it is acceptable to criticize public officials, actors, authors, restaurant owners, and car manufacturers and their laws, artistic works, products or services.

Again, in these circumstances writers can be unremittingly destructive to the career of a television producer, a playwright or a city official, and no judge will find the criticism to be libelous. Even though the statement might be defamatory, if the writer had the right to criticize, the libel suit will be dismissed.

Privilege.   This is an area judges are widening, which has further weakened the plaintiff's ability to prevail in a libel suit. Privilege originally was limited to public officials, who were protected from libel suits arising from communication they undertook as part of their official duties. As the courts interpreted it, the free intercourse of ideas during the debates of governmental bodies was so important that they didn't want to restrict it in any way.

To accomplish that end, courts in effect ruled out any libel suit brought against a public official who made a potentially defamatory statement while engaged in an official public duty. That meant that senators, council persons, judges and mayors could say anything in public debate during a council meeting or hearing or in court, and no one could sue them for libel. This was called absolute privilege.

Additionally, writers had a conditional privilege to print whatever those public officials said. The writers were protected from libel suits if they accurately repeated those statements.

However, in recent years that privilege has extended to more minor officials in government and has even been extended to business. Essentially, privilege gives people the right to talk about something they have the need to talk about to those people who have the need to hear. Now, for instance, conditional privilege can be claimed by workers whose duty or whose safety depends on evaluating other employees. Let's look at a couple of examples to see the limits of conditional privilege. Obviously, conditional privilege allows a foreman to criticize subordinates in reports to supervisors or others responsible for overseeing that worker's performance.

Even a worker has the right to criticize a fellow worker. A sawmill worker repairing dangerous machinery suspects on-the-job drug use by an operator whose performance could endanger the maintenance worker's life. The maintenance worker could report his suspicions about the operator to his foreman, and even if the charges couldn't be proven, it's unlikely the operator could successfully sue for libel because conditional privilege gives workers the right to communicate about things they need to talk about with people who need to hear. However, if the maintenance worker reported the suspected drug use to the firm's vice president for finance, the courts might not offer any protection from libel because the worker shared the message with an individual who was not in a direct position to remedy the situation.

Actual malice or negligence.   The final test for plaintiffs suing for libel is to determine whether they have to prove the libelous statement arose from actual malice or from negligence. The standard varies by state. Before they can win a libel case, all public figures, and private figures in Alaska, Colorado, Indiana and Michigan have to prove actual malice was involved in the written report. In 22 other states, plaintiffs who are private figures only have to prove the writer was negligent. The issue has not been settled in the remaining states.

Actual malice is more difficult to prove than negligence. Someone attempting to establish that a writer was negligent only needs to prove the writer didn't take the steps a responsible writer would have taken under similar circumstances to ascertain the truth. In practice, that means that if a writer wrote a controversial story using only one source, the writer would have been negligent. If the writer transcribed a taped interview incorrectly or didn't proofread a story correctly, he or she would have been negligent. Negligence might also be established if a writer wrote an article without giving the person implicated in the story a chance to respond to the charges against him or her.

Actual malice is very difficult to prove because before a plaintiff can prove a libelous statement was motivated by actual malice, he or she has to prove the writer knew the statement was false when the writer wrote it, or that the writer made the statement with blatant disregard for the truth. In effect, the plaintiff has to prove the writer was out to get him when he made the statement. That's a terribly difficult standard to establish, and many libel suits have been dismissed on that provision.

Because it's so difficult to prove a writer had malicious intent when writing a story, public figures rarely win a libel case. Therefore, a common legal strategy for those suing for libel is to avoid having to prove actual malice.

Thus, private figures have tried to file their lawsuits in states where private individuals have only to prove negligence. For lawyers representing individuals who might be considered public figures, the best strategy is to try to convince the judge and jury that the lawyer's client is a private figure.

That's a tough task, too. With minor exceptions, courts have generally held that a public figure is someone who has taken a conscious step to enter the public eye to influence opinion. The definition's key word is *conscious*. To become a public figure, an individual must take a deliberate step that will lead him or her into the public eye.

Being a public figure doesn't necessarily mean that you're the president or a senator or a film or music star. Running for a fraternity or sorority office, accepting a part in a school play or opening a restaurant could make you a public figure. The law has increasingly said that it is possible for you to be considered a public figure within those specific areas in which you have taken that conscious step to make your opinions or your talents known. You could have declined the fraternity office or the dramatic role or have become a short-order cook, but you didn't. Thus, in those respective areas, the court recognizes you as a public figure.

A couple of examples may help clarify when a person becomes a public figure. First, social or media prominence is not enough by itself to make a person a public figure. A woman who had married into the family that made Firestone tires was involved in a divorce suit. *Time* magazine falsely reported that her husband's accusations of mental cruelty and adultery had been the reasons for the divorce being granted. *Time* later conceded its report was untrue, but argued that the woman, as part of one of America's most powerful corporate families, was a public figure.

The court disagreed. People, rich or poor, fall in and out of love, the judge reasoned. It's a regular part of life, so that falling in love and marrying a socially prominent person, or divorcing one, is not the conscious step that would signal that someone was trying to use his or her position to influence opinion. According to the judge, Mrs. Firestone was a private figure.

Even when an individual is a constant presence in the news, he or she is not necessarily a public figure. In another case, a lawyer was hired by a family whose son had been killed by a policeman. As part of his duties during the trial, the lawyer represented the family when reporters were gathering information for their newspaper and television stories.

After the trial, a conservative group published an article in its newsletter that maligned the lawyer's political views and implied that he had a criminal record. When the lawyer sued the conservative group for libel, the group claimed he was a public figure and that he had to prove the more difficult standard of actual malice. The court determined that his frequent appearances on television news were simply the result of his job, and that merely agreeing to accept a case did not constitute a conscious step. He remained a private figure.

Because both the divorced socialite and the lawyer were judged to be private figures, they merely had to establish that the writers were negligent in their duties to investigate whether their statements were true before printing the story. That's a much easier task, and both individuals won their libel cases as a result.

In our society, libel is very difficult to prove. Only if a plaintiff in a libel suit can successfully pass all seven of the tests for libel will his or her libel suit be successful. If a judge or jury determines that a plaintiff has failed to overcome even a single one of the tests, the case will be dismissed. To protect the communication among people in a democratic society, the nation's libel laws have provided few easy remedies for people who think their reputations have been damaged.

Right of Privacy: The Ever-Expanding Constitutional Right

However, there is a related area of communication law that does provide much broader protection to people who feel they have been embarrassed, humiliated or used by the media, their employers or others. Many of the same incidents that might stimulate a libel suit could also result in a privacy suit. Because courts have increasingly interpreted privacy laws in favor of plaintiffs, practitioners face much greater threats from invasion of privacy suits than from libel.

It's easiest to think of a person's privacy as a property right. Whenever you purchase a home, lease an apartment, buy a car, or rent a school locker, in addition to the right to occupy and use the property you also obtain at least a partial right to be left alone while you use it. Privacy rights spring from the Constitution's Fourth Amendment, which affirms "the right of the people to be secure in their persons, houses, papers and effects, against unreasonable searches and seizures."

This principle has been applied most rigorously to private homes. With a few exceptions (for instance, police can obtain a search warrant to enter your home) no one can enter your house without your permission. For other classes of property, there still is a debate over the privacy rights you buy when you purchase or rent property. There have been a number of very bitter court cases involving drivers who objected to police roadblocks in which the drivers were forced to open trunks for inspection, or involving high school students who claimed that administrators rummaging through school lockers were violating privacy rights. The law on what constitutes privacy is still developing, but the general tendency has been to extend the right of privacy to more and more areas.

In addition to protecting property you buy or rent, privacy rights protect certain types of other intellectual and personal property an individual controls. For instance, it's valuable to view copyrights as intellectual property and copyright infringement as seizing a property right without authorization.

Privacy rights have been extended to protect unauthorized use of a person's name, appearance, voice and words. As privacy rights expand to more and more areas, public relations practitioners find their institutions threatened more often by invasion of privacy suits than by libel suits. That trend has been encouraged by the fact that many plaintiffs who think they have been hurt by communication can often seek legal redress through either libel or invasion of privacy suits. Because invasion of privacy laws favor the plaintiff instead of the defendant, privacy cases are much easier to win.

Memory Memo 4.3
Four basic types of invasion of privacy cases:

- Intrusion—physical or electronic trespassing
- False Light—false information, even if it doesn't damage a person
- Unwanted Publicity—embarrassing information that's offensive to ordinary sensibilities
- Appropriation—using a person's likeness for commercial purpose

---

There are four basic types of invasion of privacy suits that can be brought against individuals or institutions. As summarized in Memory Memo 4.3, they are:

Intrusion: You Can't Invade Someone's Property.   This is the most obvious form of invasion of privacy. Intrusion is simply criminal trespassing. No one may invade or disturb your property without your permission. At its most elemental form, that means no one may enter your home, your yard, your car, or anything else over which you hold a property right without your giving your permission for that intrusion. If they do, it's invasion of privacy.

Intrusion provisions have been extended to include high-technology methods of invading property. For example, you may not use a telephoto camera lens to shoot a photo or video of someone in a private residence, even if you're on public property when you're making the shot. Telephone bugs or other listening devices are just as intrusive as breaking into someone's home.

False Light: You Can't Lie About a Person.   This type of privacy suit protects a person's right to have his or her actions and words portrayed accurately in any medium. It is a very potent weapon when a person has been misquoted or has been accused of actions that he or she didn't do. Even if the quotations or actions attributed to the source don't damage the source's reputation, a successful false light suit is still possible.

A false light privacy suit can encompass many aspects of covering a story. In one important case, a newspaper printed a photograph and story concerning a child who had been run down by a negligent motorist. Nearly two years later, a magazine used the same picture to illustrate a story about children injured as a result of their own carelessness. The magazine's use of the photograph didn't defame the girl, but because it didn't tell the truth about the situation, the girl's false light privacy suit was successful. This legal requirement makes it that much more important that a writer confirm the accuracy of every detail and every quotation in a story.

Unwanted Publicity: You Can't Say Something That's Offensive About a Person.   This type of privacy suit, which gives people limited protection from having embarrassing private information about themselves revealed, is used rather infrequently. It's one of the hardest types of privacy cases to win because the plaintiff has to prove the actions portrayed were "offensive to ordinary sensibilities." That's a tough benchmark to reach.

Judges usually aren't prudish in determining what is offensive. They have typically used the same logic (although not the same standards) for establishing what's offensive to ordinary sensibilities as they do for judging the "community standards" that define what is obscene in a pornography case. Thus, what is offensive in New York City might not necessarily be offensive in Ottumwa, Iowa, and what is offensive today won't automatically be offensive next year.

Here are two cases that illustrate how the idea of offensiveness differs at different times and in different places. In the early 1960s a woman went through a fun house at a county fair. When she emerged from the fun house, an air jet in the floor blew her dress above her head. Among the people witnessing this private embarrassment was a photographer from the local paper. He took a photograph of the woman just as her dress blew up. The picture appeared in the local paper.

The woman sued the newspaper for invasion of privacy. She admitted the incident was true—her dress did blow over her head—but she argued that in rural America in the early 1960s, putting that picture in the newspaper was offensive to ordinary sensibilities. The judge agreed and found the paper had indeed violated the woman's privacy rights.

However, the definition of what is "offensive to ordinary sensibilities" changes. In the mid 1970s a *Sports Illustrated* photographer at a professional football game snapped a picture of a man whose pants zipper was open. When the photograph was published, the man sued *Sports Illustrated* for invasion of privacy. He admitted it was true that his zipper was open, but insisted the photograph was offensive to ordinary sensibilities. At that time and place, the judge ruled, the photograph was not objectionable and the man's privacy had not been invaded.

Appropriation: You Can't Make Money off a Person's Image.   Appropriation is the type of privacy suit that most concerns public relations practitioners. Appropriation means using a person's likeness for a commercial purpose without his or her permission.

The appropriation principle evolved from an incident in the early 1900s when a flour company placed a New York woman's picture on its advertising posters without her permission. The woman sued, arguing the company was stealing her image and gaining a commercial advantage because of it, thus entitling her to share in the benefits the company gained. The court dismissed her suit, stating there was no precedent or law that protected her privacy. The next year, New York adopted the nation's first privacy law.

Initially, appropriation was limited to situations in which there was a blatant commercial purpose in using the picture. In the years since, appropriation has been extended to include areas in which the profits are not so apparent or so immediate. In a recent case, a racetrack worker who did not give written permission to have her picture placed on a 50-cent program sold to track patrons successfully took action under the appropriation standards.

In some instances, a piece including a person's likeness doesn't even have to sell a product or service directly for the work to violate appropriation standards. Some company publication editors have found themselves involved in appropriation suits when they pictured workers in newsletters, corporate reports, and other institutional publications. Workers have successfully argued that because the publications are designed to increase company morale and production, boost sales, or promote stock purchases, the company gains from the exposure. In some instances, the courts have agreed that employees have to be paid for promoting those profit-making ends.

The principle has been taken even further so that now it's not even necessary to show a person's face in order for them to claim appropriation. For instance, there has been a successful suit in which a man who saw his name printed on credit cards shown in television or magazine advertisements sued for appropriation.

How do you deter appropriation and other types of invasion of privacy suits? Journalists can often claim that if an event is newsworthy, invasion of privacy rules don't apply. For instance, a newspaper can publish a picture of a lifeguard rescuing a swimmer without asking for permission or paying for the right to use the photograph. In some instances, public relations practitioners also have that option. In publications that are distributed internally, information about workers that is of interest to other workers can sometimes be protected by the newsworthiness defense.

To be safe, however, our main defense comes from obtaining a person's con-

scope ⟶

consideration ⟶

binding heirs ⟶
duration ⟶
no other promises ⟶
proper parties ⟶

I give permission to (*organization's name*), and those acting under its permission and authority, the absolute right and permission to reproduce, publish, copyright or otherwise use photographic reproductions in which I may be included for any purpose whatsoever. This permission is granted in consideration of _____ dollar(s), which I here acknowledge receiving. My permission given here binds me, as well as my heirs, executors and assigns, to observe the terms of this release for a period of 10 years after its execution. This agreement fully represents all terms and considerations, and no other statements, inducements or promises have been made to me.

I warrant I am of full age and have every right to contract in my own name.

_____   _____

signature of party (or guardian if underage)   date

_____   _____

signature of organization representative   date

FIGURE 4.2   Sample privacy release form

sent to invade his or her privacy. If workers sign a consent form that gives us permission to use their photographs on our product packaging, it will be very difficult for them to win an invasion of privacy suit later. As a result of the credit card advertisement example discussed above, advertisers have protected themselves by using the name of a company employee who has signed a consent form. If other people with the same name later bring suit, the company can successfully defend itself from any appropriation suits.

That makes it vitally important to the PR practitioner to incorporate consent procedures into many daily duties. Whenever photographs are taken, every person who could be identified in the photograph should sign a consent form. Figure 4.2 lists vital components of a standard release form. When presented in writing, this signed release circumvents most invasion of privacy suits. Photographers should routinely have all subjects sign release forms. Note that minors cannot legally enter into a contract.

Right of Publicity: You Own Everything You Possess

Right of publicity is a legal area related to appropriation. Simply stated, right of publicity maintains that individuals have the right to control and profit from the use of their images or their talents for a commercial purpose, even if they do not themselves appear in the commercial or company publication. That's a confusing thought but some examples will make it clearer.

The first right of publicity cases involved celebrities who objected to portions of their acts being disclosed to the public without their permission. A human cannonball whose entire 15-second act was telecast without his permission on a local news program sued, claiming his ability to draw an audience had been affected by his unauthorized appearance on television. The court agreed with him and awarded him damages.

In recent years, the right of publicity has expanded beyond this area. The newest tests have involved celebrity look-alikes or impersonators who were using their look-alike or sound-alike characteristics to endorse products or appear in commercials. In the most prominent case, comedian Woody Allen claimed his voice, appearance, and public persona were, in essence, a property right that he had worked years to gain. Because of that, any company that used a celebrity impersonator to imply that Allen endorsed a product must gain his permission and compensate him for using that property right. The judge agreed.

The case law defining right of publicity is still developing. However, the current interpretation of the law does provide warning signs for practitioners. As in all privacy cases, if you're using something that could be interpreted as someone's property, it's always wise to get a signed consent form before proceeding.

Copyright: Property Rights of the Mind

Like the privacy and right of publicity suits we've already discussed, copyright infringement suits also involve exploiting someone's property rights without their permission. However, the property rights involved in a copyright suit are often more clearly defined than the other suits we've been discussing.

Copyright is the protection given to painters, writers, photographers, film makers, composers and other artists to ensure they are compensated for the use of their works. That means that if you want to reprint a chapter from a technical book for a company report, publish a copyrighted photograph in your company magazine, reproduce a 20th-century painting in a brochure or play a popular song in a radio advertisement, you'll likely have to gain permission and pay a fee for using the works.

Current copyright law acknowledges two categories of copyrighted materials—company copyrights and creator copyrights. Company copyrights, sometimes called "work made for hire," are copyrights granted to works created by employees during their regular employment hours. Thus, a company public relations practitioner who writes an article for a company newsletter would be creating a work made for hire. Because of that, the company, and not the practitioner, would be granted the story's copyright.

Memory Memo 4.4
Protection for the two types of copyrights:

- Company copyright: shorter of (1) 75 years from publication date or (2) 100 years from creation date
- Creator copyright: creator's entire lifetime plus 50 years

A creator copyright is issued to an individual who creates a work for which he is not granted a salary. Thus, an independent artist creating paintings for a gallery exhibit would be eligible to hold a creator copyright for his or her work, as would a free-lance photographer who was paid $25 to take a portrait of a company's president, or a free-lance writer who was paid specifically to craft a speech for an executive. The most important distinction between the two types of copyrights is the length of time each is enforced, as Memory Memo 4.4 points out.

Copyright law has frequent implications for public relations practitioners. If you hire a free-lance photographer or writer to cover a company event and don't specify otherwise in the contract, your company will receive only a one-time use of the photographs or stories. If you want additional copies, or even to reprint a photograph or story you've already used, you'll have to pay the creator again for his or her permission to use the copyrighted works.

If you or your company wants to use a copyrighted work, you write to the copyright owner (which is not necessarily the creator, as copyrights may be bought and sold). You indicate what you want to use, how it will be used and the credit you will give to the copyright holder. The copyright holder can then respond, granting permission or asking for a certain fee in exchange for using the copyrighted materials. Nonprofit organizations are often granted copyright permission for a reduced fee, so it's wise to indicate if the copyrighted material will be used by a nonprofit group.

Because obtaining copyright permission can be a time-consuming process, there are a number of organizations that help to simplify the process. For instance, the American Society of Composers, Authors, and Publishers (ASCAP), which enforces music copyrights, is one of several clearinghouses for gaining permission to use copyrighted works.

Copyright laws are generally being enforced much more strictly now than ever before. Although scholars, reviewers, reporters and writers can quote briefly from copyrighted works while commenting on them, this "fair use" is a limited defense. Courts are sensitive to whether the copyright was used for a commercial purpose and whether the unauthorized use affected the potential market value of the copyright. The courts also evaluate copyright infringement cases based on what proportion of the work was used without permission. Quoting 10 lines of a novel without permission is a relatively small transgression, but if 10 lines of a 14-line sonnet were included, that is well over half of the entire copyrighted work.

After the copyright expires, works enter the public domain. Public domain works may be used by anyone for any purpose without permission or compensation. In fact, there is a brisk trade in "clip art books," which are collections of illustrations that are in the public domain and for which permission does not have to be granted before they may be used.

Financial Reporting: Telling Everything to Everybody or Telling Nothing to Anybody

Up to now, we've discussed only the laws that restrict practitioners from communicating information or viewpoints concerning their companies. However, there are also a few laws that require a practitioner to communicate certain information about his or her company or organization.

The most important one of these concerns the required reporting of information that might affect the fortunes of a company that offers stock for sale to the public. Those companies are required to provide the timely and adequate release of material corporate information, that information (such as an unfavorable court decision or a promising acquisition) that might affect an investor's decision to buy company stock. There are official forms that companies must complete and submit to the Securities and Exchange Commission (SEC) and to the markets in which their stock is sold.

News releases are held to the same reporting accuracy as the official notification. In fact, PR practitioners who have done nothing more than write news releases have been prosecuted in insider trading cases in which company officials have been accused of offering information to certain individuals that gave them an unfair advantage in investing in the company's stock. As courts now interpret the law, PR practitioners must be certain that information contained in releases or in annual reports is accurate and does not hide either bad or good news from present or potential stockholders or financial analysts. Further, practitioners are committed to communicate all material information promptly and to establish procedures so all present and potential investors can obtain equal access to the information. Finally, the courts have ruled that PR practitioners have a greater responsibility than merely reporting what corporate officers tell them. At least in the case of independent PR firms, they have an additional responsibility before issuing a news release containing material information to investigate whether corporate officers are telling them the truth. You can review the basic philosophy of corporate reporting in Memory Memo 4.5.

Memory Memo 4.5
To fulfill corporate financial reporting law, PR practitioners must

- make sure all investors have equal access to corporate news
- communicate all information promptly
- ascertain that all information is accurate

Freedom of Information: The Government of the People Telling the People

A large amount of information about the federal government's operations, as well as about the businesses and organizations that complete federal paperwork or compete for federal contracts, is available to the news media and the public through the Freedom of Information (FOI) Act. Thus, reporters or even rival companies can obtain information about a company's failure to meet Occupational Safety and Health Administration (OSHA) regulations or discover the cost overrun on a government manufacturing contract.

Organizations wishing to restrict the public's view of information they've submitted to the federal government have few protections. If the company can establish that the information requested contains vital trade or national secrets or if it invades a person's privacy or interferes with a criminal investigation, it may prevent the information's release. But even if a certain report contains information falling within these protected areas, the federal agency may delete the critical portions and release the rest of the report.

Many state and local governments have laws with similar intents. These "sunshine laws" generally require that all public meetings be open to the public, except for those portions in which personnel matters are discussed. Sunshine laws can be an opening for the public, the media and other companies to discover critical information about your organization without your consent.

ETHICS: THE SUCCESS STRATEGY OF BEING GOOD

There are few laws that require public relations practitioners to share information with the public. The more powerful motive fostering honest communication between an organization and its publics is the ethical sense of the practitioner.

As a prospective PR professional, you're probably already aware of the public's perception of public relations. When a dictator hugs children that he is holding as hostages, it's said he's doing it for public relations. If a convicted criminal quickly organizes a boys' club in a poor neighborhood and parades it before TV cameras to influence the judge's sentencing, it's called a PR move. That's not public relations. That's propaganda.

If we wish to transform the field into a respected profession, a strong ethical standard among all public relations practitioners is a must. We must first change the perception that public relations ethics is merely avoiding doing those things for which we could be sued. I would argue that adhering to ethical standards of conduct doesn't prevent PR professionals from doing their jobs. Taking pains to tell our important publics the truth provides a valuable benefit to our organization and a base of power for ethical practitioners.

At the very least, encouraging an honest relationship between our organization and its publics creates a reservoir of credibility and communication that we can tap at moments of crisis. If our company experiences a major industrial accident or an official is involved in an embarrassing personal scandal, the public perception that the incident was an aberration in the life of an otherwise honest company is vital. It can dictate how fast or even whether the company can recover and survive.

That sense of openness not only increases our credibility with our important publics, but stimulates a true communication relationship between the organization and its publics. Not only are communication channels open from the organization to the public, but even more important channels from the public to the organization are unblocked.

Those channels can be invaluable to the organization. Each day, our institution's success is predicated on the support of those publics that comprise the environment in which our company exists. Those customers, stockholders, employees and members of environmental, community, and other groups can enhance or destroy our ability to survive. Even if they are critical of our performance, we shouldn't fear them as the enemy. Instead, we should view each of them and each of their complaints or compliments as a valuable resource that can help our company to do its job better.

We should listen to employees who have suggestions about how our company can improve the way we manufacture our product. Even environmental or civil rights groups that seem radical today can help us predict societal changes. We should welcome that early warning and use it to gain competitive advantages. With that information, we can anticipate consumer tastes and societal values that can help us redesign our products, change our marketing campaigns and modify our company image. That's the raw material for a corporate strategy that will help our organization survive and prosper.

Out of an ethical sense can come not only a more humane corporation, but a new degree of power for the PR practitioner within the institutional environment. The demonstrated power of communication to transform the institution has the potential to bring the PR practitioner and his or her special talents into the highest echelons of the corporate world.

The Scope of Public Relations Ethics: Guarding Goodness Within the Gates

Inasmuch as the definition of public relations itself seems to be fluid enough to admit unscrupulous activities discussed at the beginning of this section, it's not surprising that what constitutes public relations ethics is still under debate.

The Public Relations Society of America has a 14-point code of ethics for practitioners (see Figure 4.3). Some of the rules concern the interactions between public relations practitioners and the clients they solicit and then work with. The code impels us to identify our clients and people who serve our clients in public relations communications. It prohibits practices that misuse communication channels in the news media or corrupt the way governmental processes work. Although the code provides a good starting point for the practitioner interested in performing his or her job ethically, its provisions are adopted voluntarily by public relations professionals, and its code of conduct does not apply to other corporate officials. Hence, the final course of action of any practitioner who has been asked to perform an unethical action may be to resign from his or her position.

Two articles of the code, Nos. 3 and 7, which prohibit communicating false information, seem most meaningful to our task in this text.

For many public relations writers, ethics has come to mean "I will never tell a lie." At first glance that sounds quite commendable, but on deeper examination, you see there are lots of loopholes in that simple statement. You can observe the maxim "Never tell a lie" by simply not correcting someone else's lie.

Let's say your company's president swears to reporters that a new product being manufactured by your plant won't cause pollution. However, you've read reports in environmental journals that cite several other plants using the same manufacturing process that do cause vast pollution problems. When a reporter asks you if you have any information backing your president's assurances, you reply: "I think the president's statement adequately summarizes our company's position."

You haven't lied, but you haven't told the truth either. Is that ethical? Let's modify our all-purpose ethical motto to "Always tell the truth."

Here's another situation to challenge that ethical test. Your organization's overseas development coordinator has been kidnapped by terrorists. A dangerous rescue

DECLARATION OF PRINCIPLES

Members of the Public Relations Society of America base their professional principles on the fundamental value and dignity of the individual, holding that the free exercise of human rights, especially freedom of speech, freedom of assembly and freedom of the press, is essential to the practice of public relations.

In serving the interests of clients and employers, we dedicate ourselves to the goals of better communication, understanding and cooperation among the diverse individuals, groups and institutions of society.

We pledge:

To conduct ourselves professionally, with truth, accuracy, fairness and responsibility to the public.

To improve our individual competence and advance the knowledge and proficiency of the profession through continuing research and education;

And to adhere to the articles of the Code of Professional Standards for the Practice of Public Relations as adopted by the governing Assembly of the Society.

ARTICLES OF THE CODE

These articles have been adopted by the Public Relations Society of America to promote and maintain high standards of public service and ethical conduct among its members.

1. A member shall deal fairly with clients or employers, past, present or potential, with fellow practitioners and the general public.
2. A member shall conduct his or her professional life in accord with the public interest.
3. A member shall adhere to truth and accuracy and to generally accepted standards of good taste.
4. A member shall not represent conflicting or competing interests without the express consent of those involved, given after a full disclosure of the facts; nor place himself or herself in a position where the member's interest is or may be in conflict with a duty to a client, or others, without a full disclosure of such interests to all involved.
5. A member shall safeguard the confidences of present and former clients, as well as of those persons or entities who have disclosed confidences to a member in the context of communications relating to an anticipated professional relationship with such member, and shall not accept retainers or employment which may involve the disclosure or use of these confidences to the disadvantage or prejudice of such present, former or potential clients or employers.
6. A member shall not engage in any practice which tends to corrupt the integrity of channels of communication or the processes of government.
7. A member shall not intentionally communicate false or misleading information and is obligated to use care to avoid communication of false or misleading information.
8. A member shall be prepared to identify publicly the name of the client or employer on whose behalf any public communication is made.
9. A member shall not make use of any individual or organization purporting to serve or represent an announced cause, or purporting to be independent or unbiased, but actually serving an undisclosed special or private interest of a member, client or employer.
10. A member shall not intentionally injure the professional reputation or practice of another practitioner. However, if a member has evidence that another member has been guilty of unethical, illegal or unfair practices, including those in violation of this Code, the member shall present the information promptly to the proper authorities of the Society for action in accordance with the procedure set forth in Article XIII of the Bylaws.
11. A member called as a witness in a proceeding for the enforcement of this Code shall be bound to appear, unless excused for sufficient reason by the Judicial Panel.
12. A member, in performing services for a client or employer, shall not accept fees, commissions or any other valuable consideration from anyone other than the client or employer in connection with those services without the express consent of the client or employer, given after a full disclosure of the facts.
13. A member shall not guarantee the achievement of specified results beyond the member's direct control.
14. A member shall, as soon as possible, sever relations with any organization or individual if such relationship requires conduct contrary to the articles of this Code.

FIGURE 4.3   Public Relations Society of America ethics code
—Used by permission of the Public Relations Society of America.

effort is being mounted to overpower the terrorists and rescue your employee, and you and other top managers have been told of the danger and need for complete secrecy.

At that moment, a CNN reporter sticks a microphone in your face for a live interview and says: "We've had reports a rescue effort is being mounted by army units right now. Is it true?"

Do you tell the truth and risk the chance that the kidnappers are watching CNN at that moment? Your information would endanger the rescue effort as well as the lives of your executive and the lives of the army troops attempting the rescue.

Most people would say you shouldn't directly answer the reporter's question. But how about this response: "I can't answer questions about those types of situations right now." Think again of the possibility that the kidnappers are watching CNN. That answer would appear to them to be an admission that the reporter has guessed the truth.

Is it sometimes ethical to tell a lie? In this situation, yes. I would probably tell the reporter that "I have no knowledge of any such plan." If I had later to explain why I was lying I feel I could do it in good faith.

What ethical lessons do we draw from this? As Memory Memo 4.6 reminds us, we first should use information in ways that will not unfairly hurt people or institutions. Second, we should value those people outside our organization as much as we do the people within the organization.

> **Memory Memo 4.6**
> **The guiding principles of corporate ethics:**
> - Use information in ways that will not unfairly hurt others.
> - Value those outside our organization as much as we do those within our organization.

As the asbestos saga related in the chapter introduction highlights, we have obligations to people outside the organization that sometimes outweigh the humiliation and economic costs that an ethical act exacts within the organization. As communicators we had great ethical obligations to those construction workers who were unknowingly subjected to greater cancer risks because of Manville's decision not to publicize asbestos's risks.

The costs resulting from that silence were only postponed. Manville's lack of ethics and its callous indifference to the needs of its consumers eventually brought the organization to its knees. That's a very important lesson for every public relations practitioner and every corporate manager.

The lesson to be gleaned is that public relations ethics must have a much broader role within the institution than guiding communication tasks. Should we lie for our executives? Should we cover up damaging information about our company's operations before the media? Should we participate in distorting company financial reports before our company's unions or its stockholders?

Those are standard ethical questions for public relations practitioners. But if we look at PR ethics from the perspective of the topics we are asked to defend, you'll see this is a very constricting, counterproductive view. If a nonprofit organization's supervisor is accused of sexually harassing workers, who is asked to formulate a fund-raising package that explains to socially conscious donors why the group still deserves support? If a department store chain violates the state sales tax code, who will be responsible for planning how the company will explain the situation to clamoring newspaper and television reporters? If a factory has secretly buried drums of toxic materials on company property next to a residential subdivision, who will have to develop some type of response to the environmentalists, homeowners and neighborhood children picketing the plant?

In each of these situations, company missteps or transgressions force public relations practitioners to defend indefensible positions. If these unethical dilemmas were brought on, respectively, by the personnel, finance and operations units of these institutions, do our ethical responsibilities extend to those far-flung areas of the company or organization? No—and yes.

No, I don't propose that public relations practitioners become the omnipotent czars of the institution, micromanaging in order to avoid defending shortsighted decisions by opportunistic managers trying to boost their quarterly profit statements.

Having said that—yes, I do believe public relations practitioners have the responsibility for defending the actions of all those company units. With that responsibility, however, goes a right to gather information about management practices in any area of the company, and a right to initiate serious management debates about certain units whose practices might eventually create a public relations issue.

Ethics and Long-term Institutional Success: Converting Short-term Problems into Long-term Strengths

In real life, that responsibility demands that the practitioner take a more long-term view of the company's activities than do employees who are being judged by their division's monthly productivity or their ability to generate greater profits next quarter. Our perspectives can turn to the institution's productivity, profitability and survivability over the next two, five or 10 years. That's the perspective with which all corporate managers should be concerned: Will their actions help ensure their companies will be prospering 10 or 20 years from now?

There's a natural alliance between the long-term survival and success of the organization and a systematic ethical commitment. From a short-term perspective, it may look very tempting to pollute as long as the company can get away with it, for example, because dealing with the issue would involve immediate and substantial costs.

But such a decision comes with its own cost. Would the cost of cleaning up pollution now, when the company can control the process, be less than later, when the government orders it and dictates how it will be done? Even if we can absorb and rationalize the long-term financial costs to the company, does our CEO want to risk having the company's name and reputation mangled in newspaper columns and television reports for months or years because the company defied ethics?

Yes, those are all long-term costs. Most won't appear on the balance sheet this quarter or maybe even not this year. Some, like reputational factors, might not ever be isolated as a number on a financial statement. But all of them bring substantial costs to the company's bottom line eventually, and, as we've seen, they sometimes can cost the company its very life.

Most of the strategies that contribute to long-term success are tactics that also contribute to good institutional ethics. (See Memory Memo 4.7.) Does our company offer quality products that ensure fewer consumer complaints and boycotts? Does it deal with consumers' complaints forthrightly and incorporate their concerns into new product developments? Does it enter product categories and produce products in ways that match society's new needs or concerns? Does our organization deal fairly and equitably with workers and avoid putting them at needless risk as they perform their jobs?

Memory Memo 4.7
Ethical strategies provide the following cost-effective benefits:

- They lead to new products that will meet society's new needs.
- They point the company to practices that will cut insurance costs and labor stoppages.
- They build and keep the faith of our organization's important publics that buy our products and whose political or social support may become important.

Does our institution give complete and honest information to the publics that are important to us, including friends like stockholders and seeming adversaries like consumer or public interest groups?

These ethical strategies reflect a willingness to draw management lessons from the environment. They lead to new products or adaptations of current products to meet society's new needs and allow us to compete within our industry. They point the company to quality manufacturing practices that maximize customer loyalty and minimize worker accidents, insurance costs and labor stoppages. They keep the faith of important publics on whom we depend for financial, political and social support. All these factors are vital to the organization's long-term success and profitability. Coincidentally, they are wonderful for the organization's public relations environment.

An institution that embraces these strategies would likely be progressive in the way it looks for viewpoints from its customers, its workers, and friendly and adversarial publics with which it comes in contact. It would probably launch a succession of exciting new products as the result of its market and consumer research. One would expect such a company to have fewer environmental accidents, consumer boycotts, worker slowdowns or criminal investigations. If there were crises, the public's perception of this organization would probably be positive enough that people would perceive the incident as an unfortunate fluke, rather than a systematic flaw in the institution.

Within such an organization the PR unit could reorient itself to promote positive outcomes in marketing, productivity, and public acceptance rather than put out fires prompted by negative news. That long-term orientation develops by integrating ethical procedures into all organizational levels and operations.

Ethics Is Emerging Law: Using Ethics to Predict the Future

There's one more ironic reason for introducing ethics into every institution.

Try as they might, businesses usually can't permanently avoid doing the right thing. Government rules and newspaper exposés will eventually cause the polluting plant to close or clean up. Government inspectors, industrial accidents or worker lawsuits or strikes will inevitably cure plant safety problems. Consumer complaints will eventually cause the company to improve its product.

That's because there's a link between ethics and the law. In 1955 it was merely unethical for companies to discriminate against African-Americans or any other racial group. Over the next 10 years, because of the civil rights movement's ability to focus awareness on the hypocrisy of racially based voting, housing and employment practices, such discrimination became not only unethical but also illegal. We went through similar processes to assure the rights of women in the workplace and to protect consumers in the marketplace and employees in the workplace. We're probably in the midst of an emerging struggle over privacy rights, as discussed in Sidebar 4.1.

SIDEBAR 4.1   Emerging Concerns over Privacy Issues

One of the most problematic issues of public relations concerns the right of privacy that an institution's employees, clients and customers should expect. Twenty years ago, when invading a customer's privacy largely consisted of sending an unsolicited advertisement to all subscribers to *Life* magazine or to all 15-year-old boys, it was possible for a consumer to stay fairly anonymous.

Now, with computer technology recording billions of bits of data, it's possible to link individuals with all sorts of purchases through warranty forms, subscription and donor lists, and consumer surveys.

For instance, it's now possible to match routine retail purchases with individual consumers. Those UPC bar codes on virtually every product are recorded in the store's computer, and when a customer presents a credit or check-cashing card, the store knows his or her social security number. Thus it's possible to know what brand of scouring pads a customer purchased on a certain day and whether the customer purchased them on sale or with a coupon.

Is it unethical to use that information to entice people into buying something else or to sell it to another organization that wants those people to donate to a cause? Most people would say it's within the bounds of propriety. Moreover, selling names is a big source of income for a lot of companies and organizations.

If that's acceptable, is it OK to sell information that will let political candidates know if someone supported a conservative political cause, a pro-life group or a gay political action committee? Should your marital status be made available to advertisers? Should telephone solicitors be able to find out if a woman has just had a baby, an individual has purchased a house or a person buys nonprescription contraceptives? Should a book company be able to sell the information that you buy religious books? If you think that's acceptable, should anyone be able to learn that you buy pornographic books or movies?

Is it ethical to sell the information that you missed a credit card payment four months ago? Should someone be able to buy a list of all convicted drunk drivers? Is it ethical to sell a list of women who subscribe to a service that delivers exotic lingerie every month or men who buy rolling papers for home-made cigarettes?

All this information is readily available from mailing list companies and marketing services. The ethical issues are apparent. Put yourself in each situation. There's nothing to prevent a militant anti-abortion group from harassing people who support abortion or to stop a criminal armed with knowledge of a woman's lingerie-buying habits from making obscene phone calls. There's nothing to stop police from using a compilation of people who buy rolling papers to target suspected marijuana smokers. Is that ethical?

Sometimes there's nothing criminal in the intent of the people using the information, but the information might be embarrassing to a consumer if revealed. There's nothing illegal about buying contraceptives or, in most places, sexually explicit books or videotapes, but is this something most people want to share with a business executive or telemarketing caller?

Some of the information, such as your religious or political convictions, may not be damaging or even embarrassing. However, it just doesn't seem as if it's anybody's business. Is it ethical to sell it to other businesses?

Like most ethical issues, you start accelerating down a slippery slope the moment your company or institution decides to share or sell information. Let's say your institution resolves to screen the organizations with which your company is willing to share information, and you decide to sell only to churches and charities. Does that solve the ethical problem? Not necessarily.

Here's a perfect example. In the early 1980s a Midwestern state's division of motor vehicles was asked by a coalition of churches to supply the names of the people who had certain license plate numbers. It sounded like a fairly safe request, and there wasn't anything illegal about selling the information for $2 per license plate.

Look what happened. The church members had staked out theaters that featured striptease acts and had written down the license plate numbers of the cars people got into as they emerged from the theaters. When, without revealing the reason for its request, the church coalition asked for the names and addresses of the owners of the license plates, the motor vehicle division had dutifully complied.

Then the church groups purchased a full-page advertisement in the

SIDEBAR 4.1   (continued)

metropolitan daily newspaper and, following a short printed sermon on the debasing nature of lust, printed the names and addresses of all the people who, they said, had participated in such during the past week.

As you can imagine, virtually everyone listed was humiliated. Unfortunately for the crusading church groups, not all the people listed in the paper had been at the theaters. Some of the cars had been borrowed from their owners by relatives or friends or, in a few cases, had been stolen. The churches were sued, the newspaper was sued and the division of motor vehicles was sued.

How do you protect your institution's customers and employees and your institution's reputation from the damage that can be done by sharing such information? That's the tricky part of ethics. In addition to being legal, in some circumstances sharing information probably helps the consumer while benefiting the company. How do you decide what's ethical and what's not?

The answer, I feel, comes from the boundary-spanning role of public relations. Practitioners are duty-bound to observe and study their publics and the environment in which their institution operates to discover what their audiences want from the institution.

We've often applied that philosophy to marketing new products. Companies scan newspapers and magazines for trends that might suggest new products. After developing product ideas, they conduct marketing surveys to find if people want their new products, then establish test market cities to try out advertising and merchandising approaches. They do consumer surveys to gauge satisfaction with their products and follow-up questionnaires to determine why people buy the competitor's products.

A similar research effort could be used to gather information about the ethical standards people expect from the companies and organizations they patronize. The research methods discussed in Chapter 3 could be applied to ethical issues, too. For instance, scanning publications and other media is equally useful in discerning ethical concerns. In the same way that scanning could have predicted the rise of environmentalism and women's issues, it could guide us toward emerging ethical issues and give us advance warning, so that we could adjust our institutional policies with coherence and control, rather than wait for government regulation.

What does a preliminary scan reveal about the ethicalness of transferring information? Already, Congress and the courts have placed restrictions on the information that a college can share with an employer about a student, or that a company can share with another company about an employee. Consumer-conscious companies should take steps to monitor the uses to which they put consumer information if they don't want the same governmental restrictions to be placed on them.

Initially, institutional managers dismissed each of those causes. After all, those ethical ideas were promulgated by people without power, people who weren't like them and with whom the managers had never had to deal before. However, those people without power soon forced their ideas on our entire society.

In practice, public relations ethics is an early prediction of the ethical and legal standards that will affect the entire organization. Our role in this commitment to business ethics is to involve important groups in searching for ways to harmonize business operations with the wishes of the society in which the businesses operate now and in the future. PR practitioners need to truthfully represent the rational and irrational views of various publics to their institution's managers and help managers understand the implications those viewpoints may have for the organization's life. Similarly, it's our ethical duty to truthfully explain our institution's position to society or, in cases in which we can't tell the whole story, to admit that and offer the reasons why.

Our consistent ethical question then becomes: Do we do business ethically now, and pay the costs now, or do we wait until the news media, the consumer activists, our customers, our workers and the government conspire to make us comply on their terms and after dragging our reputation through the mud?

The choice seems simple.

SUMMARY

- Conforming to ethical and legal standards makes institutions more competitive by continually compelling them to see what society values and to adapt themselves to their new environment.

- Commercial speech, the speech institutions employ to sell products and services, has many restrictions placed on it. Commercial speech is subject to libel, obscenity and invasion of privacy laws and can be restricted by government agencies, professional associations and media outlets.

- In determining whether the government can restrict commercial speech, judges apply the following five questions: (1) Does it concern a legal activity? (2) Is it misleading? (3) Is there a reason for restricting the message? (4) Are the government's actions effective in meeting the need for control? (5) Can the regulation be less restrictive and still accomplish its purpose?

- With minor exceptions, media outlets do not have to accept any advertisement they do not wish to and can refuse news coverage of any viewpoint. They can also refuse to mention any products and reject any methods of advertising they wish.

- American libel laws are interpreted to give communicators great freedom to transfer information. It's thus difficult for a plaintiff to win a libel judgment against a media outlet or other communicator.

- To win a libel suit, the plaintiff must overcome seven tests. The plaintiff loses the case if he or she fails to overcome even one of these tests: (1) publication,

(2) identification, (3) defamation, (4) truth, (5) privilege, (6) fair comment, and (7) negligence or actual malice.

- All public figures, and private individuals in four states, must prove actual malice, the more difficult standard. A person becomes a public figure by taking a conscious step to enter the public eye to influence public opinion on a subject.

- Actual malice means the writer knew a statement was false or that he or she made the statement with blatant disregard for the truth.

- U.S. right of privacy laws favor the plaintiff against media outlets and other communicators. Because a privacy or a libel case could spring from the same incident, practitioners need to be more attentive to privacy issues.

- The four basic types of privacy suits are intrusion, false light, unwanted publicity and appropriation.

- Appropriation—using a person's likeness without his or her permission for a commercial purpose—is the most likely suit practitioners may face. It, and most privacy suits, can be avoided by having subjects sign a consent form.

- Copyright is the property right that writers, photographers and other creators have over their creations. The two types of copyright, company and creator, have different lengths of protection.

- PR practitioners working for publicly held corporations must give all investors and potential investors equal access to all information that could affect the company's share price.

- The federal Freedom of Information Act and state sunshine laws allow the public access to information about the government's activities.

- The Public Relations Society of America's 14-point ethics code guides practitioners in their relationships with clients, other practitioners and the media.

- Beyond merely telling the truth, PR ethics should strive not to unfairly hurt other people or institutions, regardless of whether they are associated with the practitioner's institution.

- With the responsibility to explain organizational problems comes a right to foster good management practices so those crises don't occur.

THINK PIECES

1. Are current restrictions on commercial speech justified? If your organization were restricted from advertising its services, how would you defend its access to the media?

2. Is it possible to defend restrictions on pornography or violence in the media within the tests for controlling commercial speech?

3. Libel is difficult to prove. How does that benefit and hurt society?

4. The electronic revolution has given public relations practitioners and marketers access to people's names, addresses, income levels and buying patterns. What implications does

that have for the public's right to privacy? What should communication professionals do about it?

5. What is the public's perception of public relations? Is that attitude justified by the actions of practitioners?

MANAGEMENT PROBLEMS

D3.5

D4.4

D6.4

D7.6

ADDITIONAL READINGS

Christians, Clifford G., Rotzoll, Kim B., and Fackler, Mark. *Media Ethics: Cases and Moral Reasoning.* White Plains, NY: Longman, 1983.

Englehardt, Elaine E., and Evans, DeAnn. "Lies, Deceptions and Public Relations." *Public Relations Review* 20:3 (Fall 1994): 249–266.

Ferre, John P., and Willihnganz, Shirley C. *Public Relations & Ethics: A Bibliography.* Boston: G. K. Hall & Co., 1991.

Goldstein, Norm, ed. *The Associated Press Stylebook and Libel Manual.* Reading, Mass.: Addison-Wesley, 1994.

Middleton, Kent R., and Chamberlin, Bill F. *Key Cases in the Law of Public Communication.* White Plains, NY: Longman, 1995.

Pratt, Catharine A. "First Amendment Protection for Public Relations Expression: The Applicability and Limitation of the Commercial and Corporate Speech Models," from Larissa A. Grunig and James E. Grunig, eds., *Public Relations Research Annual,* vol. 2. Hillsdale, N. J.: Lawrence Erlbaum Assoc., 1990, pp. 205–217.

Pratt, Cornelius B. "Critique of the Classical Theory of Situational Ethics in U.S. Public Relations." *Public Relations Review* 19:3 (Fall 1993): 219–234.

Pratt, Cornelius B. "Research Progress in Public Relations Ethics: An Overview." *Public Relations Review* 20:3 (Fall 1994): 217–224.

Sneed, Don, Wulfmeyer, K. Tim, and Stonecipher, Harry W. "Public Relations News Releases and Libel: Extending First Amendment Protections." *Public Relations Review* 17:2 (Summer 1991): 131–144.

Walsh, Frank. *Public Relations and the Law.* Ann Arbor, Mich.: Books on Demand, n.d.

# part TWO

Creating: Using Receiver-centered Principles to Generate Writing Across All Media

One of the daunting aspects of teaching anything about public relations writing today is that you're expected to tell people how to write for media that may not have been invented yet.

Let's consider a relatively simple assignment first. What do you tell people about writing an annual report? Annual reports used to be produced exclusively by corporations and exclusively in printed form. It's a different world now. Many annual reports are now produced in video versions or even on interactive CD-ROM. In addition, nonprofit and governmental organizations as well as public corporations issue them.

There are more changes coming. There are already services that issue modem versions of daily newspapers and computer disk presentations of product advertisements. Further, what do you tell people about writing for what is called (at least as I'm writing this book) the "information superhighway"?

The question remains: What do you tell people about writing for media that hasn't even been invented?

Given this unpredictability, in this section I've gathered basic writing principles that can be applied to all media, so that no matter what media possibilities face you in the future, you'll have the skills to cope.

I've formulated what I call a "generative" writing system, which is designed to use what you know about the audience and its needs to help you "generate" lead sentences. Because the initial goal of any public relations document is to attract the attention of a specific audience, we'll develop an awareness of how different leads can be targeted to reach the different parts of your total audience.

Chapter 6 applies the generative writing system to the body of public relations documents. Again, it will help you generate those critical transitions that maintain your audience's attention and that help you structure your arguments clearly and efficiently so you can move your audience to take the actions that fulfill your organization's objectives.

Finally, I'll discuss how to adapt those basic writing procedures to broadcast writing by helping you understand how to add the power of sound and motion to strong prose.

It's a system that has served me well in dealing with the many changes in the field over the past 20 years. I hope it will serve you just as well in the writing challenges you'll face in your own career.

## chapter 5

Reaching the Right Audience in a Few Words: Creating the Lead Sentence in the Receiver-centered Writing Process

REAL-LIFE LESSONS

I've got a neighbor who's a business section editor of a newspaper. Combining a natural predisposition to be a pest, an inexplicable feeling of superiority over PR people, and a self-proclaimed role as the paragon of virtue on my block, he's taken it upon himself to collect and catalog every mistake made by every public relations practitioner he encounters. Every day, when news releases with misspelled words, misguided grammar or inappropriate ideas pass his desk, he remembers them, and every time we meet, he comes at me, yapping at my heels like some genetically-misdirected miniature poodle, demanding that I justify the latest transgressions committed by public relations practitioners.

One particular day, when I was in the earliest stages of conceptualizing this book, I was telling him my ideas about a public relations textbook with an entire chapter discussing how to compose a lead sentence. He assumed the look of exasperation that has marked his face since I first told him I was abandoning journalism for public relations, a decision he felt showed I had a lack of social values.

"Why do you need a whole chapter on writing a lead sentence?" he asked. "Every press release I've ever seen has started with the name of the company president and tells what the man did that day." He then began announcing in a deep voice, " 'John Smith, president of Doowhacky Enterprises, announced today that he had thought up a new product, or he was hiring a new vice president, or his dog just had puppies.' Those PR people know which side their toast is buttered on, and that means buttering up their bosses every chance they get.

"You don't need to tell PR students how to write a sentence," he concluded. "Just tell them to learn how to spell their president's name, then fill in the blanks."

Although I hated to admit it, his stereotype of PR writing isn't too far from reality. Instead of sharing information that will help our audience, we've often served as press agents for our bosses' egos. Readers, confronted with unfamiliar corporate names and even more obscure corporate officers in a story's first sentences, don't read far enough to realize that a story contains information that's important to them. Worse yet, readers may not even get a chance to see a story, because an editor or a producer didn't see the news value and didn't put it in the newspaper or on the evening news.

This chapter focuses on ways public relations writers can help assure that our PR messages are newsworthy enough to our important audiences that they will want to read them. First, I examine theories that explain why audiences are interested in information and how people use media to find that information.

I then discuss how we can increase the chances that our targeted public will read our messages by focusing important information at the beginning of a message, where people decide whether to read the story. Finally, I offer a system that can help writers generate effective lead sentences by helping them set priorities and then organize information in a story to draw an audience.

It's the first and most important step in composing prose that targets readers.

WHAT YOU KNOW

- The receivers' self-interests determine whether they'll attend to a message.
- Research helps you discover which publics you need action from to reach your organization's goals.
- You can use persuasion models to predict the decision process your audience will use to evaluate your persuasive message.
- Research will tell us what messages will motivate our audience to take action and what media will help us reach that audience.

WHAT YOU'LL LEARN

- You'll only have a few words at the beginning of every communication to get your public's attention.
- Those first few words must define the audience whose attention you want and offer that audience a benefit for attending to the message.
- It's possible to evaluate what aspects of a situation will interest a particular audience.
- When the audience for a message changes, the lead sentence will change to reflect that audience's self-interest.

KNOWING YOUR COMMUNICATION COMPETITION

The first sentence of any writing assignment is arguably the most important one in the entire piece. This first sentence, the lead sentence, provides the basic structural outline you will use to build the rest of the document. In most situations it will provide the order in which topics will be discussed in the body of the story.

The lead sentence has another purpose, as Memory Memo 5.1 reminds us: to compel the targeted audience to read it. Many of us forget that making a specific audience read what we write is the first requirement of any form of persuasive writing.

Each day your audience faces thousands of competing messages—from newspapers, magazines, memos, television, friends, family and business associates. Since the receiver-centered model reminds us that it is the receiver's prerogative to accept or ignore your message, the task becomes to win your reader's attention within the first sentence of your copy, sometimes with the very first words of the first sentence.

Memory Memo 5.1
The lead sentence's importance:

- It provides basic structure for the document.
- It is responsible for drawing the right audience's attention.

Analyze and Abandon, or Analyze and Accept: A Theory of Receiving Messages

Let's see why that is so. Think about your own response to many of the messages you encounter each day. Of the thousands of messages that confront you daily, you pay attention to a very few. Some, like the stop sign at the end of your block, you don't notice because after hundreds of trips down your street you're well aware of it. You quickly flip past a certain television comedy show because you don't think it's funny. A magazine's story on political corruption in a foreign country doesn't look very interesting after you glance at the pictures. You ignore a billboard for a cigarette brand because you don't smoke.

Let's look a little more closely at what you are doing. Did you totally ignore information from all these messages that were presented to you during the day? You might not have remembered seeing the stop sign, but you stopped. You might not remember the cigarette brand name or even the billboard, but if you drive the same route tomorrow and look at the billboard, you'll probably pay even less attention to it because you'll be thinking, "I saw that billboard yesterday and it wasn't of any interest to me."

This illustrates a concept about brain functioning that researchers have developed: We have at least some awareness of all the messages that we encounter during a day. Researchers explain it this way: When humans encounter some messages— like cigarettes ads seen by a nonsmoker—the messages are instantaneously analyzed and abandoned because they aren't interesting or relevant to the receiver. Other messages—like a threatening voice on a deserted street at night, or even a notice for a philatelic club meeting encountered by a stamp collector—are instantaneously analyzed, perceived to be more important to the receiver, and transferred to a conscious processing level in the brain. Once it's on that conscious level, you attend to the message and decide what action to take. You think it would be smart to run from the threatening voice. You decide to check your schedule to see if you can attend the stamp collectors meeting.

Memory Memo 5.2
The lessons of information processing theory:

- People ignore most of the messages they receive.
- They use just seconds to make a decision to attend to a message.
- Writers need to draw their readers' attention during this brief opportunity.

If this simplified process, reviewed in Memory Memo 5.2, is how the brain works, it means humans have the capacity at some basic threshold to notice thousands of messages around them every day. It appears we are continuously aware, on a subconscious level, of virtually all the messages we encounter. It also is evident, however, that after a cursory analysis, we ignore the vast majority of those messages and save our further attention and memory for the very few messages that we perceive as relevant to our needs.

The Race for Your Audience's Attention:
The Receiver-centered Writing Process

What's the practical meaning of this to a professional communicator? It means that we as writers have a few precious moments, a few precious words in a story's first sentence, to attract our intended readers' attention and convince them the message is important to their lives. If we don't accomplish that task within the first few words of our communication act, the reader abandons the entire message. That presents a formidable challenge for the writer, but the knowledge of what's happening inside the reader's mind helps us to design successful communication.

The story's lead must identify your intended audience, define the issues important to that audience and be phrased in a way that immediately persuades your reader to continue reading the piece. Obviously, accomplishing those tasks is critical to fulfilling your communication goal. That's why we'll spend an entire chapter on how to write the lead sentence by using what I call a receiver-centered writing process. The premise of the receiver-centered writing process is that effective public relations communication is a careful matching of audience to information.

The receiver-centered process relies on the belief that there's no such thing as uninteresting information, only information that we haven't told to the right people. The process starts with research and then analysis of audience characteristics to determine what information the audience wants and needs. Once we know what information about your organization or event will interest the reader, the receiver-centered writing process helps determine how to write a lead sentence that both persuades your audience to read it and provides a coherent foundation on which to build the rest of the document. Kenneth Carter discusses the process in Box 5.1.

BOX 5.1   Views from the Field

Kenneth W. Carter
Carter is president of Focus Communications Group, a full-service communications firm based in Dallas. Carter, formerly a director of public relations for the American Heart Association, is a member of PRSA's National Multi-Cultural Affairs Committee.

One of the criticisms of public relations is that we "shotgun" releases to every big media outlet in hopes of getting coverage. Aren't those big readership numbers what we're after?

What's wrong with that strategy is that we're not giving the client the service he or she needs—we're thinking quantity of clips instead of delivering quality of clips to our client. What the client needs from public relations is for the needle to move. Increasingly, how that is determined is at the cash register.

How do you get those quality clips that will shake your client's profit needle?

You first have to know what audience you're trying to reach. If you're trying to reach an African-American audience, you've got to abandon that broad term and be more specific. Which public within that audience will help your client? Are you looking for black social workers, black teachers, male, female, older, younger? Each one of those audiences is very distinct. We need to understand each segment of the audience we're trying to impact. If you want to reach black teachers, do you need to deal with black issues in an education publication? If you're going after black business, you'll probably want to go to magazines like *Black Enterprise* or *Minority Business Entrepreneur*. Or, depending upon the maturity level of the black business person you're trying to reach, it might be the *Wall Street Journal* is the best place to go. In any case, you need to be specific about who it is you're trying to reach and then get on their communication channel. If you want to make an impact, you've got to change your message for each segment to help them understand your company's position.

Does targeting help companies become more aware of the diverse audiences that contribute to their business success?

Sure does. That's where we get into this whole issue of cultural diversity that so many companies and institutions are talking about now. To recog-

BOX 5.1   (continued)

nize that diversity, you've got to recognize that you have to tailor your message to individual audiences. And it just makes good business sense to go after this more diverse market. We're supposed to understand profits. Well, we should understand the profits available by reflecting the total society in our company's communication efforts. If you choose to put a white male in your advertising, you're forgetting that you're turning your back on a group of people who often have the same desires for products and the same money as that white male. Businesses have been doing themselves a tremendous disservice and missing a tremendous audience because of that.

—Used with permission of Kenneth W. Carter

DO YOU REALLY WANT ALL THE NEWS THAT'S FIT TO PRINT? THE 5W-1H WRITING FORMULA

Before we can talk about a basic process for writing that incorporates a story's most important elements in the first sentence, we have to know why people are interested in certain information.

Traditionally, journalists were taught that the basic information people needed to know could be provided by answering the six questions *Who, What, When, Where, Why* and *How* (the 5W-1H questions). This formula has been widely adopted by publicity chairpersons. On bulletin boards throughout the world you will find club announcements structured thus:

WHO: CATHY SMITH, ROSE EXPERT
WHAT: WILL GIVE PRIVATE GARDEN CONSULTATIONS
WHEN: TUESDAY, SEPTEMBER 15
WHERE: WOMEN'S CIVIC CLUB, 1119 MAIN
WHY: TO BENEFIT KALIBASH YOUTH DAY CAMP
HOW: $25 DONATION REQUESTED

What is logical for a poster, however, doesn't necessarily translate well into a sentence. When converted to prose, the 5W-1H formula could create some long, tedious sentences, such as:

Assistant prosecuting attorney Trish Korman Bennett announced Wednesday that Anthony J. Edwards, the city's director for emergency preparedness, has admitted the June 1 ax murder of assistant city manager Kenneth J. Breakstone, whom Edwards said he killed at Breakstone's home after an argument over secretarial assignments in city hall.

You can see the limitations of this example of the writing formula. In a rushed world in which people have thousands of messages competing for their attention each day, this lead sentence, even though it eventually reveals shocking news, doesn't provide many compelling reasons for a casual reader to notice it.

For instance, the sentence's first 18 words identify people whom our readers probably don't know or care to know. In 18 words, the sentence has not included any details that give the reader a clue what the story is about. Those first 18 words might lead a reader to think the story concerned the city's emergency siren system or Bennett's political ambitions. The thought of reading about either would certainly discourage many readers from continuing.

Persistent readers would find some truly shocking news—who murdered a city official with an ax. That's information that would compel most people to read the story, but would a busy executive, gobbling some breakfast before leaving for the office, read far enough to discover it? Probably not. It's necessary, then, to refine our strategies for structuring a story's first sentence.

CHOOSING NEWS YOUR AUDIENCE WANTS TO KNOW: THE TIPCUP FILTER

The example demonstrates that what a writer omits from the first sentence is as important as what he or she includes. To help my students make judgments about the information that's important for drawing a particular audience's attention to a lead sentence, I adapted journalistic news theory to develop what I call the TIPCUP filter.

As the term *filter* suggests, we can predict and filter what information will or will not interest a particular group. By knowing what information to include in a lead sentence, as well as what information won't interest a particular audience, we can concentrate on different factors in a situation to create lead sentences that will involve different publics. Those six basic factors can be remembered through the acronym *TIPCUP:*

Timeliness

Impact

Prominence

Conflict

Unusualness

Proximity

Memory Memo 5.3
The TIPCUP information analysis filter:

- Timeliness: Do I need to know it today?
- Impact: Will it change what I do?
- Prominence: Do I know whom it's about?
- Conflict: Am I interested in the battle?
- Unusualness: Is it the first, last or only time it has happened?
- Proximity: Did it happen around me?

Although the basic theory behind the TIPCUP filter was developed for journalists, it's applicable to public relations writing, too. Memory Memo 5.3 presents an outline of how a reporter would evaluate a situation to see which TIPCUP news elements would make a story interesting. In addition to determining what information will interest particular audiences, TIPCUP gives a public relations writer a structure that will generate a lead sentence. Before we begin that process, let's examine those elements individually, first in the way they are applied by journalists and then by public relations practitioners.

Timeliness: Do I Need to Know It Today?

A lot of the information that interests people interests them only because they haven't heard it before. An auto wreck that killed a man yesterday may have gotten coverage on the television news last night or in the newspaper today, but it won't be included tomorrow because another accident will have replaced it in the public eye.

Remember that timeliness relies not so much on time as on the freshness of information. Stories about the FBI's treatment of Martin Luther King Jr. made headline news when the bureau's secret files were opened nearly 30 years after some of the incidents.

The same principles apply in public relations: Timeliness makes information interesting. For example, if your firm produces dry ice and a power failure that started on a hot Friday afternoon threatens to last well into the weekend, your company can't afford to wait until Monday to notify the public that it can help them save their refrigerated food. By then it will be too late and no one will care to know.

Impact: Will It Change What I Do?

Impact is the second element that determines whether people will be interested in information. Simply stated, people are interested in information that affects the way they conduct their lives. This self-interest is a powerful impetus in stimulating people to read an article. For instance, a school board debate over whether to raise the district's property taxes will likely provoke massive newspaper readership among homeowners, who will be responsible for paying the higher taxes.

Impact is probably the most powerful motivator for interest in public relations writing, too. If a news release by a national senior citizens association tells how a community halfway across the country is using visiting nurses to cut the elderly's health care costs, that's going to be interesting to many other communities nationwide struggling with the same problem. In this case, the experience of one community may help solve the problems of another, an example of impact.

Prominence: Do I Know Whom It's About?

If a young mother from your community goes to the local Kmart, it is not news. However, if a young mother picks up a few disposable diapers at a discount store clear across the country—and she happens to be a member of the British royal family—it automatically becomes news. The doings of celebrities, no matter how inconsequential, interest many readers.

The lure of prominence is not necessarily limited to film stars or royalty. If your community's mayor is charged with drunken driving, the news coverage will be much more extensive than if an ordinary citizen in the community were arrested for the same offense.

The same principle applies in public relations writing. A charity banquet for the local animal shelter probably won't get much attention from the local press, no matter how well written the press release announcing it. But if the man who trained Rin Tin Tin for the movies makes the main address, the media coverage might increase dramatically.

Conflict: Am I Interested in the Battle?

As unfortunate as it seems, conflict is a central aspect in most news coverage. People are interested when people or groups come to blows with each other, whether in ritual conflict, like sports, or in real conflict, like war. Yet conflict means more than just physical confrontation. We can find conflict in political contests, in the fight to be elected to an office, or in a battle over a zoning decision. There are conflicts such as environmentalists arguing with mining company executives over the development of a wilderness area, or a company contesting a takeover by another company.

Another form of conflict is illustrated by accident and disaster coverage. For whatever deep, dark reasons, people like to know the misfortunes of other people (which might explain the popularity of the manufactured conflicts that comprise every soap opera plot). The same morbid curiosity accounts for the high media visibility of traffic deaths, industrial and construction accidents, and other incidents where blood is spilled.

Although it's a commonly held perception that PR practitioners prefer to show their clients sailing on a calm sea of passively positive public opinion, remember that conflict is often a part of awakening an important audience's attention and inciting their support for an organizational policy. For instance, a company's effort to fend off unauthorized uses of a protected patent, or a nonprofit's fight with a governmental organization over adoption processes could bring positive attention to an organization.

Unusualness: Is It the First, Last or Only Time It's Happened?

One of the classic definitions of news was given by *New York Sun* editor John B. Bogart: "When a dog bites a man, that is not news," Bogart said. "But when a man bites a dog, that is news."

You don't need to look any further than the supermarket checkout counter (see Figure 5.1) to see evidence of the power that strange and unique events have in capturing readers' attention. The tabloid newspaper covers illustrate how unusualness is a powerful motivator of reader interest. The tabloids' frequent stories about people who communicate with Elvis Presley beyond the grave are an indication of the fascination readers have with the unusual.

FIGURE 5.1   Could this be news?
Used with permission of Weekly World News

Although public relations writers usually don't deal with such supernatural exotica, unusualness is a frequent component of their work. They are often asked to publicize projects such as the first computer shopping network in the city, production of the last model of a car by a local automotive factory before retooling, or the work of the only stained glass artisan in the state. These "firsts," "lasts" and "onlys" are relished by editors and broadcast news producers because they bring pride or a touch of whimsy to relieve the tedium of everyday news.

Proximity: Did It Happen Around Me?

The final determinant of whether an event will interest readers is whether it has a local angle. It's easy to see this at work. If a large school in your city has to be evacuated because of a bomb scare, the story will probably be included on the local newscast. However, the evacuation probably would not be included in a nearby city's nightly news and certainly wouldn't be covered by media in another state.

People are interested in many events simply because they happen close to them or involve someone from their community. For example, when a natural disaster occurs in some distant country the television news coverage often sounds like this: Nine Americans were among 3,000 people killed in an Indonesian earthquake Tuesday.

Let's look at another situation. If a couple living in a suburb of a large city has triplets, the happy news certainly won't be covered by the metropolitan newspaper or on local television. It probably won't even be included in the suburb's daily or weekly newspaper. However, if the mother works at a small manufacturing plant with an employee newsletter, the triplets might be the newsletter's lead story.

In public relations, proximity can be the greatest attention grabber. Unfortunately, it often seems to be an element forgotten by PR professionals. In fact, an Oklahoma State University poll of editors found most news releases aren't used because the releases don't have a local angle.

Every day, national corporate headquarters mail hundreds or thousands of news releases announcing hirings or promotions, but those releases generally aren't used by editors because they aren't relevant to their readers. However, the odds those releases would be printed rise dramatically if a PR person knows enough to localize releases to the new manager's hometown, to the cities where he or she previously lived, to the publications of the person's alma mater, and to other audiences that care about the fortunes of this individual.

WHO YOU ARE DETERMINES WHAT YOU'LL READ: ANALYZING DEMOGRAPHICS AND PSYCHOGRAPHICS

In examining why people are interested in certain types of information, it becomes apparent the TIPCUP formula sometimes doesn't predict if a particular group is going to be interested in a particular story. It only tells you if there is news value in the story's information. The missing factor that will determine whether your effort will be persuasive is how the receiver will react to the information you're presenting.

Let's put together a clearly ludicrous situation to prove the point. Let's say the crown prince of Monaco is visiting your city today. He's riding in a Shriner motorcycle unit in a benefit parade raising funds to restore the 70 percent of the city destroyed by a flood. His motorcycle crashes into the Luxembourg national float. Luxembourg's prime minister suffers a concussion when he falls off the float, and the two countries declare war on each other as a result of the incident.

Here we have a scenario containing every one of the TIPCUP elements. It has timeliness, proximity and prominence. His royal highness doing precision driving routines with a group of fez-topped Americans is quite unusual. The parade's proceeds will have a major impact on the mud-encrusted city. Moreover, conflict is everywhere, with Luxembourg blood flowing in the street and war clouds looming on the horizon for these peaceful little principalities.

But if you are the newsletter editor for a flour millers trade association in that same city, you will find there isn't any aspect in this story for your readers. It is obvious there is one aspect we must add to the TIPCUP formula. The final element is audience.

Unlike the other criteria determining interest, this one has nothing to do with the event itself. Instead, it is concerned with the innate qualities of the individuals receiving your message and the impact those qualities will have on each person's interest in and ability to understand your message.

This contradicts many beliefs we have about our society, because we're often told that our nation is a uniform mass society that can be persuaded and led through mass communication. That's a simplistic notion. Stanford University professor William L. Rivers says America is not really one people at all, but a confederation of citizens with very dissimilar interests, backgrounds and experiences.

Each of us belongs to many different audiences and publics: homeowners, doctors, students, stamp collectors, people from Delaware. However, no person can be defined by membership in a single audience. You are a student and belong to that public, but you also may be president of the local opera group, a member of the art gallery association and the literary study club, and an accordion player in a polka band. As Figure 5.2 illustrates, self-identity is built on the foundation of the many different publics to which an individual belongs. This complex of personal values

FIGURE 5.2   The author's audience profile

provides the perspective through which we judge our own self-interest and determines our reaction to communication events.

Every individual has a different background, a different set of interests and attributes. These personal characteristics can be defined through demographics and psychographics. As we discussed in Chapter 2, demographics classify people through quantitative information such as their age and gender, where they live, their jobs and the amount of money they earn, and their educational levels.

Psychographics describe how people define themselves—their political views, spiritual beliefs, personal values and interests. Psychographic elements are many times a much more powerful indicator of a reader's interest in a particular subject.

Public relations writers can use the knowledge of demographics and psychographics to help construct an effective communication campaign that will be relevant to a number of different audiences.

Let's take an example of a public relations writer whose job is to announce the invention of a new desktop blood diagnosis machine that eliminates the delays of sending blood samples to a large laboratory. A news release to a medical journal would concentrate on the faster diagnoses and lower costs of the new technology. Another release to a consumer health newsletter might instead emphasize the convenience and novelty of the new machine. An alumni magazine for the college of the inventor would concentrate on the person who developed the machine. A report to the president of the company marketing the device might concentrate on profits expected from the new product.

Not only do audience differences affect the material they may be interested in, but they also affect the way the material is presented. Obviously a direct-mail piece intended to recruit dropouts for a high school equivalency program would use a simpler vocabulary than a news release to a science magazine detailing a university's discovery of the effect of gravity on a subatomic field. Your audience for the first piece may not even be able to read on an eighth-grade level, whereas the second will probably have completed two decades of formal education.

Sometimes that difference in background and attitude can even cause one group of people to define the same event differently from another group. Here is one example: When the Pol Pot regime was in power in Cambodia, hundreds of thousands of people in groups opposed to the government were systematically starved by the government. Near death, the people began to eat anything that could sustain life, including household pets.

Responding to the situation, some relief agencies tried to start a fund-raising campaign to deliver food to the starving people. Others tried to organize international political opinion to force the government to end the starvation tactics.

However, some American groups viewed the atrocities and the moral response they should make, not as a situation in which people were starving to death, but as a situation that was leading to the torture of household pets. While the other groups tried to change the political environment or organize emergency food supplies to save the people, one animal rights group collected money to send volunteers to Cambodia to prevent people from eating their pets.

Because of these differences in the way different groups respond to information or perceive the significance of information, it is important to know the audience in designing a communication program. That's the fourth and final step in the receiver-centered model we discussed in Chapter 1.

Here are the practical implications of translating this theory into real-life situations:

- Every individual in our society is faced with thousands of messages each day. From those thousands of messages, a person chooses to read or listen to only a few.
- In that environment, the competition for the public relations message is intense. PR writers must first use the persuasion platform planning process to analyze the audience they wish to reach with their message.
- They must then design their message to appeal to the audience's interest or self-interest.
- Once that analysis is complete, writers must integrate that information into the message so readers immediately recognize the story is important to them.

A SYSTEM THAT GENERATES EFFECTIVE WRITING: THE RECEIVER-CENTERED WRITING PROCESS

Professional writers often think that talking about writing—developing writing theories and constructing writing models—is just pleasant conversation for people who can't write. Real writing theory? It's knowing what to write when you're stuck at the beginning of a paragraph or knowing what to do when a writing block keeps you from writing anything at all. After 20 years of getting paid to write, I still have problems in getting a story started or knowing how to begin a new section. It's to answer those frustrations that I developed the receiver-centered writing process.

The process helps generate the first few words of each paragraph when inspiration fails. It helps you analyze your audience so you'll know what information will interest your reader, and guides you in arranging that information within the sentence. Once you've got the basic pattern established by the first few words, you'll generally be able to write the rest of the paragraph.

For most beginning writers, the first sentence is the most difficult. That's understandable, since that lead sentence has to draw the right audience into the story, as well as dictate the basic structure for the rest of the document. The receiver-centered process breaks down the process of writing the lead sentence into three fundamental steps that are the same for whatever document you're asked to write. Before you begin to write, you should (1) know whom you're writing for, (2) discover what they're interested in, and (3) tell them that information as quickly as you can. For the sake of illustration, let's take a look at the process at work.

Let's say you are working as a public relations professional at the KonkreteWeave Carpet Corp. plant located in Medianville, a city in the midst of an economic slump. The company headquarters has announced that company researcher R. P. Scallion has discovered a new stainproof carpet fiber. Scallion works in the company's research laboratories in the Lesser Antilles. The carpet fiber is made stain resistant by being dipped in a high-temperature chemical bath, a lost process that had been used by the Egyptians 3,000 years ago.

Beginning Jan. 1, carpet using the fiber will be produced exclusively in the Medianville factory where you work, which will hire 900 more workers to produce the new line.

Although the Medianville plant is the first plant to make the new fiber, Scallion said this technology will soon dominate the entire industry and be used in plants throughout the world. Your public relations office asks you to produce a news release announcing the finding to the local metropolitan newspaper.

Let's look at a probable lead sentence if we were using the Who, What, When, Where, Why, How (5W-1H) method:

KonkreteWeave Carpet Corp. has announced that company scientist R. P. Scallion has discovered in tests over the past six years at the company's research laboratories in the Lesser Antilles that a new no-stain carpet can be made by soaking carpet fibers in a high-temperature chemical bath, giving consumers a much-desired feature in their new carpet purchases.

All the 5W-1H questions are answered, but it is difficult to imagine any person who would be interested in reading the sentence except KonkreteWeave's president.

We should instead start with a notion of who is going to be reading our message—our audience. That person's reaction to our message is the most important determinant of the effectiveness of our communication efforts and the one around whom we should shape our writing.

Know Whom You're Writing For:
The Audience Analysis

The first step in the receiver-centered writing process is to analyze the audience with which we want to communicate. In the case of KonkreteWeave, that means we have to take the audience characteristics we noted in the persuasion platform to find who might be interested in reading about our company's new discovery and its implications. That portrait of our important publics will guide our efforts to create a lead sentence. To accomplish that we need to learn a little more about the intended readers. Let's walk through the audience analysis in KonkreteWeave's persuasion platform.

The following case study is based in part on formal research on our audience as well as some good public relations intuition:

Audience Analysis

Demographics. The KonkreteWeave Carpet Corp. plant is in Medianville, a city of about 140,000. The city has historically been a blue-collar community, with its economy based on textile mills, shoe factories, and other relatively low-technology firms. For the past five years, a string of plant closings has boosted unemployment to serious levels.

Psychographics. The psychographic impression these economic circumstances have left on the people of Medianville is equally bleak. Unemployed workers fear tumbling into poverty. The ones still employed are wondering if their jobs will disappear. Even people who should be more secure, those with good jobs or those who have retired with comfortable pensions, are worried. They are worried about the effect of unemployment on housing values, on tax revenues, and on the quality of life in their community.

Know What They're Interested In:
The TIPCUP Analysis

Now that we have a profile of what is important to our readers, we evaluate the information through the TIPCUP filter. To do this, we estimate the strength of the information in each of the six TIPCUP categories on the basis of how important it is to our audience's needs. Knowing the economic problems of the readers of the metropolitan newspaper, which of the following TIPCUP aspects help draw an audience of Medianville newspaper readers? Our thought process would sound something like this:

Timeliness: Not really important. The project has taken six years to complete, and the news that there will be a new carpet fiber would be as interesting two weeks from now as today.

Impact: Very important. In a community filled with unemployed factory workers, the news that 900 new jobs will be created by Jan. 1 is tremendously important.

Prominence: No. There is no person connected with the story whose name our readers would recognize.

Conflict: None.

Unusualness: The story does have an aspect of unusualness: It is the first modern use of this technology. However, to most of our audience, the technological innovation is less important than the jobs created by the technology.

Proximity: Another very important element. If the jobs created would be in another state or another country, Medianville readers would not care. However, it is intensely important in a community filled with unemployed factory workers.

Tell Them Quickly: Generating the Lead Sentence

After we have discovered what information is most important to our readers, we are ready to use the receiver-centered writing process to generate a lead sentence. Memory Memo 5.4 shows the basic procedure.

Memory Memo 5.4
The receiver-centered writing process:

- Formulate your audience's demographic and psychographic profile.
- Evaluate your story information through the TIPCUP filter.
- Choose the TIPCUP elements that stimulate your receiver's interests.
- Find words that illustrate each TIPCUP element you've chosen.
- Prioritize the TIPCUP elements important to your receivers.
- Write the lead sentence, using most important TIPCUP elements first.
- Refine and tighten the lead sentence.

Take the TIPCUP elements you have determined to be important to your audience. In this case, those are impact, unusualness, and proximity. We want to get those elements, and only those elements, into the lead sentence. We also want to place the most important elements—impact and proximity—at the beginning of the sentence.

The next step is to pick words that communicate each of the TIPCUP concepts to your readers. For instance, proximity for our readers would be conveyed by the word *Medianville*. Impact for our particular audience might be stated by words like *unemployment* or *jobs*. Timeliness might be suggested by the words *soon* or *Jan. 1* or *next year*. Unusualness could be communicated by using a word like *unusual* or *new*.

Using the receiver-centered writing process, we might construct a lead sentence like this for a KonkreteWeave news release to Medianville's major newspaper:

Medianville's unemployment problems may be softened when KonkreteWeave Carpet Corp. hires 900 new workers to start manufacturing a revolutionary new no-stain carpet fiber in its local plant Jan. 1.

Now, reduced to the individual elements:

Medianville's (PROXIMITY) unemployment problems may be softened when KonkreteWeave Carpet Corp. hires 900 new workers (IMPACT) to start manufacturing a revolutionary new no-stain carpet fiber (UNUSUALNESS) in its local plant Jan. 1 (TIMELINESS).

By using this process, we have created a lead sentence that accomplishes what the first sentence in any kind of persuasive writing should. It immediately identifies the audience to which it is directed (in this case, people in a community who have been hurt by unemployment). It concentrates within the sentence's first 10 words the most important elements of the situation, the elements that will lead the greatest number of readers or the most important readers to continue reading. Figure 5.3 demonstrates the importance of those first 10 words in drawing the attention of the correct audience.

Here's a rule that summarizes the process: In the first 10 words of the lead, define an audience and provide a benefit for that audience.

Although the receiver-centered writing process does help writers produce an effective lead sentence, they are still using their individual initiative or creativity. There are always a number of different ways writers can accomplish the same communication task. In this case, for instance:

Nine hundred new jobs will be created in Medianville Jan. 1 when KonkreteWeave Carpet Corp. begins manufacturing a revolutionary new no-stain carpet fiber in its local plant.

---

or:

There will be 900 new jobs in Medianville on Jan. 1 when KonkreteWeave Carpet Corp. begins manufacturing a revolutionary new no-stain carpet fiber in its local plant.

---

or:

The new year will bring relief for Medianville's unemployment problem when KonkreteWeave Carpet Corp. adds 900 workers at its local plant to manufacture a revolutionary new no-stain carpet fiber.

FIGURE 5.3 Putting important information into the No. 1 position

ORIGINAL
Original introduces un- ⟶ Taxpayers United President Jody Carlin said the group's study of the Second
inviting topics and un- Street Bridge accident determined that "bad concrete" caused the bridge col-
known speaker. lapse.

REWRITE
Rewrite concentrates ⟶ "Bad concrete" may have caused the Second Street Bridge collapse, according
on scandal in first few to a taxpayers' advocacy group.
words and involves the
right audience.

COMPARING THE FIRST 10 WORDS

ORIGINAL ⟶ Taxpayers United President Jody Carlin said this group's study. . .

REWRITE ⟶ "Bad concrete" may have caused the Second Street Bridge collapse. . .

Although each lead sentence is different, all fulfill the basic tasks of any opening sentence. They concentrate the story's most important elements within the first 10 words of the sentence. Those elements define the audience with which we want to communicate and a benefit that will be important to the interest or self-interest of those readers.

YOU WANT DIFFERENT AUDIENCES? YOU NEED DIFFERENT LEADS

It's important to remember that a lead sentence is your strategy for reaching the greatest number of people who are united by a specific interest. It is not a static, unchanging structure. As indicated earlier, if you use the receiver-centered writing process, the lead may change when the audience changes. For instance, what would happen if you were writing about Medianville's new carpet factory for the readers of a science magazine?

First, the audience analysis in the persuasion platform certainly would change. Our audience would now comprise the readers of a scientific publication instead of the general citizenry of a specific city with a concentration of blue-collar workers. This magazine's readers are an extremely well-educated group of professionals. Even though they are scattered throughout the world, their science provides a common tie so strong that a hierarchy of personalities and reputations develops within the profession. In addition, it is a profession directed toward discovery, so that a new scientific finding might help redirect the research of many other scientists.

Once we have worked through the audience analysis, you will see the TIPCUP filter has a different result, too:

Timeliness: Of little importance. This information will be just as important to this audience next week or next month as it is today.
Impact: Yes. Scallion's discovery solves a problem many other research scientists have been working on. It may provide a new angle on research being conducted by other textile scientists.
Prominence: Yes. Many members of this select profession may know R. P. Scallion or know his reputation.
Conflict: No.
Unusualness: This is probably the most important reason. This is a first, discovering a long-lost secret of the ancient world.
Proximity: No. With readers scattered throughout the world, the specific city in which the carpet will be manufactured or where the discovery was made isn't overwhelmingly important.

When we turn to writing the lead sentence, we will use elements we've determined to be most important—impact, prominence and unusualness. After selecting words to illustrate those concepts, the lead might turn out something like this:

Solving an ancient chemical mystery, KonkreteWeave Carpet Corp. researcher R. P. Scallion has found Assyrian carpets resisted stains because they were soaked in a high-temperature chemical bath, a process that will be duplicated in a KonkreteWeave factory Jan. 1.

You'll notice how this lead differs from the one intended for the newspaper readers. Even though we are communicating information about the very same event, the audience difference dictates the difference in the lead sentences. That's because the persuasion platform audience analysis suggests this audience of scientists will demand different things to draw their attention into the story. The analysis will help us predict the audience's probable interest, its reading level and the different way a particular audience will perceive an event.

In this situation, you see all three of these predictions at work. We have targeted the message in each lead to the interests of the particular audience reading it. The research scientists want to know about a colleague's contributions to solving a perplexing technical problem. On the other hand, Medianville's newspaper readers have more interest in the jobs that may help their city recover from the economic trauma it has experienced.

You can see differences in reading level, too. The two most important determinants of reading difficulty are the number of words in sentences and the number of syllables in words within those sentences. There is a striking difference between the two example sentences. The sentence intended for the research scientists contains 39 words, 10 of which are three syllables or more. The lead for Medianville's newspaper readers, most of whom don't have the doctoral degrees held by the research scientists, contains only 29 words, of which only four have three syllables or more.

Note, too, that the story's emphasis is dramatically different for different readers. The lead sentence meant for research scientists views the story as a step in the march toward knowledge. Our lead sentence for newspaper readers in the beleaguered town views the story as an economic development, virtually the same as if an amusement park had opened in the city with the promise of bringing more money into the local economy.

THE CONSTANTS: DEFINE THE AUDIENCE, TELL THEM THEIR BENEFIT

Because the audience-centered writing process concentrates on the process a writer follows to create the writing, the same steps can be used to address any audience in any type of writing. Memory Memo 5.5 is a checklist to remind you of those points.

Let's say we wanted to create an internal memorandum to tell KonkreteWeave's chief executive about the expected benefits of manufacturing the stain-resistant carpet. The same principles apply. What does your audience (even if it's only one person) care about? What can you communicate that will be interesting to that audience? How can you get that information into the first few words of your memo's first sentence?

In every lead sentence you write you should identify the audience to which the message is addressed and then try to discover what information you can offer that would benefit that group. Finally, you should structure your lead sentence so that the information that will draw them into the story is presented to your readers immediately.

Memory Memo 5.5
Checklist for applying receiver-centered writing system to the lead sentence:

- The first few words define an audience and the benefit for that audience.
- The most important TIPCUP elements are found early in the sentence.
- TIPCUP elements that don't immediately draw an audience are lower in the story.
- Vocabulary and sentence length are appropriate to receivers' capacities.
- The lead sentence is different for different receiver groups.

The essence of good writing in a competitive world is to give your intended audience a reason to be interested in what you have to communicate and an invitation to read what you write. In the next chapter, we will examine how the audience-based writing process provides a structure for later paragraphs.

SUMMARY

- The main task of a document's lead sentence is to gain the attention of the proper audience.
- Although people have some subconscious awareness of most messages they encounter, they dismiss the vast majority of them and save their attention for a few messages they perceive as relevant to them.
- People make decisions about whether they will attend to a message within the first few words of communication events.
- Traditionally, journalistic lead sentences included all six elements of an event: Who, What, When, Where, Why and How.
- Although comprehensive, 5W-1H leads are less likely to be read because they don't concentrate information important to an audience in the first few words, in which the audience is deciding whether to attend to the message.
- The TIPCUP filter—Time, Impact, Prominence, Conflict, Unusualness and Proximity—is a journalist's compilation of elements that make an event interesting to an audience.

- An awareness of audience characteristics is essential to determine which of the TIPCUP elements will attract that audience's attention in a particular situation.
- A person's conception of self comes from his or her membership in many different publics.
- Audience characteristics will determine whether a public will be interested in a situation and should change the complexity of vocabulary, the type of medium, and other methods the writer uses to communicate with that public.
- The TIPCUP filter analyzes a situation in the context of a specific audience to see which of the TIPCUP elements will be most useful in drawing that audience's attention to the piece.
- The first 10 words of a good lead sentence define an audience and then provide a benefit that will be important to that audience.
- Using the receiver-centered writing system, when the audience changes, the lead sentence will change to emphasize those TIPCUP elements that will be most powerful in drawing that audience's attention.

THINK PIECES

1. Analyze the local and national coverage of a major news story and see how many TIPCUP elements the lead sentence of each story contained.
2. Name some situations in which an institution's objectives were gained by making people angry.
3. Describe yourself demographically, then psychographically. What media would be effective in communicating to the demographic groups to which you perceive that you belong? To your psychographic groups?
4. Analyze how different audiences might be interested in a story from today's newspaper. How would you change the lead to stimulate that interest? Which audience for the story would be most important to a particular client? How do you make this judgment?

WRITING ASSIGNMENTS

D3.10
D5.9
D6.9
D9.10

ADDITIONAL READINGS

Brooks, Brian S., Kennedy, George, Moen, Daryl R., and Rany, Don. *News Reporting and Writing*, 4th ed. New York: St. Martin's, 1992.

Hillocks, George. *Research on Written Composition*. Urbana, Ill.: National Council on Research in English, 1986.

## chapter 6

Building a Persuasive Case: Generating the Body of the Story in the Receiver-centered Writing Process

REAL-LIFE LESSONS

Let's admit it to ourselves. When we create public relations documents we are not creating literature. We needn't worry about our audience spending hours pondering the deep, hidden meaning of our writing, amazed at the lyricism of our prose and impressed by the profundity of our vocabulary. I learned that lesson the first day I was in journalism school.

I had wanted to be a writer since I first read "The Great Gatsby," and within my farmbound sequestering I had fashioned what I flattered myself was a prose style by wallowing in all the American novelists of the early 20th century. I had copied my favorite authors' prose styles, trying for Faulkner's convoluted sentences or the languorous prose of Fitzgerald. I studied vocabulary lists and weaseled long, obscure words into my writing to gain what I imagined was a sheen of intellectualism.

My newswriting teacher wasn't impressed. A crusty veteran of several South Dakota newspapers, he called my writing style "thesaurus prose." His most telling insult: He told me there were precisely two people in the world who would read a newspaper to discover how many four-syllable words I could cram into a 60-word sentence—me and my mother.

But he gave me some slight hope on that dark day when I had thought about abandoning my teenage dream of being a writer. He told me journalistic writing was not intended to show off my prose style. That's ego getting in the way of a journalist's real purpose. Journalism, he explained, exists to make sure people understand information that helps them live their lives. Anything that detracts from that is counterproductive.

What he told me is equally applicable to public relations writing. When you create PR writing, you are creating the most basic, but in a way, the most noble form of writing. You are exchanging knowledge between your organization and people important to your organization in the fastest, most forthright, and most comprehensible manner you can.

That's what this chapter is intended to foster. We are trying to use all the knowledge we have gained about our audience and the way they react to information to fashion prose that communicates directly. When we understand the difficulty and importance of our task, the adulation of our reading public isn't so sorely missed.

WHAT YOU KNOW

- Receivers quickly abandon any message they perceive is not fulfilling their needs.
- Writers need to construct messages to conform to their audiences' capabilities and desires for information.
- Persuasion is more likely accomplished when receivers are shown how a problem affects them and are given guidance on how they can act effectively to solve the problem.

WHAT YOU'LL LEARN

- Writers should put arguments in the sequence in which a receiver will most likely process and comprehend them.
- Because readers won't devote much of their available communication time reading public relations messages, practitioners have to communicate the maximum amount of information in the least reading time possible.
- The persuasion platform process can be used to guide the writing process and generate prose.

WRITING CREATED BY YOUR AUDIENCE'S NEEDS

Architect Louis Sullivan, who was responsible for transforming the Chicago skyline and the thinking of many architects, once said that "form ever follows function." Sullivan was explaining that a building's design should mirror and reveal the reason for its being. Sullivan believed a building should not be ornamented with false fronts and filigrees. Instead, the architecture should stand as a monument to the utility of the beams that support it and the tasks of the people who work or live in it.

The structure of writing, especially public relations writing, should be similar.

Writing is created to be read; public relations writing is created to persuade a public important to your organization.

That's a simple statement, but many public relations writers don't seem to adhere to that principle. They emphasize elements of their organizations that don't interest their audiences. Rather than thinking of their readers' needs, they use writing styles formed by habit or to satisfy their artistic tastes or their boss's ego.

That's not good. Public relations writers must concentrate on communicating information efficiently to specific publics in a way that satisfies their needs and helps meet the organization's management goals.

This chapter is intended to give you writing strategies that will address those needs. It will use the receiver-centered communication principles you employed in writing a lead sentence to construct the body of the public relations message, in which you'll be developing and prioritizing the arguments that lead your readers toward accepting your message. Let's begin this chapter by defining what makes good writing: Good public relations writing stems from a practitioner's knowledge of how readers react during a communication act and from a desire to satisfy the reader's communication needs. Rather than resort to a recitation of rules about writing, we will examine a communication philosophy based on what readers want from the messages they receive. It's not intended to make all public relations writers or writing alike. There are no formulas for good writing. Instead, our receiver-centered philosophy will point you toward your own writing style, one that will involve and motivate your readers and that you can employ in a wide variety of public relations media.

RELEVANT AND FAST: WHAT PEOPLE WANT FROM PUBLIC RELATIONS MEDIA

People read public relations writing not as entertainment but as a tool to find important information about an institution with which they deal. Although it disrupts my artistic self-image, I feel that the PR task of pure communication is a socially useful calling.

Two imperatives stem from that philosophy. First, remember that your audience members are reading to gather information important to their lives. That fact compels you as a public relations writer to structure information within the story in a logical flow that will allow your readers to see relationships among the facts you include. That logic should also build a story structure so your readers can retain and later retrieve the information you present. Second, your readers want to gain that information as quickly as possible. They are faced with processing and responding to thousands of messages every day, and even if they are interested in your message, they have limited time to devote to it.

If your writing is too long, or your method of offering important information too tedious, your readers will quit reading before the end of the piece. That makes it necessary to be aware of the places within stories where readers make decisions

Memory Memo 6.1
Receiver-centered writing requires that writers:

- ensure comprehension to make certain the message is transferred
- enhance reading speed to use as little of the reader's time as possible

about continuing their attention to the message. It also makes it mandatory to use a prose style and vocabulary that is as simple and direct as possible. It forces you to structure information in the piece to motivate and reward your readers for their continued attention.

In sum, the two receiver-centered considerations that drive public relations writing are the following (see also Memory Memo 6.1):

1. Make certain your message is transferred (by ensuring reading comprehension).
2. Use as little of your readers' time as possible (by enhancing reading speed).

All the prose rules we'll be discussing in this chapter derive from your readers' needs for comprehension and economy. That's a vital point, because it's important to realize prose rules don't exist simply as random, disconnected edicts issued by some junior high school language arts teacher; they stem from and should serve your readers' communication needs and make the communication process more assured.

INVERTED PYRAMIDS: THE MATCH BETWEEN WRITING STRUCTURES AND READER INVOLVEMENT

We've seen in the previous chapter how people approach the decision about whether to pay attention to a message. They usually are receptive for a few moments while they decide whether the message contains anything that interests or involves them. If it does, they decide to invest reading time in the piece. If it doesn't, they'll immediately abandon the piece. That's why I emphasized placing information that should interest your audience in the lead's first few words.

However, readers are making decisions about whether to keep reading all through a piece of writing. Think of your own experiences when you've read a newspaper article, watched a television news documentary or even been involved in a conversation with a friend. You read or watched or listened until you thought you had exhausted the information that interested you. Then you quit, even though you hadn't finished reading the article or watching the documentary. Your attention even wandered from your best friend's conversation once he quit meeting your information needs.

It's a fact of life in public relations writing that all people aren't going to attend to your whole message. Recognizing reality, the task is to communicate as much vital information to your readers as possible in the first sections of your message, reserving less important facts for deeper in the story. That ensures that the greatest numbers of readers will be drawn into the story and that even those readers who abandon the piece midway through may understand the story's most important facts.

Out of such recognition of receiver behavior comes the inverted pyramid, made famous in journalism texts all over the world (see Figure 6.1). Because readers abandon virtually any communication act if they sense they are not receiving the information they want, the inverted pyramid structure concentrates important information high in the story. Then it sets out to support the lead sentence by providing statistics, quotes and information in a coherent argumentation structure. Less important information is placed lower in the story, where dedicated readers can find historical background and miscellaneous information about the issue. It's designed to deliver the story's most important details even if the reader stops reading a story after only one or two paragraphs. It's a very practical method for newspaper and public relations writers because it adapts writing structures to reader habits. Its basic tenets are the same as the receiver-centered writing process I detailed in the last chapter. Both are designed to seize the brief opportunity writers have to capture their readers' attention and exploit that chance to involve and inform their audiences. Virtually all PR writing employs some elements of the reasoning that underlies the inverted pyramid.

In most PR writing, the inverted pyramid is constructed in the following order:

Lead Paragraph: After you have analyzed your communication purpose and your audience, you write the lead based on the receiver-centered communication principles outlined in Chapter 5.

Briefly Explain the Lead: The second paragraph of an inverted pyramid explains the lead. In most instances, it establishes the official name of the program you've introduced in the lead, highlights one statistic that gives credibility to a claim made in the lead, or offers the name of an important person who was the subject of the lead. In essence, readers should be able to leave the piece after the first two paragraphs with a basic understanding of what the story involves.

lead sentence defines audience and benefit

2nd paragraph explains lead, identifies players

3rd section uses facts and quotes to prove the lead

4th section gives background

call to action

FIGURE 6.1   The public relations version of the inverted pyramid structure

Justify the Lead: In subsequent paragraphs of the inverted pyramid, you offer quotes, facts, chronologies and other information to prove the statement you made in your lead. If you announced a concert in the lead, here's where you would tell what groups will be playing. If you said in the first sentence of an annual report's narrative that your company expects big profits from a new product, here you would offer projections and quotes from marketing experts to justify your optimism.

You develop the ideas in the same sequence in which you introduced them, and you generally use only one new idea in each paragraph. (There will be more guidance about setting priorities and structuring information for the middle section of the inverted pyramid later in the chapter.)

Background: After you have built the middle section of the inverted pyramid, the fourth section gives a historical overview of the event or issue the document discusses. For instance, if you're announcing the implementation of a new law, you might give the legislative history of the issue. A story on a leukemia cure might include earlier ineffective folk cures and drug therapies.

Call to Action: The fifth section includes any miscellaneous details that haven't been mentioned before—usually procedural information that will tell readers how they can get more information or how they can participate in the issue or event the document discusses. Here's where you would put a toll-free number or list the ticket prices for an event. You might give time and place for an antidrug rally or an address to send donations to a college's scholarship fund.

Figure 6.2 gives an example of how the inverted pyramid works in a news release. With the inverted pyramid you answer the reader's need to comprehend the

FIGURE 6.2   Example of inverted pyramid news release

Immediate news that involves readers	Local home and business owners are having to pay bigger insurance premiums because of high arson rates, according to a study released by the Hamilton Fire Department.
Source mention omitted until end of lead	
Statistics to explain lead	Hamilton fire insurance rates have increased 19 percent during the past year, largely due to arson, according to a Fire Department survey announced by Chief Robert McKintreck.
Source named	
Statement of position story will prove	McKintreck said consumers are paying insurance rates to cover fires being set for profit. Of the 82 local fires in 1990 known to be caused by arson, two-thirds involved small businesses that were losing money, McKintreck said. Another 20 percent occurred in rental homes and apartments, often buildings so old and run-down that they could no longer be profitably rented.
Most important support for position	
Less important support	
National background on problem	FBI statistics show Hamilton's problem was mirrored in other parts of the country. Nationally, arson rates were up 28 percent and fire insurance premiums rose nearly 30 percent in 1993.
Miscellaneous section, procedural items	McKintreck said the statistics show the need for more local funding for better instruments to detect traces of gasoline and other fuels at fire scenes.

story's most important elements quickly. Now we turn to guidelines for structuring successful persuasive communication within the inverted pyramid structure.

THINKING FOR YOUR READER: THE LOGIC OF THE ARGUMENT

In the body of a public relations document your job is to prove what you said in your lead. The inverted pyramid's body copy presents evidence to support your position and offers that evidence so your audience can easily understand and retain it. In persuasive communication it's important to arrange your arguments to lead readers through the evidence and clearly justify the decision you're asking them to make.

Although forms of the inverted pyramid are used almost exclusively in journalism and quite widely in public relations writing tasks, there are vital differences between the intent of each type of communication. These distinctions translate into important differences in approach.

For the most part, journalistic writing is expository, that is, writing that explains events or issues. Likewise, there are instances, like news releases announcing personnel promotions, when public relations writing uses expository writing methods.

However, most public relations writing is persuasive communication. Persuasive writing doesn't merely explain events. Rather, it asks its reader to take a definite action or adopt a certain idea.

That's an important distinction, because the goals of public relations writing make it much more important to sequence arguments properly. We are not merely trying to communicate. Instead, we are trying to tailor a communication act to help our organization reach a management goal we have spelled out in our persuasion platform plan. From a practical standpoint, we have to lead the reader in a very precise fashion through the evidence that justifies our position.

Matching Audience to Argument: Integrating the Situational Model

How do we do that? First we let the best available theories on the persuasive sequence guide our persuasion platform; then we integrate our platform's findings into our writing. What's the best way to predict whether someone will change from a communication processor to an information receiver? Grunig's situational theory, which you learned in Chapter 1, helps guide us to the information individuals use in making that change.

We also know from the learn–feel–do model that people tend to go through different steps to reach a decision, depending on whether the decision involves emotional or rational factors. In addition, if they feel there are horrific consequences if they make the wrong decisions, they'll employ a different decision sequence than they would if the decision has few negative ramifications.

Your task when you produce public relations writing is to integrate both of

---

Memory Memo 6.2
Integrating Grunig's situational theory into your writing:

- Demonstrate the problem.
- Show how readers are involved in the problem.
- Tell them how to overcome barriers to solving the problem.

---

these major persuasion models from your persuasion platform into your writing. As Grunig suggests, be sure to include information in your arguments that influences your readers to become information seekers. The following three steps (also stated in Memory Memo 6.2) integrate Grunig's theory.

Demonstrate the Problem.   Show your readers how big the problem is. Give them examples. Bring statistics into your argument. Use comparisons that make them recognize the situation you are describing is really a problem.

Show How Readers Are Involved.   Tell your readers how they are involved in the problem. Tell stories of people just like themselves who are affected by the problem. Show how similar communities are being changed because of the issue.

Overcome Barriers.   Include in your release, script or position paper the specific tasks your readers can perform to change the situation. They might buy a certain stock, write an elected official, report for a health screening, call a toll-free information number, join a protest march or change their work habits. Break down any perceived obstacles they may feel prevent them from taking action. Detail any financial or technical help, free transportation or other assistance that might encourage your audience to take action.

Finding What Comes First: Integrating the Learn–Feel–Do Model

To incorporate persuasive strategies from the learn–feel–do model into your writing you need to consider the following factors.

Rational or Emotional?   Try to analyze and predict the decision sequence your target audience will use to make a decision about the issue. If you think the issue will be decided on an emotional basis, you should use personal anecdotes and human interest stories that will illustrate how people for whom the readers care are affected by the problem. Then you can quote statistics, give histories and provide technical facts to support that emotional decision.

However, if the issue is more likely to be decided based on rational factors, you'll probably be more successful if you concentrate the strongest technical evidence early in the story and use emotional persuaders as secondary reasons deeper in the piece.

High-Consequence or Low-Consequence?   You should attempt to predict whether the conclusion you are asking your readers to make will be perceived as a high-consequence or a low-consequence decision. That will change the level of detail you will need to include in your writing. For instance, a book club direct-mail advertisement that offers a no-obligation trial membership could legitimately ask its audience to subscribe without including the hundreds of words it would take to explain all membership obligations. However, a company publication describing new disciplinary and dismissal procedures for salaried workers would need to be much more complete and detailed because it's a situation in which the consequences of not following the rules will be much greater.

Matching Story Structure to Supporting Arguments: Deciding on Argumentation Structures

Now that we have some basic idea about how to arrange information in a public relations piece and a general idea of what to include, we need to discuss specific ways to organize material within the story to make it easy for the reader to comprehend, retain and act on it. From a practical perspective, this means you need to keep in mind organizing principles that help you logically structure what I call the "position-evidence relationship" in your writing.

The position-evidence relationship describes a sequence for persuasive arguments in which the writer states a position, then provides evidence for that position. For instance, a company proposes a zoning law change so it can build a new factory. That's the position. The anticipated jobs to be created by the factory are the evidence to support the position statement. Most public relations writing uses a similar argument sequence because readers often don't pay attention long enough so we can state the evidence (arguments) first and then explain the position (conclusion) to which that evidence logically leads us.

As Memory Memo 6.3 summarizes, there are three major ways to structure a position-evidence series in writing. Because each one is used to explain a specific type of information, determining an effective argumentation pattern for a story involves assessing the information you need to present to your readers, then determining which argumentation patterns you'll need to accomplish that purpose. Here's a brief guide to those decisions.

Memory Memo 6.3
Different information is presented with different argumentation structures:

- Lists   use   Order of Importance
- Recommendations   use   Problem-Solution
- Procedures   use   Chronology
  or histories

For Lists of Reasons Use Order of Importance.   A version of the order of importance argument pattern is the zoning change example discussed above. It's the same pattern debaters use to defend their positions.

For instance, the lead of a news release announces that a steel company has been given an award for being a good corporate citizen in its community. The position statement is *the manufacturer is a good corporate citizen*. How can you justify that position? By explaining in the body of the release that the company has contributed 2 percent of its profits to local charities. The next section notes its employees volunteered more than 3,000 hours to nonprofit organizations. The final section details that the company has cut its smokestack emissions by 40 percent in the past two years. You'll notice we've listed the reasons supporting our position in order of decreasing importance, just as the inverted pyramid model says we should.

Recommendations Use Problem-Solution.   The second way to build this position-evidence relationship is to show a problem and then a solution. For instance, an alderman's position paper reveals city employees are taking an excessive amount of sick leave. In analyzing an employee survey, it is discovered that because sick leave doesn't accumulate, employees who don't use it by the end of the year lose it. Predictably, the city workers fake being sick to escape the feeling that they're being exploited.

That's the problem. What's the solution? The recommendation you propose in the position paper is for the alderman to introduce a new city compensation plan that promises cash bonuses for employees who don't take all their sick leave time.

A problem-solution pattern shows the justification for complicated decision making and helps reveal the logic of your client's position to the audience.

FIGURE 6.3   Argumentation patterns in a solicitation letter

Louisiana Parents Together

1450 Grande Dame
Shreveport, Louisiana
800–555–3940

Date
Name
Address
City/State/ZIP

Dear _____

Louisiana's parents want the best for their children—to know they're safe and happy today—and to know we've done everything we can to make sure they're prepared to make their own way in life in the future.
But in a state that *graduates fewer of its children from high school than any state in the nation,* that's not something that we can be sure we've done. In 1990, 43 percent of our public schools' seniors dropped out before their high school graduation.

THE SAD THING IS THAT IT ISN'T GETTING ANY BETTER.

We can see how these sorry statistics affect us all. Louisiana ranks near the bottom in virtually every economic category—per capita income, percentage of families in poverty, jobs created in the last five years. By failing our kids, we're hurting ourselves. In Louisiana, we're not doing all we can to help our children succeed.
What's the answer? *To meet the challenges our kids are going to face in the next century our goal is to increase our graduation rate by 10 percent in the next 10 years.*

HERE'S OUR PLAN.

Concentrate our resources on those schools with the lowest graduation rates.
We're organizing mentor teams to individually counsel students in those school districts with the most dropouts. We're organizing extra efforts to get computers and other instructional help into those schools.

Gear up the GED program to help those who've already dropped out.
This fall will see the start of our "GED on TV" program. It will be broadcast on every one of the state's public television station so any citizen can get his or her high school diploma. Plus, we've got plans to establish a GED study group in every parish so local educators can supplement the TV GED programs.

Get involved early to help those who are still in school.
We're working with 4th through 6th grade teachers to develop a career curriculum that emphasizes how job skills and educational achievements are linked.

HOW CAN YOU HELP? THERE ARE SO MANY WAYS.

We need your financial commitment.
Without our 2,000 volunteers statewide, even a small contribution $20 or $50 helps us produce new teaching materials and then broadcast them to citizens all across our state.

We need your skills and your time.
To staff our mentor program in underperforming schools and to start a GED program in every parish, we'll need another 1,000 volunteers with the commitment to help Louisiana's citizens succeed.

We need your equipment.
If your business is replacing its computers or audio-visual equipment, our neediest schools can put it to good use. We've got computer experts who can integrate it into any school's instructional system.

WHAT'S YOUR NEXT STEP?

Give us a call at 800–555–3940 to talk over how you can help Louisiana meet its commitment to its children. As a parent, how can you do anything less?

Sincerely,

Camilla Loos
President

Underlying structure is order of importance.

Another order of importance structure.

A call to action.

Overall structure is problem-solution.

Sequences of Events Use Chronology.   In the body of your story you can arrange your argument in a chronology—from what happened first to what happened next and what happened after that. Let's say you're preparing an environmental group's news release as part of its campaign to protect whales. You might structure the argument against whaling interests as a month-by-month narrative of incidents when Japan, Iceland and the Soviet Union illegally killed whales.

In persuasive writing, the structuring of the argument and the strength of the evidence is vital to effective communication. Using these argument patterns as a guide, you can plan and structure the evidence to support the position you established in the lead sentence most effectively. That scheme also helps you set priorities and sequence information in the body of the story and provides the basis for a well-organized and coherent presentation of your client's viewpoints.

A final point on argumentation patterns. You'll often discover you need more than one argument to persuade your audience in any document. That means you'll need to use more than one argumentation pattern in a single document. You'll find this demonstrated in Figure 6.3, in which several of the standard argumentation patterns are integrated into one solicitation letter. In this example, the writer's overall structure is problem-solution argumentation, but incorporates two order of importance structures within the larger argumentation pattern.

KEEPING YOUR READER READING: TESTS IN THE TEXT

With the position-evidence sequence, we've established a way to organize a story's arguments. Once you've outlined an argumentation pattern, there are other guidelines you need to be aware of in order to successfully organize information supporting your arguments.

Grouping Like Information Strengthens Arguments

The No. 1 guideline in organizing material in the body of the story is to keep similar information together. Let's say you are writing a speech for your company president about the need for more government involvement in attracting new businesses to the city. In the speech you want to make two main points: (1) business licensing and permit processes should be streamlined, and (2) city and county property taxes should be lowered.

When writing your speech, put all the supporting arguments for streamlining licensing processes in one section of your story before you begin to elaborate on the reasons for lowering property taxes. If you jump around, with one paragraph justifying easier licensing, the next discussing taxes, and the next returning to licenses, your audience has problems. That hopscotch approach hinders their comprehension of the reasons justifying your position. The constant rocking between subjects also tends to diminish the strength of your argument, because instead of an overwhelming concentration of points validating each position, you've got little clumps of isolated reasons scattered throughout the story.

Transitions Help Readers See Links
Between Arguments

So far, we've established some guidelines that help writers move readers through the story's overall persuasive sequence. Now it's time to discuss how to tie individual story sections to each other, to connect arguments so we can compound the document's persuasive effects.

Transitions are bridges between the sections of a story, showing your readers the relationship between what they have just read and what they are going to read. As such, they are vital in creating a written piece that enhances reader comprehension and builds the power of your argument.

You can think of all transitions as memory cues. In essence, what a transition does is remind your readers of the information they've already received while placing that old knowledge into the context of what they are about to read.

Writers on all skill levels are not nearly as conscious of the need for transitions as they should be. A lot of writing is weakened because writers don't communicate the links between their arguments with transitions.

When do you need a transition? You should link paragraphs with a transition when you have a change in any of the four Ts—topic, tone, time and (with apologies to more accomplished acronymic alliterators) talker. Let's review how those four transitions are used in a backgrounder on how new tax laws are going to affect your company.

Topic.   You need to bridge a paragraph gap with a transition when you switch the topic of your story. You've devoted the first part of the backgrounder to the tax savings opportunities that could come from increased investment in new machinery and manufacturing equipment. You now need to write a transition to alert your readers that a change is coming before beginning a section on tax incentives for employee training. New topics need transitions. Here's an example:

Mining and manufacturing companies that invest in new equipment will be able to take advantage of restructured investment tax credits contained in the new IRS regulations. Our company, which last year purchased over $500,000 in equipment covered by the regulations, would receive nearly $45,000 in additional tax benefits if it continues similar investments.

Investments in human capital would also be rewarded under the new tax laws. Agency officials I've interviewed speculate that the president's campaign promises will be transformed into generous tax allowances for employee training programs. News reports discussing the training tax breaks have suggested that 30 percent of all employee education expenses would be deductible.

Tone. You're working on the same piece. After you have discussed all the benefits your company will receive from the tax legislation, you want to talk about the company operations that might face higher tax bills because of the new law. Before you make that switch in tone from positive to negative you need to write a transition.

Investments in human capital would also be rewarded under the new tax laws. Agency officials I've interviewed speculate that the president's campaign promises will be transformed into generous tax allowances for employee training programs. News reports discussing the training tax breaks have suggested that 30 percent of all employee education expenses would be deductible.

However, the new regulations don't contain universally good news for the company. My research suggests the major negative impact will be changes in determining profits for the company's overseas operations. If the preliminary suggestions contained in the budget committee's recommendations are enacted, the company could see the tax liabilities for its overseas division rise approximately 5 percent.

Time. You've finished your analysis of the current situation and need to contrast this with the tax laws that have been replaced. You are moving your readers into a different chronological structure, from the present into the past, and you need to alert them to this time change with a transition.

However, the new regulations don't contain universally good news for the company. My research suggests the major negative impact will be changes in determining profits for the company's overseas operations. If the preliminary suggestions contained in the budget committee's recommendations are enacted, the company could see the tax liabilities for its overseas division rise approximately 5 percent.

The new regulations mark a dramatic change from the philosophy that governed federal tax policy in the 1980s, according to our industry association's governmental affairs director. "These regs mark a dramatic shift away from the orientation toward short-term profit strategies we saw during earlier presidential administrations," said Jerry Horsly of the American Association of Mining Companies.

Talker. In your backgrounder, you're quoting several different experts to validate your argument. When you are attributing information to one person in one paragraph, then wish to quote someone else, you need to warn the reader this change is coming. Write a transition that clearly signals that someone else's opinions are being offered when you introduce the new paragraph.

The new regulations mark a dramatic change from the philosophy that governed federal tax policy in the 1980s, according to our industry association's governmental affairs director. "These regs mark a dramatic shift away from the orientation toward short-term profit strategies we saw during earlier presidential administrations," said Jerry Horsly of the American Association of Mining Companies.

There are other experts suggesting we should be changing our tax tactics. "It's not going to be possible to compete unless we begin to capitalize on the potentialities of our workers and the newest technology," said Lawrence Chikon of the Industrial Technology Council. "These new tax laws are just a belated recognition of the new realities that will be governing our business during the next decade."

You need transitions in each of these situations to guide readers through your document and signal the connections between your arguments. As reviewed in Memory Memo 6.4, these memory-cue transitions can be formed in at least four distinct ways. Here's a brief explanation of each strategy.

Repeat a Word, Phrase or Concept. The simplest transition is to repeat a word, phrase or concept from the preceding paragraph in the first few words of the next paragraph. Figure 6.4 illustrates how these memory-cue transitions are constructed.

You will notice I could have made the memory cue work by repeating the phrase *sluggish economy* but instead I mentioned a related concept (*impact*) and showed the consequences of the statistics listed in the previous paragraph.

> **Memory Memo 6.4**
> **Memory-cue transitions can be built by including in a new paragraph's first few words:**
>
> - a word, phrase or concept from the previous paragraph
> - a definite modifier or demonstrative adjective referring to the previous paragraph
> - a connective that signals support or rejection of information in the previous paragraph
> - a time-related concept that establishes the new paragraph's chronology with previous paragraph

---

Definite Modifier or Demonstrative Adjective. Another type of memory-cue transition uses a definite modifier or a demonstrative adjective. Since even from this distance I can hear the college mind grinding away trying to remember what definite modifiers and demonstrative adjectives are, I assume it might be wise to review. Let's look at the example in Figure 6.5 first, which shows how demonstrative adjectives such as *that, this, these* and *those* point out the connections between the subjects in two paragraphs.

According to the survey, 48 percent of the executives believe the problem resulted from the sluggish manufacturing economy, while 23 percent blamed high interest rates.

The impact of the weakening economy has already been felt by members of the Kentucky Agricultural Processors Association. "A lot of our business is dependent on people having enough money to buy our products," said KAPA vice president Patty Robshear. "When other factories are closed, nobody is able to buy what we make, so we have to stop our assembly lines, too."

"Impact" refers readers back to consequences hinted at in previous paragraph's statistics.

FIGURE 6.4   Memory-cue transition

The word *that* in "that education" is a demonstrative adjective. It directs your attention to the ties between the topics in the two paragraphs and shows how the two paragraphs are related. If you had written "an education" you wouldn't have told the reader the new "education" was the same as the one in the preceding paragraph. If you used "the education" ("the" is a definite modifier) you would be more specific, but when you used the demonstrative adjective *that* you directed your reader to remember specifically the education from the preceding paragraph.

Connective.   The third way to make transitions is by beginning the following paragraph with a connective. Connectives are words like "therefore," "moreover" and "furthermore" that indicate a relationship between the two paragraphs. Although the examples I just gave are often too pretentious to use in most public relations writing, there are connectives that will work.

Different classes of connectives have different uses. Connectives like "but," "although" and "however" indicate the argument in the following paragraph contradicts the first paragraph's conclusions.

There are other connectives for other uses. If you're adding another thought,

FIGURE 6.5   Transition using a demonstrative adjective

Kyle, president of Kyle Group Inc., said training young people in the skills necessary to face a changing workplace will be the state's biggest challenge.

That education will have to involve more verbal and mathematical skills, because by the year 2000 non-technical positions will represent only 14 percent of the nation's jobs, Kyle said.

"That" directly reminds readers to refer to concept in previous paragraph. Notice we've combined it with "education," a concept-repeat memory cue.

use words like "besides" or "in addition." If you want to point out a cause-and-effect relationship between the two paragraphs' topics, there are connectives like "as a result" or "consequently." Other connectives tell your readers the succeeding paragraph will draw conclusions, offer examples or intensify the previous thought.

Time-Related Concept.   Another form of transition is a time reference. Words or phrases like "meanwhile," "afterward" or "a month before" signal to your readers that you've changed the time frame in which your writing is centered.

FIGURE 6.6   Transitions in a news release

Repeating Swain's and Gardner's names maintains links between the first few paragraphs.

Donald C. Swain will remain president of the University of Louisville until his retirement in 2003, the school's Board of Trustees announced Monday.

"We feel lucky we will be able to keep a man with Dr. Swain's talents for many years to come," said Trustee Gene Gardner after announcing Swain had signed a seven-year contract. "It's largely through his leadership that this university has grown to be one of the leading urban universities."

Gardner noted that during Swain's presidency the university funded a $40 million endowment, the largest endowment at any Kentucky university.

Connective transition "in addition" indicates further support for previous position.

In addition, Swain "has fostered mutual benefits that have made U of L a real partner with the city's business and industry," Gardner said.

"Although" suggests contradiction from information in previous paragraph.

Although Swain's contract did not expire until June, Gardner said the school did not want to lose him. "He's a top candidate whenever a leadership job at any major national university opens up."

"With that competition" combines concept cue with "that" to refer to previous paragraph.

A simple word-repeat memory cue.

With that competition, Gardner said the seven-year contract was a way for the board to tell Swain that "we're committed to him."

The long contract came less than two months after Swain was named one of America's top ten college presidents by the Higher Education Institute.

If you develop an awareness of transitions, they will help you organize your prose and your arguments much more effectively. They'll provide an informal working outline of the story as you write it, alerting you to problems in your logic patterns and guiding you to what argument should come next. (See Fig. 6.6.)

Just as important, you point out to your readers the structure of your piece, showing them how your arguments are related and providing a template on which they can build their own memory of the information in the story.

Smoothing Break Points Keeps Readers Involved

Chapter 5 discussed the decisions people make before they decide to read a story. The places where these decisions seem most likely to occur, where the reader or listener is most likely to abandon the message, are what I call break points.

The first break point, as we saw in the last chapter, is in the very first sentence of the piece, where readers decide within the first few words whether the story topic interests them. Other break points occur throughout the story, where linkages in the prose give your receivers an opportunity to contemplate whether they want to continue with the message.

Generally, you'll find break points at the start of every prose structure. At the beginning of a story, the beginning of major sections within the story, and at the start of paragraphs and sentences, readers are deciding whether to remain in the communication act. These later break points work exactly the same way as the break point in the lead. The reader will grant you just a few words in which to justify his or her decision to continue reading.

This means you must be aware of these break points and work to make the linkage as smooth and involving to your reader as possible. I asserted in the chapter on leads that one way to maintain reader attention at the beginning of sentences and paragraphs is to concentrate the most important information within the first few words of the structure.

Reading Speed Contributes to Persuasion

A reminder: Public relations writing's No. 1 goal is to communicate information coherently, simply and quickly. Because the concept of receiver-centered writing declares we should adjust our writing strategies to fit the needs of our audience, it's necessary to make our writing as short as possible, with few pauses and hesitations.

That economy contributes two things to our communication effectiveness. It requires less of our readers' time to absorb our entire message, which is important when we are competing with so many other messages for our audience's attention. In addition, it supplies fewer break points where they might decide to abandon the message.

There are scores of writing tips that help you accomplish an economy of style. For those who need to review, I've included a number of them in the Ready Reference section at the end of this chapter.

A PR WRITER'S BLOCK? NOT IF YOU KNOW YOUR AUDIENCE

After reading this chapter, you should have learned that a receiver-centered approach to communication makes writing more of a rational process. Writing is not a mysterious artistic transformation granted to only a few by a ghostly, intuitively creative spirit. Instead, it is predicated on understanding audience needs and applying scientific communication principles to meet those needs. It's that understanding of audience that makes a lead sentence easy to write. You make sure you identify an audience and tell that audience what benefit your client can share with them if they become involved.

The receiver-centered writing system provides similar guideposts for subsequent paragraphs. Writers can determine the order of material supporting the lead sentence by recognizing whether they are presenting a process, a list or a solution to a problem. Once they've determined what form of evidence they are using, they select a chronology, an order of importance, or a problem-solution argumentation pattern, respectively.

It's a generative writing system because it guides the writer in creating the first few words of each new paragraph. The memory-cue transitions described earlier in the chapter direct the writer to pull a word or a concept from the previous paragraph and then use it as an introduction to the next paragraph's topic sentence.

By using the general principles in this chapter, the writer doesn't have to wait for inspiration, but can usually apply the prose mechanics just discussed to guide the story's overall structure as well as prompt the first few words of each new paragraph. With constant vigilance to the reader's capacities and desires (and a lot of rewriting), you can learn to make the most effective use of your writing talents in all public relations media.

SUMMARY

- Public relations writing is created to persuade a public important to an organization to adopt an idea or take an action that's useful to the organization. PR writing gains a specific public's attention by communicating information that satisfies its needs.

- By knowing how readers react during a communication act, public relations writers can predict a reader's communication needs.

- Because readers generally don't read public relations messages for pleasure, receiver-centered writing should develop a logical argument pattern so that readers can (1) easily comprehend and retain information and (2) gain that information as quickly as possible.

- The inverted pyramid is a writing structure that recognizes that people will remain in a communication event only as long as it satisfies their needs. The inverted pyramid structure places information in descending order of importance to capitalize on the reader's wandering attention.

- Writers should integrate audience analysis from the persuasion platform into their writing. Grunig's situational theory dictates that we should establish that a problem exists, show how readers are involved in the issue, and demonstrate how readers can participate in its solution. The learn–feel–do model guides a writer to determine whether an emotional or rational argument will be more effective and, depending on whether an audience perceives a decision as low- or high-consequence, how extensive the writer's arguments must be.

- The position-evidence relationship defines a logical argumentation pattern for public relations writing. Order of importance is a good way to present lists. If a writer is offering a recommendation, problem-solution is recommended. Chronologies help present sequences.

- Keeping similar arguments and similar information within a single section of a document increases the power of the writer's argument.

- Transitions are memory cues to alert readers to shifts between topics, tone, time or talkers. Transitions are established in the first few words of a paragraph by (1) repeating a word or concept, (2) using a definite modifier or demonstrative adjective, (3) using a connective that signals a continuation or modification of a concept, or (4) introducing a time-related concept.

- Concentrating important information at break points, which occur at the beginnings of sentences and paragraphs, encourages readers to remain with the story.

- Modifying sentence structures and vocabulary to increase reading speed allows readers to gather information quickly and stimulates greater readership.

THINK PIECES

1. Consider an issue affecting your campus or community. What information could you offer other students that would convince them they are affected by the problem? What information might help them see that they can overcome obstacles to their solving the problem?

2. Think of a problem you solved or a purchase you made in which emotional factors were dominant in your decision-making process. Compare it to another situation in which rational reasons were more important in determining your decision.

3. You are told a story in which the events are not in chronological sequence. Speculate how the mind and memory work to reconstruct the story.

WRITING ASSIGNMENTS

D8.7
D9.9

ADDITIONAL READING

Brooks, Brian S., Kennedy, George, Moen, Daryl R., and Rany, Don. *News Reporting and Writing*, 4th ed. New York: St Martin's, 1992.

Callihan, E. L. *Grammar for Journalists.* Radnor, Pa.: Chilton, 1979.

Goldstein, Norm, ed. *The Associated Press Stylebook and Libel Manual.* Reading, Mass.: Addison-Wesley, 1994.

Hough, George A., 3rd. *News Writing*, 4th ed. Boston: Houghton Mifflin, 1988.

Kessler, Lauren, and McDonald, Duncan. *When Words Collide: A Journalist's Guide to Grammar and Style*, 3rd ed. Belmont, Calif.: Wadsworth, 1988.

Pinkert, Robert. *Pinkert's Practical Grammar.* Cincinnati: Writer's Digest, 1986.

A Quick Primer on Public Relations Writing

1. Develop story structures that reflect the way receivers process information and the way they use the medium.
   - Information important to the story's audience should be concentrated at the start of sentences and paragraphs. Here's a story for a metropolitan newspaper audience:
   Although local Democrats vastly outnumber Republicans, lower Democratic voter turnouts may cause GOP victories in city races, a poll has found.
   Here's the same story for a national public opinion polling newsletter:
   Pollsters find that local turnout percentages change election results more often than party registrations.
   - Because information about the source deadens your readers' interest before they get to the news, put the news before the source. Compare these two sentences:
   Caleb Bingham, who is a professor of history at Alpine State College, said President Warren Harding had at least three extramarital affairs while in the White House.
   President Warren Harding had at least three extramarital affairs while in the White House, said Alpine State College history professor Caleb Bingham.
   - Use short sentences and short paragraphs.
   - Keep most sentences in the active tense unless the passive tense helps identify information important to your audience. The active tense makes sentences shorter and easier to understand:
   Passive tense: *The leadership of IBM was taken over by Jones in April.*
   Active tense: *Jones took over IBM's leadership in April.*
   - Organize the inverted pyramid's third section with an argumentation pattern that will make it easiest for the reader to comprehend your information. Use one of these three argumentation structures:
   Chronological
   Order of importance
   Problem-solution
2. Use direct language and simple sentence structures that encourage fast information transfer.
   - Cut unnecessary words and unnecessary information. Compare these:
   He claimed that in the future the United States will need to ensure the implementation of plans to limit the number of immigrants entering this country.
   He said the United States will have to implement plans limiting immigration.
   - Communicate as much specific information as possible in the fewest possible words. Contrast these sentences:
   Several design improvements have been made to make the newspaper more readable. Having bigger type, shorter stories and more graphics are among the planned changes.
   Bigger type, shorter stories and more graphics will make the newspaper more readable.
   - Cut unnecessary punctuation and avoid appositives:
   John Jones, president of XYZ Corp., will attend the conference, which is intended to improve leadership skills.
   XYZ Corp. president John Jones will attend the leadership conference.

3. Build transition linkages that help hold readers' attention and show your argument pattern.
   - Transitions are needed for any changes in tone, topic, time or talker.
   - Memory cue transitions link paragraphs by repeating a key word or concept from the previous paragraph in the first few words of the following paragraph.
   - Words of opposition such as *but, however*, and *even though* signal a change in the argument.
   - Words of continuation such as *in addition, also*, and *another* signal a reinforcement of the previous argument.
4. Group like elements to aid information comprehension.
   - Placing modifying elements together within a sentence eliminates dangling modifiers. Compare these two sentences:
   An Amish woman planted potatoes in her garden as a neighbor watched near Munfordville.
   An Amish woman planted potatoes in her garden near Munfordville as a neighbor watched.
   - Grouping information about similar subjects within a paragraph or story section simplifies comprehension and increases the strength of the writer's argument.

## chapter 7

Adding Sensory Channels: Transferring the Receiver-centered Model to Broadcast Writing

REAL-LIFE LESSONS

It's 7:40 p.m. on the second night of the prestigious horse show for which I'd been hired to coordinate the media coverage. My job as public relations counselor had devolved from high-level strategy to merely trying to guard the area between the camera and the television host who is doing a remote from the horse show.

In the past 12 minutes I have almost gotten into a fight with a horse trainer who clambered over a fence to talk to his rider and nearly knocked over the camera. I've been cursed by a woman whom I had asked to step behind a rope guarding the host. I've also been accused of hastening the heart attack and resultant death of an elderly woman whom I had asked to walk 30 extra feet to her seat instead of taking a shortcut through the camera shot.

I'm not sure this is why I went into public relations. I'm squatting by the host's right knee, just out of the camera angle, speculating that the lower center of gravity will give me more leverage if I need to wrestle some aggressive horse show devotee away from the camera. Already my knees are killing me, and I've still got another 20 minutes to go before the television show is over.

The print coverage had been so simple. I had sent a few query letters and had composed several targeted versions of a release that I mailed to specific reporters. A few reporters had called back for clarifications or to ask me to schedule an interview. I had no other contact with them, but out of those few contacts poured prodigious amounts of coverage—stories in newspapers, magazines and neighborhood newsletters on all different aspects of the horse show.

The broadcast coverage had been much more complex. For just this one program, a locally produced TV magazine, I had been busy from early morning. I had met with one of the station's producers at the horse show before 8 a.m. and arranged four different interviews for his video package. Before he left, we had talked about possible sites for the on-air host that evening and had finally settled on a spot in a grove of trees at the end of the show ring.

When I presented that idea to the horse show manager, he said it couldn't be done. The satellite truck would scare the horses. It would have to be parked farther away. The cables from the satellite truck to the camera site might electrocute the horses. We'd have to dig a trench and bury the cable.

There's another problem, I mentioned. We're scheduled to play the national anthem at 7:30. The TV show is supposed to be on the air live at 7:30. Is the host supposed to do the patriotic, respectful thing and wait for 75 seconds before he gives his introduction? "Well," the horse show manager answered, "we'll have to move up the anthem and the first competition."

Virtually every available person was thrown into the effort. Workers were digging a long trench from where the truck was to be parked to the show ring. The horse show manager was alerting participants of the earlier start and changing the parking scheme for the ambulances that were usually parked in the place where the satellite truck would be. At the same time, I was negotiating a series of cues with the organist about when to start the national anthem.

In the midst of this, I was working with another television reporter who was doing a feature on the horse show for the evening news, and trying to coordinate all the arrangements for another station's weather forecaster, who was planning to do the weather report live from the horse show for the 5 p.m. news.

Finally, the magazine show crew arrived. The workers laid the TV cables and re-sodded the horses' staging area. Eventually, aided by two fearsome-looking employees, the show was finally completed without a single person walking into the shot.

I wondered if all the work had been worth it. This, after all, was nearly 10 hours of work for one single media placement. However, when I dragged myself home that night and watched the videotape, it was stunning. The horse show, which was just another event in the print stories, shone on television. Unlike the newspaper stories, television captured the sun settling over the nearby trees, throwing dappled shadows onto the flamboyant colors of the show ring. You could see the attractive women in their stunning riding habits and hear the sounds and verbal commands they used to control their powerful horses.

Television captured the event's sophisticated beauty by supplementing words with sight and sound. This is the power and challenge of broadcast writing, to integrate those sounds and those sights with persuasive, well-written prose. Overlaying those other appeals to the senses onto your writing will be the focus of this chapter.

WHAT YOU KNOW

- People process and use different media in different ways.
- The basic elements of communication in all media are dictated by the same communication principles.

WHAT YOU'LL LEARN

- Broadcast communication effectiveness can be helped or hindered by the audience's perceptions of the message's deliverer.
- Broadcast writing is an additive medium, in which auditory and visual messages are overlaid on strong written prose.
- Broadcast writing, like all writing, has to be structured to compensate for the medium's weaknesses and exploit its strengths.

BROADCAST WRITING: THE SAME . . . BUT DIFFERENT

Many people in the profession think broadcast writing is completely different from writing for the print media. That's a vast exaggeration. Writing is communication, and communication—no matter what the medium—is governed by many of the same principles and procedures.

There are, however, important differences in each medium for which you write. Even though you have examined the basics of persuasive writing that apply just as well in broadcast as in print writing, it's the purpose of this book to help you adapt your writing techniques for different media, to exploit the strengths of a medium, and limit the impact of the weaknesses a medium brings with it.

In broadcasting, there are both formidable weaknesses and significant strengths. Some of the distinctions are outlined in Table 7.1. In deciding on a medium, consider the capacity of each medium to communicate your message cost-effectively.

This talk about the weaknesses of broadcast communication may surprise you. For decades, we've had to endure both celebrations and condemnations of the power of broadcasting and especially of television. We've been told that television is so powerful it can brainwash us. Television has been blamed for everything from children talking back to parents to children murdering their parents. Experts featured on this or that talk show claim it can make us buy what we don't want to buy and convince us to do what we don't want to do.

I don't believe that. Television and radio do have great power but they also have profound weaknesses. Let's talk about their strengths first.

Both radio and television use the print medium's communication capability of language. But radio and television add additional sensory channels that PR writers have to learn to integrate into their creative processes.

Radio should take the words that comprise a print message and add sound—voice, on-site recordings, sound effects and music. Television should take those words of print, add the sound of radio and then supplement those communication methods with motion. I say "should" because all too often writers merely take a prose message and create a radio message by having an announcer read it into a microphone. For television, they use a video camera to tape the announcer as he or she reads the message out loud. That may be broadcast production and distribution, but it is not broadcast writing.

TABLE 7.1   Advantages and disadvantages of broadcast media

Radio	
Advantages	**Disadvantages**
1. Tightly focused psychographic selection possible.	1. Listener can't review message.
2. Relatively inexpensive to produce.	2. Time restrictions limit message.
3. Message can be delivered anywhere.	3. Listener may not be engaged in message immediately.
4. Adds power of audio channel to dialogue.	4. Can't use visuals or print to reinforce message.
5. Announcer's personality and voice add to power of message.	

Television	
Advantages	**Disadvantages**
1. Combines power of motion, sound and dialogue.	1. More expensive to produce.
2. Announcer's personality and appearance add to message's power.	2. Broad, untargeted audience.
3. Huge audiences.	3. Time restrictions limit message.
4. Most effective in communicating emotional messages.	4. Viewer can't review message.
5. Print can be added to reinforce message.	5. Viewer may not be engaged in message immediately.

As in the case of all writing, broadcast writing exploits the strengths of the medium and tries to minimize its weaknesses. Those strengths are the power of sound for radio, and of sound and motion for video, to reinforce the impression of the words or even to create new impressions that words are not capable of delivering. (See Memory Memo 7.1.) If you don't use that power, you've merely got an overly expensive and usually less effective version of print communication.

> **Memory Memo 7.1**
> **Broadcast writing should emphasize the medium's strengths:**
> - sound, sight and motion
> - the receiver's relationship with the message's deliverer
> - its portability and pervasiveness

I counsel writers to think of broadcast writing not as a completely separate type of writing, but as a process of overlaying additional communication channels on solid prose. That process of maintaining the print medium's ability to transmit information efficiently while adding the emotional and persuasive power of the broadcast media will be the focus of this chapter.

EXPLOITING THE STRENGTHS OF BROADCAST MEDIA

Although broadcast media are not the all-powerful communication narcotics we are led to believe, there are persuasive tasks that radio or television can accomplish very efficiently. As with all communication, the intelligent practitioner begins by examining the communication objective he or she wants to reach and selecting an effective medium to accomplish those tasks.

Broadcast Involves the Senses

In some ways, broadcast has powerful advantages over print. With broadcast, you can involve other senses in communicating your message, letting your audience hear the excitement of a crowd before a riot or witness a demonstration that proves your product is better than its competitors. On radio, you can hear the pop of bacon sizzling, the crack of a rifle firing or the happy squeal of children playing.

On television, to those sounds are added sight and movement. The emotional power on the human psyche of seeing a whimpering child or a basketball player soaring high above the rim for a dunk is profound in motivating interest and involvement.

Broadcast Has Strengths of Personal Media

Broadcast writing, because it is often delivered by announcers with whom we become familiar, has many of the advantages of more personal media. We grow to trust the judgments of our favorite personages on radio and television and often develop some form of relationship with them. We like this personality or think another is funny or sincere or committed. That sense that we know and have a relationship with a broadcast announcer provides extra persuasive power for a message.

Broadcast Is Inescapable

Perhaps the broadcast media's most profound power is its pervasiveness. We wake up in the morning to a clock radio, eat breakfast while watching a television news program, drive to work or school listening to a favorite disc jockey, and perform many of our daily tasks to the accompaniment of an FM station or a soap opera, only to come home at night (listening to the car radio again) and perhaps put in several hours in front of the television watching sports or other shows with our family and friends. For many people in the world today, there are few waking moments without the din of a radio or television show in the background.

OVERCOMING THE WEAKNESS OF BROADCAST MEDIA: THE PASSIVE RECEIVER

That word *background* suggests the broadcast medium's most profound shortcoming. Think how many times you've heard someone say he or she turns on the television "for some background noise." It's there, but we often aren't really tuned in to it.

That's because radio and television are passive media, and as Memory Memo 7.2 points up, you've got to surmount that essential weakness. With print media, you have to commit time and mental energy to receiving the message; you can't vacuum the house and read the newspaper at the same time. You can't drive to school and study a textbook. Print media demand the receiver's active participation. Broadcast media just "happen," whether or not you are engaged in receiving and processing the message.

Memory Memo 7.2
Broadcast writing has to overcome the medium's passive nature:

- People can receive but not consciously attend to broadcast messages.
- Receivers can't review a broadcast message after they've received it.

Think of your own attention level to your car radio as you drive to school. Let's hope for the safety of the world that you're paying more attention to the cars merging into traffic ahead of you than to the intricate rhythm of a song you're hearing. Of course, when the traffic report comes on, you may actively process that information, adjusting your route to avoid a traffic jam. When there's news of your favorite band you'll probably pay much closer attention than you do while the disc jockey is prattling to the weather man. That's natural, because we're very selective about the communication events to which we attend. It's the same with broadcast as with all other media.

Thus, even though broadcast is always there, it doesn't mean we're always paying attention. The relative certainty you have in print that people who see a story that interests them will read it isn't such a certainty in broadcast media. Although an issue may be vital for a consumer, and he may be listening to the radio when a pertinent news item is aired, he may not attend to the message.

Broadcast communication appears to be received continuously by the brain at some very low level but not transferred to a conscious level unless there is some receiver interest involved. So with that great power of broadcast media, its omnipresence, comes a massive weakness. Because people aren't consciously attending to your message a good portion of the time, it's up to the broadcast writer to break into the reverie induced by this steady hum of broadcast messages.

In addition, the receiver's attention has to be captured immediately, because broadcast, unlike print, doesn't give the receiver an opportunity to review the message if he or she didn't understand it initially. Once a broadcast message is on its way, it speeds past the receiver's eyes and ears, never to return. You can't review it—you can't file it in a drawer for later reference. You can't even refer to it again for a phone number. For the writer striving to make broadcast communication effective, overcoming the transience of a broadcast message is the central effort in writing for broadcast media.

THE IMPORTANT NO. 1 POSITION: TIPCUP BROADCAST LEADS

All broadcast writing must strive to capture the attention of a passive audience very likely engaged in some other activity and not highly involved in the medium. But as we dismiss our rapture with the broadcast medium, we also have to acknowledge its power. We often realize we are entranced by the images on television, watching raptly as fast-paced commercials flip visuals before our eyes and imagination. We unconsciously tap our toes to songs and advertising jingles on radio.

How do we transform a passive processor into an active participant? By integrating the same persuasive, receiver-centered writing principles already discussed into broadcast messages and then adding the power of sound and motion. Here are some guidelines.

That process starts by recognizing that we have to drag our audience's attention into a broadcast message. To do that, we again have an imperative to sculpt the initial phrase of the broadcast message, that No. 1 position I discussed in the previous two chapters. Although we are in a different medium, the task is still the same: to capture the attention of an elusive audience so we can successfully communicate. By concentrating elements of interest into that No. 1 position of the broadcast story's lead, we are more likely to attract the public we need to reach.

Using the TIPCUP elements, we should be able to judge the information that's likeliest to interest that particular audience. Is the element *impact*, such as on animal activists, of news about new ways of testing cosmetics without animals? Is it *prominence*, such as the news of a Hollywood actor's participation in a civil rights demonstration? Is it *unusualness*, such as a first-time use of an exotic technology that could reduce air pollution?

No matter which TIPCUP element you pick, your task is virtually the same as in the simplest news release. You must signal to your targeted reader that this particular message is intended for him or her by placing the most important information into the No. 1 position. As before, you are looking for words that communicate a TIPCUP concept to your audience, and you are looking for ways to place them into the No. 1 position.

But in broadcast writing, we have to contend with a big conundrum. We know that when people read newspapers, or magazines, or letters, they are involved in the message. It may take them only a second to decide whether the message affects them or not, but for that split second we can be assured they aren't mowing the yard, cooking supper or settling a fight among the children.

There aren't any such assurances in broadcast media. In fact, broadcast audiences are notoriously inattentive. Let's see what happens when a print lead sentence encounters a typical broadcast audience.

Jefferson County residents who use a private trash hauling service can get a $1,000 tax refund if they make their application today, the county's tax assessor announced.

Memory Memo 7.3
Strategies for involving receivers in the broadcast lead:

- Use sound effects to draw receiver's attention before starting text.
- Use trigger words to alert people in the desired audience that the story is for them.
- Use setups as auditory headlines to give audience time to attend to the story.

You might notice a problem. A person eligible for the refund who is only half listening to the radio would probably focus attention on the message when he or she hears the $1,000 refund being mentioned. But by that time, 14 words into the story, the person has already missed a vital part of the story—who is eligible for the refund. Without a way for the receiver to review the story, you've failed in your communication task.

Memory Memo 7.3 summarizes some strategies that we'll review in the following section.

Trigger Words

There are several specialized leads used in broadcast writing to overcome this problem. All use what's called a "trigger word" to alert the target audience that the story is intended for them. The trigger word or words suggest the story's significance in the first sentence, so the audience is primed to listen to the second sentence. Here's how to use trigger words to convert the above lead into a stronger broadcast lead.

There might be a *one thousand dollar tax refund* in your future.

Jefferson County residents who use a private trash hauling service can get a one thousand dollar tax refund if they apply today, the county's tax assessor announced.

Or:

The county is giving *money back* to people who take care of their own trash.

Jefferson County residents who use a private trash hauling service can get a one thousand dollar tax refund if they apply today, the county's tax assessor announced.

Setups

Both of these leads alert listeners to the story topic that is approaching and let them decide whether to attend to the message. You might consider them as broadcast versions of newspaper headlines, a few brief words that tell your receivers what to expect in the following story.

In fact, another type of broadcast lead is structured exactly like a headline. These broadcast leads, called setups, are usually incomplete sentences without articles like *a* and *the*. A setup for the above story might look like this:

Tax refunds for some Jefferson County residents.

    Jefferson County residents who use a private trash hauling service can get a one thousand dollar tax refund if they apply today, the county's tax assessor announced.

Break Points: Using Memory Cues to Build Transitions

Broadcast prose must also lead the receivers from one topic to the next as effortlessly as possible. That's quite a task because broadcast reports are not freestanding stories, as print works usually are. Broadcast stories are shorter, and the coverage in a newscast might bounce from a city police roundup of white-collar criminals to hurricane coverage from Indonesia, war in Africa and a local dog show. That's a broad range of subjects, and receivers could very easily get lost in the jumble of topics. The broadcast writer has to ease that transition and signal the receiver when the topic changes.

Sometimes you can find relationships between topics that will lead naturally from one story to the next. For instance, a story on a presidential trip to Europe could be linked with another story on federal budget appropriations for social issues with a sentence like this:

The president will be thinking about the budget on his European trip.

Two sports stories, one on a football player's arrest on drug charges and another on an antitrust case against major league baseball, might be linked like this:

Major league baseball might be finding itself in court, too.

Finding these thematic elements to tie individual broadcast stories together is often very useful, but there are some situations when they shouldn't be used. In fact, some of the worst moments of broadcast journalism arise from embarrassingly awkward attempts to link stories together. I'm sure at one time or another you've heard an exchange like this on your local radio or television news as the anchor introduces the weather forecast:

I hope it's not going to be as warm here over the weekend as in those Mideast hot spots, Don.

There's really no need to humiliate yourself this much, because there are alternatives. The memory-cue transitions discussed in Chapter 6 work as well when you are moving between stories in broadcast writing as they do when you are moving between paragraphs in print writing.

If you are making a shift in time or topic, alert your audience with a memory-cue transition in the first few words of the new story. For instance, if you're moving between events that happened the same day, this might work:

Meanwhile in Washington, tempers were flaring over a Supreme Court decision.

If you're trying to link happenings from different parts of the world, this transition would be effective:

Across the Pacific, there was a new outbreak of violence in the Philippines.

It's the same if you are moving between stories about two different individuals.

George Bush wasn't the only retired politician making news today.

In each case you are merely signaling to your audience that they should be ready for another topic and orienting them to their new surroundings.

BROADCAST PROSE: TIPS ON KEEPING THE RECEIVER INVOLVED

The need to deal with the transient elements of broadcast media isn't limited to the opening lines of stories. It creates problems that have to be confronted all through the story.

Simplifying Prose: Helping Receivers
Who Can't Review

Because you don't have the option of letting your audience review a sentence in case they initially miss its meaning, you have to simplify. You must simplify vocabulary, choosing more understandable and accessible words for the broad audience that broadcast media usually draw. You must simplify and shorten sentences too.

Putting the News First.   You even need to simplify sentence structures. Don't separate subjects and verbs from each other, because receivers relying completely on aural memory can forget the sentence's subject by the time they encounter a verb. For instance, this is a bad broadcast sentence.

The measure, which will be debated on the Senate floor today, will place new inspection standards on packing plants,

---

In fact, you need to be careful whenever you use a dependent clause in broadcast writing. As you can see from the example above, they usually don't work in the middle of a sentence. Don't put them at the beginning, either.

Because of new weather service data, forecasting tornadoes will be much more accurate.

A sentence structure like this forces your audience to remember the qualifying information, then place it in context of the sentence's main point when they finish hearing the statement. As we've discussed before, try to shape your writing to fit the way your audience will cognitively process the message. Communicate the sentence's main topic, then give the reader any qualifying information.

The measure will place new inspection standards on packing plants. It's headed for a Senate debate today.

Here's another example:

Forecasting tornadoes will be much more accurate because of new weather service data.

What else should you do to overcome the receiver's inability to review broadcast copy?

Simplifying for Comprehension.   You should adjust your presentation to acknowledge the great reliance you're placing on your audience's memory as it processes the story. Avoid strings of numbers and even the names of sources if they aren't imperative to understanding or giving credibility to the story.

Instead, simplify complex numbers into more understandable concepts. Sixty million Americans could be translated into "one of every four Americans." If a source's name is not as important to bringing credibility to the story as the position he or she holds, give only his or her title. Of course, simplifying the information you're presenting to your audience not only helps relieve the audience of some formidable memory feats but also eliminates words, which is critically important when you're trying to cut an 800-word print article to 80 words for a broadcast report.

> *Memory Memo 7.4*
> *A checklist: Overcoming the audience's inability to review broadcast messages*
> - Put the news first, then put qualifying information later in sentence.
> - Simplify sentence structures and vocabulary.
> - Highlight the person-to-person communication of broadcast with less formal language and more facial and voice inflection cues.

In case you forget any of these elements, you can review them in Memory Memo 7.4.

Showing Your Strengths: Prose That Shows Broadcast's Immediacy and Personalities

Although we've been discussing how to deemphasize some of the weaknesses of broadcast media, there are two other factors that should be integrated into broadcast writing to accentuate the medium's strengths.

As I mentioned before, one of the strengths of broadcast is its immediacy. That is emphasized in broadcast writing by using present tense and present perfect verb tenses. For instance, when you attribute a statement to a source in broadcast copy, you usually would use "she says" (present) or "she has said" (present perfect).

Another strength of broadcast is its ability to add the effect of an announcer's personality and humanity to a communication effort. That power is exploited in a number of ways in broadcast writing. First, public relations writers can select on-air or on-camera announcers with whom their target audiences can identify and who can bring credibility to their information. For instance, a pharmaceutical company's video news release on an advanced breast cancer detection system would be better narrated by a woman than a man. The announcement of a social agency's counseling program for senior citizens might be received more favorably by the program's target audience if you have an older person making the announcement.

You need to capitalize on other personal characteristics. In addition to age, race or gender, the announcer's clothing or accent can also contribute to drawing and then communicating to a certain audience. Public relations consultant Natalie Wester discusses some of those cues that are so important to successful broadcast communication in Box 7.1

There are other ways to exploit broadcast's personal strengths. Broadcast writers generally use more informal, conversational language than print writers, more contractions, such as "don't" or "can't," and shorter sentences.

However, that informality and casualness has to be perfect on the air. Because you are using a fallible human being to read your copy, you have to make major changes in preparing copy for broadcast. Ready Reference sections at the end of this chapter highlight those differences.

BOX 7.1   Views from the Field

Natalie Wester
Wester is the founder and owner of Cleveland's Wester Com-
munications Group. Previously, she was vice president and
the manager of media training at Edward Howard & Co.,
another Cleveland-based public relations firm.

Public relations practitioners have traditionally made statements
for their institutions on television. Is that still desirable?

You can still see public relations practitioners on camera during a newscast representing their organizations' positions as the "company spokesperson." But more and more, CEOs and other top-level executives are being cast as spokespeople before the media. Corporate mergers and massive layoffs, environmental disasters and charges of criminal activity, bankruptcies and personnel scandals—with today's volatile business climate, it is increasingly important that the leaders of organizations be prepared to face the press as the most credible bearers of information to the public. Instead of hiding behind PR professionals, the wise CEO or manager will rely on them as crucial, behind-the-scenes coaches and counselors on strategy, approach, and message content.

What special skills do institutional managers need to communi-
cate effectively in the broadcast media?

Clarity, consistency and the ability to crystallize key messages into sharp, clear, captivating nuggets of easily understood information. You have to

BOX 7.1   (continued)

know what you're talking about, be quotable when you're talking about it, and be able to convey a sense of comfort—no matter how nervous you are—because television is all about impressions. There's a definite skill to handling on-camera interviews, but it's a skill that can be learned with proper media training.

This seems to be just dressing up the message. Can this type of training help managers become more effective leaders?

Absolutely. First, because effective media training forces managers to think in terms of key messages, it can help a manager determine and clarify his or her institution's position on important issues and situations. Second, the same ability to crystallize those captivating nuggets of information for the media is also effective in communicating to and motivating a company's employees. Finally, successful media training forces a manager to plan, think through, and find answers to all the "what-ifs" that might occur in an organization, fostering sharper insight, on-target preparation, and more control. All of these are attributes of a good leader.

We've talked about language up to now. Should we be concerned about nonverbal impressions, too?

Second to verbal preparation comes visual preparation, or making sure the "window dressing" is in order. Remember those job interviews—nonverbal impressions count. Your dress, mannerisms, posture and surroundings can say quite a bit. Be sure they communicate the appropriate messages as well: credibility, believability, comfort. For example, when doing an on-camera interview, dress as you normally would for your position and avoid distracting accessories; stand or sit up straight and avoid nervous fidgeting; maintain eye contact with the interviewer. If the interview is taking place at your institution, pick an appropriate location that is tidy and free of offensive or controversial signage. These are just a few of the nonverbal cues that can leave either a good or bad impression.

—Used with permission of Natalie Wester

OVERLAYING SOUND ONTO BROADCAST COPY

The final and most profound strength of broadcast media is their ability to supplement with a human's additional sensory channels the information that can be communicated through prose. Radio can add the power of sound to prose, and television should integrate sound and movement with language. Any radio or television message that neglects those powerful tools would be better communicated through print media. If your broadcast writing is merely reading copy into a microphone, it's not broadcast writing.

In radio, the tools to create this sensory complement to your message are voices, recordings at a site, sound effects, and music. Each can play an important part in making a broadcast report effective.

In its simplest use, sound can draw the receiver's attention from whatever he or she may be doing. The explosive sound of a shuttle launch, followed by the words "We have liftoff," are very effective in drawing attention to a story on the space program. The scream of an African lion is an attention-grabbing opening for a story on efforts to stop zoos from capturing wild animals. In Figure 7.1A, the radio feature lead (the script is included in its entirety in this chapter's Ready Reference 7.5) signals a story about water with the squeaking sound of a shutoff valve to pull inattentive listeners into the piece.

Sound can also be used to indicate to an audience that a particular piece is for its members. Cows mooing might signal that a radio report is intended for farmers, the roar of stock cars might draw auto enthusiasts, and the squeaking of sneakers on hardwood might attract basketball fans.

Sound can also be used to create a mood or establish a time period for a story. Big band music quickly signals a story about World War II. The peal of a single church bell might alert listeners to a story on small-town life. A cacophony of bells might set the scene for a story on the Vatican.

Music and sounds can even be used to identify concepts in broadcast writing. One copier company's radio ad had its high-speed copier identified by pulsing, majestic, harmonious symphonic music, while its slower competitor was represented by out-of-tune music played by a single tuba.

The most important and powerful use of sound is to help tell the story you need to tell. Any words you use to describe the agony of babies born to addicted mothers are overwhelmingly reinforced by the wailing of the scores of abandoned babies in big-city nurseries devoted to their care. You are better able to persuade listeners that industrial machinery noise is harmful if instead of spending the entire report

FIGURE 7.1A   Example of radio script lead

Dry Weather Corn

Time	Aural Channel	Narration: John Masterman
0:00	**NATURAL SOUND: 3 seconds, then fade** gurgling water, then a squeaking wheel controlling the water flow being shut off.	
0:03	**MASTERMAN**	That's the sound of water—water that has created bumper crops in Travis, California, and water that's now being turned off. That's worrying farmers, who depend on irrigation to produce huge harvests and big profits.

saying "the machinery is loud enough to damage your hearing" you devote several seconds of the sound track to the narrator yelling over the equipment's racket.

Use every opportunity to tell your story with sound. A story on how Japanese culture contributes to the country's industrial might would be made much more effective by hearing factory workers performing early morning calisthenics and singing the company song before beginning work.

The two-column script format shown in Figure 7.1B will help remind you to integrate sound into your radio writing. (See also the audio format in this chapter's Ready Reference section.) One column contains the narrator's words, and the other makes sure that those sound effects, music and other auditory cues that reinforce the narrator's speech are integrated into the story. You'll see how the two-column format reminds you not to let one source speak too long and to stitch sound effects and quotes (called actualities) from other speakers into the story.

You should also be conscious of integrating voices into your radio reports. Just as in print stories, outside sources bring credibility to broadcast work. They demonstrate that someone else supports the conclusions you are making in the story.

Also as in print stories, other sources help relieve the tedium of listening to only one voice. Even more important, the audience can often perceive the source's emotion or sincerity or insincerity from his or her words, which makes the report that much more persuasive.

FIGURE 7.1B Example of two-column radio script format

	But that is a lot in Africa's and Asia's dry areas. There, corn crops failed three of every five years until they started planting Kalmar's dry weather variety. Now they have a return almost every year.
1:43 <u>**SONG: 3 seconds, then fade under**</u> cue on "We've Got to Feed the Children"	
1:46 <u>**MASTERMAN**</u>	Kalmar's role in feeding Third World countries got extra attention when the Musicians Hunger Project took money from their best-selling record and bought 15 thousand bushels of Kalmar's seed corn for western Africa farmers. Until recently, America's farmers didn't need to copy Third World methods. But those practices are looking profitable to Travis farmer Larry Quick, who just planted 800 acres of Kalmar's drought-resistant corn.
2:13 <u>**QUICK ACTUALITY: 6 seconds**</u> "With so few farmers able to pull off a corn crop this year, I think prices are going to be high. Even a hundred bushels an acre is going to make for a sweet payday."	
2:19 <u>**MASTERMAN**</u>	For Quick and other farmers a sweet payday has usually been tied to the sound of sweet water from this pipeline.

2:23 <u>**NATURAL SOUND: 2 seconds**</u>
squeaky water spigot being turned

2:25 <u>**MASTERMAN**</u>

But before the spigot watering Travis farms is turned on again, farmers in this dry sea of dust may have to make some drought-resistant decisions to keep their farms afloat. From Travis, California, this is John Masterman reporting.

2:30

FIGURE 7.1C Memory-cue transition in radio script story

Integrating these auditory elements into broadcast copy is indispensable in exploiting the power of the broadcast medium. But while sound elements are important, it's equally important to use sound, music and voices with a purpose. As in all communication, every word, every sensory element, has to contribute to one central communication goal.

For example, if your story is about new ways to set broken legs, but your report begins with sounds from a football game (which you include because it's an activity in which a person might get a leg broken), you've already got two problems. First, it's very likely that you discouraged the audience you wanted—the doctors who might adopt this procedure—from attending to the message. They won't understand the message is intended for them. Second, you're going to confuse the sports audience you have drawn by presenting a story on medical technology when they wanted and expected a story on football.

That integration of messages is equivalent to "keeping like elements together," a guideline that is just as important in broadcast communication as in print communication. You are just adding an audio channel to a message in which those same basic principles of communication apply.

However, remember that you are relying on just the audio channel to communicate your message, because your audience can neither see what you're discussing nor review the message. For that reason, your prose needs to be a little more descriptive. Use word play and alliteration to make the language more interesting and involving to an audience that totally relies on auditory cues for an understanding of the story. Figure 7.1C is an example from our drought-resistant crop story that demonstrates how to use a memory-cue transition to link the story's final words (which feature a lot of alliteration) with the preceding sound effect.

You need to describe, where relevant, whether your speakers are old or young, whether they are factory workers or business executives, whether the action of the story is taking place in a factory or a wheat field. If a sound effect is not obvious, identify it to your read-

---

Memory Memo 7.5
A checklist for integrating sound into radio writing:
- Use sound to identify an audience and draw its attention into the piece.
- Use sound to establish a mood or time period for the story.
- Use sound to help tell the story.

ers. If you are alternating between speakers, you need to identify each source every time he or she speaks, unless the voice is very distinctive. In other words, you must replace visual elements with descriptive writing and sound effects to create a visual element within the story. Use the checklist in Memory Memo 7.5 to see that you're accomplishing that task.

OVERLAYING MOTION ONTO BROADCAST COPY

When you write for television or video, you're trying to apply all the strengths of print and radio while adding the power of sight and movement. You want to use every persuasive force of the print medium: the power of printed words and pictures, subtitles and lists, graphs and charts, quotes and written excerpts. To that, you want to add the capability of sounds, voices and music to create a mood, add credibility, gather attention and draw a targeted audience. You want to startle an audience into interest in a story on urban renewal with the sound of an explosion demolishing an old building. You want to use music that signals an exciting story on a pro football player's assault on the single-game rushing record. You want to use the angry voice of an unemployed auto worker to communicate how easily frustration can turn into self-destructive behavior.

Once you have these elements of words and sound in a television story, you can think about pictures. That's different from the way most of us think about television stories. Too often we believe that pictures are enough to make a good television story. That attitude is what contributes to the general vacuousness that characterizes a lot of what we see on television.

For television to be as effective as it is capable of being, it has to incorporate all three sensory channels into its presentation. That's why it's impossible to talk about television independent of the other communication media.

Once you have the strengths of print and audio in place, you can create a tremendously effective piece by adding motion. Showing a slow-moving column of peasants trudging through a narrow cemetery gate as they mourn an assassinated Third World politician creates a stirring picture. Showing that film to the audio accompaniment of hecklers from a rival political party makes for powerful drama.

In a different way, showing fast cuts of the hyperkinetic energy of auditioners for a clown college to the accompaniment of the song "Be a Clown" provides an experience that you can't achieve with the video alone.

Memory Memo 7.6
A checklist for writing video copy:

- Make sure you've got effective text and sound to which you can add visuals.
- Coordinate the communication effects of text, sound and motion.
- Make sure you're adding motion and not merely sight to your message.
- Be careful not to distract from powerful images with unnecessarily descriptive text.

You notice we talk about the power of television as the power of motion, not of sight. That's intentional. You can use the power of sight in print stories with photographs and charts, sidebars and illustrations. The one new element that video adds is motion. Memory Memo 7.6 summarizes your thought process to guarantee you're using this last sensory element effectively.

For that reason, you shouldn't be content merely to pose an announcer in front of scenery and shoot video of him or her reading copy. That's not what video is for. In fact, magazine photographers wouldn't be able to keep their jobs if they tried to illustrate articles with such boring visuals.

Instead, you need to emphasize motion in the pictures accompanying your story. For a story on a famous rock group's concert in your town, show ticket holders sprinting toward the stadium gate for the best seats. Illustrate a story on taxes by following legislators through a day as they meet with special interest lobbyists, encounter protesters outside the Capitol, and finally take their place in the chamber to vote.

There are thousands of such procedures and possibilities for visual storytelling. There are volumes and volumes written about video techniques and the mental images they can evoke. It takes directors years of study and experience to begin to master them. Luckily for us, we have an audience that's been wonderfully trained by movies to know what some very simple shots mean.

Want examples? What is happening when a shaky handheld camera follows a character down hallways or across dark alleys? From your experience with horror movies, you probably know the character is most likely in extreme danger of undergoing a most gruesome and bloody demise. What is happening when a man and a woman run toward each other in slow motion? They're usually in love. When two men approach each other in slow motion, there is usually going to be a fight employing rather savage forms of martial arts.

There are thousands more of these cinematic conventions. Handheld camera shots usually suggest realism or tension. The camera swiveling on its base indicates speed. Black and white gives a gritty, documentary feel to a scene. Shooting a subject from below emphasizes size and power. Shooting someone from above communicates a sense of vulnerability and timidity. Some basic terminology describing these techniques is included in the Ready Reference section at the end of this chapter.

Writing copy for video production closely follows the principles outlined for print and radio media. After establishing your thesis in the first few seconds of the piece, you've got to explain precisely the issues you'll explore in the report. That's the same routine that you would follow in the first two paragraphs of a print story. Figure 7.2A shows the lead of a video feature story that illustrates this conception. Figure 7.2B shows the rest of this video news release, which was prepared by a brokerage firm to showcase its advice for a changing stock market. Notice how the writer uses a thematic visual, the lonely Santa Claus, to anchor the beginning and end of the package. It's also interesting to see how she uses cash register sounds as an aural asterisk to draw attention to her three main points about the weakening economy. Finally, note how she mixes graphics and live action to involve the viewer.

The same principles apply to the body of the story. As indicated in the discussion of radio writing, don't let one scene or one speaker dominate for too long. The three-column format is used as a reminder to fill all the sensory channels available.

sound effects	video	dialogue
:00 MS: Santa sitting by himself HAVELOCK VO NAT SND	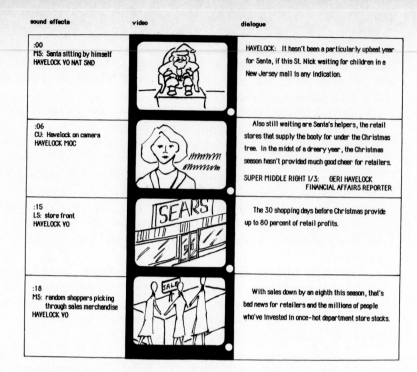	HAVELOCK: It hasn't been a particularly upbeat year for Santa, if this St. Nick waiting for children in a New Jersey mall is any indication.
:06 CU: Havelock on camera HAVELOCK MOC		Also still waiting are Santa's helpers, the retail stores that supply the booty for under the Christmas tree. In the midst of a dreary year, the Christmas season hasn't provided much good cheer for retailers. SUPER MIDDLE RIGHT 1/3: GERI HAVELOCK FINANCIAL AFFAIRS REPORTER
:15 LS: store front HAVELOCK VO		The 30 shopping days before Christmas provide up to 80 percent of retail profits.
:18 MS: random shoppers picking through sales merchandise HAVELOCK VO		With sales down by an eighth this season, that's bad news for retailers and the millions of people who've invested in once-hot department store stocks.

FIGURE 7.2A   Example of a television feature story lead

:27 MS: Havelock on camera in front of store entrance HAVELOCK MOC	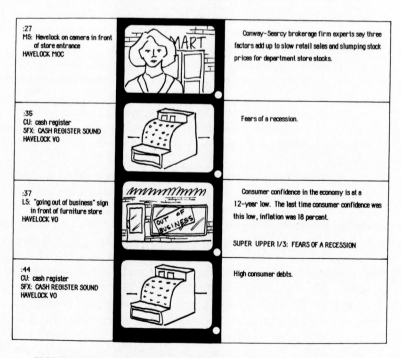	Conway-Searcy brokerage firm experts say three factors add up to slow retail sales and slumping stock prices for department store stocks.
:35 CU: cash register SFX: CASH REGISTER SOUND HAVELOCK VO		Fears of a recession.
:37 LS: "going out of business" sign in front of furniture store HAVELOCK VO		Consumer confidence in the economy is at a 12-year low. The last time consumer confidence was this low, inflation was 18 percent. SUPER UPPER 1/3: FEARS OF A RECESSION
:44 CU: cash register SFX: CASH REGISTER SOUND HAVELOCK VO		High consumer debts.

FIGURE 7.2B   Television feature storyboard

sound effects	video	dialogue
:46 CU: credit card going through machine HAVELOCK VO NAT SND		Shoppers may be taking a breather to pay off credit card bills, which now total over one trillion dollars. SUPER UPPER 1/3:: HIGH CONSUMER DEBTS
:54 CU: cash register SFX: CASH REGISTER SOUND HAVELOCK VO		High unemployment.
:56 MS: "not hiring" sign in front of business HAVELOCK VO		Fears of rising joblessness, which is 25 percent higher than last year, may be scaring people away from the stores. SUPER UPPER 1/3: HIGH UNEMPLOYMENT
1:02 CU: cash register SFX: CASH REGISTER SOUND HAVELOCK VO		The Total?
1:04 graphic: shopping bags representing total retail sales wipe to expose each years totals HAVELOCK VO		It adds up to the lowest retail sales in eight years. After steady growth for over a decade, department store sales fell 12 percent since last year.
1:10 MS: Havelock on camera in front of Conway-Searcy building HAVELOCK MOC		For investors, this means holding those once-glittering retail stocks is like finding a lump of coal in a Christmas stocking. A Conway-Searcy brokerage firm analyst says to think about recession-proof stocks.
1:20 CU: Farrier at desk FARRIER ACTUALITY		FARRIER TAPE: There's nothing but a downhill slide for retailers for at least the next two years. We're advising our clients to move into SUPER LOWER 1/3: JOHN FARRIER CONWAY-SEARCY ANALYST
1:25 graphic: icons representing medical, technology, energy wipe to show each icon FARRIER ACTUALITY		medical stocks, technology and energy issues that are at historic lows. With careful picks, we think investors can lock in on the stocks that will be the first to make a comeback. SUPER LOWER 1/3: MEDICAL/TECHNOLOGY/ ENERGY CONWAY-SEARCY PICKS
1:35 LS: Santa walking down nearly empty hallway of shopping mall HAVELOCK VO NAT SND 1:45 END		That comeback seems like it may leave retail stocks, and people holding retail stocks, out in the cold. From Bayonne, New Jersey, this is Geri Havelock reporting. END

191

Remember as well that you still have the responsibility to create solid argumentation structures using chronology, order of importance, or problem-solution. In addition, you have to link each of them together with memory-cue transitions that orient your viewers to what they'll be seeing next.

Be conscious of how easy it is to confuse your viewers, who are receiving information simultaneously from a number of sensory channels. For example, you shouldn't show scenes of your institution's president jogging in a company-sponsored charity event while the narrator is talking about the president's problems coping with a recession in your industry. Viewers will be confused because the information they're receiving from the auditory channel doesn't support the visual message. Similarly, if you display a slide or supertitle of a quotation on-screen, the voice-over has to repeat the words on the screen exactly. Any deviation again confuses the viewers and distracts them from the message you're trying to communicate.

Much of video writing is essentially the same as for the other media we've discussed. In fact, the major distinction is not so much a matter of knowing what to write as knowing what not to write.

It bears emphasizing that video is powerful because of its ability to focus the effectiveness of sound and motion in communicating a message. All too often, words disrupt that process. It's true that in radio and in print, you need words to create a vision in the receiver's mind. For instance, in a radio story you might reinforce the cracking voice of an elderly nursing home resident by a word portrait mentioning his weathered face and uncertain walk.

But such visual prompting is unnecessary in video. If you are showing video of a blizzard, it's both redundant and infuriating to have a voice-over telling the viewers they are looking at a blizzard. If you are attempting to communicate the emotion of a local sports hero's retirement, don't say "It was an emotional time for Old Buck" as you show footage of the retirement ceremony. To communicate that sentiment, it's probably going to be much more effective to have no narration as you show Old Buck fighting back the tears as he faces the home crowd for the last time.

Instead of describing the scene, the words should supplement the power of the video. Obviously, use words to identify speakers and explain the context of action the video is showing, but don't try to compete with the power of your image. If it's necessary to orient the viewers to a scene, make the points before the film begins or against scenic shots. If you are talking when the filmed action is at its height you may detract from the visual's strength and confuse your viewers as they attempt to absorb complex information from two channels at one time.

Again, I suggest a scripting format that reminds writers to incorporate all three channels into their video writing as well as coordinate sound, visuals and words with each other. You'll see an example of this scripting format in the Ready Reference section following this chapter.

NO DIFFERENT—JUST MORE

It's important to remember that as we move from one medium to the next, from print to radio to television, we don't have to completely alter the principles that guide good writing. Instead, each medium represents an additional communication channel that supplements the power we've already gained from the others. Using that knowledge, we can exploit the vast communication power of broadcast media most effectively.

SUMMARY

- Writers need to adjust their writing styles to accentuate the strengths and deemphasize the weaknesses of each medium in which they work.
- Broadcast writing is not totally different from writing for the print media. Instead, it involves overlaying messages and stimuli from additional sensory channels onto well-written prose.
- Broadcast media have powerful advantages over print media: (1) They reinforce a message with input from other human senses, (2) they exploit the identification receivers have with personalities who deliver the message, and (3) they are pervasive.
- Broadcast media also have significant weaknesses: (1) Audiences receive the messages passively, and (2) audiences cannot review the message after it has been broadcast.
- To overcome the transience of a broadcast message, writers use trigger words to introduce information immediately that will capture the audience's attention. They also simplify vocabulary and sentence structures and include less detailed information.
- Because broadcast reports are generally shorter than print stories, writers must develop transitions between different stories by using memory-cue transition methods.
- Broadcast writing emphasizes the immediacy of the medium by employing present tense verbs. Writers reinforce the medium's person-to-person communication strength by using contractions, shorter sentences, and informal language.
- Both radio and television writing should involve the receiver's auditory senses by integrating sounds, voices and music. They (1) draw the receiver's attention, (2) identify an audience for a story, (3) create a mood or establish a time period, (4) identify participants or concepts, (5) bring credibility and additional power to the message, and (6) introduce variety into a story.
- Video should add visual elements to print's prose and radio's auditory messages. Visuals should emphasize motion and not merely sight.
- Video script writers should not repeat in the script the details that the viewer can see in the visual. That detracts from the power of the visual.

THINK PIECES

1. Why is there a difference in how much information people retain from print and broadcast media? Does the involvement of other sensory channels overcome the inability to review?

2. Compare the memorability and persuasiveness of emotional and rational appeals. What types of messages are better portrayed in the different media?
3. What sounds could you use to illustrate a radio story on homelessness? What sounds might help communicate a story on housing values?
4. What's the importance of mood over plot in music videos? How has that changed video storytelling?
5. Recall your reactions to your city's newscasters. What sort of personal images do they and their stations try to establish for them? How does that change your perceptions of the news they present?

WRITING ASSIGNMENTS

D1.10

D8.8

D9.11

D10.14

ADDITIONAL READING

Arnheim, Rudolf. *Visual Thinking*. Berkeley: University of California Press, 1980.

Cohler, David Keith. *Broadcast Newswriting*. Englewood Cliffs, N.J.: Prentice Hall, 1990.

Greenberg, Keith E. "Radio News Releases Make the Hit Parade." *Public Relations Journal* 48:7 (July 1992): 6.

MacDonald, Ronald, ed. *Broadcast News Manual of Style*, 2d ed. White Plains, N.Y.: Longman, 1994.

Marlow, Eugene. "Sophisticated 'News' Videos Gain Wide Acceptance." *Public Relations Journal* 50:7 (August/September 1994): 17–21, 25.

Shell, Adam. "VNRs: Who's Watching? How Do You Know?" *Public Relations Journal* 49:12 (December 1993): 14–16.

Phonetic Spellings for Broadcast Copy

Broadcast copy preparation is intended to make the announcer's job as simple as it can be. Part of that task is to provide guidance on pronouncing unfamiliar words. Pronouncers are placed in parentheses after the word. Accented syllables are capitalized, as in this example: *Mackinac (MAK-ih-naw) Island hosted the festival.* Obviously, if your copy contains too many pronouncers, review it. You may need to simplify it for your audience. Here are the symbols used in broadcast copy:

Vowel Sounds

A   ah——father, arm
     a——bat, apple
     aw——raw, talk
     ay——fate, ace
E   ee——feet, tea
     eh——get, bed
     ew——few
I   eye——time, ice
     ee——machine
     ih——pit, middle
O   oh——note, oval
     ah——hot
     aw——fought
     oo——food, two
     u——foot, took
     ow——how, clout
U   ew——mule, hue
     oo——rule, fume
     u——put, curl
     uh——shut, puff

Consonant Sounds

g——got, beg
j——general, job
k——keep, cat
ch——chair, butcher
sh——machine, shut
z——disease, visit

Broadcast Copy Style Rules

The style rules governing broadcast copy preparation derive from the reality that the copy is intended to be read aloud by an announcer. Because of that, broadcast copy is written to appear precisely as it would be spoken.

ABBREVIATIONS

Because it is difficult for an announcer to instantly recognize and translate abbreviations into their spoken form, abbreviations are generally not used. There are a few exceptions. For organizations and countries that are known by their initials, make sure you write them exactly as they would be spoken. Thus, U.S. Senate becomes the *U-S Senate*. FBI is written in broadcast copy as *F-B-I*. Maintain exact oral pronunciation in your broadcast copy. NAACP is written in broadcast copy as *N-double A-C-P*. But when an acronym is pronounced as a word, don't use hyphens. Thus, broadcast copy uses *NATO* and *NASA*.

SYMBOLS

Symbols are also difficult for an announcer to convert into spoken English. Again, spell out all symbols in exactly the way they would be pronounced. Thus, in broadcast copy $7 is written as *seven dollars*.

NUMBERS

The style rules for handling numbers are different for broadcast, too. Write out the numbers one through ten, just as you would in print copy. Also write out eleven, as it might be mistaken for two letters. Use figures for 12 through 999. But write the words *thousand, million* and *billion*. It sounds confusing but it becomes simpler if you think about writing broadcast copy to duplicate spoken language. Thus, 2,603,000 is written *two million, 603 thousand*. That principle extends to decimals—8.6 is written *eight-point-six*.

Although there are some exceptions to the preceding rules (for addresses, times, sports scores and stock reports), you'll still adhere to the need for exact spoken language. For that reason, 6004 Hite St becomes *60-0-4 Hite Street*. Dates are also converted into spoken style. Dec. 7, 1941, is written *December seventh, 19-41*.

Format for Radio Script

Note: If this copy were being prepared for a newscaster to read, it would be double- or triple-spaced.

my pr firm

123 Main Street / Hometown, Any State / 12345 / 505 555-1234

Title of Story

Time	Sound effects	Narration: Victor Voice Talent
<u>0:00</u>	**NATURAL SOUND–2 seconds** Sound of old-fashioned radio being tuned. Narrator's voice flashes in, then comes in clearly.	
<u>0:02</u>	**TALENT NARRATION**	Audio feature stories often begin with a sound effect. It helps draw listeners' attention to the story before the narration begins so they don't miss any important information. Second, if it is chosen carefully, it can identify the subject and audience for a story. Because the sound of the narrator's voice and sound effects are all you've got to communicate your ideas, you need to use them wisely. Here's public relations practitioner Moe Howard to tell you how the listener's needs are factored into radio writing.
<u>0:24</u>	**HOWARD ACTUALITY (12 seconds)** "It's true that the broadcast writer has to think about the capabilities of the people listening. Since they can't review any facts, radio stories have less complex and shorter sentences. The writing should be more conversational to take advantage of the listeners' identification with the human being reading the copy."	
<u>0:36</u>	**TALENT NARRATION**	What about the announcer reading the story? How does copy change to reflect the person reading it aloud?

<u>0:41</u> **HOWARD ACTUALITY (14 seconds)**
"The broadcast writer needs to double-space the copy and use special broadcast style rules when writing the script. That makes it much easier to read. Just as importantly, the writer needs to give the narrator some help with other sounds so he or she doesn't have to carry the whole story alone."

<u>0:55</u> **TALENT NARRATION**   And how do you use sound to tell your story?

<u>0:58</u> **HOWARD ACTUALITY (8 seconds)**
"You need to use all the sound resources you can to communicate, switching back and forth among the narrator's voice, actualities from other speakers and sound effects that help tell your story."

<u>1:06</u> **TALENT NARRATION**   The multiple-column format you're looking at helps you accomplish that. The first column is the running time—the total the story has run so far. It reminds you if you've used a particular narrator's voice or sound effect too long, or if you haven't given enough time for a sound effect to be understood. And since radio reports are usually very short, it also reminds you if you've run over your limit.

<u>1:27</u> **SFX: Blaring horn (1 second)**

<u>1:28</u> **TALENT NARRATION**   Newly out of time, this is Victor Voice Talent reporting.

<u>1:30</u>

Full Text of a Radio Feature Story

Radio copy should build on the strengths of written prose. Instead of having an announcer simply read narrative prose, use the aural channel radio provides. Add natural sounds, taped quotes from sources, music, and sound effects to involve the listener. In addition, think about the different emotional effects the narrator's gender and vocal qualities add to your message. This story was produced on audiotape, then distributed to stations.

Dry Weather Corn

Time	Aural Channel	Narration: John Masterman
0:00	**NATURAL SOUND: 3 seconds, then fade** gurgling water, then a squeaking wheel controlling the water flow being shut off.	
0:03	**MASTERMAN**	That's the sound of water—water that has created bumper crops in Travis, California, and water that's now being turned off. That's worrying farmers, who depend on irrigation to produce huge harvests and big profits. No one's predicting big profits this year. It hasn't rained in Travis for 47 days, part of a three-year drought. That's nothing new. There have been droughts here before. But always before, when Mother Nature didn't provide water, man could. In the drought of 1970, farmers used over 800 million gallons of water. However, expanding cities around the farms are now crying for

water that used to go to farmers. This year, the local

water district cut 90 percent of the farmers' irrigation

water.

Although the sound of the water being turned off is

making for some uncomfortable times in Travis, it's

stimulating another sound in Nordorff (NAWR-duhf),

South Dakota.

0:42   NATURAL SOUND
corn grinding through auger 2 seconds, then
fade under

0:44   MASTERMAN

At the Kalmar (KOWL-mahr) Seed Company plant in

Nordorff, thousands of bushels of drought-resistant seed

corn are pouring through the auger on their way to fill

orders in the parched western U–S.

Kalmar's hybrid corn was developed to meet another

period of bad weather—the 1930s Midwest dust bowl.

Kalmar founder Gard Kalmar was a South Dakota

farmer then. Like thousands of others, he was pushed

off his farm by the dry winds.

After three years on the road, Kalmar started working

at a small Wyoming research farm. His son, Leif

Kalmar, said it was there he found a small cornlike

grass that could exist in Wyoming's harsh climate.

1:16   KALMAR ACTUALITY: 7 seconds
"Scientists still can't believe he got a cross
between that grass and a corn plant. But with an
eighth-grade education and a big stubborn
streak he proved them all wrong."

1:23 **MASTERMAN**

By the early 1950s, Kalmar had developed a corn strain that yielded 120 bushels per acre. That's not a lot by American standards, where top farmers sometimes squeeze over 200 bushels per acre from rich soil and ample rain.

But that is a lot in Africa's and Asia's dry areas. There, corn crops failed three of every five years until they started planting Kalmar's dry weather variety. Now they have a return almost every year.

1:43 **SONG: 3 seconds, then fade under**
cue on "We've Got to Feed the Children"

1:46 **MASTERMAN**

Kalmar's role in feeding Third World countries got extra attention when the Musicians Hunger Project took money from their best-selling record and bought 15–thousand bushels of Kalmar's seed corn for western Africa farmers.

Until recently, America's farmers didn't need to copy Third World methods. But those practices are looking profitable to Travis farmer Larry Quick, who just planted 800 acres of Kalmar's drought-resistant corn.

2:13 **QUICK ACTUALITY: 6 seconds**
"With so few farmers able to pull off a corn crop this year, I think prices are going to be high. Even a hundred bushels an acre is going to make for a sweet payday."

2:19 **MASTERMAN**

For Quick and other farmers a sweet payday has usually been tied to the sound of sweet water from this pipeline.

<u>2:23</u>   <u>**NATURAL SOUND: 2 seconds**</u>
squeaky water spigot being turned

<u>2:25</u>   <u>**MASTERMAN**</u>   But before the spigot watering Travis farms is turned on

again, farmers in this dry sea of dust may have to

make some drought-resistant decisions to keep their

farms afloat. From Travis, California, this is John

Masterman reporting.

<u>2:30</u>

Glossary of Video Terminology

Video production has its own language. Writers need to understand it so that they know the communication possibilities of different camera angles and movements. Although there are thousands of different combinations of visual techniques that can create innumerable emotional effects, these constitute the basic building blocks for video writers.

PRODUCTION METHODS

Your first task is to decide whether film or tape (and the associated costs and problems of each) is most suited to your task.

film: Uses same equipment as movies, so film has to be developed after it is shot. Generally better quality photography and softer look than videotape. More control over filming process. More expensive.

videotape: Records sound and motion directly onto electronic tape. Fastest and most inexpensive process. Editing, special effects, and supertitles are easier than with film.

CAMERA SHOTS

Don't be afraid to use close-ups and extreme close-ups. They provide variety in a video report and help your readers concentrate on what you want them to see.

long shot (LS): Shows the entire setting. Sometimes called an establishing shot because it establishes the location for the rest of the action.

medium shot (MS): Far enough from subject so that we can see subject as well as the setting behind the action.

close-up (CU): The subject fills the screen. This shot emphasizes one specific subject without distractions from the background.

extreme close-up (ECU): The camera focuses on one specific item—the detail in a picture, a serial number on a product, or a healing wound on a finger.

PLACING AND MOVING THE CAMERA

The way you place and move the camera can emphasize certain emotional effects.

eye-level placement: Putting the camera at eye level of a normal person establishes the viewer in the same emotional position as the person in the shot.

high-angle placement: In addition to being a standard angle for establishing shots, a high-angle shot creates a psychological impression belittling the shot's subject.

low-angle placement: As you might guess, a low-angle shot emphasizes the power and dominance of the scene's subject.

panning: The camera base remains stationary while the camera swivels. A pan recreates the position of a spectator.

203

truck: A truck shot has the camera rolling sideways to stay alongside the action. This is the perspective you have while you're looking at the driver in a car travelling beside you on the highway.

zoom: While the camera base remains stationary, the zoom lens rotates to bring the image closer or move it away. With a zoom, you can rapidly change the viewer's orientation to the subject.

dolly: In a dolly, the camera rolls toward or away from the subject. This gives the same impression as walking toward a scene and is a more natural movement than a zoom.

TRANSITIONS BETWEEN SHOTS

As in print writing, video transitions help show the viewer the links within your story and demonstrate the argumentation pattern that proves your thesis.

cut: A cut is an instantaneous switch from one scene to another. It is by far the dominant transition used in news coverage.

dissolve: When you need a softer transition between shots (for example, to suggest romance during a wedding scene) you might consider a dissolve. A dissolve also is used to evoke dream sequences, passages of time, and other more disjointed transitions in a sequence.

wipe: In a wipe, the screen appears to peel or erase the image and substitutes another one on the screen. A wipe lets the viewers view one image as another image is entering the screen and suggests a more direct linkage between the images in the transition.

SPECIAL EFFECTS

Because they can sometimes overwhelm the message, special effects should be used sparingly. However, where appropriate, they can create a very powerful emotional impact.

supertitle (SUPER): A supertitle is lettering superimposed on the screen to identify a speaker or present statistics or other information. It should be used to bring the power of print to reinforce an aural or visual message.

split screen: This is a wipe that stops halfway across the screen. It's used to compare before-and-after scenes and other transformations.

key insert: In a key insert, an image is placed over another scene. Thus, you could show a product and then place a corporate logo onto the image.

matte: A matte is used for much of the trick photography you see in movies. In film, a matte is a shield that prevents part of the film from being exposed. There are generally two mattes made, one for the live action and one for the painting or special effects that will occur around the actors. Thus, actors running down a darkened corridor could be filmed with a matte eliminating all the other elements in the scene. Then a director could place a matte over the part of the film the actors occupied in the first filming and paint a mountain scene over the space occupied by the original matte. By filming the scene again, it appears the actors are actually running through a cave in the mountain.

Format for Video Storyboard

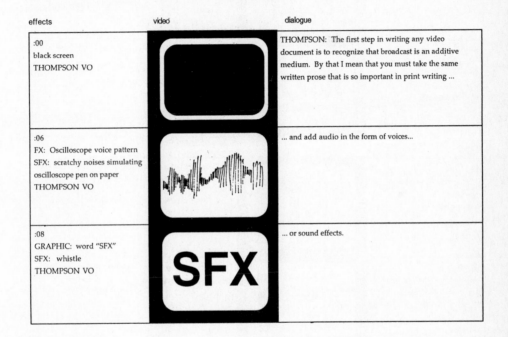

my pr firm

Client: Practitioners of the Future
Title: "Video Writing Format"

Time: 1:06
Date: Aug. 16, 199_
Writer: Thompson

effects	video	dialogue
:00 black screen THOMPSON VO		THOMPSON: The first step in writing any video document is to recognize that broadcast is an additive medium. By that I mean that you must take the same written prose that is so important in print writing ...
:06 FX: Oscilloscope voice pattern SFX: scratchy noises simulating oscilloscope pen on paper THOMPSON VO		... and add audio in the form of voices...
:08 GRAPHIC: word "SFX" SFX: whistle THOMPSON VO		... or sound effects.

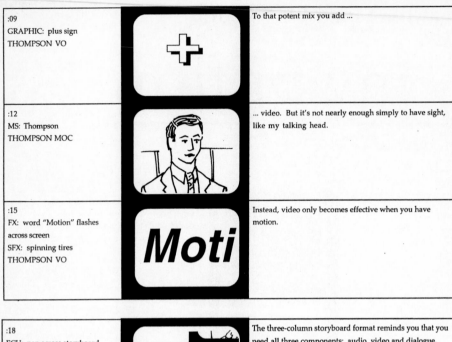

:09 GRAPHIC: plus sign THOMPSON VO		To that potent mix you add ...
:12 MS: Thompson THOMPSON MOC		... video. But it's not nearly enough simply to have sight, like my talking head.
:15 FX: word "Motion" flashes across screen SFX: spinning tires THOMPSON VO		Instead, video only becomes effective when you have motion.

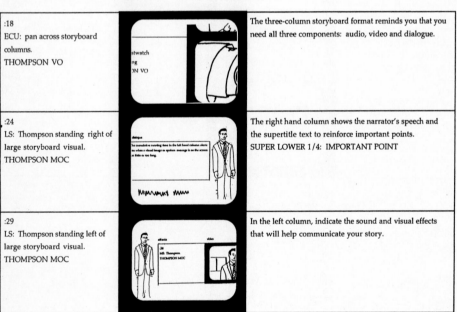

:18 ECU: pan across storyboard columns. THOMPSON VO		The three-column storyboard format reminds you that you need all three components: audio, video and dialogue.
:24 LS: Thompson standing right of large storyboard visual. THOMPSON MOC		The right hand column shows the narrator's speech and the supertitle text to reinforce important points. SUPER LOWER 1/4: IMPORTANT POINT
:29 LS: Thompson standing left of large storyboard visual. THOMPSON MOC		In the left column, indicate the sound and visual effects that will help communicate your story.

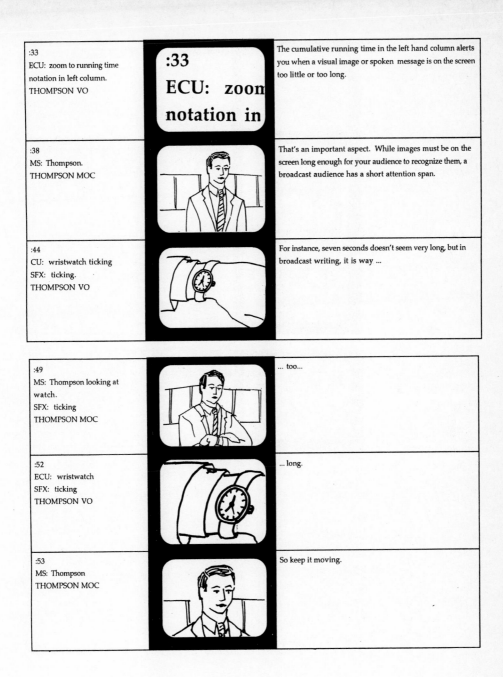

:33 ECU: zoom to running time notation in left column. THOMPSON VO	**:33** **ECU: zoom** **notation in**	The cumulative running time in the left hand column alerts you when a visual image or spoken message is on the screen too little or too long.
:38 MS: Thompson. THOMPSON MOC		That's an important aspect. While images must be on the screen long enough for your audience to recognize them, a broadcast audience has a short attention span.
:44 CU: wristwatch ticking SFX: ticking. THOMPSON VO		For instance, seven seconds doesn't seem very long, but in broadcast writing, it is way ...
:49 MS: Thompson looking at watch. SFX: ticking THOMPSON MOC		... too...
:52 ECU: wristwatch SFX: ticking THOMPSON VO		... long.
:53 MS: Thompson THOMPSON MOC		So keep it moving.

:55 FX: Numeral "1" shrinks, then explodes SFX: pop THOMPSON VO		One last point:
:56 CU: Thompson THOMPSON MOC		You don't have to illustrate every single camera shot in the storyboard's middle column.
:59 MS: Thompson THOMPSON MOC		For instance, if you are doing a pull-back shot to end this video, ...

1:02 LS: Thompson THOMPSON MOC 1:06 END		... it's not necessary to show every view as the camera pulls back. Just give sufficient written instructions.

Targeting: Applying the Receiver-centered System to Deliver Messages to Targeted Publics

You're now entering into a lifetime enterprise of learning the tactics of public relations.

My education has not stopped yet. Virtually every day, I discover a new magazine or radio talk show that I didn't know existed. I read about a colleague who has developed a unique PR presentation to an audience. I hear the comment of a reporter that suggests I might have more placement success if I changed the format of a document. I find a new computer delivery system for my public relations messages.

This part of the text tries to cut a few years off the beginning of your learning curve. We'll be talking about how to format different types of public relations documents. You'll learn how to apply the basic writing and communication principles we've already learned to writing speeches, feature stories, position papers, advertising copy, and other PR tasks.

There's another component of your PR education that we'll work on in this section. It's in answer to one of my first editors, who told me not to waste my time writing something if I couldn't find an audience to read it. Keep focused on an audience, he said. Make sure you are writing with a particular media outlet in mind.

That's why you'll notice an unusual presentation in this section. For each of the four writing process chapters, on internal, external, face-to-face and advertising writing, you'll find a corresponding chapter that tells you how to deliver your message.

There's information on the inside workings of media outlets, with discussions on new applications of media to foster two-way communication between organizations and their publics. We'll look at alternative electronic media that are expanding our communication channels exponentially, and we'll be examining new ways of tracking the effectiveness of our communication efforts.

As you read this next section, you'll probably sense my enthusiasm for relationship marketing, database overlays, multivariate audience analysis and the other new techniques of media placement. They are possibilities that didn't even exist when I began my career, but they have become just as important as excellent writing skills for the practitioner.

Throughout this part of the book, keep this in mind: excellent writing, skillful placement. It's a combination that will make you a successful professional.

chapter **8**

The Audience That Should Be on Your Side: Applying Receiver-centered Writing to Reach Internal Audiences

REAL-LIFE LESSONS

Internal communication seems to be the hot topic in the business press now. It's hard to pick up a business magazine or executive's self-help book without finding an article on new ways to handle the suddenly fashionable internal communications role within the company.

The list of recommendations seems endless. In one audiotape, the narrator talks about how one company has tried to stimulate contact between workers and managers by moving all its executives' desks out of their offices and into the middle of the factory floor. A magazine article details how another company's executives stimulate more communication among workers by building a new corporate headquarters in which people from different divisions come into more frequent contact with one another as they go to conference rooms, cafeteria areas and bathrooms.

An executive's biography tells how he attempted to foster new commitment among the company's workers by visiting loading-dock workers at 3 a.m. Another popular management self-help book detailed how one company flew the several hundred workers of its European division to the United States to visit the company's factory and visit with U.S. coworkers.

There's no disputing the value of these largely symbolic acts, for they show some commitment by American business executives to communication with their workers and to fostering interplay among their workers. They are important because they show some tiny degree of movement toward a genuine commitment to two-way communication by organizational leaders. It's one of the first times it's entered the consciousness of mainstream business and so even these first steps are welcome.

Public relations, and internal public relations especially, is in a wonderful position to turn these symbolic flourishes that represent communication into fundamental, workable innovations for real communication within institutions. That means we need to provide more than occasional symbolic gestures from the company president to the minions on the factory floor that hint that there are opportunities for workers to talk to the president.

Internal communication means formalized ways of getting information from the newest hire on the factory floor to the company president every single working day of the year, and not just when the organization's president feels particularly magnanimous. It means the CEO will hear problems and complaints and bellyaching about his or her own performance, and not just the respectful gratitude for the boss's wonderful gesture.

Moreover, it's not just the CEO's job to communicate and be communicated to. Internal PR also means encouraging structures and opportunities for engineers to share their innovations with marketers, for assembly workers to tell their ideas about equipment purchases to procurement officers and for payroll workers to inform personnel executives that their new forms aren't getting the information the company needs to process newly hired employees.

Out of that unruly cacophony of voices comes an organization with a real capacity to solve its problems. It may not fit into an organizational chart, but it works because everybody knows the problems the organization faces and every worker and executive has a chance to add his or her expertise to the solution, even if it's not his or her department's responsibility.

It's a brave new world out there. Internal communication will have to be a part of the renaissance.

WHAT YOU KNOW

- A clear understanding of an organization's objectives is necessary to design an effective communication program.
- Messages must be constructed to answer the needs and wants of the audience, not of the sender.
- Providing a clear argumentation structure in a document helps readers comprehend and act on a message.

WHAT YOU'LL LEARN

- Internal communication systems should not only deliver messages to employees, stockholders, customers and other internal audiences but be designed for those audiences to respond and become involved in the institution's decision processes.
- The process necessary to create internal documents can be quite effective in isolating and resolving institutional problems.
- Internal documents not only communicate to internal audiences but can be used to guide the creation of documents intended for external audiences.

HELPING THE ORGANIZATION UNDERSTAND THE ORGANIZATION

In Chapter 2, we discussed the role of management-by-objective planning in public relations practice. As I indicated there, the first step in MBO planning is discovering the institutional problems a communications program can help solve.

But there's one natural area in which institutions and practitioners have been remiss in using management-by-objective techniques to solve communication problems. That area is internal communication, the part of the PR mission that deals with an institution's relationship with its employees, managers and stockholders. The employee newsletters, management reports, and annual stockholder reports that inform and influence the actions and attitudes of people within an organization are all forms of internal communication.

As Memory Memo 8.1 details, a well-founded internal communications program is the foundation of any complete public relations effort. Not only does an effective internal communication program help motivate and involve the energy and talents of an institution's shareholders and employees; it also helps the institution come to an understanding of itself.

> **Memory Memo 8.1**
> **A good internal communications program can**
> - build a shared view of institutional goals among all important publics
> - help discern an institution's problems and discover solutions
> - serve as communication media to all individuals within the organization
> - provide the foundation for an effective communication campaign with external audiences

That understanding is critically important to the institution's success. Out of it comes a shared conception among workers, executives and stockholders about the goals for which the institution is striving. At its most basic level, that understanding provides a formalized structure for finding an institution's strengths and weaknesses and then communicating that information to the individuals within the organization who can help exploit those strengths and correct those mistakes. A company's self-understanding also provides the foundation for planning campaigns to inform outside audiences.

However, the value of that information to the institution's success is dependent upon our honestly communicating our findings to those internal publics that can help correct the institution's mistakes. That honesty is hard to come by in some organizations because internal communication is what is known as "controlled" communication, messages that don't have to pass through a newspaper or broadcast media editor before they reach an audience. PR practitioners don't have to conform to an outside editor's requirements, but can write what they want and put it directly into the hands of the people whom they want to read it.

Controlling the Message but Ignoring the Audience

That would seem to give a lot of power to internal communication. Let's contrast that with our external communication efforts. Instead of having, as we're often told by our bosses, the truth of our institution's position "distorted by misinformed reporters," our message twisted and turned against us by editors "biased by their liberal viewpoints," or our executives "tricked and surprised" into filmed misstatements by ambushing television film crews, we would be allowed to tell our stories to employees and stockholders calmly, intelligently and truthfully.

That's the promise of internal communication. It's supposed to be an unbiased forum to tell the institution's story to active publics who, because of their identification with the institution, want and need to know about the organization's triumphs and the way it is trying to turn problems into triumphs. The ability to give an organization a forum to tell its story the way it wishes is one reason why internal communication would seem to be ideal for solving an institution's problems.

Unfortunately, many institution managements have used their unfettered control over internal communication to turn out publications just as biased as those newspaper and television exposés they rail about. The resulting newsletters, position papers and institutional reports have often ignored their primary audience, the thousands of employees or stockholders to whom they could be delivering accurate information and from whom they could be eliciting the communication and commitment that could resolve problems.

Bringing Insider Commitment into the Organization

In many companies, internal communication exists to stoke the egos of institutional management. Workers seem to be minor functionaries in the background of the exciting lives of executives, who are pictured shaking hands with important dignitaries, announcing initiatives or receiving plaques honoring the institution for its workers' contributions to a charity drive. The chance to discover and deliver important information about the institution has been lost in creating a personality cult.

In addition, the vital feedback workers and executives need to help solve an institution's problems is lost in the rush to burnish the organization's image. Often, internal audiences are either not told of institutional problems or the news about them is so sanitized that readers have no idea their input might help. The "propaganda sheets," as Crable and Vibbert describe them, are filled with good news about the institution. Yet they often lie abandoned and unread at the bottom of many an employee's locker or desk.

If internal communication media were merely unread, the major waste would be that lots of trees would have fallen needlessly to produce an ego rush for management. Unfortunately, that's only a minor part of the problem. The more damaging part is that internal communications' immodestly complimentary portrayal of an organization and its management isolates executives even more completely in their institutional towers.

Because of the nature of their business and social relationships, executives more often talk to other business and governmental leaders than to their employees, the public, or even their own customers. Despite the perception that organization executives are the institution's eyes and ears to the outside world, organizational research has shown that lower-level employees have more contact with outsiders than do higher-level employees.

The implications of this are frightening. Research suggests accurate information will not flow from outsiders to subordinates and through to superiors. Instead, studies show lower-level employees routinely distort information to make it conform to what the superior wants to hear. As one industrial trainer put it, it's as if an airplane pilot asks, "What's the height?" and hears the altimeter reply, "What would you like it to be?"

The isolation, and the seemingly sanitized world view executives receive because of it, often helps create egocentric traits in institutional managers. As news reports of institutional excesses suggest, an organization's executives sometimes adopt an imperial attitude about the validity of their decisions and the value of other people's opinions, desires or needs. That attitude implicitly sends a message to stockholders and subordinates that institutional management doesn't want news about problems in the organization and doesn't need or want input from people who want to deal with those problems.

Indeed, the Burston-Marsteller report on institutional communications compared many American corporations to totalitarian states. Traditional internal communication programs, the report concluded, "run counter to the nature of our [democratic] society, which is based upon the right to air grievances, express opinions and voice disapproval."

In an organization that asks for and depends on the cooperation and commitment of every member, from janitor to major stockholder, that's a damn poor attitude to take. That can be a critical flaw in an executive's ability to integrate the talents of his or her employees into the organization and indeed to gather a realistic picture of the organization itself.

In a well-managed internal communication program, we're trying to develop a communication environment that encourages commitment, talent, knowledge and energy so that these can be brought to bear on institutional problems. Institutional managers isolated from the factory floor, the small-investor's home or the middle-manager's tiny office cannot marshal the total expertise needed to run a massive organization without the help and insight of their employees and stockholders. That's not an indictment of management—it's just a recognition of the capabilities of any individual human being.

An honest appraisal of institutional strengths and weaknesses, the type of evaluation that is a part of the process and product of a well-conceived internal communication program, is a necessary component of any management process. An organization's executives must deal with the concerns of stockholders, stakeholders, and employees and integrate them into their management plans. They must recognize the company's inherent production capacities and how they match their customers' emerging desires. Finally, they need to understand how changes in society itself, and its concern for the environment or civil rights or consumer affairs, may change the very expectations of the organization.

Internal communication should be a systematic forum for honest, open, two-way communication between an organization's internal publics and management. Because public relations interfaces with the institution and its important internal and external publics, it breaks down the walls isolating institutional officers from the concerns of workers and stockholders. That focus can expedite the flow of knowledge about new social trends into the management information process. Public relations can be the catalyst that brings these influences into focus.

INTERNAL COMMUNICATION FINDS AND SOLVES PROBLEMS

This discussion of internal communication is put first among the writing chapters because of its central position in any communication process founded on management-by-objective principles. That attention to the world outside the organization, oriented by the research discussed in Chapter 3, starts the process through which the institution discovers its identity, its institutional culture. Beginning with MBO planning and the persuasion platform, it can then communicate that sense of itself to employees, managers and stockholders.

Internal Communication in the MBO Planning Process

The foundation of the MBO process, and the first step in any management process, is to isolate organizational problems that need to be addressed. You'll remember that the first step of the persuasion platform is to find organizational problems that can be cured through communication.

This isn't necessarily the way the professional world operates. Many organizations simply write news releases and brochures or buy advertising time and call their activities a communication program. However, unless they know why they're spending money on those activities, it's most likely money wasted. Unless you know the audience and the attitudes you hope to change by communication, you'll be unable to justify your efforts or your costs.

Two-Way Communication Restarts the PR Cycle

Internal communication plans involve more than telling publics what the institution wants them to hear. It also means encouraging those publics to tell PR practitioners about their relationship to the organization. We use that information as a vital input for making business decisions, solving institutional problems and bringing the unique and valuable perspective of our employees and stockholders into management decisions.

For instance, if your organization is considering demolishing a group of historic vacant buildings it owns to build a new employee parking garage, it may seem to be only an economic and employee relations decision. After all, the buildings are a drain on your company's resources, and employees are always complaining about the lack of downtown parking. However, to the local historical society and the many organization stockholders who sympathize with their movement, those decrepit 100-year-old storefronts preserve the neighborhood's character and signal something important about the city's identity.

Sensitivity to those cultural currents is the unique contribution public relations practitioners can make to the input management needs for its decision-making process. A carefully conceived program of internal communication forces managers to confront the ramifications of their decisions before they are fought out on the front page of the city's newspapers.

The compromise reached in a situation similar to the one above led to the organization building a four-story parking garage behind the restored facades of the century-old buildings. This solution solved the company's economic and employee relations problems while enlisting the support of the community and the historical preservation group.

Citizen and governmental groups are increasingly interjecting themselves into what were formerly private business decisions. Because of that, it's become more important to explore the social, employee and public relations implications of all organizational decisions in management reports. Even if it is presenting information that management doesn't want to hear, such communication can save the organization time and money in the long run, and establishes the public relations person as a valuable member of the management team.

WRITING THAT HELPS LEADERS LEAD:
THE POSITION PAPER

Most of the internal management documents you'll be writing will be position papers. Whether it's an informal summation of the reasons to have an organization's picnic in the city park instead of at the lake outside town, or a recommendation about spending $1 million retooling a factory for a different product line, the position paper can be adapted to fit your purposes.

Position papers are relatively formal and structured documents that collect information and assess its impact on the organization. They serve an important function as institutions decide on policies for communication areas and in all other organization activities. A position paper, as the name implies, advocates a particular position, using research to support a decision the organization should make or has made. It's an advocacy document, and not only supports a particular decision, but also disputes the alternative courses of action.

Some organizations use multiple position papers in their management decision processes. Instead of assigning a comprehensive background report to one writer, management assigns a different writer or team to defend each side of an issue. After executives have a strongly argued response from each side, they make a decision. Once a decision has been made, the organization often adopts a final position paper for the issue, distributes it to interested parties and files it for future use.

There are frequent opportunities to use position papers in deciding on and then announcing organizational decisions, but don't limit the effect of your internal communication efforts by rigidly separating your internal and external communication programs. The information you collect and analyze to make and support internal decisions can also be employed effectively in an external communication program. For instance, if your plant has an accident, you'll find it valuable to be able to tell the press why you chose a particular manufacturing process or machine. If a citizen's group concerned about higher taxes attacks your nonprofit organization's proposed program that's being considered for public funding, having a position paper detailing a similar program's success in another city may save your appropriation. Now that a company's position on an issue can be stored in a computer file for easy retrieval, the ability to respond to consumer and media concerns is much more efficient.

A U.S. senator's office developed such a computerized system to keep up with the hundreds of constituent letters it receives each week. As a public issue gains attention the senator and his advisers draft a written position on the issue and store it in the computer. When a constituent writes asking about the senator's stand, the senator's position is retrieved from the computer file and integrated into a computer-generated "personal" letter to the voter. This method enables the senator to maintain an otherwise impossible volume of correspondence, and the voter receives a quick, specific answer to his or her question.

Some companies extend the uses of internal management documents beyond reacting to consumer and media requests. The advertisements that Mobil Oil Corp. has used to influence public policy (see Figure 8.1) are basically restructured position papers. A growing number of corporations are publicly communicating their viewpoints on important political and social issues through such paid "advertorials," which often start as internal position papers.

That's a demonstration of the power of internal communication. Formalizing the decision-making process leads managers to consider a much wider range of ramifications from their decisions. It establishes a procedure to deliver exact information on organizational policy to internal audiences so they are well informed and feel part of the team. Just as important, it provides a mechanism for dealing with public concerns about institutional issues. In the absence of prompt and well-considered information from the organization, those concerns could erupt into a firestorm of rumors and ill will.

Your Side and Their Side: Researching Position Papers

Position papers are meant to assist managers in making decisions and thus are structured to approximate an individual's decision process. Following is the format:

Position Paper

1. Position statement
2. Background and current situation
3. Positive implications of decisions
4. Negative implications of decisions
5. Recommendation

How big is BIG?

Bridge explains lead. →

△ identifies points
that support idea
stated in bridge. →

✓ shows repetition of "BIG": →
reinforces transitions
between supporting
arguments.

Call to action urges calm →
in face of big profit reports
and restates main thesis
in last sentence.

We've said, from time to time, that we make a lot of money. Even BIG money. But we have to.

Have you seen our investments? They, too, involve BIG money.

Here's what we mean:

△ To continue developing energy supplies around the world requires a lot of different projects in a lot of different places. In the U.S., for example, we're pumping heavy oil from the ground in California with state-of-the-art, environmentally sound technology we didn't have years ago. Today, these supplies are adding thousands of barrels of crude oil a day to America's production. But it took an investment of $400 million over the last three years to get us where we are today.

△ In the U.K., we'll be spending some $300 million as our share of a pipeline and processing facilities that will deliver gas from the North Sea to Scotland. And a major project offshore Nigeria to produce condensate will carry a $400-million price tag for Mobil.

Put those three projects from just one segment of our business together and the number adds up to $1.1 billion.

✓ That's BIG money.

Mobil operates, or has major interests in, 20 refineries around the world, turning out some 1.8 million barrels of products a day. We're not planning to build a new refinery, which would cost $2 billion or so to process 150,000 barrels of crude a day. But we have recently expanded or upgraded six of our refineries, with similar plans under way at five others. Total cost for these refinery programs—a "mere" $2.3 billion.

✓ We're talking BIG money.

△ The costs associated with pumping gasoline can also add up. Ever wonder what it costs to build a service station? They are bigger and better today than ever before. With your gasoline, you can get your morning newspaper, coffee and donuts, along with any other products you might want to purchase at the mini-mart. On average, today's stations are capable of pumping 2 million gallons of gasoline a year, and allow more customers to be served at one time. And a typical station, from the underground tanks to the hose at the end of the pump, generally runs well in excess of $1 million, mini-mart and land included.

△ Then there's the cost of doing all these things—finding and producing oil and gas and selling gasoline and other products—in an environmentally sound way. Let's add in the $315 million we spent last year in capital expenditures on anti-pollution requirements and other environmental activities.

✓ More BIG money.

We're not complaining. But, the next time you see those BIG numbers in our earnings statements, remember: The numbers are big because the business is big. And the capital investments to stay in that business are tremendous.

FIGURE 8.1 Advocacy advertising

The position paper starts with strong and comprehensive research. In the preliminary research, you'll usually be gathering a balanced selection of arguments that examine various sides of the issue, because you can't advocate a particular decision until you know why it's the best decision.

Your research should be based on the research process described in Chapter 3. To save time and limit your frustration, succinctly define the research area. If you're unsure about specific sources for your information, start with general sources such as encyclopedias and general interest periodicals. They'll often cite journal articles or specific research studies you can pursue for more detail.

Even though you need to define your research topic narrowly, you need to think expansively within that narrow subject. As a public relations practitioner, you are the bridge linking divisions, examining not just the financial or productivity implications of a decision but broader ramifications. Your education and your sensitivities should enable you to know and apply social science research to your problems. What public sentiments about your issue have the Harris or Gallup polls discovered? According to psychology or management journals, how have other organizations been affected when such decisions have been implemented? Are there cultural trends you need to integrate into your analysis? Do you need to do your own research using focus groups, employee questionnaires or telephone polls?

The strategy you follow depends on the type of organization for which you work and the importance of the document on which you're working. Sometimes the depth of your research and the documentation of your sources will be exhaustive, equaling the formal level of an academic research paper. At other times, when the stakes are lower, your research may be much more informal and unstructured.

In all cases, you are gathering information not only to prove your arguments, but to counter the well-meaning objections of those who don't agree with your position. Because you are the source of all the information your management will convey to workers, the media and the public, it's your responsibility to be both complete and fair in your search and presentation of relevant facts.

Creating a Working Document

Virtually all internal communication pieces are what I call "working documents." They are not meant to be read once and abandoned like a newspaper story. Instead they become important references for everyone, from the organization president making a presentation to the company's board of directors to the institution's switchboard operators who answer questions about the times and dates of organization events.

Because they are working documents, the information in them needs to be as accessible as possible for the people who use them. That means you need to structure the document so people can find the information they need.

So, instead of writing page after page of unbroken paragraphs, find ways to segment the information and label it to help readers find what they're looking for. The first step is to divide the document into different sections and identify each section with a subhead. This not only helps your audience but helps you structure the story logically and gather similar information within each subhead. You'll see what I propose in Figure 8.2. The same copy is presented with and without subheads in the

Communication   Consultants:
A   Quick   Study

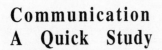

To New Associates:

 As a Communication Consultants associate, you're expected to ably represent the company in all your interactions with the public. We expect every person in the firm, from receptionist to board president, to know the company's philosophy, goals and capabilities. To that end, we've prepared this short guide to help you learn about the company.

Communication Consultants
Management solutions through
integrated communication

Box 4188
Louisville, KY 40204
(502) 584-1932

PHILOSOPHY - A HOME-TOWN EXPERT

 Communication Consultants concentrate on fund raising for non-profits in the greater Louisville area. Now, we don't have anything against the national fund raising consulting groups. But if you've been in Louisville any time at all, you know personal relationships are vital to accomplish anything. That's given the town a unique fund raising environment, where networking is a preeminent factor in fund raising.

OUR MARKETING QUESTIONS - DO YOU NEED RESEARCH ... OR RESEARCH AND SERVICE?

 Here are the questions we ask every potential client:
1) Wouldn't your firm rather have your research done by someone who knows the corporate, personal and family interrelationships that permeate the fund raising climate?
2) Wouldn't your firm feel more comfortable if you had something more than a stack of paper to help you as you execute a national consulting group's 20-page fund raising plan?
3) Wouldn't it be nice to have a home-town expert on which your firm can call as you gear up your board for the fund raising push, prepare your solicitation materials and design a media relations campaign and special event schedule to support your development efforts?

That's what Communication Consultants offers its clients. We'll not only provide the specialized services they need to conceptualize their organization's fund raising efforts, but will help see them through to a successful completion.

CAPABILITIES - FUND RAISING IN AN INTEGRATED COMMUNICATION CAMPAIGN

Development Services -fund raising success means planning and research
 Our firm doesn't believe it's possible to plug the outlines of a fund raising plan that worked in Chicago or Cleveland into Louisville's unique corporate, political and social culture. We start our work with strategic studies of our client's organization to establish discrete and well-focused institutional goals they want to reach.

(continued)

FIGURE 8.2 Subheads make prose more readable

We then examine, through focus group studies, interviews and other research, the community's perception of the client's organization and its possible support of their goals. With that information, as well as our extensive and successful experience in local capital and general fund raising campaigns, our firm uses computer data-bases and other means to identify the most cost-effective target audiences for their fund raising appeals -- the local and national corporations, foundations and individuals who are the best prospects for major gifts -- and guide our clients in writing the grants and proposals to reach them.

We develop long-term plans to integrate annual, planned and memorial giving into their fund raising campaign. And we can help them plan and develop cost-effective direct mail and telemarketing plans to identify and gain the support of small-gift donors that might be developed into long-term funding sources for our client's organization.

Management Consulting - fund raising starts with a strong organization

Communication Consultants has an integrated approach to an institution's management. We don't believe a development campaign is a separate, isolated task that can be conducted irrespective of what is happening elsewhere within the organization. Instead, we at CC think development activities need to be an integral expression of the organization's management philosophy. Our firm's partners have broad experience in board development and have conducted many communication campaigns for non-profit associations. It's this systematic management philosophy, integrating basic financial and management tactics to communication campaigns, that makes Communication Consultants different.

Media Relations - gaining the media's support for development efforts

We back up these efforts with an integrated public relations campaign that gives our client's fund raising effort its best chance of success. Communication Consultants has an excellent track record with national and local media, and the firm's innovative step of targeting news releases and media is a method for communicating specific information to key publics that prompt them to action.

Special Events - injecting excitement into fund raising

Carefully planned special events can be intensely valuable in strengthening the commitment and shared goals of individuals already within the organization and can prompt valuable media coverage and increased awareness that leads to broader community involvement. Our firm's partners have had extensive experience is planning, budgeting, designing and supervising all forms of special events, from fund raising dinners and concerts to press conferences and media events.

SUMMARY - A UNIQUE PERSPECTIVE FOR A UNIQUE COMMUNITY

At Communication Consultants, we believe our integrated communication management philosophy, our broad experience in public relations and development areas and our knowledge of Louisville's unique corporate, political and social culture makes our firm extremely qualified to prepare an organization's strategic plan, identify donors and implement a comprehensive public relations and development operation.

It's a set of skills and knowledge that make us unique in our area and help the support and commitment of important publics in the Louisville area.

FIGURE 8.2 (continued)

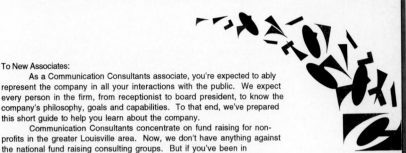

To New Associates:

As a Communication Consultants associate, you're expected to ably represent the company in all your interactions with the public. We expect every person in the firm, from receptionist to board president, to know the company's philosophy, goals and capabilities. To that end, we've prepared this short guide to help you learn about the company.

Communication Consultants concentrate on fund raising for non-profits in the greater Louisville area. Now, we don't have anything against the national fund raising consulting groups. But if you've been in Louisville any time at all, you know personal relationships are vital to accomplish anything. That's given the town a unique fund raising environment, where networking is a preeminent factor in fund raising.

Here are the questions we ask every potential client: 1) Wouldn't your firm rather have your research done by someone who knows the corporate, personal and family interrelationships that permeate the fund raising climate? 2) Wouldn't your firm feel more comfortable if you had something more than a stack of paper to help you as you execute a national consulting group's 20-page fund raising plan? 3) Wouldn't it be nice to have a home-town expert on which your firm can call as you gear up your board for the fund raising push, prepare your solicitation materials and design a media relations campaign and special event schedule to support your development efforts?

That's what Communication Consultants offers its clients. We'll not only provide the specialized services they need to conceptualize their organization's fund raising efforts, but will help see them through to a successful completion.

Our firm doesn't believe it's possible to plug the outlines of a fund raising plan that worked in Chicago or Cleveland into Louisville's unique corporate, political and social culture. We start our work with strategic studies of our client's organization to establish discrete and well-focused institutional goals they want to reach.

We then examine, through focus group studies, interviews and other research, the community's perception of the client's organization and its possible support of their goals. With that information, as well as our extensive and successful experience in local capital and general fund raising campaigns, our firm uses computer data-bases and other means to identify the most cost-effective target audiences for their fund raising appeals -- the local and national corporations, foundations and individuals who are the best prospects for major gifts -- and guide our clients in writing the grants and proposals to reach them.

We develop long-term plans to integrate annual, planned and memorial giving into their fund raising campaign. And we can help them plan and develop cost-effective direct mail and telemarketing plans to identify and gain the support of small-gift donors that might be developed into long-term funding sources for our client's organization.

Communication Consultants has an integrated approach to an institution's management. We don't believe a development campaign is a separate, isolated task that can be conducted irrespective of what is happening elsewhere within the organization. Instead, we at CC think development activities need to be an integral expression of the organization's management philosophy. Our firm's partners have broad experience in board development and have conducted many communication campaigns for non-profit associations. It's this systematic management philosophy, integrating basic financial and management tactics to communication campaigns, that makes Communication Consultants different.

We back up these efforts with an integrated public relations campaign that gives our

Communication Consultants
*Management solutions through
integrated communication*

*Box 4188
Louisville, KY 40204
(502) 584-1932*

FIGURE 8.2 (continued)

client's fund raising effort its best chance of success. Communication Consultants has an excellent track record with national and local media, and the firm's innovative step of targeting news releases and media is a method for communicating specific information to key publics that prompt them to action.

Carefully planned special events can be intensely valuable in strengthening the commitment and shared goals of individuals already within the organization and can prompt valuable media coverage and increased awareness that leads to broader community involvement. Our firm's partners have had extensive experience is planning, budgeting, designing and supervising all forms of special events, from fund raising dinners and concerts to press conferences and media events.

At Communication Consultants, we believe our integrated communication management philosophy, our broad experience in public relations and development areas and our knowledge of Louisville's unique corporate, political and social culture makes our firm extremely qualified to prepare an organization's strategic plan, identify donors and implement a comprehensive public relations and development operation.

It's a set of skills and knowledge that make us unique in our area and help the support and commitment of important publics in the Louisville area.

FIGURE 8.2   (continued)

figure. Notice how including frequent subheads makes the text less formidable to read. In addition, the reader who scans nothing more than the subheads gets an outline of the main points the report is presenting.

Within each section of a document, consider marking important argument points by underlining or boldfacing the copy. Identify reasons justifying your argument with asterisks or bullets that help show the weight of evidence backing up your point of view. Remember to keep paragraphs and sentences short to aid comprehension.

Don't hesitate to use an alternative presentation for statistics and other data. Narrative prose (such as what you're reading here) isn't the optimum way to relate numbers, especially those that you're asking your audience to compare with other numbers. A much better way is to place that statistical information in tables, or better yet, in charts or graphs. Remember that your value as a writer is ultimately whether you communicate well—and one of the strengths of a professional writer is to know when writing isn't the best way to convey information. Memory Memo 8.2 reminds you of some of those tactics.

Memory Memo 8.2
Converting text into a "working document":

- Divide the text into distinct sections; label with frequent subheads.
- Use graphic elements like bullets or underlining to define important points.
- Convert complicated information into tables or graphs where appropriate.
- Simplify: Keep sentences and paragraphs short and vocabulary appropriate for the audience.

In addition to structuring the document to make it easy to use, remember to utilize your prose and vocabulary to gain the same result. In too many position papers and annual stockholder reports, writers forget their purpose is to communicate important information to their audience. Too often, they write in a way that's intended to impress rather than communicate.

Always remember to target your writing style to your audience. If it is comprised exclusively of technical people, technical language is just fine, but if you're dealing with the nonspecialist public, use language they can understand. Although there are a few instances in which complex vocabulary can be appropriate for a particular audience, there are even fewer in which complex sentences are necessary. They don't add to comprehension. Whether you're communicating to high school dropouts or doctoral graduates, long sentences aren't impressive if people can't understand them. Your duty is not to your ego, but to your audience.

Writing Position Papers

The Position Statement: What Should the Organization Do?   The start of a position paper states a management decision you think your research justifies. It's like the lead statement in an inverted pyramid. It is one simple, declarative sentence that informs your audience immediately of the conclusion you will attempt to prove with the document.

Background and Current Situation: How Did We Get Here?   A position paper's second section should provide a fairly complete historical portrait of the issue so that even those readers unfamiliar with the topic can understand how the current situation came to be. The background section describes the economic, social, political and, if necessary, the scientific history of an issue. It also includes past company policies and decisions relating to the subject. The current situation details why those factors lead to the need to take action today.

As in all writing, you organize your prose so your readers can logically process and understand the information. In the background section, that structure will usually be chronological, tracing the issue's development. An appropriate structure for the current-situation section is more problematic. However, order of importance (discussed in Chapter 6) is the likely choice.

That need to organize the document logically is true at the sentence level, too. Just because you're researching technical journals, academic reports, and business writing doesn't mean you need to mimic their prose. Simply because scientists, historians and other experts have certain talents in their individual fields, they don't necessarily know how to write. You do.

Instead of blindly copying their vocabulary, their sentence structures and their organizational patterns, think of your audience. It's a challenge to take an expert's technical article and transform it into prose and presentations your readers can comprehend. If necessary, shorten their sentences and reorder their paragraphs. Translate the expert's jargon into language your audience can understand. Convert statistics into charts or graphs. As I've suggested before, segment and identify the information with subheads, boldface, bullets and underlining. Your goal is efficient communication to your audience through fidelity to the experts' ideas, not loyalty to their prose.

Benefits: Why Should We Listen to You?   Once you've established the problem, your task is to justify why the actions you've put forth in your position statement will help the organization. As you present the various arguments, use a structure that makes it easy for readers to comprehend your reasoning and to follow the
logic of your decisions. As you move through your thought process and writing
process, order your conclusions and justifications for those conclusions so your readers can logically process them. First, group all the reasons that support your position in the benefits section, and summarize all the possible arguments against taking this action in the later consequences section.

To find an internal logic for the information you're presenting, you'll need to
choose among the position-evidence sequences discussed in Chapter 6. Depending
on the proof you're presenting, different argumentation patterns will be effective.
Generally, however, you'll build a structure similar to the following example, in
which the writer states a positive benefit, then presents the evidence that leads him
or her to that conclusion.

Preserving Mountain Music

The increased public attention to mountain music in our region may
help preserve the art form. Because area young people have less and
less exposure to mountain music, it is in danger of being lost as a living art. WMMT's ability to transmit mountain music into its traditional
home may prove the impetus for youngsters to imitate, preserve and
develop the art.

As in all other presentations, you must keep related reasons and evidence
grouped together and show with transitions how one piece of evidence is related
to the next. Following these few guidelines will help establish a unifying format
and an internal logic that will make your arguments appear stronger. They will
also help establish a flow that will encourage your audience to read the entire
document.

Consequences: What Bad Things Might Happen?   A position paper attempts
to justify a particular decision, but that doesn't mean you can or should ignore evidence that supports alternative decisions. In addition to giving strong reasons to
adopt the position you suggest, you should present and then argue against the evidence supporting alternatives. As both you and your management will be expected
to answer these objections when they are voiced by the press or the public, you
should prepare for those confrontations by presenting all the arguments completely,
both pro and con.

That makes it imperative that you not only play devil's advocate by stating what
bad things might happen if you adopt your position, but also present a counterar-

gument that will be effective in justifying the risk you're asking the organization to take. Here's an example of that argument sequence:

Tired Volunteers

As part of the agreement with the agency, WMMT has agreed to more than double its broadcast hours each week. That vastly increased broadcast time may strain our relationships with our disc jockeys, all of whom are volunteers. However, we expect the broader anticipated audience will also stimulate more volunteers to staff the station's expanded transmitting times.

Recommendation: What Do We Do Now?   As in all persuasive writing, the final section of a position paper asks readers to take an action. In a position paper, where you are arguing for a specific decision, you'll conclude by summarizing the rationale you've already presented in the body copy. You're summarizing why those reasons make your conclusion the right one. The summary should be only a few sentences long.

You're also asking for action in the recommendation. You'll propose certain actions for management to take toward implementing your conclusion, such as approving new worker training courses, authorizing a full-fledged feasibility study or adopting a new program.

Of course, an approved position paper usually leads to a persuasion platform plan that establishes a formal list of activities, a timetable for their completion and an evaluation system to see if the project was a success. It's a continual process that stimulates other position papers that begin the sequence again.

Effective position papers are the first step in this ongoing process. They compel organization leaders to confront all important ramifications of their decisions. Equally important, they place public relations practitioners at the center of many management decisions, bringing them into the management team and introducing their heightened sensitivity to social, environmental and other public opinion considerations. Memory Memo 8.3 provides a checklist for creating position papers.

Memory Memo 8.3
Checklist for writing the position paper

- Position statement should be one sentence that explicitly states the action you want institution to take and the main persuader for taking that action.
- Background should provide enough history to establish a need for action and let readers evaluate effectiveness of your recommendation.
- Benefits section should group like information, establish benefit for the institution and present evidence to justify that conclusion.
- Consequences section should demonstrate what could go wrong if institution took recommended action, then present counterargument stating way institution could overcome that problem.
- Recommendation should advise administrators of initial actions to implement the plan.

TELLING THE FACTS AND DISCOVERING
A PHILOSOPHY: THE ANNUAL REPORT

The annual report, a statement that tells investors and others about the organization's current financial condition and its performance during the past year, came into being because of a legal requirement. Publicly held corporations must truthfully report to stockholders information about the organization that will affect whether they decide to become or remain stockholders in the organization.

This is an important communication task. We are asking stockholders and stakeholders to make an investment in the organization, not just with their stock purchases, but as customers, contributors, supporters and friends in times of crisis. For well-run companies, the information in an annual report builds confidence among investors, analysts, and the financial press in the organization's prospects as well as confidence that the institution's management decisions will sustain that growth. When confidence is high, stocks are worth more and borrowing costs less.

Many nonprofit groups have voluntarily adopted annual reports to communicate to their important publics, too. For well-run nonprofits and associations, an annual report can build trust that its publics' contributions are being spent wisely and the problems and priorities the organizations have identified are still important. In both cases, this important public confidence is built on the candid communication of triumphs and the rewards they've brought, as well as problems and the way the organization plans to solve them.

Creating Company Value from a Company's
Biggest Communication Expense

The candidness and clarity that contribute to this confidence are sometimes in short supply in institutional reports. Sometimes reports reflect a false, pompous dignity so that an institutional officer can feel more important. At other times, the tendency to obfuscate is simply meant to cover up bad news. In either case it detracts from the objective of internal communication, which is to offer important information to insiders so they will place their loyalty, commitment, talents and, in the case of investors, their cash in the service of the organization.

That task is defeated when an institutional report reads like this:

Under certain circumstances, such as when there has been a change in the amount of dividend payout or a fundamental change in investment policies, it might be appropriate to annualize the dividends paid over the period such policies were in effect, rather than using the dividends during the past twelve months, although the current distribution rate may differ from the current yield computation for a variety of reasons. Average annual total return reflects the hypothetical annually compounded return that would have produced the same total return if the Company's performance had been constant over the entire period.

This would merely be poorly written copy except for one thing: For most companies, the institutional report is its most expensive and expansive communication effort during the entire year. American companies spend over $200 million a year on annual reports, and the per-copy price of some institutional reports can be more than $10. Compared to other public relations efforts during the year, that is a massive expenditure. Since corporations are spending investor funds to produce these expensive reports, an ineffective report tends to throw the judgment of the corporation's executives into doubt.

For certain institutions, however, the annual report has become a means for CEOs and public relations managers to develop and communicate a strong organizational identity—in effect, to determine why the organization exists. They answer the questions: How do the corporation's activities contribute to its stockholders' economic well-being? How does the institution contribute to its community's economic and social growth? How does the organization's product or service show its concern for the public's needs and safety? How do its policies indicate a commitment to the environment and other social concerns?

Out of that formative communication audit comes an institutional philosophy that not only informs and directs the annual report but serves to guide all the corporation's communication efforts. That's the proper use of the massive resources that go into producing an institutional report. With that guiding philosophy you can use the power of communication to integrate the talents of managers, employees and contributors or stockholders into a unified organizational vision. That task, which I'll discuss in the next section, is encapsulated in Memory Memo 8.4.

> **Memory Memo 8.4**
> **Checklist for writing the annual report**
>
> - Obtain necessary approvals from administrators, lawyers, accountants.
> - Develop and carry out central theme throughout report.
> - Translate all information into vocabulary or graphics audience can understand easily.
> - Employ working document strategies to make information more usable.

Getting Everybody on Board: Researching the Annual Report

The annual report is one of the few collaborative writing efforts many public relations people perform. Because legal regulations dictate some information that has to be included, the organization's lawyers are intimately involved in preparing the corporate report. Since most reports include a letter from the chief executive officer, he or she is usually involved. Extensive financial information is a major portion of any annual report, which means the organization's accountants and economists are part of the collaboration. Because it is the focus of the organization's formal and legal reporting, the report usually has to be approved by managers all through the institution. Adding photographers, graphic designers and other production people brings a multitude of voices into the creative process.

It's usually the public relations person's responsibility to keep the production process timely and efficient. Above all, it's the practitioner's responsibility that there emerge from this gauntlet of legal, economic and management specialists a coherent, readable report that's appropriate for its audience.

A word of encouragement and advice is in order. While a lawyer's expertise is the law, and an accountant's is finances, the public relations person's profession is communication. Thus, although the PR person should yield to the lawyer and accountant in their areas of expertise to guarantee accuracy, the PR practitioner's counsel should be final on elements of prose style and presentation.

Writing the institutional report starts with research. What has your organization done well in the past year? Have certain product lines or services been particularly successful? How will you exploit those opportunities?

Just as important, what weaknesses does the organization have? Are there diminishing markets, protesting advocacy groups, diminishing resources or labor unrest with which your organization will have to contend in the future? What are your organization's responses to those concerns?

Once you've done your internal research, you can turn your attention to your audience. As in all public relations writing, receiver-centered principles should dominate your writing process. What do you know about the investors who will read your report? Are they rich or middle class, old or young? Are a substantial number employees of the organization? From those questions, you'll be able to determine how your needs to communicate coincide with your audience's need to know. You'll notice that many of these questions will be answered with your persuasion platform.

It's important to assess past efforts, too. How well did last year's report satisfy those communication needs? Will a different presentation help communicate the issues to your important publics?

Discovering the Tale the Numbers Tell: Developing an Objective and a Theme

Out of this research and contemplation will emerge a communication objective for the new report. Within an overall goal of wanting stockholders to buy more stock are some meaningful questions that will point you toward a realistic communication objective.

Do you want to show how your organization dealt with problems that caused a drop in earnings or contributions last year? Do you want to show how savvy managers anticipated the business or social environment and beat the competition to the market with an outstanding new product or service? Do you want to show how the organization dealt with a damaging takeover bid? Do you want to answer the criticism of an environmental group? Do you want to detail changes that have made a contentious labor environment more workable?

Once you've established your communication objective, you can begin thinking about producing a new report. The challenge of writing an annual report is to maintain the reader's interest and the report's coherence as you move through a thicket of information, much of which is legally mandated. Among the elements either required or expected in an institutional report are:

- financial summary
- letter from the chief executive officer
- institutional description
- narrative section describing operations
- balance sheet and income statement
- statement of sources and use of funds
- notes to financial statement
- auditor's statement
- 10-year statistical summary

The report may also include the organization's history, a discussion of organization policies, request for support of the organization's stance on a political issue, results of any stockholder surveys, and other reports.

To help the reader move through this mass of information, it's often advisable to decide on a theme to anchor all the annual report's sections. Often this theme springs directly from the communication objective you developed earlier. At other times, you might integrate that communication objective in a unifying message. Has there been or will there be a significant anniversary for your organization? Has your organization reached some major milestone in terms of production, ranking within the industry or sales? Has it made a major commitment to a new product line or added a new division that looks as if it will change the direction of the organization? You'll see an example of a unifying theme driving graphics and text in the annual report shown in Figure 8.3. It shows the way one organization integrated a light-hearted concept to unify its annual report and establish an affirming self-image among its donors and supporters in the community.

You can use any of these elements to bring unity to the report, announcing the theme on the cover, more fully introducing it in the CEO's letter, then detailing it in words in the narrative report and showing it graphically and numerically in the financial section.

Although a major proportion of the institutional report will be devoted to charts and numbers showing the organization's financial progress, the public relations writer generally has direct responsibility for two sections, the CEO's letter and the narrative report.

Showing a Human in Control: Writing the CEO's Letter

The CEO's letter sometimes is initiated by the president, who writes the letter, then passes it to the PR writer for review and suggestions. In other organizations, after interviewing the CEO, the writer composes the letter, then sends it back to the CEO for his or her approval.

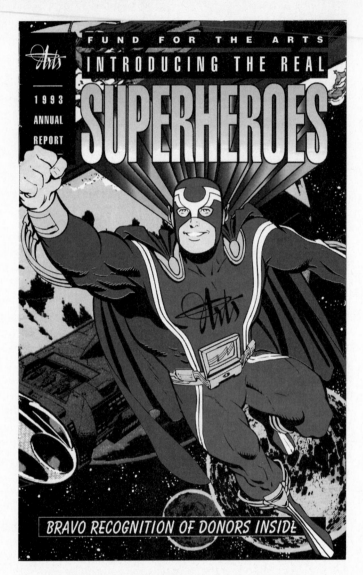

FIGURE 8.3 A unifying theme in an annual report
Used with permission of Greater Louisville Fund for the Arts

The subjects discussed in an executive letter vary from organization to organization, but don't dwell on detailed financial data or the minute areas of management within the organization. Those will be covered in depth in the financial report. Concentrate instead, as your CEO should, on the overall factors of planning for the organization's success. What does he or she think was the organization's greatest success of the past year? What is going to have to change to put the organization in the most

his past year was one which took the heroic efforts of all of us working together to ensure that the Fund for the Arts would truly be Too Big To Ignore. It was a challenging year, in which some companies combined their forces with mergers, while others divided their resources to become new entities. It was a year in which our area continued to combat some very real economic trends in funding for the arts. Your support of the Fund for the Arts continued to bring greater returns, as we added a new agency, with Music Theatre Louisville officially becoming a member on July 1, 1993.

Being successful took the commitment and participation of our entire community. Contributions from individuals were the cornerstone of our campaign, as businesses and employees joined together to show their support for the quality and quantity of arts in our area.

Our regional campaigns grew by leaps and bounds last year. Partnership campaigns in Southern Indiana, Shelby, Oldham and Hardin Counties brought over $160,400 to the campaign. We began implementing our strategic plan, Vision 2000, by extending access to Fund member groups through touring and residency programs and by providing grants and technical support to local exemplary programming. The beauty of these partnerships was that we were able to extend the reach of the Fund campaign through targeted support...

Support for projects like Hardin County's Arts Fair on the Square and Pops in the Park, Shelby County Community Theatre's performances, and Floyd and Clark Counties' Arts Councils in Southern Indiana. In addition, we provided transportation assistance to bring school children from each of the counties to a variety of performances and activities throughout the year.

The Fund for the Arts continues to take a leadership role not only locally, but nationally and internationally, as well. One example of this was the fact that we were selected to bring our message and tradition of arts support to a major international conference in Nagoya, Japan and then were selected by the National Arts Council of Singapore to present an overview of our Fund's success story. Representatives from cities all over the world look to us as a model for community support of

the arts. They are in awe of the fact that the economic impact of the Fund and its agencies exceeds $70 million annually. They want to know how the Fund creates a campaign that supports programs attended by over 350,000 school children annually. And they are amazed by the fact that Fund member agencies sponsored 1,600 downtown event nights; thus supporting not only the arts groups, but ancillary businesses like hotels, restaurants and print shops, as well.

Each year's successful campaign provides us with the incentive for developing an even more creative, innovative campaign for the following year. As the 1994 Campaign year begins, we know that only through out-of-this-world superhero efforts will we be able to maintain the high standard that each of us has come to expect from the Fund and our member agencies. We invite you to stay tuned for ways in which you can join us in our quest to ensure that the arts in our community inspire and enrich the lives of us all.

Bertram W. Klein
1993 Chairman of the Board

Stephen T. Bow
1993 Campaign Chairman

Allan Cowen
President

FIGURE 8.3 (continued)

THE CAMPAIGN

At the beginning of the 1993 Campaign year we asked what King Kong, Godzilla, John Wayne and Elvis all had in common with the Fund for the Arts. As the campaign progressed, we found that it took the heroic efforts of great campaign leaders to make the answer to that question a reality, and we've certainly had our share of larger-than-life heroes during this campaign.

Our heroes were people like County Judge/Executive David Armstrong, Mayor Jerry Abramson, and the Board of Aldermen. They were companies like Blue Cross Blue Shield of Kentucky, Philip Morris USA, Brown-Forman Corporation, Jewish Hospital HealthCare Services, and South Central Bell. They were old friends like Humana Inc., and Liberty National Bank and old friends with new names like PNC Bank, Galen Health Care, Inc. and National City Bank. They were innovators like Louisville Gas & Electric Company and IBEW Local #2100 whose efforts in working as a team on last year's campaign have become a model for the future. And they were the campaign's real superheroes, like 1993 Campaign Chairman Stephen Bow and his army of volunteers, who made a lasting impression on the arts in our community by leading the Fund campaign to a victorious year. Despite all the odds, Bow and his forces rallied to produce a record-breaking $4,583,375.00, a 5% increase, for the Fund for the Arts campaign. So BRAVO to the campaign leaders and their results which played such key roles in ensuring that the 1993 Fund for the Arts Campaign was, indeed, Too Big To Ignore.

AMAZING 100 CAMPAIGN
The Amazing 100 Campaign Division includes the Fund's leading major donor groups.

Campaign Chairman:
Stephen T. Bow,
Blue Cross Blue Shield of Kentucky

Campaign Division Facts:
Amount Raised: $1,749,395
# of Donors: 122

INDIVIDUALS CAMPAIGN DIVISION
The Individuals Campaign Division includes the Boards, BRAVO and Encore Divisions whose campaigns take place at the beginning of the campaign year. Their consistent performance laid the foundation for the success of the campaign year.

Campaign Chairman:
John P. Knight, Jr.,
Liberty National Bank & Trust Company

Campaign Division Facts:
Amount Raised: $497,749
# of Donors: 1,280

Boards Campaign Division
The Boards Campaign Division, which includes all board members of the Fund for the Arts' member agencies, was the first campaign to kick-off the 1993 campaign season.

Campaign Chairperson:
Mary Michael Steele

Campaign Division Facts:
Amount Raised: $131,418
# of Donors: 444
% of Goal: 100.5%

Bravo Campaign Division
The Bravo Campaign Division provides the traditional base for the Fund for the Arts campaign. It includes Fund for the Arts board members and other individual donors who generally contribute $500 and above. Volunteers for this division are Fund for the Arts board members.

Campaign Chairman:
Philip M. Lanier,
Middleton and Reutlinger

Campaign Division Facts:
Amount Raised: $209,527
# of Donors: 221
% of Goal: 102%

Encore Campaign Division
The goal of the Encore Campaign Division is to extend the Fund campaign to include individuals not included in the employee campaigns. The Encore Division, which includes donors contributing between $100 and $499, targets donors by demographics, prior giving history and personal contact with donors.

Campaign Chairpersons:
Martha Dunbar
Dixie Rounsavall
Rhonda Goodall
Woo Speed Meyers
Debbie Holloway

Campaign Division Facts:
Amount Raised: $96,561
# of Donors: 616
# of New Donors: 48

THE FUND FOR THE ARTS' SUPERHEROES SOARED HIGH IN SUPPORT IN 1993.

The Fund for the Arts is now the second highest in the nation in dollars raised from workplace giving campaigns.

Fund for the Arts Giving History 1980-1993

MILLIONS

5 4 3 2 1 0

80 81 82 83 84 85 86 87 88 89 90 91 92 93

The Fund for the Arts rates third in the nation in total dollars raised from individuals.

BUSINESS CAMPAIGN DIVISION
The Business Campaign Division involved hundreds of volunteers from the area's leading business community. Their efforts resulted in eighty-two new donors who contributed a total of over $13,500.

Campaign Chairman:
Ronald Murphy, PNC Bank

Campaign Division Facts:
Amount Raised: $154,429
# of Donors: 408
# of New Donors: 82

PREMIERE CAMPAIGN DIVISION
This new division took on the task of raising $100,000 primarily from donors new to the Fund campaign.

Campaign Chairman:
Tom Schifano,
Blue Cross Blue Shield of Kentucky

Campaign Division Facts:
Amount Raised: $129,475
# of Donors: 26
% of Goal: 129%

EMPLOYEE CAMPAIGN DIVISION
This year the Fund for the Arts conducted nearly 160 workplace giving campaigns, resulting in fourteen new campaigns. Fifty campaigns raised 10% or more than they had in 1992, with fifteen companies contributing more than $50,000.

Campaign Division Facts:
Amount Raised: $1,881,665
# of Donors: 26,684
% Increase: 5.23%

REGIONAL CAMPAIGNS DIVISION
The basic strategies in conducting regional campaigns in Southern Indiana, Shelby, Oldham and Hardin Counties included the following:

- Increasing support for the Fund for the Arts' member groups.
- Extending access to Fund member groups through touring and residency programs.
- Providing grants and technical support to local exemplary programming.

Campaign Chairman:
W. Fred Hale,
PNC Bank, Indiana

Campaign Division Facts:
Amount Raised: $160,446
# of Donors: 1,570
# of Employee Campaigns: 41
# of Corporate Donors: 152

FIGURE 8.3 (continued)

profitable position? What shadows are on the horizon portending success or failure? And what are your CEO's plans to exploit those opportunities and avoid those failures?

In short, the letter should be visionary, conveying your executive's intelligence, commitments and passions concerning the organization. There will be plenty of pages of dry statistical presentations totally without your help. The letter should introduce a human being and establish a personality that guides the organization's decisions. Figure 8.4 (on pp. 236–237) compares two letters from the same bank's annual reports for two years to see how it's possible to draw the chief executive's personality into the CEO letter. The letter from 1987, with its tabular recitation of financial information, does not capitalize on an opportunity to calm the fears of stockholders about the emerging problems in the nation's banking institutions. The 1990 CEO letter, by comparison, shows stockholders and potential investors the bank's savvy management decisions in the face of an uncertain economic environment. It's this personal involvement that we need to showcase and exploit in letters.

So, as much as you are able to guide the CEO's writing, try to reveal his or her personality by using direct, forceful language, personal references and even anecdotes. Integrate the annual report's theme into the writing as well.

The CEO's letter is a truly collaborative effort. It can't be you revealing your personality. It must be you drawing out your executive's personality and revealing it through writing. You may want to refer to the speech section on person-to-person writing. The techniques for capturing personality in language are much the same. It's sometimes a frustrating period of schooling for your CEO but often it is a valuable first step toward the organization locking on its institutional image. If it leads to that, it's been a very valuable exercise.

The Story Inside Your Organization: Writing the Narrative

The narrative is the other area in which the PR writer will be directly involved. The narrative serves many purposes. For potential stockholders it describes the organization, its products or services and its related activities. For financial analysts and current stockholders it reports the results of the previous year and plans for the future. It also serves as a statement of record, discussing the major management decisions, sales, mergers and even the social conditions that affected the organization. It should be forward-looking, too, detailing prospects for expansion into new markets and new products.

Again, recognize the institutional report as a motivator for candid appraisal and hard decisions within the organization. The narrative, with an army of financial analysts and thousands of anxious investors poring over it, is not the place to invent a glowing tale of success when the organization has major problems.

The narrative should discuss the problems as well as triumphs the organization confronts now or may face in the future. Is a major union agreement coming to an end? Are the natural resources your organization depends on to make your product running low? Has a major division shown weak earnings because of foreign competition? Has a scandal in your fund-raising unit caused contributions to drop?

Those are valid questions for the organization's stockholders and stakeholders to ask. The thought of publicly airing those problems should motivate both you and your executives to formulate some good answers. Let the process of creating the institutional report aid in that process of self-analysis and decision making.

FIGURE 8.4   A comparison of CEO letters
Used with permission of Mark Twain Banks

To the Shareholders of Mark Twain Bancshares, Inc.

Nineteen eighty-seven was an historic year for Mark Twain Bancshares.

It was a period of unprecedented growth and profitability. Our assets exceeded $1.6 billion, and our corporation posted record earnings for the fifth consecutive year.

At Mark Twain, 1987 witnessed:

- record earnings of $10.4 million, an 18% increase over 1986 results
- record levels in every major balance sheet category: total assets increased 11%, total deposits 12%, and net loans 14%
- a 9% increase in the common stock dividend
- a three-for-two common stock split
- the acquisition of Bankers Trust Company of Belleville, Illinois, now Mark Twain Belleville Bank
- the acquisition of Edwardsville National Bank and Trust Company of Edwardsville, Illinois, now Mark Twain Edwardsville Bank
- the acquistion of Accredited Premium Acceptance Corporation of St. Louis, an insurance-premium finance company
- $15 million long-term debt refinancing, saving $1 million a year for the next seven years
- $15 million in convertible debt (equity contract notes) issued to assist in acquisitions

Your management has spent considerable time in planning for 1988 and beyond. We expect 1988 to be a year of again record earnings, continued growth—internally and by acquisitions—and ever increasing products and services for our customers.

Our rapidly changing industry is creating many opportunities. We intend to take advantage of these challenges and continue to enhance shareholders' value.

John Dubinsky
President and Chief Executive Officer

Alvin Siteman
Chairman of the Board

*To
Our
Shareholders*

Nineteen hundred and ninety was a challenging year for the banking industry. Most financial services companies directly or indirectly experienced the effects of the Savings & Loan crisis, major bank failures, FDIC insurance increases and a softening in the economy. Many banks that had previously been considered top performers experienced significant declines in both their earnings and their stock price. Despite the forces that influenced the market in 1990, we are pleased to report that the performance of Mark Twain Bancshares, Inc. remained strong.

Mark Twain earned $16.099 million in 1990, comparable to the $16.156 million earned in 1989. Fully diluted earnings per share reached a record $1.96. Return on shareholders' equity was 14.37%, which was higher than any of Mark Twain's major competitors in Missouri. Loan charge-offs were consistent with historically low levels, and non-performing assets declined from 1989 levels. While we are proud of these achievements given the difficult environment, Mark Twain is challenged to produce even better results in the future.

By sustaining the sound performance of the Company's basic banking business and expanding the capabilities of related fee businesses, Mark Twain has built the foundation for continued growth in earnings. During 1990, Mark Twain's banking businesses grew earning assets by an average of 9.0%. This was achieved in a weaker economy and with no deterioration of asset quality. Mark Twain's related fee businesses - Capital Markets, Trust, Mortgage and International - continued to produce double-digit increases in revenues. Consolidated revenues for the divisions were up 34.2% for the year and have been growing at a five-year compound rate of more than 22%. Mark Twain believes that these growth trends will continue in the future and that they will translate into higher earnings for the Company and solid returns for Mark Twain shareholders.

The problems that plagued the entire banking industry in 1990 severely pressured bank stock prices throughout the year. While price declines were warranted in some cases, other companies like Mark Twain were impacted by

being a participant in the industry. In Mark Twain's third quarter 1990 report, we stressed that in time, banks with strong records of performance should be differentiated from weaker institutions. We stated that this differentiation could initiate an appreciation in stock price. During the first ten weeks of 1991, the price of Mark Twain stock has in fact risen substantially. We maintain that Mark Twain's ongoing superior performance will continue to separate the Company from weaker institutions and increase shareholders' value.

John P. Dubinsky
President and
Chief Executive Officer

Alvin J. Siteman
Chairman

FIGURE 8.4   (continued)

Although the narrative won't be as personal as the CEO's letter, even here there is no need to obscure your meaning behind a wall of huge words and massive sentences. The report is intended to help inform stockholders—people like your parents and grandparents (and maybe even you)—who own stock in an organization. Stockholders are generally not accountants and engineers, but that financial background and technical expertise seem to be expected, judging from the vocabulary and prose style of many institutional reports.

The report's overall structure should make the information accessible. As when writing a backgrounder or position paper, structure the document so your readers can find the information they want. Provide a table of contents and use graphic and organizational elements like subheads, bullets and label tabs to identify topics in the report.

You may even want to segment the institutional report for your different audiences, providing a short summary of all relevant financial information for the casual observer and another section for the financial analyst or for the stockholder looking for specific, detailed information about the organization.

Although the institutional report is necessary to fulfill the legal necessity for reporting to stockholders, remember that it can help foster the loyalty, commitment and investment that stockholders and supporters bring to the institution. In exchange, they deserve a clear and candid assessment of the institution's accomplishments and aspirations. That's the goal of the annual report.

CAPTURING THE COMMITMENT OF INSIDERS: INTERNAL PUBLICATIONS

I've been emphasizing the capacity of internal communication to unleash the creativity, commitment and efficiency of people within the organization. In the section on backgrounders and position papers, the emphasis was on bringing other viewpoints into management decision making. In the previous section, we talked about how the annual report process helps an organization discover its identity and then reveal it to an active public of stockholders and stakeholders who play an active role in the institution's success.

This section will deal with perhaps the most important public of any organization—its employees. Although employee relations encompasses many areas, such as union management, compensation levels and benefit and pension management, that are far beyond the scope of this book, PR communication programs contribute many vital services in the institution's relationship with its employees.

The importance of an institution's employees cannot be doubted. It's through their direct efforts that goods are produced or services provided. It's only through their increased commitment and cooperation that productivity can be increased. Those things are taken for granted. But employees contribute to the organization's success, or failure, in other ways, too. In many companies, employees are heavily involved in stock purchase plans, actually contributing capital back to their employers.

It's not wise to forget that employees are often considered by the outside world to be the most credible judges of an organization. Many times, it's through their experiences that people outside the organization develop an image of the institution—either as an arrogant bumbler or as a principled, efficient organization.

I'm not going to discuss specific writing strategies for employee publications in this section. Writing style for employee publications, whether mimeographed newsletters or slick, full-color magazines, is essentially the same as for newspapers and magazines. Within the theory of receiver-centered communication, the same rules apply for internal audiences as for external audiences. Most of the writing for employee publications follows the basic forms of the news release and the feature story (examined in Chapter 10). The task is the same: You need to analyze your audience, their interests and abilities, and sculpt your writing style, vocabulary choice and choices of topics accordingly.

Newsletter Content: Keeping the Focus on Employees

Even though there's not a lot to say about employee publication writing, there is plenty to say about employee communication and the way we communicate through employee newsletters.

Employee newsletters are an example of what is called a controlled medium. As explained earlier in the chapter, this means that unlike the information PR people place in newspapers, which may be changed by an editor, information in a controlled medium, like advertising or employee publications, is exactly what the organization decides.

That control should be very valuable to the institution, because we want our employees to know information that's most beneficial to the institution, presented in a way that will help the institution. But many institutional managers, with the cooperation or at least the acquiescence of public relations practitioners, often confuse control with censorship. Employee publications that could serve as credible communication outlets between management and workers have instead become little-read and less-believed shouters of happy news about the institution for its managers.

If you work in an organization that has a newsletter, you probably already know what I'm talking about. Many institutional newsletters seem to be almost exclusively devoted to pictures of the CEO shaking hands at the stockholder meeting or a long, glowing biography of the new organizational president. When employees are mentioned, rarely are their contributions to the institution highlighted. Instead, employee news (and seemingly employee achievements) are limited to who has had a baby, who is engaged and who practices an interesting hobby.

Institutional managers should realize the readers of an employee publication are employees, employees who want to read about themselves and, to the surprise of many executives, about their role in making the institution successful. What's really heartbreaking about this situation is that the news employees want in their newsletters is information that will make them more productive and committed to the organization and more knowledgeable about its operations.

Employees don't want a Pollyannaish view of their institution filled with news of weddings and pregnancies and employees who carve napkin rings in their spare time. They don't want to be subjected to an egocentric tour-de-force of their institution's management, with every issue plastered with pictures of the president and his or her lieutenants. They want the information about the skills, knowledge and attitudes that I constantly hear institutional leaders bemoan that today's workers won't adopt.

Does that sound incredible? Let's look at Foehrenbach and Rosenberg's survey of employees who were asked what information they wanted from their organizations. The top 10 types of information employees wanted were:

1. Future organizational plans
2. Productivity improvement
3. Personnel policies and practices
4. Job-related information
5. Job advancement opportunities
6. How external events will affect my job
7. How my job fits into the organization
8. Operations outside my department
9. How our institution is doing against the competition
10. Personnel changes and promotions

That information shows a work force that wants to be involved, that wants to improve its own performance and wants to share in the rewards a productive and successful institution can bring.

Can you guess the two things employees least wanted in an internal newsletter? Here they are, coming in at the bottom of the 17 items on Foehrenbach and Rosenberg's list:

16. Human interest stories about other employees
17. Personal news (birthdays, anniversaries, etc.)

What's the result of this ill-conceived internal communication strategy? People don't read internal publications. A study by Grunig found employees at the National Bureau of Standards spent only 30 minutes a week reading the organization's 21 different internal publications. A mail survey by Morgan and Schiemann showed employees believe they have to rely on the grapevine for information because they cannot rely on management to keep them well informed.

Why do supposedly enlightened, well-managed and profit-centered organizations continue to invest resources in employee communication programs that don't add to the institution's productivity and success? Richard Nemec offers a possible explanation of that attitude: "If you had to condense modern corporate communication problems into one word," he said, "it would be 'fear.'"

What are managers afraid of? According to the Burston-Marsteller report previously cited, it appears they are scared of their own employees' opinions. "We don't view an employee publication as some sort of 'free press' where employees can bitch at management," said one industrial relations manager about his institution's newsletter.

From those quotes, and others like them, it appears most newsletters are private presses for executive egos that preserve, if only on paper, the cozy idea of happy, smiling workers (pregnant and carving napkin rings, no doubt) who are grateful for their jobs and filled with praise for their management.

It's not as if employees want only happy news. From the workers' list included above, that's apparent. To add to that evidence, a survey by Surlin and Walker shows employees strongly favored in-depth coverage of bad news by an organization's newspaper. However, they didn't expect to get it.

Should we abandon internal publications? Of course not. If planned to fulfill organizational objectives, they can become well read and serve extremely valuable purposes within the organization.

A study by Grunig found that young, well-educated workers, the type of workers who can bring a creative impetus into an institution, use internal communication media more than any other group. Unfortunately, a survey of newly hired employees at the Bank of America found that group was more dissatisfied with employee publications than any other group.

Newsletter Control: Employee Publications That Spring from Employees

What can we do to create better employee publications? First, there has to be much more employee involvement in selecting the subject matter of internal newsletters. In addition to integrating those 10 types of information employees want to see in publications, some companies have begun to involve employees directly in controlling internal communication media.

One company has established a newsletter editorial board that's largely comprised of employees from all areas of its factory. Some employers have given space for columns written by regular employees. Others have encouraged and then published letters from employees to top management along with the management's replies, even when those letters were very critical of management performance.

Encouraging communication from employees to management is the key to effective employee communication programs. Executives who want to encourage creativity and commitment must become comfortable with the idea that frank and sometimes critical comments are often the first step to changing bad situations for the better. This two-way communication must be encouraged. That means not just telling employees what we want them to believe (which companies have been very good at). We also need to stimulate employees to tell management their gripes as well as their satisfactions. Through that we can discover and cure problems before they become major disruptions to the harmony and efficiency of the workplace.

Unfortunately, although certain strategies can be integrated into employee publications to encourage two-way communication, newsletters aren't really the most productive way to foster that interplay. We'll talk in the next chapter about "interactive" media whose purpose is exactly that.

SUMMARY

- Internal communication is intended to motivate the involvement and talents of stockholders, employees and supporters to promote the institution's goals. It can also foster processes by which an institution can come to a greater understanding of itself.

- Internal communication is controlled communication, messages that don't have to pass through a newspaper or broadcast media editor before reaching an audience. Thus, practitioners can be assured their institution's message will reach its intended public unabridged and without distortion.

- One problem with most internal communication efforts is that managers use them to communicate "at" employees and stockholders, rather than "with" them. That implicitly sends a message to employees and stockholders that corporate management doesn't want negative input from them and increases the isolation of top managers.

- Internal communication programs should encourage internal publics to share their unique perspectives and talents with institutional managers. Gathering this information on the wide-ranging economic and social ramifications of a particular decision is vital to effective management processes.

- Position papers summarize information to advocate a specific decision. They inform internal publics about the rationale for organizational decisions and can also be used as high-credibility information to respond quickly to public concerns and institutional issues.

- Position papers are working documents, that is, reference sources for employees and stockholders as they do their jobs. That means we should make the information in them accessible by including frequent subtitles, boldfacing copy and highlighting important points with bullets and charts or tables.

- Annual reports are legally mandated for public corporations, but many nonprofit institutions voluntarily produce them for their employees, contributors and communities.

- The information in an annual report should build confidence that an organization's managers can detect and effectively respond to problems and opportunities in the environment. That demands a truthful exposition of the institution's triumphs and failures.

- The PR practitioner collaborates with an institution's lawyers, managers and accountants to produce the annual report. It's the practitioner's job to produce a coherent, readable report from this mass of technical information.

- The annual report writing process begins with research to determine the company's problems and opportunities and how those factors will affect the institution's internal audiences. From that initial research, the practitioner should be able to develop a theme that coherently communicates those major institutional messages.

- The CEO's letter in the annual report should be a more personal document, concentrating on the manager's vision for the organization.

- Many institutional newsletters are oriented toward coverage of corporate executives and personal news about employees. But research shows employees most want information about the company's decisions, its competitive environment, and ways workers can do their jobs better and gain more benefits from their involvement.
- Employee publications are more successful in stimulating creativity and commitment if workers recognize that managers want internal communication outlets to be a frank and truthful forum for positive and negative opinions.

THINK PIECES

1. Name some environmental, political or social battles fought recently in your community. Could some of the furor have been dampened if the affected organizations had gathered more information from the affected publics before taking action?
2. How are rumors begun and sustained? How can an organization use information to control that process?
3. How does integrating position papers into the management process change the ways institutional decisions are made?
4. How can an effective CEO letter in an annual report contribute to institutional innovation?
5. Will an institution that doesn't control and censor internal publications be a more contentious or less contentious work environment? Give reasons for your answer.

WRITING ASSIGNMENTS

Position Papers

D4:5

D5:5

D8:5

D10:8

Annual Report Letters

D8:6

D9:4

ADDITIONAL READING

Bernays, Edward L. *Crystallizing Public Opinion.* New York: Liveright, 1961.

Bernays, Edward L. *Public Relations*, rev. ed. Norman: University of Oklahoma Press, 1977.

"The Bottom Line in Public Relations." *Burston-Marsteller Report No. 46*, November 1977.

Broom, Glen M. "Co-orientational Measurement of Public Issues." *Public Relations Review 3* (Winter 1977): 110–119.

Broom, Glen M., and Dozier, David M. *Using Research in Public Relations: Applications in Program Management.* Englewood Cliffs, N.J.: Prentice-Hall, 1990.

Center, Allen H. *Public Relations Practices: Managerial Case Studies and Problems*, 5th ed. Englewood Cliffs, N.J.: Prentice Hall, 1995.

Drucker, Peter. *Management: Tasks, Responsibilities, Practices.* New York: Harper Business, 1993.

Gootnick, David E., and Gootnick, Margaret M., eds. *The Standard Handbook of Business Communication.* New York: The Free Press, 1984.

Heath, Robert L., Leth, Steven A., and Nathan, Kathy. "Communication Service Quality Improvement: Another Role for Public Relations." *Public Relations Review* 20:1 (Spring 1994): 29–41.

Hendrix, Jerry A. *Public Relations Cases.* Belmont, Calif.: Wadsworth, 1988.

Meyer, John W., and Scott, W. Richard. *Organizational Environments: Ritual and Rationality.* Thousand Oaks, Calif.: Sage, 1992.

Peters, Thomas J., and Waterman, Robert H. *In Search of Excellence.* New York: Warner, 1982.

Pincus, J. David, and Silvis, Donn. "How CEOs View Their Communication Roles." *Communication World* 4:12 (December 1987): 18–22.

Standard Format for a Position Paper

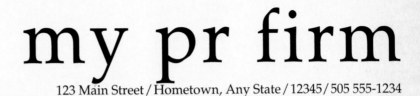

my pr firm

123 Main Street / Hometown, Any State / 12345 / 505 555-1234

Title Identifying Client and Project

Position

The position statement should be one declarative sentence that recommends an action and gives the main reason your client should undertake the action.

Background and Current Situation

The background section is a brief explanation of the historic, economic or sociological reasons that make necessary the actions you've recommended in the position statement. It is usually structured using a chronological argumentation structure. One warning: This should not be a history of the company, just a discussion of the events relevant to the action you've recommended.

Benefits

Give reasons to act
The benefits section tells your readers all the reasons they should do what you recommend. An effective structure within each benefit section is to establish a direct benefit from taking the action, then discuss the ramifications of that benefit at greater length. However, remember that this is a working document, so keep each benefit distinct from other benefits and write as concisely as possible.

Use subheads
Give your readers every chance to see your argumentation pattern clearly. Provide frequent subheads and use other graphic devices like bullets, indentations or boldfaced copy to emphasize important points and break up the copy so that it's less intimidating to read.

Consequences

The drawbacks section should be an honest appraisal of what could go wrong if the organization undertakes the actions you've recommended. Organization leaders need to know those consequences. After having identified the negative potential, offer a counterargument that will help your organization minimize those repercussions.

Recommendation

The recommendation statement restates the position and then, as every persuasive document should, indicates the specific actions that readers need to take to implement the policy you've recommended.

Full Text of a Position Paper

POSITION PAPER

WMMT TRANSLATOR TRANSMITTERS

Position

WMMT should purchase eight translator transmitters to increase its listenership in remote mountain areas of Kentucky and West Virginia.

Background and Current Situation

Appalachia's hills and hollows are a natural barrier for radio signals. Signals from WMMT's present 1000-watt transmitter on Letcher County's Pine Mountain can reach as far as Kingsport, Tenn., and areas in western North Carolina.

However, mountain ridges prevent the signals from reaching many listeners within the eastern Kentucky and western West Virginia mountains who should be served by WMMT's mix of mountain music and local public affairs programming.

That's more important since the area's five other radio stations have been purchased by outside corporations within the past three years. In each case, the stations' new owners have oriented their programming to either rock or country music. WMMT is the only station that still features mountain music, music that was largely created by the people within our listening area.

Benefits

Bigger audience

The translators will increase the station's potential audience. This bigger audience will provide greater public support for the station's fund-raising campaigns, which in turn will give us a stronger platform in our presentations for our corporate development efforts.

Higher profile

Buying the translator transmitters will increase the station's profile in the region and in the nation. As the most powerful mountain music station in the traditional home of the art form, WMMT will be looked upon as an authority. We might logically hope to build upon that foundation to solicit a National Endowment for the Humanities grant to produce a weekly mountain music show using local talent that could be simulcast to stations throughout the nation.

Preserving mountain music

The increased public attention to mountain music in our region may help preserve the art form. Since area young people have less and less exposure to mountain music, it is in danger of being lost as a living art. WMMT's ability to transmit mountain music into its traditional home may provide the impetus for youngsters to imitate, preserve and develop the art.

Drawbacks

Shaky finances

Buying the translator transmitters may strain the financial resources of the station. While the station has received a $73,000 grant from the National Telecommunications and Information Agency (NTIA), the eight translator transmitters will cost the station approximately $97,000. However, since the transmitters will extend the station's reach into West Virginia, we anticipate receiving adequate funding from the West Virginia Arts Council to cover the shortfall.

Tired volunteers

As part of the agreement with the agency, WMMT has agreed to more than double its broadcast hours each week. That vastly increased broadcast time may strain our relationships with our disc jockeys, all of whom are volunteers. However, we expect that the broader anticipated audience will also stimulate more volunteers to staff the station's expanded transmitting times.

Recommendation

To increase WMMT's public exposure and potential funding sources, I recommend the station move immediately to issue a contract for the first four translator transmitters and invite bids for installing them in Pikeville, Harlan and Prestonburg.

READY REFERENCE 8.3

Full Text of an Annual Report Introduction

This introduction to the corporate report from the H. J. Heinz Co. shows how powerful and confidence-provoking internal writing can be. The writer has directly confronted major problems facing the company and has shown how a coherent, far-seeing corporate philosophy is helping the organization meet its challenges.

WHAT IS QUALITY MANAGEMENT?

by Philip Crosby
Founder, chairman and creative director,
Philip Crosby Associates, Inc.

Quality has become the subject of a great deal of concern by shareholders and corporate executives worldwide. Heinz, for one, has been taking effective action to make certain that quality management will always be an integral part of the policy, even though quality has long been a hallmark of the company.

To better explain the complexities of dealing with quality in today's business world, I like to relate it to another aspect of real life: health.

The traditional way of dealing with personal health has been for individuals to recognize when they were not feeling well, obtain medical treatment, recover, and then wait for the next thing to come along. With this concept, people's lives and general well-being were placed in the hands of technology. It was not felt that individuals could do much to change or prevent what would happen.

Now, we have learned that people can prevent many illnesses and identify signs of others. We can prevent heart and lung disease by proper diet, exercise and lifestyle. We can be vaccinated against epidemic diseases such as small pox, diphtheria, poliomyelitis and others. We can prevent accidents by wearing safety belts and by learning about hazards.

As individuals learn to take change of their own wellness, technology adds support through early detection and preventative aids. People willing to work at it are living longer, healthier and more fulfilling lives.

Corporations have traditionally handled quality in much the same way people dealt with illness. Constant measurement of the products or services—after they were made or supplied —let management know when something was going wrong. Then, everyone would leap onto the identified problem and solve it, usually for the umpteenth time. Management operated on a reactive mode, based on assumptions

---

Total Quality Management (TQM) represents a new Heinz culture and reflects the Founder's motto: "To do a common thing uncommonly well brings success."

6.

---

that now serve proven to be incorrect.

Today, quality is seen as conformance to requirements. This means that we define precisely what we are going to give the customer, then we all work together to make it come out exactly so, the first time.

The conventional system of attaining quality has been one of appraisal. This is much like taking a complete physical several times a day in order to see if everything is still functioning. It is very expensive and time consuming, while having no effect on the future—everything is past history.

Now, we have learned that prevention means concentrating on a process that routinely produces products that conform to our customer's expectations. When we are eating right, managing stress, sleeping properly and getting exercise, we are working on the process, NOT on the product.

The quality performance standard of industry has always been "acceptable quality levels." This standard is based on the assumption that it would cost too much to do things right all the time. The standard that Heinz is using in its new Total Quality Management (TQM) process—a standard called "defect-free"—is much less expensive and highly productive. After all, it's always cheaper to do things only once.

The measurement of quality used to be indexes and other subjective or comparative evaluations. Now, companies like Heinz have learned to determine the price of nonconformance (PONC), or what it costs to do things wrong. This PONC represents a large amount of money in any business and can be reduced dramatically when the culture of the company changes.

When Heinz began its TQM journey about three years ago, the company started with what some executives characterized as a "rather unsophisticated self-examination." The study told them that at Heinz, the cost of quality was somewhere near $475 million per year. They also discovered that well over $300 million of that was due to failure to do things right the first time and then trying to find and correct mistakes. Now that the Heinz TQM process is more sophisticated, company

managers are finding that the real price of non-conformance is much, much higher. Although Heinz management initially found these numbers staggering, the figures aren't all out of line with those of other companies.

Changing the culture, by plan, is required to put quality in its proper place. Quality is the foundation of an organization. It is the platform holding everything else. It is the integrity that makes for profit and appreciation. Competing in this world economy requires that customers see a company as completely reliable in every respect. Heinz understands this and is working hard at creating a new culture through Total Quality Management in fact Heinz is believed to be the only major food processor with a global quality effort. TQM is a part of the business plans for all Heinz affiliates, regardless of their size or location. The objective of the Heinz process is continually to improve customer satisfaction and eventually reduce its price of non-conformance to zero.

Heinz has been working hard to take advantage of its new understanding of quality and has been succeeding dramatically. Some examples: A voluntary team of hourly workers in the U.K. corrected a problem of loose-fitting labels. One-lab personnel discovered the reasons for broken french fries when they detected microscopic cracks that appeared in now potatoes during handling. Starkist greatly improved productivity in a tuna filleting operation by adding workers and slowing the line.

Heinz management has taken TQM seriously and has been formally educated in our Quality College. A clear corporate policy has been issued. It says, in part: "Heinz is committed to providing products and services that fully satisfy customer requirements... through the mobilization of everyone in the corporation in a relentless and continual search for improvement" Management at all levels provides consistent personal witness and dedication to this policy, knowing that the job, of course, will never be finished.

The quality of a corporation's goods and services, like personal wellness, is to our benefit as shareholders, employees, suppliers and customers.

8.

© 1990 Philip Crosby Associates, Inc. All Rights Reserved.

chapter 9

Delivering Internal Messages:
A Practitioner's Practical
Tactical Guide

REAL-LIFE LESSONS

A local bank's vice president in charge of its personal banking division recently retired after over 15 years of service. This vice president provided the bank's largest depositors with individualized banking, investment and loan services and had built strong personal relationships with these most important customers.

To announce the change, the bank's public relations plan consisted of mailing news releases to business newspapers and the major metropolitan newspapers detailing the old vice president's retirement and his replacement's promotion to the position. The external communication campaign got a good reception. All the local business-oriented publications included a brief mention of the change in their personnel changes section.

But consider the bank's communication goal. It wasn't really as important that the city's businesspeople know the personnel change as that the bank's best clients know and support the new vice president. The bank's concentration on an external media campaign didn't meet the bank's goal. Over 30 percent of the bank's personal banking customers defected to other banks or brokerage houses. Why?

The problem here is that the bank wasn't solving the right problem, not talking to the right audience. The bank really didn't need to communicate to people in the general audience nearly as much as it needed to deliver the news to the bank's most important clients that their contact with the bank had changed. Although most of its clients probably saw the newspaper story, clients who believed they had a special, personal relationship with the bank may have questioned that belief if they first heard about the personnel change by reading it in the newspaper. In effect, these customers had come to think of themselves as insiders.

That's why the bank made a mistake when it assumed it could effectively communicate with all its customers, even its most important ones, with an external media campaign. The bank could have communicated the importance of these clients by including them in an internal communication campaign.

Many institutions have found it's good business to expand their definition of internal publics. Instead of restricting their special internal communication campaigns to employees and stockholders, some organizations are including other publics that have the capacity to make or break them. By giving customers and even consumer activists, union officials and environmental protesters the attention of an internal communications effort, those organizations are finding they are better able to meet their main goals.

New technology has made those tasks easier. We now need to adjust our perceptions of internal communication to admit those important publics into our communication strategies.

WHAT YOU KNOW

- Communication has not occurred until a writer's intended audience reads and reacts to the message.
- Messages that are personalized to a specific audience have a much greater likelihood of being acted on by that audience.
- Audiences have to both receive information and find its source credible before they will act on it in the desired way.

WHAT YOU'LL LEARN

- Interactive media let receivers be active participants in creating messages that match their precise information needs.
- Desktop publishing techniques have made it possible to target smaller and smaller subgroups of internal publics economically.
- Receivers have to perceive internal publications as sources of honest, nonmanipulated information before the publications will have a persuasive effect.

HEARTS AND MINDS: THE HUMAN SIDE OF ORGANIZATIONAL SUCCESS

A constant topic in our nation's business magazines, in our newspapers, and perhaps even at your family's own dinner table has been the nation's seeming inability to compete with the United States' international economic rivals.

There is ample evidence confirming those worries. In the routine production jobs of manufacturing, low-cost overseas labor has seriously eroded our ability to deliver competitively priced goods to customers in other countries, or even to our own consumers. Even our nation's undeniable strength as a technological innovator has often gone substantially unrewarded. For instance, although computer chip technology was essentially an American development, we've been much less successful in capturing and then maintaining our market share in this lucrative field.

It's not a pretty situation. But instead of consoling ourselves with reminiscences about our once-dominant industrial culture, we must reassess how we can compete with our international rivals. Despite the jingoistic ring of the sentiment, what I propose is a battle for the hearts and minds of the people who have the capacity to resurrect our industrial standing.

Why is this a communication task? It's because a faith in creativity and innovation to keep us competitive is essentially a faith in our human resources. But I'm proposing a new and more encompassing faith in human resources that employs human resources in a way different from the past.

Surprisingly, the proposal doesn't involve a retraining program for our nation's CEOs. There seems to be little excess creative capacity among those well-paid, high-profile men and women. The overlooked resource—the people whose advice has been discouraged and ignored, and the only people with the untapped potential to lead our industries back from this brink—are those people who design, make and buy our products. Our workers, managers, engineers and even our customers are the people whose hearts and minds need to be won.

Public relations, through internal communication programs, should be given a significant responsibility in that quest. Winning their hearts would mean we've helped win the commitment of our workers and the good faith of our customers. If we win their minds, we'll have gained the benefit of their interest and intellect in solving our problems. If we succeed, we'll have stimulated the creativity, innovation and loyalty that in the American legend is supposed to distinguish the nation's people.

TWO-WAY COMMUNICATION: DEMOCRACY IN THE WORKPLACE

For too many years, business leaders have felt that creativity and innovation rested exclusively within themselves. In their own minds, those old boys in the executive suites were the only ones who came up with the sparkling ideas, the unique business plans and the great deals necessary for business success. What about workers? Well, workers provided the bodies that mechanically carried out the creativity of executives.

It might have worked that way once upon a time, but in a new, competitive America, merely exploiting the bodies of workers and extracting the maximum number of routine actions per eight-hour day won't work. Instead, those thousands of minds that are connected to those thousands of workers must be involved. Not only their bodies but their intellects, their creativity and their commitment must be harnessed. That's a new view for business, and one in which communication has a vital role. Practitioner Matthew Gonring discusses his views on this subject in Box 9.1 (pp. 252–253).

However, within many companies, that change in communication tactics dictates a fundamentally different management philosophy. As I pointed out in the pre-

BOX 9.1   Views from the Field

Matthew P. Gonring
Gonring is director of corporate communications for USG Corp., a Fortune 500 building products manufacturer. Prior to joining USG, he headed United Airlines' external communication operations and was director of public relations for Northwest Airlines.

What's the connection between better institutional performance and efforts to communicate to internal audiences?

Employees of any organization are a critical communications link in the organizational chain contributing to its success. They are more than people producing, selling and distributing products or services. They are important ambassadors in their workplaces, in their communities and among a broad spectrum of constituents. Through employees having a clear understanding of the goals, challenges, mission and strategy of an institution, they become more focused, effective contributors to the organization. The bottom-line rationale for employee communication and worker involvement is that an informed employee has a better opportunity to be productive than an ill-informed worker.

How can PR practitioners transform an institution's stated commitment to internal audience involvement into practice?

A commitment to internal communications runs as deep as the visibility of top management's willingness to communicate. The PR practitioner must have a good grasp of the business and the demographics, attitudes and opinions of the internal work force. He or she must take a structured, planned, program approach to communications and must be able to sell and implement the elements of the program throughout the organization. After these pieces are in place, the PR practitioner can promote and utilize every opportunity to visibly portray top management's commitment to communication. In the final analysis, no amount of promotion can take the place of substance.

What methods can practitioners use to open up communication channels to and from internal audiences?

To effectively communicate with an internal work force, the PR practitioner must understand work force demographics, opinions and attitudes. Through complementing top-down communications with effective bottom-up communications, the practitioner can be certain that information delivered is in line with what the audience needs and wants. Most effective internal communications programs contain a multimedia mix and a two-way mechanism for frequent adjustment of the media message.

What are the roles of formal and informal communication to involve internal audiences?

Communications, in its broadest form, is simply a critical component in every aspect of modern-day business. The role of the communicator should not be limited to the in-house publication. Rather, internal and employee communications should be viewed as an ongoing mechanism that can support, promote and encourage virtually every marketing, operations, human resource or finance initiative or program planned for the organization. An organization's PR practitioners must take the lead role in involving the communications function in every division and selling its abilities to enhance organizational effectiveness throughout the organization.

—Used with permission of Matthew P. Gonring

---

ceding chapter, many organizations more closely resemble totalitarian governments than institutions in a free and open democracy. Like totalitarian governments, they centralize decision making at the top of the organization and discourage initiative and free-thinking that dispute the official orthodoxy. You only have to observe the informally enforced dress codes in many business organizations, where even a white shirt with a tiny colored stripe is considered a symbol of rebellion, to know how tightly controlled those organizations are.

In communication, too, the similarities to totalitarian governments can be seen. In many organizations, communication isn't used to encourage employees to express different points of view, but to convince employees that the constraints the company enforces are good for them. Just like the media of any totalitarian government, they display only the organization's good side, showing happy employees overjoyed at the prospect of being controlled by a paternalistic overseer. This isn't public relations. It's propaganda.

As the people of Eastern Europe who were forced to believe officially sponsored lies found, that leadership style infects workers with inaction and passivity. When employees are never given chances to influence decisions that affect them, they retreat into themselves. The commitment that administrators think they are receiving from a quiet work force is merely the blind, unthinking obedience employees perceive that management wants.

This creates an organizational culture that is actually counterproductive to the institution's well-being. Communication researchers have found that in highly structured organizations in which decision making is reserved for only those at the top of the hierarchy, employees virtually ignore internal publications. That's the medium that is supposedly creating a work force with high morale and commitment to the organization.

So is the vast amount of money that corporations sink into internal communications wasted? Yes, if the company's only task is to enforce employee conformance to authority. But internal communication, if used in innovative and constructive ways, can have a formative impact on the organization's efficiency, creativity and profitability.

This chapter will examine innovations in communication tactics that can mobilize the valuable talents of workers all through the organization, creating an atmosphere in which creativity and commitment can occur. Encouraging creativity and commitment sounds like an inexact art, but corporate managers and communication researchers are discovering that certain communication environments foster those transformations.

> *Memory Memo 9.1*
> *Creativity and communication are closely related.*
> *Creativity happens when*
>
> - managers make decisions based on the broadest possible information from workers and customers
> - formal organizational barriers are removed and workers in different units share information about how they can work together
> - workers have more power to experiment with the procedures that govern their individual units

As Memory Memo 9.1 reminds us, they've found creativity happens more frequently when workers are given responsibility for the success of their units and real power to change policies and techniques in order to reach that success. They've found creativity happens more frequently when formal organizational barriers are broken down and people from different areas and levels of the institution are encouraged to communicate with each other. They have found managers are more creative when they have the broadest possible information base about their products, gained by soliciting input from their workers and customers.

FORMAL SYSTEMS TO STIR TWO-WAY COMMUNICATION

This idea of empowering workers is not a utopian dream. These procedures have already shown results in bottom-line-oriented institutions. For instance, instead of imposing top-down management, Corning Glass organized workers into small groups to encourage communication and creative problem solving. During the program's first eight years, profits went up 250 percent.

As an experiment in management techniques, Eastman Kodak allowed factory workers to assess and reform the professional-film manufacturing unit, which had been suffering from $1 million annual cost overruns. After the workers were given the responsibility and the power to tackle the task, the division's costs came in $1.5 million under budget.

These triumphs, which managers often evaluate as purely administrative successes, are in reality communication successes. By giving workers responsibility for their professional lives and credit for their successes, they become committed to the organization's future and dedicate their skills and creativity to making the organization work. Yet that management environment, in which workers share their knowledge with supervisors, engineers and other workers, happens only as the result of systematically encouraged communication.

This demands pledging undying allegiance to a traditional American ideal more often honored in words than in deeds. That ideal is that innovation is a byproduct of American democratic values. That's easily said, but for innovation to occur at every level in the organization, some form of democracy has to prevail at every level of the organization. In many organizations, that's akin to advocating subversion.

This new administrative environment, with all its disruption of the corporate executive's safe, egocentric world, is built upon two-way communication. Sometimes encouraging communication to foster creativity instead creates situations in which workers criticize management and dispute executive decisions. In a communications program that stimulates innovation from workers, managers will invariably lose some of their authority and will most certainly lose their arrogance about their omnipotent control over their workers.

General Motors' Saturn manufacturing plant is a multibillion-dollar experiment in this management philosophy. Their top factory managers share office space with union officials. Saturn's small work teams have great discretion over hiring team members and even over the type of industrial equipment the company buys for the work team's use.

Saturn's managers exchanged authority for quality. They chose to pull in tandem with a work force that pulls in big profits and solves many management problems on their own. The authority they lost over workers was more than replaced by the power they gained by delivering high profits and consistent innovations to their stockholders.

Internal communications can encourage that environment. But it's no longer possible to just say we want all employees to contribute to the company's efforts. A commitment to two-way communication is more than sponsoring a company picnic, hanging a few suggestion boxes or having the president present a speech to a group of employees once a year. Communication, as we will discuss throughout this book, is not merely words.

Organizations have to demonstrate every day that management wants input from workers, stockholders, consumers and all those publics that can contribute to the organization's ability to compete. In addition, practitioners must develop procedures and media that give those publics constant opportunities to communicate their concerns. Most important, organizations have to accept those compliments and complaints openly and abide by the changes they dictate even when they aren't flattering to managers and their policies.

Low-Tech Two-Way Media in Employee Communication

Those techniques to encourage employee and consumer communication vary from the timid to the revolutionary and from the simplest media to the most high tech. (Because the developments in this area are very new, this list is necessarily tentative.) Sometimes the institution merely makes a public commitment to open communication with employees. For instance, Connecticut Mutual Life Insurance employees regularly eat breakfast with executives and participate in a discussion session in which no questions are barred. Although this is not very substantive, it does help establish a perception of open communication channels among workers and administrators.

At other companies, administrators more systematically demonstrate that employee input is gathered and used. For instance, AT&T employees are given two-part postcards requesting employee comments and questions. When the employees submit the cards, the questions are directed to the most appropriate manager for an answer. With the two parts, the manager can retain a permanent record of the comment and then compose a written response on the second part that is returned to the employee. In addition, questions with general interest are published in the employee newsletter.

High-Tech Two-Way Media in Employee Communication

Some institutions take a more high-tech approach to sharing information within the company. Many companies with interactive computer systems are designing electronic methods that enable employees to talk to each other and the institution to talk to its employees. For instance, many companies have computer mail systems, called e-mail, that simplify the burdensome paper memo system of dictating, typing, duplicating and mailing. With e-mail, a message is typed on the computer and electronically sent to its receiver or receivers. Electronic mail encourages more frequent exchanges of information among workers and extends the range of contacts to include a company's international employees.

Memory Memo 9.2
Techniques for two-way communication:

- Reorient employee publications to cover news about employees rather than about managers.
- Give employees input into and control over internal media.
- Target internal media toward more focused audiences.
- Use e-mail, the Internet and accessible database systems to allow employees to create individualized information resources.

There are other uses for electronic mail systems. At many companies, the public relations staff creates a daily summary of important company news that employees can access immediately on their own computers. One computer company has set up a computer bulletin board that lets employees share information ranging from rummage sale announcements to an open forum on how to solve software programming and technical design problems.

A vast extension of this simple, companywide e-mail system is occurring through the Internet system. The user groups set up on the Internet enable experts and enthusiasts on thousands of subjects from all around the world to engage in informal conversations and exchanges of information. Some techniques to stimulate two-way communication are summarized in Memory Memo 9.2.

Worker Involvement Stimulating Two-Way Communication

In other institutions, the solutions are a little more radical, and some even involve (gasp!) turning over to workers some of the power of public relations practitioners. That's the point of two-way communication. In relinquishing part of the management of internal communication to employees, we are only giving a voice to those people for whom internal communication is intended—the employees.

For instance, workers at the Tucson Medical Center produce a monthly TV news program, staffed by employees, that is broadcast to hospital employees. Employees are featured on the program, and only if there is no other news source for a story are managers allowed to appear on the program.

At Ohio Bell, instead of PR staff members running the internal publications, the company has appointed a seven-member task force drawn from all divisions that decides editorial content for publications.

This seemingly passive role is becoming an increasingly common task for public relations practitioners in these new communication contexts. It's no longer a situation in which we control communication or even communicate ourselves. Instead, often our role now is to encourage and facilitate communication among others, to apply the things we know about communication to encourage all forms of formal and informal contact among our employees, customers and publics.

Hence, we increasingly find ourselves helping implement innovative office configurations, rearrange worker groupings, change employee compensation programs and integrate computer technology into the real-world communication among individuals.

Stimulating Two-Way Communication Through Desktop Publishing

Employee control over internal communication is much easier to rationalize because new technology has made electronic, broadcast and print media much less expensive and much more accessible to all personnel. In print, one of the most important developments has been the emergence of desktop publishing technology that uses a personal computer to write, design, typeset, illustrate and assemble a publication for printing.

To someone who is not familiar with printing, those computer tasks might not seem so miraculous. But, believe me, they are. This cheap technology has dramatically decreased the costs of internal publications. Those lower costs have allowed more specific targeting of publications to specific publics within large institutions and have allowed much smaller organizations to begin internal communication programs.

Traditional publication preparation is very complicated, very time-consuming, and very expensive. Before desktop publishing so radically changed the scene, every publication, from the simplest brochure to a catalog or magazine hundreds of pages long, had to go through much the same procedure.

Most publications started with what was called a layout, which were sheets that showed the approximate design of each page. A layout sheet included relatively accurate approximations of all the photos, headlines and margins that would appear on each page. While constructing the layout, the designer would also have to estimate the space the typeset story would take up. That meant using a complicated formula to convert double-spaced typewriter copy on lines 6 inches wide into much smaller typeset letters that were single-spaced and set in columns that might be only 2 inches wide.

The layout was intended to give clients a chance to review the designs before they spent too much money on typesetting. If the client didn't like the design, the designer started over and created a new design. Preparing pages of new designs might add days of production time and many more dollars in staff costs.

Once the layout was completed and approved, another artist usually constructed what's known as a keyline. A keyliner took the dimensions of photos, illustrations and headlines on each page and created an exact representation of the elements to ensure that everything fit. Keyliners would laboriously draw boxes on the page representing the height and width of each line of headline copy and even every line of body copy and photo captions. If certain elements were too big or too small, the keyliner would consult with the designer and change the type or photos to solve the problems.

When all the design elements fit together, a pasteup artist would order properly sized typefaces for the headlines and body copy and would reduce or enlarge photographs and illustrations so they would fit the designer's specifications. The typeset stories and headlines were returned from the typesetter in long, single-column strips called galleys.

Both the galleys and the photographs then had to be manually pasted onto boards to create what's called a mechanical. The mechanicals, exact representations of what every finished page would look like, were then photographed by a special camera in order to make a printing plate from which the page would be printed.

As you can imagine, because this tedious process could take days or even weeks to complete and involved major staff-time expenditures, every individual mechanical represented a significant investment. Design and pasteup costs for even modest publications could easily run into thousands of dollars.

Desktop publishing has radically simplified this task. With a desktop publishing system, creating a mechanical essentially becomes a one-step procedure. In seconds, the designer can experiment with and then establish a basic format for column widths and margins that can be duplicated again and again. The designer can determine where in a design a photograph or a headline would look best by moving the element from one side of the page to the other or even from one page to the next. Figure 9.1 shows how desktop production systems save hours of staff time.

Those frightful calculations to choose the proper type size for the headlines and body copy are not necessary either. As all the stories have already been generated and saved in a computer file, the designer can bring the story into the desktop publishing software's memory, then lay it into the space he or she has reserved for it. If the story is too long when it's set in 12-point type, one small adjustment can make it 10 point or 9 point, or whatever size is needed to fill the hole. If there's a typographical error in the copy, the story doesn't need to be typeset again. Because the desktop software also contains some primitive word processing capacity, the designer can correct a word or punctuation mark on the computer screen.

Photographs and illustrations are much easier to accommodate in a desktop publishing system, too. A scanner can convert a photograph or illustration into digital data that a computer can reproduce. A scanner does this by taking a tiny section of the photograph and analyzing whether that minute square is dark or light. By combining hundreds or thousands of these tiny segments that comprise a photograph, the computer can reconstruct the photo and then place it in a publication electronically.

Because the photograph is now in a computer format, it can be manipulated in a number of ways. If the hole the designer has reserved for the photograph is too large, the computer can expand the photo to fill the space. The same applies when

FIGURE 9.1 Traditional Production vs. Desktop Production

Traditional production
1. Writer types copy.
2. Editor edits copy and selects art.
3. Copy and art are sent to designer.
4. Designer makes up dummy.
5. Designer sketches rough layout.
6. Keyline artist sizes copy and art.
7. Keyline artist produces keyline.
8. Copy specifications sent to typesetter.
9. Typesetter keyboards copy.
10. Type galleys proofread by editor.
11. Type galleys to typesetter for revisions.
12. Galleys corrected and sent to pasteup artist.
13. Photos screened to size and sent to pasteup artist.
14. Pasteup artist assembles mechanical.
15. Mechanical is converted to a plate.
16. Plate is placed on press for printing.

Desktop production
1. Writer keyboards copy into computer.
2. Copy is edited and art is selected.
3. Designer scans art and photo in scanner.
4. Designer assembles and resizes art and copy in desktop program.
5. Mechanical is printed on laser printer.
6. Mechanical is converted to a plate.
7. Plate is placed on press for printing.

the photograph is too small. The computer can also cut out portions of the photograph to make it smaller, or eliminate the photo's background to highlight its main subject. If it's not practical to cut something out of the photograph to make it fit into a hole, or if the designer wants a different artistic effect, it's also possible to stretch or squeeze the photograph along either the horizontal or vertical dimension to fit into the space.

In addition to using a scanner to convert original photographs and illustrations into a computer format, there are scores of commercially available computer disks containing illustrations that can be placed in any computer document. There is other software that will construct graphs, charts, balance sheets or that even let you create your own drawings to be inserted into publications.

Because the story is recorded in the computer, it's possible to use the computer to chisel the copy to fit around an irregular photograph or illustration. Of course, if the designer needs to make any adjustments, he or she is able to make changes on the computer screen that the client can instantly see and decide on.

It's only after all the changes and experiments are completed on the computer that the design emerges onto a piece of paper. Here, too, the desktop publishing system saves you and your staff a lot of time and effort. Instead of having to systematically prepare a mechanical by pasting all the elements onto a board that can be photographed for a printing plate, most desktop systems are connected to a high-quality laser printer. The laser printer produces a print that usually surpasses the quality of a manually prepared mechanical and that can just as easily be used to produce a printing plate.

Obviously, a desktop publishing system saves enormous amounts of staff time and leaves some of your communications budget for more important tasks. However, there's an equally valuable contribution the technology can make to an effective PR program. Because design and preparation costs are nearly negligible for slightly different versions of the same document, PR professionals can target different messages to different audiences. Sometimes that means one version of a brochure or publication for assembly workers and another for employees in the shipping department, each emphasizing issues of particular interest to that public.

One company, for instance, publishes four versions of its stockholder report, respectively directed toward employee stockholders, institutional investors, general investors and the retired people who comprise a high percentage of its stockholders.

The power of desktop publishing can take you even further. In one publication on which I worked, a chamber music group needed to recruit audience members to concerts and solicit interest from potential concert sponsors. Instead of producing two totally different publications, I preserved the general design format and illustrations but emphasized different elements in the copy for the different audiences. For the local audience from which the chamber group wanted season ticket sales, the brochure copy emphasized the chamber group's accessible music, affordable ticket prices and convenient ordering procedures.

For the publications directed toward potential concert sponsors in other cities, the philosophy changed, thanks to desktop technology that increasingly allows PR professionals to economically target smaller and smaller concentrations of people. Because the potential income from each possible concert sponsor was in the thousands of dollars and there were only 50 sponsors on the mailing list, it became quite cost-efficient to target a single individual with a specific brochure. This new trend is called targeting "an audience of one."

For each potential concert sponsor, a brochure was individually crafted to include the name of the city, the sponsoring organization, a list of local halls into which the group might be scheduled and even attendance figures in similarly sized cities to prove the group's drawing power. With a field-formatted computer program that inserted all the individualized information into the specific brochures, each different brochure could be produced in a matter of minutes. The resulting publication, individualized for a specific organization, was printed by a laser printer, folded and mailed. The results of this tightly targeted marketing campaign were very impressive.

Stimulating Two-Way Communication with Consumers

Of course, in a two-way communication system, this audience-of-one concept isn't limited to our company telling people what we want them to know. In fact, one of the most stunning developments in internal communication within the past few years has been the trend to consider individual consumers as important sources of information for improving products and the corporation's knowledge of the business environment.

Many companies have established toll-free consumer hotlines, phone lines that were originally intended to distribute recipes, dosage advice and other product use information. However, a number of companies saw them as a way of collecting consumer complaints and suggestions quickly enough that the company could resolve product defects before huge numbers of customers were dissatisfied, and before well-publicized and embarrassing product recalls were necessary.

Over time, companies using the toll-free lines found customers were often calling to tell them about their satisfaction with certain product features or to suggest product changes. That information allowed many companies to discover popular product features that could be emphasized in advertising campaigns, giving them an advantage over their competitors.

To those companies that have wholeheartedly adopted a system of soliciting information from consumers via toll-free numbers, the benefits are enormous. General Electric Co. credits its toll-free line with defusing potentially destructive consumer dissatisfaction. Simply giving customers some method for venting their anger helps, the company's management says. But it also helps that knowledgeable customer service agents have been given great discretion in awarding coupons, free service calls and other incentives to answer consumer complaints. Often the most soothing comment the GE operators can make is that they will refer the caller's complaint, compliment or suggestion to the company's engineers. By empowering GE customers and making them a part of the company's design and review process, the company thinks it can gain long-term consumer commitment to GE products and create a valuable early-warning system allowing the company to correct complaints and exploit popular product features in marketing campaigns.

Now many companies are pursuing the same interactive strategies on the Internet.

A CALL TO ACTION

The empowerment of people important to the organization is at the heart of any internal communication program. As has been demonstrated time and time again, the creativity so valued by institutions doesn't develop in an environment in which communication from employees to employees and even employees to supervisors is discouraged. With a genuine commitment to two-way communication, and by applying creative solutions and the new, accessible and inexpensive technology that encourages two-way communication, PR practitioners can create that new environment that will help involve the human resources we must rely upon for our organization's success.

SUMMARY

- Two-way internal communication is intended to gain the benefit of the interest and intellectual talents of an institution's workers, stockholders, customers and supporters.
- Leadership styles that discourage worker participation and communication create organizational cultures characterized by employee inaction and passivity.
- Researchers have found employee creativity is fostered when people from all areas and levels of the institution communicate with one another and are given power to change company policies to achieve success.
- Effective two-way communication doesn't come from the institution merely saying it wants all employees to contribute to the company goals. Instead, it comes from systematically developing media that encourage communication throughout the organization and then honestly using the information generated from that process to integrate real changes into the institution.
- Electronic mail (e-mail) systems encourage informal communication as well as the personal interaction of employees from all divisions to bring their talents to bear on company problems.
- Two-way communication is stimulated when managers transfer responsibility for internal communication media to workers.
- Desktop publishing radically simplifies the process of producing publications, making it possible for institutions to target messages to specific internal publics.

- Companies using toll-free information lines have been able to use input from customers and others to defuse consumer dissatisfaction and to gain valuable information about desired product features.

THINK PIECES

1. Can an individual's personal commitment to solving a problem be transferred to an organization that's also committed to the issue?
2. How can you rationalize a decision to remove PR practitioners from a company's publication editorial board?
3. Name ways PR practitioners can stimulate workers and consumers to offer their evaluations of a company's products and procedures.
4. What should be the goals of internal publications? Do those goals change after employees have been with the company for a number of years?
5. Evaluate each of the 10 most wanted types of newsletter information in terms of their appeal to self-interest.

MANAGEMENT PROBLEMS

D1:4

D2:1

D4:1

D4.2

D4.3

D6:1

D7:2

D7:3

D7:4

D8:3

D8:4

D9:2

D10:2

ADDITIONAL READING

Beach, Mark. *Editing Your Newsletter: How to Produce an Effective Publication Using Traditional Tools and Computers*, 4th ed. Cincinnati, Ohio: Writer's Digest, 1995.

"The Bottom Line in Public Relations." *Burston-Marsteller Report No. 46*, November 1977.

Calloway, Linda J. "Survival of the Fastest: Information Technology and Corporate Crisis." *Public Relations Review* 17:1 (Spring 1991): 85–92.

Druck, Kalman B., ed. *New Technology and Public Relations: A Guide for Public Relations and Public Affairs Practitioners*. Ann Arbor, Mich.: Books on Demand, n.d.

Grunig, James E. "Implications of Public Relations for Other Domains of Communication." *Journal of Communication* 43:3 (Summer 1993): 164–173.

Hutchins, Holly R. "Annual Reports: Earning Surprising Respect from Institutional Investors." *Public Relations Review* 20:4 (Winter 1994): 309-318

Pavlik, John, Vostyan, John, and Maher, Michael F. "Using Readership Research to Study Employee Views." *Public Relations Review* 16:2 (Summer 1990): 50-60.

Shell, Adam. "Annual Report Portfolio: Corporate Speak." *Public Relations Journal* 49:8 (August 1993): 18-20.

Shushan, Ronnie. *Desktop Publishing by Design*, 3rd ed. Redmond, Wash.: Microsoft Press, 1993.

White, Jan V. *Editing by Design: A Guide to Effective Word-and-Picture Communication for Editors and Designers,* 2nd ed. New Providence, N.J.: R. R. Bowker Co., 1982.

## chapter 10

The Audience to Reach an Audience: Applying Receiver-centered Writing to Media Relations

REAL-LIFE LESSONS

Public relations has been identified in the public's mind with publicity for so long that we practitioners sometimes start to judge ourselves by how many stories we can place, and how prestigious the media outlets are in which we place them. However, as I've emphasized throughout this book, our task is really to accomplish the client's overall goals. Sometimes that involves getting a story placed in the *New York Times,* sometimes in a union newsletter. Here's a story that illustrates that lesson.

A local bakery owner hired me to develop a media relations program to support a marketing effort. He excitedly explained to me, complete with blueprints and patent application, how he had invented a mechanism that would precisely center the layers of a wedding cake atop one another. Although that didn't seem terribly important to me, he explained that it might be very important to caterers and bakeries. By using a series of what appeared to be giant protractors and centering guides, he could keep a cake from tilting as it climbed to four or five layers. Getting that job right the first time could eliminate a lot of a baker's worry and a lot of wasted effort in restacking the layers.

He had already gotten one small mention of his invention in our metropolitan area's biggest newspaper and was very proud of the attention. He wanted me to conduct a national campaign that would send hundreds of releases to big newspapers all over the country. When I examined the local article, however, I found its tone was much like my initial response: Here's a farfetched item from the local loony inventor.

Although I could probably get some national media placements for him, I feared he would face more of the same mocking attention. So, before agreeing to run a nationwide campaign for him, I asked him what he really wanted from his invention. Somewhat predictably, he said he wanted to "sell a whole lot of them and make a whole lot of money."

I thought about it for a moment. "Then you don't want to run a national media program," I said. I told him if he wanted to sell the cake-centering devices, he needed to direct his messages to people who actually believed that centering a wedding cake was a serious issue. Instead of risking ridicule in big-city newspapers, I suggested, releases should go to specialized journals that went to professional caterers and bakers. I could tell he was disappointed. He really craved the exposure of well-known newspapers, but he accepted my advice and gave me a few suggestions of bakery magazines.

I explored sources in the Standard Periodical Directory and cut his list from several hundred media outlets to only six small professional journals and newsletters for bakers. They represented not millions of readers, but slightly over 4,000. But those six publications, those 4,000 readers, were the ones who made buying decisions for their bakeries and were the people able to make my client's objective of "selling a lot" come true.

The huge national campaign was reduced to just one release, mailed to six publications. The printing and production costs: about 80 cents. The mailing costs: $1.50. The response: gratifying.

The other part of the campaign? I suggested he make personal appointments with the presidents of three major bakery products companies to see if he could find a national distributor for his product.

The moral of the story? In most situations, publicity in and of itself is generally not the final goal of a communication campaign. In designing external media campaigns, practitioners can't let their focus stray from the organizational objectives the institution actually wants to reach. If it helps your client more to gain a placement in a small-circulation specialized magazine than a feature on the network news, pass up the prestige in order to reach the client's goals. If it helps your client more to have a dinner party with six people who are important to his or her success, recommend that. Of course, if it will most help your client to get a story in your city's metropolitan newspaper, strive to do just that.

This chapter is about making that final goal as successful as possible by producing prose that fits the needs of the media for which you are writing and satisfies the objectives of the organization for which you are working.

WHAT YOU KNOW

- You need to keep the focus of your communication on the needs of the person who can influence your audience.
- You modify the format of your communication act so your audience can most easily use the information.
- Knowing the variety of media and their needs helps you target information to specific audiences and assemble a coalition of publics to support your cause.

WHAT YOU'LL LEARN

- News releases are used too often in media relations situations in which photo opportunity teasers, feature teasers or query letters might be more effective.
- Feature stories written by journalists bring more credibility and usually provide more in-depth coverage that a news release could provide.
- A focus feature story can show why a person is involved in an issue and encourage commitment from others.
- A feature story has the inverted pyramid as its core structure.

YOUR ROUTE TO READERS

There are times when we need the support and commitment not only of our employees, customers and stockholders, but of people and groups outside the institution. This is external communication.

External communication is not as simple as internal, because there's an intervening level through which our information must pass before it can reach people outside the organization who are important to our mission. These so-called gatekeepers, the editors and producers and writers who control the flow of information through their media outlets to their audiences, have an enormous influence over whether the practitioner will succeed.

Thus, gatekeepers, should they so desire, can effectively shut down a public relations campaign directed toward external audiences. With that power, they can alter the tone of your messages and place your institution in a negative light. They can even refuse to place your information in their publications or broadcast stations at all, crippling your ability to communicate important messages to vital publics.

That power over PR messages creates a great deal of suspicion of journalists by public relations professionals, who believe journalists are often anti-business and antagonistic toward the role of PR people in disseminating information.

Unfortunately, I'm afraid it's a situation public relations practitioners have had a major role in creating and perpetuating. All too often, we've done our jobs in ways that have made journalists' jobs much more difficult. We've flooded editors and news directors with information that's totally unsuited to their audiences. We've sent releases about freeway traffic control devices to small-town editors and hints on applying eye shadow to financial news reporters.

At one point or another, we've violated every style and grammar rule and have given editors poorly written copy. Journalists have often had to labor for hours to make our prose readable and presentable to their audiences.

We've also been guilty of ignoring the formats in which journalists expect information. Instead of presenting information about events to calendar editors in an abridged, tabular form, we've given them two-page releases. They've had to wade through reams of paper and millions of words to find the information they need to share with their readers.

It's no wonder the relationship between journalists and PR practitioners is sometimes stormy and filled with mutual distrust. Yet bad as it is, it's the environment in which you'll have to work. However, it's not a situation you need to aggravate by your lack of knowledge and professionalism.

The purpose of these next two chapters is to detail what journalists expect from writing they place in their publications and on their stations, whether the writing comes from their own staffs or from a public relations writer. By meeting their needs with your writing, you can create a mutually beneficial relationship with the journalists with whom you work and help establish and then benefit from a new reputation of public relations professionalism.

THE RECEIVER-CENTERED RULES OF YOUR RELATIONSHIP WITH JOURNALISTS

Effective communication with journalists is based on the same principles that govern all other communication. To be effective, all messages have to answer some need of the receiver for whom it is intended. In the case of journalists, they need information they think their audience will find important.

There are two keys (listed in Memory Memo 10.1) to help the public relations practitioner accomplish that task. First, we need to understand the obligations editors perceive they have toward their audience. What information do they think their readers, viewers or listeners want or need to receive? Second, we must provide that information in a format journalists can easily integrate into their communication with their audience. In other words, how can we structure our work so journalists have to expend the least effort to use it in their publications?

Memory Memo 10.1
Our receiver-centered relationship with journalists demands that we:

- understand what editors feel their audiences want
- provide that information in a way that is easy for journalists to use

---

NEWS RELEASES: NOT THE AUTOMATIC ANSWER TO MEDIA RELATIONS

Our initial task is to determine if the information we want to communicate will fulfill the editor's duty to inform his or her audience. It's the same principle discussed in Chapter 1. As stated there, the first step in any communication process is to find if the receiver wants or needs to hear what we have to say.

For instance, if a newspaper focuses on business news, it's stupid to waste paper, postage and staff time to mail the editor news on food or fashions, unless they relate specifically to the business aspects of those fields.

That sounds like simplistic advice, but many practitioners send every release they produce to long lists of newspapers and broadcasters, regardless of whether they are interested in the subject. This lack of discrimination in choosing when to communicate clogs the communication channels and besmirches the reputation of public relations practitioners.

Remember that there's another component in the first step of our communication model. Not only do you have to tell your audience something it wants to hear, but you must communicate something that fulfills your client's interest. Misjudging that results in practitioners using news releases in the wrong situations.

In Chapter 2, we discussed the folly of initiating communication campaigns until we had isolated some institutional problem we could solve by communicating. If you start communicating before you have a goal for that communication, you risk generating contradictory interpretations of your message. That's an even greater problem when you use the mass media, where diverse audiences can receive the message.

The situation discussed in the chapter opening shows that problem. Most big-city newspaper editors and their readers weren't interested in the cake-centering invention for the reason the client wanted them to be interested. They only wanted to mock the invention's seemingly misguided inventor.

What would be a better strategy? First, don't restrict your external communication strategies to the mass media, because information presented in mass media is usually less persuasive than information presented in more personal types of media like phone calls, letters and specialized publications. A personal letter or meetings with top company officials can send a message to the most important audience in a way that emphasizes the audience's importance. That's something the news release can't do.

What's the second lesson you can draw from this? As sacrilegious as this sounds, you might not even want to send a news release. To repeat: News releases are not the automatic answer to every communication need. There are many other options, some of which are listed in Memory Memo 10.2, that can be very effective in stimulating news coverage.

News releases have value in certain situations—when you are making routine announcements about institutional changes or special events, for instance. Although larger media outlets will usually shorten the release dramatically, smaller newspapers and broadcast stations may use a release in close to its original form. Releases can also be useful in providing background information for reporters preparing feature stories.

Memory Memo 10.2
Your alternatives to news releases for getting news coverage:

- Calendar announcements
- Photo opportunity teasers
- Feature teasers
- Query letters

However, even when you need to deliver information to the mass media, the news release format is often an inappropriate choice. If you announce a personnel promotion to a publication that prints a single line or two for 20 or 30 local executive promotions, it's counterproductive to your long-term communication purpose to send a four-page release detailing everything in the manager's life from his birthplace and high school athletic record to the name of his spouse. You're only making more work for an editor you need to keep on your side if you hope to be successful. If the outlet will only use three or four lines and a photo, encapsulate the four-page release into three or four lines and send it along with a photograph.

If you are providing information that will be placed in a calendar section, it makes both your job and the editor's job harder if you bury those dates in narrative prose. Make it easy on everybody by sending a short, tabular calendar announcement with that important information listed prominently.

If you're sending public service announcements to a radio station that no longer broadcasts full public service announcements (PSAs) but instead weaves a few seconds of information into their announcers' between-record dialogue, provide information in a way they can use. The formats shown in Figure 10.1 can be used as a formal 15-second PSA (upper version) or can be adapted by announcers as brief filler material (lower version). In addition, the listing can be integrated easily into newspaper and magazine calendar sections and television supertitles.

If the intent is to get coverage by a photographer, a quick summary with the time, date, photo subject and significance of the event would be easier for you to produce and easier for the photographer to use than a news release. A two-page release would force a photographer to examine and analyze it to discover an interesting visual and then find a date, time and location. By matching the photographer's needs with your coverage request, this teaser provides enough information for the photographer to make a decision about covering the event and then to write a caption (or as print journalists would say, a "cutline"). See Figure 10.2 for an example of a "photo op" teaser.

If your intent is to stimulate a feature story, instead of a news release send a query letter. We'll be discussing tips for writing query letters later in the chapter. No matter what the communication task, match the message to what you expect to receive from it.

Writing the News Release

Although I feel practitioners write too many news releases, I'll concede they are useful in certain situations. Small specialty magazines and small-market newspapers and broadcast outlets often accept and place print and video news releases announcing an institution's events, promotions and achievements.

In larger markets, releases can sometimes be used to prompt a feature story or provide background for a reporter producing his or her own story. In addition, large-market outlets often print or show news releases when they announce routine bureaucratic information. Your local newspaper undoubtedly includes releases about changes in the trash pickup day, or application procedures for a hospital's class on high blood pressure. Health care reporters for your city's television stations may routinely include videotape footage from a video news release in their own stories.

Let's say you have determined your situation fits into one of those categories

Singing

AMERICA'S
P · R · A · I · S · E · S

PUBLIC SERVICE ANNOUNCEMENT

Start October 27, 1989   Contact: William Thompson
Stop November 11, 1989   456-2465 or 588-6976

15 seconds reading time

FIVE TOP CHORUSES
IN VETERAN'S DAY CONCERT   Five of Louisville's top choirs,

including barbershop champion The

Thoroughbred Chorus, will be on one stage

on Saturday, November 11th for a patriotic

songfest called "Singing America's

Praises." Tickets for the 8 p.m. concert in

Memorial Auditorium are $12 and $15, and

are available by calling 584-7777.

-30-

SUMMARY
     "Singing America's Praises" choir concert
     Saturday, November 11th, 8 p.m.
     Memorial Auditorium
     Tickets: $12 and $15   Call: Kentucky Center Ticket Office: 584-7777

A Veterans Day Concert on November 11, 1989,
presented by the Coalition of Dedicated Artists, Inc.

P.O. Box 5343 / Louisville, Kentucky 40205 / 502 456-2465

FIGURE 10.1 Public service announcement/calendar section fact sheet

MISSOURI REPERTORY THEATRE

4949 Cherry ● Kansas City, Mo. 64110-2499 ● 816/276-1579

REQUEST FOR MEDIA COVERAGE   MEDIA CONTACT

Saturday, March 26, 1988   Rendall Himes
2 to 3 p.m.   (276-1579)

JOIN THE WHITE RABBIT AT THE REP FOR "ALICE'S EGG HUNT"

WHO: Area children and costumed characters from Missouri Repertory
        Theatre's production of THE CURIOUS ADVENTURES OF ALICE

WHAT: A free Easter Egg Hunt at The Rep. Participating children will
        meet some of the Wonderland characters from THE CURIOUS
        ADVENTURES OF ALICE, find hidden prizes and have an opportunity
        to win a grand prize drawing for the "golden egg." The White
        Rabbit will serve as master of ceremonies. Also joining the
        festivities will be Alice, the Mad Hatter, the March Hare and
        Humpty Dumpty.

WHEN: 2 to 3 p.m. Saturday, March 26, 1988
        (Rain date - noon Sunday, March 27)

        Scheduled Activities:

        2:05   Alice and the White Rabbit will cut the ceremonial
                ribbon to start the egg hunt

        2:25   White Rabbit's egg-in-spoon race for older children

        2:35   Opportunity for children to have their photos taken
                with Humpty Dumpty "sitting on a wall."

        2:45   The Mad Hatter and the March Hare will draw the name
                of the grand prize winner for the golden egg

WHERE: On the northwest lawn adjoining the UMKC Center for the
        Performing Arts, 50th and Cherry streets, Kansas City, Mo.

NOTE: Good visuals for a pre-Easter story. Approximately 100 children
        (ages 3 to 12) are expected to attend the egg hunt. The event
        is free, but space is limited and reservations are required.
        (Just to make sure every child gets a prize.)

Used with permission of Missouri Repertory Theatre

FIGURE 10.2 Photo opportunity teaser

and you need to write a news release. Because they are meant to be used by the media, they need to be in the format the media uses. For print media, the accepted format is that journalism classic, the inverted pyramid. Although the use of inverted pyramids in news releases was discussed in Chapter 6, let's briefly review it here.

The inverted pyramid stems from the recognition that many people aren't going to attend to your whole message. The task then becomes communicating as much vital information as possible to your readers, even if they stop reading a story after one or two paragraphs. The inverted pyramid meets the receiver-centered test we've been offering as a standard for good professional writing because it adapts writing structures to the ways readers will be using the medium. When a practitioner decides a news release is a cost-effective method of getting publicity, it's still vital to target specific messages to each important public. The release in Figure 10.3 (pp. 274–275), directed toward veterans' organization newsletters, was only one in the campaign. Other specialized releases went to historical preservation group newsletters and fine arts editors.

To write an inverted-pyramid story, begin by analyzing your purpose and your audience. Once you know why you're writing, the lead is composed based on the TIPCUP principles outlined in Chapter 5. The lead in Figure 10.3 excites veterans' interest within the first few words by defining them as the audience and the benefit they'll get.

The pyramid's second paragraph explains the lead. In most cases, it completes any information omitted from the lead that is needed for the most cursory telling of the story. Here's where you include the names of any individuals or organizations that didn't make it into the lead. If you've introduced a play on words or any other creative element in the lead, in this paragraph you explicitly restate your main idea for those readers who didn't understand at first.

The inverted pyramid's third section presents information that supports the statement presented in the lead. If your lead says new taxes would hurt your industry, you offer the evidence that supports that contention. That might be employment statistics, quotes from economists, or government studies.

Develop a structure that will demonstrate the logic of your arguments and that matches a mental template your audience can use to process your information. We discussed that concept in Chapter 6. Depending on what evidence you're presenting, you need to develop an argumentation pattern that lets the reader understand your reasoning. If you're presenting a sequence of events, a manufacturing process or a series of legislative actions, for example, you should probably use a chronological sequence. If the best way of presenting your evidence is to show a perplexing situation and how your proposal will make it better, a problem-solution argumentation pattern may work best. If you're simply presenting a list of reasons justifying how your proposal will make something better, an order-of-importance presentation is logical.

Limit yourself to one new idea per paragraph and keep paragraphs short. Paragraphs that can be easily digested are more inviting to readers. As we discussed before, concentrate enticing information for your readers in the break points—those first few words of each paragraph in which readers make their decisions about continuing to read. Readers will also be more likely to push through the break points if you offer smooth memory-cue transitions that show how each paragraph's ideas are linked with the ideas in the preceding paragraph.

After you have built the inverted pyramid's middle section, the fourth section provides a historical overview of the event. This section gives the background that helps the reader place the current issue in perspective. If you're justifying a com-

AMERICA'S
P·R·A·I·S·E·S

Sept. 22, 1989   Contact: Leslie Buddeke
FOR IMMEDIATE RELEASE   (502) 555-2465

MEMORIAL AUDITORIUM REDEDICATED DURING VETERANS DAY CONCERT

First five words define the audience for veterans' newsletter, gives them benefit.

Louisville's veterans will be honored when the city's Memorial Auditorium is rededicated during "Singing America's Praises," a Veterans Day concert presented by five major Louisville choruses on Saturday, Nov. 11.

Second paragraph gives brief explanation of overall event.

Memorial Auditorium, which was originally named the War Memorial Auditorium in memory of World War I veterans when it was completed in 1929, will be rededicated in a patriotic performance featuring over 300 performers. The event will be punctuated by displays of color guards from area military units and a series of patriotic readings accompanied by a special dramatic presentation.

Representatives of major veterans groups will be present to receive the rededication of the auditorium during a finale that will include all 300 singers in a full-throated patriotic tribute.

The singers are from five of Louisville's best known choral ensembles. Included in the concert will be performances by the Thoroughbred Chorus, the seven-time world champion barbershop chorus; and The Motet Singers, which has appeared in concert at the White House.

These two paragraphs listing choirs arrange them in order of importance.

The concert also includes the Louisville Youth Choir; The Derby City Chorus, which has already competed in two international women's barbershop competitions in its seven-year existence; and The Louisville Chorus, which has represented Louisville on a European sister-cities tour.

(more)

A Veterans Day Concert on November 11, 1989,
presented by the Coalition of Dedicated Artists, Inc.

P.O. Box 5343 / Louisville, Kentucky 40205 / 502 456-2465

FIGURE 10.3   One news release in a targeted campaign

Memorial Auditorium
page 2

The concert will be held in Memorial Auditorium at 970
Fourth St. in Louisville. The building is one of Louisville's most
historically and artistically significant sites. Since its 1929
dedication to the dead servicemen and women of World War I,
the auditorium has hosted some of Louisville's greatest artistic
performances. The auditorium has greeted such famous stars as
George Gershwin, Helen Hayes, Marian Anderson, George M.
Cohan, Ethel Barrymore and Mikhail Baryshnikov.

However, the building remains a tribute to America's
veterans, with a massive collection of battle flags and campaign
banners, some of which were donated by Gen. Dwight D.
Eisenhower, Gen. Douglas MacArthur, Gen. George Patton and
Gen. James Doolittle. All flags will be on display before and
after the Nov. 11 concert.

The patriotic concert is sponsored by CODA, Inc., a
coalition of the five groups performing during the concert.
Proceeds from the concert will go toward arts education and
arts scholarships in the area.

Tickets to Singing America's Praises are $12 and $15 and
are available now at the Kentucky Center for the Arts box office
or by calling the box office at 555-1344. People outside the
Louisville area can call the box office toll free at 1-800-555-1344.

-30-

Background section in these two paragraphs establishes history of the building, paying particular attention to audience of veterans.

Full call-to-action information in final paragraph.

pany's lawsuit, this section might discuss a past lawsuit that has some bearing on
how the court might decide your case. A release announcing a charity fund-raiser
could include the total amount the charity has raised in previous campaigns.

The fifth section includes procedural information that will be important for readers who want to take some action based on the information in the release. This call
to action is a vital part of almost all public relations writing because the job in persuasive writing is to have your audience take a specific action as a result of your
message. The fifth section states explicitly what that action is. It could be a toll-free

phone number for information on a product, ticket information and times for an event, or a senator's address to stimulate a lobbying campaign.

Look at Figure 10.4 for another example of how the inverted pyramid is used in a news release. This announcement release on a new use for a sewage treatment plant is intended to defuse some potential anxiety over the new owners and their operations.

With the inverted pyramid you answer the reader's need for fast comprehension of the story's most important elements. Although its most common use in public relations writing is in news releases, the inverted pyramid is used in virtually every other type of PR writing, including writing that is much more effective in fulfilling PR communication tasks. One of those more effective forms is the feature story.

FIGURE 10.4   A release with a purpose

Lead quickly establishes proximity and impact to local readers. Notice mayor's name held until final position.

Second paragraph establishes location and names of major players in deal. Outlines overall plan for the plant.

Mayor's quote validates No. 1 reason for deal.

Second most important reason for city's deal with IWC.

IWC
Industrial
Water Company

June 28, 1993
For immediate release

Contact: Kelly Corbin
            (418) 555-09811

Monville Finds New Use
For Old Sewage Plant

The sale of Monville's old sewage treatment plant will give the plant a new lease on life as a recycler of non-hazardous wastes from industry and restaurants, Monville Mayor Joyce Parker announced today.

The sewage treatment plant, which is in an industrial area at 10th Street and I-735 adjacent to the Mallgate manufacturing plant, was sold to Louisburg-based Industrial Water Company, Inc. on Saturday. The company plans to install and refurbish existing equipment to make the plant operational within 90 days. It will employ about 10 people.

The property, which was due to be sold at public auction Tuesday, was instead purchased in a negotiated sale, a move Parker said made very good financial sense for the city. "Selling the property to a company that wants to use most of its existing equipment and capacities meant we got a higher price than if we had sold it at auction to someone who would have had to clear the property for another purpose," she said. "In addition, the negotiated sale let us specify that Industrial Water Company provide certain funds for landscaping and odor control." According to IWC president Neil A. Cora, the company will use containment buildings, filters and the latest technology to control possible odors from the recycling process.

- more -

3480 Old Jonesburg Pike • Louisburg, Pennsylvania • 42039 • 418-555-3469

New Use of Old Plant
page 2

> The plant will accept water laden with non-hazardous greasy wastes from restaurants and non-hazardous industrial process waters from other commercial establishments, remove 99 percent of the contaminants before discharge, then recycle useful materials.
>
> The plant will help local businesses and sewage systems meet more stringent federal clean water standards. New regulations require municipalities to bring all businesses into compliance with tougher pollution standards. Many local businesses have been forced to ship their wastes great distances for treatment because the nearest treatment facility was 150 miles away. As the first commercial plant in the area to treat these wastes, the IWC facility will provide area businesses with a local source for this environmental service.
>
> Industrial Water Company, which will operate the Monville plant, brings extensive experience in environmental engineering to the project. Since 1980, IWC president Neil Cora has been engaged in research and consulting on non-hazardous waste with sewage and water districts throughout the United States as president of Cora Environmental Associates. A former process control manager of the Metropolitan Sewer District's Callahan Wastewater Treatment Plant in Louisburg, he is a nationally certified waste water treatment plant operator.
>
> Industrial Water Company, Inc. will begin accepting wastes from local businesses and restaurants within three months. The company is already operating a 24-hour service line to deal with environmental emergencies and schedule service calls. The service line number is (418) 555-3460.
>
> -30-

Full explanation of what plant will do. Notice emphasis on countering citizen fears of pollution.

This paragraph is example of "information as needed" concept. Without previous paragraph, this paragraph telling of local business benefits wouldn't make sense.

Background paragraph focuses on expertise of company president, again countering citizen fears.

Call to action focuses on business customers the company will serve.

Again, information focused on company's environmental concerns.

FEATURE STORIES: MORE AND BETTER COVERAGE

I've already stated that you can transfer the skills we've learned among internal and external media, between print and broadcast techniques. The inverted pyramid structure is at the heart of all journalistic and persuasive writing processes, including the feature story. Whereas the news release is structured to deal with breaking news, to cover events, and to make announcements, those event-oriented messages don't encompass all the types of external communication that can help meet organizational goals. If your nonprofit institution's objective is to recruit more volunteers, you could send a simple release requesting volunteers to the local newspaper or television station. Most likely your release, if it is printed at all, would be reduced to a sentence or two in a listing of other organizations that want volunteers. It's unlikely there would be any mention of what your organization stands for, the important contributions your volunteers have made to the community or the personal rewards volunteers gain from their association with the group. On television, your request probably wouldn't get mentioned at all.

The newspaper and the TV station won't run that information because they don't have enough space or time to do that for every organization. Even if they did have the resources, communicating that information would violate their duty to be objective and independent of all the community's groups. Those are the realities of journalism.

But there's another reality here. You need volunteers and you are depending on a communication campaign to help your organization meet that institutional objective. However, without background about your organization's philosophy and commitments, your appeal for volunteers won't be very effective.

What if you could get the newspaper or TV station to produce a story about an older woman who has been a volunteer for the organization for 40 years? That story of her dedication to the cause would communicate all your organization's positive qualities—everything you wanted to tell the public to support your call for volunteers.

That's what a feature can do. As Memory Memo 10.3 highlights, a feature can communicate those intangible factors of an organization that often can't be captured in a news release announcing an event or a new program. Feature stories can show the personality, the passion, the humor and the commitment that propel an organization to its goals. For many PR communication tasks, those are the most important components of the story we need to tell our publics. Thus, in formulating a media relations campaign, we should often concentrate on obtaining feature stories from a few media outlets rather than attempting to send news releases to scores of newspapers and television stations.

Memory Memo 10.3
Feature coverage vs. releases: Features win.

- Features can communicate intangibles of the organization and its people.
- Features gain credibility by journalists' perspective.
- Features are generally longer than coverage from releases.
- Features save staff time, since journalists write them.

Conducting a media relations campaign based on placing feature stories is not an impossible task. Feature stories are a prominent part of every journalistic medium, including newspapers, magazines, radio and television.

In magazines, virtually all the stories are features except for departments (those short sections that recur each month). Newspapers, recognizing that they are losing the battle with broadcast media for breaking news, are increasingly using features to provide their readers with a more in-depth look at the news and information. Even internal media, like employee newsletters, newspapers and even stockholder annual reports, use the feature form quite frequently.

What Is a Feature Story?

It's hard to define what a feature story is because there are so many different types. Basically they can be divided into two kinds: a news feature and a special interest feature.

A news feature probes behind the scenes of daily news events to show the human involvement or the social or ethical ramifications of an event. For instance, a story that examined the political effects of legalizing a controversial new birth control drug would be a news feature. A story showing the motivations driving the drug company president who wants to market the drug in the face of a consumer boycott would also be a news feature. A story that followed anti-abortion activists on their weekend schedule of protests at family planning clinics might also be considered a news feature.

A feature can also be on a topic that isn't breaking news. These special interest features include stories like the history of the dill weed or an interview with a popular entertainer. Those stories on exotic beach resorts in the Sunday travel section fit into the same general interest feature category. So does the humorous story that's structured like a consumer report on the best snow sleds for adults.

There are many opportunities for public relations practitioners to place feature stories in media outlets. You might see practitioners working with reporters and editors to produce feature stories profiling a company's productivity teams or a ballet company's apprentice dancers. Historical features might highlight the 50th anniversary of a company's local plant or a horrible epidemic that led to establishing a certain research hospital.

An airline's public relations person might suggest to an editor an adventure story on mountain climbing in a remote area of South America, which his or her airline flies to, of course. Seasonal features are frequent PR placements, too, with expensive adult toys a likely Christmas placement for an upscale catalog outlet's PR practitioner.

A PR consultant for a security firm could propose a how-to feature on selecting among the many burglar alarm systems on the market. An industrial union wanting to gain public support for striking workers might profit from a feature explaining the pressures from companies to lower wages and cut fringe benefits.

As you can see by the range of subject matter, feature stories aren't defined so much by their topic as by their method of presentation. Because of their format, feature stories aren't used for spot news coverage. Newspapers, employee newsletters and broadcast stations don't have the space for every news item to be a feature, nor do writers have the extra time that's required to research and compose a feature. Whereas a spot news story usually answers little more than the who, what, when, where, why and how of an event, a feature story involves much more research, sometimes extensive library or document searches, and hours or even weeks of interviewing subjects and following them through their normal activities.

Finally, feature stories are generally united by their more descriptive language, including such literary devices as metaphors and similes, that help bring readers an in-depth understanding of the topic and the people involved in it. Whereas spot news stories and news releases rely exclusively on independent sources to verify the stories' facts, feature stories generally allow reporters to draw some form of supported judgment from information they collect. In a feature story, a writer might draw the conclusion that the man he interviewed is funny or serious or offbeat. A writer might suggest in the article that a particular issue might be the most important one of the next decade or even that a celebrity is vastly overrated.

However, before the enthusiasm of touting or trashing your most and least favorite causes overtakes you, note this caveat: All these must be supported judgments. You must have facts gleaned from your research or interview sources to back your opinions. The only difference is that in a news story with a public relations use, you need sources to build your case and then you have to get someone else to voice your conclusion. In a PR-generated feature story, you need sources to build your case, but then you may choose to voice your own conclusion from those facts.

Writing the Feature Story

Although some writing texts stress that the feature story is a completely different story format, there are many more similarities with basic journalistic writing than there are differences. Structurally, most features, at least most features with public relations uses, employ a modified inverted pyramid format with a different style of opening and ending.

Some newspaper features called "brighteners"—humorous slice-of-life stories of weird accidents, mistaken identities, and other of life's little absurdities—are often told in chronological order without an inverted pyramid, but that type rarely has public relations value. Instead, because there are few public relations feature stories intended merely to entertain, feature stories in PR contexts almost always use the inverted pyramid as a core structure.

If you are writing a feature story for a medical society's cardiopulmonary resuscitation (CPR) training program, it's not enough to tell the story of someone whose life was saved because someone else performed CPR. We want to inform our publics of how many lives are lost because of a lack of training, how easy the training is, when local classes start and how our audience can enroll. An inverted pyramid is an effective way to communicate that message by grabbing our audience's attention with the drama of a life being saved, educating them in the value and availability of training, and then moving them in a call to action to enroll.

The Feature Lead.   Even though most PR features use an inverted pyramid as their core structure, they can have significantly different openings (see Memory Memo 10.4). Instead of beginning with a rapid-fire recital of all the elements of self-interest that seem to characterize news release formats, features more often develop reader interest with inventive language or interesting situations. Also unlike the inverted-pyramid style of news releases, which load the least important information into the final paragraphs and don't include any summary statements, features generally include some sort of resolution.

Memory Memo 10.4
Types of feature story leads:

- summary
- shocker
- anecdote
- description
- question
- quotation
- focus

There are a number of types of feature leads that are placed atop an inverted pyramid. The lead that is most similar to the news release lead is called the summary lead. The summary lead immediately introduces an important fact that identifies the story topic and involves the reader's interest or self-interest. Sometimes the lead merely identifies what the story will be about:

Three recent disasters in high-rise buildings are forcing hotels to reevaluate their fire warning and protection devices.

Sometimes the facts are much more shocking:

Sex isn't dirty anymore—it's dangerous.

Some feature stories begin by describing the situation in which the story will take place:

Imagine a lawn, beautifully green, mowed a uniform inch-and-a-quarter high, stretching unbroken by household fences or subdivision streets from Maine to California, from Washington state to Florida.
  That's a fantasy for people who like yards. I don't.

This is also a description lead:

Outside a tidy South Miami house bordered by yellow flowers crouch six men wearing camouflage jumpsuits, their faces mottled with black paint. Each clutches an AK-47 automatic rifle next to his chest.

Among the easiest feature leads to write (and unfortunately also the least effective) are question and quotation leads. If they grab reader interest with a provocative question that has some relation to the reader's life, question leads can be acceptable. These two question leads, for instance, have some merit. They too use shock to lure a logical target audience for the PR message into the story.
  Here's one for recruiting participants for a marriage counseling class:

How do you rate as a lover?

Here's another question lead, this one recruiting people for a charity's amateur sleuth weekend:

Could you kill someone in cold blood?

But all too often question leads sound more confounding than compelling. For instance, if you were a stamp collector, would you know this story was targeted to you?

What do Walt Disney, baby buggies and killer whales have in common?

Could you imagine an audience that would still be interested in the no-iron properties of knit fabrics after this lead?

Why are knit fabrics so important to the woman of today?

Quotation leads are often equally obscure, a counterproductive factor as a reader decides whether to read a feature. Because quote leads don't define what the story is about, it is difficult to make sure you are attracting your target audience into the piece. Here's a story promoting a hospital's neurosurgery department that illustrates this problem:

"One moment I saw the truck in front of me and I knew we were going to crash. The next time I woke up it was six weeks later."

Although all these types of feature leads have their place in journalistic writing and in public relations tasks, too, there's one type of lead, the focus feature lead, that seems well suited to the persuasive communication tasks we often have in public relations.

The Focus Feature

One of the more popular and easily mastered feature structures is the focus feature. (A checklist for writing a focus feature lead is contained in Memory Memo 10.5.) The effectiveness of the focus feature is based on the premise that we as human beings are sometimes overwhelmed by the enormous problems facing us. However, if we can reduce a problem to the effect it has on one human being ("that could be me"), each reader can develop a sympathy and empathy that lead to understanding.

Let me give an example. The Christian Children's Fund, which advertises constantly to find sponsors for poor children, doesn't base its campaign on asking you to help the millions of children who need to be schooled, clothed and fed. Instead, the fund asks you to help one child,

> **Memory Memo 10.5**
> **What makes a good focus lead?**
> - It contains only one person's story.
> - That story reflects a connection to a larger issue.
> - It tells the whole critical incident, but no more.
> - It uses quotes or anecdotes to tell that story.

a child much like your own little brother or sister, or your own child. Flashing pictures of individual children with their big eyes and pleading expressions helps persuade us that we could forgo a cup of coffee a day to make this one child's life better. Even if we haven't responded to the message, we've felt its persuasive tug: Although I'm not rich enough to feed all those millions of starving children, I can give enough money to help one child.

That's the premise of the focus feature. It asserts that if we can show a huge problem through the eyes of one human being, we can get people to care about the problem and begin to understand the relationship of that problem to their lives, or at least to the lives of human beings like them. (You may recognize how that sequence is similar to the steps of Grunig's probability of communication model.)

There have been focus features showcasing new research on the effect of positive thinking for people recovering from diseases. The complex research was made accessible to the audience by focusing on one man who had battled back from cancer by using what he called "humor therapy." In Ready Reference 10.4 at the end of this chapter, you can study in full a focus feature that examines farm safety through an incident in which a child witnesses his father being hurt in a serious farm accident. We'll also look at it in this section.

The focus feature is an extremely powerful formula for persuasive writing. During the deep recession of 1981, President Ronald Reagan publicly complained that business confidence necessary for a recovery would never come because every night there was a story on the evening news "about some worker in South Succotash, Texas, who can't find a job" because of the recession. That was a focus feature making Reagan's life uncomfortable.

As shown in Figure 10.5, the focus feature has the inverted pyramid at its heart, but it starts and ends with a focus on one individual, a person who through his or her own struggle or triumph represents all the people affected by the issue. Here's the first sentence of the farm safety story included in the Ready Reference section:

Larry Milchewski was a little boy of seven, isolated on a large western Nebraska farm, when he saw the violence of the farm for the first time.

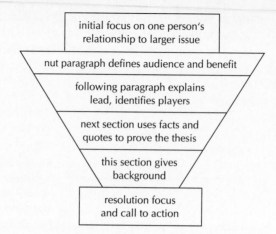

initial focus on one person's
relationship to larger issue

nut paragraph defines audience and benefit

following paragraph explains
lead, identifies players

next section uses facts and
quotes to prove the thesis

this section gives
background

resolution focus
and call to action

FIGURE 10.5   Focus feature structure

The Critical Incident.   By the end of the first paragraph we're already involved in Milchewski's personal tragedy. This is what I call a critical incident, and every print or video feature story will be helped by including one. A critical incident is an identifiable instance in a person's life in which he or she is confronted with the manifestations of a much larger reality. In Milchewski's case, the critical incident is the story of his father's death, a memory that draws us into caring about the issue of rural health care.

"I remember that it was a warm, late spring twilight and I was sitting on the tractor's fender," Milchewski said. "My dad was rushing to get several more rounds plowed before we lost the sun behind the hills surrounding our bottom ground."

As the tractor picked up ground speed, suddenly and without warning, the hitch holding the plow onto the tractor's underside shattered. No longer anchored to the tractor, the plow pivoted on the lift arms, swung out of the ground and, in a rapid arc, those several hundred pounds of cast iron and steel came down on Milchewski's father in the seat beside Milchewski.

"I still get sick thinking about the sound," Milchewski said. "There was this loud snap, this chilling scratching of metal against metal. I saw the blur of the plow fly in front of my face, and then the plow recoiled like a cannon and fell back onto the ground."

Although Milchewski, inches away from his father, was unhurt, the plow's impact snapped eight of his father's ribs and drove his face into the 3/8-inch iron spokes of the steering wheel.

"Dad had the presence of mind to shut down the tractor, but when he turned to me there was blood covering his face," Milchewski said. "He spit some blood out of his mouth, then told me to run and get my two older brothers who were working in another field about a half mile away."

The three boys were able to pull their father off the tractor. They placed him as gingerly as possible in the family's pickup truck. But without an ambulance service and with the nearest hospital 60 miles away, the boys' father died at the town's doctor's office.

It's vital for a critical incident to show a human being's personal relationship to the larger issue. In a story on a back-to-nature movement, the critical incident might be a humorous experience of five city-bred people trying to milk a cow. For a report on racism against Asian-Americans, it might be a childhood reminiscence of the first day in a new school. Remember that you're not writing someone's life story, just the critical incident that led them—and hopefully will lead your readers—to a larger truth.

Once you've identified the critical incident, you need to slip, at least temporarily, from your terse news style into a storytelling style. That's a completely different task from news writing, because in a focus feature you are demanding attention not because of self-interest in the subject but because of a shared empathy and interest in another human's life.

Thus, in a focus feature, you don't have to try to stuff the most important elements of the story into the first sentence. Instead, spend the first sentence introducing the reader to the focus individual. Identify him or her with a title or description. Whatever you do, don't talk about groups of people in the initial focus. As soon as you begin to talk about a group of people or a situation, your readers instantly lose their ability to empathize with the individual.

Also within the first sentence, try to mention one important element that helps us frame what the story might be about. In the paragraph we've included above, you'll see that after the first sentence we know Milchewski has farm ties and a tragic story to tell about a farm accident. There's nothing there that defines the self-interest that the TIPCUP news formula demands. If we are interested in the story, our attention is instead dictated by our curiosity about another person's life and our shared humanity.

The remainder of the initial focus is different from the news style, too. Because you are telling a story, the focus will almost always be in chronological order. You won't need to worry about the order of importance. Instead, these are the questions you need to answer: What happened first? Then what happened? What did that cause?

The most common problem writers experience in dealing with the critical incident is that they tend to leave out important intervening events, so that it's difficult to develop an empathy for the focus individual or understand the motivation for his or her feelings or actions. Sometimes that initial scenario demands one paragraph, sometimes five or six.

Because you're trying to establish the sense of a person so your readers can identify with him or her, you may sometimes use more details that personalize and describe the focus individual. If it adds to your readers' understanding and empathy, tell how tall or old your subject is. What does he look like? How long has she worked at the company? What does he wear to work?

It's also important to try to link the paragraphs in the initial focus with strong transitions. By concentrating on the "what happened next" questions of the chronological structure, you'll do that naturally. However, some writers also try to develop a theme that unites the story. Look at the opening of a story on a group of people who were fooled by a prank call.

The holidays came early for Holly Gingiss when she received a call Tuesday night telling her she had won a new car, a car she could pick up the next morning at a local car dealership.

"Waiting for my car was just like being a kid on Christmas Eve," Gingiss said. "I couldn't sleep at all that night."

That holiday feeling ended early Wednesday morning when she, along with 28 other people, showed up in front of Foss Ford only to discover they had all been victims of a prank caller.

The writer has developed a theme from Gingiss's quote, "a kid on Christmas Eve." From that initial suggestion, the writer has drawn a unifying concept of "holidays," with which she introduces each paragraph in the initial focus. You'll notice the similarities of this technique and the memory-cue transitions we discussed in Chapter 6. Memory Memo 10.5 (p. 283) summarizes important considerations in writing a focus feature lead.

Transition to Larger Issue.   After the initial focus is completed and you've finished telling the story of the critical incident, you are ready to move to the next step of the focus feature: the transition to the larger issue.

This is a very simple, nearly mechanical step that demonstrates how the critical incident and the person you described in the initial focus are related to the story's main issue. The transitions invariably use phrases like "Friedman is only one of 3 million Americans who suffer from this disease" or "Bhutto's mechanical flyswatter was only one of the 200 wacky inventions at the French industrial trade show."

Here's the same principle at work in the farm safety story:

That's Milchewski's horror story. It's a frightening experience that is shared in some fashion or other by virtually every person who's been around farming for very long.

But now there's evidence that there aren't going to be so many of these horrible stories to tell in the future.

In the transition, you are making an explicit tie between your focus subject and the main issue. Although there are slight variations (notice in the hoax story the transition is ". . . she, along with 28 other people"), the vast majority of the transitions to the larger issue use some variation of the words *one of.*

The Body of a Feature Story.   Once you've established the transition, you're basically writing an inverted pyramid, with all the pyramid's components. First, there's what some writers call a "nut" paragraph, which is basically the same as the lead paragraph of a typical inverted-pyramid story. In the nut paragraph, you tell the reader what the story is about, just as you would in an inverted-pyramid lead paragraph. Notice in the farm safety story that the nut paragraph is a summary lead and could stand independently as the first paragraph of a regular news story.

According to government experts and reports from the National Safety Council, farming is becoming safer because of better equipment design, more professional emergency medical services in rural areas, and a greater awareness among farmers of the dangers all around them.

Sometimes, however, the nut paragraph is introduced and combined with the transition to the larger issue.

Following the nut paragraph, as you might expect, is an explanation of the information in the lead, immediately giving readers enough information to understand the context of the story. That's exactly what the second paragraph of the inverted pyramid accomplishes, as discussed in Chapter 6.

In subsequent paragraphs you present the proof of the nut paragraph's statement: those anecdotes, quotes and statistics that fit one of the pyramid's argumentation structures (order of importance, problem-solution, chronology) also described in Chapter 6. Background and procedural information are saved for lower paragraphs, just as in the pyramid.

The feature story's final element, and the major element that distinguishes a feature story from straight news style, is that the feature story's ending brings the story to a resolution.

The Ending of a Feature Story.   In a focus feature, the resolution focus returns the reader's attention to an individual and exploits the powerful empathy the focus feature can develop to suggest solutions in which the reader can participate. Sometimes the resolution focus returns to the same person whose story was told in the initial focus, sometimes to a different person who is involved in the same issue. The same principles you used in selecting the initial focus apply to the resolution focus. You're looking for a quote or a scenario involving an individual that effectively resolves the discussion of the larger issue. As such, it serves the same purpose as the call to action in a regular news story.

Obviously, a resolution focus sometimes presents itself when the individual involved in the initial focus has solved the problem that was afflicting him or her at the beginning of the story. Sometimes the ending focus will come from a quotation that suggests a new governmental policy or a new social or personal action that will resolve the conflict.

For instance, in a feature story on the experience of traveling on standby airline tickets, the resolution section depicted a young couple who had hoped to catch a flight to Alaska boarding a plane to Cancun instead. The farm safety story returned in the final section to Milchewski's emotional response to seeing farmers' children in the audience of his safety meetings. Here's that story, showing the final paragraph of the inverted pyramid and the memory-cue transition into the resolution focus:

"That's why the new labeling requirements for pesticides and farm chemicals the council has gotten are so important," Newberg said. "The public has to be made more conscious of health hazards that might not kill you in one horrible accident, but whose long-term consequences are just as deadly."

That new attitude toward safety may be the biggest improvement the council can claim, according to Milchewski. "That's where I've personally been most successful," he said. "Every time I go out to a farm group to speak and talk about my father dying on that tractor, I look at the boys and girls out in the audience. They've already seen so many near-tragedies in their lives that they can immediately project themselves into a situation where they've almost lost a parent. And the parents know of times when they've almost left their kids as orphans."

In Milchewski's case, there was hope that there would be a solution because of his involvement. At other times, the resolution focus is simply a discouraged shrug of the shoulders with the discovery that there isn't any resolution. The phone hoax story mentioned earlier ended with a dejected "winner," her body bent down by a cold rain, trudging back to her old car.

Finally, remember that because virtually all public relations writing is persuasive writing, it's necessary to integrate a call to action into the focus feature's final section. Establish the important lesson you want the reader to take away from the story. Repeat a vital statement and suggest a course of action the reader can follow to remedy the situation. An effective way to accomplish this is to integrate a powerful quote showing your source's courage, commitment and passion into the feature's final paragraph. You'll see this in Milchewski's quote in the last paragraph from the farm safety story:

"It's that new awareness I'm most proud of," Milchewski said. "Farmers have to be involved enough in the political process and in their own personal actions so there will never again be another kid who is forced to see his father killed in a farm accident. We just can't accept that nightmare as a normal part of farm life anymore."

INTERVIEW ATTRIBUTION

Many print and broadcast writers have one main problem to overcome when they begin producing features: They have trouble deciding which of a source's statements to quote. It's very typical for a writer to fill paragraph after paragraph with interminably dull quotes. It's almost as common for a writer to paraphrase vast tracts of quotes, with only one or two actual quotes salting six or seven paragraphs of paraphrased conversations.

Both of those approaches are wrong. When you write in a journalistic form, you have a definite prose voice—certainly professional and correct, and hopefully lively. But your prose voice, charming as it may be, gets tedious after awhile. In the same way, your source's voice gets tiresome if the reader has been subjected to it for several paragraphs. What you want is to balance your own voice with that of your interview sources so your reader can enjoy both of them.

Deciding What to Quote

Which quotes do you pick? That's a question with no easy answers. When you quote someone, you want to bring the essence of his or her personality into the story. You want to show another human being dealing with the problems and prospects of the day.

What does that uplifting language mean in the real-life decisions of selecting what to quote? Here's one: In general, don't quote procedures. For instance, this is a bad quote:

"If our city has over 100 applicants for the supplemental rental program, the federal housing office will approve a waiver for new housing construction," Percy said.

This is just as bad:

"The children who are entering kindergarten need to have their doctors give them their measles shots before they'll be allowed to attend," Downs said.

I don't think this is any better:

"Danny Sullivan will be starting on the inside of row 1, and next to him, driving the green Chevrolet-powered car, will be Michael Andretti," the race steward announced.

None of these show humanity or humor or life. They show bureaucracy and tedium. As a writer, you've got the responsibility to distill just the information your audience needs to know, and you can generally say it more quickly and more interestingly than your source. Paraphrase procedures.

If you've used some of the interviewing techniques discussed in Chapter 3, however, you'll often get quotes that contain colorful language or reveal a pleasant, or even a disagreeable, personality trait. If that occurs, consider using the quote. Let's look at the preceding quotes for instances in which you could quote those very same thoughts.

If Percy said, "Those idiots at the federal housing office won't let us build a single new apartment house until we've got 100 families screaming for places to rent," you should quote him.

Use Downs's words if he gives you a quote like this: "After that boy died of measles in Los Angeles last year, I vowed that not one single 5-year-old child will enter the doors of our schools until he or she is vaccinated."

Those quotes sing with human exuberance and passion. They bring a personality and a new voice into your story that a reader welcomes.

There's another time when you need to quote. When the information revealed in the quote is so unbelievable that your credibility would be doubted if you paraphrased it, you must quote. That holds true even if you're quoting procedural information.

For instance, let's say you were interviewing a national crime expert. You get this quote:

"Instead of the estimated 50,000 child kidnapping cases last year, my research of police files finds only 48 children were kidnapped by strangers during the last 12 months," Calibrini said.

That is news so unexpected by your readers that you need to highlight the accuracy of your reporting by quoting it.

Integrating Quotations into a Feature Story

Now that you know a little bit about selecting quotes, you need to know how to integrate them into your story.

A common mistake of writers is relying too much on the phrase *when asked* to introduce quotes. The role of the journalistic writer is to stay out of the reader's view, but "when asked" puts the reporter into the story by making him or her a conscious presence in the reader's mind. You'll often see a paragraph with this opening:

When asked why he keeps trying to escape from prison, Jones replied, "I look at every prison wall like it's Mt. Everest. I climb over it because it's there."

You've buried a wonderful quote within this sentence, a quote that could keep your audience in the story for at least another paragraph. "When asked" doesn't give any hint to the reader of the intriguing quote to follow.

There's a better way to do this. As television's "Jeopardy" game show illustrates, any question can be rephrased as a statement. Thus, instead of saying "when asked," you could turn the questionlike phrase into a statement:

Breaking out of jail is like a mountain-climber's quest, Jones said. "I look at every prison wall like it's Mt. Everest," he said. "I climb over it because it's there."

Rephrasing the introduction to the quote in this way allows you to emphasize the information that is going to keep readers interested in the story. You'll note that it uses the same principle as the memory-cue transition discussed in Chapter 6.

One final warning about quotes. Every quote, just like every word in a story, is supposed to push the story to its logical conclusion, to add one more bit of evidence to prove your thesis. There will be times in your professional writing life when you'll be presented with a wonderful quote brimming with backwoods wisdom, a mother's love, or the hard-edged glint of a corporate manager. Although it might be a wonderful quote from the story's main source, if it doesn't have anything to do with the story you're writing, you can't use it. Everything has to add to the story's central effect. If it doesn't, drop it. Memory Memo 10.6 should help remind you of your responsibilities in handling quotes.

Memory Memo 10.6
Guidelines for handling quotes:

- Don't quote procedures.
- Use quotes that show personality.
- Avoid "when asked" in transition into quotes.
- Don't use a quote unless it contributes to telling the story.

VIDEO NEWS RELEASES AND FEATURES

An increasingly important part of a practitioner's duties is to prepare news releases not just for print media, but for radio and television outlets, too. Even though they're called video news releases, they're prepared more like the feature stories discussed in this chapter. But remember that we have to integrate the basic principles of broadcast writing we examined in Chapter 7 within the fundamental standards of good communication.

It's still important to find a critical incident, except now it's imperative to find one that you can illustrate with sound, vision and motion. Just like print writers, broadcast writers need to examine their source materials critically for those quotes that display the speaker's passion and commitment about the subject.

You must support your thesis with sound arguments. It's just that now you need to find sound effects or visuals to accompany and reinforce your reasoning.

Transitions are just as important in broadcast writing as they are in print, except that now, you must weave identifying sound effects or video footage in with the announcer's narrative.

Even the basic structural elements of video news releases and features are the same. Focus feature structures are as common in radio and video features as in print.

It's just that now you are presenting your stories in dramatically abridged versions. A 1,200-word print feature may be truncated to a 500-word video feature that will run for only one minute and 45 seconds. The same feature story prepared for a radio newscast might last only 35 seconds.

In addition, as we've discussed, the presentation is dramatically different. The script and storyboard format guide you to include the sounds and visuals to exploit the powers of the medium. You might want to review the radio and video news release examples we examined in Chapter 7.

WRITING QUERY LETTERS

As a public relations writer, you'll often be writing feature stories for internal publications. You might be successful in placing feature stories you've produced in small city newspapers and television stations and in some specialty magazines and journals. For those outlets, editors consider feature stories for publication in the same way they evaluate news releases.

However, most feature stories seen in major daily newspapers and in bigger circulation magazines are written by staff members of the respective newspaper or magazine. The same goes for feature stories produced by major television and radio stations. You've still got an excellent chance of placing feature stories in those media outlets, but you often need to use other strategies to bring them to the attention of editors so they'll assign their own writers to do them.

The easiest way to try to place the story is with a telephone query. If you've got a good professional relationship with an editor, you might be able to telephone him or her, briefly describe the proposed feature, and have it assigned to a reporter. That is possible if you've successfully worked with an editor before. If you haven't, you must use a little more formal approach. That's called a query letter.

A query letter is a composite creation, essentially an abridged feature story of three to five paragraphs melded to a sales letter. The query letter tells an editor or reporter what your story idea can offer, how information about the subject will meet the needs of the editor's readers, viewers or listeners, and how the editor can get the story.

Let's look at the structure of a query letter (see Figure 10.6). The query letter's first paragraph has no social niceties, no "How are the kids?" A query's first paragraph is essentially a feature story lead attached to a statement that acknowledges the editor's self-interest. Here's the first sentence from our example:

I thought your health-conscious readers might be interested in St. Vincent's newest health care worker, one that is a super laboratory technician, nurse and consulting physician.

FIGURE 10.6   A query letter

St. Vincent's
Medical   Center

June 24, 1994

Mr. George Liston
Malmouth Voice
1829 Foster Avenue
Malmouth, Nevada 73899

Dear Mr. Liston:

Lead shows knowledge of editor's audience and states story thesis. →

    I thought your health-conscious readers might be interested in St. Vincent's newest health care worker, one that is a super laboratory technician, nurse and consulting physician.
    This multitalented worker is a specially programmed medical computer that is assisting doctors and nurses in increasingly complex medical tasks.
    For instance, in the hospital's pathology department, the computer diagnoses diseases using a program modeled after the logic that expert doctors use. After an examination has isolated symptoms, the computer compares the patient's conditions against the over 30,000 disease traits stored in its memory banks. If the computer needs additional information to make a firm diagnosis, it can ask the doctor additional questions through a display terminal.

Middle three paragraphs follow computer through chronology of patient care. →

    After it makes the diagnosis, the computer provides treatment recommendations, even estimating blood and fluid needs by calculating the dimensions of interior body cavities from a patient's height, age and weight.

–more–

Call to action restates → reason for acting, states desired action.

Postscript is one of let- → ter's most read sections. Use it!

St.Vincent's
page 2

In St. Vincent's experimental intensive care unit, the computer even takes over routine patient care from overworked and scarce nurses. There, the computers are programmed to automatically administer blood if a patient's closely monitored blood pressure level indicates blood loss. Because available nurses are used more efficiently, mortality has dropped dramatically.

If you think your health-conscious readers might want to know about this high-tech health care professional that will serve them during their next hospital stay, I'd be glad to put you in contact with the hospital's doctors and technicians who are finding new computer health applications every day. I'll give you a call within the next several days to check on your plans.

Sincerely,

Cammy Davis

Cammy Davis
Public Relations Manager

P.S.: We've just received word that Dr. Rod Randall, St. Vincent's chief pathologist, will head the AMA's Technology in Medicine conference next year. That's quite an honor for us and might be something to anchor your story on.

FIGURE 10.6   (continued)

As Memory Memo 10.7 reminds us, the query letter's first sentence must grab the editor's attention and immediately speak to the editor's readers and their interests. Because there is so little space, a query letter usually does not use a focus feature's initial focus structure but a more traditional feature lead.

The second paragraph is equivalent to the second paragraph in a news release. It explains the lead and the story explicitly so the editor will know precisely what the rest of the letter will contain.

The next one, two or three paragraphs summarize the body of the feature story, giving a few snappy facts, statistics or attributed opinions that support the statements you've made in the first and second paragraphs.

Up to now, you've merely shortened a feature story into three or four paragraphs. Now the structure turns from a feature story to a sales letter. The next paragraph usually contains a very explicit statement telling how the story's information can satisfy the editor's responsibilities to his or her readers.

Because a query letter is persuasive communication, the final paragraph or two is reserved for call-to-action details. In this case, there's information telling how the editor can give such a wonderful story to his readers. Usually, this paragraph names the person or organization that is particularly knowledgeable in this field (your client, of course) and offers a reporter an interview or other research opportunities. The final sentence usually states that you'll call the editor for his or her response to the query letter.

Memory Memo 10.7
Guidelines for writing query letters:

- Establish story lead and journalist's benefit in first sentence.
- Explain lead completely in second paragraph.
- Give highlights of feature story in middle paragraphs.
- Restate benefit to audience and give call to action in last paragraph.

Here's how our example involved the editor's self-interests and includes call-to-action details:

If you think your health-conscious readers might want to know about this high-tech health care professional that will serve them during their next hospital stay, I'd be glad to put you in contact with the hospital's doctors and technicians who are finding new computer health applications every day. I'll give you call within the next several days to check on your plans.

FEATURE TEASERS

There are other methods for introducing feature story ideas to editors. Many institutions use "feature teasers," which are single-paragraph summaries of possible feature stories arising from institutional activities or research. Each paragraph shows how the story idea applies to the medium's audience and gives necessary details about dates, places and contacts to pursue the story, and, therefore, does not require too much of the practitioner's or editor's time. Figure 10.7 shows an example from a university's public affairs department.

Some organizations take this concept even further. Noticing that media outlets tend to use more feature stories to commemorate holidays, special events and citywide festivals, some practitioners prepare special feature idea sheets coinciding with those peak times. For instance, one university's PR unit collected feature story ideas from around the campus four to six weeks before Christmas, Easter, spring graduation and Black History Month. Those feature story suggestions resulted in extensive coverage in the city's major media outlets.

June 1991

Dental laser takes pain out of trip to the dentist

A new type of dental laser being tested at the
University of Louisville may eliminate the anxiety
and pain people associate with dental visits.
Pediatric dentist Frederick Parkins and a team of
colleagues compare procedures done with a Neodymium
YAG laser to those performed using traditional dental
instruments.
The laser eliminates pain and bleeding that results
from common dental procedures. Patients, especially
children, also find the noiseless laser less intimidating
than a drill.

UofL

Population decline is defense against poverty

The national decline in youth population is more a
result of couples defending themselves against poverty
than of yuppie decisions to put careers before
childbearing, says a University of Louisville researcher.
Kentucky State Data Center Director Ron Crouch says
a major predictor of poverty in the 1990 census was whether a
family had children. Birth dearth figures indicate two-worker
families under 35 have a harder time making ends meet and
therefore limit their family size, he says.

*The SOURCE
News and Feature
Service*

Enzyme replacement therapy gives hope to Gaucher's patients

An enzyme replacement therapy used at the University of
Louisville offers new hope to victims of Gaucher's disease.
Victims of the rare disorder can't produce an enzyme that
disposes of fatty substances known as lipids. As a result,
lipids accumulate in the spleen, liver and bone marrow,
preventing them from functioning properly.
Pediatric oncologist Salvatore Bertolone replaces the
enzymes with a drug called Ceredase. The new method, which
received Food and Drug Administration approval in April, may
replace spleen removal and bone marrow transplantation as the
treatment of choice.

Math teaching methods add up to fun, improved learning

Forget the chalkboard. If you want children to learn
math, you've got to let them get their hands on it.
So says University of Louisville education professor
Charles Thompson. Thompson is working with local public schools
to introduce new teaching concepts in the classroom.
He says teachers should bring math to life by using hands-on
demonstrations. For instance, when teaching measurements,
teachers should have students pour liquid into measured
cylinders to help them better understand the lesson.

*Public Information
Office
University of Louisville
Louisville, Kentucky
40292*

(502) 588-6171

FOR MORE INFORMATION ON ANY OF THESE STORIES, PLEASE CALL JOHN
DREES AT U OF L, (502) 588-6171.

FIGURE 10.7   A feature teaser
Used with permission of the University of Louisville Office of News and Public Information

WORKING WITH MEDIA GATEKEEPERS

The news media will continue to be an important outlet for public relations practitioners. However, we need to recognize journalists' goals and how they function if
we want to improve our relationship and our performance. We must limit the prodigious number of news releases with which we've been flooding their desks and con-

centrate our efforts on delivering feature story ideas that fulfill their duties to their readers and complement our organizational goals.

Our task with gatekeepers is the same as our task with any other audience: to target our messages precisely to fulfill their goals and our goals. With the writing techniques you've learned in this chapter and the delivery techniques you will discover in Chapter 11, our relationship with journalists could be much more pleasant in the future.

SUMMARY

- Media editors and producers are the gatekeepers who control the flow of information from PR clients to media audiences. Because gatekeepers can effectively stymie a PR campaign, it's necessary for practitioners to anticipate the gatekeeper's information needs and provide that information in an easily usable format.

- Releases are valuable when you are making routine announcements about institutional changes or special events. They are used fairly frequently by small market media outlets and are helpful in providing background information for feature story writers. Video releases with feature topics are finding broader usage on large market TV stations.

- There are alternatives to news releases that can more readily meet a gatekeeper's needs for information: query letters, photo opportunity teasers, and summary fact sheets (such as feature teasers and calendar announcements).

- News releases use the inverted-pyramid structure. The one difference is that the release's final section includes procedural information—a call to action—that permits readers to participate in the issue the release discusses.

- Because feature stories can communicate a broader view of an institution's vision and commitments, they are an important component in a public relations campaign.

- There are two types of features: A news feature is an in-depth exploration of some aspect of a news event, and a special interest feature is on a topic that isn't breaking news.

- Although the feature story uses the inverted pyramid as its core structure, it contains a more developed opening and an ending resolution section. Common feature story leads are the summary, shocker, description, question, quotation, anecdote and focus.

- The focus feature captures the audience's interest and involvement by capitalizing on readers' ability to empathize with an individual. The focus lead concentrates on an individual's involvement in a critical incident in which a person confronts a larger issue.

- Writers should vary their own prose voice with those of their interview subjects. However, paraphrase, don't quote, procedural information.

- A query letter invites feature coverage from a media outlet. It combines a summary of the feature story with a sales letter that demonstrates the value of the story to the media outlet's audience.

THINK PIECES

1. Compare a feature story and a news story in their impact and ability to motivate people to action.
2. Why is a feature story that is stimulated with a query letter and written by a reporter more credible than one written by a PR practitioner?
3. Why should a focus feature story detailing a worker's personal experience with a company program be more persuasive than a news story on the program?
4. What are the limitations of a media relations program in fulfilling all an organization's communication goals?

WRITING ASSIGNMENTS

Print News Releases

D1.6
D1.7
D2.4
D3.6
D3.7
D5.6
D6.6
D7.7
D9.5
D10.6
D11.4
D12.5

Print Feature Stories

D5.4
D6.5
D6.7
D10.7

Radio

D5.7
D10.6
D10.12
D11.4
D11.6
D12.5
D12.7

Television

D3.7

D5.8

D6.6

D6.8

D9.5

D9.7

D10.14

D11.4

D11.7

D12.5

D12.8

ADDITIONAL READING

Brady, John. *The Craft of Interviewing.* New York: Vintage, 1976.

Brooks, Brian S., Kennedy, George, Moen, Daryl R., and Rany, Don. *News Reporting and Writing*, 4th ed. New York: St. Martin's, 1992.

Goldstein, Norm, ed. *The Associated Press Stylebook and Libel Manual.* Reading, Mass.: Addison-Wesley, 1994.

Hough, George A. 3rd. *News Writing*, 4th ed. Boston: Houghton Mifflin, 1988.

Metzler, Ken. *Creative Interviewing*, 2nd ed. Englewood Cliffs, N.J.: Prentice-Hall, 1989.

Morton, Linda P., and Warner, John. "Proximity: Localization vs. Distance in PR News Releases." *Journalism Quarterly* 69:4 (Winter 1992): 1023–1028.

Standard Format for News Releases

my pr firm

123 Main Street / Hometown, Any State / 12345 / 505 555-1234

NEWS RELEASE
(date)
FOR IMMEDIATE RELEASE

For information contact: (your name)
Work phone: (your phone number)

(Descriptive Title)

The body copy of a news release is double-spaced, with a five-space indentation beginning each paragraph.

News releases should be keyboarded carefully to eliminate all mistakes. However, if a mistake remains in a copy that will be delivered to an editor, it is quite acceptable to use standard journalistic proofreading marks to indicate the mistakes on the final copy. Those proofreading marks can be found in the Associated Press Stylebook or in the annotated stylebook in Section A of the Applications Workbook at the end of this text.

Writers should not hyphenate a word at the end of a line, nor break a paragraph at the end of a page. If a release goes more than a single page, write the word *more* centered underneath the story at the bottom of all pages if more pages follow. At the end of the release, center the symbol *–30–* below the story's final line.

–30–

Standard Format for Public Service Announcements

my pr firm

123 Main Street / Hometown, Any State / 12345 / 505 555-1234

PUBLIC SERVICE ANNOUNCEMENT
Start date: (date PSA should begin)
Stop date: (last date PSA should run)

For information contact: (your name)
Work phone: (your phone number)

(Descriptive Title)
Reading time: ( ) seconds

Nonprofit groups use public service announcements to obtain publicity from radio and television stations.

The PSA's narrower margins and shorter sentences make it easier for an announcer to read it on the air.

A PSA can be 10, 15, 20 or 30 seconds long, but longer PSAs are less likely to be used. Note that you include the PSA's reading time in the top margin.

The reading time of a PSA must be determined, because it must fit into a station's programming schedule. It takes about 10 seconds for an announcer to read 25 words.

–30–

Standard Format for Query Letters

my pr firm

123 Main Street / Hometown, Any State / 12345 / 505 555-1234

(date)

(contact name)
(firm name)
(address)
(city, state, ZIP)

Dear (name):

The first paragraph of a query letter should be nearly identical to a feature lead sentence. It should also demonstrate that you understand the nature of the publication or station's audience and how information about your topic will serve the audience.

The second paragraph defines the story exactly, as any second paragraph in an inverted pyramid structure does.

In the two to five subsequent paragraphs, you should present reasons that your story will interest the intended audience by including facts, statistics, anecdotes or quotes that support your original thesis.

In the letter's final paragraph, you need to restate how you think the media outlet's coverage of your story idea will serve its audience. You should include all call-to-action information that tells how you can help the editor write about the issue and indicate the action the editor needs to take to pursue the issue.

Sincerely,

(Your Name)
(Your Title)

P.S. Because postscripts are among the most-read sections of letters, it's usually productive to place one more interesting fact here to entice the editor.

Full Text of Focus Feature Story

FARM SAFETY FEATURE STORY

First paragraph introduces focus individual to audience. ⟶ Larry Milchewski was a little boy of seven, isolated on a large western Nebraska farm, when he saw the violence of the farm for the first time.

"I remember that it was a warm, late spring twilight and I was sitting on the tractor's fender," Milchewski said. "My dad was rushing to

Next five paragraphs are narrative of critical incident. Quotes help establish focus individual's personal involvement. ⟶ get several more rounds plowed before we lost the sun behind the hills surrounding our bottom ground."

As the tractor picked up ground speed, suddenly and without warning, the hitch holding the plow onto the tractor's underside shattered. No longer anchored to the tractor, the plow pivoted on the lift arms, swung out of the ground and, in a rapid arc, those several hundred pounds of cast iron and steel came down on Milchewski's father in the seat beside Milchewski.

"I still get sick thinking about the sound," Milchewski said. "There was this loud snap, this chilling scratching of metal against metal. I saw the blur of the plow fly in front of my face, and then the plow recoiled like a cannon and fell back onto the ground."

Although Milchewski, inches away from his father, was unhurt, the plow's impact snapped eight of his father's ribs and drove his face into the three-eighths-inch iron spokes of the steering wheel.

"Dad had the presence of mind to shut down the tractor, but when he turned to me there was blood covering his face," Milchewski said. "He spit some blood out of his mouth, then told me to run and get my two older brothers who were working in another field about a half mile away."

The three boys were able to pull their father off the tractor. They placed him as gingerly as possible in the family's pickup truck. But without an ambulance service and with the nearest hospital 60 miles away, the boys' father died at the town doctor's office.

Transition to larger issue, showing that individual's experience is shared by others. ⟶ That's Milchewski's horror story. It's a frightening experience that is shared in some fashion or other by virtually every person who's been around farming for very long. But now there's evidence that there aren't going to be so many of these horrible stories to tell in the future.

The "nut paragraph"—a lead sentence for a standard news release. ⟶ According to government experts and reports from the National Safety Council, farming is becoming safer because of better equipment design, more professional emergency medical services in rural areas, and a greater awareness among farmers of the dangers all around them.

Formally identifies client and shows client's involvement in issue. ⟶ Milchewski has had some personal responsibility in bringing this new and more hopeful outlook. As executive director of the Midwest Rural Health Council, a group that studies and works for higher farm health and safety standards, he transformed that childhood experience into a forceful advocacy for other rural residents.

"In only four years," Milchewski said, "the council has helped win federal funding to upgrade rural ambulance services, has pushed manufacturers to voluntarily upgrade farm equipment safety standards, and has forced new U.S. Department of Agriculture regulations changing labeling directions for farm chemicals."

Despite the improvements, farming is still one of the most dangerous professions in America today.

Government figures list farming as the most hazardous American industry. Statistics compiled for 1988 show there were 56 deaths per 100,000 farmers. This compares with an accidental death rate of 52 per 100,000 workers for mining, 38 per 100,000 for construction workers, and only five deaths per 100,000 factory workers.

Problem/solution argumentation structure. Problem is solved by client's involvement.

But through the work of Milchewski and other committed advocates, there's growing evidence that life on the farm isn't quite so dangerous any more. "We have to say that farming is safer today than it was 10 or 20 years ago," said Larry Brisley, a Midwest Rural Health Council agricultural engineer who specializes in farm safety.

The figures seem to back up Brisley's statement. Since 1960, farm accidental deaths have plummeted by nearly 50 percent. Although this figure is misleading because there are fewer farmers today, the death rate has also fallen.

Establishing first problem organization is trying to solve.

Brisley said the improved farm safety picture was made possible by improvements in many areas. But tractor and machinery accidents, which a Department of Transportation study claims are responsible for 60 percent of agriculture's accident deaths, have been the top priority for study.

"Farming accidents have decreased because machinery design is much better today than it was before," Brisley said. "Today's equipment does a better job of what it is supposed to do. There's been a decrease in tractor accidents because of the roll frames and cabs as well as improved machinery shields."

Although government studies pointed out specific problems in machinery design, one of the most powerful arguments convincing farm equipment companies to improve equipment safety were the lawsuits brought by farmers hurt because of improperly designed equipment.

"Product liability is our organization's most persuasive argument to convince manufacturers they need to make safety changes," Brisley said. "The industry cannot afford any longer to put out equipment without safety in mind. That's been a major factor in our success in changing machinery design."

Second problem our client is attacking.

Another reason farming is safer is the improved emergency medical service in rural communities. Since 1974, the federal government has pumped more than $80 million into emergency medical services programs in rural areas.

The council has helped upgrade those services, according to council legislative director Sonia Newberg. "We were one of the leading players in the fight for federal funding that gave rural hospitals more money to provide traumatic care units. Until we educated the feds about the frightful dangers farmers face from machinery, that funding had been exclusively devoted to central city hospitals where gunshot wounds were the norm. Now we've gotten our share."

But Newberg said that while the death rate from farm machinery is being whittled down by better design and health care, other dangerous elements of farming are being discovered. "Our technology is changing," she said. "Things we were not even aware of even a few years ago are going to be our biggest source of problems in the future.

"That's why the new labeling requirements for pesticides and farm chemicals the council has gotten are so important," Newberg said. "The public has to be made more conscious of health hazards that might not kill you in one horrible accident, but whose long-term consequences are just as deadly."

Transition from inverted pyramid back to focus individual.

That new attitude toward safety may be the biggest improvement the council can claim, according to Milchewski. "That's where I've personally been most successful," he said. "Every time I go out to a farm group to speak and talk about my father dying on that tractor, I look at the boys and girls out in the audience. They've already seen so many near-tragedies in their lives that they can immediately project themselves into a situation where they've almost lost a parent. And the parents know of times when they've almost left their kids as orphans.

Last paragraph suggests actions readers may take if they want to continue the organization's efforts.

"It's that new awareness I'm most proud of," Milchewski said. "Farmers have to be involved enough in the political process and in their own personal actions so there will never again be another kid who is forced to see his father killed in a farm accident. We just can't accept that nightmare as a normal part of farm life anymore."

-30-

## chapter 11

Delivering Messages to the Media: A Practitioner's Practical Tactical Guide

REAL-LIFE LESSONS

Early in my career, I was lucky enough to taste true humiliation—frightful, gut-wrenching embarrassment. No, I didn't feel lucky at the time, but in retrospect I've discovered that my true understanding of public relations theory has more often been reinforced by repeated blows to my head, and my ego, than through any book-borne logic.

One of the first lessons I was taught at the point of a sharp comment came after I had been in public relations about two years. I had been relatively successful in getting coverage for the large conservatory of music for which I worked. In addition to good attention by the local newspaper, I had scored feature stories on National Public Radio and in *Time* magazine. I was 24 years old and life was sweet.

But one evening I was invited to a dinner party and introduced to an older man who told me he was the editor of a rural weekly newspaper on the outskirts of the city. I know your name, I told him. His newspaper was on my media mailing list, and every week I sent him a packet of releases, one news release for each classical music concert the conservatory was doing.

He met my friendly reply with a stony stare. "Do you send me all those releases because you have some relative working for the post office that you're trying to send business to?" he asked. "Or are you just trying to tick me off?"

As I stood there looking the way that only a young man who's had his heart ripped out of his chest can look, he lectured me on media relations. His newspaper's readers were more interested in "Waylon and Willie and the boys" (quoting a famous country music song of the day) than in Wagner and Wolfgang, he said. Why was I wasting the taxpayers' money to send him stuff his subscribers weren't interested in?

Let's suppose for an instant, he said, that someday I might have something that he would be interested in. Why was I so stupid to make him waste hours of his valuable time ripping open envelopes containing releases that I should have been able to predict he wouldn't be interested in? It's never good to mess up the lives of the people from whom you'll eventually want kind treatment, he said.

Let's make a wild speculation, he said. Let's say my school did finally sponsor a concert artist his audience would want to see. Why didn't I know enough about his paper's format to realize he only put calendar listings for entertainment events in his newspaper? Isn't it pretty stupid to spend your time writing a three-page release on the event, just so an editor will have to pore through it in order to assemble a four-line listing of name, date, time, place and ticket prices?

The meal didn't go down very well that evening, but I learned a lot from that encounter. What seems easiest from the practitioner's viewpoint—spending an extra few dollars to mail full releases to every media outlet in the market in the hope that they might eventually print one—is really counterproductive to our final goal. It wastes money, paper and the working relationship with editors that is the key to success in any external communication program.

WHAT YOU KNOW

- Messages organized for ease of use will be acted upon more frequently than those that are more difficult to use.
- Every situation involves different audiences, and each of those audiences may have a different motivation for being involved in the problem.

WHAT YOU'LL LEARN

- Few communication goals can be satisfied by the participation of a single audience, and multiple audiences almost always have different motivators that drive them to action.
- Reporters and editors are gatekeepers, separate audiences whose separate communication needs have to be factored into the information practitioners offer and the format in which they deliver it.
- The enormous growth of media outlets and delivery systems enables practitioners to deliver precisely targeted messages to very specific audiences.

IF YOU CAN'T PLACE IT, WHY ARE YOU WRITING IT?

In previous chapters, we've learned the basic techniques of writing effective public relations messages. Your goal in writing is to fit the message to the audience to which it is directed, to fashion prose that is efficient and well-structured, and to make sure that your writing's style and presentation do not detract from your communication purpose.

The same principles apply to delivering public relations messages to the external media. Television and radio stations, newspapers, magazines and other media need and want PR writing that is intended for their specific audiences. Your job as a public relations professional is to research your subject so you'll know what relevant information you have to offer to certain audiences, and to research the media covering your subject so you'll know all the outlets interested in your message and their specific needs. You'll also need to know the technology available to help you tailor those messages to specific media, to help you select the appropriate media and then to deliver it effectively.

The purpose of this chapter is to explore your relationship and responsibilities to the media. Then we'll examine how you can use research and technology to target, and then deliver, your public relations messages. It's a strategy that will build your credibility with journalism professionals, which will make your communication campaigns more effective and improve your long-term relationships with the media.

THE NEW MEDIA RELATIONS RELATIONSHIP

Let's explore that relationship with the journalists who are so important to your success. It's first necessary to correct a few misinterpretations of the PR person's role in media relations. According to some of PR's critics, media relations at one point (in a past that even predates my own career) meant a back-slapping, influence-peddling, old-boys network of exchanged favors.

Among the stories I have heard have been tales of public relations practitioners lavishing expensive lunches, prime sports tickets and other favors on reporters and editors during the year, then ending the annual gift grab by delivering cases of liquor to newspaper offices at Christmas. In exchange for those gifts (the theory went), journalists gave generous public relations practitioners preferential treatment in newspapers and newscasts.

Such gift exchanges are becoming increasingly rare. At most major newspapers, national magazines, and radio and television stations, journalists are under specific instructions to refuse gifts or other favors that might be viewed as creating a conflict of interest. In most situations, editors and reporters insist on buying their own lunches, and concert reviewers buy their own theater, opera and symphony tickets.

That doesn't mean you can't have a warm personal friendship with the media people with whom you work. Sharing lunch can help you discover in an unpressured environment the type of stories a reporter is interested in and helps the reporter understand the strengths and structure of your organization. Nevertheless, by following the principles listed in Memory Memo 11.1, it's possible to have good relationships and frequent, positive coverage from reporters without ever buying a lunch.

You don't need to apologize for not lavishing gifts on reporters—because you are already helping them do their jobs. Journalists and public relations people who are involved in media relations are necessary for each other's existence. A survey of media outlets in one large city found that about 45 percent of the news items in newspapers and about 15 percent of the news items on radio and television newscasts originated from public relations sources. In another poll, business and financial editors considered public relations people to be their most important source of information. The media would have to hire many more reporters to obtain anything close to the coverage they currently provide with the help of public relations people.

As that relationship of mutual benefits suggests, your success in media relations shouldn't depend on your generosity to reporters. Instead, you should strive to create a professional environment in which you structure your media relations efforts to help journalists do their job better. That means helping editors and reporters find stories that genuinely interest or help their readers and providing that information in a way that allows them to accomplish their jobs most efficiently.

When you provide that sort of consistent delivery of services structured with the media's needs in mind, you'll find your relationship with your media contacts will be very warm, and you'll be able to fulfill your organization's communication objectives effectively.

But you also need to understand the professional environment you enter as a newly minted PR professional. The practitioners who have preceded you haven't necessarily established a sterling reputation for the public relations field. Journalists are naturally frustrated by the estimated 100 to 150 news releases that pile onto each editor's desk each working day. PR people working for national corporations hoping for coverage have often simply dumped a release on the desk of every major newspaper and every television and radio station in the nation.

Editors regularly complain about the complete disregard for a local angle in news releases and about the bad writing and poor attention to journalistic style. They say there's too much self-serving puffery instead of news in many news releases. That's one of Jane Anne Wilder's points in Box 11.1.

Memory Memo 11.1
Factors in a successful media relations relationship:

- Media decision makers: Adapt messages and delivery routines to accommodate their interests and work schedules.
- News hole: Plan events and news release timetables to coincide with slow news days.
- Market dynamics: Modify delivery systems to capitalize on placement opportunities in smaller markets or media outlets with specialized needs.

RECEIVER-CENTERED MEDIA RELATIONS: KNOWING YOUR AUDIENCE'S AUDIENCE

It helps to look upon your relationship with media people as a communication act, distinct and independent of your final goal. Applying the communication model we discussed in Chapter 1, you'll see the first thing we have to do is find situations in which the information we have to communicate coincides with the editor's interests and needs. Why are editors interested in your information? They aren't trying

BOX 11.1   Views from the Field

Jane Anne Wilder
Wilder is media relations manager for Swedish Medical Center, the Pacific Northwest's largest hospital. Previously, she was the public relations director for Washington's statehood centennial and is the coauthor of a book on children's nutrition.

Is a news release the correct strategy for every media relations situation?

It used to be that the news release was the answer to everything. News releases are still important, but I do far fewer of them than I used to. I'm much more likely to call or write a personal note. I also do a lot of follow-ups. If I read something off the wire service in the morning paper, I'll call the paper or the TV stations and ask them if they want a local angle on the national story.

Is it possible to target specific publics with a media relations program?

Not only is it possible, but you darn well better be doing it. Media people resent it when the releases you send them don't have anything to do with their audiences. They are human beings and sometimes their biases show in their coverage. You keep them biased toward your side by taking the time to do your job right. It's when we can see what services we have to offer and what audiences will be interested in them that we can find the best fit between messages and audience.

Let's say you've done all these things and have a great media relations program. So you've accomplished your institution's public relations goals, right?

I'll have to disagree. There are some publics that we PR people tend to forget about if we get caught up in thinking our only job is media relations. You've got to remember that your board is a public, your staff is a public— even your boss and your administrators are publics. We've got 4,000 employees in the hospital, and in theory, every one of them could be a good-will ambassador. We have over 800 hospital beds at the hospital and literally hundreds of thousands of visitors through our doors every year. Every one of them is a candidate to hear the messages we want to share.

BOX 11.1   (continued)

It sounds like there are so many publics we can talk to and so many messages we can communicate. How do you decide what your priorities are?

Any effective external media campaign has to dovetail with management goals. If you as a PR practitioner are sitting there alone in your little office coming up with what's important to the institution, both you and the administrators are going to have some unpleasant surprises. But administrators can't think their problems are their own and the PR department needn't worry their little heads about it either, because everybody has a problem then, too. I view an important part of my job as getting all of us singing from the same sheet of music.

—Used with permission of Jane Anne Wilder

to do you a favor by printing information from your release; they are trying to deliver important information to their readers.

That means you need to evaluate the audience editors are serving. What are the audience's interests? How much education do they have? Where do they live? From that information, and more like it, you can begin to predict messages that will satisfy those needs.

After you decide on a message, you select a communication medium that will most effectively transmit your message to the publics you need to inform to fulfill your institutional objectives. This is where many public relations people need to think more creatively.

As we've discussed before, the most persuasive communication tools are those that are the most highly targeted and the most personal. That means specialized journal articles are more effective than newspapers and broadcast stations, letters are more persuasive than journal articles, and personal meetings are more persuasive than anything else. It might be logical to concentrate your communication efforts on speeches, letters, personal phone calls, roundtable discussions or even a dinner party bringing together your managers and your target public. Those too are forms of external media and should be considered as you plan a communication campaign.

THE DAY-TO-DAY MECHANICS OF MEDIA RELATIONS

But let's say you determine that mass media newspapers and TV and radio stations are the most effective way to reach your important public. In those circumstances, you need to structure your presentation to meet the needs of the editor and the audience both you and the editor are serving. That means more than personalizing the story for those readers. It also means adapting the methods and even the times you present the story to editors.

Here's an example: All editors, whether working in newspapers, magazines or broadcast media, have daily peak work periods when they are completely engaged in putting their product together. To deliver a quality newscast or newspaper on time, their total attention has to be turned to fulfilling their production responsibilities during those hours. It's only common sense that a public relations person presenting his or her pitch for a story during those times will get a decidedly icy reception. You need to schedule your presentations to key media people when your presence won't be so unwanted.

Those peak times come at different moments during the day or on different days, depending on the medium's publication cycle or broadcast time. For wire service reporters and morning newspaper people, peak time is usually the late afternoon and evening. For evening newspapers, morning is the busiest time.

Television journalists, as you might expect, are busiest during the two or three hours before airtime at noon, early evening and late night. Radio news personnel need to fit any contact for story ideas from PR people in between newscasts.

The writers, editors and photographers who produce weekly newspapers and weekly and monthly magazines have more irregular schedules. Employees on weekly newspapers and magazines generally have one or two days during which their main jobs are the needed production work to design, lay out and print each week's publication. For monthly magazines, that production sequence will usually stretch for a full week. To keep a pleasant professional relationship with them, plan your visits and calls to them around their essential work.

Even if you're merely sending a release for an item to be placed in a community calendar section of a newspaper or radio station, consider the medium's deadline schedules. Those deadlines vary widely, but it's not uncommon for daily newspapers that publish schedules in their Sunday edition to require all calendar items by Tuesday or Wednesday of the preceding week. Radio and television stations often have even longer deadlines. Quite frequently, their deadlines for their community calendars are three or four weeks before the event.

When you anticipate coverage by a reporter or camera crew prompted by a news release, observing those deadlines becomes even more important. Although an assignment editor can send a reporter or camera crew for breaking news at almost a moment's notice, most PR placements don't warrant that type of response.

For nonemergency news items, you need to deliver a news release about your event far enough ahead of the deadline that a reporter can be assigned, interviews can be scheduled and conducted, and the print story can be written or the broadcast story produced before the deadline. Sometimes it is also necessary to include time for the reporter to conduct extra research for background information or visuals. That often stretches the required delivery date for news releases to three weeks or more before the optimum time for your story to run.

You should also recognize that feature stories or stories by columnists or special correspondents require even more time. Newspaper columnists or television reporters who specialize in humorous or special features might have scheduled the specific stories they will produce for weeks in advance. Magazine feature story deadlines can be four to six months before publication.

Media Relations Planning with the Media Analysis Form

What's the practical solution to this confusing and complex mix of deadlines for the scores of media outlets with which you're likely to be working? Obviously, you need to gain some degree of control. Without it, you won't be able to provide media members with information when they need it, or communicate with important publics when their support will be most helpful in solving institutional problems.

To that end, I recommend a media analysis form that encapsulates deadline and other information for important media outlets. That information includes the names, titles and areas of responsibility of editors, as well as the names, interests and special deadline information of reporters who cover areas related to your PR efforts. You'll see an example in Figure 11.1.

The media analysis form can be written on paper or notecards, which you'll review every time you conduct a media relations campaign in order to select media outlets and plan the production schedules for your news releases and query letters. Even better is to put such a media list into a computer file. As we will discuss later in the chapter, a computer program can be structured to assemble all the media outlets devoted to a particular subject, to select the names of writers and editors who deal specifically with that area, and even to generate address labels for those individuals. It can also help you plan your media campaign by grouping all your contacts by their respective deadlines. Thus, you can get a printout listing editors who need the information three months, one month, or one day before the event.

By working from a media analysis form and then integrating those deadlines into a persuasion platform, you'll be able to avoid missing deadlines or forgetting to include an important reporter or editor in your mailings, the most common problem of every media relations plan.

Information for this media analysis form comes from personal contacts with media representatives, from a publication's listing of personnel, from the credits of TV newscasts and from observing reporter bylines. You'll supplement those local sources with information from the media reference books we'll specify later in this chapter.

You'll quickly learn some general media relations guidelines as you compile the media analysis form. You'll discover it's usually inefficient to try to place a story nationally by sending releases to individual newspapers or broadcast stations. National coverage comes most easily by placing a story on one of the wire services, of which the Associated Press is the largest. Most towns and cities have a newspaper or television or radio station that subscribes to one of the wire services. Most cities have an Associated Press bureau where you can submit a story, and where the approval process through which wire stories are selected begins.

There's another route to national placement. A number of commercial services

Reporter's first name:	Natalie
Reporter's last name:	Halperin
Title:	music critic
Media outlet:	Kansas City Chronicle
Address:	1729 Main Street
City:	Kansas City
State:	Missouri
ZIP:	64109
Office phone number:	816-555-1394
Best calling time:	Monday–Thursday: 11 a.m.–Noon Friday 9:00 a.m.–4:00p.m.
Media opportunities:	Weekly arts calendar; major artist interviews in Sunday arts section; weekend highlights column for Saturday features section; radio interview with local arts figures on Friday.
Deadlines:	Sunday arts section: Noon Wednesday weekly Daily features: 3 p.m. previous day City desk: 10:45 p.m. previous day for breaking news
Special editions:	Fall arts roundup–August 1 deadline Holiday arts special–November 1 deadline
Special interests:	Likes: administrative intrigues in arts organizations Dislikes: interviewing singers
Work background:	Feature writer for Peoria paper after college. At present position since 1986. Has had stories published in Music America magazine. Does half-hour interview program on classical station each week.
Personal background:	Took lessons from our school's junior division; bachelor's and master's degrees in music from Northwestern University. Father is Gene, who was on school's board through 1950s. Plays cello in community orchestra. Into skiing.
Prospective stories:	Interview with one of our students who goes to Aspen Music Camp? Give chance to ski and highlight our music program.

FIGURE 11.1   Media Analysis Form

operate a wire service exclusively for public relations placements. Operating similarly to the Associated Press wire, these services (such as PR Newswire and Business Wire for print, and Medialink and News Radio Network for broadcast stories) screen print and broadcast releases offered to them before transmitting releases to news outlets via wire service machine or satellite feed.

Factors in Media Relations Decision Making

Media Decision Makers.   In compiling your media analysis form, you'll learn how each individual media outlet operates, which editors have the power to assign stories, and which writers are allowed to pick and choose their own stories. In broadcast media, you'll discover whether a producer or a host decides who will be interviewed on the radio and television talk shows that are noticed by your important publics.

The News Hole.   There will be other important information you'll notice as you study your potential media outlets. For instance, because more newspaper advertising is sold for certain days, the news hole (the amount of space a newspaper has available for news coverage) is generally smaller in newspapers published on Mondays, Tuesdays, Wednesdays and Saturdays.

Although television newscasts are generally the same length every day, you'll notice that on certain days there are generally fewer breaking news events. Although heavy news days vary depending on the schedule of local government meetings, Saturdays, Sundays and Mondays are generally slow news days in most cities. Releasing your news on those slow news days might boost your broadcast coverage if your information is marginal enough to be pushed out of the media by more prominent events.

Large-market vs. Small-market Placement.   You'll also quickly develop an awareness of the differences between your ability to place information in major metropolitan print and broadcast outlets, and the newspapers and TV and radio stations in smaller markets. Because of smaller staffs, fewer production dollars, and, quite frankly, less local news, smaller markets are more willing to accept and place information from public relations sources.

Thus, a story that wouldn't be placed in a major metropolitan newspaper might very easily be run verbatim in a community weekly. Photos that would never appear in a big-city newspaper might make the front page in a small-city daily. A videotape news release that a television station in a major market would never run might be a prominent feature during a small-city newscast.

Don't discount those outlets merely because they aren't in a major market. Those consumers, those votes or those voices outside metropolitan areas can be just as valuable, and at times, more valuable to you and your organization's success.

BEYOND THE SHOTGUN: PR DELIVERY SYSTEMS

Now that you know a little about your relationship with media members, we can begin to talk about operating within that role. Already, you've discovered that there are several important components that have to be considered in the design of any successful public relations communication campaign.

First, it's important to know the characteristics of the audience with which you are trying to communicate. Second, you should know the information in your message that is important for that audience and structure your information to most effectively involve that audience with your message. Third, it's most important to employ a delivery system that credibly presents your message to people to whom it is important. Finally, the delivery system should do all this in the most efficient way possible.

Too frequently, little attention has been devoted to planning a PR delivery system. Traditionally, a PR practitioner might prepare a news release on an event or an issue, make copies of it and send it to scores, or hundreds, or even thousands of media outlets. The same release might go to the editor of a major metropolitan newspaper, the producer of news programming at a rock music station, the managing editor of a wire service's regional bureau and the editor of a small-town newspaper.

That shotgun approach of sending the same release to every media outlet no matter what its interests wasn't a particularly good communication strategy 30 years ago and still isn't.

THE EMERGING DYNAMIC: THE UN-MASS MEDIA

The shotgun strategy is valid only if you believe that there are no differences among communication media outlets. Some media critics tend to support that position, pointing to the decreasing number of competitive newspapers in big cities and the increasing number of media outlets owned by media conglomerates.

There's also the perception articulated by many conservative political leaders that the media has a single voice—a consistency of message and outlook—that deprives some viewpoints from gaining access to the media and makes the difference between a Los Angeles television station and a small newspaper in rural Georgia negligible. They claim the media now speak with one, harping voice. The frequent purchases of newspapers, television stations and magazines by media conglomerates seem to support their position.

Those producers, those editors, represent every kind of person, from the farmers and small-business owners served by a weekly newspaper to the intellectuals and arts-oriented people who listen to a classical music station. So is there a mass media? There's surprisingly little evidence to support that viewpoint. In fact, over the past 40 years the world has undergone a communications explosion that has made it possible for more groups to express themselves in the media. During that time the media have become much more diverse, not less. You'll see that trend in Table 11.1.

TABLE 11.1   Number of media outlets in the United States, 1945–1995

Type of Media	1945	1965	1985	1995
Newspapers	11,877	11,353	9,134	10,972
Periodicals	8,880	8,990	11,090	10,387
Radio stations	936	5,279	9,642	11,701
TV stations	6	586	1,194	1,520
Cable systems	0	945	7,230	11,800
TOTAL	18,699	27,183	38,110	46,380

SOURCES: Gale Directory of Publications; Broadcasting/Cablecasting Yearbook

Look at how much more competitive all the communication media have become. In television, many more choices are available to the typical viewer since cable television has become a common feature in communities. In practically every market, the variety of cable outlets dwarfs the number of channels available just a few years ago. Special-interest cable networks like the History Channel, the Fashion Channel, and Court TV counter the argument of those who claim the nation is being subjected to an increasingly uniform mass media. Local access cable channels and low-power local broadcasting stations have also increased the options available to TV viewers.

Among periodicals, too, we can see a stunning new diversity. Since 1940, the number of magazines has increased substantially. As that roster of magazines has grown, the amount of specialization has also increased. Supplementing the general-interest publications that dominated journalism 30 years ago, we're now seeing publications targeting smaller and smaller audiences. There are now glossy city magazines ranging from *New York* magazine to a magazine published for St. Joseph, Mo., residents. There are publications written for skateboarders, for Armenian-Americans, for women in Madison, Wisc., for users of certain models of computers, and for cigar smokers.

The level of specialization is also evident among trade publications, which cover specific industries, occupations and other economic activities. There are trade publications for vending machine operators, French-Canadian missionaries, eyeglass frame wholesalers, police dog handlers, and more.

There may be even more specialization in the future. The publishing explosion discussed above was in full force before small-time publishers began exploring the low-cost possibilities of desktop publishing. Desktop publishing (discussed in Chapter 9) has radically cut the cost of publishing by cutting the time it takes to prepare copy for printing and dramatically reducing the number of people it takes to do it. That is only going to weaken the claim that there is less media diversity.

Targeting Specialized Audiences

Unfortunately, public relations professionals often act as if none of this diversity has happened. All too frequently we've produced one single release on an event, and expected it to satisfy the needs of every publication editor, every broadcast producer. But those producers and editors represent increasingly specialized audiences who look to public relations sources for more and more specialized information. How have all these new media outlets, this new specialization, changed the way you as a public relations professional should design and conduct your communication campaigns?

First, you need to realize that those publications, radio stations, and regular, pay and cable television outlets are tools you can use to build your communication campaigns. You should view each of those media outlets not merely as addresses to which to send releases, but as representatives of particular groups of individuals united by a common interest or quality.

Today's increased publication and broadcast specialization makes every outlet more valuable, because now you can increasingly target only those audiences for whom your information is vital. Because of the increasingly narrow audiences media outlets serve, it is likely you can predict what information a particular publication or broadcast outlet will want to communicate to its customers. Where previously you might have mailed hundreds or thousands of news releases, you can now send releases to only those media outlets that have a particular interest in your message. That can help you cut the cost of your PR campaigns.

Specialization also means you can increase the credibility of your message. For men and women interested in technical fields like computer programming, information they receive from a publication like *Byte* magazine is going to be much more believable than the same story appearing in a metropolitan newspaper. That additional credibility is a bonus to any communication campaign. To take advantage of the media's new specialization, we must deliver the information wanted by the editors and producers managing each outlet.

Getting Maximum Coverage: Story Splitting

As a PR professional, you have the tools that will help you target individual messages to individual audiences. That's the way to maintain your credibility and effectiveness.

You've already learned one way to target audiences. In Chapters 5 and 6, we discussed strategies to determine what would interest particular audiences and how to construct lead sentences and inverted pyramid structures to emphasize that information. But although the structure of a news release demands that it focus on one main topic, that doesn't mean a PR professional has to send the same release to every media outlet.

For one thing, most stories have more than a single interesting aspect. Let's look at an example. A coal company announces the use of a new university-developed technique to replant trees on a number of exhausted strip mines. Where previously there were gaping, ugly gashes in the mountains, there are now grassy slopes with young trees. The company is donating the land to the state parks department and is building a new backpacking trail that will meander through the growing forests. What is interesting about this story? Who is interested in it?

We can see that environmental publications are going to be interested in the commitment this company has made to restoring the wilderness it disrupted. Magazines for backpackers and campers will want to share information about the new recreation area that has been developed for its readers. Scientific magazines might be interested in the application of new technology to this real-life problem. Newspapers in the towns and cities around the restored mine will be happy that tourism dollars might replace some of the wages lost when mining operations closed. The university's publication will revel in the knowledge that its academic efforts are paying off for the state's citizens. The newspaper in the small town where the inventor grew up will be interested in the success of a hometown product.

Those are only some of the possible stories within this one event. I call this technique "story splitting." Virtually every situation has a similarly varied set of news elements.

Taking each of the story's facets and structuring several specialized releases tailored to particular media outlets seems like a simple, reasonable goal for public relations practitioners, but it has too frequently been ignored. It has always been argued that customizing releases is impractical because writing multiple releases is too time-consuming and labor-intensive. However, the task of individualizing releases for particular groups isn't overwhelming, because it doesn't necessarily mean rewriting the entire release.

Because the receiver-centered writing process is built around the inverted pyramid, it is very likely the main body of individualized news releases on a single topic will remain fundamentally identical from release to release, even if releases are directed to different audiences.

The TIPCUP process forces writers to concentrate information important to a specific audience within the story's first few paragraphs. The PR writer adapts the first paragraph to target the individual editor or producer for whom it is intended. The rest of the release, concentrating on background information about the event, can stay essentially the same. Figures 11.2 and 11.3 show examples of the process.

FIELD-FORMATTED RELEASES: USING TECHNOLOGY TO INDIVIDUALIZE PR MESSAGES

When I started using story splitting to target versions of news releases to specific media, I taped an opening paragraph to the release's body copy, photocopied it, then pulled off the tape, placed another targeted opening paragraph on the body copy and photocopied the new release. I did this again and again, as many times as necessary.

Luckily, you don't have to repeat this drudgery. Computers and wordprocessing programs make adapting PR messages to individual audiences easy. Every word processing program has a feature that allows a writer to make multiple copies of a document in the computer memory. With that capacity, you can make changes in only those sections of the document that need to be altered to individualize the story for its particular market. After that, the computer will print out each separate version, preserving the common elements from one version to the next.

Computer and electronic technology can be used in other ways to simplify the individualization of news releases. Often, situations arise in which a number of people receive a similar honor or award. An announcement of a college's graduates or the Army's announcement of enlisted personnel who have been promoted often involves thousands of individual names whose owners hail from thousands of communities.

Although many hometown newspapers might be interested in the news of a local citizen's accomplishments, no editor has the time to search through thousands of names for news of the people who might interest the paper's readers. Few public relations staffs have time to individualize thousands of news releases to increase the possibility of their being used. However, most word processing software programs let PR people individualize releases on a vast scale. The writer can create a

ARS FEMINA ENSEMBLE

WRITING WOMEN BACK INTO MUSIC HISTORY

NEWS RELEASE

Special to New Albany Tribune

Feb. 14, 1994   Contact: Susan Reigler

For immediate release   Phone: (502) 555-5119

New Albany Teacher

Soloist at U of L Concert

    A New Albany High School teacher will be the featured vocalist in a free concert devoted entirely to chamber music composed by women.

    NAHS choir director Linda DeRungs will join fellow members of the Ars Femina Ensemble to perform in a Women's History Month concert at the University of Louisville. DeRungs, who has been teaching at New Albany for eight years, is part of one of the leading forces resurrecting and restoring women's music to its proper place in the repertoire. She and the other Ars Femina members recently released a compact disc recording devoted to music written by women before 1800.

    Thousands of women, most of whom were ignored by the men who wrote music history, have created a treasure trove of technically excellent, emotionally compelling music through the centuries that Ars Femina has discovered. In research trips through Europe and North America, Ars Femina members have unearthed over 235 diverse chamber music works written by women, most of which were unpublished and had to be prepared directly from the original manuscripts.

(more)

P.O. BOX 7692 • LOUISVILLE • KENTUCKY • 40257 • (502) 897-5719

FIGURE 11.2 Version of news release targeted to one performer's local newspaper

New Albany Teacher
page 2

That original scholarship has turned Ars Femina concerts into important events, since in virtually every performance the group's four instrumentalists and one vocalist bring to light a work that has languished unperformed in European archives for hundreds of years. The works are performed on original 17th century instruments or historically accurate recreations and performances are accompanied by short talks describing the works' histories.

The March 6 concert will include three 20th century premieres of works by Isabella Leonarda, Hildegard von Bingen and Marianne Martinez. Leonarda, an Italian, was the 17th century's most published composer, publishing from the time she was 22 until she was 80 years old. Germany's von Bingen was credited as the inventor of the medieval morality play in the early 1100s. Martinez, the daughter of the Spanish ambassador to the Austrian court, was Vienna's first woman Kapellmeister, studied under Haydn and played in piano duets with Mozart.

The March 6 concert by the Ars Femina Ensemble is free and open to the public. Held in the University of Louisville School of Music's North Recital Hall, it will begin at 7:30 p.m. The concert is part of a monthlong series of lectures, films, plays, poetry readings and art exhibits focusing on women's history that is sponsored by the University of Louisville.

-30-

Calendar Information:

The Ars Femina Ensemble

"Music by Women"

Wednesday, March 6—7:30 p.m.

University of Louisville School of Music North Recital Hall

Free—Call 555-5119 for information

FIGURE 11.2 (continued)

standardized news release (for instance, announcing the members of the first semester dean's honor roll at a college), leaving blanks where the individualized information would go. These blanks, called "fields" in computer terminology, are for information like name, address, city, state, high school graduation year, and parents' names.

After just the few words are typed in each release listing information on an in-

ARS FEMINA ENSEMBLE

WRITING WOMEN BACK INTO MUSIC HISTORY

ENSEMBLE:

William Bauer

Linda DeRungs

Lynda Hurd

Jim Oxyer

Susan Reigler

Katherine Whiteside

BOARD OF DIRECTORS:

Elizabeth Stith, Chair

William Bauer

Myrtle Bingham

Jerry Eifler

Nancy Evans

Sarah Febish

Eric Graninger

Randall Holden

Kathryn Johnson

Mary Kuhns

Fran Lewis

Mary Ann Lundy

David Lunsford

Beth Niblock

Susan Reigler

Barbara Sandford

Marcia Segal

Mary Ann Stenger

Terry Weiss

Nick Wilkerson

NEWS RELEASE

Special to Louisville Woman magazine

Feb. 14, 1994   Contact: Susan Reigler

For immediate release   Phone: (502) 555-5119

Women's History Month

Honored with Special Concert

    Women's History Month will be celebrated in song by the Ars Femina Ensemble during a March 6 concert devoted entirely to chamber music composed by women.

    The Louisville-based Ars Femina Ensemble, comprised of William Bauer, Linda DeRungs, Lynda Hurd, James Oxyer and Katie Whiteside, is one of the leading forces resurrecting and restoring women's music to its proper place in the repertoire. The group recently released a compact disc recording devoted to music written by women before 1800.

    Thousands of women, most of whom were ignored by the men who wrote music history, have created a treasure trove of technically excellent, emotionally compelling music through the centuries that Ars Femina has discovered. In research trips through Europe and North America, Ars Femina members have unearthed over 235 diverse chamber music works written by women, most of which were unpublished and had to be prepared directly from the original manuscripts.

(more)

P.O. BOX 7692 • LOUISVILLE • KENTUCKY • 40257 • (502) 897-5719

FIGURE 11.3   Version of news release targeted to women's magazine

Women's History concert
page 2

That original scholarship has turned Ars Femina concerts into important events,
since in virtually every performance the group's four instrumentalists and one vocalist
bring to light a work that has languished unperformed in European archives for
hundreds of years. The works are performed on original 17th century instruments or
historically accurate recreations and performances are accompanied by short talks
describing the works' histories.

The March 6 concert will include three 20th century premieres of works by
Isabella Leonarda, Hildegard von Bingen and Marianne Martinez. Leonarda, an Italian,
was the 17th century's most published composer, publishing from the time she was 22
until she was 80 years old. Germany's von Bingen was credited as the inventor of the
medieval morality play in the early 1100s. Martinez, the daughter of the Spanish
ambassador to the Austrian court, was Vienna's first woman Kapellmeister, studied
under Haydn and played in piano duets with Mozart.

The March 6 concert by the Ars Femina Ensemble is free and open to the public.
Held in the University of Louisville School of Music's North Recital Hall, it will begin at
7:30 p.m. The concert is part of a monthlong series of lectures, films, plays, poetry
readings and art exhibits focusing on women's history that is sponsored by the
University of Louisville.

-30-

Calendar Information:

The Ars Femina Ensemble

"Music by Women"

Wednesday, March 6—7:30 p.m.

University of Louisville School of Music North Recital Hall

Free—Call 555-5119 for information

FIGURE 11.3 (continued)

dividual, the computer will insert all the information into the appropriate fields, then
print a personalized release. See an example of this type of release in Sidebar 11.1.

MEDIA DIRECTORIES: KNOWING YOUR OPTIONS

You now know some strategies for individualizing PR messages to specific audiences.
But how do you find, and then reach, all the people to whom your message is important? What media outlets offer the most credibility for your message to the audience with whom you most want to communicate?

SIDEBAR 11.1   Field-formatted News Releases

A field-formatted computer process can be used to add individual elements to thousands of similar news releases. After just the personalized information is typed for each field, the computer will insert it into the appropriate locations in each release. The following illustrates the process, from identifying the field to an individual version of the final product.

Merge Information for Co-op News Release

student's first name:

student's last name:

gender:

degree level:

degree program:

name of high school:

graduation year:

hometown:

parents' names:

co-op company name:

co-op location:

MACRO INSTRUCTIONS:

1. In <<gender>>, "M" will print "his" in paragraphs 1 and 2;
        "son" in paragraph 5.
    In <<gender>>, "F" will print "her" in paragraphs 1 and 2;
        "daughter" in paragraph 5.

2. In <<degree level>>, "B" will print "bachelor's";
        "M" will print "master's".

3. In <<degree program>>, "C" will type "communication";
        "D" will type "business"; "E" will type "engineering".

(continued)

SIDEBAR 11.1   (continued)

Merge Information for Co-op News Release

student's first name:	Mary
student's last name:	Portledge
gender:	F
degree level:	B
degree program:	C
name of high school:	Thomas Jefferson High School
graduation year:	91
hometown:	Corning
parents' names:	John and Anna Portledge
co-op company name:	V-J Energy Services
co-op location:	Chattanooga, Tenn.

MACRO INSTRUCTIONS:

1.   In <<gender>>, "M" will print "his" in paragraphs 1 and 2;
        "son" in paragraph 5.
     In <<gender>>, "F" will print "her" in paragraphs 1 and 2;
        "daughter" in paragraph 5.

2.   In <<degree level>>, "B" will print "bachelor's";
        "M" will print "master's".

3.   In <<degree program>>, "C" will type "communication";
        "D" will type "business"; "E" will type "engineering".

There are many reference books that can help with that task. Probably the two best reference works for finding American and Canadian newspapers, magazines and more general publications are the Standard Periodical Directory and the Gale Directory of Publications.

The Standard Periodical Directory groups more than 85,000 publications either by type (newspapers, house organs, etc.) or by subject matter (genetics, cosmetics, babies, horses, etc.). The Gale Directory, which indexes more than 38,000 publications, groups magazines and newspapers by the city in which they are produced.

---

news from

Kalifer University

<<current date>>   contact: April Joiner

FOR IMMEDIATE RELEASE   phone: 555-1359

Corning Graduate Complete Co-op Program

A <<name of high school>> graduate has completed a co-op work internship at <<co-op company name>> as part of <<gender>> work for a <<degree level>> degree in <<degree program>> at Kalifer University.

<<student's first name>><<student's last name>>, a 19<<graduation year>> graduate from <<name of high school>>, finished the internship at the <<co-op company name>> offices in <<co-op location>> and has now started on <<gender>> last semester of course work.

Kalifer University's co-op program, which has won two national awards for university program innovation, is designed to give practical experience and professional contacts to Kalifer students before they enter the job market.

As part of Kalifer's job placement program, it has been very successful. Since the program began in 1990, 85 percent of the Kalifer students completing co-ops have received job offers from their co-op sponsors. Among the 35 participating companies are Veterans Chemical Bank, KaliCare Health Services, Dow Smith Electric Co. and Rumanian Federal Insurance Co.

<<student's last name>> is the <<gender>> of <<parents' names>> of <<hometown>>.

-30-

(continued)

Thus, if you want to find every print media outlet in New York City or in Marshalltown, Iowa, it's possible to do that with the Gale Directory.

If you're looking for even more specialized publications, there are resources that can help you with that task. The Newsletters Directory lists more than 11,500 newsletters, digests, updates and bulletins in the United States, indexing them by

SIDEBAR 11.1 (continued)

news from

Kalifer University

November 22, 1995   contact: April Joiner

FOR IMMEDIATE RELEASE   phone: 555-1359

Corning Graduate Complete Co-op Program

    A Thomas Jefferson High School graduate has completed a co-op work internship at V-J Energy Services as part of her work for a bachelor's degree in communications at Kalifer University.

    Mary Portledge, a 1991 graduate from Thomas Jefferson High School, finished the internship at the V-J Energy Services offices in Chattanooga, Tenn., and has now started on her last semester of course work.

    Kalifer University's co-op program, which has won two national awards for university program innovation, is designed to give practical experience and professional contacts to Kalifer students before they enter the job market.

    As part of Kalifer's job placement program, it has been very successful. Since the program began in 1990, 85 percent of the Kalifer students completing co-ops have received job offers from their co-op sponsors. Among the 35 participating companies are Veterans Chemical Bank, KaliCare Health Services, Dow Smith Electric Co. and Rumanian Federal Insurance Co.

    Portledge is the daughter of John and Anna Portledge of Corning.

-30-

subject area. Thus it's very easy to find the names and addresses of newsletters, along with a detailed description of the publications' editorial interests, circulation and editors. The subject categories listed in Newsletter Directory are even more specific than those found in the Standard Periodical Index. For instance, there are 10 subject categories listed under the general term *politics*. Figure 11.4 shows typical entries from the Gale and Newsletter directories.

    With the Encyclopedia of Associations you can find communication sources even more specific than those in the Standard Periodical Index. The Encyclopedia of As-

BIXBY (L3), pop. 6,934.

Tulsa Co. (NEC). 15 m S of Tulsa. Elevator. Gasoline, naptha manufactured. Oil wells. Farming. Pecans, grain, truck crops.

Print

★24545★ Bassin'
NatCom. Inc.
15115 S 76 E Ave.   Phone: (918)366-4441
Bixby, OK 74008   Fax: (918)366-6250
Bass fishing magazine featuring articles on the proper use of equipment, techniques the experts use, and suggestions for the best locations to fish; including profiles of bass fishermen who have landed a prizewinning catch, product reviews of what's new and old standbys, and regular columns by the experts. **Founded:** 1974. **Frequency:** 8x/yr. **Printing Method:** Web offset. **Trim Size:** 8 x 10 7/8. **Cols./Page:** 3. **Col. Width:** 30 nonpareils. **Col. Depth:** 140 agate lines. **Key Personnel:** Thayne Smith, Executive Editor; Gordon Sprouse, Managing Editor; Gerald W. Pope, Publisher; Ellie Shimer, Advertising Mgr. ISSN: 0884-4739. **Subscription Rates:** $13.95. $2.50 single issue.
Ad Rates: BW: $4,955   Circulation: ★220,211
              4C: $6,442
              PCI: $240
Formerly: PRO BASS.

★24546★ Bixby Bulletin
Seven W Dawes
Bixby, OK 74008   Phone: (918)366-8260
Community newspaper. **Founded:** 1905. **Frequency:** Weekly (Thurs.). **Printing Method:** Offset. Uses mats. **Cols./Page:** 6. **Col. Width:** 26 nonpareils. **Col. Depth:** 294 agate lines. **Key Personnel:** Robbie N. Boman, Editor; Dave Fordonski, Publisher. **Subscription Rates:** $14.88.
Ad Rates: SAU: $4   Circulation: 2,400

★24547★ Winning!
NatCom. Inc.
15115 S 76th E Ave.   Phone: (918)366-4441
Bixby, OK 74008   Fax: (918)366-6250
Magazine covering lotteries, contests, sweepstakes, and Las Vegas style gaming. **Founded:** 1976. **Frequency:** Monthly. **Printing Method:** Offset. **Trim Size:** 8 x 10 3/4. **Cols./Page:** 3. **Col. Width:** 2 1/4 in. **Col. Depth:** 10 in. **Key Personnel:** Simon McCaffery, Editor; Gerald W. Pope, Publisher; Ellie Shimer, Advertising Mgr. **Subscription Rates:** $12. $1 single issue.
Ad Rates: BW: $2,305   Circulation: ‡225,000
              4C: $2,875
              PCI: $77

Fruit (*See also* Produce Trade)
  Apricot Quarterly Roundup **4134**
  California Strawberry Report **4161**
  Calyx Newsletter **4165**
  Cranberry Station Newsletter **4189**
  Fresh Facts **4248**
  Fresh Facts for Foodservice **1781**
  Fruit Growers Newsletter **4251**
  Fruit Situation and Outlook
    Report **4252**
  IAI Apple News **4287**
  Indoor Citrus and Rare Fruit Society—
    Bulletin **4300**
  Kiwifruit Growers Newsletter **4321**
          ・ ・ ・

Fuels, Synthetic *See* Synthetic Fuels

Fundraising
  Channels **798**
  Christian Management Report **595**
  Dimensions **5749**
  Endowment Builder **5755**
  501(C)(3) Monthly Letter **638**
  Foundation Giving Watch **5767**
  FRI Monthly Portfolio **5770**
  FRM Weekly **5772**
  The Fund Raising Forum **5774**
  Healthcare Fund Raising
    Newsletter **5787**
  LRE Project Exchange **9302**
  Membership Matters! **5832**
  National Catholic Development
    Conference—Monitor **5844**
          ・ ・ ・

Funeral Supply Industry
  Casket Manufacturers Association of
    America—Newsletter **1717**
  Cemetery Business & Legal
    Guide **6923**
  Funeral Service :Insider: **1784**

Funerals
  Continental Association of Funeral and
    Memorial Societies—Leader **7666**
  ICS Newsletter **9596**
  Toronto Memorial Society—
    Newsletter **1995**

Fungi
  Mycological Society of America—
    Newsletter **4692**
  North American Truffling Society—
    Newsletter **4379**

FIGURE 11.4 Research resources for targeting specialized print media
These two examples from the Gale Directory of Publications and the Newsletter Directory show how tightly focused many publications are. With that information, PR professionals can effectively target messages to very specific audiences. By appearing in specializing publications, your message gains higher credibility with a target public.

sociations is a multivolume reference source listing the names and addresses of more than 20,000 organizations, associations, fraternal clubs and lobbying groups. It includes a truly broad scope of associations. There are large, well-known organizations like the American Bar Association, which conducts research and educational projects for its 326,000 members, and slightly less celebrated groups, such as the American Council of Spotted Asses, which maintains a breeding registry and conducts competitions for this rare type of donkey. Most important for the PR professional, it lists the publications each organization produces and their frequency of publication.

There are similar publications for broadcast outlets that not only help you in targeting releases but can give you specific information about desired topics and guests for radio and TV talk shows. Although specific strategies for booking talk show guests are beyond the scope of this book, the same principles apply as those that guide the placement of releases. As a PR practitioner you must do the research to know what audience is interested in your message, then justify to the appropriate broadcast outlet your organization's expertise to discuss that subject. Those hours and hours of broadcast talk shows can be a valuable resource for a complete public relations campaign. See the Ready Reference section at the end of this chapter for a list of media reference books and their features.

Computer Searches to Find Special Audiences

Obviously, there are many, many publications that can help you learn about possible media outlets for your PR message. However, you might see a practical problem in using these many different reference books. With this wealth of resources, it becomes a daunting task to examine every one of them for possible media outlets for our PR messages.

Again, computer technology can help. An increasing number of the media directories are in database format accessible to computer searches, which allows the computer to go word by word through each reference database looking for specific topics.

For example, let's say you are looking for all publications that have a major focus on raising chickens or that serve areas where chicken ranches are a significant industry. If you were conducting a manual search, that would mean examining the cross-indexes in all the reference books for publications about poultry and then examining individual entries to determine if the publication covers chicken ranching. That would give you a list of the most obvious publications that deal with raising chickens.

However, it would be nearly impossible to locate publications in areas that grow chickens. Even though the Gale Directory lists primary industries in each city's entry, it would be necessary for you to examine every town and city in the entire directory in order to find those communities that listed chicken farming as one of their main industries.

However, a computer database search of the reference books could go through each reference looking for mentions of the word *chicken*, and, for each mention, the computer would print the name of the media outlet and the reference book entry. By using a computer database search, a PR professional could obtain a complete list and description of all publications that have any interest in chickens. Then the practitioner could examine each of those entries to see which would be most appropriate for a given PR message.

Media Surveys: Knowing Who's in the Audience

Knowing the media resources available to us still won't do us much good unless we know what those editors and broadcast producers want and unless we can deliver the things they need. As stated earlier in the chapter, a generalized release that's sent to a metropolitan newspaper editor, a television news producer and a small-town newspaper editor often won't get the response it should because each of those journalists is looking for something specific, some news that will interest or help his or her readers.

Therefore, it's necessary for a PR practitioner to know the particular characteristics of the medium with which he or she is supposed to be communicating. A knowledge of those characteristics will enable you to deliver the specific message to the specific target audiences.

Again, research will provide many of the answers. Many publications and broadcast outlets commission research organizations to provide a demographic profile of their readers. These profiles are intended for potential advertisers who need to know what audience they will be reaching by advertising in a particular medium. Those demographic profiles can provide much the same information about audience interests to the PR practitioner. Generally, stations and publications are quite willing to share this information with PR professionals. Figure 11.5 shows an example of one publication's demographic analysis of its readers.

In addition to these media-sponsored audience surveys, there are several publications that compare audience penetration, market share, and other factors among print and broadcast outlets. Publications like Simmons Study of Media & Markets and the International Demographics Media Audit (discussed in Chapter 3) can give you additional information about a media outlet's characteristics. Its research analyzes audiences to such a degree that you can tell, for example, what publication or television show is seen by the greatest number of men over the age of 25 who don't have a high school education. For a public relations practitioner who wants to know how to reach an appropriate audience for a high school diploma equivalency program this type of specific information could be very valuable.

How do you find audience characteristics for media outlets that don't take part in these rating services? Although the evidence isn't quite as scientific as found in formal audience surveys, every media outlet offers major clues about the characteristics of their audience.

What can you infer about a publication's audience by examining the publication? Let's look at two senior citizens' magazines that seem pointed toward the same audience—older adults. The senior citizens' magazine that includes a stock market column obviously is meant to appeal to older people who have enough extra income that they can afford to invest some of it. The magazine also has advertisements for ocean cruises and luxury household items. It's reasonable to think the primary readers of this magazine are healthy and free of financial worries. The other publi-

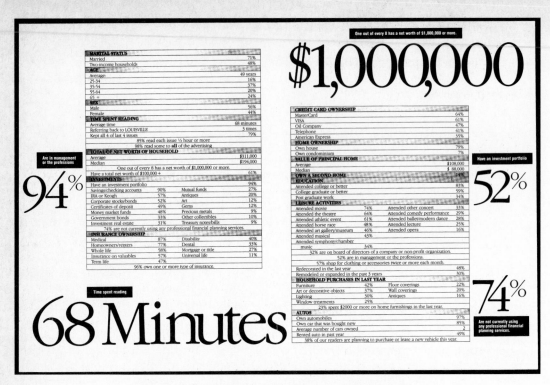

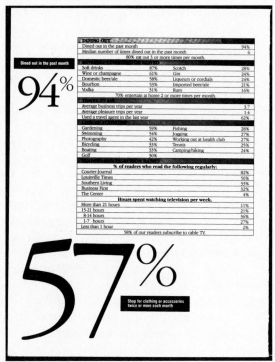

FIGURE 11.5 Demographic report for a city magazine
Used with permission of Louisville Magazine

cation includes a monthly feature on how to make inexpensive meals from macaroni, and advertisements for basic medical products or free transportation services. You can bet that magazine has as its readers older adults with much lower incomes.

HIGH-TECH PR DELIVERY SYSTEMS

Any individualization in the writing process won't be effective unless you can strategically target and economically and efficiently deliver those specific messages to specific media outlets. With the thousands of specialized media that are available to PR professionals, that's certainly one of the more complicated aspects of the communication task.

Computer technology can also help in managing the delivery of those individualized messages. An efficient news release program often involves maintaining mailing addresses or fax numbers for hundreds of different publications and being able to pull them together in certain combinations on short notice, which a computer can expedite.

For instance, if you were a PR practitioner announcing a new brand of yogurt, you might want to mail or fax a release to all food editors across the nation. Or, if the product was going to be test marketed only in a two-state market, the release should go only to food editors in those two states, or just to those two states' food editors who did regular reports or columns on natural foods.

A computer program allows you to make any of these distinctions and, as Memory Memo 11.2 shows, many others. Certain geographical areas can be selected by asking the computer program to search for and select only media outlets in certain ZIP code areas.

For instance, if you wanted all media in Missouri, you would ask the computer program to select publications and radio and TV stations whose addresses included ZIP codes with the first two digits 63, 64 and 65. If you wanted media in just Kansas City, you would ask the computer to select only the ZIP codes beginning with 640 and 641. You could pick specific neighborhoods by specifying the last two digits. If it would be useful, you could even target individual blocks or office buildings by using the nine-digit ZIP code.

Memory Memo 11.2
By using computers in media targeting you can

- create multiple versions of a release by substituting different lead sections targeted to individual media interests.
- search media databases to assemble targeted media mailing lists for individual campaigns.
- deliver documents to media outlets through modems.
- create individualized field-formatted releases in situations in which many people have been involved in the same activity

---

Overlaying Databases for Targeted Distribution

The computer can also be programmed to build media lists with characteristics that are much more specific than geographic location. By assigning certain designations (usually numerical or alphabetical codes) to certain types of characteristics, and then matching those codes with the appropriate publications, a PR person can compile a list to target certain types of editors or audiences. For example, within a master list of newspapers, a PR professional can establish a coding system that designates weekly newspapers, daily newspapers, and newspapers that have automotive reporters, farm reporters, or other specialized writers.

It is also possible to code each media outlet in terms of its total circulation, the primary industries of its service area, the average income or educational level of its subscribers, the average water hardness of the region it serves, or any of thousands of other characteristics. Once those categories have been assigned to the media outlets, the computer can be easily programmed to select those with certain characteristics or even with a combination of characteristics.

Let's say you were in charge of a public relations campaign announcing new sunglasses designed specifically to prevent snow blindness. Obviously, few people in Virginia or Texas are going to need such a product, but it will interest people in areas where there is a lot of snow, and where people remain outside in the snow's glare for long periods. That means that people across the northern United States and Canada might want to know about the new product. Our market research might show, for example, that the product will be especially appealing to people with a special interest in snowmobiling, skiing and other winter sports.

Given a task like this, a computer can quickly examine the characteristics of every media outlet that has been entered into its files, then review them for a given combination of characteristics. After the computer completes that search, it can assemble a list of every media outlet that has every one of those distinguishing codes.

In this situation, for instance, you might instruct the computer to search for only those publications and media outlets (1) in areas that have over three feet of snow annually, (2) in areas that have skiing or other winter sports as a major economic base (because some ski resorts make their own snow, every skiing area isn't necessarily included in the first category), and (3) that have winter sports as their major interest (e.g., skiing magazines), no matter where they are located. The computer will automatically examine each and every media outlet within its memory and compile a list with only those publications and broadcast stations that have any of those three characteristics.

The computer could then give you a total count for the media outlets meeting those specific criteria, print mailing labels for each of them, and even personalize the mailing label or news release to print the name of the editor or broadcast producer. That can save you hours of work and help guarantee a much more effective and economical communication campaign for your organization.

Using Alternative Media to Distribute PR Messages

Once a public relations practitioner has discovered the particular markets he or she wants to target, it's necessary to develop efficient methods to deliver the information. It's easy for the best-planned campaign to fall apart if the delivery system is faulty.

If you talk to any experienced PR practitioner, you are sure to hear stories of hours-long car trips to deliver news releases personally, or of a missed mail drop that seriously hindered a campaign. There would probably also be tales of broken copying machines or dubbed-over videotapes, sick secretaries, or other misfortunes that destroyed any chance of executing an effective campaign or that forced emergency measures to complete a publicity effort.

There are always going to be some misfortunes in the public relations business, but high technology has helped ease some of the problems in delivering both written and broadcast PR messages. For printed news releases and other written communication, computer technology has made it possible to send news releases instantaneously to newspapers and other media outlets. Using a computer modem, a device that allows computer language to be transmitted via telephone lines, you can transmit words or data directly from your public relations office to almost any other computer terminal anywhere in the world that also has a modem. Many public relations offices have established just such a network with their major print media outlets. That makes it possible for newspaper editors to bring news release copy directly onto their screens, edit it and then send it to their typesetting equipment without ever retyping the release copy. There are also commercial firms that will deliver their clients' news releases to major media outlets in the same manner.

Another aspect of high technology that is commonly employed in public relations is the facsimile, or fax, machine. This relatively inexpensive piece of equipment can be used to transmit instantaneously what looks like a photocopy of writing, typing, or even illustrations from one fax machine to another anywhere in the world. Almost all PR units use faxes to deliver news releases to media outlets, and features allow releases to be "broadcast" to scores of media outlets simultaneously.

In broadcast media, public relations professionals also have more delivery tools at their disposal than when they were limited to mailing or using messengers to deliver news releases, audiocassettes and videotapes. In what is now a fairly common practice, PR professionals record an audio message, then invite radio producers or news editors to telephone the PR office and record the taped message for a radio report. A method like this, even though it is an advancement over mailing or delivering cassettes, is still a fairly primitive way to deliver broadcast public relations material.

It is space technology, not telecommunications and computers, that has changed the face of radio and television broadcasting and, thus, public relations vis-a-vis the broadcast media. Using satellite transmission has brought public relations practitioners the same sort of instant access to radio and television broadcast media that computer modems have given PR people sending print news releases. Using transmitting dishes similar to the satellite dishes homeowners use to get additional television signals, public relations professionals can instantly send audio and video transmissions to virtually any broadcaster or any other person or institution having a satellite dish. Although the technology is still relatively expensive, it is being used more frequently every year.

One of the most successful uses of this method has been by representatives in the U.S. Congress. With a transmitting dish located on the roof of one of the congressional office buildings, each member can daily broadcast his or her comments on important issues at a specific time. The radio and television stations in the home districts have been alerted about the transmission time and are thus able to integrate a Washington interview into their local nightly news broadcast.

The growth area of communications technology is likely to be fiber-optic telephone lines, which should give public relations people the capacity to transmit words, data, audio and video to other telephones and computers. It should give us more potential for interactive communication not only with other institutions but also with individuals who have a computer or television set in their home.

MATCHING DELIVERY STRATEGIES TO ORGANIZATIONAL OBJECTIVES

After learning about all these delivery methods, an important clarification needs to be made. Up to now, we've talked about reaching the maximum number of media outlets, without regard to your organization's communications goals. Remember that in all the uses of technology we have discussed, our purpose has been to fulfill our communication goals by providing specific information to media that connect us to people who have some desire to know it.

It's true that every event or issue has many possible publicity angles and that publicity could be obtained in many different media outlets. By doing research into your subject, you can find all the facets and all the outlets. But not every story that you could generate from those angles has any relevance to your communication goals. As we discussed in Chapter 2, your task is to analyze your communication needs and then design a strategy to meet those goals. So your campaign effectiveness should not be judged by how many placements you get, but in how well the placements you do get inform and persuade the audiences important to your communication objective.

That management philosophy reinforces a responsible attitude toward the journalists who have the power over whether our media relations efforts will succeed or fail. In practice, that means finding situations in which the needs of journalists and our organization's communication goals coincide. We can do that by providing journalists with story ideas that closely adhere to their perception of what their audiences need. Just as important, we can provide them with written copy that follows the same standards for accuracy, style and content they would expect from their own reporters.

That strategy means trying to avoid the shotgun, saturation public relations of earlier years that emphasized sending releases to every editor and producer, regardless of their interest in our message. By carefully selecting media and the messages we want to communicate, we can maintain our organization's credibility and ensure our releases will not be subject to an editor's automatic toss into a wastebasket.

SUMMARY

- Because PR practitioners are important sources of information for journalists, practitioners should strive to create a professional working relationship with journalists instead of trying to obtain better results by bribing them with gifts.

- Practitioners can develop a better working relationship with editors if we help them find stories with angles that interest their readers, present information in a format editors can readily use, and follow accepted journalistic writing styles.

- Because personal communication media are the most persuasive, public relations practitioners should integrate speeches, letters and personal meetings into an external communication program.

- A media analysis form encapsulates information about a media outlet, editor or writer so that practitioners can compile a list of media that could help the institution meet its communication objectives.

- A huge growth in the number of media outlets since 1945 has resulted in greatly increased specialization among print and broadcast media. This offers practitioners opportunities to target precise messages to specific audiences.

- Practitioners can obtain maximum media coverage by story splitting—crafting a release or feature story idea for each of the many facets that comprise a story—and then placing each story with the medium most interested in that story element.

- Writers can use computer word processing programs to exploit story-splitting techniques. Although the first few paragraphs will be targeted to different audiences, the body copy will often remain essentially the same.

- The Standard Periodical Directory, the Gale Directory of Publications, the Newsletter Directory and the Encyclopedia of Associations are sources for information about media outlets.

- A computer database search of media characteristics from media reference books and other sources can help the practitioner compile tightly focused media lists for targeted communication campaigns.

- There's been tremendous progress in electronic delivery methods for PR messages, including computer modems, fax machines and satellite transmission.

THINK PIECES

1. Why do specialized media have more credibility than general media? What are other elements that help to form a message's credibility? What is the connection between message credibility and audience acceptance and action?

2. What are the advantages of placing your organization's personnel on radio and television talk shows? What are possible disadvantages?

3. What is the potential harm in trying to obtain the maximum number of media messages without regard to your organization's communication goals?

4. How does video's live transmission capability help improve the credibility of public relations messages?

5. What are some skills that company personnel who speak to the media for the company need to develop?

MANAGEMENT PROBLEMS

D1.1

D1.2

D1.3

D2.3

D3.1

D3.2

D3.3

D9.1

D10.1

D11.2

D12.2

ADDITIONAL READING

Berkowitz, Dan, and Turnmire, Kirk. "Community Relations and Issues Management: An Issue Orientation to Segmenting Publics." *Journal of Public Relations Research* 6:2 (1994): 163–184.

Druck, Kalman B., ed. *New Technology and Public Relations: A Guide for Public Relations and Public Affairs Practitioners*. Ann Arbor, Mich.: Books on Demand, n.d.

Ross, Stevens S. "Public Relations in Cyberspace." *Public Relations Journal* 51:1 (May 1995): 36–39.

"Technology Transforms Media Relations Work." *Public Relations Journal* 49:11 (November 1993): 34.

Weiner, Richard. *Professional's Guide to Publicity*. New York: Public Relations Publishing Co., 1982.

Wiesendanger, Betsy. "Plug Into a World of Information." *Public Relations Journal* 50:2 (February 1994): 20–23.

Wilcox, Dennis, Agee, Warren, and Ault, Phillip. *Public Relations: Strategies and Tactics,* 3rd ed. New York: HarperCollins, 1990.

Selected Resources for Targeting Print and Broadcast Media

The media directories listed here show the wide range of media placement opportunities, including those with broad coverage and specialized foci. In addition, many medium-sized and large cities have their own local media directories. Directories can help guide the practitioner's media choices when the practitioner is unfamiliar with a medium or a market. However, reporters and editors are a notoriously mobile group, so the directories are only a preliminary guide to media contacts. Practitioners must continually research and update their own key media contacts.

Alternate Press Index	Underground publications of Marxist, feminist and ethnic groups
Bacon's Publicity Checker	List of types of publicity used, specialized editors' names
Cable Contacts Yearbook	Host names for local cable talk shows
Encyclopedia of Associations	List of association purposes and publications of over 20,000 organizations
Gale Directory of Publications	List of publications and city's primary economic activities
National Publicity Database	Database-searchable source of publicity outlets
Newsletter Directory	List of highly specialized, low-circulation publications
Newspaper Op-Ed Pages Directory	Listing of newspapers offering opposing editorial viewpoints
Talk Show Directory	Listing of local and national talk shows on radio and television

Looking Them in the Eye: Applying Receiver-centered Writing in Face-to-Face Media

REAL-LIFE LESSONS

After the University of Missouri extended the definition of "cannon fodder" to encompass participants in team sports, I found myself on my university's lacrosse team for a season. The player who had recruited me for this unique sport that mixed contusions and humiliations in equal measure was the team's goalie, Stephen.

Thus I met Stephen's mother. She was a tiny woman and a devoted fan of the lacrosse team, following us to games all over the Midwest. Probably because I looked like the player most prone to injury in the mayhem-filled sport, she took it upon herself to build me into an appropriately sized hulk. She decided to feed me alfalfa pellets.

Alfalfa pellets aren't candy-coated vitamins filled with the essence of alfalfa or tasty natural snacks molded in the shape of an alfalfa leaf. Alfalfa pellets are pellets made from alfalfa, dark green with a sort of rank grass smell. I was familiar with alfalfa pellets. On the farm, we fed them to underachieving pigs. A girl I dated fed them to her hamster. From my past experience, I had never really considered myself as a likely alfalfa pellet prospect.

One afternoon after a game, Stephen's mother approached me and told me she always worried about me because I was so thin. She handed me a large brown bottle. The label proclaimed that there were 750 alfalfa pellets inside. Thinking about choking down 750 of the nasty things convinced me I could be forthright in telling her that my health wasn't important enough to me to contemplate eating these vile-smelling pellets.

But before I could say anything, she put her hand around my waist. "You're just like another son to me," she said. "I just don't think I could face your mother if anything happened to you and I knew I hadn't done what I could to help."

Her concern didn't change the fact that alfalfa pellets are nauseating pig food. So what did I do? I started taking eight alfalfa pellets every day.

I offer this incident to show the power of person-to-person communication. No medical journal staffed with world-famous physicians, no newspaper public education campaign, no television commercial featuring film star endorsements could have convinced me to put one alfalfa pellet in my mouth. Yet this tiny farm woman had me taking 56 a week, 240 a month. What was the difference?

The difference is the power of one individual talking to another individual. Even in an age in which we idolize mass communication and its celebrities, person-to-person remains the most potent, persuasive form of communication. Unfortunately, it's the one PR practitioners most often neglect. Through neglect, it's become the form in which we're least proficient. The purpose of this chapter is to rediscover some of the circumstances in which we can employ person-to-person communication and review some of the techniques that can make it effective for our institutions.

WHAT YOU KNOW

- As media become more personal, their persuasive power becomes greater.
- Practitioners need to be aware of and choose the most effective communication path among the many media available.
- Writing for a medium demands that practitioners not only communicate their messages clearly but that they capitalize on the strengths of the deliverer of the message.

WHAT YOU'LL LEARN

- In person-to-person writing, the writer must integrate the personality, mannerisms and personal experience of the speaker into strong prose.
- Practitioners need to break away from their adherence to mass media channels as the near-exclusive answer to all public relations problems.
- Because person-to-person communication, like broadcast writing, relies on human memory, complex issues must be reduced to a limited number of clearly explained points.

PERSON-TO-PERSON: THE PERSUASIVENESS OF FACE-TO-FACE DELIVERY

Person-to-person communication is an often overlooked area in our field. We tend to concentrate our resources on mass media outlets and internal publications through which our message can reach thousands or millions of people with one stroke.

Although those broad-based programs will be a major component of most public relations programs, we should remember the tremendous power of personal communication. As we've discussed in previous chapters, the power to persuade becomes greater as you use more personal media. For example, you are more likely to see a certain movie if your friends recommend it than if you read about it in a newspaper. All mass media are relatively unimpressive in their persuasive power; letters, telephone calls, and conversations are much more effective.

There are many public relations duties in which the persuasive powers of personal media can help fulfill our institution's objectives. Executives often need to make speeches and other presentations to key publics like stockholders and industry peers. They meet with activist publics, including environmental and citizen groups, where precise oral communication can defuse crisis situations. Top executives have to be groomed to deal effectively with reporters. Managers and supervisors need training to hold dialogues with workers to explain new company programs and involve workers' talents in the company's goals.

All too often, we discount the importance of this communication to our company's success and the skills required to perform them well. This discussion of face-to-face communication comes late in the book because its great potential for helping our institution is matched by its difficulty.

It's fortunate that the same principles that you've used in other PR writing tasks are involved in personal messages. Throughout the book, we've discussed matching the message, the medium and the purpose of the words to the audience's wants. You need to plan everything from the opening sentence to the call to action to satisfy a particular audience's communication needs.

That's still the case in personal communication tasks. Remember your feelings of despair as you sat through the lecture of a professor who didn't even give you anything you could use on the upcoming test, let alone in your life? No matter what the medium, the audience and its needs are still of prime importance.

Writing for personal communication tasks is different. Now, there is one more audience member you need to consider for your message. It's not merely you as a PR person communicating directly to an audience. Now, you are writing for another human being, who will convey your message to the public.

That's a big responsibility, because you are not using your own prose voice in your prose. Instead, even if you're a 110-pound, 24-year-old woman fresh in the enthusiasm of your youth and your career, you must shape your writing, your examples and your expressions to emerge from the mouth of a 58-year-old, overweight, aggressive corporate president.

Personal communication writing brings together every writing skill we've discussed in this book. You need the ability to communicate information solidly, as in a news release. It's necessary to present anecdotes and examples that reinforce those points, as you would do in a feature story. There are often times, as in broadcasting, when pictures or charts add valuable emphasis to your message.

Out of this interplay comes personal communication, the most forceful in its ability to persuade an audience. Transforming that potential into power will be the subject of this chapter.

SPEECHES: WRITING FOR SOMEONE ELSE'S VOICE

Public relations writers often are responsible for writing speeches for institutional officers. In addition to the usual perils of any writing task, composing a speech is doubly difficult because speeches offer an additional element of failure. Not only do you have to adapt your message to the information needs, background and interests of the audience, but you have to weave the experiences and talents of the speaker into the speech.

You have no doubt been victimized by speakers who have selected a topic completely inappropriate or uninteresting for their audience, written in language either too simple or too complex for the audience's background. Added to that definite handicap, they've plodded through an uninspired and lifeless reading of information in which they seem as uninterested as the audience, the majority of whom by this time are practicing their origami skills with their paper napkins.

How do you as a PR writer help speakers, and their listeners, avoid this fate? Part of your task involves the same skills you've been developing all through this text. You need to evaluate your audience first. What interests them? What type of technical background and language do they bring to the subject? What information or approach can your speaker bring that might be new and might help audience members cope with their own experiences? Is your audience likely to be combative or supportive when faced with your speaker's view of the subject?

Evaluating Your Speaker

Even before you begin developing an exact topic, you must shift your attention to the speaker. In developing a speech, the speaker, with his or her strengths and passions and failings, is just as important as the audience that will hear the presentation.

It seems to me the most common problem with speeches and other oral presentations is that speakers ask their writers to create a person on paper who doesn't exist in life. Speakers seem to believe that no one would be impressed by the real-life struggles they've gone through, the obstacles they've faced and overcome, and the talent (and luck) around which all success revolves.

When developing a speech, nearly all speakers want to be more humble, more calm, more studious and more reflective than they actually are. Yet the people most often asked to give speeches aren't those who've been encased in a shrine contemplating life and humility. They are men and women of action, people whose energy and anger, commitment and contrariness have taken them to the top of their fields. Speeches that intend to entertain, inform and persuade should reveal, not obscure, those human traits that have made them human beings—and successful human beings.

That quest to impress instead of inform begins with the topics most speakers select for themselves. In effect, they program themselves for failure by picking a topic that sounds better listed on a résumé than delivered from a rostrum.

You can help your speakers succeed. It starts by helping them pick topics to which they can contribute a new understanding and about which they can demonstrate the passion that has made their own prominence possible.

This means you might guide a small-business executive away from topics like "The Future of the American Enterprise System" and into topics in which her own experience provides anecdotes and real-life understanding. For that executive, a better topic might be "How a One-Woman Company Pulls Off a High-Powered Corporate Look."

That woman's tale of hiring answering services by the day or offices by the hour to disguise the lack of staff and facilities until she landed a big contract would provide a wealth of funny stories. In addition to being entertaining, that in-depth knowledge would help ensure the speaker would present a valuable message for other businesspeople who are considering starting their own businesses.

This type of insight into what makes a person interesting obviously can't be imposed from a distance. Even if you're writing a speech on "The Future of the American Enterprise System" for the head of the Federal Reserve Bank, those personal insights and observations are important. They make the difference between listening to a human being and reading an encyclopedia article. To get those insights, you need time with the speaker before you write the speech.

These initial sessions should be like a feature story interview. If the person for whom you're writing the speech is barking orders at you instead of answering questions, your ability to write an effective, informative speech will be severely compromised. Elizabeth Cheever has some revealing suggestions for getting cooperation and support from your speaker. You'll find her ideas in Box 12.1 (pp. 346–347).

As Cheever points out, in these initial sessions you're looking for the speaker's objective in giving the speech. Is it to inform, to challenge or to get the audience to undertake some specific action? You want to know the philosophical orientation through which the speaker approaches the topic. Which side of the issue will the speaker argue? Why does the speaker believe that? What incidents in the past were important in bringing him or her to that conclusion?

Perhaps you noticed similarities between the pattern of questions here and the GOSS interviewing formula we discussed in Chapter 3. The GOSS formula is designed to show how the human element contributed to the success or failure of a project, and that's precisely what you're trying to do here.

Integrating the Speaker into the Speech: Recreating a Real-life Person on Paper

But you're after more than information and anecdotes in your meeting with the speaker. You're there to study the idiosyncrasies and cadences of his or her speech. If the speaker is fresh from the backwoods and rock hills of Missouri (as I am), there's little you can do to put a continental veneer on that drawl.

Yet a speaker who carries the burden of a doctorate from Oxford University provides you with similar challenges. She may have enormous advantages with your audience as they evaluate her sophistication and intelligence, but she may be perceived as lacking sincerity and humor.

BOX 12.1   Views from the Field

Elizabeth F. Cheever
Cheever is president of Cheever Communications, a Boston-area consulting firm specializing in executive coaching. She has an advanced degree in clinical psychology and has 20 years of communication experience in training and coaching professionals in Fortune 500 companies worldwide.

When you're writing a speech, are you thinking not only about the audience to which the speech will be delivered, but about another audience—the person making the speech?

Absolutely. If you don't focus on the speaker's interests initially, you are wasting a tremendous amount of time and energy writing something that the speaker really doesn't want to say. This could also make the speaker's delivery of the speech both uncomfortable and unnatural. Most speakers have had such bad experiences delivering speeches that they conclude speeches are supposed to be boring. They think: "I'll just go in and deliver this lifeless, external thing that doesn't belong to me." Writing the speech from the speaker's viewpoint can do away with these problems.

It seems an institution's CEO wouldn't have time to spend with a speechwriter. How do you get him or her involved?

The chances of a writer in isolation writing something that's going to work for an individual CEO are almost nil. You've got to be more assertive with these CEOs who claim they don't have the time to work with a speechwriter. You need to present your case very rationally to them. You should explain to them that time spent now is going to save time and money later, and it will give them the chance to look good. It's useful to get their ego involved because people tend to open up if you focus on them. If you phrase your questions in a way that makes them believe you want to create a speech that matches their strengths and diminishes their liabilities, they're going to believe you're on their side. They will be very impressed when you indicate you want to create a speech to express their personality. This understanding gives you a better relationship with the speaker and helps make sure you get their cooperation and commitment.

Even in the best of circumstances, you've only got a few minutes to develop some personal impressions of the speaker. How do you do it?

You start by finding out how they want to be perceived. Do they want people leaving the speech thinking of them as a strong leader, an intellectual, a pal, a visionary? You have to coax them into revealing personal things they've done. Let's say your speaker wants the thrust of his speech to be "Why downsizing is going to benefit the people in the company." You lead him into a discussion: "Well, why do you think downsizing is going to help? Do you think that's realistic? Do you know of some examples of where it has worked before? Can you tell me where you're going to implement this in the company? What's the name of a contact person in that division so I can get some more support for your position?" By leading them through this path of questions you tend to find the vignettes that you can't find merely by asking them to tell you all they know about the subject. Ask them that abstract question, and they'll give you an abstract answer.

Can a good speechwriter make someone a better speaker?

No, not directly. However, if the writer can involve the speaker in a creative partnership, the content is going to be tremendously better because it reflects the speaker's personality. In addition, the speaker is going to be more willing and able to make the delivery something meaningful. When you start to get speakers engaged in creating the speech in this way, you sell them on telling stories. Since they generated the germ of every story, they are going to tell them better, with more confidence and conviction.

—Used with permission of Elizabeth F. Cheever

Each of these speakers presents you with a challenge. Your task is to reveal the intelligence and humanity beneath the diction by integrating the speaker's background and traits into the speech's sentence structures and vocabulary, as Memory Memo 12.1 details. Your speaker's background will provide several benefits when you're ready to write the speech. First, it will bring a level of humanity and empathy that will increase the audience's interest and attention to the message. Second, it may bring you a wealth of stories that will help illustrate your speaker's involvement with the topic.

Memory Memo 12.1
Integrate the speaker into the speech:

- Include allusions to the speaker's personal background and experiences in the speech.
- Adapt the speech's vocabulary, sentence structure and diction to fit (or to compensate for) the speaker's habits.
- Synthesize the speaker's argument structures into the speech's structure.

Just as important, that insight will help you create a speech that fits the speaker's actual diction patterns. This will eliminate a lot of the fumbling and mistakes that occur when someone is trying to read sentences that don't fit his or her normal speaking style. Many writers not only observe speech patterns, but record their conversations with the speaker so they can review both the information and the way the speaker delivers that information.

What should you observe in that interview and recording? First, you hope to discover whether the speaker is more comfortable telling personal anecdotes or building a logical construction of evidence block by block.

You're also interested in the way the speaker makes a point or draws a conclusion. Does the speaker draw conclusions by marshaling a summary of facts? Does he or she ask a rhetorical question, then answer it? What type of technical jargon or slang does the speaker use? Are sentences short or long? Does the sentence length change when the speaker is excited? Are sentence patterns subject-verb-object, or does the speaker use a lot of complex sentence patterns in which an introductory clause precedes the main sentence kernel?

Depending on the speaker, there are many other mannerisms you might note. You'll notice very quickly that there are certain speech patterns you will want to use in the speech to make the speaker feel more natural, and there are other traits you will want to deemphasize. It's just as important to discover those negatives during this planning phase as it is to find the patterns you want to emphasize.

Perhaps the speaker has a slow, monotonous delivery. Over the course of a 45-minute speech, you know the audience will be driven into a collective coma if you mimic his natural speech patterns in your writing. While preserving the speaker's vocabulary and argument style, you might push his delivery speed higher by inserting more short sentences than the speaker commonly uses.

There are many other such techniques to emphasize the speaker's natural delivery while making it palatable for audiences. Long sentences generally slow delivery speed. Words beginning with certain consonants, like t, p, f and d, usually leave a psychological effect of harshness or power, whereas consonants like m, w, n and s are usually considered more soothing and soft.

Integrating the speaker's verbal traits with what you know about the speaker's views of the subject and his personal background and involvement gives you many tools with which to work when you begin writing the speech.

Researching the Topic: Bringing Authority to Personality

Once you've done research on the speaker and your audience, it's time to turn your attention to the general subject on which you've been asked to write. If you haven't already selected a specific topic, your interview and research should help you select a subject that's interesting to the audience, appropriate to the speaker and tightly focused so the speech can be finished within your time limit. Your research should also provide logical arguments to accompany those strong personal opinions you obtained from the speaker during your interview.

After you complete your research you're ready to isolate the main conclusion you want to establish. Don't try to establish more than one major theme in the speech, with three or four major arguments supporting it. Because you're communicating in an oral medium in which your receivers are not taking notes, they won't be able to remember more than a few items of information.

Writing the Speech: Every Medium in One Message

The Opening. With those points in mind, you're finally ready to write the speech. Although different writers use different creative methods in writing speeches, I liken speech writing to broadcast feature writing. I've included a checklist for the task in Memory Memo 12.2.

As in feature writing, you're trying to create an involving and unusual opening that quickly communicates your speaker's view of the topic. You're also trying to develop a strong ending that will bring listeners to that same level of involvement and point of view your speaker has, a powerful impression that will be implanted in the audience's memory for a long time. Those are exactly the motives of a feature story.

Memory Memo 12.2
A checklist for speech writing

- Have you limited your speech to establishing only a few main points?
- Have you written effective transitions that reinforce your main points and guide the audience to the connection between your major arguments?
- Have you simplified complex concepts and facts so they can be understood orally?
- Have you used all sensory channels?

There are similarities to broadcast writing, too. You're trying to capitalize on the identification your listeners have with another human being and exploit the power of the speaker's appearance, voice and emotion for a communication purpose. As broadcast writing emphasized, you should integrate visuals to reinforce your message.

It's useful to create a speech just as you would a broadcast feature story. The opening remains the most important part of any communication event. It's there that you need to involve the listeners before their attention wanders, to take advantage of that brief period of time when they are receptive to the new information. It's in the opening that the audience is still eager to learn the personality and viewpoint of a new acquaintance.

You want to put the best information you've collected from the speaker and the library into the lead. Assess the anecdotes, personal experiences, surprising facts or provocative questions your fact-finding process has uncovered. In doing your research, you likely uncovered some information you didn't know, some story that illustrated the problem, some anecdote that brought a smile. Look for the best one and build a feature lead around it.

If you want to highlight the story of a person affected by his or her involvement with your topic, you might want to develop a focus feature structure. If you're writing a travelogue, a descriptive lead might be better. If you're trying to startle your audience from complacency into awareness, an unimagined fact in a shocker lead might be best. See Chapter 10 to review the different feature leads.

Remember the lead will not be effective if it merely grabs the attention of the audience without starting to build the persuasive structure upon which your story will rest. Too many speeches begin with a clever story or joke that isn't relevant to the topic.

The Argumentation Structure.   To be persuasive you must offer a clear thesis in your lead section, then construct a body of evidence in the speech's main section so your audience can believe the conclusions you suggest in the lead. That means the middle part of the speech must be like the inverted pyramid, building a case of facts, quotes and anecdotes that prove those three or four recommendations you've isolated as the main points of your speech.

I usually create a speech using the three-column broadcast writing format in Figure 12.1. I write each of my three or four main conclusions on a separate script sheet. In one column, called "human support," I place the anecdotes or examples I've gathered in my research and conversations that are real-life illustrations of those points. In the second column, labeled "visual reinforcement," I include a slide, a cartoon, an overhead listing important ideas, or some other visual that will emphasize the conclusion I'm trying to draw. In the final column, labeled "objective evidence," I write all the facts, statistics and quotes supporting that specific conclusion. The three-column format reminds me to fill all the sensory channels that can contribute to communicating the message.

FIGURE 12.1   Outline plan for a speech

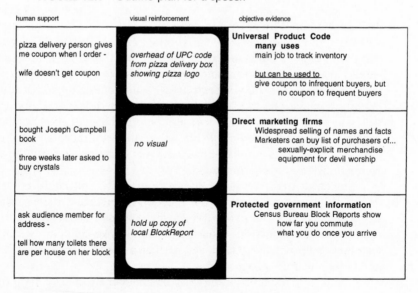

Speech Title: Ethics of Tracking Consumer Purchases
Topic Outline: How much do marketers know about you?

As in all writing, transitions are enormously important in speech stories. Because you are working in an oral medium, well-developed memory-cue transitions allow the speaker to make the argumentation structure clear and unobtrusively review prior arguments the audience might have forgotten, while leading them to the next point.

Because you've only got the spoken word to hold your audience's attention, employ the rhyming and other wordplay stratagems broadcast copywriters use to maintain interest. Alliteration (repeating an initial sound in nearby words) draws attention to a phrase. Repeating a key word or phrase provides continuity that helps the audience organize the material and recognize major dividing points in the speech. Here's an example from the speech you'll find in the Ready Reference section at the end of this chapter:

So marketing is not some foreign element in your business plan, sucking up resources that should be going to feed your children. Marketing is the central element of your business plan. Marketing is the central element in your business's ability to make money.

Now, I'm sounding like a robber baron here, some sort of rapacious captain of industry gone bad. But it's not that way. In these times, it's not possible to make money if you ignore the needs of your customers.

It's also wise to follow the style rules of broadcast writing. Spell out numbers and abbreviations. Include pronunciation for hard-to-pronounce words and names. Some speechwriters even include cues to guide the speaker's gestures and the inflection or volume of his or her delivery.

There's another similarity to television: Because there's no chance to review facts, it's necessary to keep your facts simple and understandable. For instance, if you tell your audience a defense contracting company had cost overruns of $16,186,234, your speaker and your audience are likely to get lost in the jumble of numbers. To simplify their task, present that statistic as a cost overrun of "over 16 million dollars."

If you have more complex concepts to present, don't hesitate to incorporate charts, graphs, slides or photographs. But remember as you choose and prepare those visual aids to consider the size of the audience and the room so every person can see.

A visual element is important because it's another sensory channel you can use to present information and persuade your audience. It's all too often neglected. We tend to think of every oral presentation as a traditional speech, with a well-dressed man or woman seemingly rooted in concrete behind a tall podium with only their words to tell their message. That was generally true in the 1800s, in the time of Henry Clay and the great orators. But with electronics, video and other ways to present information visually, we needn't think of audiovisual presentations as being something separate from speeches.

Although I'll talk about audiovisuals as a separate component, you should force yourself to think visually in every situation of face-to-face communication. Even when your client has been asked to give a speech, think about illustrating it with charts, photographs or a written list of important points. Integrating the two presentational styles will give your words more impact.

AUDIOVISUAL PRESENTATIONS: NO SUBSTITUTE FOR A HUMAN FACE

Audiovisual presentations are useful in many situations. After being produced, they can be used repeatedly before large numbers of people without any additional effort. They communicate their messages precisely and without alteration, time and time again, and don't depend on the changing behaviors and moods of a human being for their effect.

Audiovisual presentations are often poorly produced or used in the wrong situations, however. Those that don't have excellent production values have the same emotional impact as bad home movies or videos. You feel embarrassed for the person responsible for the product and you feel pity for the people having to sit through it.

Even those institutions with money and talent to produce the slick graphics and style of an expensive AV presentation sometimes use them incorrectly by substituting an electronic presentation for a live speaker.

Remember the effectiveness of personal communication. As we examined earlier, one human being talking to another can be more powerful in changing a person's mind than the slickest magazine or the most dazzling television news report. As you shy away from those personal forms of communication, you are also relying on media that, no matter how costly, will likely be less effective in convincing your audience.

When to Use Audiovisual Presentations: Serving Your Purpose, Solving Your Problem

Audiovisual (AV) presentations are vital in certain circumstances—for instance, if your personnel or financial resources do not make individual presentations possible or if pictures are better at conveying your message. In many circumstances, audiovisuals can provide incredible punch to supplement and drive home the personal message a spokesperson is charged with delivering.

Too many institutions, however, create audiovisual presentations in place of trusting the passion and commitment of their personnel to tell their story. For some reason, they believe an expensive film or series of slides can replace that human emotion and that human ability to change the presentational style to accommodate a different audience or to respond immediately to an audience's questions, enthusiasm or mood.

Your first consideration when you're asked to do an audiovisual presentation is to decide what type of medium will support your message. That's an important question because with our emphasis on cost-effective communication, the expense of producing a technically sophisticated video presentation can quickly overrun any expected benefit your organization could receive from it.

Sometimes, with a talented speaker, the most effective audiovisual presentation is also the simplest—an easel tablet that lets the speaker note key points, draw pictures or demonstrate concepts to the audience. Depending on such factors as the number of people in the audience, the speaker's skills, and the need to repeat the presentation, effective audiovisual media could consist of large, prepared charts or graphs, or transparencies on an overhead projector. It's only after you've determined that these options are inappropriate that you should move to consider the expense and impersonality of slide-tape, video or film presentations. (Slide-tapes, which combine slide presentations with sound tracks, are discussed in Chapter 13.)

In every case, however, you should start planning any audiovisual presentation with a clear statement of what purpose your communication will serve. Too often I've heard colleagues say they've gotten instructions to put together a "flashy AV presentation for the 60th anniversary."

Even when you are dealing with person-to-person communication, the task always begins with an understanding of the institutional problem you're trying to solve through your communication effort. Without a notion of what the institution wants to communicate and hopes to gain from the message, the final result will more often be flash than substance.

Writing the Audiovisual Presentation: It Says Audio and Visual

Once you've established that purpose, creating an audiovisual presentation uses many of the concepts and skills associated with video writing. Again, you're trying to use the additional sensory input of sight and sound to reinforce your message.

First, you need to recognize that because you're communicating through a medium that doesn't allow you to review claims, you generally need to keep your message simple and direct. What are the two or three main points you want the audience to understand and remember from the presentation? For the simplest of audiovisual media, getting those points onto an easel board or an overhead transparency to reinforce the message may be all you have to do.

If you need more evidence to demonstrate those points, think of ways you can visually reinforce a point that's already being made in words. Just as in advertising writing and all forms of broadcast writing, you shouldn't indiscriminately use visuals that simply repeat the speaker's words. In too many cases, AV writers use slides merely to present words or numbers that are communicated just as effectively using oral channels. Instead, your visuals should reinforce and give additional resonance to the words presented by the speaker.

Remember that you're using visual communication channels, so exploit the power of sight. If you're talking about hunger in Africa, don't limit yourself to presenting a slide saying "5 million go hungry every night." Instead, present the hungry face of one starving 4-year-old girl and tell her story as a way of showing the plight of those 5 million. If you're comparing numbers, don't simply display numbers on a slide. Illustrate them graphically with a pie chart or a graph.

You can also employ video production techniques and effects that add emotional power to your visuals. If your task is to convince stockholders of your company's solidity and strength, take a cue from television advertising and shoot low angle shots of your office tower, products or people. If you are trying to portray excitement, rush the pacing of your visuals. If you want to show the erection of a building or transformation of a product over time, fade out each visual as you fade in the next picture.

In all cases, look for the striking visual that pounds your message home and gives your audience a key for remembering the major points and attitudes you want them to take from the presentation.

If you're using a slide-tape presentation or video production, don't forget sound effects. Many slide-tape shows or industrial films have silent backgrounds or music so sterile that it sounds like elevator music in a white-bread factory. Use that added sensory channel to help emphasize your message. If it will help communicate the message more effectively, have factory machines churning or insects chirping. Even if you're using a slide-tape format, add the recorded voice of the person pictured on the screen. As always, exploit every sensory element of the medium in which you're working. If you can't integrate both sound and visuals, you're probably using a medium inappropriate for your task. Reconsider why you're doing a film or a slide-tape presentation.

You prepare an audiovisual presentation in much the same way as you do a television commercial storyboard. Although some professionals use one column for the spoken presentation and another describing the visual, I prefer the storyboard's three-column format even for a slide-tape presentation because it reminds the writer not only to consider the visual but to plan for sound effects and other special effects such as fading an image.

Memory Memo 12.3
A checklist for writing for audiovisual presentations:

- Do you have a situation in which an AV presentation is more appropriate than a personal presentation?
- Have you chosen the proper AV medium for your communication purpose and for the person who will be presenting the presentation?
- Have you used broadcast writing principles when appropriate?
- Have you employed all sensory channels effectively?
- Have you used emotional as well as rational arguments if appropriate?

In addition, the running time notation forces you to consider the pacing of the visuals and keeps you from holding some slides on the screen for two or three minutes, while other important images have to zip by to keep up with the narrative, straining the human capacity to comprehend them.

A checklist in Memory Memo 12.3 guides your preparation of audiovisual presentations.

USING THE POWER OF PERSONAL PERSUASION

Person-to-person communication is an often neglected area of public relations writing. However, its effectiveness in persuading audiences and moving them to action cannot be denied.

Both speeches and audiovisual presentations demand sophisticated writing skills from practitioners, but if planned to satisfy organizational objectives, both can be powerful components in an institution's overall communication program. By defining highly targeted publics, then exploiting the proven persuasive power that individuals have when communicating to individuals, you can make great strides in encouraging actions that will support the company's mission.

SUMMARY

- Person-to-person communication is often overlooked by public relations practitioners more intent on placing communication in mass media outlets. Yet person-to-person is probably the most vital type of communication for organization executives who deal with activist publics, reporters and peers.

- Person-to-person communication demands that we integrate the talents and weaknesses of the person delivering the message.

- To craft a powerful speech, practitioners need to study a speaker's interests and intents as well as his or her speaking cadences, vocabulary and thought patterns and then integrate that knowledge into the writing process.

- Speechwriting employs many of the techniques of broadcast feature writing. Use wordplay, repetitive language, visuals, anecdotes and personal experiences to reinforce key points.

- Audiovisual presentations should exploit all the sensory channels available, including movement and sound.

THINK PIECES

1. You're working with a speaker whose delivery is rapid and hard to understand. What can you do to make the presentation better?

2. Remember some instances in which an audiovisual presentation was very effective. Why was it powerful? Would it have been enhanced or hurt by including a speaker before, during or after the presentation? Can you draw some conclusions about instances when personal communication can make an audiovisual presentation more persuasive?

3. Recall a memorable speech or lecture you've heard. What did your personal interest in the subject have to do with your response to the presentation? What's the importance of matching material to audience?

4. What's the worst speech or lecture you've ever had to sit through? What problems did the speaker have? Why did those problems hurt his ability to communicate with the audience? What would you have prescribed to improve the presentation?

WRITING ASSIGNMENTS

Letters

D1.9

D4.7

D6.5

D7.8

D8.6

D9.4

Speeches and Audiovisual Presentations

D2.5

D4.8

D9.6

D10.8

D11.3

ADDITIONAL READING

Beckham, James A. "How to Make Speeches Work." *Public Relations Journal* (August 1985): 29–30.

Dunkel, Jacqueline, and Parnham, Elizabeth. *Effective Speaking for Business Success: Making Presentations with Confidence, Using Audio-Visuals and More.* Bellingham, Wash.: Self-Counsel Press, 1993.

Ehrlich, Henry. *Writing Effective Speeches.* New York: Paragon House, 1992.

Neal, James E., Jr., and Neal, Dorothy J. *Effective Letters for Business, Professional and Personal Use,* 2nd ed. Perrysburg, Ohio: Neal Publications, Inc., 1994.

Verderber, Kathleen S., and Verderber, Rudolph. *Using Interpersonal Communication Skills,* 7th ed. Belmont, Calif.: Wadsworth, 1992.

Standard Format for a Speech

Note: If the speech copy below were being prepared for delivery, it would be double-spaced.

my pr firm

123 Main Street / Hometown, Any State / 12345 / 505 555-1234

A speech format should help turn the speech text into a working document for the person using it—in this case, the person delivering the speech. To accomplish this task, I recommend that writers use a format similar to a radio script.

PLACE OVERHEAD
"Dialogue into one narrow column"

Place the **dialogue into one narrow column**. That makes it less likely that the speaker will lose his or her place while reading the speech. Double-space the text, too—that will make it easier to read.

mispronounce "phonetic"
PLACE OVERHEAD
"Give broadcaster's phonetic spellings"

Remember, as well, that you are trusting a fallible human being to deliver these words orally to your audience. If necessary, **give** the broadcaster's (fony TIC)—no, that's **phonetic** (fah NEH tihk)—**spellings** to help your speaker pronounce difficult words, or consider modifying the speech's language to eliminate words the speaker finds difficult to pronounce.

PLACE OVERHEAD
"Use left column to give cues to the speaker"

I use the **left column to give cues to the speaker**. For instance, it might help to remind the speaker of an appropriate time to show a visual to the audience, or to emphasize an important issue with a gesture or by coming from behind the podium.

Use different type presentations to give different instructions to the speaker. In this case, I've used italics to give instructions to the speaker and boldface to indicate the overhead text. Of course, since the consequences of the speaker losing his or her place are so great, clearly label each page with a page number.

PLACE OVERHEAD
"Highlight the exact words the audience sees"

It also helps the speaker if the text boldfaces or **highlights the exact words the audience sees** in the visual so the speaker cannot distract the audience by saying words that are slightly different from those they are seeing.

Full Text of a Speech

To effectively use the power of personal communication, speeches need to emphasize the speaker's personality, experiences and conversational style. In this speech format, the bold-faced passages remind the speaker to display an overhead transparency on the screen.

Boldface signals speaker to place slide or transparency on screen. →

A frank and provocative statement of the speech's topic. →

Summation of main point of speech. →

Thank you for that flattering introduction, Leo.

This presentation is called **"Marketing on the Cheap."** I call it that so I won't scare too many people away. It's many a small-business executive who thinks marketing involves having such a dominant market share that he can throw vast sums of money at advertising agencies so an agency can tell him how he should run his business. For cash-strapped organizations, that's not realistic. So, understandably, many small-business people expect the same sort of payback from marketing as they anticipate from sending their children off to college. Both cost a lot of money, and who knows if you'll get back anything that's useful.

But marketing, done right, is something very different from that. In fact, you might find you and marketers have very much the same goals. To explain what I mean I'll need to reverse some preconceptions you may have about marketing.

Marketing is something different from moving the product. Moving the product can mean selling the product two cents cheaper than your competitor, who has the option to sell it two cents cheaper than you. The famous story in marketing circles concerns two competitors. One guy asks the other guy, "How do you sell it so cheaply?" The second guy says, "Well, I lose 50 cents on every deal, but I make up for it on volume."

That's a ruinous strategy. That's also not marketing.

So marketing is different from moving the product. Marketing is fulfilling the objectives of the organization. If you think about the purpose of your organization, it isn't to move the product. It isn't even to control a market segment. If you set your prices low enough you can control a market segment—for just as long as you've got spare money in your bank account to cover your losses.

No, the purpose of your organization is to make money, enough money to support you, to support your family and to invest enough in your business to expand it. It's the capitalistic dream.

So let's look at a definition of what marketing is all about. **Marketing is directing all the resources of the organization toward determining and satisfying consumers' needs and desires in the ways that will best enhance the profitability of that organization.**

So marketing is not some foreign element in your business, sucking up resources that should be going to feed your children. Marketing is the central element of your business plan. Marketing is the central element in your business's ability to make money.

Now, I'm sounding like a robber baron here, some sort of rapacious captain of industry gone bad. But it's not that way. In these times, it's not possible to make money if you ignore the needs of your consumers.

In fact, I want to offer an alternative definition of marketing that helps clarify its role a little better. Here's what Peter Drucker has to say about marketing:

Marketing is . . . the whole business seen from the point of view of its final result, that is, from the customers' point of view.

For most people, this is almost exactly the opposite of their original perception of marketing. For most people, marketing is telling consumers the company's point of view. But that's not what marketing is. In reality, marketing tells us that it's not really our vision of our company that is important—instead it is the customer's perception of us.

Conversational language that helps draw listeners into message. That's strange, isn't it—the customer's perception is the important view. So the questions become not what you want to tell your customers. These are the questions: What is it that those customers see when they look at your company? What do they see when they see your sales force? What do they perceive when they think of your services? How do they think your product fits into their lives?

So here's the first mistake many people make in marketing. They think marketing is an advertising campaign to say what they want to say about their company. But that's not marketing—that's bragging. That's because it talks about you, but doesn't say a thing about your audience.

So let's look at that first definition of marketing again. It says we're supposed to satisfy a customer's needs and desires.

You'll notice there are two components here. Some products satisfy needs. Needs are based on rational thoughts. This is a rational thought—I need to eat. To satisfy that rational need I buy food. Macaroni and cheese satisfies a need.

Slide helps reinforce main points of speech. But let's look at **the second component of the definition of marketing. There we talk about satisfying a desire. In fact, the most powerful element in marketing is desire.** Where macaroni satisfies a need, veal cordon bleu satisfies a desire. And, as the man who sells veal cordon bleu could tell you, satisfying desires is generally more profitable than satisfying needs.

Examples that explain abstract principle. Let's look at the American Express card. Here's a credit card that costs 55 dollars more than most other credit cards. Here's a credit card that even discourages you from charging anything! Yet when I got out of college, I shelled out the money for one. Why? What good is a charge card that you have to pay off every month? What's the point? How do you account for its success?

The American Express card is a success because it caters to the emotions and the fantasies of the customer. I remember the feeling of going into a restaurant and slapping down my American Express card as if it meant something.

So what is it that they are selling? They are selling a fantasy. Their commercials state that. . . . I'd like to apply for membership. With your 55 dollars, you join Paul Newman and all the other famous people in a prestigious fraternity. They're saying that by paying 55 dollars a year you join this exclusive club, a club whose privileges and rank can only be

359

exceeded if you pay 75 dollars a year for a gold card or 105 dollars a year for a platinum card. That fantasy costs.

Pointing intellectual principle to needs of audience.

What does this expensive advertising campaign that is targeted to prestige customers mean for the person who is marketing on the cheap? That means there are profits to be made by offering each customer a chance to buy a self-image. Those self-images aren't necessarily restricted to the upper-echelon consumer. If you are selling coffee service to someone who prides himself on getting the best value for his money, then you need to offer that cheapest, most basic coffee service. But when you're selling to the doctor's lounge in the medical clinic, you're giving someone the opportunity to buy a bit of esteem, a bit of prestige, a bit of a reward for being important.

That's an important thing to emphasize—the emotional reasons people buy products. People buy things not only to satisfy a need for coffee or food or clothing. They are buying something that projects an impression of themselves to others. The guy who wears the Hank Williams Jr. belt buckle is announcing something to the world about himself as surely as the business executive who wears blue power suits and red power ties. They are each announcing a message to the world, a communication about what is important to them, and how they want us to perceive them.

Another real-life example.

You can play these games with clothes, beer, even cars. A few years ago, Buick decided to abandon its "doctor's car" image that had served it so well. A Buick was what you bought to reward yourself after you spent 20 years in a Chevrolet. A Buick was a status item, a way to feel superior to your former peers who could only afford a Chevrolet. But when Buick, in order to gain a bigger market share, started promoting itself as a low-cost luxury that even working people could afford, they lost that aura. They lost the image that people bought when they bought a Buick. They lost the desire that drove their sales.

Those desires are important. Those desires are profitable. But you have to be conscious of your customers' impressions of your company, those impressions that help match the desires fulfilled when people buy your product.

There are several components to this image. At the simplest level, there's the appearance of your personnel. If I go back to my small town and walk into the feed store with a suit coat on, they would know I didn't belong, that I wasn't their type of people. If I walk into a bank representing a business concern with my suit coat off, they would know I was someone they couldn't do business with. So something as simple as appearance can help fulfill those desires.

Returning to listener's needs.

That image of your organization is also reflected by your product line. If you go into selling crackers and peanut butter when your main product line is gourmet coffee, you run the danger of sending a message that you are a peanut-butter cracker firm, instead of a gourmet coffee firm.

It also involves the way you present yourself to your client. Can you project an image of stability, success and innovation to your customers? We do that with our appearance and the appearance of our equipment. We also do that with the presence of sales materials that suggest we'll be in business past next Thursday.

This is the part of marketing that always scares people in small business. When they start to look at sales support literature, they get scared at the cost, frightened by the time, intimidated by the process of putting together their own material.

A call to action, just like we find in all other types of persuasive writing.

But that's a process that's no longer so daunting, nor so expensive. You're lucky that you have come into business at a time when you can put together darn good-looking printed pieces at next-to-nothing prices. With desktop publishing, color copying and other technical marvels you can produce targeted, low-cost, good-looking publications and sales support literature. With that, you can project that image and foster that desire that's so important to your success and so profitable to your company.

Signal to put example onto screen.

Here's a marketing piece in full color that we assembled out of our supplier's sales brochure and a laser printer. We've included individual pricing information for a specific client, pricing information that, using a computer spreadsheet, we can change in about six seconds for the next client. The price? One dollar 15 cents per copy. Are you going to be able to get a dollar fifteen payback from having individualized information for a sales call? My bet is that you will.

Let's say you have to make up a more original printed presentation. **This is a brochure, printed on both sides, that is completely original.** It's designed in three columns, just like a professional design. It's got photographs, headlines, charts and graphics just like a professional design. Its cost? On my equipment, with the desktop publishing software, the laser printer, and the scanner, the design costs about four dollars.

But what if you don't have the three thousand dollars worth of equipment that I have? Are you cut out of this?

Nope. Down at Kinko's they have all this equipment. The computers and desktop publishing software you can rent at six dollars an hour. That's right. Six dollars an hour. The laser printer gives you typeset copy at 99 cents a page. The cost for the design there is 12 dollars.

So let's review a few steps that summarize marketing on the cheap.

Signal to put example on screen.

MARKETING ON THE CHEAP

Reinforcement and summation of main points of speech.

From a practical standpoint, what can you do?
- Offer a unique service
- Audit your business; be creative in what your company could do, then tell customers about it
- Reflect your audience's self-image in your marketing
- Offer levels of service a company can buy
- Keep the product line you offer one type of customer consistent
- Modify your own appearance to match your customer's expectations
- Reflect your audience's needs in marketing and sales materials
- Emphasize what makes your company different

361

- Target different audiences with different pieces
- Do your own . . .
     desktop publishing
     color copying

So this is what we're talking about when we talk about marketing on the cheap. With a strong marketing strategy and today's technology, you can come off looking like the big boys. You can project a much higher-price image than you may have thought possible. You can satisfy those desires that help your customers gain a self-image. And with that, you can satisfy your own desires—for profits and success.

chapter 13

Delivering Face-to-Face Messages: A Practitioner's Practical Tactical Guide

REAL-LIFE LESSONS

There's a paradox about face-to-face communication. Although it's an ancient type of communication—Neanderthals grunting at each other were engaging in face-to-face communication—there's now more experimentation happening in face-to-face media than in any other type of communication.

Here's an example. While writing this book, I toured a company's new headquarters and manufacturing plant. My guide, the corporation's director of training, proudly escorted me through the manufacturing plant's training facility. There, in a large room encrusted with computer terminals and large video monitors, was where the company trained its assembly workers and service staff to work with the small engines the company manufactured. The training director showed me a line of computers that ran the interactive multimedia training programs the company had just installed and brought on-line.

The computers were a response to a problem concerning person-to-person communication. Because of budget cutbacks, the firm's senior repair technicians had limited periods to spend one-on-one with their new service personnel. Yet without that type of personal contact, it was difficult to train new technicians about the idiosyncrasies of the company's many engines. That led to more complaints and product returns from angry customers. The problem: How to bring the skills and expertise of a master technician to each trainee when understaffing made that impossible.

To solve the problem, the training supervisor had designed a software package that allowed workers, using the computer simulations, to peer inside the housing and examine cross sections of the engine and exploded views of all the engine's parts. They could even zoom in on small technical elements and assembly procedures for specific engine parts. The program contained computer animation to show trainees how the pistons could snap the connecting rods if they weren't installed correctly. More amazingly, the service workers could listen to a malfunctioning engine, type in their diagnosis of the problem, and then be led through a video presentation that showed the repair procedures to fix the problem.

It was an ingenious high-tech solution to an interpersonal communication problem, and it allowed the few master technicians to spend their time dealing with trainees' specific questions and problem areas beyond the software's scope.

As the training director and I walked from the training area, I asked him about the company's new headquarters, a rambling, intersecting series of offices that was a dramatic departure from its previous building, a thin, gleaming skyscraper. With a dismissing tone, the engineer told me the less imposing expression of corporate power stemmed from the company president's desire to have company workers "talk to each other more often." The training supervisor said the president quoted research that found if workers were located more than two floors from each other, they rarely had any contact. The president believed that lack of contact prevented the types of informal conversation that contributed to problem-solving creativity. If someone from marketing heard about a product feature a customer wanted, the president believed she would be more likely to share it with someone from engineering if she had a chance to see an engineer during her workday. It would take much more effort and moxie to write a memo or a letter to a relative stranger in another division suggesting she had a way to do the engineer's job better.

That seemed logical to me as I looked through the new offices and saw short stairways connecting each division's work areas and common areas, where people from different divisions could encounter others and congregate on their way to conference rooms, dining areas and work places.

I asked the engineer if the new office layout worked: Did it encourage an environment where workers worked together on problems? I could tell he was about to ridicule the concept when he paused. "You know," he said, "I was on this very landing when a guy from corporate communication first told me about multimedia. I was the guy who applied it to the training program, but he was the one who gave me the idea."

Here were two different experiments, one high-tech and one decidedly low-tech, in how to foster interpersonal communication. Both were responses to the knowledge that person-to-person communication is a very powerful engine of adaptation and creativity in an organization. It's a force we can encourage in an institution by developing instruments and procedures that encourage people to "talk to each other more often."

WHAT YOU KNOW

- Technology can be used to transform impersonal media into much more targeted media.
- The opportunity to be engaged in two-way communication increases a

receiver's attention to a message and commitment to decisions arising from that exchange.

- Technology that lessens the interaction between sender and receiver reduces the persuasive impact of the message.

WHAT YOU'LL LEARN

- Audiovisual technology should not be used to replace person-to-person messages but to supplement that personal message.
- Integrating computer technology into person-to-person communication lets practitioners increase the interactive possibilities of traditional personal messages.

MEDIA ASSISTS FOR FACE-TO-FACE MESSAGES

When using different media to supplement face-to-face messages, your goal is to effectively use the power the personal contact gives you. The force of the speaker's personality, presence and commitment can be supplemented but must never be hidden by the tricks and flashiness of the media you use.

This doesn't deny the power of slide-tape presentations, videotapes or overhead projector presentations to enhance the message of a speaker. Visual reinforcement of a spoken message can reinforce the power of the words and the personality of the speaker as you communicate your message.

For hard-to-understand claims, visual evidence can add an invaluable confirmation. You can show a product performing a remarkable task, demonstrate calculations that are too difficult to comprehend, or point out statistical relationships that are complex. By using the power of sight and movement, you can involve other sensory channels in communicating your message.

This chapter will examine some of those alternatives a speaker can use to reinforce his or her message during a presentation.

TRADITIONAL AUDIOVISUAL MEDIA: FIXED MESSAGES FOR CHANGEABLE AUDIENCES

As you're probably aware, there are a lot of available options for reinforcing the speaker's message with a visual component. At the very simplest, the speaker can write or draw on a chalkboard, display board or a large pad of paper on an easel. In circumstances in which the speaker wants to emphasize the spontaneity of his or her thoughts and have plenty of opportunities for unexpected turns in the presentation to accommodate audience needs, these simple methods can be very effective.

Visual components work best when speakers are exuberant and can sustain the energy and pacing of the presentation even while they are writing or drawing. For that reason, these methods are most effective when the material to be presented can be executed very quickly. As students, you probably know the boredom of trying to maintain your attention as a professor writes sentences and sentences on the chalkboard.

When more complex material needs to be communicated or when the speaker needs some help in maintaining the audience's interest, there are other, more involving media you can use to supplement the speaker's words.

Opaque and Overhead Projectors

Opaque and overhead projectors are the next level of technology. Most opaque projectors are clunky, heavy pieces of equipment that will project an image of a book page, a photograph or some other type of object that for some reason cannot be photocopied. Although they are nearly indispensable in some situations, they are rarely used and increasingly hard to locate.

A more common form of equipment used in person-to-person presentations is the overhead projector. The overhead projector sends light though a transparent sheet of acetate that has an image on it. Although the image can be drawn or written on the acetate by hand using special pens, most transparencies are created with photocopying machines. Instead of using the copying machine to place an image of a typed page, a photo, chart or news clip on paper, the image is transferred to a sheet of acetate.

The advantage of a projector is that the visuals can be created very easily. However, changing transparencies on the projector, or materials in the opaque projector, can be tedious and distracting to the audience. Color reproduction in either medium is either nonexistent or of very poor quality.

Slide Presentations

Photographic slide presentations relieve some of these problems. Color reproduction is usually superb. Like an opaque projector, even those items that can't be photocopied can be photographed for slides. In addition, slide presentations can be presented to an audience with much less fuss than is the case with overhead or opaque projectors. With remote-controlled units to advance from one slide to the next, the speaker can concentrate more completely on his or her presentation and spend less time changing the visual.

Slide presentations can also be supplemented with synchronized sound tracks that automatically advance the slides to the accompaniment of music, dialogue and sound effects. These are called slide-tape presentations. Some directors have synchronized several or even scores of slide projectors to create dazzling visual effects.

Of course, slide-tape presentations have certain disadvantages. Although new computer technology that produces slides may make costs somewhat lower, taking and developing photographs can become quite expensive, especially for presentations that might contain hundreds of individual slides. Moreover, although multiple-slide-projector shows can simulate the movement of video productions, the slide-tape is essentially a static medium.

There are also problems associated with moving equipment to a different location to make a presentation. The trays necessary for sequencing the slides into the projector are somewhat bulky, and enormous amounts of luggage space can be taken up when transporting two or three slide trays. In addition, because the coordination between projectors must be exact in shows using several slide projectors, those shows can be transported only with great care and difficulty.

Film and Videotape Presentations

Some of those problems are solved by using films or videotapes, both of which exploit the power of movement. Although film was once a relatively common medium for industrial, training, and image films for institutions, it is used less often now. Although film has excellent color reproduction, it is very costly to produce and very expensive to duplicate multiple copies. Film reels are also bulky and not easily transportable.

Videotape is the medium of choice for most public relations and industrial applications. Compared to film equipment, videotaping equipment is inexpensive. Videotapes are relatively cheap to produce, and multiple copies are very inexpensive. Videotape is also very transportable, as up to eight hours of video can be placed on one video home system (VHS) format videotape.

Sound and color quality are not quite as high in videotape as on film, however. Despite improvements in large-screen television projection systems, the technology for showing videos to large numbers of people erodes the transmission quality even further.

INTERACTIVE PERSON-TO-PERSON TECHNOLOGY: AUDIENCES MAKING THEIR OWN MESSAGES

The main problem with traditional support media for person-to-person communication is that as media become more sophisticated, they tend to separate the receiver from the presenter.

Yes, video or film can be involving and even thrilling, but the viewer can't manipulate the image or ask a question. Yet it is the power of person-to-person communication to persuade that we try to capitalize on. Every additional level of complexity and impersonality that we inject between the message and our receiver may hurt that quest.

This text has repeatedly emphasized the power of interactive communication to involve receivers and make PR practitioners' persuasive abilities more effective. Fortunately, we have some newly developed techniques that bring interactive communication and a high degree of technical sophistication into our person-to-person messages. (See Memory Memo 13.1.)

Memory Memo 13.1
Your audiovisual media options

- easels and blackboards
- overhead projectors
- opaque projectors
- slide
- film
- videotape
- computer projection systems
- CD-ROM multimedia systems

Computer Projection Screens

One of the most accessible of these new interactive-communication technologies is the computer projection screen. A computer projection screen is a device that allows whatever information is on a computer monitor to be projected through an overhead projector onto a wall screen.

It's a small device, about the size of the box in which a medium pizza would be delivered. The projection screen is a frame in which is mounted a transparent plastic screen. The screen is placed on an ordinary overhead projector just as if it were a transparency sheet. The computer projector plugs into the back of a computer monitor.

Any words or graphics on the computer monitor appear on the transparent film of the computer projector. The light passing through the overhead projector displays the computer screen's image onto a wall screen. To the audience, it looks exactly like a overhead transparency, but it has one important difference. Because it is projecting exactly what is on a computer screen, it can simultaneously show a computer's calculations to an audience. That may not seem very exciting, but it can give you great power in involving the audience in your message.

Let's say you're trying to demonstrate the profit potential of small changes in efficiency. You could prepare slides showing how a 0.3 percent productivity increase could lead to a $500,000 increase in profits. To get this figure originally, you would probably have done calculations using a computer spreadsheet, which is something like an electronic accounting balance sheet.

Think how much more involving it would be for your audience if you could show them instantaneously how one tiny improvement in efficiency could dramatically boost profits. While the audience watches, the computer can recalculate profit figures and deliver the projections. It has the quality of immediacy that makes the demonstration much more affecting.

It can also lead to greater audience involvement. I've been in meetings of sales representatives where the sales manager has asked for each representative's sales figures. As each representative makes his or her report, the manager enters the figures into the computer. After the reports, the manager instructs the computer spreadsheet to calculate total sales figures. The immediate and ongoing nature of the report brings an involvement that's akin to the excitement during a telethon as a charity campaign nears its goal.

I've also witnessed presentations in which the computer projection screen has seemed to increase involvement and commitment, just as an interactive medium should. In one meeting I attended, workers were asked to commit their work units to an increased number of units produced. With the spreadsheet recording and calculating the results, each group of workers was able to see how the group's individual commitment to higher goals was a part of the company's overall effort to become more efficient.

Presentations using computer projection screens are not limited to spreadsheet programs. Any program that can appear on a computer screen can be projected. If you want a committee to review and compare changes in an employee magazine article, word processing programs that provide a split screen can enable everyone to see and agree on editing changes.

Using a computer program that converts data into bar graphs and pie charts can graphically and instantaneously illustrate voting results at stockholder or association meetings. You can make instant changes in publication designs and get them approved if you use a projection screen with a desktop publishing system. You might even liven up a meeting or presentation by projecting and playing a video game that simulates business competition.

Up to now, we've talked about just creating a changing image from one single computer program. You can also use any number of word processing, graphics, or spreadsheet programs to prepare an entire series of visuals, much as you could present a slide show or an entire stack of overhead transparencies. With a scanner, you can even convert photographs into a computer image that can be projected onto a screen. This method of creating a presentation can be much cheaper and faster than using more traditional methods, because you can avoid typesetting and photography charges by integrating different computer typefaces and graphics.

In addition, it's a lot more convenient and portable, because instead of having to travel with a slide projector tray for slides or a stack of transparencies, several full visual presentations can be placed on one computer disk. Once you're at the speech or presentation site, you merely pop the single disk into a computer that's outfitted with the computer projector equipment and open the file. Most computer projectors even come with a remote control unit that lets you move between the visuals.

Multimedia Computer Presentations

You can use computers to create even more exciting visual presentations. A number of computer companies now market multimedia programs. These multimedia programs allow a computer operator to integrate graphics programs and word processing into a video presentation that can be shown on a television or computer monitor instead of an overhead projector. Although the medium is different, that's basically the same result as a computer projection screen.

However, a multimedia program can take the graphs, illustrations and typefaces that a computer projector can produce and integrate moving video pictures as well as music, narration and sound effects with the visual presentation. Figure 13.1 is an example of a screen from a multimedia program.

In effect, you can create and edit a fully formed video production using just a desktop computer. It's very impressive technology. What's more important is that it can be made interactive with the people who otherwise would be passively viewing the results.

That power can be useful in training workers. By integrating touch-sensitive areas onto the computer screen, you can present decision options to people viewing the presentation. This is the training system in the technical facility described at the beginning of this chapter.

In that factory, they used the presentation to help train inspectors to recognize

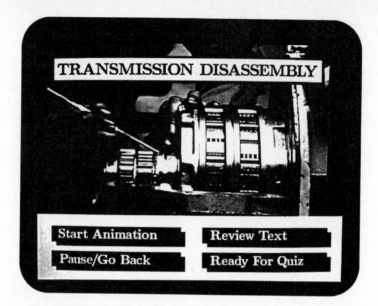

FIGURE 13.1   Sample screen from a computer multi-media program

faulty workmanship. After examining a three-dimensional view of a part and even hearing the noise it made when it needed repairs, the computer presented a number of possible solutions to the inspector.

The inspector chose a repair option by touching an area on the screen, either with a light pen, a computer cursor or a computer mouse. The computer then told the inspector if he or she made the right choice and moved step-by-step with narration and visuals through the repair process. Technical specifications on the part as well as ordering information could be reviewed on the screen by accessing the information from a CD-ROM file.

There are millions of other possible uses. Potential homebuyers could conduct searches without long car trips by browsing through a computer video file of homes. The homebuyer could ask the computer to look only at homes with a certain number of bedrooms or a patio and a two-car garage. The search could be narrowed further by limiting it to certain neighborhoods and certain price ranges. Once those parameters have been established, the homebuyer could see a video of only the homes that fit those characteristics, electronically strolling from one room to the next with an accompanying narration and a supertitle telling the number of square feet in each room. Using the software's number-crunching capabilities, homebuyers could discover the estimated closing costs or monthly mortgage payments by telling the computer how big a down payment they could make.

The possibilities of multimedia computer programs for training and for worker and consumer communication are endless. It's something that will be explored much more thoroughly during the next few years.

The Internet

The Internet, a worldwide computer network, hooks millions of computer users together. It lets them exchange mail with individuals, engage in discussion groups with other like-minded individuals, find information from public databases, and play games with other users.

The important unifying characteristic of all these users is that for each interaction on the Internet, an individual has chosen to discover information on a particular topic or with a particular person or institution.

Unimpressed? You shouldn't be. A consumer indicating that he or she is interested in a product solves a problem that advertisers and media buyers have been trying to solve for centuries. A scientist specializing in radio astronomy who joins an Internet discussion group comprised of researchers and students throughout the world has created her own scientific conference from her office.

The Internet has become one of the most effective person-to-person media outlets ever, primarily because the thousands of different user groups provide for very tight targeting, and the people who cruise the Internet select themselves based on their own interests.

The Internet has already been used in thousands of fascinating ways. The union representing thousands of orchestra musicians scattered through scores of cities throughout North America has established a news group sharing information about the union's efforts with its otherwise isolated members.

A company that makes golf course equipment has set up an on-line service that allows golf course managers to play on computer versions of famous golf holes that the company maintains. Each time they sink a putt on the computer green, the managers see a billboard advertising the company's products and are then invited to explore the technical capabilities, prices and delivery timetables of the company's equipment in depth by clicking on a billboard icon.

A car company lets car shoppers examine different cars' performance numbers, read magazine reviews of the cars, check on prices for different options, figure financing plans, or even take a computer-simulated test drive.

The Internet is fun and a perfect way to offer a message that can reach millions of potential customers who can find an almost unlimited amount of information in an interactive form. It will probably be one of the most important media public relations practitioners will deal with in the 21st century.

CAPITALIZING ON PEOPLE POWER IN INTERACTIVE MEDIA

The important concept to remember in using all these media is that you need to exploit each medium's particular power to draw personal involvement and interaction from the people for whom the messages are intended. The medium itself doesn't create one person's identification with another that is so important to cost-effective communication. Even with the most advanced medium, it is still necessary to create an environment and a message in which those human-level exchanges take place. That's a lesson we can apply in virtually every communication task we undertake. Let's look at one of MCI's direct-mail efforts that could have been another impersonal and uninvolving marketing campaign.

MCI's "Friends and Family" program deserves special note for its success in integrating powerful person-to-person communication tactics in a mass marketing campaign. In the promotion, MCI promised sizable discounts to individuals who set up calling circles with family members and their closest friends. When consumers enrolled in the service, they gave MCI a list of names and phone numbers of friends and family members, who would share in the discounts if they also signed up for MCI long-distance service.

MCI's telemarketing people then called the friends or relatives whom each individual submitted and asked them if they would like to save Great Aunt Sadie (or their good friend Hank) and themselves money by enrolling in Friends and Family. Or (the implication was) would they just like to thumb their nose at their relatives and friends by refusing. A tough pitch to turn down, isn't it?

Keep that lesson in mind and don't merely create a message that reinforces a passive, deadened audience. Instead, at every opportunity think about the ways you can use creativity or technology to make receivers active participants and involve them in actions that will stimulate the actions that signal true persuasion.

SUMMARY

- Traditional audiovisual media include chalkboards and opaque, overhead and photographic slide projectors. Even though all have shortcomings, they are useful in certain circumstances.

- Because videotaping equipment and production are relatively inexpensive, videotape is replacing film in most organizational audiovisual applications.

- A computer projection screen displays information from a computer monitor onto a wall screen. It is useful in involving audiences by displaying spreadsheet calculations and other software program manipulations to audiences in real time.

- Multimedia computer programs can integrate standard computer programs with video, music, narration and sound effects to create interactive presentations for worker training and consumer communication.

THINK PIECES

1. Does the novelty of new communication technology hurt or help your ability to get an audience to respond to and retain a message?

2. How are the retention and persuasion of a message improved by a receiver's participation and involvement in creating the message? How does that involvement help make interactive multimedia technology very effective?

MANAGEMENT PROBLEMS

D5.1

D5.2

D8.1

D8.2

D10.4

D12.1

D12.3

ADDITIONAL READING

Bobbitt, Randy. "An Internet Primer for Public Relations." *Public Relations Quarterly* 40:3 (Fall 1995): 27–32.

Druck, Kalman B., ed. *New Technology and Public Relations: A Guide for Public Relations and Public Affairs Practitioners*. Ann Arbor, Mich.: Books on Demand, n.d.

Dunkel, Jacqueline, and Parnham, Elizabeth. *Effective Speaking for Business Success: Making Presentations with Confidence, Using Audio-Visuals and More*. Bellingham, Wash.: Self-Counsel Press: 1993.

Horton, James L., and Shinbach, Peter L. "Shrink-wrapped Presentations From Your Desktop." *Public Relations Journal* 50:4 (April 1994): 11–12, 18.

Katzman, Jodie B. "Interactive Video Gets Bigger Play." *Public Relations Journal* 51:1 (May 1995): 6–8, 10, 12.

Major, Michael J. "How Tech-Friendly Companies Communicate." *Public Relations Journal* 51:1 (May 1995): 24–27.

Masterton, John. "Discovering Databases." *Public Relations Journal* 48:11 (November 1992): 12–17, 19.

Miga, George P. "Quality Presentations Boost Decision Making Power." *Public Relations Journal* 50:2 (February 1994): 24–25.

Spector, Shelley J. "Interactive Multimedia Comes of Age." *Public Relations Journal* 51:1 (May 1995): 42–45.

Verderber, Kathleen S., and Verderber, Rudolph. *Using Interpersonal Communication Skills*, 7th ed. Belmont, Calif.: Wadsworth, 1992.

Wiesendanger, Betsy. "Electronic Delivery and Feedback Systems Come of Age." *Public Relations Journal* 49:1 (January 1993): 10–14.

## chapter 14

The Integrated Message: Applying Receiver-centered Writing to Advertising

REAL-LIFE LESSONS

Until fairly recently, few practitioners, especially those in PR agencies or corporate settings, would ever deal with advertising. Conversely, few advertising people would ever find themselves working on a project with public relations professionals.

Advertising, it was thought, had vastly different goals and purposes from public relations. Public relations practitioners didn't do anything as base as sell toothpaste or farm machinery, underwear or automobiles. Advertising, we thought, was manipulative communication to trick people into buying products they didn't want. Public relations, on the other hand, was persuasive communication to convince people to adopt ideas that would improve their lives and, at the same time, help our clients.

But increasingly, public relations professionals in all disciplines are finding themselves engaged in either creating advertising, critiquing and buying advertising, or evaluating its effect in meeting organizational objectives. Corporations have begun to address public and regulatory issues facing them, not only by communicating to government officials through their lobbyists, but by appealing directly to the public through purchased advertisements (advertorials) explaining the corporation's position. Some corporations have begun to expand the reach of their traditional PR image-building activities into advertising space.

That appears to be only the start of public relations' involvement in advertising. Because of the consumerism movement, consumers have become increasingly suspicious of advertising claims. That has caused companies to complement their advertising with the validation provided by media coverage prompted by PR practitioners.

This closely merged public relations and advertising effort is called integrated marketing, and its increasing use has meant that all public relations professionals, including corporate, agency and nonprofit areas, have begun to encounter more advertising assignments.

Although advertising and public relations practitioners have often viewed themselves as offering very distinct services, the ends to which they are dedicated are similar. Each is trying to solve specific problems for a client by using communication. Each uses persuasive communication, and the goals each strives for—even through creative advertising writing—can be stimulated and generated through a management-by-objective planning process.

The gulf that separated advertising from public relations has begun to narrow as practitioners from each discipline have begun to note their common purpose. That first step makes our knowledge of advertising important.

WHAT YOU KNOW

- All persuasive communication should be oriented to solving an organizational problem.
- Communication effectiveness is not judged by the number of people you communicated with, but by whether the people who you wanted to take an action took that action.
- Each medium has certain strengths and weaknesses in its effectiveness, and one of the practitioner's jobs is to choose the best medium for a particular task.

WHAT YOU'LL LEARN

- Although advertising is usually distinguished by a creative introduction, the objectives and structure of the body copy are essentially the same as for all persuasive communication.
- The boundary between the roles of public relations and advertising practitioners is becoming indistinguishable.
- Judgments about media choice and persuasion strategy rest upon a clear determination of the problem confronting the organization and the audience whose involvement can help solve the problem.

THE ADVERTISING CHALLENGE: PERSUADING THEM AFTER YOU'VE CAUGHT THEIR ATTENTION

Throughout this book, I've emphasized the competitiveness of communication—the battle for attention and access to the receiver's mind. Writing advertising copy means entering into the same battle, with some crucial differences.

Some of those differences make the competition easier. Because advertising is a controlled medium involving the purchase of space or time in a mass medium to promote a product, service or idea, your message is ensured of gaining access to a medium through which a receiver can encounter it. Unlike a news release, advertising doesn't have to pass the gauntlet of an editor's judgment as to his or her audience's needs and desires before it can ever reach the public.

However, an advertising message has other, formidable barriers to overcome in gaining a public's attention and action. One problem is the sheer volume of advertising messages against which an advertisement is deployed. By the time a typical individual is 21 years old, he or she has encountered between 1 million and 2 million advertisements! In that roar of advertising claims and counterclaims it's not surprising that many people simply ignore a vast majority of the advertising they encounter each day.

It's not just the number of messages that creates an enormous challenge for the advertising copywriter. Even if people notice the message, there's no guarantee they'll believe it. One study showed that over two-thirds of all Americans think advertising claims are exaggerated or misleading.

Therefore, unless an advertisement is carefully conceived and creatively executed so that it can emerge from the cacophony, that lonely little commercial merely contributes to the confusing clutter of messages that are routinely doubted or ignored. What's worse yet is that the advertiser has paid hundreds, or maybe even hundreds of thousands, of dollars for the privilege of being ignored.

How does an advertisement gain attention in the midst of this confusion of voices? Some argue that the commercials that are noticed are those more outrageous in their premises, more outlandish in their presentation, and more overstated in their production. Out of this theory come commercials in which the meticulously photographed wriggling of a rock star's back pants pocket is connected with a soft drink's attributes.

The underpinnings of this advertising theory date back to those high school student council elections almost everyone remembers, in which one intellectually impoverished candidate would spell SEX across the top of a poster. In smaller letters would be, "Now that I've got your attention, let me tell you about my plans for the school lunchroom monitors." In essence, those advertising theorists claim the main part of communication is capturing attention.

Yet those people should be reminded of the basic premise that underlies all persuasive communication, including advertising. Persuasion, by its very definition, is moving people to take an action. Without an eventual action, attention does not help us.

However, those advertising messages against which an advertiser is competing do change the way advertisers conceive and structure their message. It is necessary, as the soft drink campaign illustrates, to gain attention for the message in the midst of scores of other messages and with the memory of millions more.

In essence, the advertiser must introduce the message more creatively than ever before. But that attention-getting device (what I call a conceit) has to be closely related to the eventual message the advertiser is going to tell. The conceit has to logically lead to the benefits to be gained by buying a product or adopting an idea. To help formulate that conceit, many advertising writers begin their writing by composing a persuasion platform.

INTEGRATING THE PERSUASION PLATFORM
INTO ADVERTISING WRITING

As discussed in Chapter 2, a persuasion platform guides writers in developing a plan for solving an organizational problem. But more important for advertising tasks, the persuasion platform helps stimulate the creativity that leads to a conceit, which is a new and interesting way of presenting an advertising claim that brings a fresh outlook and renewed attention to the claim. Generally, the conceit appears in the headline and illustration of a print ad or the scenario of a broadcast ad.

The platform stimulates the writer's creative process by first isolating the one major selling idea the product can promise the intended audience. Then the platform tries to place that main selling idea within the context of audience characteristics to create a new presentation. This conceit will invite the target audience's attention while forcefully communicating the most important message to tempt the reader to buy the product.

It's the same basic planning process recommended for every persuasion task we've faced in our public relations duties. There are only a few distinctions we need to discuss, distinctions that respond to the different problems faced in marketing activities.

Isolating the Institutional Problem: What Are You Trying to Do Beyond Selling?

In the platform, the section detailing the client's problem briefly touches on all those historic, social, economic or perceptual elements that have caused the problem affecting our client's organization. We develop a reason for communication before we communicate. That's as important in advertising as it is in all other institutional communication.

Let's say the appliance company for which you're writing copy has just been purchased by another company. The new company has poured money into a retooling effort to correct your product's awful service record. How would you structure an ad campaign for this situation? Would you picture a product spokesperson gazing lovingly at a refrigerator and saying how wonderful it is? Would you show a happy, active family being more happy and more active because of your new refrigerator? Would you have the company's new CEO come on screen and say how fortunate he feels to head a company with the reputation of your company?

I don't think any of those will work very well, because none of them attacks the basic problem—that people know you've made a lousy product in the past. To succeed, you've got to overcome that reputation, and hiding behind slick advertising presentations that ignore your former transgressions won't accomplish that.

When you realize your problem, your options become clearer. Perhaps you should have the CEO appear on TV to say you've made an inferior product but that you've changed. That's what Ford did, and invited people to take a test drive to see the improvement for themselves. Maybe you need to bury the problems along with the brand name and start over. That's what General Motors did with its Saturn Division; GM tried to create an entirely new impression with a new car line. It even went so far as to not mention in its advertising campaign that Saturn was a GM division.

Determining the Objective: Solving the Problem

Once you've established the problem, it's important to formulate an advertising objective that will solve that specific problem. When the advertising project is in the formative stage it's best to think of the persuasion problem as a challenge to change the mind of one typical individual in the target audience. Most advertising experts recommend that during the creative stage, ad copywriters try to communicate about the product to accomplish one of the following:

1. establish a use
2. stimulate trial
3. position the product
4. build brand awareness

Establish a Use.   If your audience is likely to respond to highly rational arguments, your most logical goal is to try to establish a use or a new use for the product. Selling a lawnmower to a homeowner, heavy manufacturing equipment to a corporation president, or a box of salt to a homemaker all involve considerations of cost or efficiency for the user. For this type of product or idea, you're going to use a hard, no-nonsense appeal.

This is probably the simplest advertising appeal, because you're showing your audience how buying the product will directly benefit it in the most practical ways. It can be effective for new products with new functions because it emphasizes the function and not the brand name. Thus, a series of commercials promoting a collapsing hanger set that saves closet space would barely mention the product's brand name.

It can also be effective for an established product with a unique feature. That explains the number of commercials touting "new, improved cleaning power" or a "new, easy-pull starter."

It can be equally effective if a manufacturer discovers a new use for an established product. Think of the plight of Arm & Hammer baking soda. A one-pound box of baking soda makes, according to my calculations, over 19,000 chocolate chip cookies. You can't make much money if you're selling an inexpensive product that lasts for years. If that isn't discouraging enough, the number of people who bake from scratch is declining in this age of microwave ovens and store-bought snacks.

What's a manufacturer facing these discouraging prospects to do? It finds new uses for the product, a task at which the Arm & Hammer researchers have been extraordinarily successful. They promote baking soda as toothpaste and as an antacid.

It even cleans battery acid from car batteries. In their most remarkable selling job, they've been able to convince consumers to buy a full box of the product, then pour it down their drains as a deodorizer. These are all examples of convincing the customer of the solid benefits of using the product, new uses they might not have imagined possible.

Stimulate Trial.   If you predict the persuasion sequence will involve low-consequence decisions, your most likely selling objective may be to stimulate trial. Encouraging a consumer to experiment with a new product works best when the ramifications of making the wrong decision are small. Thus, stimulating trial is a logical objective for a campaign selling $2 raffle tickets for an animal shelter's fund-raiser.

Conversely, if you want to convince a town's residents to approve locating a nuclear reactor in their vicinity (a high-consequence decision), you're ill-advised to try to stimulate trial among people who might be profoundly affected by a wrong decision.

However, trial works well for all sorts of products. We're equally willing to try a new brand of soap or cereal that largely satisfies rational appeals, as well as inexpensive jewelry or candy or toys that satisfy emotional cravings.

For public issues campaigns in which we're asking people only to sign a petition or mail a postcard to a legislator, it can often work as well. What's important is that the consequences of making the wrong decision be manageable.

Position the Product.   Positioning is a way of communicating which segment of the market a particular product intends to fill. This type of campaign generally works best in decisions that are high-consequence. For the high-income auto buyer trying to decide whether to buy a Mercedes or a BMW, the decision generally doesn't turn on performance, maintenance records or even price. Commercials for each of these products tell us what statement we are making to the world when we buy a particular luxury automobile. From their commercials, we understand that BMWs are intended for younger people who want to display an unharnessed sophistication. The Mercedes, on the other hand, seems to appeal to older buyers who want to buy dependability and communicate stability to others.

This appeal is often seen in corporate image campaigns, in which a company claims it gives good service just like its competitors, but it has a concern for the environment of the community that its competitors can't match.

Build Brand Awareness.   These are campaigns for products that have been on the market for years and are in a marketing environment where there are few distinctions among products offered by competitors and little new product information to offer consumers. Almost all decisions about these types of products are based on emotionalism.

The classic example of this is the decades-long battle between Pepsi and Coca-Cola. After years of advertising and consumer trials, there is very little more to say about either product. Each of us knows how each product tastes, and early in our lives we usually establish a favorite. The task of a brand image commercial is just to keep the brand name in the consciousness of the user and reinforce those attributes the user associates with the product.

Predicting the Probable Persuasion Sequence

After you've isolated the demographic and psychographic factors that will motivate the target audience's behavior, it's necessary to discover the probable persuasion sequence. This information will help the writer decide whether emotional or rational appeals will most effectively motivate the audience to take the desired action. Here are the most common persuasion sequences for each advertising objective:

If the Objective Is:	*Persuasion Sequence Chosen Will Be:*
to establish a use	learn–feel–do or do–learn–feel
to stimulate trial	do–feel–learn or do–learn–feel
to reposition the product among its competitors	feel–learn–do or do–feel–learn
to build brand awareness	feel–learn–do or do–feel–learn

Discovering the Main Persuader: What Can You Say That No One Else Can?

The main persuader is the central concept that drives the creation of all copy in the advertising, a conception that is introduced in the headline, then repeated in the body copy, and reinforced in the final few words of the advertisement. In short, the main selling idea should be your best judgment of the one message that will most effectively convince the target audience to take the desired action.

Sometimes that message is simply that the product has a new ingredient that makes it a good buy. At other times the central message is that the product has a reputation for quality, or that people view you with respect if you own the product. Then there are other times when the main selling idea might be to convince the buyers that they are saying something about themselves—that they are sophisticated, or frugal, or technically knowledgeable—when they use the product.

The main selling idea should distill the many hundreds of things that you could say about the product into one central idea. For that reason, it's usually best to refine the main selling idea to one declarative sentence. For instance: Crylon paint's better covering capacity saves time by letting you paint anything with one coat. Or: Drinking Pepsi shows that you are young and adventurous. Or: Buying Michelin tires shows that you value your children's safety.

In each of these cases, the main selling idea isn't a slogan or a headline (although don't be surprised if the main selling idea you generate is the germ for a very good headline). Instead it is a selling strategy, the one idea that will be significant for your target audience as it decides whether to attend to your message.

Composing the Creative Strategy Statement: How Can You Say It Differently?

The creative statement develops the main persuader into a conceit. It starts with a summation of the platform's main conclusions. Will an emotional or a rational appeal be more effective with your audience? How can you structure the message to best emphasize those appeals to your audience? Can you expect your audience to make a snap judgment about the issue or will they need to contemplate before they decide to accept or reject your proposal?

After that, you determine the form of your advertising strategy. Will you use humor? How sophisticated will the language need to be to communicate with the intended reader? What do you want the reader to think or feel after reading the ad? If you're trying to position the product, how should your reader feel about competitors?

The strategy statement is often a free-form, stream-of-consciousness play of ideas and thoughts until a central conception for the ad comes into focus. It should be a method of generating a creative communication of your main selling idea to a particular public.

This central conception is what I call a conceit. It's important to realize that after 200 years of American advertising, there are very few new advertising claims left. Laundry detergents from time immemorial have claimed they get clothes cleaner. Adding machines and calculators and now computers have promised to make office workers more productive. Advertisements for the Pony Express offered the fastest communication across the country; fax machine ads make the same promise today.

So you need to give up on coming up with a new advertising claim. What you want is to emerge with a new conceit, a way of communicating your claim that makes it different from the way that message has been communicated hundreds of times before.

Hardee's, the restaurant chain, mounted an ad campaign that is a good example of this. Hardee's selling point was that they have more sandwich choices than other hamburger chains. The chain could have said simply, "You can order more types of sandwiches at Hardee's than you can at McDonald's," but that statement, although good for a main selling idea, isn't very effective at drawing attention amid the sea of ads that swells around consumers.

Hardee's needed a different way to make the claim. The conceit Hardee's advertisers emerged with—"Sometimes you gotta break the rules," combined with descriptions of all kinds of unusual sandwich combinations—essentially communicated the main selling idea. However, the challenging language and slang were also effective in sending a message of unconventional behavior and rebellion the advertisers thought would be effective in luring the teenage customers Hardee's wanted.

At its best, your advertising strategy statement should do just that—forcefully convey the main selling idea in a new and interesting way, while suggesting the product will fulfill a psychological need. It is from this conceit that the advertisement is built. But each advertising medium uses this conceit in a different way to involve the audience in its message. Knowing that, we'll talk about each major advertising medium separately.

PRINT ADVERTISING: AN ACTIVE BUT SELECTIVE AUDIENCE

The print advertising medium has many of the same strengths and weaknesses that print has in accomplishing all other tasks. Print advertising is usually the best choice when trying to communicate rational arguments about a product. Because it is in a permanent medium (unlike radio or television), the product can be studied and complex claims can be reviewed at the reader's own pace. At the present stage of technology, print messages can be targeted to particular audiences much more precisely because of the multitude of special interest newsletters, newspapers and magazines.

Print's advantage, as discussed in Chapter 7, is that readers are more active participants in receiving print messages. People listening to their car radio or watching television while eating a meal tend to be much more passive in attending to broadcast messages than are print readers, who have to be much more involved in the communication event. Hence, readers are more involved in the messages to which they attend.

Print advertising has certain weaknesses, too. For instance, there's a negative element in the reader's actively attending to print messages. Whereas broadcast commercials reach consumers whenever they turn on a radio or television whether they want them or not, print ad readers can simply turn the page if they aren't interested in an advertisement.

Most important, print has none of the sensory elements inherent in radio or television advertising that make broadcast emotional appeals so effective. You can't see a product work, as on television, or hear an authoritative voice talking, as on radio.

An important initial task, as it is with every communication event, is to select the proper medium for transmitting your message. If you want to send a rational or complicated message, you'll usually be better served using a print medium. If you need more precise targeting of your message, again, print is usually better.

Writing Print Advertising: Steps in Moving an Audience to Action

A print ad, like all persuasive communication, is intended to state a proposition, explain the proposition, and then give reasons for the proposition. Finally, following the definition of persuasion, it offers a specific action the receiver can undertake to participate in the benefits the proposition promises. Virtually every print ad is comprised of five elements that move the reader through just those steps: (1) the headline-visual, (2) the bridge, (3) the statement of benefits, (4) the wrap, and (5) the logo and baseline.

The Headline–Visual: Grabbing Attention While Keeping the Focus. One of the more difficult tasks for advertising copywriters is to compose persuasive prose and then establish a strong visual message that complements their words. Advertising research has shown that ads that present information graphically, either through illustrations, photos or the graphic presentation of text, draw audience attention much better than text alone. Part of this attraction is that people like to look at pictures. However, it's important to think of advertising illustrations as something more than finding pictures that will draw attention.

For instance, if your company is running a series of informational ads to calm environmentalists' fears over a new factory building, it's not enough to put a picture of an attractive, swimsuit-clad woman or man over the advertising text. Sure, a lot of people will look at the picture, but then will be disappointed that the ad text is about environmental issues and not about swimsuits or the bodies inside them.

Contrary to many of the advertising maxims you may have heard, the best advertising illustration isn't necessarily the one that attracts the most people; it's the one that attracts the right people. The right people are the ones who are legitimate prospects for buying your product. The right people are the ones who can help you accomplish your organizational goal if they adopt your idea. So the idea is not to get attention; it is, once again, to get results.

A. Jerome Jewler, a University of South Carolina advertising professor, writes of a necessary headline–visual synergy, a melding of illustration and text that creates an effect greater than the effect either one would have individually. Your intent should be to meld the visual and the words to convey a unified message growing from your main selling idea and creative strategy statement. That said, there is very little further direction to offer you in choosing illustrations, because in advertising virtually anything can work in the right situation. But here are a few personal guidelines.

Think of your illustration as an extension of your headline, and the headline as an extension of your illustration. They should support and complement each other. Thus you should avoid illustrations that are not an integral component of your advertising copy.

This very mistake marred the introductory ad campaign for the Infiniti luxury automobile. In a series of ads narrated by Clint Eastwood, dreamily photographed video of rocks, trees and cows were used to proclaim the natural inspirations that led to the engineering and design of this radically new car. Consumers were confused and unimpressed. An Oklahoma City Infiniti dealer, discouraged by slow sales, said, "The car is real quality, but it's hard to convince someone of that when all you do is show a bunch of cows rubbing against a tree." The moral of the story: Keep your communication objective in focus and don't disrupt the single-mindedness of the message that leads from the visual into the copy.

Because most effective advertising copy, as we will see later, involves showing how the consumer's life will be made better by using a product or adopting an idea, illustrations showing consumer transformation are often quite effective. Show how the product works better than its competition, how the consumer's life is made better by adopting your ideas, or how envious the neighbors would be of the purchase your reader has the chance to make. This consumer transformation is as powerful a motivator in the visual as it is in the body copy.

Another guideline for advertising illustrations ties in with a central rule for writing advertising copy: Avoid advertising cliches. For instance, ever since advertising writers and artists first put pen to paper (or perhaps even chisel to stone), there have been illustrations of a happy suburban housewife in a happy suburban home happily holding the product box next to her smiling face. We've seen it before. It doesn't draw your readers' attention from the din of advertising messages and all sorts of other communication events around them. Another cliche is to show the product, standing noble and solitary on the page. Automobile ads are legendary for this. This presentation has been around too long to draw any attention. It doesn't show the customer being helped by the product, or his or her self-image being transformed by owning it. A better idea? Show a young couple in an off-road vehicle excitedly pounding over rocks in a beautiful and remote valley or show the exhilarating handling of a sports car on a twisting mountain road.

In short, don't show the advantages of the product. Show the benefits to the consumer—the consumer transformation that will overtake the reader when he or she buys your product or adopts your idea.

The Headline: The Lead Sentence of an Advertisement.

Because the headline should complement the visual, many of the same principles apply. (See Memory Memo 14.1.) Having said that, however, let me caution you that just as in choosing a visual, a similar lack of rules about what works applies to headlines. There is no minimum number of words that a headline has to contain, nor are there any prescriptions that tell what a bad headline is.

It may help to remember that the headline essentially serves the same role as the lead sentence in a news release. It's the limited opportunity your reader gives you to involve him or her in the story. Within those few words, you've got to interest a reader who has been assaulted by hundreds of thousands of advertisements in the past. To do that, you need a stimulating idea that involves the reader's self-interest or curiosity in the main selling idea, and you need to structure it within a format that your reader hasn't seen before.

Memory Memo 14.1
Checklist for creating advertising headlines

- Has your headline identified a specific audience?
- Have you demonstrated a consumer transformation that has given the reader a rational benefit as well as a self-image improvement?
- Has your headline stated your audience's benefit in a unique way?
- Does your headline complement the advertisement's key visual?

There are many types of headlines. There are headlines in which the writer offers a benefit:

What does this bunny have to do with Sleepy Hollow products? Nothing.

This ad for a cosmetic company that doesn't use animal testing is paired with a picture of a fat white rabbit and the story of the company's commitment to not hurting animals in their testing and manufacturing process.

There are headlines that select a particular audience:

Impotence.

This one-word headline for a hospital's sexual dysfunction clinic is quietly effective in drawing the attention of men who desire help for a sensitive problem.

There are headlines that offer news:

On July 12th, there'll be a South Seas port in the center of Iowa.

This ad for a Polynesian arts and food festival offers information about an exotic entertainment option for the landlocked residents of a medium-sized Iowa town. A pig and a cow with leis around their necks communicate the Polynesian concept and the local angle.

There are headlines that show the problems if you avoid using the product.

There'll be a lot of red faces in your family if you don't use High PF sunscreen.

This ad, using an appeal called the reverse benefit, pictures three sunburned children and suggests that you'll be a better parent if you buy this sunscreen brand.

In all these headlines, you see informational appeals that stem from the TIPCUP formula outlined in the beginning of the text. Three of the headlines show reader impact, whereas the Polynesian festival ad combines proximity, unusualness and time factors.

The thing that is different is that each of these headlines offers a conceit, a way of provoking curiosity that will lead the audience into the advertising copy for at least a brief time. The conceit, as explained before, is a different and creative way of making the same claim, of saying the same thing that has been said a hundred times before. Note an example of that in Figure 14.1, in which a striking photo is paired with an appropriate, creative headline to make a combination that's more effective than the headline or photo would be individually. Remember that you're communicating with a typical consumer who has read thousands of ads and is wary of every cliche.

There are limitless ways to escape cliches and to discover a conceit, but one of

FIGURE 14.1 Headline–visual synergy
Used with permission of Image Printer Inc.

the most common is through wordplay. By rhyming or alliterating (repeating vowel or consonant sounds), you make the same claim a little more fun to read, and give an advertisement a touch of the fun we had as children listening to our parents read children's books to us. Sidebar 14.1 shows an example of this repetition. This is an advertisement for a master's in business administration program that students could complete with evening classes: "You could spend your evenings watching Thirty-Something, or learning how to make eighty-something."

Advertising copywriters also often use what I call reversals. A reversal is contrasting the first example in a headline with the second example. A reversal using an outdoor clothing company claims its clothes are "For the outdoors inside each of us."

Another technique of creating a headline conceit is the pun. A pun is a way of replacing words with other words of similar sounds but different meanings. "He wasn't a Wright Brother, but he had the right idea." This ad for General Dynamics is about Edson Gallaudet, an airplane pioneer who founded an aircraft company that later became part of General Dynamics.

In all these cases the final result is that you've brought just a little more interest to the headline, so that even if the self-interest of the subject discussed in the headline isn't enough to get someone to read, the entertainment and curiosity value of the wordplay may bring the reader in. Finally, you're also hoping to introduce multiple meanings that not only introduce the benefit but add an emotional statement about the product and its manufacturer.

The Bridge: Explaining the Lead Sentence.   The problem with most conceits, this elaborate interplay of words and meanings in the headline, is that no matter how clearly you think you have established the true meaning, a certain proportion of your audience just won't get it. That's where the bridge comes in.

The bridge is the advertising equivalent of the news release's second paragraph. The bridge is the opportunity to explain the headline and directly state the main selling idea in terms your audience can understand. Here's where you use plain language to tell readers what you're going to prove in the body copy. It's generally a one- or two-sentence paragraph. See Sidebar 14.1 for an example of a bridge.

The Statement of Benefits: Justifying the Actions You Want.   The main body of the advertisement presents the statement of benefits. The statement of benefits is, again, very much like the third section of an inverted pyramid, in which you use facts, testimonials and histories to prove your thesis. In the Webster University ad, the thesis is contained in the bridge.

The benefits in an advertisement are usually segmented much like those in a news release, too. Information supporting certain points is grouped together. For instance, an advertisement for a car might spend the first section of the benefit statement supporting the car's reliability, the next section discussing its performance, and the final section talking about its low price. Transitions are important, and memory-cue transitions are useful in showing readers the linkages among the product's many benefits.

SIDEBAR 14.1   Example of a Print Advertisement

This print ad illustrates the basic structure of advertising writing: (1) headline–visual, (2) bridge, (3) statement of benefits, (4) wrap, and (5) logo and baseline. Notice how closely the primary argumentation patterns follow the structure of the other persuasive writing we've discussed in this book.

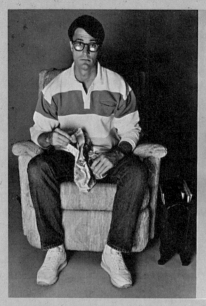

You could spend your evenings watching ThirtySomething, or learning how to make eighty-something.

Bridge equivalent to pyramid's second paragraph. It explains lead. →

Statement of benefits functions as ad's justification of lead. Here, writer uses order of importance to list benefits. →

Start statement of historical background. →

This, plus coupon, functions as call to action. →

Webster University has programs that can take you much further than those you're watching now. Our degree programs offer convenient evening and Saturday classes, designed for working professionals like you.

At Webster, you'll find smaller classes, so students receive more personalized attention. Our faculty includes part-time teaching professionals with a "real world" perspective. In short, Webster offers a quality education from an outstanding learning institution.

To learn more about Webster, return our coupon. It just might get you off that couch and onto the fast track.

UNIVERSITY

SAINT LOUIS, MISSOURI
GENEVA · LEIDEN · LONDON · VIENNA

Webster University admits students of any race, creed, color, age, sex, nondisqualifying handicap or national ethnic origin.
Webster University is accredited by the North Central Association of Colleges and Schools.

Webster University, Dept. M
470 East Lockwood
St. Louis, MO 63119-3194
968-7000 (BA & BSN)
968-7100 (MBA, MA, MAT, Dr. App. Mgmt.)

Please send me information about the following degree program(s):

BA Programs
☐ Business & Management
  ☐ Accounting
  ☐ Business Administration
  ☐ Health Care Administration
  ☐ Human Resources Management
  ☐ Marketing
  ☐ Real Estate
☐ Computer Studies
  ☐ Information Management
☐ Media Communications
  ☐ Public Communications
  ☐ Selected Production Courses
☐ Paralegal Studies
☐ Psychology
☐ Selected Liberal Arts Courses
☐ Nursing (BSN Completion)

Certificate Programs
☐ Paralegal Studies
☐ Writing As A Profession

MA & MAT
☐ Business
☐ Computer and Information Resources Management
☐ Counseling Services
☐ Finance
☐ Gerontology
☐ Health Services Management

MA & MAT (continued)
☐ Human Resources Development
☐ International Business
☐ International Relations
☐ Legal Studies
☐ Management
☐ Marketing
☐ Media Communications
☐ Procurement and Acquisitions Management
☐ Real Estate Management
☐ Teaching (MAT)

MBA
☐ Business
☐ Computer and Information Resources Management
☐ Finance
☐ Health Services Management
☐ Human Resources Development
☐ International Business
☐ Management
☐ Marketing
☐ Procurement and Acquisitions Management
☐ Real Estate Management

Dr. App. Mgmt.
☐ Doctor of Applied Management

Name _____

Address _____

City _____ State _____ Zip _____

Class locations: Webster Groves, St. Peters, Northwest Plaza, Downtown.
Five terms a year.   NCJ 9W

As in internal writing, emphasizing the weight of evidence is very important, too. In an advertisement, the main selling idea should be enough to convince a logical prospect to purchase the product or adopt the idea. However, you want to show your readers reason after reason after reason to justify that decision, so subheads, bullets and other physical structuring of the copy help show those added values to your readers.

The Wrap: Reminding Your Audience of Why They Started Reading.   The final section of the body copy in an advertisement is called the wrap. The wrap is the persuader, the invitation that moves the consumer from absorbing information into taking action—to buy a product or adopt an idea. Very much like the inverted pyramid's call to action, the wrap restates the main selling idea and then gives you some specific call to action, a way of gaining all the benefits the product promises.

The wrap then makes a definitive suggestion to the readers—that they call a toll-free number for information, or go to their nearest store, or write their legislator, or redeem a coupon. The wrap should explicitly move readers from merely processing facts to the point that they are ready to make a commitment.

The Logo and Baseline: Calling Your Audience to Action.   An ad's logo and baseline generally reestablish the brand name and reinforce the main selling idea. The logo area often pictures the product's store packaging and the company's logo so the consumer will be able to identify it on the shelf. The logo and baseline component also often contains the store's address and/or phone number so that readers who have decided to take action will have definitive information to accomplish that action. Finally, a baseline generally employs a corporate slogan to reinforce the ad's or corporation's emotional image.

Memory Memo 14.2
Purpose of each section of an advertisement:

- Bridge explicitly restates the headline's conceit.
- Statement of benefits builds the weight of evidence, explaining the main persuader and including secondary persuaders.
- Wrap restates the main selling idea in a way that reminds reader of the headline.
- Logo and baseline establish the mechanics by which the reader may take action.

As a final check of your advertisement's body copy, review the standards listed in Memory Memo 14.2

MODIFYING PRINT ADVERTISING PRINCIPLES FOR OTHER MEDIA

The volume of print advertising in media other than newspapers and magazines is growing tremendously. All print advertising is united by the same advertising principles we saw in our earlier discussion of magazine and newspaper ads. In print advertising, you are trying to display a proposition about your product that involves your audience's attention and self-interest, that shows evidence that your proposition is true, and that then moves people to take a definitive action that will benefit them and your client. That's what unites all persuasive communication, so there's no overwhelming difference between mailed direct-response copy and a poster inside a bus. Because the principles of writing are essentially the same, this section will look at the peculiarities of each type of advertising and then discuss the implications as you write for each medium.

Outdoor Advertising: Your Two Seconds of Selling

Outdoor advertising, the billboards located along streets and highways, presents one of the hardest advertising writing tests for the copywriter. Not only do you have to communicate a selling message and hook it with a brand name, but you have to do it in the approximately two seconds that a person driving along the highway can devote to your efforts. What a task!

Obviously, the consumer's maximum attention span dictates that your message be simple. Therefore, if you have a complex message you should be presenting it in some other medium. But if your message can be reduced to a simple set of bright graphics and a few words, outdoor advertising can punch home a message to commuters.

Because of the severe time restrictions that govern the way outdoor ads can communicate their messages, it's possible to think of an outdoor ad as a self-contained headline. As we noted in the section on headlines, most headlines seem to gather attention through wordplay. It's no different for outdoor advertising. One billboard for a luncheon meat advertised cold cuts with a visual of a submarine sandwich, complete with a conning tower and flag. The headline: "Launch a Great Lunch."

Although billboards are effective in delivering simple messages about brand names to commuters, concerns about the aesthetics of U.S. highways have increased legal restrictions on billboards. Despite protests from outdoor advertising firms, stricter federal highway funding rules have limited billboard placements in virtually every state so that billboards may become an increasingly small proportion of total advertising.

Transit Advertising: The Long Message on the Long Road Home

Transit advertising is advertising placed on and in buses and subways as well as in the shelters and terminals that serve them. Transit advertising is also seen in airport terminals. Transit advertising is generally comprised of posters or placards that are very similar in presentation to billboards—just an illustration and a few words, or perhaps a short, simple message.

That's a shortsighted view of the medium, because there is a vast difference in how consumers use billboards and the way they use transit advertising. True, the placards on the outside of buses and on bus shelters can capture only the few seconds of attention to a billboard, but the cards inside buses and subway trains and stations are vastly different. A survey of riders on commuter trains found the average time bored commuters read subway cards was measured in minutes and not seconds.

That means advertising messages on the cards inside buses and subway cars can be much longer and more involved than those on the outside. Of course, the limiting factor is type large enough to be read from across a subway car. A complicating factor is that the socioeconomic and educational levels of mass transit riders are generally lower than those of the population in general. However, this emphasizes once again how a medium's characteristics and the way people use it dictate the way you produce messages.

Point-of-Purchase Advertising: Reminding Them They Wanted to Buy

Point-of-purchase (POP) advertising is the advertising placed in restaurants and retail stores to help convince customers to make certain purchases after they reach the store. POP ads range from window posters to "shelf talkers," the tiny posters located beneath the product shelves in food and drugstores.

POP advertising has been one of the growth areas of advertising, as retailers try to extract more revenue from every store operation. Ads have found their way onto shopping carts and above cash registers.

Point-of-purchase ads have been called "last resort advertising." That generally describes the way consumers use them and dictates the strategies for creating them. Because of space considerations and the hurried atmosphere in most retail stores, complex messages won't work in point-of-purchase ads. Instead, because they serve mainly as reminders of a buying impulse triggered by advertising the customer has seen in other venues, POP is generally tied closely with the main campaign. It generally repeats a slogan or visual and brand name that spurs customers to make the purchases they had resolved to make when they saw the first advertisement.

Following the same trend, many other items in our daily lives have become covered with advertising in the past few years as advertisers have tried to expand the reach of their ads. Posters have begun to adorn college and high school newspaper distribution boxes and to be displayed as part of educational materials displayed on grade school bulletin boards. Advertisements are on the back of theater and movie tickets and are mounted on parking meters, on bus shelters, and even above the urinals in men's public restrooms.

Even more surprising has been the willingness of consumers to spend money to buy advertising specialties, those T-shirts, hats, pencils and other notions that businesses used to give away to promote their products. Now, there is a multibillion-dollar market for clothing featuring the logos from movies, rock groups or television shows.

Direct-Response Advertising: Trackable Advertising

Direct-response advertising is advertising that asks you to make an immediate response: to call a toll-free number to enter your name on a petition, to mail a magazine coupon in order to donate to an arts group, or to complete a catalog order form to order shoes, lawn tractors, or even dating services. Direct-response advertising also has a formidable presence in broadcast media, with hundreds of individual direct-response ads selling records, telephone services, collectibles and household appliances appearing each day. In addition, there are many more broadcast hours devoted to direct response through networks like the Home Shopping Club, and half-hour advertiser-sponsored programs selling real estate courses, cosmetics and household cleaners.

Direct response is the fastest-growing segment of the advertising industry and one in which public relations people often find themselves employed. PR practitioners in nonprofit organizations often plan and write direct-response pieces to sell arts tickets and solicit donations or memberships. Corporate public relations personnel and individuals in governmental relations are increasingly writing direct-response copy to solicit stockholder and public support for company decisions that affect governmental and citizen groups.

Although executives handling traditional advertising have often had a patronizing attitude toward direct-response advertising, the creative strategies of the two forms have been moving closer together. That's been demonstrated as more and more mainstream companies, such as AT&T, Time Warner and American Express, use direct response as part of their marketing efforts. In addition, direct-response advertisers have begun integrating more sophisticated graphics into their presentations.

As a result, there are now very few major differences between direct-response advertising and traditional advertising in support of retail outlet sales. Both attempt to draw attention to a proposition through a headline–visual conceit, develop evidence supporting that promise, and then try to propel the reader into a definite action to take advantage of the company's promise. The major difference is that direct-response advertising prompts a consumer action and immediately tries to convert it into a sale by giving the consumer a way to complete the transaction, either through a mail-in coupon, a phone call or even direct contact through a computer modem or fax machine.

That final consummation of the sale is the only real difference between direct-response and general advertising. But that difference has several ramifications for the copywriter, the most important being that the consumer has to make a decision without being able to touch or see or examine the product. From the advertisement, and from the advertisement alone, the consumer has to be able to know every important detail about the product, from its size and color to its guarantee. In direct response, you're not selling just the product but also a sense of trust, because the buyer is sending money with nothing more than the advertiser's word that the product will be delivered. Because it's admittedly difficult to convince someone to order something by phone or mail, direct response often includes premiums for ordering, a free gift or a substantial discount from regular prices.

That's a lot of information to communicate and usually means that direct-response advertising has longer and more extensive copy. Whereas most TV ads using general advertising methods last only 30 seconds, the usual length for a broadcast direct-response ad is one, two or even 30 minutes. In print, a single newspaper retail ad is often replaced by a direct-mail package comprising an outside envelope with a teaser message, a large foldout color brochure, a four-page letter, a card offering a free gift, and a postcard order form. You'll see an example of a two-page sales letter in Figure 14.2. Some direct-response advertising, like that for Publishers Clearing House Sweepstakes magazine sales, is even more voluminous.

The Renaissance Consort
of Harletsburg

September 16, 1995

Mr. Nick Harner, Catering Manager
River House East
Fourth Street & River Road
Riverside, Kentucky 40553

Dear Mr. Harner:

As in all lead sentences, present a benefit immediately.

Holiday-time festivities are coming up soon—and perhaps you've been wondering what new entertainment idea you can present at your holiday banquets.

Why don't you consider going back 400 years for a new idea?

Why not transport your banquet patrons back to the rich sumptuousness of a Renaissance royal court this holiday season? That trip is possible for a limited number of groups this Christmas—since the Harletsburg Chorus is sponsoring a Renaissance Consort for private performances.

The Chorus' Renaissance Consort is a small ensemble of five to eighteen highly trained choristers costumed in the 16th Century's authentically rich tapestries and silky fabrics. They recreate the entertainment that would have been presented during a royal feast, the intricate and haunting madrigals as well as the traditional Christmas carols that would have been familiar to the royal families of the period and that are still familiar to families today.

Use graphic elements to highlight important points, make the copy more inviting.

The Renaissance costumes and the entertainment provide your guests a novel fantasy escape from the cares of the 20th century, as well as providing you with a novel suggestion to offer banquet patrons who are looking for a sophisticated and entertaining alternative to standard holiday events.

Use the power of personal persuasion in your letter. Use "I," "you," "we."

With this musical entertainment at the core, I can help you add as many details to recreate the tastes and sights of the Renaissance court as you and your staff want. I've successfully produced full-fledged madrigal feasts throughout the Midwest, and can add dramatic presentations and comic skits to the evening as well as advise you on authentic menu items like game-bird pie, wassail and flaming plum pudding.

P.O. Box 3890 / Harletsburg, Kentucky 40295 / 502–555–1992

FIGURE 14.2 Sales letter for direct-response advertising

You can be assured of a top-level musical performance by this group from the Harletsburg Chorus, a professional choir that has been in existence for nearly 50 years. The Renaissance Consort, which is composed of Harletsburg Chorus singers, recently made a most successful appearance at the Shakespeare Institute sponsored by Shakespeare in the Park.

The Renaissance Consort will be offering only a limited number of private performances this season, so I urge you to call Renaissance Consort Managing Director Catherine Davis at 555-1992 to discuss dates, program details and performance fees for bringing this delightful escape to a Renaissance royal court to some of your holiday events.

Restate main selling idea and give reader way to respond. →

I hope we'll have the opportunity to help you and your clients have a successful and enjoyable holiday season. Call us at 555-1992 to learn more about transporting your guests back 400 years to a delightful land of music, food, and entertainment.

Sincerely yours,

Linda DeRungs
Consort Coordinator

The postscript is one of the most-read parts of the sales letter. Use it! →

P.S.: Remember that The Renaissance Consort's services include not just the entertainment for your holiday banquet, but also my professional consultant services to make your guests feel right at home in a sumptuous Renaissance court.

Almost all direct-response ads place more emphasis on physically describing the product than does general advertising. In addition, although both hammer on consumer benefits, direct response spends more time on testimonials from satisfied customers to gain consumer trust. Finally, direct response always has some form of response mechanism—a coupon, phone number or order blank.

This response mechanism has to be carefully crafted, because it fulfills two vital functions. First, it is the formal contract that exists between the consumer and the advertiser. That means it has to give full details of the offer, including the manner of payment, the goods promised, and even what a consumer has to do to get the free gift. See an example of a coupon in Figure 14.3.

Second, although you are composing what is in essence a quasi-legal document, you also must keep in mind you are trying to persuade the consumer to make a buying decision. That means repeating at least the main selling benefit as a reason to take the buying step, with a statement like this: "Yes, I want to profit from proven financial forecasting by ordering the Money Advocate today." Remember, because

detach here ↘

Go Ramblin'

I'm going to enjoy Ramblin' Through the Night!
... let me experience it all with tickets to all seven Jazz Series concerts for just $50 for each subscription.

I'm ordering _____ season tickets at $50 each. My total is $_____. I prefer _____ orchestra _____ balcony.

Three easy ways to order:

> * Call 989-5939 to charge your tickets by phone. We'll mail your tickets the same day.
> * Visit Jazz Series Office at 1307 Oak weekdays between 10 a.m. and 6 p.m.
> * Complete and mail this form. We'll mail your tickets within five days after we get your order.
>
> _____ check enclosed (made payable to Jazz Series)
> _____ please charge VISA/MasterCard # _____
>
> expiration date _____ signature _____

Name _____ Phone _____

Address _____ City _____ State _____ Zip _____

Mail to: Jazz Series / P.O. Box 3890 / Kalley KS 78359

FIGURE 14.3 Coupon copy for direct-response advertising

your task is to motivate action now, you need to be conscious of using every opportunity to display your main selling idea and ask for action.

Although direct-response advertising in magazines and newspapers has a similar format to general advertising, direct response often uses what is called the "classic mailing package." This advertising combination, which you have received in the mail hundreds of times, adds to the copy and coupon basic to the magazine ad a letter, an outside envelope with a few words of copy designed to "tease" a reader to look inside, and secondary pieces offering free gifts, contests and the like.

The letter is the most important component in the classic package because it's there that you can talk to the reader in the most personal and persuasive way. The direct-response letter uses many of the structural tactics of the backgrounders and administrative communication forms we examined in Chapter 8. By indenting whole paragraphs and using bullets and subheads to emphasize the weight of evidence supporting your promise, you can highlight your claims and make them seem more persuasive. Direct-response letters may even go beyond this, with certain key paragraphs printed or underlined in different color ink or with a big check mark or a handwritten notation scrawled beside them. Because the main selling idea is so important, it's sometimes stated in short form even before the letter's salutation. As in all writing, you'll group arguments supporting your claim, separating them from the points telling readers what they'll miss if they don't respond to your offer.

The direct-response letter has a few other distinctions from ordinary business communication. It is at its heart a selling letter, so that the persuasive techniques used in advertising writing are equally valuable here. That means making a promise of benefits early in the letter and then offering a multitude of reasons supporting that benefit. After you support the main benefit, you mention even more reasons to respond, including secondary benefits, free gifts and guarantees.

After all the selling points have been presented, you write a wrap summarizing the key points and telling your reader how to take action. You explicitly tell him or her to mail a card or coupon or call a toll-free number. Then, after the closing signature, you repeat the key selling idea and again ask for a response in a postscript. As I've emphasized before, the whole purpose of direct response is to persuade the consumer to take an action this very minute. For that reason, you can't neglect an opportunity to communicate the main selling idea.

The last vital difference between direct-response and general advertising is the way that the response to a particular advertisement can be measured. By using specially coded post office box numbers or telephone operators, advertisers can measure the number of responses from one particular advertising outlet or even one specific ad. This capability, which we'll discuss at length in the next chapter, has generally become known as database marketing. It has greatly increased the capacity to target advertising and public relations messages to consumers. Memory Memo 14.3 gives you a checklist of the principles that should guide you as you create direct-response advertising.

Memory Memo 14.3
Checklist for writing direct-response advertising copy

- Does the copy adequately describe a product the consumer can't examine?
- Does the copy list multiple reasons to take the requested action?
- Does the response mechanism include all information the reader needs to take action?
- Does the coupon list all conditions for buying the product, such as getting premiums?
- Does the system let you track the results of your advertising?

BROADCAST ADVERTISING

As mentioned in Chapter 7, the broadcast medium is often portrayed as an all-powerful motivator. That stereotype is applied even more rigidly to broadcast advertising, which is painted as a subtle, sinister communicator transforming young children into violent, crazed little monsters; teenagers into foul-mouthed, disrespectful, disenchanted rebels; and their parents into quiet, submissive, consuming beasts of burden.

It seems impossible for one medium to bring all that misery into the world. Those pervasive radio and television ads have some degree of power in creating and socializing us, but like every other communication medium, both radio and television, in addition to having seductively persuasive powers, have overwhelming weaknesses.

There are persuasive tasks that radio or television can accomplish most efficiently. Likewise, there are persuasive tasks much more logically undertaken by print advertising. As with all communication tasks, the intelligent practitioner begins by examining his or her communication objective, and then selecting an effective medium to accomplish just those tasks.

Even though broadcast communication is pervasive in our life, it is a passive medium and doesn't command our full attention. That passivity causes problems, because if listeners and viewers discover halfway through a commercial that they're interested in the message they don't have any chance to review the commercial. They can't simply turn a page and see the ad again, as they would a magazine. For that reason, complicated messages are sometimes not as effective in the broadcast media.

Broadcast advertising does, however, have one major advantage over print. With broadcast, you can involve other sensory channels in communicating your message, letting your audience hear the excitement of a crowd before a sale or witness a demonstration that shows your product is better than its competitors. In broadcast advertising, just as in all broadcast writing, you need to exploit the powers of the medium and minimize the weaknesses. If your broadcast ad consists of simply reading copy you prepared for a print ad, then you have failed in your task. We will look at those distinctly different strategies for radio and television in the following sections.

Writing Radio Advertising: Creating a Visual with Sound

Radio advertising, like magazine advertising, allows you to be quite selective in targeting audiences. In your area you can probably listen to radio stations that specialize in news or sports or Spanish language programming. Other stations may cater to listeners interested in 1940s big band music or popular music. Even among rock stations catering to teenagers and young adults, there is probably at least one that plays heavy metal, another that plays lighter rock, another that specializes in rap music, and possibly one other that dredges up classic rock. Each of those stations is serving a tightly defined psychographic identity, and radio advertising lets you reach those targeted audiences. In addition, radio advertising can communicate to potential customers in situations that no other medium can reach, because it can influence consumers while they are working, driving or even exercising.

But as discussed in Chapter 7, to be a successful writer in a particular medium, you have to exploit the strengths and minimize the weaknesses of that medium. On first examination, radio advertising seems burdened with extraordinary weaknesses, in that your listeners can't see the product or the spokesperson or even review your advertising claims if they miss them the first time. But I would argue with those people who contend sound is the strength that radio advertising adds, if sound only means you're reading the words that you wrote for a magazine ad's audience. Yes, radio is a powerful medium, but it doesn't gain its power from sound—it gains its persuasive strength from your ability to exploit the power of the human imagination.

Radio is often called the theater of the mind. Out of the fabric of words, sounds and voices, the human brain can construct fabulous stage pieces that can transport the listener into an environment that would be very difficult and very expensive for a movie director to create: A pilot can land a plane on the city's biggest outdoor restaurant deck; a business executive can be transported from coast to coast through a fax line in three seconds; an orchestra can be in the car's backseat to show the fidelity of an auto stereo system.

That's a lot of power at your disposal. The theater of the mind doesn't depend on what you can imagine but on what you can make your audience imagine. From those four elements you have to work with—words, music, sounds and voices—you must make your audience believe in the world you create. From the formality or informality of your language and the accent of the voices you select you suggest to your readers a mental image of the characters who populate your world. From the scenario you establish with sound effects and dialogue you create the physical environment of this private world.

All this requires what I call translation skills—the ability to translate a striking visual concept into words that evoke that world for your listeners. Thus, radio advertising, like all other advertising, starts by establishing a central conceit communicating a main selling idea that's important to your intended audience and that is unusual enough to draw your audience's attention to the advertisement. Establishing that central conceit, the unique presentation that communicates your main selling idea in a unique way, seems harder to do in radio than in any other medium.

It's often helpful to initially visualize the radio advertisement as a magazine ad, because the most effective radio ads are those that establish a powerful visual image, that make people imagine the characters who are talking and the physical environment where they are located. If you were creating a magazine ad, what illustration would you use to help your audience understand your concept? Would it be a character whose clothing or appearance communicates a certain occupation or nationality? Would it be the teeming streets of a city or a quiet lake at sunset? Once you've visualized a scene that would help your audience understand your main selling idea, the fun begins, because in radio advertising you aren't limited by what you can photograph. The scenarios you can establish are virtually unlimited because you're using the imaginative power of the listener's mind.

I'll give you an example. A rural county's economic development commission wanted a radio ad targeted toward relocating businesses. The commission decided to highlight the county's solid financial advantages and pleasant country lifestyle. Obviously, a magazine ad could have shown an idyllic country farmscape or a clean-cut worker or presented a photo of a well-dressed business executive. But a radio ad isn't limited by reality.

The commission's radio commercial was structured as a media interview. With nature sounds in the background, the reporter's first comment was: "I've never interviewed a cow wearing a business suit before." The cow, answering in an authoritative voice, lists the county's many benefits. It's a fun, unique concept that shocks the audience from its inattention immediately but always keeps the image of the advertiser (an efficient, business-centered group) and the message of the commercial (the benefits of locating in a rural area) up front.

That's the key to effective radio advertising. You must provide the thread of words, sounds and voices so the human imagination can weave a complete and believable world in which your audience accepts your advertising claims as a natural part of the conversation.

Most of the time it takes only the most primitive type of suggestion to engage that creative spirit. Sometimes it's as simple as identifying the scenario. When Ford wanted to advertise the advantages of its sound system, custom designed for each car interior, the commercial began by the narrator asking a customer what he was doing lying on the rear floorboard. The customer explained he was testing whether Ford's engineers had placed the speakers in the right location for perfect sound. The customer then contorted himself into a whole series of positions as he moved around the car listening to the superb sound. The commercial ended with the customer requesting the narrator to climb atop the car with him and hold his feet while he lowered himself over the side to listen to the speakers from outside the windows. A simple concept, but one that instantly enlisted the radio listener's mind in constructing a wild scene that gathered attention and illustrated the main selling idea.

At other times sound effects are enough to establish the scenario. The sound of a car's screeching tires, followed by an explosion of glass and the crunching of metal, is quite enough to communicate a car wreck to an audience. Music is often a potent imaginative stimulus, too. Balinese finger cymbals and Japanese kotos accompanying the United Airlines theme music quickly and powerfully helped communicate the company's expanded service to the Orient.

Figure 14.4 shows how even simple sound effects can add to a radio commercial's effectiveness. The commercial to raise funds for a nonprofit organization opens with a suspense lead and the special effect of a child crying, which gets the attention of its targeted audience. Notice how the sound effects and text show a transformation from crying to laughter as a result of the consumer responding to the call to action.

Client: National Children's Committee **Title:** "Seconds"	**Time:** 30 seconds **Writer:** Tweeddale
Sound effects	Narration
:00	NARRATOR (firm yet reassuring woman): Here are two statistics you might not know:
:03 SFX: sound of child crying	NARRATOR VO: There are one million, 314 thousand seconds in a year.
:06 SFX: crying is louder and more insistent	And in every second of every day, three children are sexually or physically abused in the United States.
:13 SFX: crying crescendos, then stops abruptly	You can stop the hurt.
:15	NARRATOR: You've got over a million seconds this year. Spend 45 of them calling 1-800-524-HEAL. Your contribution to the National Children's Committee pays for violence intervention programs that can . . .
:22 SFX: child giggling	NARRATOR VO: . . . stop the hurt and start the healing. Making a child laugh is one of the best ways to use the next 45 seconds. Call 1-800-524-HEAL today.
:28 SFX: ends with final giggle END: 30 SECONDS	

FIGURE 14.4   Example of a radio commercial

There's one surprising thing about an audience's reaction to radio advertising. They will believe almost any outrageous scenario you establish—a man going to work naked because he's not using a one-hour dry cleaner or even a space alien buying tie-dyed sweatshirts at a local T-shirt shop. What an audience will not buy is a radio commercial filled with actors who sound like radio announcers acting as if they are in a normal situation reciting unrealistic dialogue comprised of hackneyed advertising claims. An ad similar to the following ran hundreds of times on a major market's top radio station. The characters are two deep-voiced radio announcers who can't act:

"Hello, Harry. I haven't seen you for months. And now to see you here in the Terrace Restaurant of the Ambassador Hotel. What a surprise."

"Joe, what could be more natural? The Terrace Restaurant of the Ambassador Hotel is just the place for business meetings. I've got a big client over in one of the leather upholstered booths and he is so impressed by the surroundings and the food. I'm sure he's going to sign the contract today."

"So, Harry, the main dining room of the Ambassador Hotel is the key to your success? Why, I'll have to come to the Terrace Restaurant of the Ambassador Hotel more often. I hear it's open on Saturdays and Sundays now, too, so I can treat my family by bringing them here for the elegant atmosphere."

"Joe, I bet the kids will love the desserts."

"Harry, I can be a hit at the office—and at home. All I need to remember is the Terrace Restaurant at the Ambassador Hotel."

Yes, it's OK to hiss.

This atrocious commercial offers a lot of clues about writing a radio commercial's body copy. First, either create a visual concept in which it's natural to talk about your client's products, or create one so unbelievable that your audience will accept that in your imaginary world people actually do talk about a product's benefits. Second, when composing dialogue, write like your audience talks. Use contractions, slang and jargon where appropriate. For the sake of credibility, be very careful not to put a trite, overused advertising cliche into the mouth of a speaker.

Now let's look at this very simple piece of radio copy and note the differences:

PLUMBER: I'm not a fancy guy now. I don't wear a tie to work or Calvin Klein jeans on the weekend. But I do own a car phone. Yup.

Now you've seen those guys in their big cars stopped at the stoplight with their phones stuck in their ears and you say—"What a jerk!"

But that's just not how it is.

Now I drive a '73 Ford pickup, buddy, with empty Styrofoam coffee cups on the dashboard and everything. And I need that phone.

I'm a plumber, OK, nothing too glamorous. People with clogs, little drips, calling me at all times, beeping me. I got to call home, say where I am, say I'll be late. Otherwise, whoa.

So I call this BellSouth Mobility. And that's when I found out you don't have to be some big shot to own a car phone. 'Cause with BellSouth Mobility's $78-a-month package all it takes is a clog and one leaky elbow joint and buddy, that's paid.

NARRATOR: For details, call 1–800–331–1800. BellSouth Mobility— we're the phone company for your car.

Reprinted with permission of BellSouth Mobility, Inc.

You'll notice the striking visual images that are quickly established. The main character is a working-class Joe in his pickup truck who is unimpressed by and even resentful of pretension. Using slang and the common complaints of a working man who's on the road all day, the dialogue identifies the intended audience and lets the discussion of a mobile phone's benefits come naturally and unobtrusively.

Notice how few words are in this 60-second commercial. That's also important for luring the audience for this commercial, because the slow drawl of the Southern target audience has to be integrated into the dialogue. No matter what the accent, it's usually a very good practice to write fewer words than is possible to stuff into a commercial. As a rule of thumb, writing about 60 words in a 30-second commercial or 125 in a 60-second commercial will give your actors a better chance to capture the realistic rhythms of natural speech and milk the copy for humor and drama.

You'll also notice how many times the company's brand name is mentioned. Because there's no chance to review the copy to establish the company name, it's necessary to keep repeating it. Copy experts say that as long as it's not forced, three mentions in a 30-second ad or five mentions in a 60-second ad are not too many.

Remember, this need to communicate visually on radio also extends to establishing a picture of the product that would normally be in the logo-baseline section of a magazine ad. Often you'll include some description of the packaging in the call-to-action section at the end of the commercial, such as: "Look for Mineral-Ice in the ice-blue package at your local drugstore."

Finally, as Memory Memo 14.4 reminds us, all advertising has the same basic goals. The BellSouth ad, like all good advertisements, communicates the real-life benefits of the product while establishing a definite emotional image for the user. By the end of the commercial, we know how the product will help this man, and he understands that having a car phone won't change him into one of those egotistical executives he sees on the highway. By buying the product, he is purchasing benefits and a self-image. That's a powerful combination, no matter the medium in which it's communicated.

Memory Memo 14.4
Checklist for writing radio advertising copy

- Have you established the product you're advertising and the audience for which it's intended?
- Does your copy create a strong visual image for the listener?
- Have you created a scenario in which talking about the product doesn't seem stilted?
- Have you established the product name and other product identifiers in the copy?
- Have you written the proper number of words to let actors personalize the copy?
- Are your vocabulary and diction appropriate for your audience?

Writing Television Advertising: Using Every Channel That's There

Television shares many traits with radio. It, too, is a passive medium, so you need to arrest the attention of your audience immediately to involve it in your message. In television, too, it is not possible to review advertising claims.

But television has the strengths of capturing all the sensory attributes of the other advertising media we've discussed. Like a magazine ad, a television commercial can present information through pictures and written text, capturing the visual nature of print and at least some of the credibility people ascribe to print messages. Like radio, television can portray the personality of an announcer or the sound of the product being used through voices, music and sound effects. However, television adds the wonder of movement and captures all the storehouse of rational and emotional associations we've gained from a lifetime of watching movies and television.

Involving all those senses simultaneously in an advertising message is the challenge of television advertising copywriting. Making decisions about camera angles and camera movement, sound effects and music, accents and actors, charts and captions are added to basic skills in presenting benefits in your copy. Memory Memo 14.5 presents a simple checklist of all those writing skills you have to add.

Memory Memo 14.5
Checklist for writing video advertising copy

- Do you establish an audience and a benefit for that audience?
- Have you included motion as well as visuals?
- Have you used all the sensory channels available to you?
- Are visual, aural and text messages coordinated?
- Have you established a definite viewpoint and followed it throughout the ad?

Creating a Visual Memory: The Central Visual

The initial steps in creating a television commercial are very similar to the beginning of any other advertisement. Your persuasion platform should lead you to a central visual, the conceit that is going to demonstrate your product's main selling idea to your target audience in a way that will first involve and then persuade the audience.

That central visual conceit, like all other conceits, should be a striking, unique presentation that will draw an audience that's become jaded after viewing thousands of other television commercials. You can probably remember a small number of television ads that startled you when you first saw them with the originality of their presentation, and then presented a selling idea that established or solidified your knowledge of the product's main benefit.

I recall a tire company's commercial claiming its tires maintained traction on wet roads better than any other tire. That's a common claim, but the commercial's central visual conceit planted that claim firmly. In the commercial, an exotic sports car sped down rainy, narrow, mysteriously dark German streets onto a wet dock, where workers attached grappling hooks to the car's body to load it onto a ship. The ship's crane pulled the cables tight to lift the car into the air, but the tires held so well that the car's body ripped from the car's axle and undercarriage, the tires still firmly planted on the wet dock. That's a great central visual conceit, one that captures attention and communicates a selling point important to the product that lingers in the memory even years later.

In print and radio advertising, that central conceit is usually at the beginning of the ad. However, the conceit in a television ad can occur in the beginning or even at the end of the ad. The challenge of writing a television ad is to fit all the visual, aural and language stimuli into a narrative structure that will effectively communicate the visual conceit and the main selling idea.

Here's where the staggering variety of choices and options you have in designing a television commercial unfold. You could structure the ad to demonstrate your product or to show an elegant, romantic or efficient lifestyle of which your product is a part. You could have a user or a celebrity present a testimonial or compare your product to its competitors. You could present a problem, illustrated by tragic or humorous situations, that your product could solve.

Once you decide how to structure your presentation, you're still presented with a staggering range of choices, all of which affect the writing strategies you'll undertake. First, there are choices to make about your narrators. Young or old? Woman or man? Upper-class, lower-class or someplace in between? On-camera or off-camera? If on-camera, what message can you convey by their clothing, their hair color, their race? Each of those decisions will affect the dialogue you choose to write to fit your characters.

How are you going to photograph the commercial? Sometimes black and white is appropriate because it conveys the credibility of a documentary or the gritty realism of a 1940s detective movie. Is the commercial going to be animated or use real-life action? Are you going to use hard focus or soft focus? Are you going to use videotape, or do you need the better resolution qualities of film?

Adding Visuals and Sound to Text

Once you've made these decisions about the structure, theme and presentation of the commercial, you're ready to write the ad copy. (However, as in all creative work, sometimes at least part of the ad copy or even a great camera angle comes to you before these matters are decided, so don't worry if your creative process doesn't follow this sequence every time.)

Television advertising copy is very similar to all other advertising copy. You're trying to write realistic dialogue for your actors while demonstrating the product's main selling idea. Because of the inability to review claims, you want to break down your ideas into short, simple sentences and repeat your main selling idea and the product name often. At the end of the commercial, you try to compel the customer to make the desired buying decision. To accomplish that, you need to write a wrap summarizing your main points, then give specific information about store locations and other procedures so that the customer can take advantage of the offer. That's exactly what we discussed in the print and radio sections of this chapter.

There are some writing modifications you make because of the medium. Above all, you need to think visually—not only in the scenes you choose to show in your ads, but also in the ad copy you write. First, be sure that you don't overwrite the copy. In many places, the strength of your visuals can communicate many of the adjectives you're tempted to use. Words will simply distract from the visuals or sound effects.

Of course, there will be instances in which you can reinforce the visuals with words. When you make that decision, be certain your words and descriptions merge precisely with the visual. For instance, if your corporate information ad copy is discussing your company's reforestation efforts you shouldn't be showing a visual of your factory smokestacks or of your corporation's president shaking hands with your state's U.S. senator. Creating two different messages, one visual and one aural, will certainly confuse your viewers as they try to choose which one to process. Coordinating your visual and aural messages is simplified by the TV commercial storyboard format that matches narration, sound effects, and visuals. See Sidebar 14.2 for an example.

There may also be places where you want to really punch your message home by not only using the visual and aural channels but by adding print in the form of supertitles on the screen. Used sparingly, supertitles can be very effective in reinforcing your main selling ideas. Employ them when you have a list of product benefits or when you want to establish the brand name or a corporate baseline slogan forcefully. But when you do use supertitles, be sure your voiceover is exactly the same as the supertitle so you won't confuse your viewers.

Scripting the Television Commercial

Once you've got the copy written, it's necessary to merge the prose with the television medium's technical capabilities. Again, the first point to remember is that movement is the greatest strength of the medium. You need to use it well or you're doing nothing more than filming someone reading a print ad.

It's helpful to think of the camera as a character in your commercial's narrative. Does the camera represent one of the participants in the commercial, for instance, an office worker who runs through the office trying to avoid a coworker who has bad breath? Once you've established that viewpoint, you've restricted yourself to only those shots a human could experience. Unless you do some explaining, you won't be using wide helicopter shots or fancy special effects. However, in certain situations this human viewpoint is very persuasive because viewers feel they are involved in the action, and the characters are speaking directly to them.

However, if the camera is a disinterested observer, a wide variety of shots and camera movements can be used. The camera as objective observer can witness the tension between husband and wife over his grass-stain encrusted slacks, then record the next-door neighbor's advice on which laundry detergent to use, and float away to a far-off research laboratory to hear a scientist explain the technical reasons why the detergent is best. This viewpoint gives you the possibility of showing people on all continents using the product, or proving a product's germ-fighting ability with microscopic views of a toilet bowl. Through special effects, it can show a little girl maturing into a beautiful woman before our eyes.

After you've picked a viewpoint you can decide on specific shots and specific camera movements. The commercial's subject can be photographed in every way, from an extreme close-up to a long shot from the top of a building or an airplane. Long shots are often used at a commercial's opening to establish whether the commercial is at the beach or in the mountains, at the office or in a restaurant. Then,

---

SIDEBAR 14.2　Storyboard for a Television Commercial

This commercial uses all sensory channels to involve and inform its viewers. The ad reinforces the dialogue by using supertitles to list the three major warning signs of teenage depression. In addition, the music helps create a mood of tension and foreboding that is then relieved by a final, soothing chord. The commercial is made even more effective by using two types of film that help communicate different moods. In the student sequences, the director uses grainy, low-speed film that blurs all movements to emphasize the disorientation felt by young people who suffer from depression. During the parent-teacher discussions, the director uses film that permits a sharper focus.

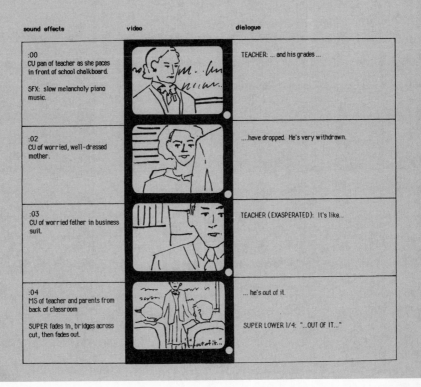

(continued)

SIDEBAR 14.2 (continued)

sound effects	video	dialogue
:05 MS of boy in white T-shirt, denim jacket and torn jeans. Dolly in front of student as he walks through school hallway. SFX: dissonant bass chord rises and ends with increasingly louder hissing sounds.	*"...out of it..."*	SUPER LOWER 1/4: "...OUT OF IT..."
:08 MS of mother and father. SFX: higher pitched chord while teacher talking. Replaced by despondent bass chord accompanying mother's answer.		MOTHER: He just won't talk to us.
:09 CU of mother. SUPER fades in, bridges across cut, then fades out.	*"...alienated..."*	MOTHER (ANGUISHED): We feel so alienated. SUPER LOWER 1/4: "...ALIENATED..."
:12 MS of student pushing past friendly classmates in front of lockers. SFX: dissonant bass chord rises and ends with increasingly louder hissing sounds.	*"...alienated..."*	SUPER LOWER 1/4: "...ALIENATED..."
:15 LS from back of classroom SFX: higher pitched chord while teacher talking. Replaced by despondent bass chord accompanying father's answer		TEACHER: Is he acting differently at home?
SUPER fades in, bridges across cut, then fades out. :17 CU of father.	*"...time alone..."*	FATHER: Well, he spends a lot of time alone. SUPER LOWER 1/4: "...TIME ALONE..."
:19 CU of boy slumped on floor in front of lockers. Jerkily zoom out to MS. SFX: dissonant bass chord rises and ends with increasingly louder hissing sounds.	*"...time alone..."*	SUPER LOWER 1/4: "...TIME ALONE..."
:23 Slide of logo and hospital phone number. SFX: same melancholy piano at beginning but last note blooms into major chord. END :30	CHARTER HOSPITAL	ANCR: Depression. Don't let your teenager fight it alone. Call Charter Hospital. SUPER FULL-FRAME: Hospital logo and phone number END

depending on what's being communicated, closer shots are used. A commercial for a dress shop might use a medium shot to show the overall design of a dress, then move in for an extreme close-up to show detailing on a pocket or collar, and then pull back to a close-up of the model's face to show how pleased she is with the store's low prices for stylish fashions. (If you need to review television terminology, please see Chapter 7.)

After you've reached this stage, you again can consider the contributions that music and sound effects can make to your persuasive efforts. As in radio, you can use aural cues to accentuate the mood you're trying to create or simply to draw the viewer's attention to the commercial. It's even possible to differentiate the quality of two products you're comparing, as was demonstrated in a television ad for a small, four-wheel-drive car. The ad characterized the tiny car as a small version of an expensive Range Rover by playing the "Hungarian Rhapsody" every time either vehicle appeared. When the Range Rover was shown, the music was played by tubas. When the smaller car was pictured, the rhapsody was performed by flutes. Clever idea.

REMEMBERING THE FOREST AND THE TREES: CONCENTRATING ON YOUR COMMUNICATION PURPOSE

Creating advertising is a long and complicated process that is beyond the capacity of a book like this to cover fully, but we can examine how it looks when it all comes together. A commercial for a product that removes women's leg hair doesn't have any celebrities, million-dollar sets, casts of thousands, overly fancy production values, or a famous movie director controlling the action. It's just a well-designed commercial using a good central visual and the power of movement and the medium to communicate the main selling idea.

This commercial opens with the central visual, a comparison about how a woman's legs feel as her hair grows. Comparing a three-day growth (a scrub brush) with a five-day growth (a cactus) and a seven-day growth (a porcupine) establishes a problem that will be solved by the product. Each stage of the hair growth is accompanied by a short sound effect that gets increasingly deep and more annoying as the leg hair gets longer.

The brand name is established quickly, but instead of being shown in a static slide, the brand name is shown being written in script. This exploits the movement and not merely the visual aspects of the television medium.

As the woman spreads the product on her legs, a series of magnified animated inserts shows how the product works to remove hair below the skin. The animated sequence exactly follows the live action as the model demonstrates the product. The woman again runs her hand along her smooth legs, with the camera trucking alongside as the narrator repeats the main selling idea.

Then the key visuals—the brush, cactus and porcupine—are repeated along with the annoying music identifying each disgusting day of hair growth. After the problem is reestablished, the brand name is displayed, and harp music replaces the disgusting sound effects to accentuate the customer's transformation. The packaging is shown so the consumer can identify it in the store. At the end, instead of having all three varieties in the frame initially, there are only two. A long, sleek hand enters the frame to place the last box, again emphasizing the medium's movement.

There should be a steady change of shots, not allowing the viewer's attention to wander by lingering on one scene too long. Remember, however, to consider your viewers' mental capacity. There's a fine balance to maintain between keeping viewers' interest and confusing them. An auto service center's ad, for example, tried to create a sense of anxiety about using other repair shops by using very rapid cutting of shots. But the commercial, which displayed text slides containing six to eight words on the screen for less than one-fourth of a second, outdistanced the audience's capacity to comprehend it. After a few months, the ad was pulled and the text slides reedited so that they remained on the screen long enough to be read.

There are thousands of permutations that can be used to combine all these elements of text, pictures and sounds to create exciting and innovative looks. But remember that in advertising, as in all public relations activities, you are trying to solve institutional problems through communication. That means keeping in mind the reason you're communicating and not getting lost in slick techniques. That's an especially appropriate warning in advertising, where the creative urge sometimes overwhelms the commercial's original message and communication purpose.

An example of this phenomenon was the Spuds McKenzie campaign for Anheuser-Busch's Bud Light beer. Bud Light was a very late entry into the light beer category, in which Miller Lite beer held a commanding position. Obviously, Bud Light had to establish brand awareness and reprogram beer drinkers to not associate all light beer with Miller Lite.

The company's ads introduced the lovably ugly Spuds McKenzie dog and surrounded him (although it later turned out Spuds was female) with beautiful women and exotic locations. What happened? Spuds McKenzie became one of the most recognized figures in America. He was constantly mentioned in comics' monologues and caused a revival of the bullterrier breed in America. There was less certainty whether in the frenzy over the cute dog anyone could remember that Bud Light was the beer associated with Spuds.

It seemed the individuals most affected by the campaign were dog-loving kids. The thousands of Spuds T-shirts worn by thousands of grade school and junior high school students brought the wrath of anti-alcohol groups down on Anheuser-Busch. The company was asked, quite appropriately, whether the cute-dog campaign was to convince adults to buy beer or was intended to create a market of teenagers who thought beer drinking was cute. The company was lambasted on the floor of the U.S. Senate, in editorial pages, and at school meetings. After one of the most extensive ad campaigns in history, Bud Light's ads had resulted in good sales, but had provoked one of the biggest consumer protests ever against a marketing campaign.

To solve the problem, the company abandoned a highly visible campaign (Spuds was used almost exclusively for anti-drinking spots for several years) and went back to its original communication problem. What did the company want to accomplish in the marketplace? The answer: It wanted beer drinkers to remember there was another light beer, a beer made by the respected brewer of popular Budweiser beer.

Out of that reworking came the highly successful "But I asked for a Bud Light" campaign. In a memorable series of commercials, people who merely asked for a light beer instead of Bud Light suffered humorously horrible fates involving light bulbs, lamps, hydroelectric dams, and other lighting appliances. My personal favorite portrayed a caveman traipsing across the tundra carefully carrying a burning torch. When he returns to a dark cave and announces he has discovered fire, the chieftain thanks him for this great technological gift, then screams, "But I wanted a Bud Light." The new campaign solved the company's communication problem, the lack of brand recognition, with a message targeted to an audience that could buy the product, the young sophisticated adults Anheuser-Busch was trying to attract with the campaign.

Solving particular institutional communication problems and objectives through targeted communication is the essence of good public relations and good advertising. Keep it in mind as you perform all your writing tasks.

SUMMARY

- All advertising and all public relations communication should begin with a realization of the organizational problem it is intended to solve.
- Advertising is a controlled medium in which time or space is purchased to promote a product, service or idea.
- Even though advertising doesn't have to be approved by an editor or producer to gain access to its audience, it does have to overcome the resistance of an audience that has been subjected to millions of commercials.
- To overcome the audience's inattention to advertising, writers develop a conceit, which is essentially a new and creative method of presenting an advertising claim the audience may have heard hundreds of time before.
- Advertising writers often use a persuasion platform format to help them develop a knowledge of their audience, what persuaders would be most effective for that audience, and then what conceit might capture that audience's attention.
- There are four basic advertising objectives: (1) Establish a use for the product, (2) stimulate product trial, (3) position the product among its competitors, and (4) build brand awareness. Each objective is usually associated with a different persuasion sequence.
- Practitioners need to choose different advertising media to solve different institutional problems. Print advertising, for instance, is usually considered more effective when making complex arguments because readers can review the claims at their own pace. Television advertising, on the other hand, is effective in establishing new claims for a product because it can show the product in action.
- Print advertising generally follows this basic structure: (1) the headline–visual,

(2) the bridge, (3) the statement of benefits, (4) the wrap, and (5) the logo and baseline.

- The advertisement's headline and visual should grab the attention of the ad's intended audience as well as communicate a benefit that's appealing to that audience.

- There are many ways to develop an effective headline conceit. They include wordplay, reversals and puns.

- The structure of an advertisement contains many of the same components as an inverted pyramid. An advertisement's bridge is similar to the pyramid's second paragraph. The bridge explicitly explains the main selling idea the headline conceit attempts to establish. The statement of benefits supports the ad's original thesis. The wrap and the logo and baseline, like the pyramid's call to action, move the audience to action and tell the audience how to take advantage of the benefits the writer is offering.

- Other types of print advertising, like outdoor, transit or point-of-purchase, must be written to adapt to the way the audience uses the medium.

- Direct-response advertising is a rapidly growing segment of advertising in which public relations practitioners are often involved. Unlike other advertising, it immediately tries to convert consumer interest into a sale by offering the consumer a way to respond directly to the message through coupons, toll-free order lines, or other response mechanisms.

- Direct-response advertisements usually have more copy because the writer's copy has to instill the consumer confidence normally established by examining the product. Because of that, writers must fully establish the product's characteristics in the copy and illustrations.

- The response mechanism for a direct-response advertisement must be carefully constructed because it is considered a contract between the consumer and the advertiser.

- Broadcast advertising has value because it lets the writer use the receiver's aural and visual senses to reinforce the message.

- Radio advertising can be directed to more precise target audiences than can television advertising.

- Radio advertising writing establishes a theater of the imagination, that is, the power of the listener's imagination constructs a scenario from the sounds, voices and words the commercial uses.

- Radio advertising, like all other persuasive communication, must lead the receiver to action. By repeatedly mentioning the client's name and providing enough details at the commercial's end, the ad leads the listener to recognize the product in the store and take the appropriate action.

- Good television advertising writing should involve the receiver's senses by exploiting the power of words, sounds and motion. The TV advertising writer must make decisions about narrators, on-camera actors, camera shots, editing techniques, and other strategies to fully involve the receiver.

THINK PIECES

1. What advertisements or commercials have been most memorable to you? What product did they advertise? If you remember the brand name, how did the commercials establish a brand name? If you don't remember the brand name, what did the commercial do wrong?

2. Compare the credibility of purchased advertisements versus editorial coverage by the media of the same products or ideas.

3. What types of audiences are you more likely to reach using radio instead of television; newspapers instead of magazines?

4. How does the composition of a radio or television audience change at different hours of the day?

5. Formulate an argument defending integrating messages from both PR and advertising sources into one campaign.

6. Name a product that could be advertised effectively with a positioning campaign; a new-use campaign; a brand image campaign; a trial campaign. Defend your answers.

7. Reconstruct a television ad you remember. Analyze it in terms of a central visual. Did the central visual help you remember the major selling idea?

WRITING ASSIGNMENTS

Print Advertisements

D1.8
D2.6
D3.8
D5.3
D10.10
D10.11
D11.5

Radio Advertisements

D1.8
D2.6
D10.10

Television Advertisements

D3.9
D10.10

Direct-marketing Advertisements

D12.6

ADDITIONAL READING

Barrett, Gavin. *Forensic Marketing: The Professional's Guide to Optimizing Results from Marketing Communication*. New York: McGraw-Hill, 1995.

Bendinger, Bruce. *The Copy Workshop Workbook*. Chicago: The Copy Workshop, 1993.

Berkman, Harold W., and Gilson, Christopher. *Advertising: Concepts and Strategies*. New York: Random House, 1987.

Broom, Glen M., Lauzen, Martha M., and Tucker, Kerry. "Public Relations and Marketing: Dividing the Conceptual Domain and Operational Turf." *Public Relations Review* 17:3 (Fall 1991): 219–225.

Burton, Philip Ward. *Advertising Copywriting*, 6th ed. Lincolnwood, Ill.: NTC, 1990.

Goldman, Jordon. *Public Relations in the Marketing Mix*. Lincolnwood, Ill.: NTC, 1994.

Jewler, A. Jerome. *Creative Strategy in Advertising*, 5th ed. Belmont, Calif.: Wadsworth, 1995.

Nelson, Roy Paul. *Design of Advertising*, 7th ed. Madison, Wisc.: Brown and Benchmark, 1994.

Stone, Bob. *Successful Direct Marketing Methods*, 5th ed. Lincolnwood, Ill.: NTC, 1995.

## chapter 15

Delivering Advertising Messages

REAL-LIFE LESSONS

When I made a recent trip to Chicago, I found myself in a grocery store walking behind a shopping cart that had a small television screen mounted on the handle. As I strolled around the store the screen flashed advertisements for Pepsi and Nabisco products and informed me what store items were on sale and what aisle they were in. By pushing a button, I could call up a detailed map of the market or find the exact location of a particular brand-name item.

That was what was happening in front of my eyes. What was happening without my knowledge was even more amazing.

As I walked around the store, sensors in the store's ceiling were tracking my shopping habits as I took my trip through the aisles. It timed how long I spent squeezing the melons, price-checking bread, reading product claims on shampoos, or selecting cuts of meat. By the time I finished, the system had recorded that I spent more time at the liquor counter than in the baking products section. It knew I had run past the baby food and the laundry soap.

That information can be very useful to merchandisers. National figures show that shoppers spend over 3 minutes in the produce section, versus just 42.3 seconds among the breads. Should the store owner try to jazz up the bakery to get people to linger a little longer, or would it be better to stock fewer brands of bread and bring in more types of fruits and vegetables?

You see what's happening? Not only do we have another way of delivering advertising to shoppers, but we are using the process of advertising to gather information about the people to whom we're advertising, while we're advertising.

This technique, as intrusive and encompassing as it seems, is nothing uncommon in advertising today. It's relatively easy now to track a specific consumer's purchases from a wide variety of retailers and direct-marketing firms.

Although it introduces some ethical questions, that knowledge has given advertising and public relations people better ways to predict and then measure communication success. Using new advertising techniques, it's possible to pinpoint people who have very specific needs or characteristics. Most importantly, it is now becoming possible for communication professionals to track individuals so we can see the effects and the profits from a communication campaign over an extended time period.

These new techniques and technologies help guide our energies into those efforts that are most valuable in helping our organizations meet their communication objectives. They also help public relations practitioners redefine the traditional duties and expectations of our field. Both of those are important developments that will change the perception of public relations in the future.

WHAT YOU KNOW

- Public relations practitioners are increasingly being asked to be involved in marketing communication campaigns.
- It's important to concentrate your communication dollars on high-potentiality publics and to be able to track the effects of communication on them.
- The research capabilities of computer databases allow practitioners to formulate increasingly complex portraits of individual consumers.

WHAT YOU'LL LEARN

- With purchase and media tracking techniques, we can develop a very precise cost-effective comparison for communicating with specific individuals.
- New techniques that calculate the lifetime value of an individual can justify devoting greater resources to certain individuals.
- Having a well-developed psychographic profile of an individual can help predict the consumer's actions in areas of his or her life.

TIGHT TARGETING IN THE AGE OF INTEGRATED COMMUNICATION

I began this book by indicating that the PR practitioner's role is to solve institutional problems by targeting specific messages to individuals or publics that could help solve those problems. In this final chapter, we'll examine how advertising and marketing are providing advanced methods that help PR practitioners reformulate their communication tasks and reassess their communication success.

As Aaron Cushman discusses in Box 15.1, those reforms could have a profound effect on the way public relations is practiced and, indeed, in the way institutions are run. With new technology it is possible to more accurately isolate and reach the members of target publics who are most likely to respond to a specific message.

That technology also makes it possible to assess the results of communication, replacing short-term goals with parameters that force us to view the effects over sev-

---

BOX 15.1   Views from the Field

Aaron D. Cushman
Cushman is founder and president of Chicago's Aaron D. Cushman and Associates agency. Cushman formerly was president of Cushman, Veeck Public Relations in association with former Chicago White Sox owner Bill Veeck, and he joined Veeck as a partner-owner of the White Sox in the late 1970s.

What's behind this new movement to integrate public relations into advertising and marketing campaigns?

I'm not so sure it's new. I've been espousing the conception of public relations as a marketing vehicle for years. The key element is that people are becoming so sophisticated when it comes to advertising that they no longer anticipate getting 100 percent of what an ad promises. But when something appears editorially, people tend to believe what they read as being the truth. The practicality of the situation is this: Public relations messages have a 4-to-1 ratio of credibility over advertising.

But can we make bottom-line claims for the effectiveness of public relations efforts that support marketing?

There is no comparison when you put the cost of consumer-oriented advertising against an editorial approach. I was brought into the Keebler cookie company when they were going to introduce their soft-center cookie. Keebler's president told me even though Keebler had close to a billion dollars in total sales volume, they couldn't compete in a wide-open advertising fight with Procter & Gamble and Nabisco, who already had their products on the retail shelves. So he was looking for a public relations program that could get the type of coverage he couldn't afford to buy. We came up with the idea about how little Keebler was engaged in this fight with a $2 billion market at stake. After the *Wall Street Journal* put the story on the front page, we got business page and television coverage nationwide talking

BOX 15.1   (continued)

about this David and Goliath situation where Keebler was taking on these giants. After making all the network appearances with an award-winning press kit, we calculated we spent $10,000 for a $3.3 million value in television time. More important, Keebler got a 31 percent market share. That's the bottom line.

Isn't there a lot more creativity involved in writing advertising copy versus public relations copy?

That's absolutely ridiculous. In advertising you do see wonderful copy lines that ad people come up with periodically. But Coke has had its "real thing" slogan for years. Nike will run its Air Jordan ads for as long as Michael Jordan is successful. Any time an advertiser buys media, he controls that space or time. The challenge in public relations is that you won't have a chance to tell your story unless you have a creative concept that will get you media acceptance. That means you've got to keep something new cooking all the time because an editor isn't interested in something that is three weeks old, let alone three years old. That's a lot more than an advertising media buyer has to think about.

—Used with permission of Aaron D. Cushman

eral years of communicating, or not communicating, with a particular public or individuals. Sometimes that assessment method examines not years, but the lifetime of the members of that public.

Being able to examine the long-term ramifications of communication may radically change the procedures we use to plan communication campaigns and may have a startling, positive impact on the way organizations are administered. That makes our ability to translate MBO procedures into PR communication tasks much more practical and effective.

Although all the media and methods discussed in this chapter may not have been applied in traditional public relations tasks yet, it's probably only a question of time before they are used in one form or another in our duties. These, and undoubtedly many more, will be available to you and your colleagues soon. Let's first look at new media options.

IT'S EVERYWHERE, IT'S EVERYWHERE! NEW ADVERTISING MEDIA

Technology has given advertisers new media in which to place their messages. Advertising is now placed on electronic signs that hang over the aisles of supermarkets, by the checkout lanes of discount stores, and in the windows of hair stylists.

A video network uses a satellite to beam news, information, and, of course, advertising into school classrooms. There are also plans afoot to launch a network that would broadcast commercially sponsored programs on health care, travel and entertainment into medical office waiting rooms. Small video monitors are being stationed at self-serve gasoline pumps to show commercials as you fill your car. Memory Memo 15.1 lists some of the media through which advertising is finding its way into places where people shop, stand or wait.

> *Memory Memo 15.1*
> *Some emerging advertising media:*
> - In-store television commercials
> - Low-power television stations
> - Computer disk advertisements
> - Computer modem shopping services
> - World Wide Web

There are also a number of more fundamental changes that have created new media for advertising messages. One change has been a proliferation of what are called "low-power" television stations. These stations, which broadcast with a few thousand watts instead of the millions of watts of VHF and UHF channels, rarely reach viewers more than 25 miles from their transmitters. There are now about 800 low-power stations. Some experts predict there may be 4,000 by the end of the 1990s.

As the projected numbers of these stations and their limited ranges suggest, low-power stations were designed to provide tightly focused programming. Often, an individual station's entire programming will be devoted to local foreign-language talk shows, or farming programs, minority affairs programming or local government meetings. To give you some idea of how specific the programming is: Some individual stations are devoted to a single high school's sports, instructional programs and graduation ceremonies.

Low-power stations provide two major advantages for advertisers. First, advertising rates are much, much lower than for regular full-power stations. That makes television advertising possible for many more companies and institutions.

Second, low-power stations give an advertiser or public relations practitioner the capacity to tightly target a message. If you are trying to reach a very specific audience that is represented by a low-power station, it could be a very effective advertising option.

There's another area in which technology has created what is essentially an additional medium for advertising messages. With the increasing number of personal computers in homes and an entire generation of computer-literate youngsters nearing adulthood, a number of companies have begun computer-based shopping services.

One American automobile company sends potential customers a computer disk instead of a sales brochure. The disk is programmed so customers can research each of the car company's model specifications and then custom-design their own car by selecting among models and available optional features. The computer can then calculate a sticker price. That's a lot more information for the serious car-buying customer than any traditional advertising medium can offer.

Whereas the car company's disk is essentially an advertisement, other computer systems compress the advertisement and the store into one service. Most of these services provide a modem that uses a residential telephone line to hook a personal computer into the shopping service's computer. At this stage in the technology's development, the modem allows personal computer users to review and order from the video catalogs of major retailers of clothing, computer accessories, tools and kitchen utensils. Users can even order flowers or book airline reservations via computer.

Although the technology is proven, consumer response to the services is still being tested. Obviously, the computer monitor can't reproduce the color and sharpness of catalog photographs, and unfamiliarity and fear of the technology probably discourage some shoppers. However, the immediate customer response that's possible and the increasing number of home computers (15 million American homes now contain home computers) make the medium intriguing for advertisers.

These new technological advances in advertising have simply created new forums in which to put what are basically traditional advertising messages. The more radical changes technology has fostered in advertising stem from new techniques for analyzing customer data and testing advertising effectiveness. We'll look at some of these now.

MEASURING COMMUNICATION: NEW WAYS TO TEST PERSUASION EFFECTS

PR practitioners have not always looked to advertising to find ways to target audiences and evaluate communication success. That's not to say advertisers haven't expended tremendous effort and money to guide and evaluate their campaigns. For most of their history, however, advertisers have been as relatively inefficient as public relations practitioners in developing systematic methods for directing communication campaigns.

For instance, most research evaluating advertising effectiveness asked consumers if an advertisement had given them a positive attitude about the product, or if they could remember the product name associated with a slogan, or if they had read most of an advertisement. That's hardly enough evidence on which to gauge whether a communication campaign has been effective. Such tests don't prove there's a direct correlation between the selling message and the sale. A product pitched as "made by Americans for Americans" might elicit positive responses from extremely patriotic people, but if you're trying to sell champagne, where the perceptions of French elegance and quality are important factors, Americanism isn't going to help. Similarly, if your tests find that most people can remember the name of the product when confronted with a slogan, it proves only that the advertiser has successfully fulfilled a memory task, not created a sale.

As you'll remember from Chapter 1, these secondary measures of communication aren't true measures of persuasion. For a professional communicator, persuasion has only occurred when the receiver takes an action as a result of hearing a message.

In some instances, even sales figures don't give a true picture of an advertising campaign's effectiveness. In mass market advertising campaigns, in which there may be coupon incentives, in-school promotions, and sponsored music videos running simultaneously, it's virtually impossible to tell the sales effect of a single part of the advertising campaign.

Did It Really Work? Tracking Back-End Performance

Some newer advertising tests, largely adopted from direct marketers, are beginning to establish a solid research base that can be used to evaluate advertising expenditures. Although they have yet to be used extensively in public relations, those new procedures have tremendous potential to reform the methods we use to judge the effectiveness of our PR communication efforts.

One of the evaluation procedures that are being applied to advertising and direct marketing help determine what is called "back-end performance." Examining back-end performance lets a business know not only the number of responses to a particular marketing message, but whether an individual consumer is a repeat customer of the company.

That's important to many direct-response marketers because they often go to enormous expense to get a prospect to make an initial commitment to a product. Magazines offer trial issues of their magazines or clocks, radios, calculators or other premiums. Many other marketers provide deep discounts and other incentives to entice the consumer to try the product.

Because of that substantial outlay just to get a customer, many direct-response marketing campaigns don't make money from the customer's initial order. To break even, the company first has to satisfy the customer with the initial purchase. At that point, the company may be in a position to make a profit by getting the customer to buy the product again and maybe even buy other company products.

For such marketers, merely looking at the initial response to a communication campaign can bring an inaccurate assessment. There have been many cases in which customers like the free premium so much that even though they didn't want the product, they would order it just to get the free watches, food canisters or other premiums. After the customers have the premiums, they never order company products again.

This has created some problems for those marketers who have merely examined the results from split-run tests, a concept briefly discussed in Chapter 3. Split-run tests, you will recall, let advertisers determine which of many different options for advertising—illustrations, copy, design formats, premiums, or even envelope colors—deliver more sales. Advertisers can make these judgments by changing one element in the advertisements delivered to one portion of a mailing list. By comparing the sales figures of audiences who receive the different versions, it's possible to predict which version will be more effective in delivering a response from a particular mailing list.

Split-run tests are a good method to determine which advertising strategy will be most effective in stimulating a customer to initially respond to an advertisement. But by concentrating only on one response, the tests neglect the capacity of some members of our publics to be more important to our eventual success. One customer might respond to our initial ad, then never buy another product from our company. Obviously, that customer is much less valuable to us than the customer who buys the product as a result of the initial advertisement, then continues to buy other items from the company.

So companies look at back-end performance, or the payback the company might get from its relationship with an individual customer after one or two years or even five years. You'll see in Sidebar 15.1 how tracking buying behavior for an extended period changes the marketer's decision about which audience is most profitable to communicate with.

Relationship Marketing: Calculating a Receiver's Lifetime Value

Because these long-term marketing assessment strategies are so important, many direct-response marketers are now talking about "relationship marketing" and "relationship payback," thus emphasizing the long-term profits from a continuing rela-

---

SIDEBAR 15.1   Calculating Back-end Performance

Tracking back-end performance compels us to consider the long-term implications of our communication management decisions. Although it was first used by direct marketers to compare the efficiency of different mailing lists, it can also test the payback from offering a premium to encourage sales or determine whether an employee-retention program would contribute to overall productivity. This back-end performance calculation projecting long-term profits for a financial services company shows that our evaluation of the profitability of communicating with different audiences could change dramatically if we extend the payback period. This back-end calculation is very simplified. A more sophisticated analysis might include comparisons of account maintenance costs, the effects of inflation, bad debts, and income from new customer referrals.

age of enrollee	number of enrollees	solicitation costs per 100 enrollees	income generated in year 1	year 1 profit	income generated through year 5	5-year profit	income generated through year 25	25-year profit
60	100	$500	$6,000	$5,500	$30,000	$29,500	$37,000	$36,500
35	100	$2,000	$2,400	$400	$16,800	$14,800	$203,000	$201,000

tionship instead of the immediate payoff. Relationship costs and relationship marketing are intriguing ways to track direct-response advertising. As you probably already realize, relationship marketing describes the goals of public relations practitioners: to use cost-efficient communication processes to gain and sustain the support of publics that are necessary for the immediate and long-term success of our companies. As summarized in Memory Memo 15.2, that's relationship marketing in a nutshell.

> *Memory Memo 15.2*
> *Relationship marketing:*
> - orients the organization toward ethical behavior and long-term goals
> - justifies extra communication spending to reach the best prospects
> - helps set priorities for communication tasks

To formalize and quantify a concept as nebulous as a relationship, direct-response advertisers have developed a calculation called "lifetime value." The concept of lifetime value means that some people, over the duration of an information campaign or even the duration of their lives, are more valuable to communicate with than others. If we concentrate our communication efforts on those people who have the ability to substantially help or hurt our institution, we have a chance of getting much better paybacks from our communication campaigns than if we use an equally costly campaign intended to reach everyone.

Here's an example from marketing to illustrate lifetime value. A food processing company sells canned corn. In planning its advertising campaign, it obviously wants to concentrate its commercials, advertisements and other promotions on people who buy canned corn.

In analyzing the broad market for a product like canned corn, which almost every family buys, the company's marketers probably rationalize that their most likely target audience will be the women over age 21 who do the food shopping for their families. That audience for messages about canned corn will include a 26-year-old homemaker with three small children who is barely able to make ends meet, an affluent 44-year-old woman with three teen-age daughters, and an extremely rich 73-year-old retired widow. They all buy canned corn and so are part of the target audience.

That's what a traditional marketing campaign might conclude. However, a campaign using lifetime value principles doesn't give equal weight to those three women. Instead, lifetime value argues that at different times in his or her life, a consumer's loyalty has a different value to a company. Instead of analyzing that customer's value to the company in terms of what he or she can buy during the next three weeks or three months, lifetime value tries to project the customer's value to the company during his or her lifetime. By estimating how many purchases customers might make during shopping trips for the rest of their lives, we can determine how much we can invest in a communication effort to win their loyalty.

For canned corn, it's easy to see that a 73-year-old retired widow doesn't have much lifetime value to the company. No matter how rich she is, there's only a limited amount of canned corn she can buy during the rest of her life. The analysis of the other two women is very interesting, however. Normal advertising campaigns usually focus on high-income middle-aged people because they generally have the most buying power. But it's easy to see that although the 44-year-old woman may be buying a lot of canned corn for her three teen-age daughters now, within a few years her children will have left the house. At that point, even though she has another 30 or 40 years on the planet, the amount of value she has to the company will go down dramatically.

The young, struggling homemaker with her three small children is another case altogether. She's got another 15 to 20 years in which she will be making food decisions for four or five family members, and then 30 or 40 more years in which she'll still be buying canned corn, although in much smaller quantities. In the eyes of a lifetime value marketer, she's the richest consumer lode to mine, because the buying decisions she makes now could establish a pattern that would keep her buying the company's products for 50 or 60 years.

Because of that immense payback value she represents, lifetime value marketers can justify quite generous expenditures to communicate with that 26-year-old woman about canned corn. Although general advertising expenditures might be cost-effective for the 44-year-old woman, the food company can offer the young woman free samples of its product, free recipe books, generous coupons, and other premiums. If it can win the product loyalty of that woman, it can balance the costs of those enticements against the value of what she will buy for decades.

Lifetime value represents a healthy trend for American business. It shifts the emphasis away from short-term profits and back to products, conduct and messages that will pay off for the company for a long time to come. That is also the essence of the value that public relations represents to an institution. It's our job to build an environment of public support that's only obtained by a long-term commitment to corporate responsibility and ethics.

Lifetime value is more than an ethical reminder with which to educate corporate executives. It also is a tool we can use to plan our public relations communications campaigns and justify higher-than-average expenditures to reach particularly valuable target groups. Let's look at how lifetime value concepts can be applied to PR communication situations.

Let's say you work for a company that, because of a history of environmental abuses, has gotten a bad reputation among environmentalists. Consequently, every time the company needs a permit to do business or expand, a group of young environmentalists seems to camp in legislators' offices to lobby against the company's plans.

However, new management has brought a new, conscientious attitude. The company has begun cleaning up the environmental problems it caused. As a PR manager, you've communicated the company's environmental turnaround in the company's newsletters and corporate reports. You have gained prominent press coverage on the company's pollution control innovations and have taken out advertisements in the state capital's newspaper during the legislative session extolling your company's new attitude to lawmakers. Unfortunately, all the efforts of you and your company have not changed the minds of the young environmental lobbyists, who still harass the company at every turn.

Lifetime value concepts might indicate that communication to townspeople where the company is located, even to the legislators and regulators who vote on the government permits, won't be the most cost-effective way to communicate. The townspeople and stockholders already know the many advantages the company brings to the community. The legislators are responsive to voters and other pressure groups, but they aren't necessarily the people to whom we should devote the greatest communication resources.

Instead, lifetime value concepts suggest that over their lifetime, those dedicated young environmental activists are going to make the company's existence miserable. They not only have the ability to involve the company in many drawn-out legal and regulatory battles, but they are capable of stimulating a lot of negative media coverage for the company. Worst of all, they might be causing havoc for the next 40 years.

Lifetime value argues that it might be wise to spend substantial resources now to communicate with the members of that environmental group. Those tactics might include plant tours for group members, informal letters to key leaders, and personal consultations between environmental leaders and company management.

Relationship marketing is a useful perspective from which to look at public relations communication as well as PR budgeting. It weans us from thinking in terms of simply "getting stuff in the newspaper." It compels us to think about the people with whom it is important for us to communicate. It segments those publics from the general mass of people who comprise a society and forces us to rank the importance of those publics. Once we've established those rankings, we can begin to set priorities on our expenditures for communicating to each of those groups, basing our budgets on the importance of their support to the institution's success.

By extending the period during which we look for a payback on our communication efforts, lifetime value forces organizations to confront the short-term and long-term advantages and disadvantages of company initiatives and communication campaigns about those initiatives. That's a very positive outlook for institutions that are planning to survive and prosper in an ever-changing environment.

TARGETING ADVERTISING MESSAGES TO INDIVIDUALS: DATA-DRIVEN MARKETING

Whereas lifetime value principles can be applied to publics, there are exciting developments in data-driven marketing that let us focus that targeting power on individuals. It's called data-driven marketing because it's possible only because of the vast amount of information marketers are collecting about consumer purchases and putting into computers, where it can be manipulated. Data-driven marketing can just as easily be applied to public relations communication.

As Memory Memo 15.3 shows,

Memory Memo 15.3
New sources of audience information

- Universal product codes
- Credit card and debit card purchase tracking
- Product use and media use surveys

direct marketers have easy access to your buying decisions. When you order an item through a catalog or television offer, the seller can directly connect your name, address, credit card number, and eventually a social security number (through your credit card application) to a specific purchase. Those individual mail-order or direct-marketing purchases provide a lot of information about your lifestyle and habits. If you order gourmet cookware, exercise equipment, jazz recordings, and books on mystic philosophy, marketing experts can begin to piece together a portrait that helps them predict certain other purchases you might make.

We Know What You've Bought: Universal Product Codes

Those direct-marketing purchases in which you've voluntarily given your name aren't the only source of personal purchasing information in this high-technology era. You're probably familiar with supermarket and department store cash register tapes that list and describe purchases. These register tapes are generated by the universal product code (UPC) bars printed on product packaging. Those UPC bars were originally intended to tell stores what items were almost sold out so the store could restock its inventory. However, marketing people are finding other uses for that information.

Because so many purchases are made or validated with credit cards, debit cards (plastic cards that take the place of bank checks), and check-cashing cards, retailers have a record of the customer's name, address and social security number.

All those payment methods give retailers and marketing and public relations practitioners the opportunity to directly link an individual name with specific retail purchases. That pattern of purchases provides wonderfully detailed information that allows communicators to develop detailed profiles of current customers. Those profiles also let PR practitioners predict potential customers with whom to communicate our message.

In addition, profiles give marketers opportunities to conduct communication campaigns based on lifetime value principles. Let's go back to the canned corn example. Let's say you are marketing Brand A canned corn. You discover from cash register tapes and debit, credit or identification cards that Mary Jones buys Brand A canned corn and Jane Smith buys Brand B canned corn. In designing a marketing communication campaign this is extremely important information. Because Mary Jones is already buying our product, we may want to reinforce her present buying behavior, but we don't need to communicate basic product quality or features with our advertising claims. On the other hand, Jane Smith is a person we need to convince of our message.

Offering free product samples or cents-off coupons to Mary Jones simply cuts into our revenues (in that she is simply spending less for purchases she would make anyway), but those incentives to buy our product could move Jane Smith to become a loyal, long-term customer. With current technology we can isolate people who don't buy our products and mail them coupons and other inducements. That ability to concentrate our financial and communication resources on just the individuals we need to convince is very valuable to us.

An Audience of One: New Capabilities to Target Print Advertising Media

We have a greater ability to target specific audiences today. As we've seen, we can reach a very selective audience through direct mail and telemarketing. But until recently, targeting in general advertising has been dependent on whatever special interest the media outlet served. Obviously, it's impossible to target television commercials so they'll go only into homes owned by white-collar professionals or people who like to fish.

General interest magazines, in trying to compete with specialized magazines, have been employing more and more technology to give that kind of selectivity to advertisers. For several decades, it's been possible to buy magazine advertising that appears only in certain regions of the country. Thus, it was possible for a beer company that marketed its product only to certain regions to buy advertising that had the prestige of a national magazine but was limited to only a certain geographic area.

Now general interest magazines like *Time*, *Newsweek* and *Sports Illustrated* have gone beyond this selectivity. Advertisers in these magazines can place advertising to reach subscribers in specific zip codes. Moreover, although it's not widely used, new computer-coordinated binding and addressing equipment makes it technically possible for advertisers to bind specific advertisements into individual copies of those magazines.

That means that if your company sells expensive boats, you could bind an advertisement for your $100,000 cabin cruisers into copies of Sports Illustrated magazine that are going to high-income individuals who own a boat valued at $30,000 to $70,000 but who have certain psychographic traits that make you think they are looking for more status items in their lives.

Letting the Customer Drive the Communication: Information-as-Needed Techniques

Other companies that have recognized the benefits of targeting communication to logical customers have taken a more low-technology approach. I call these strategies "information-as-needed" techniques because they are structured so that your organization doesn't offer a message to important receivers until it has determined that the information will be relevant to those receivers at this particular time.

Here's an example of information as needed. One national retailer found that an average family spends more than $3,500 on household and yard items in the six months after moving to a new home. Unfortunately, those high-volume customers are relatively limited in number and are scattered across the entire landscape. It was just not practical to conduct a major advertising campaign to advertise the company products to this dispersed market segment.

Instead, the company purchased a small number of advertisements in major magazines and on television that offered a relatively expensive, multipage booklet on organizing a move, including tips on selecting a moving company, turning off and reconnecting utilities, and other hints. As you might imagine, each family's booklet also contained a personalized section giving directions to the company's retail store in the family's new hometown. (See Sidebar 15.2 for an example of another communication campaign that's designed to concentrate advertising on high-potentiality customers.)

Because the retailer had the customers' names, new addresses, and approximate moving dates, the company was able to follow up its initial contact by blanketing its customers' new addresses with appropriate catalogs, coupons and other offers to entice them into the company's local store. That personal service, even though much more expensive than a normal advertising campaign, brought huge returns. It was effective because it identified customers just before they were making major buying decisions and then delivered information that helped them with those decisions.

A luxury car company took the concept even further. Although car dealers advertise virtually every day of the year, the majority of people ignore the ads. Why? Except for brief periods every few years, most customers simply aren't in the market for a new car.

To help control its advertising expense, the car company studied its potential customers and found the average luxury car buyer replaced his or her car every three years. With that knowledge, the company examined auto registration records to discover when people had purchased their luxury cars. The company then established a program that started mailing glossy catalogs, personal letters, and incentives to luxury car owners approximately two and one-half years after they had purchased their last automobile. By concentrating its advertising effort exactly when car owners were beginning to make decisions about their purchases, the car company was able to justify a much more expensive and personal advertising campaign, a campaign that was much more effective.

Knowing What You've Done, We Can Tell What You'll Do: Multivariate Descriptors and Customer Twins

The information-as-needed strategy can be employed using even more powerful marketing tools. New computer capabilities are giving us the power to collect and study vast amounts of information about millions of individuals. This extensive information on individual consumers includes demographic, psychographic, lifestyle and purchasing behaviors, which are called multivariate descriptors.

Here's how the services that compile multivariate descriptors function. Marketing research services, including Lifestyle Selector, Select and Save, Donnelly's Carol Wright, CSI Telemarketing and JFY, have collected data on millions of individual consumers. In addition to standard demographic information such as name, address, phone number, household income, and number and age of family members, the services have collected extensive psychographic information, including data on hobbies, reading interests, and past purchases.

Let's examine Lifestyle Selector's list of consumer information in Sidebar 15.3. After collecting demographic data that allow communicators to identify specific consumers, Lifestyle Selector develops a lifestyle profile for each of about 14 million

SIDEBAR 15.2   Collecting High-potentiality Customers

MCI's Friends & Family® program's initial success was built on advertisements that offered customers who joined MCI the opportunity to create personal calling circles. The customer benefit was additional savings to the numbers he or she selected. The benefit to MCI was that customers themselves were assisting MCI by providing names and numbers of customers who may wish to join MCI. MCI sales representatives had the perfect pitch: A brother or friend had thought so much of the prospective customer that he wanted him in his calling circle so they could talk more frequently. By joining Friends & Family, that referral customer could achieve the same additional savings.

While the current Friends & Family program no longer requires that a customer provide names to MCI, MCI has retained the concept of providing additional savings on calls to other MCI customers.

William Thompson's Friends & Family℠ Tree

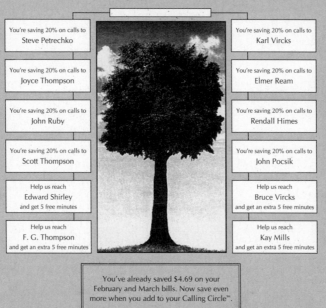

You're saving 20% on calls to
Steve Petrechko

You're saving 20% on calls to
Joyce Thompson

You're saving 20% on calls to
John Ruby

You're saving 20% on calls to
Scott Thompson

Help us reach
Edward Shirley
and get 5 free minutes

Help us reach
F. G. Thompson
and get an extra 5 free minutes

You're saving 20% on calls to
Karl Vircks

You're saving 20% on calls to
Elmer Ream

You're saving 20% on calls to
Rendall Himes

You're saving 20% on calls to
John Pocsik

Help us reach
Bruce Vircks
and get an extra 5 free minutes

Help us reach
Kay Mills
and get an extra 5 free minutes

You've already saved $4.69 on your February and March bills. Now save even more when you add to your Calling Circle™.

Your Friends & Family Calling Circle Status.

CIRCLE MEMBERS: Your 20% bonus discount is active on all calls to the following friends and family including your own home number:

Steve Petrechko	(314) 555-2134
Karl Vircks	(515) 555-1341
Joyce Thompson	(703) 555-4569
Rowena Ream	(708) 555-9765
Pam Ruby	(713) 555-0865
Rendall Himes	(816) 555-5862
Scott Thompson	(816) 555-9470
John Poscik	(816) 555-5845

Help us to reach these people and you save even more!

UNABLE TO REACH: We'd like to add these friends and family to your Calling Circle, so you can increase your savings, but despite many attempts we've been unable to reach them. Maybe you'd like to call them yourself and invite them to join your Calling Circle. We'll even give you a free phone call to each one. Then have them call 1-800-388-5272 to join.

Edward Shirley	(512) 555-8629
Gary Thompson	(206) 555-7153
Kay Mills	(816) 555-0074

NEED ENCOURAGEMENT: These are the friends and family that have chosen not to join or have left your Calling Circle. Use a free call to invite them back into your circle so you both can save.

Bruce Vircks	(515) 555-3796
Randy Thompson	(816) 555-8678

To add to your Calling Circle, return the enclosed reply card or call 1-800-388-5272.

* Number is within your local calling area – 20% discount to this member will apply only to your MCI Card Calls.

—All references to MCI and Friends and Family used with permission of MCI Communications Corporation.

SIDEBAR 15.3 Targeting an Audience by Multivariate Descriptors

The Lifestyle Selector collects billions of individual facts about consumers, from how old they are to what they do on weekends for fun. These lists provide practitioners with a wealth of targeting options.

THE LIFESTYLE SELECTOR

Location ID: 10 DCLS 552   Mid 019107-000
NDL/The Lifestyle Selector.
1621 18th St., Denver, CO 80202. Phone 303-292-5000, 800-525-3533, FAX, 303-294-9628.
Specific list selections are located in each appropriate classification in their normal alphabetical sequence.

1. PERSONNEL
VP Grp Mgr—R.S. Wotkins, III.
Pres—Tim Prunk.
Branch Offices
New York 10010—One Madison Ave. Phone 212-481-9200. FAX 212-213-2976.
Carlsbad, CA 92008—Opus Plaza I, 1921 Palomar Oaks Way, Suite 305. Phone 619-431-0300. FAX 619-431-5730.

2. DESCRIPTION
Database of buyers of consumer goods who voluntarily complete and mail a detailed customer questionnaires packed with the products, providing information about their individual and household lifestyles, hobbies and demographics.

3. LIST SOURCE
Self-reported questionnaires packaged in consumer goods.

4. QUANTITY AND RENTAL RATES
Rec'd May 20, 1993.

	Total Number	Price per/M
Total list (24 months)	27,805,673	65.00
Art/antique collecting	2,491,327	"
Automotive work	3,998,635	"
Bible/devotional reading	4,337,054	"
Bicycling	4,026,686	"
Book reading	10,236,701	"
Buy pre-recorded videos	1,508,905	75.00
Cable TV viewing	5,095,378	65.00
Camping/hiking	5,805,431	"
Career-oriented activities	1,153,983	"
Casino gambling	1,198,595	75.00
Charities/volunteer activities	1,145,491	65.00
Collectibles/collections	3,130,144	"
Community/civic activities	1,492,993	"
Crafts	7,898,677	"
Crossword puzzles	2,104,936	"
Cultural/arts events	3,272,417	"
Current affairs/politics	1,637,558	"
Dieting/weight control	3,192,621	"
Dining out frequently	105,558	"
Donate to charitable causes	2,869,951	75.00
Electronics	2,228,889	65.00
Fashion/clothing	3,387,196	"
Fishing	6,476,963	"
Flower Gardening	4,464,566	"
Foreign travel	3,225,581	"
Frequent flyer club members	3,275,208	75.00
Gardening	9,947,157	65.00
Golf	5,267,062	65.00
Gourmet cooking/fine foods	4,895,586	"
Grandchildren	5,343,281	"
Health/natural foods	3,257,539	"
Home/personal computers	5,057,093	75.00
Home video games	1,506,005	65.00
Home workshop	6,992,769	"
House plants	6,844,326	"
Household pets	10,439,453	"
Hunting/shooting	4,440,078	"
Moneymaking opportunities	1,187,331	"
Motorcycling	963,462	"
Needlework/knitting	5,024,280	"
Our nations heritage	1,090,655	"
Outdoor gardening	2,783,377	"
Own a cat	3,648,172	"
Own a dog	4,985,409	"
Own a CD player	5,123,107	"
Photography	5,082,345	65.00
Physical fitness/exercise	8,735,805	"
Power boating	1,917,058	"
Real estate investments	1,601,112	75.00
Recreational vehicles	2,114,528	65.00
Running/jogging	2,774,728	"
Sailing	873,758	"
Science fiction	1,707,328	"
Science/new technology	1,826,622	"
Self improvement	3,737,747	"
Sewing	5,028,231	"

	Total Number	Price per/M
Snow skiing	1,954,425	"
Stamp/coin collecting	1,903,514	"
Stereo/records/tapes/CDs	11,956,132	"
Stock/bond investments	3,246,788	75.00
Sweepstakes/contests	4,260,710	65.00
Tennis	1,680,518	"
Travel in U.S.A.	4,314,335	"
Vegetable gardening	3,346,315	"
Veterans benefits/programs	425,259	"
Walking for health	7,825,069	"
Watching sports on TV	10,036,358	"
Wildlife/environmental issues	3,997,376	"
Wines	1,616,610	65.00
Sex:		
Males	13,427,297	"
Females	13,920,868	"
Age:		
18-24	1,802,907	"
25-34	5,204,107	"
35-44	5,788,440	"
45-54	4,699,652	"
55-64	3,977,165	"
65+	5,573,471	"
Marital status:		
Married	18,749,501	"
Unmarried	8,187,215	"
Income:		
Under 15,000.00	1,681,537	"
15,000.00-19,999.00	2,194,381	"
20,000.00-24,999.00	2,165,289	"
25,000.00-29,999.00	2,133,305	"
30,000.00-34,999.00	2,080,097	"
35,000.00-39,999.00	2,043,941	"
40,000.00-44,999.00	1,897,906	"
45,000.00-49,999.00	1,529,504	"
50,000.00-59,999.00	2,257,163	"
60,000.00-74,999.00	2,276,883	"
75,000.00-99,999.00	1,373,449	75.00
100,000.00+	1,332,449	"
Home ownership:		
Owner	19,805,422	65.00
Renter	6,253,535	"
New movers	619,129	75.00
Occupation:		
Professional/technical	6,007,151	65.00
Upper mgmt/administrative	1,267,192	"
Middle Management	1,601,516	"
Sales/Marketing	1,365,008	"
Clerical	1,935,444	"
Craftsman/blue collar	2,206,529	"
Student	1,286,961	"
Homemaker	4,002,848	"
Retired	4,617,834	"
Working Women	10,529,964	"
Self-employed/Business Owner	1,591,471	"
Religion/ethnicity:		
Catholic	2,304,014	"
Jewish	570,104	"
Asian	230,584	"
Hispanic	679,351	"
Protestant	21,169,602	"
Children:		
By exact age	17,547,608	"
Credit card holders by type of credit card:		
Travel/entertainment	3,973,244	"
Bank	18,077,301	"
Gas/Dept. Store, etc.	8,884,154	"

Selections: 6-month hotline, ZIP Code, 5.00/M extra; state, SCF, 3.50/M extra; each additional selection, 7.00/M extra; keying, 1.00/M extra; 60-day hotline, scoring surcharge, 10.00/M extra.
Minimum order 10,000.

5. COMMISSION, CREDIT POLICY
20% commission to all recognized brokers; 15% to agencies and lettershops. Advance deposit may be required. Net 30 days.

6. METHOD OF ADDRESSING
4-up Cheshire labels. Pressure sensitive labels, 5.00/M extra. Magnetic tape (9T 1600/6250, 38K cartridge), 15.00 nonrefundable fee.

7. DELIVERY SCHEDULE
3-5 working days.

8. RESTRICTIONS
Sample mailing piece required for approval.

11. MAINTENANCE
Every two weeks.

people it surveys each year. Thus, a PR practitioner is able to identify if a particular individual has a pet, plays tennis, goes boating, collects stamps, enjoys gourmet cooking, goes to baseball games, or even dabbles in the occult.

At the simplest level, the capacity to capture all these audience characteristics provides you with the ability to build a mailing list of people who pursue particular activities. For instance, if you want people who invest in real estate, you can get a list of about 1.4 million Americans who might be likely prospects for your organization's newsletter on real estate limited partnerships.

You can also find more tightly focused concentrations. Let's say, for example, that you are putting together a prospect list for an Atlanta caterer who specializes in bar mitzvahs. With a list of multivariate descriptors, you can select a mailing list that comprises only the parents of 12-year-old Jewish boys with mailing addresses in the zip codes surrounding Atlanta.

Here is the amazing thing you can accomplish with this multivariate list. Let's say you are working for a national nonprofit agency striving to place teen-age orphans with new families. Because there aren't any mailing lists specifically of people who want to adopt teen-age children, you have to look for other methods to find an audience that is going to be interested in your message. You try to think about some characteristics that are common to the foster families who are already involved in your program, but there don't seem to be any. The foster families come from all sections of the country and represent many different income levels, faiths and races. So how can you find promising prospects? You can use what's called a back-through run.

Here's how a back-through run works. With the Lifestyle Selector data, you can submit your entire list of families who have already adopted a teen-ager. A computer program checks the entire Lifestyle Selector list and selects every one of your foster families that also appears on the Lifestyle list.

The computer then compiles all the lifestyle and demographic characteristics of the families who have already adopted children and takes that information to create a composite profile of people who have participated in your program. That portrait might reveal a concentration of foster families from certain age groups, occupational groups, or lifestyle interests. That profile is valuable in itself, because it gives the adoption agency an idea of appropriate vocabulary, benefits and premiums to use in its recruitment materials.

But more important is that the group of psychographic and demographic qualities that characterizes the agency's present customers can be used to expand its list of prospects by running the typical adopter profile "back through" the database. Taking those characteristics, a computer program selects every consumer in the entire Lifestyle Selector data bank who exhibits that cluster of characteristics held by people who have already adopted a teen-ager. That list of names of so-called "customer twins" contains potent prospects for the next recruitment campaign the agency mounts. That's an exact way of picking an audience for your message.

This power is even more accessible now that one computer software company has produced an extremely inexpensive lifestyle data file for a desktop per-

> **Memory Memo 15.4**
> **Steps in a customer twin back-through search:**
>
> - Compile all customers who have taken the desired action.
> - Develop a profile of those customers from a multivariate list.
> - Examine the multivariate list for other customers who fit that profile.
> - These names are customer twins of those who have taken the desired action.

sonal computer. For under $1,000, you can buy up to 26 pieces of demographic and psychographic information on thousands of individual consumers. Having this type of information at our fingertips would have been inconceivable to a practitioner even five years ago. Memory Memo 15.4 summarizes the process of finding this prospective customer.

INTEGRATED COMMUNICATION'S CHALLENGE TO PUBLIC RELATIONS

In no other area are the expanding duties and powerful tools of public relations shown as clearly as in integrated marketing. Here we see the increasing reliance institutions are placing on their PR practitioners to solve problems through communication. Here we see how much technological and research competence is demanded of practitioners, who must now analyze and prescribe remedies that often employ computer database searches and other high-technology methods.

Here, finally, we see the future of public relations. We see the ability not only to target specialized messages to specific publics but to send personal messages to individuals within our audiences. The knowledge of an individual's purchasing patterns and psychographic characteristics makes that possible. What public relations practitioners need now is the knowledge to employ those methods and the courage to convince administrators of our leadership and professionalism.

Finally, we need the vision to understand the break with past practices that these newer methods represent and to understand the good—and the harm—of which we are now capable. That is the true challenge of targeting the message.

SUMMARY

- Many emerging media are being used for advertising, including in-store television commercials, low-power television stations, computer disk advertisements, and computer modem shopping services.

- Most traditional advertising research methods use polling techniques to determine if consumers have a positive attitude about a product, remember the product slogan associated with a brand name, or have read most of an advertisement.

- Back-end performance evaluates communication effectiveness by judging not just the responses to a particular marketing message, but whether individual consumers continue to buy from the company.

- Relationship marketing, an extension of back-end performance tracking, is readily adaptable to public relations tasks. Relationship marketing, like public relations, uses cost-efficient communication to sustain the long-term support of important publics.

- Calculating an individual's lifetime value—the value of the receiver's support of an organization over an extended period—gives practitioners guidance in segmenting audiences and then justifying spending greater resources to target communication programs to them.
- Lifetime value concepts deemphasize business decisions based on short-term profits and encourage decision-making processes that focus on products, conduct and messages that will pay off in the long term.
- Universal product codes give retailers the ability to link individuals with specific purchases so that marketers can develop detailed customer profiles and predict who will become new customers.
- "Information-as-needed" techniques estimate when customers will enter the market for a product and target more detailed information to them at that point.
- Multivariate marketing statistics can help compile a composite profile of people who use certain product categories. After that profile has been established, it's possible to compile a list of "customer twins," consumers who share characteristics with customers who've already bought a certain product.

THINK PIECES

1. Why should extending the payback period for communication activities improve a company's management?
2. What are some nontraditional communication media that can be used to involve and inform children about a company's product?
3. Describe a long-term, high payback prospect for a computer manufacturer. What would be a high payback prospect for the Democratic Party? the Republican Party?
4. What negative perceptions does a direct-marketing ad writer have to overcome? How can you overcome those prejudices?

MANAGEMENT PROBLEMS

D6.2

D9.3

D11.1

ADDITIONAL READING

Dilenschneider, Robert L. "Marketing Communication in the Post-Advertising Era." *Public Relations Review* 17:3 (Fall 1991): 227–236.

Kotler, Philip, and Andreasen, Alan R. *Strategic Marketing for Nonprofit Organizations*, 5th ed. Englewood Cliffs, N.J.: Prentice Hall, 1995.

Masterton, John. "Discovering Databases." *Public Relations Journal* 48:11 (November 1992): 12–17, 19.

Petrison, Lisa A., and Wang, Paul. "From Relationships to Relationship Marketing: Applying Database Technology to Public Relations." *Public Relations Review* 19:3 (Fall 1993): 235–245.

Rapp, Stan, and Collins, Thomas L. *The New Maximarketing*. New York: McGraw-Hill, 1995.

Stone, Bob. *Successful Direct Marketing Methods*, 5th ed. Lincolnwood, Ill.: NTC, 1995.

Spector, Shelley J. "Interactive Multimedia Comes of Age." *Public Relations Journal* 51:1 (May 1995): 42–45.

Warner, Carin I. "Applying Integrated Marketing to Brand Positioning." *Public Relations Journal* 48:10 (October 1992): 15–16.

Applications Workbook Section A

Annotated Associated Press Stylebook

Because of the close professional interaction between public relations practitioners and journalists, most PR people follow the writing style rules observed by journalists. *The Associated Press Stylebook and Libel Manual* is the journalist's source for that information.

Although the following pages summarize the rules most commonly used in public relations tasks, the stylebook covers an amazing variety of topics. Do you *rear* or *raise* a child? What's the difference between a *blonde* and a *blond?* Is it *Kmart, K-Mart* or *K mart?* Is there such a word as *afterwards?* Is *nylon* capitalized? What does a *Buddhist* believe? All those questions are answered in the AP Stylebook, and all practitioners should own a copy of this inexpensive, valuable reference book.

Please note that many companies and organizations supplement or supplant certain features of the *Associated Press Stylebook* with a company style book. That's not necessarily negative, but remember that style rules that conflict with Associated Press rules can discourage editors from using a certain release that might have been placed if it hadn't demanded extra attention.

The style section begins with an explanation of the proofreading marks journalists use to correct written copy (Workbook Figure 1). Immediately following the six style rule sections are self-quizzes for each section. This material from *The Associated Press Stylebook and Libel Manual Fully Revised and Updated*, © 1994 by the Associated Press, is reprinted by permission of Addison-Wesley Publishing Company, Inc.

Proofreading   Symbols

Two kentucky gubernatorial candidates   indent paragraph, capitalize

will respond to questions from reporters   insert words

in a debate at 7:30 p.m. Friday the at University)   transpose letters or words

of Louisville.   no   paragraph

The debate, featuring Democratic candidate   replace letter

Christine Helm and three time GOP candidate John   insert   hyphen

Forbes, is sponsored by the Lou. Business Forum.   don't   abbreviate

Questioning the candidates will be WHAS-TV   insert   colon

reporter Mike Cass, business editor Carol Tompkins   insert   comma

of The Courier-Journal and and The Shively   delete letter or word

Newsweek's Jason Calley.   insert   apostrophe

This debate is the fourth in a series of debates   delete   punctuation

spotlighting eight of The state's most important   lowercase

political contests. The 3 previous events have   spell it out

showcased candidates for lieutenant governor,   insert and remove space

secretary of state and treasurer. The free   period

event is at the university library, the address   insert   semicolon

is Fiftyfive Corndine Plaza in downtown   use   figures

Louisville, Kentucky.   abbreviate

Workbook Figure 1

PART 1: PUNCTUATION

A. Commas

Commas are generally overused by most student writers. Too many commas cause slower reading speed and needlessly interrupt copy flow. Generally, commas should be used to indicate a pause a speaker would naturally make as he or she reads copy aloud.

1. Series.   Use commas to separate elements in a series, but do not put a comma before the conjunction in a simple series. *The dog had fleas, ticks and lice. She refused to marry Jack, Kevin or Mick.*

2. City, State or Nation.   Place a comma between the city and state or nation in which it is located, and another comma after the state or nation name. *His flight left Cancun, Mexico, at 1 p.m. and landed in Kansas City, Mo., seven hours later.* However, if there is no modifying state or nation name, do not use a comma. *He flew from Paris to Chicago in a 747.*

3. Appositives.   An appositive is a phrase or clause that describes another word. When the information contained in the appositive could be dropped and not radically change the meaning of the sentence, the appositive must be enclosed in commas. If the appositive's information is vital to the meaning of the sentence, it must not be set off by commas. Here's an example: *The cat, which was sitting on my bed, belongs to Tom.* This sentence implies there is only one cat and it belongs to Tom. Compare it with this sentence: *The cat that was sitting on my bed belongs to Tom.* In this case, the sentence suggests there are many cats in the room and the reader must understand that it was the cat on the bed that belonged to Tom. Because it's essential to the sentence's meaning there are no commas. Also, note that *which* is used only for nonessential clauses or phrases, whereas *that* or *who* is used for essential clauses or phrases.

4. Quotations.   Use a comma to separate a complete quotation from its attribution. *Jones said, "If I wanted to hear music that sounded like that, I would put my head next to a jack hammer."* The same rule applies if the attribution is placed at the end of the sentence. *"This rock music is just like having your temporal lobes removed through your nose," Jones said.* No commas before partial quotes: *He said the food was "darn tasty."* Notice the comma and period go inside the quotation marks.

5. Ages.   Separate an individual's age from his or her name by commas. *Killed in the accident was John Kelly Maupin, 8, a pupil at Regis Primary School.*

6. Numbers.   Numbers larger than 999 need commas. The major exceptions are street addresses, telephone numbers and years.

B. Colons

The colon's most frequent use is at the end of a sentence to introduce a list, tabulation, text, and the like. But remember that a colon signals a dramatic pause and needs substantial information on each side of the colon; otherwise it will sound very unnatural. This next sentence shows a colon used improperly. *My mother's list is:*

bread, milk and eggs. You'll notice you can easily drop the colon and the sentence sounds even better. The following sentence shows when the dramatic use of a colon is effective. *The invasion was threatened by the weather: blowing winds, fierce rain and rough seas.* One final point: Capitalize the first word after a colon only if it starts a complete sentence.

C. Semicolons

If you're making a second point in your sentence, a semicolon can take the place of an omitted coordinating conjunction. *The package was due last week; it arrived today.* Semicolons are also used to separate elements of a series when individual segments contain material that also must be set off by commas. *He leaves a son, John Smith of Leavenworth, Kan.; a daughter, Mary Smith Sanders of New York City; and a sister, Martha Smith of Omaha, Neb.* Note the semicolon is used before the final *and* in this type of series.

PART 2: TITLES

A. Courtesy Titles

In general, do not use the courtesy titles *Miss, Mr., Mrs.* or *Ms.* on first reference. On second reference, use only last names unless people in the story have the same last name. Generally, if they are within the same family, most publications use only first names. If they don't belong to the same family, both first and last names are generally used.

B. Job Titles

1. Capitalization. Formal titles that could be used to address a person are capitalized when they appear before an individual's name. Thus, titles such as *professor, president, sergeant* and *doctor* are capitalized. But job descriptions are not capitalized: *singer George Jones, farmer Lance Smith* or *astronaut Buzz Aldrin. Secretary of State George Marshall* is upper case but *senior secretary/stenographer Miles Kelly* is not capitalized.

2. Abbreviations. When used before a full name outside direct quotations, abbreviate courtesy titles such as *Mr., Mrs., Sen., Gov.* and *the Rev.* (note it is always *"the" Rev.*) as well as military and police titles such as *Pfc., Sgt., 1st Lt.,* and *Gen.* If the name is being used in direct quotations, spell out all except *Dr., Mr., Mrs.* and *Ms. "Sergeant Cameron and Dr. Smith were in the burning building,"* said Sgt. David Kelly.

3. Capitalization. The title is spelled out and is written in lower case if it appears alone or after a name, or if it is separated from the name by a comma. Here are three examples that illustrate the rule: *He saw A.F. Hill's president, Carrie Sweeny, at the grocery store. He saw A.F. Hill President Carrie Sweeny at the gro-*

cery store. He saw Carrie Sweeny, president of A.F. Hill, at the grocery. Do not repeat a title the second time or subsequent times when you use a name. On second reference, *Sgt. Sam Hill* would be called *Hill.*

C. Compositions

Capitalize the principal words in the titles of books, movies, operas, plays, poems, songs, television programs, lectures, speeches and works of art. Put quotation marks around the names of such works. Do not underline the titles of any of these works.

D. Periodicals

Capitalize magazine and newspaper names, but do not underline or place in quotes. Observe the periodical's preferred usage. Lowercase *magazine* or *newspaper* if it is not a part of the publication's formal title and capitalize *the* if it is part of the title: *The New Republic magazine.* If a newspaper's location is needed but is not part of the official name, enclose the state in parentheses. *The Chillicothe (Mo.) Constitution Tribune.*

E. Reference Materials

Capitalize, but do not use quotation marks around books such as almanacs, directories, dictionaries, handbooks and encyclopedias that are primarily reference manuals.

PART 3: NUMERALS

Generally, spell out whole numbers below 10 and use figures for 10 and above. However, there are notable exceptions. Figures are used for all ages, dates, dimensions, percentages, speeds and times. *The boy, only 9 years old, has a 5 percent chance of survival.* In a series, apply the appropriate guidelines. *The millionaire gave the three 8-year-old girls six dogs, 13 cats and 10 three-room houses.* Spell out all numbers, except for a calendar year, if they appear at the beginning of a sentence.

A. Money

For dollars, use figures and the $ sign in all except casual references or amounts without a figure. *The book cost $4. Dad, please give me a dollar.* Spell out and lowercase the word *cents* for amounts less than a dollar. *The gum cost 7 cents.*

B. Percentages

Always use figures: *1 percent*, and use decimals, not fractions: *2.5 percent.* For amounts less than 1 percent, precede the decimal point with a zero. The word *percent* should be spelled out. Repeat *percent* with each individual figure: *He said 10 percent to 30 percent of the electorate may not vote.*

C. Fractions

Spell out amounts less than one in prose, using hyphens between the words: *two-thirds, seven-sixteenths*, and so forth. For precise amounts larger than one, convert to decimals whenever it is practical. Fractions are preferred, however, in stories about stocks and are used exclusively in tabular material.

D. Million/billion

For large numbers, use only two decimals and the words *million* or *billion: 246.32 million Americans, $5.46 billion* instead of *246,323,325 Americans* or *$5,459,430*. Decimals are preferred where practical.

E. Ages

Use figures for all ages. Ages expressed as compound adjectives before a noun use hyphens: *A 5-year-old boy*, but *the boy is 5 years old. The woman is in her 30s and has a 2-month-old daughter.*

F. Dimensions

Use figures and spell out inches, feet, yards, and the like. Hyphenate adjectival forms before nouns. *He is 5 feet 6 inches tall* (no commas). *The 6-foot-2-inch man. He bought a 9-by-12 rug. The rug is 9 feet by 12 feet.*

G. Scores

Use figures exclusively for scores, placing a hyphen between the totals of the winning and losing teams: *The Reds defeated the Red Sox 4-3. The Giants scored a 12-6 victory over the Cardinals.* But remember to distinguish between scores and actions within a game. *She fired a 5-under-par 67. She was four shots off the lead. He made seven field goals to lead his team to a 21-7 victory.*

PART 4: ABBREVIATIONS

Because space is at a premium in most print writing, professional writing style sanctions many abbreviations.

A. States

Spell out the names of all states when they stand alone in textual material. Abbreviate the names of most states when they appear in conjunction with the name of a city, town, village or military base in datelines and in text. Place one comma between the city and the state and another comma after the state: *He is grateful to*

Claremont, Calif., and all the citizens of Nevada. All states with the exception of *Alaska, Hawaii, Idaho, Iowa, Maine, Ohio, Texas* and *Utah* are abbreviated. Note the difference between postal abbreviations (*OK* and *MO*) and Associated Press usage (*Okla.* and *Mo.*). The state abbreviations are as follows: *Ala., Ariz., Ark., Calif., Colo., Conn., Del., Fla., Ga., Ill., Ind., Kan., Ky., La., Md., Mass., Mich., Minn., Miss., Mo., Mont., Neb., Nev., N.H., N.J., N.Y., N.C., N.D., Okla., Ore., Pa., R.I., S.C., S.D., Tenn., Vt., Va., Wash., W. Va., Wis.* and *Wyo.*

B. Acronyms

Although it's acceptable to use the initials of organizations and government agencies that are widely recognized, names not commonly before the public should not be reduced to acronyms solely to save a few words. Do not follow the first mention of an organization's full name with an acronym in parentheses. If an abbreviation would not be clear on second reference without this arrangement, do not use it.

C. Addresses

Use figures for all street addresses. Spell out all street names except *Ave., Blvd.* and *St.* in all usages. Use the above abbreviations and compass (e.g., *south*) abbreviations only with a numbered address. Examples: *He lives on South Korbel Avenue. He lives at 4 S. Korbel Ave.* Spell out and capitalize *First* through *Ninth* when used as street names; use figures with two letters for *10th* and above: *15 E. Fifth St., 12344 W. 112th Road.*

D. Companies

Abbreviate and capitalize *company, corporation, limited, incorporated* and *brothers* if a business uses these words at the end of its proper name: *Ford Motor Co.* but the *Corporation for Public Broadcasting*. Do not capitalize or abbreviate when used alone.

E. U.S./U.N.

Spell out *United States* and *United Nations* when used as nouns. *U.S.* and *U.N.* are permissible when used as adjectives. Examples: *He lives in the United States. She's a U.N. delegate.*

F. Do Not Abbreviate

The following are not abbreviated: days of the week; *president, association, professor, superintendent, assistant* and *district*. Do not replace *and* in text with the *ampersand (&)*.

PART 5: CAPITALIZATION

Professional writing attempts to be as unpretentious as possible. Since we're trying to avoid writing like William Wordsworth, don't capitalize words like *truth*, *beauty*, *freedom* and *justice*. Capitalize a word only if you can justify it within the context of the following rules.

A. Proper Names

Capitalize proper names or proper nouns that constitute the unique identification for a specific person, place or thing, such as *Alice*, *Michigan Avenue*, *Boston*, *Indiana Power Co.*, *Columbia River*. But if a common noun is part of a proper name, lowercase those common nouns when they stand alone in later references: *the avenue*, *the power company*, *the river*. Lowercase the common noun elements of names in all plural uses: *the Democratic and Republican parties*, *lakes Erie and Ontario*.

B. Government

Always lowercase broad references to government: *the federal government*, *the administration*, *the presidency*, *the state government*, *the city government*. But capitalize *city*, *county*, *state* and *federal* as well as *city council*, *legislature* and *assembly* when part of a formal name: *Federal Trade Commission*, *Indiana General Assembly*. Capitalize *Army*, *Navy* and all other branches of the U.S. military, even when standing alone. However, lowercase references to other nations' military forces: *the French army*. Capitalize all references to the *U.S. Congress* and the *U.S. Constitution*, even if they appear without the U.S. modifier. Lowercase *congressional* and *constitutional* unless they are part of a proper name.

C. Buildings

Capitalize *capitol* when referring to the buildings where the legislative branches of state governments or the federal government meet. Remember that *capitol* refers only to a building. The city in which government resides is the *capital*. Capitalize proper names of buildings, including the word *building* if it is an integral part of the proper name: *the Empire State Building*. Capitalize the names of specially designated rooms: *Blue Room*, *Lincoln Room*, *Oval Office*, *Persian Room*. Capitalize *room* when used with a figure: *Room 7*.

D. Historic or Public Events

Capitalize historic events and periods (*the Great Depression*, *Prohibition*), holidays (*Thanksgiving*, *Christmas Eve*, *Father's Day*), and wars (*World War II*, *the War of 1812*). An apostrophe precedes the numbers in designating a decade: *the Roaring '20s*, not *the Roaring 20's*.

E. Directions/Regions

In general, lowercase *north, southeast, northern*, and so forth when they indicate a compass direction. However, capitalize these words when they designate geographical regions. *The train rolled south along the East Coast. Although she was from western Texas, she had a Northern accent. Leaders of Eastern Europe met with South Pacific executives in eastern Saudi Arabia.*

F. Do Not Capitalize

Do not capitalize seasons of the year (*spring, summer, fall, winter*) or years in school (*freshman, sophomore*, etc.). Do not capitalize *priest* in any usage. Capitalize *pope, president* and all other formal titles only when they directly precede the person's name. *Pope John Paul II spoke to the crowd. The pope went inside the building.*

PART 6: TIME

A. Dates

Use *Monday, Tuesday*, and so forth for days of the week within seven days before or after the current date. Use the month and a figure for dates beyond this range. Do not use *st, nd, rd*, or *th* after the date. Many public relations practitioners include both the day of the week and a month and figure: *Monday, June 14.*

B. Time

Use a colon to separate hours from minutes. Lowercase *a.m.* and *p.m.* and use periods: *2:17 p.m.* Use figures except for *noon* and *midnight.* Do not put a *12* in front of them. Avoid redundancies such as *8 a.m. Tuesday morning.* If a period starts precisely on the hour, the hyphen and two zeros are not necessary: It's *7 p.m.*, not *7:00 p.m.*

C. Months

Capitalize the names of all months in all uses. When a month is used with a specific date, abbreviate only the following months: *Jan., Feb., Aug., Sept., Oct., Nov.* and *Dec.* Spell out when using alone, or with a year alone. When a phrase lists only a month and a year, do not separate the year with commas. When a phrase refers to a month, day and year, set off the year with commas. Examples: *August 1991 was the state's hottest month. Jan. 15, 1961, was her birth date. The exhibit will open March 15 in the Flinen Museum.*

SELF-QUIZ ON AP STYLEBOOK PART 1: PUNCTUATION

May 19, 1996

FOR IMMEDIATE RELEASE

Contact: _____

Office Phone: 555-1234

NEIGHBORHOOD WATCH MAY
HAVE SOLVED VANDALISM CASE

The city's worst vandalism spree which resulted in over 100 broken lawn statues may have been stopped when three men were arrested after a tip to the Louisville Police's Neighborhood Watch program.

The three men: Calvin Thomas Cronston, 18 of 3,486 E. Calgary Pike; Samuel Jay Dallas, 19, of 708 Jackson Lane and Jacob Lee Penner, 18 of Clarksville, Ind. were arrested about midnight on Thursday, May 18, after Deer Park residents reported to police that four plaster dogs and two stone jockeys had been broken by gunfire. One of the callers gave a detailed description of the car.

When the three youths were arrested, police found a .22-caliber rifle, a .32-caliber pistol, a pellet gun, and 2100 rounds of ammunition in Penner's car. All three men were charged with 87 felony vandalism counts.

Deer Park residents have reported nearly 100 broken lawn ornaments since June. "We didn't really care about the statues but we were really fearful that a child was going to accidentally get in the way of these gun-happy nuts" said Deer Park resident Carlin Sweet.

Detective Gene Hill said the Louisville Police were, "real happy to get these people off the streets".

"The police are so pleased the Neighborhood Watch program continues to be effective in helping us fight crime," Hill said. "I'm familiar with programs in Cincinnati Ohio and in Memphis, Tenn. and I don't know any of them as effective as the one we have in Louisville. This proves once again that if we work together we can stop crime."

-30-

SELF-QUIZ ON AP STYLEBOOK PART 2: TITLES

Nov. 12, 199__   Contact: _____

FOR IMMEDIATE RELEASE   Office phone: 555-1234

SOUTH AFRICAN POLITICS
FOCUS OF CONFERENCE

Former South African prime minister P.W. Botha and Rev. Desmond Tutu will be among political figures from four continents who will be highlighted speakers at the second annual Vital Issues Conference Dec. 5. The topic of the conference, sponsored by the National People's Rights Organization and local Businesswoman Mrs. Joyce Dunne, will be Moral Response in South Africa: A Black American Perspective.

The opening session will feature speeches by Mr. Botha; "Time Magazine" editor Grant Fowler; and Eleanor Kalish, author of the book, Storm Over Southern Africa.

The conference's second session will concern South African human rights issues, including a panel discussion by four men who were illegally detained for six months in 1991 by South African police.

The next session will explore law enforcement issues, and will include a showing of The Naked Fist, a film about Soweto Township Police Capt. Corza Cantow. Capt. Cantow has been implicated by the Amnesty International human rights group in the kidnapping and deaths of at least 40 people involved in civil rights demonstrations. Tutu will introduce the film.

The final session will be devoted to the international response to South African unrest, with speeches by Al Gore, Vice President of the United States, and University of Johannesburg professor Kalibar Koweta. Afterward, there will be a presentation of the conference's proceedings to editors of "The New World Political Dictionary," which will issue a special volume on the conference in next year's edition.

-30-

SELF-QUIZ ON AP STYLEBOOK PART 3: NUMERALS

Aug. 10, 199__   Contact: _____

FOR IMMEDIATE RELEASE   Office phone: 555-1234

HELTON LEADS TEAM
TO YOUTH SOCCER TITLE

Tiny Jim Helton scored 7 goals to lead the Bloomfield Beanpoles to an eleven to seven win over the Lexington Lizards in the final game of the Missinois Youth Soccer League Saturday.

The three foot seven inch Helton scored 5 of his goals with free kicks that snaked past Lizard goalie Bruce McComb for scores. "I guess the 99¢ my dad spent for that practice goal really helped me tonight," said Helton, who is nine years old.

Helton said his occasional workouts with St. Louis Spirits forward George Krenschicki, who is 5 feet, 4 inches tall, have helped his confidence. "When we first started practicing a lot of people would stop and stare at these two short people playing," Helton said. "But since George has proven he can play pro ball, I don't let my being short bother me any more."

Helton may be part of a dynasty in the 21st century if he follows his early plans to enter Bardstown's Holy Heart High School for his freshman year in 2001. Holy Heart's soccer team holds a national record for losing only four percent of its contests in the last ten years.

Holy Heart soccer coach Kelly Phillips is excited at the prospect. "Jim only came to about 1/3 of our practices this season," Phillips said. "But if I got five cents for every goal he scored on our high school boys, I'd be rich. He's the kind of player a coach needs if he wants to make two million dollars a year coaching."

The championship game was the first played in Callam Stadium, the county's new $1,173,342 arena. 12 members of the city council who had voted to build the stadium were honored in ceremonies before the game.

-30-

SELF-QUIZ ON AP STYLEBOOK PART 4: ABBREVIATIONS

April 18, 199__   Contact: _____

FOR IMMEDIATE RELEASE   Office phone: 555-1234

CALIFORNIA SENATOR
GETS ILLEGAL CONTRIBUTIONS

California Sen. Neil Edleniot received nearly $170,000 in illegal campaign contributions from a single businessman, according to an investigation by People Concerned by Political Corruption (PCPC).

Despite laws limiting individual campaign contributions to $2,000, the United States senator received $168,000 from California business owner Aris Braldow, the watchdog group has discovered. The organization has turned over its evidence to the FBI.

According to the organization's evidence, Braldow's money snaked all through the U.S. as he tried to stay under the $2,000 limit for political contributions. The investigation found that Braldow funneled his contributions to Edleniot through three companies and 84 individuals in five states, who claimed they contributed the money to the senator.

Braldow's primary company, the Korforn Raisin Corporation of Barstow, CA, distributed $112,000 to two other Braldow-controlled firms, Reform Company of Colorado, located in Denver, and Braldow Brothers, Incorporated, based in McNaughton, Michigan. Each of the three companies then paid $56,000 to Braldow's daughter, Jeanne Benson, in Wichita, Kansas. Jeanne Benson deposited the $168,000 in her bank account on Tuesday, Aug. 14.

On Wed., Aug. 15, Edleniot received $2,000 from each of 84 individuals who listed addresses in Hawaii, Maine, Texas, Ohio and Michigan. But each $2,000 contribution had been wired from Wichita, and from one single address: 16 North Anderson Ln. Braldow's daughter lived at that address on Aug. 14.

(more)

ILLEGAL CONTRIBUTIONS
page 2

Braldow and his daughter would not comment on the investigation. Edleniot and his office staff did not return repeated phone calls from the citizens' organization. The Los Angeles division of the FBI is continuing the investigation.

The People Concerned by Political Corruption is a nonprofit organization located in Orono, Maine. It is funded by contributions from individuals and is not affiliated with any political party or other group.

-30-

SELF-QUIZ ON AP STYLEBOOK PART 5: CAPITALIZATION

Jan. 19, 199___
FOR IMMEDIATE RELEASE

Contact: _____
Office phone: 555-1234

WASHINGTON PARADE
HONORS CONSTITUTION

Bill Clinton and members of his Presidential Administration will be among the celebrities appearing in a Washington parade honoring the Constitution's 210th birthday.

The March 23 parade will attract bands and floats from throughout the south and midwest for the City's world-famous Cherry Blossom Festival, which begins during the first week of Spring each year. The parade units will assemble by the treasury building near the Potomac River, then travel east along the River until reaching the Capitol.

There the parade will be joined by Congressional leaders from the Democratic and Republican Parties, who will lead the procession past the Washington city hall and on to 1600 Pennsylvania Ave. Once at the White House, the president will present a medal to the parade's grand marshal, army Gen. Norman Schwartzkopf, in a private ceremony in the oval office.

"This celebration of the freedoms gained from the constitution is going to be the biggest thing the capital city has seen since prohibition was lifted," said Charles Burke, the president of Freedom 1787, the organization sponsoring the parade.

Freedom 1787 is a nonprofit organization founded in 1972 to direct the 200th anniversary of the documents upon which the United States' Federal system of government was built. In addition to his duties with the Freedom 1787 organization, Burke is director of the federal election commission.

–30–

SELF-QUIZ ON AP STYLEBOOK PART 6: TIME

June 26, 199__   Contact: _____

FOR IMMEDIATE RELEASE   Office phone: 555-1234

DAVIESS WOMEN GET
FREE CANCER SCREENINGS

Daviess County women who want to protect themselves from breast cancer can get a free breast cancer examination in their own neighborhoods during the next three weeks.

Beginning Jul. 17th, the Daviess County Health Department will sponsor a countywide visit by the state's mobile mammography van as part of its health awareness campaign.

The mobile mammography unit is a large van that contains high-technology equipment designed to detect breast cancer in its earliest stages. If a breast tumor is found early, 95 percent of all patients survive for five years or more. The van, which was placed in service in February, 1989, is staffed by two doctors and four nurses. It has direct communication links to diagnostic computers at the state university's medical center.

The mobile mammography van's Daviess County schedule is as follows: July 17th, Galt Community Center; July 20, Gilman City High School; July 27, Lexington City Hall; August 2nd, Kingston Public Library; and August 7th, Chula Courthouse. Screenings will be conducted at each site between 9:00 A.M. and 12 noon each morning.

The mobile mammography van is returning two years after its last successful visit to Daviess County, when nearly 400 women were screened for breast cancer. On one day during that tour, January 23, 1994 93 women were examined for the early stages of breast cancer.

For more information or to schedule an appointment, call the Daviess County Health Department at 555-1234.

-30-

Applications Workbook Section B

Writing Diagnostic Exercises

The following sections are not meant to take the place of formal instruction in grammar or usage, nor can they make a good writer out of a lousy writer.

Instead, this section is meant to help individual students polish certain weak elements in their writing. It's designed to provide quick instruction in specific areas that often trouble student writers. The parts are designed so that your instructor can assign specific ones to combat particular problems. In other situations, you may recognize particular elements in your writing you want to polish. Others may want to complete each section to review basic writing principles.

PART 1: APOSTROPHES

Many students have difficulty distinguishing situations in which they should use an apostrophe. Apostrophes have three basic uses. They are used to take the place of missing letters in a contraction: *He'll stop the ne'er do well*; to indicate possession: *It was Joe's dog*; and to form the plurals of single letters: *Mind your p's and q's. He got two A's and two B's.* Although the third rule is quite simple, there are more complications in dealing with contractions and possessives. Let's look at each individually.

A contraction uses an apostrophe to indicate that a word or figure is missing. Thus, *don't* is the contraction for *do not*, *I'll* is the contraction for *I will*, and *'73* is the contraction for *1973*. Also remember that if there aren't any letters or figures missing, you don't use an apostrophe: *the 1950s, the Roaring '20s*.

Although this sounds like a simple rule, the field is fraught with danger. Let's start with simple elements. *Won't* is the contraction for *will not*, whereas *I'd* could be the contraction for *I had* or *I would*. In addition to these problems, there are too many instances in which a contraction can be confused with a possessive. For instance, *it's* is the contraction of *it is*, but many people confuse it with the possessive *its*.

As we've seen, apostrophes are also used to indicate possession: *Susan's courage, the employee's injury, chemistry's principles*. The rules you learned in grade school still apply: Just add apostrophe-S to a noun to make it possessive. This rule also applies when the word ends in a double S: *the witness's testimony*. When a plural noun ends in an S, you generally add an apostrophe but no S: *the cities' mayors*.

Although other style guides recommend omitting the S after the apostrophe for possessives ending with S sounds like *ce*, *x* and *z*, Associated Press style doesn't confuse the writer with those exceptions.

Remember that most pronouns have their own possessive forms and don't require apostrophes: *yours* and not *your's*, *hers* and not *her's*. The real problem with possessives comes in distinguishing possessives from similar sounding contractions. Is it *it's* or *its*, *your* or *you're*, *they're* or *their* (or perhaps *there*), *who's* or *whose*? The first rule is that the pronouns *its*, *his*, *her*, *ours*, *theirs*, *yours* and *oneself* never take an apostrophe, but other pronouns like *another's*, *anyone's* and *others'* do include apostrophes.

The only way to correct these mistakes is to read the sentence and insert the uncontracted word where the contraction stands: *They are game is at 2 p.m. It is dividend is bigger.* These sentences obviously need the possessives *their* and *its*, respectively.

EXERCISES

Rewrite the following sentences, using apostrophes correctly.

a. Its our friends home that she bought three years ago.

_____

b. Hes the class's president for 92.

_____

c. Whose got the most As among the fraternity's members?

_____

d. Its friends who'll be important to you're lifestyle in the 1990's.

_____

e. Until the final minute it was anyone's game, but now the trophy is our's.

_____

PART 2: DANGLING MODIFIERS

It's important to eliminate dangling modifiers from your writing, because the ridicule and humiliation from which you'll suffer if you have dangling modifiers is perhaps unequaled by any other mistake. Beyond that personal reason, your readers will likely be confused if your writing is filled with dangling modifiers.

Here's an example of a dangling modifier and a demonstration of its ability to confound your readers. *The burglar was arrested by county police after she had been stabbed in a marshy, undeveloped area by her accomplice.* In this sentence, it appears the woman was stabbed in some marshy, undeveloped part of her body. I don't think that's what the writer intended to say.

The sentence would be much clearer if related information were grouped together within it. Thus: *The burglar was stabbed by her accomplice and then arrested by county police in a marshy, undeveloped area.* Or: *After escaping into a marshy, undeveloped area, the burglar was stabbed by her accomplice and then arrested by county police.*

The general principle in curing the tendency to write dangling modifiers: You need to make sure you keep related information together within the sentence. Often a dangling modifier occurs because a prepositional phrase is placed in the wrong position within a sentence. *Because of his body odor, the principal sent the student home.* Although it's difficult to tell whether the principal was irritable because he hadn't had time to take a shower that morning, it's unlikely that's the intended meaning. By repositioning the modifier, we can make the principal seem a bit more worthy to be passing along our society's standards of cleanliness: *The principal sent the student home because of his body odor.*

The other major cause of a dangling modifier occurs when the thing a modifier is supposed to modify isn't even in the sentence: *After studying for 14 hours, the test was postponed.* It's obvious the test wasn't studying for 14 hours, but there is nothing else the phrase could be modifying. *With our tranquilizer gun poised, the lion crept toward us.* The obvious question is how the writer could have been so careless as to let the lion get his tranquilizer gun in the first place?

In both of these instances, you can cure the dangling modifier by simply adding a referent the modifier can modify. *After I had studied for 14 hours, the test was canceled. With our tranquilizer gun poised, we watched as the lion crept toward us.*

Sometimes, the problem occurs because the writer hasn't precisely defined the modifier: *Charging toward the basket for a last-second shot, the player's head crashed into the rim.* In this example, we've got a decapitated head performing round ball heroics. It's an impressive show of character and tenacity from the skull in question, but it's probably not what the writer meant. If you define the modifier precisely, you can cure this particular problem. *As the player charged toward the basket for a last-second shot, his head crashed into the rim.*

EXERCISES

Rewrite the following sentences, eliminating the dangling modifier or misplaced phrase.

a. Looking over her shoulder, the angry hog was chasing Denise.

_____

b. I shot an elephant in my pajamas.

_____

c. After turning in the assignment late, the professor yelled at me.

_____

d. Having only a month to live, the orphanage's children presented poor little Tammy with her Christmas presents early.

_____

e. After playing the stock market for six months, the firm's bank account was empty.

_____

PART 3: FRAGMENTARY SENTENCES

This section discusses one of the most serious mechanical problems a writer can have. Even one sentence fragment in a piece can blight your reputation as a professional writer. Eliminating these horrors from your writing is a basic step in your progression as a writer. Luckily, the problem is easily distinguishable and easily correctable.

In identifying a sentence fragment, there's one important principle to remember. Don't think that a sentence fragment is merely a grouping of words that isn't long enough. Just adding words won't change a fragment into a sentence. A sentence fragment can be a single word, a phrase or a long, long clause. What does a sentence have that a fragment doesn't? A fragment sometimes lacks a subject or sometimes a predicate. Sometimes a fragment contains a subject and a predicate, but doesn't create a complete thought.

There's a two-part test to determine if a group of words is a complete sentence: (1) Does the sentence contain a subject and a verb? and (2) Does the group of words make sense when it stands by itself? Let's look at some examples of sentence fragments: *I found it. The body of a 3-year-old, blond, blue-eyed boy.* The first group of words is a complete sentence, but even though the second sentence is much longer, it never includes a verb. Read in isolation, the second grouping doesn't make any sense. By both tests, it is not a sentence.

Let's look at another example. *I forgot the ingredients for my cake. Although*

I had gone to the tiny grocery store to get flour and sugar. In the second grouping of words, there is a word that appears to be a subject (*I*) and words that appear to be verbs (*had gone*). It passes the first test for a complete sentence.

However, this sentence fragment doesn't state a complete thought when read in isolation. That's because it is a dependent clause and depends on an independent clause to make its meaning clear. Dependent clauses can be recognized because they begin with a subordinating conjunction that qualifies the information that follows. Words such as *because, even though, since, during* and *whatever* are subordinating conjunctions. Dependent clauses are also introduced by relative pronouns such as *who, which* and *that*.

Here are some more examples of dependent clauses that are sentence fragments: *Who graduated from college. When he was good. That saw the emergence of the working class from poverty.*

How do you correct a sentence fragment? If the fragment is a dependent clause, it's very simple. Simply combine the dependent clause with an independent clause to make a complex sentence. Here's how to correct the sentence about the cake: *I forgot the ingredients for my cake, even though I had gone to the tiny grocery store to get flour and sugar.*

In some instances, it may be necessary to make minor modifications to rearrange or combine the sentence elements. Let's look at this example again: *I found it. The body of a 3-year-old, blond, blue-eyed boy.* By replacing *it* with its exact referent, we make a complete sentence: *I found the body of a 3-year-old, blond, blue-eyed boy.*

EXERCISES

Rewrite the following sentence fragments.

a. When pigs fly and buttercups dance. That's when John will be welcome in this house.

_____

b. I froze. Walking through the rain and sleet and snow.

_____

c. Although there was a cat in the tree. John did nothing.

_____

d. When I went through the gate and into the woods to see the birds. That's when it became apparent there had been an accident.

_____

e. There. Over the hilltop just to the right of the building. Dixie saw the plane.

_____

PART 4: PARALLEL STRUCTURES

Many students' writing suffers from a lack of parallelism, yet they often don't even know that such a prose transgression exists. Here's the principle: All sentences that contain a coordinating conjunction (like *and, but, or, nor, so, for* and *yet*) must have the same grammatical structure on each side of the coordinating conjunction. If the sentence doesn't, it suffers from a lack of parallelism.

For instance, there's a lack of parallelism in the following sentence: *He is wanting water and to eat excessive amounts of cheese.* You cure it by eliminating the infinitive *to eat* after the conjunction. That gets the same grammatical structure on each side of the coordinating conjunction: *He is wanting water and excessive amounts of cheese.* Or: *He is wanting to drink water and eat excessive amounts of cheese.* Or: *He wants to drink water and eat excessive amounts of cheese.*

However, the rule against creating a nonparallel structure doesn't come from the same source as the rule against comparing apples and oranges. The two things on each side of a coordinating conjunction don't have to be like each other. It's just fine to say: *I'm comparing apples, oranges and bright chartreuse bulldozers.* You do have to have the same structure on each side, however. Thus, it's not just fine to write: *I'm comparing apples, oranges and two pears are in the basket.*

So, parallelism is merely being sure that you have the same structure on each side of the conjunction. There are a lot of ways you can violate this rule. For instance, a lack of parallelism can occur in a series. *He hates potatoes, cheap wine and going to restaurants.* You can cure this by establishing a consistent verb pattern in each element of the series: *He hates eating potatoes, drinking cheap wine and going to restaurants.* Depending on your intended meaning, this could also be correct: *He hates potatoes, cheap wine and restaurants.*

Sometimes a lack of parallelism occurs when a writer mixes different types of verbals. That was the problem in the first example. The clause in front of the conjunction was a gerund (*wanting*) and the phrase after the conjunction began with an infinitive (*to drink*). Again, you fix it by getting the same form on both sides of the conjunction.

Another type of parallelism mistake is when a clause suddenly appears in the midst of what the reader thought was a list. *The organizational communication text emphasized fairness, consistency and that managers need to listen to workers.* Again, the solution is to get the same structure on each side of the conjunction: *The organizational communication text emphasized that managers need to practice fairness, promote consistency and develop good listening skills.*

By being conscious of parallel structures in your writing, you're giving your readers an orderly sequence of information. That means they don't have to spend any extra effort translating your messy prose into a coherent thought.

EXERCISES

Rewrite the following sentences to correct the lack of parallelism.

a. He hates pitting avocados, squeezing oranges and bananas.

_____

b. Either tell your teacher how much you like this course or how you could drop it.

_____

c. The actor had blue eyes, a winning smile and was well-built.

_____

d. The city's alternatives are to shut down the polluting incinerators or finding a cleaner technology.

_____

e. The team's goals were improved play, increased attendance and that a new stadium would be built.

_____

PART 5: PASSIVE VOICE

Despite what many of my English composition friends claim, the passive voice isn't Satan manifesting himself in prose. The passive voice is an effective strategy when what is being done is more important than who is doing it. That doesn't happen very often, but the exceptions to that rule can create striking and effective sentences.

Let's review what passive voice is. A sentence can be written in either active voice or passive voice. In an active voice sentence, the subject of the sentence acts upon something else. A passive voice sentence occurs when the object of a sentence appears to be acting upon the subject. Thus, *The football was kicked by John* is a passive sentence. *John kicked the football* is active.

It's relatively easy to spot a passive sentence. Your first warning sign is when you see verb forms of "*to be,*" like *am, are, is, was, were* and *been*. Once you see those verb forms, examine the sentence to determine if the subject of the sentence was performing an action. For instance, *The car was moving* is active but *John was pushed* is passive.

Passive sentences can make the reader's job much more difficult. If your sentence reads: *The unemployment law so important to our suffering workers will be written by Sen. Taknas*, the reader must reconstruct the sentence to find who was doing what to whom.

The complex structure can sometimes confuse not only the reader, but also the writer, and even make him or her forget to put an actor into the sentence. Look at this sentence: *It was evident the software program was the best on the market.* Who or what made that judgment? Many such holes in your argumentation sequence will make your story fall apart.

Finally, passive sentences tend to be flabby, because a prepositional phrase usually follows the passive verb. That makes the sentence longer and weakens the sentence still further.

In most sentences, the subject is acting upon an object, so the active voice is the logical choice. *The corporation sold its subsidiaries. The opera company will move into its new auditorium.* In each of these cases, the subject will draw more readers than the object, so it deserves its No. 1 position within the sentence. In addition, the passive voice sentence sounds ridiculous: *The auditorium will be moved into by the opera company.*

But remember that in the receiver-centered writing system, there are situations in which your readers may identify more with the fate of a sentence's put-upon object than with the powerful actor. These active and passive versions of the same sentence illustrate my point. *A Senate revenue bill introduced Tuesday will hit homeowners with higher taxes. Homeowners would be hit with higher taxes in a Senate bill introduced Tuesday.* In the second, passive version, the message's most important audience and the effects it will suffer are placed in the No. 1 position within the sentence. That helps draw an audience and immediately communicates its involvement in the issue.

Converting a passive sentence into an active sentence is quite easy. Find the sentence's verb, then determine who is performing the action. Put the actor into the sentence's subject position. In the sentence *Blue gowns will be worn by all graduates*, the verb is *will be worn* and the actor is *graduates*. After putting the actor in the subject position, this active voice sentence results: *All graduates will wear blue gowns.*

In some sentences in which the passive voice seems to be the logical construction, it's possible to recast the sentence in the active voice by emphasizing an action the object will take as a result of the process. The sentence that we decided earlier was acceptable as a passive sentence, *Homeowners would be hit with higher taxes in a Senate bill introduced Tuesday*, can be converted into an active voice sentence while retaining homeowners in the No. 1 position. What action will the homeowners perform that is linked with the Senate's action? By changing the verb to one emphasizing the homeowners' actions, the sentence becomes active: *Homeowners will pay higher taxes if a Senate bill introduced Tuesday becomes law.*

EXERCISES

Convert the following sentences into active voice sentences.

a. The new safety standards were approved by the Industrial Standards Board.

b. A woman was killed Tuesday by former Mayor John A. Killebrew.

_____

c. That milk was purchased last week by me.

_____

d. The people most affected by the legislature's decision will be uninsured motorists.

_____

e. Four former congressmen will receive awards given by a citizen's panel.

_____

The following sentences are taken from an employee publication. Are they active or passive? If they are passive, change them to active. Would the active or passive voice be more effective in drawing an audience into the piece?

f. The 42 employees contributed $6,516 to the charity.

Active or passive?

_____

More effective as passive? Yes/no.

Why?

_____

g. The firm's vice president imposed an unpaid suspension on each of the striking workers.

Active or passive?

_____

More effective as passive? Yes/no.

Why?

_____

h. The company was the recipient of a $6 million federal contract.

Active or passive?

_____

More effective as passive? Yes/no.

Why?

_____

i. Company officials were still negotiating as this issue went to press.

Active or passive?

———————

More effective as passive? Yes/no.

Why?

———————————————————————————————————

j. Employees rated in the top 10 percent will receive a $500 bonus.

Active or passive?

———————

More effective as passive? Yes/no.

Why?

———————————————————————————————————

k. The company's main generating unit was destroyed by lightning.

Active or passive?

———————

More effective as passive? Yes/no.

Why?

———————————————————————————————————

l. It was decided that employees working overtime would receive extra pay each week.

Active or passive?

———————

More effective as passive? Yes/no.

Why?

———————————————————————————————————

PART 6: REDUNDANCY

Obviously, if you are trying to be an efficient, effective communicator, one of the worst things you can do is to make your receiver read the same thing twice. That's exactly what redundancy forces your readers to do. The following points summarize some of the more common causes of redundancy in student writing.

Be critical of prepositional phrases. Examine every prepositional phrase you write to determine if it is really needed. Prepositions are words that indicate the relationship between words in the sentence. That relationship might be position or direction, such as *with, on, at, aboard, under, toward* and *around*. Sometimes prepositions imply possession (*of, from, among*) or a logical relationship (*because of, concerning, in spite of, contrary to*). A prepositional phrase is the preposition plus its object.

Prepositions such as *after, below* and *toward* are often precise and productive in sentences. However, prepositions such as *from, by* and *of* can often be replaced by a possessive. The routine is to transpose the object of the preposition in front of the referent and then switch the object into a possessive form. For instance, *the cat of Anjanette* becomes *Anjanette's cat.*

Many prepositions that imply logical relationships require more words to say less. It's usually a wise choice to eliminate compound prepositions such as *with reference to, on account of* and *in consequence of. Because* is generally a better substitute.

Watch out for adverbs. Words that often introduce prepositional phrases, such as *up, off* and *out*, sometimes become adverbs. Unfortunately, they have the same regrettable consequences on tight writing whether they are adverbs or prepositions. Forms such as *rise up, round off* or *find out* are redundant, taking the place of *rise, round* and *find.*

Select nouns and verbs carefully. Writers also need to be aware how verb choice can make their prose leaner and better. As I stated earlier in this section, active voice sentences are usually more powerful and are invariably shorter than sentences written in the passive voice.

A more unforgivable redundancy problem stemming from verb use is when a strong verb has mutated into a pudgy noun. For instance, words that end in *sion, tion* and *ing* are often powerful verbs that have been fattened into noun forms. *He will take it under consideration* can be energized by converting *consideration* into a verb: *He will consider it. The store opening was Thursday* is stated more efficiently as *The store opened Thursday.*

Another clue that a verb has been changed into a noun is when *occur* or *happen* appears in a sentence. Both words communicate little action. *The man's hanging occurred Nov. 17, 1884* is better stated *The man was hanged Nov. 17, 1884.*

Carefully choosing your verbs can also eliminate unnecessary adjectives and adverbs. In their book *When Words Collide*, Kessler and McDonald discuss how careful writers can replace adverbs with more inventive and considered verbs. *Walk gracefully* is stated more succinctly as *glide*, and *walk aimlessly* is communicated more efficiently as *wander.* The same principle can be used to eliminate boring, imprecise intensifiers such as *completely, very* and *extremely.* Thus, *He hit Joe extremely hard* becomes *He slugged Joe. She patted the cat very affectionately* might be better stated *She caressed the cat.*

There's one more way in which being conscious of how you're using verbs can help make your prose sleeker and more powerful. Words such as *now, then, currently* and phrases like *in the past* are usually redundant because the correct verb tense tells when the action happened or will happen, past, present or future. It's not necessary to write *John is currently at the exhibit.* The verb *is* tells when the event is taking place: *John is at the exhibit.*

Use common, precise language. Many developing writers think their writing will be better and they'll sound more intelligent if they use longer, more complicated words. Basically, if you use long words you're (1) just as stupid as you ever were and (2) handicapped by the additional problem of not being able to pronounce any of the words you are using.

Be conscious as well of common words or phrases that can be shortened or eliminated without changing the sentence's meaning. *That* is a classic example of a word that's a common part of virtually everyone's language and that is unnecessary in a vast number of uses. An example, *He knew that he would be in the movies*, just as easily becomes *He knew he would be in the movies. This is the issue that will win the election* can be stated more effectively as *This issue will win the election.*

Examine the rest of your vocabulary as well. Do you write *He is in need of* when *He needs* is a much better way to say it? Are any of the following in your prose: *on the decline, in the course of, hold the belief that, will take under consideration,* and *made a denouncement of*? They should be replaced with *declining, while, believe, consider* and *denounced*, respectively.

EXERCISES

Rewrite the following sentences to eliminate the redundancies they contain.

a. The store is in the vicinity of the fire station at Charledown Heights.

_____

b. A total of six people currently serve on the board.

_____

c. If the pier is built elsewhere, building costs could fluctuate up and down.

_____

d. Her bank balance had been on the decline until it had reached a current total of $6.

_____

e. The estimated cost of the pound was in a report prepared by an expert consulting firm that was funded utilizing the receipts of an American Humane Association grant the city was a recipient of.

_____

_____

_____

PART 7: RUN-ON SENTENCES

A run-on sentence occurs when a writer jams two or three independent clauses together. The most common type of run-on sentence is called a comma splice. That's when two independent clauses are joined with a comma: *The home was bright and sunny, the people who lived there were in debt.*

The other major type of run-on sentence is caused by linking two unrelated independent clauses with the conjunction *and.* Here's an example: *The company announced a 15 percent dividend increase and company scientists have developed new manufacturing processes.* Whether hooked with a comma or not, a run-on sentence is a confounding mishmash of thoughts.

However, run-on sentences are extremely easy to correct. Because a run-on sentence is comprised of independent clauses, the easiest way to solve the problem is to break the run-on sentence into two sentences and place a period after each independent clause. *The home was bright and sunny. The people who lived there were in debt.*

If the independent clauses are closely related, you can insert a semicolon after the first clause. *The home was bright and sunny; the people who lived there were in debt.* If the independent clauses have parallel constructions, you can connect them with a comma and a coordinating conjunction. *The home was bright and sunny, yet the people who lived there were in debt.*

With related thoughts, a fourth possibility is to use a subordinate conjunction to make half of the sentence into a dependent clause and signal the correct relationship between the clauses: *Although the home was bright and sunny, the people who lived there were in debt.* Here's how the other example sentence might be corrected: *Because company scientists have developed a new manufacturing process, the company announced a 15 percent dividend increase.*

Beware of a too mechanical solution to ridding your prose of run-on sentences or sentence fragments. Writers who have only recently discovered they write run-on sentences tend to write monotonously repetitive 12-word sentences. Make sure you vary the length and sentence pattern of your prose. At one point or another in your writing, you'll find that the pacing and cadence of your prose will be improved by occasionally inserting a dependent-independent clause construction, a longer sentence, or a passive voice sentence. It will improve the readability of your prose.

This brings up one final and important point. Run-on sentences are found most easily not by analyzing the grammar of each sentence but by reading your prose after you write it. If you conscientiously do this, you'll soon develop a critical ear for grammatical mistakes. That action will immediately isolate the sentences you'll need to examine more critically. You'll soon gather a sense of the rhythm and sound of good prose that will allow you to concentrate your energies on writing engaging and even exciting prose.

EXERCISES

Correct the following run-on sentences.

a. Cammy felt the water slide down her neck, she backed away from the pump.

_____

b. The factory shut down for a month the workers collected unemployment.

_____

c. The girl was declared the contest winner and her singing was wonderful.

_____

d. The two men went to the game, they were attacked in the parking lot, the two were hospitalized.

_____

e. The arts association announced next year's season the stars of the Metropolitan City Opera will be the highlight.

_____

_____

PART 8: SENTENCE SHIFTS

Sentence shifts are related to subject/verb agreement. Once you begin a sentence with a passive voice, the entire sentence should remain in passive voice. If you start a sentence with a singular pronoun, you shouldn't use a plural antecedent (the thing to which it refers) later in the sentence. That's a simple principle, but writers often make mistakes when too many words, phrases and clauses intervene between the beginning and end of a sentence.

Let's look at some examples of a pronoun shift. *Jacob, Teddy and Sam are the ones that were sent to the principal's office.* Do you see the problem? *Jacob, Teddy and Sam* are humans but *that* is used only when referring to nonhumans. For example, *Bossy is the cow that gives me the most trouble.* In addition to assuring that if there are humans at a sentence's beginning there are humans at the sentence's end, you need to make sure the same number of things are involved throughout the sentence. Here's an example: *All campers should wash your hands before eating.* You'll notice that there's a crowd at the beginning of the sentence, but there seems to be only one pair of hands to be washed at the sentence's end. The correct form is: *All campers should wash their hands before eating.*

A related problem is called an orphan noun. An orphan noun occurs when the antecedent to which the pronoun refers is not readily apparent. Here is an example. *Kevin sang as he examined her jewelry and this made Kelly so angry she shot him.* In this case, it's not really certain if it was Kevin's singing that stimulated Kelly's homicidal frenzy or whether it was Kevin's coveting Kelly's jewelry. You can fix this sentence by definitely establishing why Kelly shot Kevin. *Although Kevin was examining Kelly's jewelry, it was his singing that made her shoot him.*

Here's another instance of an orphan noun: *The quarter is in the fur coat in the gold cabinet; do you want it?* In this sentence, the desired object could be the quarter or the coat or the cabinet. With fuzzy prose like this, your generosity is only limited by how much the listener wants to take from you. The solution: *Do you want the quarter that's in the fur coat in the gold cabinet?*

You also need to be conscious of changing voice midway through the sentence. This isn't good: *Warren plastered the hallway, and the wallpaper was finally hung by Kelly.* The sentence's first clause is in the active voice, but the second clause is in the passive voice. You lose the sentence's momentum and force the reader to re-examine the sentence to find the object of the action. A better way: *Warren plastered the hallway, and Kelly finally hung the wallpaper.* Now the sentence is in the active voice on both sides of the conjunction.

How do you cure these problems? Remember that good prose is always balanced. Once you establish a singular pronoun, you need to have a singular referent later in the sentence. If you have an undefined pronoun in one place, you need to explicitly define the referent somewhere else in the sentence. Similarly, if you start a sentence in the active voice, the sentence's second clause must also be active.

EXERCISES

Rewrite the following sentences to avoid sentence shifts.

a. Each boy wants to see their projects approved.

_____

b. Sales were destroyed by the recession, but the company's president saved the business.

_____

c. Every person that has to be immunized should report to the clinic.

_____

d. The girl's cats, who were all black and white, climbed on the bed.

_____

e. Mac's pride and arrogance were apparent and it was what led to his problems.

_____

PART 9: SEXIST LANGUAGE

Practitioners should be constantly alert to social trends so that they can adjust their organization's attitudes and actions to those movements. Nowhere is that more important than in a sensitivity to sexist implications in writing. It is a matter of fairness to half the world's population.

The simple prescription to eliminate sexism in writing is to treat both men and women the same. For instance, it's difficult to justify using courtesy titles such as *Mrs.* and *Miss* for women and *Mr.* for men. What's the problem? Women shouldn't be labeled by their marital state when men are identified only by their gender.

Does *Ms.* solve this problem? Yes, but it introduces a new set of problems in identifying women who think using *Ms.* implies a political endorsement of the women's movement. Because of these problems, the *Associated Press Stylebook* suggests eliminating all such courtesy titles to avoid the appearance of sexism.

There are other possible problems with titles. Words such as *fireman, anchorman* or *postman* inaccurately portray the people who do those jobs. More sensitive and sensible people have suggested replacing those titles with *firefighter, anchorperson* and *postal carrier.* You should copy that practice.

Another problem arises from traditional grammar rules that specify that masculine pronouns such as *he, his* and *him* be used when referring to a noun that could either be a man or a woman. Here's an example: *A truck driver is responsible for keeping his safety equipment accessible.* A woman could be a truck driver, too, and we're perpetuating a stereotype by using the masculine pronoun *his* to describe an occupation.

An even more onerous stereotype is created when writers begin speculating about the gender of certain occupations that have been traditionally held by females. Here's an example: *When a secretary closes the office, she must shut down her computer and switch off her office lamp.*

How do you handle this problem? A number of ways have been proposed. Some scholars have advocated that writers use forms of *he/she. When a secretary closes the office, he or she must shut down his or her computer and switch off his or her office lamp.* To prevent this awkward, wordy form, other editors have suggested supplanting *he* or *she* with *s/he.* I don't think it helps.

The most workable solution has been to use the plural noun form and a version of the plural pronoun, *they,* if possible. *When secretaries close the office, they must shut down their computers and switch off their office lamps.* Remember that once you change a singular noun to plural, you need to switch to a plural verb. In this sentence, *closes* is replaced by *close.* Because it's impossible for a number of people to turn off one computer or one office lamp, you need to change the referents, too.

There are other problems that are more difficult to identify. Writers often describe women using terms that would not be included if the story were about a man. Here's an example: *The city manager candidates are attorney Jack Kelly and Cynthia Corbett, an attractive blonde who was the county's first female corporate lawyer.* The better way? *Two attorneys, Jack Kelly and Cynthia Corbett, are the city manager candidates.*

A more perplexing problem results from changing standards of what certain groups consider to be sexist writing. A recent dictionary suggested that the sex-specific terms *waiter* and *waitress* be replaced by *waitron*. At this point, that still sounds contrived and awkward.

Some dictionary editors, concerned about the possibly sexist origins of certain words, have made even more profound suggestions. In addition to repeating the well-worn (and as yet unaccepted) *womyn* for *woman* and *herstory* for *history*, the editors attacked such words as *seminal*. That is despite the fact that *seminal's* origin is the Greek word for *seed* and not the English word *semen*.

What's the lesson you need to take from this? (1) You should avoid the presumption of maleness in your writing unless you truly are speaking only of men. (2) You should treat men and women equally in your writing by avoiding courtesy titles, job titles that imply gender, and descriptions that are applied only to women. (3) You need to stay current of society's changing beliefs of what is sexist and adopt those standards that have gained acceptance by the audiences for which you write.

EXERCISES

Correct the following sentences to remove the sexist implications.

a. A receptionist should correct her own errors before her messages reach her boss.

_____

b. Seeing her attorney, Mrs. Jones mentioned the divorce.

_____

c. Each lawyer has to present his best evidence or he'll lose his case.

_____

d. The workmen's compensation laws were responsible for employee safety.

_____

e. The company's new lawyer is Joyce Herbert, a perky 42-year-old blonde.

_____

PART 10: SUBJECT-VERB AGREEMENT

English is fraught with perils that stem from agreement problems. As you negotiate your way through a sentence, you've got to make decisions that assure that the subject and the verb agree.

It's made more complicated by the fact that there are many exceptions to the hide-bound agreement rules we were taught in grade school and high school. So let's first discuss principles. Once you establish a verb tense, a subject number, or a pronoun number within a sentence, you generally have to preserve that tense or that number all through the sentence.

Here are some examples of how it should be done. For subject/verb agreement, if you've got a plural noun, then you need a plural verb. Most of us are very proficient with singular and plural verbs: *He is the world champion. They are the world champions.* You wouldn't say *They am the world champions.*

That's easy, but you must remember some very confusing idiosyncrasies for certain nouns. They are made easier to remember because of a logic that guides the rules. For instance, here's a correct subject/verb agreement that may make you scratch your head: *Little Emily, along with four other children, was found in the cave.* Your first response probably is to pair the plural verb *were* with *four other children.*

What's the principle here? Remember this is subject/verb agreement. As *Emily* is the subject and *along with four other children* merely a modifier, you use a singular verb. By the same token, if a singular subject is followed by phrases such as *together with* or *as well as*, you use a singular verb.

There are other equally frustrating peculiarities about subject/verb agreement. For instance, is *everyone* plural or singular? Is *politics* plural? How about *herd? Three hours? $10,000?* What about *The Stars and Stripes? Peanut butter and jelly?* To solve these problems, here's another rule you can apply. If the subject indicates that people or things are working together as an identifiable unit, then the subject takes a singular verb.

Using that principle, *everyone* is singular. So is *politics, herd, $10,000* and *three hours. The Stars and Stripes*, if it refers to the U.S. flag, is singular. *Peanut butter and jelly* is a bit more problematic. If you are referring to *peanut butter and jelly* as separate items you use a plural verb: *Peanut butter and jelly are in the cabinet.* But if you mean to suggest the messy combination of the two that's used to make a childhood ambrosia, then it is singular. Thus, *Peanut butter and jelly is my favorite sandwich.*

You can extend this rule further. Would you use a singular or plural verb with *a number of bankruptcies?* Which would you use with *the number of bankruptcies?* Because *a* is an indefinite article, it suggests an undefined amount. *The* seems to represent an organized unit. So here's the proper format: *A number of bankruptcies are . . .* and *The number of bankruptcies is. . . .*

Here's another example of the principle. Even though you generally use a plural noun with a compound subject (e.g., *Dick and Jane are going*), when the parts of a compound subject refer to the same person or thing, the verb is singular: *The family's best reader and bicyclist is Billy.*

EXERCISES

Establish the correct subject/verb agreement in each sentence.

a. He (is, are) the duke.

b. Penelope, the pig, and Bessie, the cow, (is, are) the basis of tonight's meal.

_____

c. Everyone, including my three sisters, (is, are) going to the movie.

_____

d. Without fail, the number of students dropping out (is, are) sure to rise.

_____

e. Every worker (has, have) the power to belong to the profit-sharing plan.

_____

f. Bacon and eggs fried over a campfire (is, are) my favorite meal.

_____

Answer Keys

ANSWER KEY TO AP STYLEBOOK PART 1: PUNCTUATION

May 19, 1996   Contact: _____

FOR IMMEDIATE RELEASE   Office Phone: 555-1234

NEIGHBORHOOD WATCH MAY
HAVE SOLVED VANDALISM CASE

The city's worst vandalism spree which resulted in over 100 broken lawn statues may have been stopped when three men were arrested after a tip to the Louisville Police's Neighborhood Watch program.

The three men Calvin Thomas Cronston, 18 of 3,486 E. Calgary Pike; Samuel Jay Dallas, 19, of 708 Jackson Lane and Jacob Lee Penner, 18 of Clarksville, Ind. were arrested about midnight on Thursday, May 18, after Deer Park residents reported to police that four plaster dogs and two stone jockeys had been broken by gunfire. One of the callers gave a detailed description of the car.

When the three youths were arrested, police found a .22-caliber rifle, a .32-caliber pistol, a pellet gun and 2100 rounds of ammunition in Penner's car. All three men were charged with 87 felony vandalism counts.

Deer Park residents have reported nearly 100 broken lawn ornaments since June. "We didn't really care about the statues but we were really fearful that a child was going to accidentally get in the way of these gun-happy nuts" said Deer Park resident Carlin Sweet.

Detective Gene Hill said the Louisville Police were "real happy to get these people off the streets.

"The police are so pleased the Neighborhood Watch program continues to be effective in helping us fight crime," Hill said. "I'm familiar with programs in Cincinnati Ohio and in Memphis, Tenn. and I don't know any of them as effective as the one we have in Louisville. This proves once again that if we work together we can stop crime."

-30-

ANSWER KEY TO AP STYLEBOOK PART 2: TITLES

Nov. 12, 199__   Contact: _____

FOR IMMEDIATE RELEASE   Office phone: 555-1234

SOUTH AFRICAN POLITICS
FOCUS OF CONFERENCE

Former South African prime minister P.W. Botha and the Rev. Desmond Tutu will be among political figures from four continents who will be highlighted speakers at the second annual Vital Issues Conference Dec. 5. The topic of the conference, sponsored by the National People's Rights Organization and local businesswoman Mrs. Joyce Dunne, will be Moral Response in South Africa: A Black American Perspective.

The opening session will feature speeches by Mr. Botha, Time Magazine editor Grant Fowler, and Eleanor Kalish, author of the book Storm Over Southern Africa.

The conference's second session will concern South African human rights issues, including a panel discussion by four men who were illegally detained for six months in 1991 by South African police.

The next session will explore law enforcement issues, and will include a showing of The Naked Fist, a film about Soweto Township Police Capt. Corza Cantow. Capt. Cantow has been implicated by the Amnesty International human rights group in the kidnapping and deaths of at least 40 people involved in civil rights demonstrations. Tutu will introduce the film.

The final session will be devoted to the international response to South African unrest, with speeches by Al Gore, Vice President of the United States, and University of Johannesburg professor Kalibar Koweta. Afterward, there will be a presentation of the conference's proceedings to editors of The New World Political Dictionary, which will issue a special volume on the conference in next year's edition.

ANSWER KEY TO AP STYLEBOOK PART 3: NUMERALS

Aug. 10, 199__   Contact: _____

FOR IMMEDIATE RELEASE   Office phone: 555-1234

HELTON LEADS TEAM
TO YOUTH SOCCER TITLE

Tiny Jim Helton scored ⑦ goals to lead the Bloomfield Beanpoles to an ~~eleven~~ 11-7 ~~to seven~~ win over the Lexington Lizards in the final game of the Missinois Youth Soccer League Saturday.

The three foot seven inch Helton scored ⑤ of his goals with free kicks that snaked past Lizard goalie Bruce McComb for scores. "I guess the 99¢ my dad spent for that practice goal really helped me tonight," said Helton, who is (nine) years old.

Helton said his occasional workouts with St. Louis Spirits forward George Krenschicki, who is 5 feet 4 inches tall, have helped his confidence. "When we first started practicing a lot of people would stop and stare at these two short people playing," Helton said. "But since George has proven he can play pro ball, I don't let my being short bother me any more."

Helton may be part of a dynasty in the 21st century if he follows his early plans to enter Bardstown's Holy Heart High School for his freshman year in 2001. Holy Heart's soccer team holds a national record for losing only (four) percent of its contests in the last (ten) years.

Holy Heart soccer coach Kelly Phillips is excited at the prospect. "Jim only came to about one-third ~~1/3~~ of our practices this season," Phillips said. "But if I got five cents for every goal he scored on our high school boys, I'd be rich. He's the kind of player a coach needs if he wants to make $2 ~~two~~ million ~~dollars~~ a year coaching."

The championship game was the first played in Callam Stadium, the county's new $1.17million ~~$1,173,342~~ arena. (12) members of the city council who had voted to build the stadium were honored in ceremonies before the game.

-30-

ANSWER KEY TO AP STYLEBOOK PART 4: ABBREVIATIONS

April 18, 199__   Contact: _____

FOR IMMEDIATE RELEASE   Office phone: 555-1234

CALIFORNIA SENATOR
GETS ILLEGAL CONTRIBUTIONS

California Sen. Neil Edleniot received nearly $170,000 in illegal campaign contributions from a single businessman, according to an investigation by People Concerned by Political Corruption (PCPC).

Despite laws limiting individual campaign contributions to $2,000, the United States senator received $168,000 from California business owner Aris Braldow, the watchdog group has discovered. The organization has turned over its evidence to the FBI.

According to the organization's evidence, Braldow's money snaked all through the U.S. as he tried to stay under the $2,000 limit for political contributions. The investigation found that Braldow funneled his contributions to Edleniot through three companies and 84 individuals in five states, who claimed they contributed the money to the senator.

Braldow's primary company, the Korform Raisin Corporation of Barstow, CA, *Calif.* distributed $112,000 to two other Braldow-controlled firms, Reform Company of Colorado, located in Denver, and Braldow Brothers, Incorporated based in McNaughton, Michigan. Each of the three companies then paid $56,000 to Braldow's daughter, Jeanne Benson, in Wichita, Kansas. Jeanne Benson deposited the $168,000 in her bank account on Tuesday, Aug. 14.

On Wed, Aug. 15, Edleniot received $2,000 from each of 84 individuals who listed addresses in Hawaii, Maine, Texas, Ohio and Michigan. But each $2,000 contribution had been wired from Wichita, and from one single address: 16 North Anderson Ln. Braldow's daughter lived at that address on Aug. 14.

(more)

ILLEGAL CONTRIBUTIONS
page 2

Braldow and his daughter would not comment on the investigation. Edleniot and his office staff did not return repeated phone calls from the citizens' organization. The Los Angeles division of the FBI is continuing the investigation.

The People Concerned by Political Corruption is a nonprofit organization located in Orono, Maine. It is funded by contributions from individuals and is not affiliated with any political party or other group.

-30-

ANSWER KEY TO AP STYLEBOOK PART 5:
CAPITALIZATION

Jan. 19, 199__   Contact: _____

FOR IMMEDIATE RELEASE   Office phone: 555-1234

WASHINGTON PARADE
HONORS CONSTITUTION

Bill Clinton and members of his Presidential Administration will be among the celebrities appearing in a Washington parade honoring the Constitution's 210th birthday.

The March 23 parade will attract bands and floats from throughout the south and midwest for the City's world-famous Cherry Blossom Festival, which begins during the first week of Spring each year. The parade units will assemble by the treasury building near the Potomac River, then travel east along the River until reaching the Capitol.

There the parade will be joined by Congressional leaders from the Democratic and Republican Parties, who will lead the procession past the Washington city hall and on to 1600 Pennsylvania Ave. Once at the White House, the president will present a medal to the parade's grand marshal, army Gen. Norman Schwartzkopf, in a private ceremony in the oval office.

"This celebration of the freedoms gained from the constitution is going to be the biggest thing the capital city has seen since prohibition was lifted," said Charles Burke, the president of Freedom 1787, the organization sponsoring the parade.

Freedom 1787 is a nonprofit organization founded in 1972 to direct the 200th anniversary of the documents upon which the United States' federal system of government was built. In addition to his duties with the Freedom 1787 organization, Burke is director of the federal election commission.

-30-

ANSWER KEY TO AP STYLEBOOK PART 6: TIME

June 26, 199__   Contact: _____

FOR IMMEDIATE RELEASE   Office phone: 555-1234

DAVIESS WOMEN GET
FREE CANCER SCREENINGS

Daviess County women who want to protect themselves from breast cancer can get a free breast cancer examination in their own neighborhoods during the next three weeks.

Beginning Jul 17th, the Daviess County Health Department will sponsor a countywide visit by the state's mobile mammography van as part of its health awareness campaign.

The mobile mammography unit is a large van that contains high-technology equipment designed to detect breast cancer in its earliest stages. If a breast tumor is found early, 95 percent of all patients survive for five years or more. The van, which was placed in service in February, 1989, is staffed by two doctors and four nurses. It has direct communication links to diagnostic computers at the state university's medical center.

The mobile mammography van's Daviess County schedule is as follows: July 17th, Galt Community Center; July 20, Gilman City High School; July 27, Lexington City Hall; August 2nd, Kingston Public Library; and August 7th, Chula Courthouse. Screenings will be conducted at each site between 9:00 A.M. and 12 noon each morning.

The mobile mammography van is returning two years after its last successful visit to Daviess County, when nearly 400 women were screened for breast cancer. On one day during that tour, January 23, 1994, 93 women were examined for the early stages of breast cancer.

For more information or to schedule an appointment, call the Daviess County Health Department at 555-1234.

-30-

SECTION B ANSWERS

Part 1: Apostrophes

    a. It's our friend's home that she bought three years ago.
    b. He's the class's president for '92.
    c. Who's got the most A's among the fraternity's members?
    d. It's friends who'll be important to your lifestyle in the 1990s.
    e. Until the final minute it was anyone's game, but now the trophy is ours.

Part 2: Dangling Modifiers

    a. Looking over her shoulder, Denise saw the angry hog chasing her.
    b. While I was still in my pajamas, I shot an elephant.
    c. After I turned in the assignment late, the professor yelled at me.
    d. Because Tammy had only a month to live, the orphanage's children presented her Christmas presents early.
    e. After Joe played the stock market for six months, the firm's bank account was empty.

Part 3: Fragmentary Sentences

    a. John will be welcome in this house when pigs fly and buttercups dance.
    b. I froze walking through the rain and sleet and snow.
    c. Although there was a cat in the tree John did nothing.
    d. When I went through the gate and into the woods to see the birds it became apparent there had been an accident.
    e. Over the hilltop just to the right of the building is where Dixie saw the plane.

Part 4: Parallel Structures

    a. He hates pitting avocados, squeezing oranges and peeling bananas.
    b. Either tell your teacher how much you like this course or ask him how you could drop it.
    c. The actor had blue eyes, a winning smile and a stunning physique.
    d. The city's alternatives are to shut down the polluting incinerators or find a cleaner technology.
    e. The team's goals were to improve play, increase attendance and build a new stadium.

Part 5: Passive Voice

    a. The Industrial Standards Board approved the new safety standards.
    b. Former Mayor John A. Killebrew killed a woman Tuesday.
    c. I purchased that milk last week.

    d. The legislature's decision will most affect uninsured motorists.

    e. The citizen's panel will present awards to four former congressmen.

    f. Active. More effective as active, unless your audience was the charity that received the contributions.

    g. Active. Passive is more effective because the audience would more likely be interested in the workers in the sentence than in the suspension bureaucracy.

    h. Passive. The active voice is shorter and still keeps the audience in the No. 1 position. *The company received a $6 million federal contract.*

    i. Active. More effective as active because the main players are in the No. 1 position.

    j. Active. More effective as passive because a major benefit is hidden at the end of the sentence. *A $500 bonus will be given to employees rated in the top 10 percent* would be better.

    k. Passive. More effective as active. *Lightning destroyed the company's main generating unit.* Sentence is shorter and emphasizes nature's violence.

    l. Passive. More effective in active voice because the employee audience's benefits are emphasized early in the sentence. *Employees working overtime learned they would receive extra pay each week.*

Part 6: Redundancy

    a. The store is near the Charledown Heights fire station.

    b. Six people serve on the board.

    c. If the pier is built elsewhere, building costs could fluctuate.

    d. Her bank balance had declined until it reached $6.

    e. The pound's estimated cost was in a consulting firm report funded by an American Humane Association grant the city received.

Part 7: Run-On Sentences

    a. As Cammy felt the water slide down her neck, she backed away from the pump.

    b. When the factory shut down for a month the workers collected unemployment.

    c. The girl, whose singing was wonderful, was declared the contest winner.

    d. The two men who were attacked in the parking lot at the game were hospitalized.

    e. The stars of the Metropolitan City Opera will be the highlight of next year's arts association season.

Part 8: Sentence Shifts

    a. Each boy wants to see his project approved.

    b. The recession destroyed sales, but the company's president saved the business.

c. Every person who has to be immunized should report to the clinic.

d. The girl's cats, which were all black and white, climbed on the bed.

e. Mac's pride and arrogance were apparent and they were what led to his problems.

Part 9: Sexist Language

a. Receptionists should correct their own errors before their messages reach their bosses.

b. Seeing her attorney, Jones mentioned the divorce.

c. All lawyers have to present their best evidence or they'll lose their cases.

d. The workers' compensation laws were responsible for employee safety.

e. The company's new lawyer is Joyce Herbert.

Part 10: Subject/Verb Agreement

a. He is the duke.

b. Penelope, the pig, and Bessie, the cow, are the basis of tonight's meal.

c. Everyone, including my three sisters, is going to the movie.

d. Without fail, the number of students dropping out is sure to rise.

e. Every worker has the power to belong to the profit-sharing plan.

f. Bacon and eggs fried over a campfire is my favorite meal.

Case Studies for Management Problems and Writing Assignments

The following case studies are designed to test many aspects of your public relations management and writing ability. The information from which you'll be required to compose a coherent and well-structured document is often disorganized and haphazardly worded. That's similar to situations you'll encounter in professional life. They will sometimes contain information that would be boring or unnecessary to communicate to certain audiences. Occasionally, the case studies will contain organizational information that, while vital for internal planning, might be better left unsaid to external audiences. The case studies will sometimes require you to make judgments about objectionable language, idiomatic quotations and other problems inherent in a process that requires the practitioner to gather information from a variety of sources.

CASE STUDY 1: ANNOUNCING A CONCERT

You work as a public relations assistant for your local Fine Arts Council. The council is sponsoring a concert by Felipe Jones, a classical guitarist. He'll be playing "Fandanguilla," by Joaquin Turina; "Prelude No. 2," by George Gershwin; and "Pleasant Despair," by Erik Satie. Jones, who is 87 years old, has performed in New York's Carnegie Hall, in the Kennedy Center in Washington, and, according to his press booklet, has just returned from a triumphant tour of 17 European cities. The concert will be two weeks from Friday at 8 p.m. in the Midtown Community Auditorium. The site of the auditorium is 1756 Nall Avenue in your town. It's been 70 years since Jones first made his professional playing debut. Tickets to the show are $7. They are available at the door the evening of the show. Jones is a 1924 graduate of Central High School, the biggest high school in your town, and grew up on the west side of your community. Jones has been certified as the oldest active professional performer in the United States by the American Federation of Musicians. "I ain't seen anyone older than me playing for the last 20 years," Jones is quoted as saying in his press materials. Jones has only returned to your town to play one other time. That was in 1952. This concert is to raise funds for the arts council's annual Easter party so that the group can entertain your city council members two weeks before the vote on allocations to the city's arts budget.

Management Problems

1. What are the possible audiences toward which you could direct your organization's marketing efforts?
2. How would the emphasis of your marketing communication change as you tried to reach each audience?
3. If you placed only one message in a mass medium to reach all your possible audiences, how could that disrupt your ability to attract individual audience segments within the total ticket-buying public?
4. How could information about the concert's proceeds be harmful to your organization's purpose? What would be your advice to the organization about this issue?
5. What combination of demographic factors might you choose to compile a targeted mailing list to attract concertgoers for this event?

Writing Assignments

6. Write a news release announcing the concert to older adults in your community.
7. Modify the previous release to target classical music fans in your area.
8. Compose a print or radio ad for the concert.
9. Write a personal letter from the arts council director, Monica Torrence, to area art supporters to raise money to fund the Jones concert.
10. Prepare an outline of visuals and sound effects for a video news release that might help you tell the story and draw concertgoers for the event.

CASE STUDY 2: A HOMEBUYING SCHOOL

You are working for a public relations firm employed by Paul Cremona, the owner of the Paul Creason Realty Co. You work the Creason account. Cremona has noticed many first-time homebuyers are not very knowing about real estate. That causes two problems for him. Often they waste his agents' time because they can't figure out if they can afford a home or not until they find that the down payment they can put on a house is way too inadequate. If this happens, by the time they abandon the search an agent has spent hours showing them houses. In addition, he finds the first-time buyer often is working with three, four or even five agents, and Cremona often loses the sale to another agency, again after investing a lot of his agents' time in the quest. You suggest a homebuying school, where people in a group could systematically learn about buying a house instead of having it given to them one-on-one by a real estate agent. You also suggest a gift or something like that would be nice to get people to join the program and would be especially appropriate if the students bought a home from Cremona's agency. Cremona is enthusiastic about your plan. The Creason Home-ownership School, he calls it, and offers four weeks of night classes. He said the program will give help in explaining the disadvantages and advantages of fixed rate and adjustable mortgages, the No. 1 complaint Cremona says he hears homebuyers complaining about. The classes are every Monday night next month from 7–9 p.m. There won't be any cost for the class, and people can enroll by contacting the agency at 587-3432. By the time the pupils get through they should know how to deal with home improvement contractors after they move into their home and movers and bankers before they move in. Among other things, the program, to be held at Creason's main office at 1763 Taylorsville Rd., will, among many, many other things that will be of interest to people who have the potential to be homeowners, cover aspects of the homebuyer's relationship with real estate agents and what elements of a home's infrastructure should be examined in order to avoid later costly and complex jobs, such as replacing plumbing and other water outlets, electrical power wiring, roofing or even structural supports. In addition, the program, for which only first-time home-buyers are eligible, will tell people how to manage a budget and save on taxes through the use of home equity loans in the years after you buy a home and have built some equity in the house. Participants will also learn how to read sales contracts. Cremona said he will teach the class himself. He has 23 years' experience in the business and has been a speaker at many national real estate conventions. He said the program will even tell people how to figure closing costs when completing the purchase of a house. In addition, he agrees to give each graduating student the amount of $1,000 apiece off the cost of their home if they buy it from the Creason agency. The course is also intended, with luck, to help a person adjust their spending patterns so that they can keep up with their house payments and save enough for a down payment.

Management Problems

1. How do the communication goals of the school help solve some of Cremona's organizational problems? How much should the release discuss the underlying organizational problems that the school is supposed to solve?
2. How does the free gift help in the persuasive sequence?
3. What problems might a practitioner encounter in getting an editor to run an announcement of the school in his or her publication? How would this change if Cremona decided to charge for the school?

Writing Assignments

4. Compose a news release to be sent to your local newspaper that announces the homebuyers school. Be sure to target an audience and emphasize a benefit for that audience in the release's No. 1 position.
5. Compose a short oral presentation for Cremona to give to his sales agents that will help convince them of the value of the program.

6. Write a newspaper or radio advertisement for the school.

7. Compose a persuasion platform for the intended audience, omitting the budget section.

CASE STUDY 3: FASHION HOUSE INTRODUCES HOLLYWOOD LINE

You work for April Apparel, a New York-based clothing company owned by April Ormand, a former cabaret dancer whose father was a French Resistance fighter in World War II. Ormand has been in this country since 1971. The company has developed a new clothing line that will be modeled after clothing worn by characters from major movies released by Calbaer Pictures. The clothing will be sold by better department stores. Calbaer Pictures has exclusive, multifilm contracts with some of Hollywood's major stars, including Keifer Sutherland, Julie Harris, Kevin Costner, Daryl Hannah, Bruce Willis, Meryl Streep, Julia Roberts and Tom Cruise. The adult pictures represent a further expansion of the apparel lines April Apparel already has established with the Cobalt Warriors and Deep Forest Baby Bunnies. Both lines, inspired by children's films of the same names, were outrageously popular. As the exclusive licensed apparel manufacturer, April sold more than 300,000 apparel items linked with each of the two films. Calbaer, with which April has entered into the agreement, is run by producer Max Baer, a successful Hollywood producer and the man who portrayed Jethro Bodine in "The Beverly Hillbillies" television program during the 1960s. April has already had a successful design history of converting movie looks into popular fashions. The company developed a line of nylon jackets and pants in neon colors inspired by the Tom Cruise film "Days of Thunder," released in 1990. Among the apparel April designers is creating as part of the Calbaer agreement are tight-fitting, naturally aged leather leggings inspired by the costumes Julia Roberts will wear in next summer's Calbaer release, "Foxtail," a comedy set in the old West. Another clothing line will be based on corsets that figure prominently in scenes from the Daryl Hannah movie "Rebel Ecstasy," a Civil War epic to be released at Christmastime. Other anticipated looks, according to Ormand, will be appropriate for office and formal wear. Before beginning her own company, Ormand had been a designer for Clien Fashions, Gallante and Korbal, U.S.A. The first designs will be unveiled next spring.

Management Problems

1. To what editors would you communicate in order to support the company's sales effort directly?

2. What general publication editors might be useful in helping to get your message to consumers interested in movies?

3. What are some specialized and more personal media that could let you communicate to a highly targeted audience of individuals interested in each of the film stars?

4. What would be the learn–feel–do sequence for the owners of the major retail store that is buying 15,000 of this company's items?
5. What might be some of the legal implications if you formally announce to investors that actor Keanu Reeves has agreed to have his movie role costumes featured in this company's clothing line before he signs a release statement?

Writing Assignments

6. Ormand wants you to write a print news release that will help support the company's marketing effort.
7. Compose a video news release to support the company's sales effort.
8. Compose a print ad for the company's products.
9. Write a television commercial about the product.
10. Determine the TIPCUP elements that will be most important to include in the lead sentence of a release directed to potential customers.

CASE STUDY 4: STREAMLINING AN INDUSTRIAL PERMIT PROCESS

In researching possible sources of information on the industrial recruitment process for your job at the Cornwell Chamber of Commerce, you find two cities that have apparently been very successful in recruiting new businesses: Norfolk, Virginia, and Monmouth, New Jersey. The two cities are about the same size as Cornwell and have problems similar to those of Cornwell—an inner city decaying after major heavy industries closed up. In an article in *Manufacturing Quarterly*, the development directors of both the two cities were interviewed. Each said they felt they had lost a couple of potential industries because of a long and lengthy permit process. Executives who had located in the cities complained that they had to go through between 14 and 20 different city and county agencies to connect utilities, get construction, zoning and sign permits, and other things like that. Both cities set up a business expansion clearinghouse, making it possible for executives to stop in one office and collect all the forms they needed for permits and licenses. The clearinghouse provided a central location where all the experts from each permit office were available so that people weren't bumped from office to office in search of answers for their questions. Obviously, shortening the review and application process enabled businesses to make money sooner and thus pay taxes sooner. The new procedures gave the two cities a competitive advantage over other cities that they could push in their meetings with executives and in promotional materials. The two cities were also able to reduce their permit staffs by 85 people (38 in Monmouth and 47 in Norfolk), which meant quite a bit of savings on salaries. If Cornwell wanted to do this, you would immediately have to find and rent office space to house all the permit offices. In addition, all office personnel would have to meet to coordinate their application forms so that businesspeople would not have to fill in the same information on application after application. At the very least, this policy might show a change in the city's attitude toward business and communicate that the city can provide a good environment for business. There's also the possibility that businesses now in the city center would stay rather than move to adjacent rural counties where they think the bureaucracy will be less than what it is here. That would mean more tax dollars would stay in the city. One problem is going to be that there are entrenched bureaucracies within all the permit offices that won't be glad to give up their accumulated powers. In addition, the mayor campaigned on this issue, that of reducing the bureaucracy. If the city payroll is reduced through the bureaucratic consolidation, the mayor stands to lose votes and support from the city bureaucracy but should gain support from non-city employees. Hopefully, these procedures will help reverse the decline of the city. The city, just last year, was in the running for three major industrial plants, but lost all three to other cities. Unemployment is now at 8.3 percent, up from 5.9 percent two years ago. In 1970, Cornwell was one of the nation's 15 largest industrial centers, with auto, steel and other manufacturing plants located here. For the past 15 years, businesses located in the central city have increasingly been moving way out in the country in the areas surrounding Cornwell rather than expand in the city that gave them birth. Chamber of Commerce President Merle Bryant thinks the plan would be very popular with what he describes as "tough-minded, no-nonsense executives who want everything they do to run as efficiently as their businesses."

Management Problems

1. What internal public may need prior notice before this policy change takes place?
2. What medium might be most effective in convincing this public of the need for the new policy?
3. What interaction might there be between external opinion about the changes and the internal public's acceptance of the policy?
4. What are some possible legal implications if your news release in Cornwell highlighting this policy includes a quote from a Norfolk business owner who is using her city's clearinghouse, but the quote was invented by a Norfolk city employee?

Writing Assignments

5. Compose a position paper for the chamber of commerce. Structure the piece so that readers can readily find and share information.
6. Write a news release announcing the proposed changes in city procedures.
7. Write a personal letter from the chamber's Bryant to business executives who are prospects to move to Cornwell.
8. Write a short speech for Bryant to deliver to a convention of business relocation experts.
9. Omitting the budget section, write a persuasion platform for the business owners the city hopes to attract.

CASE STUDY 5: A MAGAZINE'S RECYCLING EFFORT

You're working as a public relations practitioner for *Ballou*, a big-circulation women's fashion magazine. In response to some environmental activists who happen to be Ballou employees, the company reluctantly put together a committee to examine ways the magazine could be involved in recycling and other environmental and social issues. The company's task force is comprised of administrative assistant Carol Underwood, production supervisor Jackson Norman and assistant vice president Linda Goodwin. Among the programs they established is one that collects soft drink cans from offices and sells them to aluminum recovery firms. The company uses the proceeds, which were $350 during the first month, to help the homeless. The task force also recommended, among its many suggestions, that all internal communication, whether internal memorandums, story manuscripts, policy reports, announcements or letters, be placed on the company's electronic mail system that's been a part of its computer network for the past three years. In the past three months, the volume of messages transmitted on the e-mail system has increased 325 percent. It's estimated that this one policy saves about one-half ton of paper each month. Among the e-mail messages is a 15-minute course, which employees can call up on their computer screens, explaining what materials can be recycled and the procedures for recycling them. The magazine has also replaced its regular desk wastebaskets with green and gold wastebaskets that have three tiers. The tiers allow employees to separate trash into categories that aid recycling. Trash is still picked up every night but it's stored in three holding areas for later sale to recycling concerns. Magazines, of course, use tremendous volumes of paper. Thus, there are many opportunities, many, many opportunities to save big amounts of paper. Through exact computer calibration of the magazine's photographs and layout boards, the production department has been able to reduce the number of spoiled and unusable magazines by 87 percent. That represents savings in the amount of one ton of paper each month. The designers have made the three outside margins of each page three-sixteenths of an inch smaller. By the time 400 million copies of the company's magazines are produced, printed and distributed every year, that tiny area will amount to nearly 90 tons of paper that the company will have saved. Following the lead of many other magazines, your company's publications will, starting this summer, be printed on lighter-weight paper. That's another 135 tons of paper saved over the next year. Following research, the magazine has discovered that not nearly as many subscriber-reply cards as estimated before are needed. Previously, the magazine has included four subscriber reply cards in each copy. Research found that although significant numbers of new subscriptions come from the cards bound into magazines sold at newsstands, only 1 percent of all new subscriptions come as a result of subscriber cards in home-delivered magazines. Knowing that, the magazine will no longer include subscriber reply cards in home-delivered magazines, and will place only one reply card in newsstand copies. That action alone will save 95 tons of paper per year. The magazine's task force has also been instrumental in conceiving and implementing an industrywide effort to encourage paper manufacturers to produce even lighter-weight paper for color magazines. Among the magazines in this effort are *Time, The New Republic, The National Review, The Atlantic Monthly* and *Newsweek*. By starting an industrywide effort, the hope is that manufacturers will realize there is a market demand for new, environmentally sound products. The total savings in paper represent a sizable business advantage for the magazine. With the total paper savings, the company will save over $110,000 in paper costs this year. All told the recycling efforts cost the company about $8,000 for initial start-up costs and can be maintained for less than $3,000 each year. On an individual level, there have been some dramatic changes. Domika Lewis, who is a senior fashion writer for the magazine, is one of those people who has had to change her attitudes since the recycling effort started. During the orientation period two months ago, task force member Underwood passed through the editorial department at the magazine. Lewis, who has been with the magazine for 17 years, commented: "I'd been working at my desk all day transcribing interviews, so the floor around my wastebasket looked like there had been some sort of volcanic eruption in my trash can. Carol, who I didn't know at that time, came up to my desk trailing this line of blue-suited executives. So this woman I've never seen in my life is digging through my trash. At first I figured it was some rather indiscreet fashion house spy looking for the new spring designer lines. When Carol announced she was going to demonstrate how wasteful the company had been by using my trash, I was kind of offended. I figured she was going to give me some sort of holier-than-thou environmental sermon before pulling out a couple of pieces of paper that could be recycled. But Carol floored me when she separated all my trash into three recycling piles. There was cardboard in one, coated paper in another, and stationery paper in a third stack. By the time she got through, there were only two items left that couldn't be recycled. I was convinced. In those three minutes, she had reduced my part of the trash problem by over 90 percent. With these three-tier wastebaskets it's really easy to be involved in the program. After all, it's what the world is coming to. I don't like to sound like a sap, but each of us has got to develop a commitment to keeping the world in some kind of shape for our kids. It's got to be a part of how we live our lives forever."

Management Problems

1. What additional media can we use to remind people at the point of action about the company's recycling program?
2. What's a possible danger of using traditional media to reinforce the company's recycling messages?

Writing Assignments

3. Produce an advertisement to be placed in *Ballou* magazine that extols the company's commitment to environmental issues.
4. Compose a feature story for the company's internal newsletter.
5. Prepare a position paper advocating that the company retain the recycling program and allocate $3,000 for next year's operating expenses.

6. Write a news release directed toward environmental publications discussing the company's recycling effort.
7. Write an audio news release to be distributed to all-news stations.
8. Write a video news release to be distributed to midday news programs.
9. Write a lead sentence for a news release directed toward environmental magazines and another lead sentence for a release directed toward *Ballou* stockholders.

CASE STUDY 6: HIGH-TEMPERATURE ENGINE PLASTICS

You work for an advanced technology plastics firm called Britlim Ltd. It's located in Indianapolis, Indiana, and its best known work was fabricating specialty parts for Indianapolis 500 race cars. Britlim just successfully tested new plastic engine components and sold them to Ford Motor Co. Your scientists have been working on this concept for the last 12 years. The first parts of this series will be placed on Ford's cars during the next model year from now. The parts aren't the plastic parts that many manufacturers put in dashboards or bumpers and exterior things many auto manufacturers use plastic for. Instead, the first batch of these new plastic parts is for plastic intake manifolds. These parts act as chambers in which the air needed to burn fuel is drawn into an engine. The problem with using plastics in cars before has been that they melt in the high temperatures that are within engines, which sometimes reach 350 degrees Fahrenheit in engine compartments. That's why most engine parts were made of iron or steel. Plastics still aren't strong enough for moving parts within engines like camshafts and crankshafts. Recently, to save weight and thus save gas, manufacturers have been making more parts out of aluminum. Plastics are lighter than aluminum, however, and thus can save more gas. Britlim has already proved plastics will work. It has already produced plastic valve covers (a cover on the top of the engine that covers the valves, of course) that have been installed in Ford cars. Just with the plastic valve covers, gas mileage is 1 percent or 2 percent better than with the aluminum covers. There are other advantages. It is much cheaper to make plastic parts than metal parts because plastic is smooth coming out of a mold, whereas metal parts are rough and often have to be machined to smooth out edges. That roughness hurts engine performance and gas mileage, too. It causes turbulence as air flows through the manifold. That causes friction and bad engine performance. That rough interior is caused by a difference in the way plastic and aluminum parts are cast. Aluminum parts are made out of melted aluminum that is poured into casts that have sand cores. After the aluminum hardens, the sand is flushed out. The sand leaves a rough surface inside the intake manifold. Because the sand casts are unstable, large metal parts normally have to be cast separately as two or more pieces and then joined together. That adds to the manufacturing costs. Plastic parts are different. They use metal cores that melt at between 150 degrees and 450 degrees Fahrenheit. The plastic resin is then injected into the mold, where it hardens. The metal core leaves much smoother edges than does the sand. The metal core is then melted out by submerging the entire mold in hot oil. The metal melts, leaving behind a one-piece plastic shape with very precise dimensions. That procedure demands plastics that can withstand very high temperatures. Such plastics are achieved by using a type of plastic resin called phenolic plastic, which actually undergoes a molecular change in the molding process. When the plastic is melted for the mold, the molecules link up differently. In fact, they bind together irreversibly so that once the plastic sets, it cannot melt again and can resist temperatures even higher than aluminum. The plastic parts weigh about 25 percent less than the metal ones they replace. The plastic parts put Britlim in a very lucrative position looking forward to the next few years. The company has already received contracts totaling $50 million from Ford and, if the other automakers also latch onto the parts, those figures could soar even higher. Company accountants estimate, for example, that if General Motors converted exclusively to the plastic valve covers and intake manifolds, the total contract would be in excess of $150 million. Britlim Ltd. President Benton Harlert is enthusiastic about the coming business: "We could bury everyone else in the business if we could get the GM contract. It's the wave of the future since the car companies have to bring their mileage up. They've sliced the weight off the body and the interior. The only heavy thing left on a car is the engine, and Britlim has the solution to that problem." Britlim researcher Kyle MacGlothlin developed the plastic forming process and was present when Ford tested the product. "It's funny," MacGlothlin said. "They had all these tests lined up—there were steam rollers to try to crush it, explosives to try to tear it apart—all sorts of things. We were out on this airport runway, but it looked like a medieval dungeon with all its instruments of torture. They had a very negative attitude coming into the test, and they were really surprised when they couldn't destroy it. It validated all the work, all the years of backbreaking work we've put into this product. In fact, now that we've solved this initial problem of heat resistance, there's absolutely nothing that will prevent us from converting maybe 50 percent of every engine into plastic components. We could solve the energy crisis almost singlehanded."

Management Problems

1. What are some of the important messages about this new product to communicate to Britlim employees and stockholders?
2. How important will reliability be in helping establish consumer acceptance of these parts? What special events might you coordinate and publicize to communicate this property?
3. Using the GOSS formula, compile a set of questions for an interview with the inventor of the process.
4. What are some of the legal implications if your public relations department shares the news release announcing this discovery with your company's top 10 investors before you issue it to the financial media and other investors?

Writing Assignments

5. Compose a query letter trying to interest an automotive editor in doing a feature story.

6. Write a news release to science editors about the new technology and the energy savings it represents.

7. Write a feature story for the company newsletter highlighting the research initiative and competitive advantages the company has gained with the new development.

8. Write a script for a video feature that will be distributed to cable television auto racing shows.

9. Write the lead sentence for a news release directed to a magazine read by automotive engineers and another lead for a release directed toward a newsletter that alerts investors to good stock buys.

CASE STUDY 7: A NEW SICK LEAVE POLICY

Catharine Rios is a council member in your town. After months of study she and her staff finished writing a 12-page report today. The report discusses sick leave and its use by city employees. The report notes that it cost city taxpayers $4,007,232 last year for the sick leave taken by employees of your municipality. The employees accumulate sick leave at the rate of 2 hours for each week they work, or a total of 13 days of sick leave a year. The average city employee, according to the results of Rios' study, uses 10 of those sick days each year. Rios adds that that number is about twice the national average for all adult workers employed full time in the entire nation. In the report, Rios writes: "It must be suspected that much of the sick leave time claimed and used by city employees is used not to recuperate from illness, but to extend weekends or just to take time off. The problem is particularly acute on the days just before or after a holiday. It's also a serious problem on Mondays and Fridays, as many employees seem to take those days off in order to extend their weekends to a total of 3 or 4 days." Rios added that she is working on a possible solution to the problem and will present her corrective solution to the city council for its approval sometime during the next week. The solution she will propose is to pay retiring employees in cash for 1/2 of their unused accumulated sick leave so that they would have an incentive not to use sick leave but to save it. They might receive an extra payment of hundreds or even thousands of dollars upon their retirement. She noted that currently when city employees retire, they are not paid for their accumulated unused sick leave. They lose it all, so there is an attitude among city employees that as long as it is given to them they should take as much of it as they can. Rios explained that it would be cheaper to pay the employees a portion of their unused sick leave than to have to hire substitutes at full salary when someone is sick or to have to hire additional full-time city employees in order to have enough employees on hand at all times, as a number of city employees are likely to be out sick on any given workday during the year. Rios estimates that the plan could save the city 1/4 of the costs it is currently spending on overtime. Rios asks you to prepare a news release to send to the Better Government Association, a vehement anti-tax, anti-government spending group that launched a vicious attack on Rios during her last election campaign. The association publishes a monthly newsletter for its 600 members. The association has criticized Rios many times in the past for her "free-spending ways."

Management Problems

1. Why will the taxpayers group's preconception of Rios make your communication task more difficult?
2. Will it be more effective to try to place this release in the taxpayer's publication before announcing it to the general public? Why or why not?
3. What are some of the other audiences with which you will need to communicate about Rios' proposal?
4. Will you need to frame different arguments to convince city employees to support Rios' plan? What would those arguments emphasize?
5. Name at least three ways you could quantitatively measure success in this campaign.
6. To illustrate the problems with deadbeat city workers during a news conference, Rios shows the picture of a municipal employee who had taken an average of 36 sick days a year for the past three years. Later it is discovered that the employee had been suffering from leukemia and that more than half of those days were taken as unpaid leave of absence. Discuss the legal implications for the city.

Writing Assignments

7. Write a news release for this specialty membership newsletter. Make sure you structure the lead so these disgruntled taxpayers can see a money-saving benefit from what appears to be just another government giveaway.
8. Compose a personal letter from Rios to key individuals in the anti-tax group.

CASE STUDY 8: COOPERATING WITH A STRATEGIC PARTNER

You work for BioloGene, a small, 4-and-one-half-year-old company that is working on gene-splicing technology. Started by three former university researchers, your small biotechnology company has one very commercially viable idea, but ordinary product development procedures may mean another four to six years before the product can go on the market and start returning the company's investment. The company's idea is something called homologous recombination, which allows doctors and scientists to replace certain genes within cells. It also allows them to activate or deactivate specific genes within cells. All these actions permit the cells to react more favorably to drugs or allow the cells to accomplish some purpose themselves that will eliminate or fight a disease. Unfortunately, company cash reserves are down to $826,500, which is much too little to finance the company during the development process. That process will consume about $1.331 million, and establishing a viable marketing effort will take even more money, maybe as much as $7.598 million, before the product is fully established. Because of the company's high level of debt and uncertain short-term cash flow, taking out a bank loan is not likely to be a wise decision. Because of this need for financing, BioloGene is contemplating taking in a strategic partner, a larger, better-funded firm with which to share some of the product development costs and risks. The firm would like to hire a business broker by Jan. 1 to help it discover five to eight possible partnerships. Obviously, by sharing those risks, BioloGene is also going to lose a portion of the huge financial windfall that may come from selling the product. It's also true that the addition of a strategic partner is going to rob BioloGene's three founding partners of some of their autonomy and independence in making business decisions, because the strategic partner will want some significant control over company decisions in exchange for its capital contributions. The rather congenial environment the three partners (who are also friends) have enjoyed may be somewhat strained by the increased formality demanded by the strategic partner's bureaucracy. The alternatives to all this are that BioloGene wouldn't have enough money to take the product to market, so that the company would probably go bankrupt before the product reached the market or would have to sell the homologous recombination idea to another firm. That would mean BioloGene would lose control of the technology and the potentially huge profits that could be made from it. There are other advantages to the strategic partner idea. A larger pharmaceutical firm as a partner could bring legal expertise and political contacts that might hasten the Food and Drug Administration approval process. That sort of firm could also bring marketing expertise and a distribution network to BioloGene's product. That's a definite weakness in BioloGene's business plan. The arrival of some marketing and business minds might also let BioloGene's three partners concentrate more on basic research, which seems to be their strength.

Management Problems

1. What types of persuasion tasks will have to occur within the company's management hierarchy before this strategy is transformed into policy?
2. What are some of the possible consequences of not gaining full support of the present partners before undertaking a strategic partnership?
3. What further writing tasks are going to be necessary before BioloGene's offer is presented to potential partners?
4. What continuing communication is needed to smooth the business relationship if the strategic partnership is formalized?

Writing Assignments

5. Compose a position paper advocating that BioloGene investigate forming a strategic partnership.
6. Draft a simple letter that could be used by the president of a potential strategic partner to inform and persuade his stockholders that the strategic partnership with BioloGene would be advantageous. Assume the letter is for Robert McKillip, president of McKillip Genetics, Inc.
7. Compose an outline of the middle section of a news release justifying this course of action to BioloGene employees. Compose another outline of a release directed to stock market analysts. Does the order in which major persuaders are presented change between the two versions?
8. Convert all the numbers in the story to how they would appear in a print story as well as in a broadcast story.

CASE STUDY 9: ANNOUNCING AN ART EXHIBIT

You are the public relations specialist for your city's art museum. In "an artistic coup of tremendous proportions," as your museum's director terms it, your museum has snared an exhibit of paintings by the famous Russian painter of the early 20th century who was Jewish and eventually had to emigrate from Russia after the Communists took power in 1917, Marc Chagall. The director got the chance to examine the paintings originally because he was a former student of an important Russian art curator, Benrikh Kalisniykov. Chagall was an enormously important figure in 20th century art as one of the pioneers of 20th-century fantastic art. His paintings, like "Self-Portrait with Seven Fingers" from 1912, melded brilliant colors and the delightful imagery of Russian-Jewish folk tradition with the fragmented forms of Cubism and led the way for artists like Salvador Dali, who would later found Surrealism. The exhibit will be shared with seven other museums in the United States (including the Metropolitan Museum of Art in New York City and the National Gallery in Washington, D.C.), Mexico, Belgium and the Louvre in France before going back to Russia. For your exhibit, tickets will be $10 each, and people wanting to see the exhibit should reserve tickets by calling 555-1343. During the exhibit, the museum will not be open for general viewing, and only people who make reservations will be admitted to the museum's galleries. Tickets will probably be as rare for this exhibit as for the exhibit of Grecian gold that dated to Alexander the Great's time. That exhibit was mounted at the museum in 1987. There were 150,000 visitors to the museum during that 40-day exhibit, including a record of 11,000 visitors in a single day. Chagall was born in 1889, the same year as Adolf Hitler. Chagall, however, was born in Russia. He moved to Paris in 1910, but returned to Russia in the excitement over the Russian Revolution in 1917. He became disenchanted and returned to Paris in 1922. In fact, it is the nature of that disenchantment that led to the paintings that are going to be in the exhibit coming to your museum. The paintings were done as murals for the Moscow Jewish Art Theater. Chagall created the seven large panels in 1920 and 1921. The panels, Chagall said in a 1953 interview, "were a summation of the Jewish life of my youth in the White Russian town of Vitebsk." The paintings (each of which is 6 feet tall and 8 feet wide) portray a wedding scene, a Torah scribe, musicians, dancers and acrobats, in his usual pattern of bright colors and distorted perspective. They are meant, Chagall said, "as a metaphor for the travail of art in the Soviet Union, as well as the fate of that country's Jews." The paintings' history came to demonstrate that, according to your museum's director, Christian Kroner. Kroner said the paintings were taken from the theater's lobby in 1929 on Stalin's order. Stalin made the order because he viewed them as examples of decadent, non-Socialist art. They were moved to the theater's rehearsal hall. When the Germans attacked Moscow in 1941, the theater's actors carried the murals to safety in Siberia until the war ended. The scene was described in a book by one of the actors, Vladimir Kosrekov:

> It was a cold December night. The temperature was about 15 degrees Fahrenheit. The German artillery flashed on the horizon like popping light bulbs at the edge of a stage. The three buildings on one side of our theater and the two buildings on the other side had already been destroyed. There were three hulking holes in our theater's backstage area already, and you could see these lacy, delicate sets done in pastels that we had made up for "Cinderella" through the blackened holes in the bricks. As an actor, it was hard for me to tell which was the reality and which was the fantasy, because the scenery was so much closer to what we had known as reality until just a few months before. But that was over now. We knew the paintings, these wonderful, priceless works of art that were the symbol of our theater and of our faith, would be immediately destroyed if the Germans reached the city. They knew it was of the Jews. We knew the paintings might be destroyed by the artillery even if the soldiers didn't reach us. We knew just as well that if we tried to get them from the theater we put our lives in danger too. But we were young and death meant nothing to us. Fifteen of us, four men and eleven women, waited until after midnight and then moved them from the theater. Our way was lit by the fires burning in the buildings. That night over 600 buildings in the city were on fire. We moved the paintings, two to each painting, the three blocks to the railway station. There, one of the actress's brothers, who was in the army and being sent to the Manchurian front, hid the paintings in camouflage screens for our own artillery pieces. After an 11-day ride, he hid them in caves behind the battle lines and did not tell anyone where they were until after the war.

In 1947 the paintings were brought back to Moscow and placed back into the theater. But after the war, Stalin pushed his anti-Semitic campaign, and one night in 1952 the paintings were removed from the theater's rehearsal hall and taken to the cellars of the Tretyakov Gallery in Moscow. Although Stalin died in 1953, the paintings were never seen again until two years ago, when Kroner, after much pleading, was given access to the paintings. The exhibit at your gallery, from June 8 through July 21, results from that first viewing. Kroner said the paintings looked awful. "Paint was flaking from the paintings and you could see only the ghosts of these wonderful images that I had fallen in love with in art school. I was simply furious." Kroner spent that fury on Benrikh Kalisniykov, who is the chief of all fine arts in the Russian Republic. Kroner offered to have Western museums restore the paintings if the institutions could exhibit the murals. Kalisniykov initially refused, saying that it would be unfair to the Russian people to have them exhibited first in the West, because their people hadn't had a chance to see them since Stalin pulled them from the theater lobby in the 1920s. "I quickly put him straight about that," Kroner said. "I told him that it is the fault of the Soviet leaders that the Russian people haven't seen these paintings. Then I told him he had the choice of letting us restore them to again be a glory of the Russian people or watch them rot away in his cellars. The responsibility for destroying a glorious work of art would be his, and his alone." Kroner went on: "Kalisniykov eventually relented and the paintings were brought to New York where expert art restorers spent eight months getting them into shape for our show. We had the honor of exhibiting them first because I was the one, among all the other museum directors of the world, who had enough clout and moxie to get them out of Russia." You find that Vladimir Kosrekov is still alive and you call him. You find he will be flown into your city by the museum to participate in the opening. He's now 87 years old. You call him at his home in St. Petersburg and get this quote: "I will be there for the opening day. It is my first trip into a western country and I will be seeing my sister-in-law in Boston on my way to your city. It will be nice to know that I'm still alive to see my paintings again. Stalin is dead. Hitler is dead. All those who tried to destroy them are dead. But the paintings and the hopes of little people like me still are alive. Is life all bad when this happens?" The exhibition is already drawing widespread attention from sources across the country. The *New York Times* art critic, who is named Dash Riprock, wrote, "You've seen these pictures in art history books your entire life. They're considered treasures of the world. And the surprising thing is that no one has seen them for forty years. It will be an exciting time when they hit our shores."

Management Problems

1. What might be the implications of quoting Kroner's frank language concerning the Soviet policy?
2. In addition to selling tickets to the Chagall exhibit, how could the museum take advantage of this important show to build its institutional strength?
3. What audiences in addition to art lovers are potential marketing targets for your communication campaign?

Writing Assignments

4. Write a fund-raising letter from Kroner to the museum's members and local corporate supporters to bring in money to stage equally impressive shows.

5. Compose a news release announcing the show to local and regional newspapers and television stations.

6. Write a short introduction of the paintings' history that will be delivered orally by the museum's tour guides.

7. Write a television public service announcement for the exhibit.

8. Write a persuasion platform that will guide your efforts to draw members of your city's Russian Orthodox churches, which include a large number of recent Russian immigrants. Omit the budget section.

9. Which argumentation structure will you most likely use to present the paintings' history? Which one will be most appropriate for listing the other museums in which the paintings will be exhibited? What argumentation structure should you use to present the Russian museum director's rationale for sharing the paintings with Western museums?

10. Write two lead sentences—one for a release directed to art historians and another directed toward local art museum members. Compare the vocabulary of the two sentences.

11. Prepare an outline of sound effects that might draw your receivers' attention to the lead of a radio story about the art exhibit as well as other sound effects that might help you tell the story.

CASE STUDY 10: AN INDUSTRY TRIES TO IMPROVE ITS IMAGE

As a freelance public relations specialist, you've been hired to coordinate a new program that is being started by a group of companies that make liquor, beer and wine. You have this conversation with John Clark, a one-time Hollywood actor whose most notable role was in "Psycho." He was president of the Screen Actors Guild, the same office held by Ronald Reagan before he became president. Clark later became ambassador to Mexico and is now the chairman for this group of alcohol producers. Clark said: "The company leaders recognize that they have been getting destroyed in the press and in public opinion during the past 10 years. Every drunk driving death spurs a whole new round of negative press attention to the problem. And there have truly been some disasters. The Carrollton, Ky., wreck where a driver hit a church bus and killed 25 teen-agers and two adults was simply a catastrophe for us. The negative public opinion fostered by such goings-on has led to movements to increase taxes on alcoholic beverages, warning labels on packaging, and has undoubtedly contributed to the vastly decreased consumption of the coalition companies' products. We've also had this increased attention to the role of alcohol in domestic violence between husbands and wives and between parents and children. Clubs have sprung up in schools that encourage abstinence from alcohol altogether. The manufacturers felt they had to do something to reinforce the idea that some drinking of alcoholic beverages isn't a bad thing and that the liquor, beer and wine industry isn't against arresting drunk drivers or sponsoring alcohol awareness programs. In fact, they hope that by becoming actively involved in sponsoring and funding alcohol awareness programs, that they can head off some of the most radical measures that some of the anti-alcohol lobbying groups are lobbying for, and point their efforts in more reasonable directions that accept that some drinking is OK but that alcohol abuse is not; that social drinking is fine but that getting drunk and hitting schoolchildren is not what alcohol makers are in favor of. We want responsible use of our products and we're tired of looking like the bad guys in this whole debate. We've got a big job ahead of us, because we know we've got to stimulate some fairly substantial changes in the way our society views drinking and driving. But I've got the commitment from the presidents of all the liquor, beer and wine companies. We're dedicated to this task. We want to stop being against efforts to control alcohol and start being for responsible individual and social actions to encourage responsible drinking." The coalition's goals are very ambitious, you find out, for they involve cutting drunken driving in half within the next 10 years. That's a big job, because alcohol-related traffic deaths have gone down from 57.3 percent of all fatal accidents seven years ago to 49.2 percent today, which is about a 1 percent drop each year. But obviously, nine more years will only take the accident rate down to 40 percent, which is a heck of a long way from the 25 percent rate the council claims it wants to achieve. The coalition plans to run an extensive alcohol awareness advertising campaign. The first step in that campaign is a set of commercials due to run before Labor Day in September. The radio ads will be run in 77 cities. The time was chosen because about 300 Americans die in alcohol-related car wrecks each Labor Day. The council members have also agreed not to target advertising to anyone under the drinking age. That prohibits them from using characters, celebrities or active sports figures to promote alcohol, or from sponsoring events on college campuses. The council members have also agreed to work to enact into legislative law those state proposals that would immediately strip the licenses from drivers who are caught behind the wheel drunk, and would urge states to issue driver's licenses and identification cards that are harder to forge to help stop the black market in illicit ID cards that underage minors use to get liquor. Clark is going to be responsible for $40 million in expenditures for the coalition of makers of beer, liquor and wine, which is known as the Century Coalition. The coalition's plans came from studying the successes that have already reduced deaths attributed to alcohol. Most experts attribute those successes to various lobbying citizen groups that have undertaken massive efforts to beef up drunken driving laws and enforcement and to heighten public awareness of alcohol abuse. The groups have worked hard to tighten enforcement of present laws forbidding alcohol sales to people under 21 years of age. The coalition plans to copy and reinforce these plans. In addition to the other measures outlined, the coalition also has agreed to find community alcohol awareness and enforcement programs that work and then work to duplicate those programs in other places.

Management Problems

1. What are some of the difficulties the Century Coalition has to overcome to coordinate efforts with anti-alcohol lobbying groups? What might be the positive effect of that collaborative effort?

2. What type of internal communication efforts may become necessary when organizations decide upon a radically new direction in their public stance on an issue?
3. How may the participation of this industry group change the way elected officials view groups trying to pass laws regulating alcohol use?
4. What are some of the consequences in the choice of this particular spokesperson for the industry group?
5. If the campaign were directed toward combating teen-age drinking, would a different campaign kickoff date be more effective?

Writing Assignments

6. Write a news release announcing the new program.
7. Write a news feature for an industry newsletter that discusses the philosophy for the new program.
8. Compose a position paper that will support a company's efforts to involve and educate its employees in the rationale for the new program.
9. Write a short speech that could be used as a model for high school presentations.
10. Compose a print, radio or television ad pointed toward an under-21 audience that urges proper alcohol use.
11. Compose a print ad that would run in a political magazine read by legislators that highlights the alcohol manufacturers' efforts to regulate themselves and the use of their products.
12. Write an audio public service announcement to be placed at the end of recordings released by leading country music stars.
13. Using one of the marketing statistics references mentioned in Chapter 3, write a demographic and psychographic description of liquor buyers.

CASE STUDY 11: ADVICE TO CONSUMERS

You're a public relations person working for the American Union of Conscientious Consumers. The research staff of the union has been noticing a startling increase in the number of calls concerning insurance companies that are safe, propitious investments. Your organization's financial research analyst, Marybeth Danaher, prepares a list of guidelines that a person wishing to buy life insurance would be well advised to follow when contemplating the need to buy said insurance. "The most important thing," Danaher said, "is to check the ratings. There are over 2,600 companies in the United States that sell life insurance, so that's a lot of ratings." She notes that there are four ratings services, the A.M. Best Co., Standard & Poor's Corp., Moody's Investors Service, and Duff & Phelps, Inc. All but A.M. Best ratings were begun within the last 10 years; Best has been rating companies since 1899. Most of the companies rate on a scale from A+ to C−. It's not terribly difficult to get the ratings of insurance companies from the ratings services. You can get the Best ratings from the Best Insurance Reports volumes that are in most libraries. Duff & Phelps has its rating guides available in libraries, too. Moody's has a guide in a book form, but it isn't available in very many libraries. There are electronic services, too, including Best, which charges $2.50 a minute while you ask for ratings. That number is a 900 number, 900-420-0400. To make a phone call to Moody's, you have to pay a long distance charge but you don't have to pay the charges to Moody's, as you do to Best. Its number is 212-553-1653. Standard & Poor's rating desk, whose phone number in New York City is 212-208-1527, also gives free ratings. The problem of life insurance companies is more of a problem now more than ever. The savings and loan crisis has brought to the fore the notion that there may be many problems in a number of our nation's financial institutions, of which insurance companies are one form. Indeed, that problem has washed over into that area of endeavor. Two major insurance companies have been put under government regulatory control in the past two years. The problem with them, and with a lot of other insurance companies, is that they have a lot of high yield, so-called junk bonds in their portfolios, which were used for leveraged buyouts and forced mergers during the 1980s. Those investments went bad in the recession of the early 1990s. Now a lot of insurance companies are in trouble. "There are some ways to tell if your insurance company is one of the ones in trouble or not. Obviously, you can look at the ratings from those ratings services. But there are some differences between the ratings services, for you can find that one service might give an insurance company an A+ and another service might give the self-same company a Double B," said Danaher. "If you're concerned about safety, it's usually best to look at all the services. Traditionally, Best will give the highest ratings, and the others tend to be more critical. But none of the services should have given any rating lower than a Double A for you to be fairly certain that your investments are going to be safe. Another thing you're looking at when you're looking for a good company is to look at the company's financial report. A sound company will have at least $100 million more in assets than liabilities. The best companies are also going to be licensed in New York, which has the toughest licensing laws for insurance companies of any state in the entire United States. Because of that, a lot of companies are licensed in every state but New York. That makes a New York company a safe bet."

Management Problems

1. Describe the advantages the union obtains by publicizing this information to consumers who are not already members.
2. What would be the likely result if Best issued a news release discussing its 900 ratings service?

Writing Assignments

3. Write a letter to union members from Marybeth Danaher informing the members of these ratings services.
4. Write a news release to financial editors.

5. Write a magazine ad for Best that advertises its 900 service.
6. Prepare a script for a radio feature story to be distributed to financial affairs shows on local stations.
7. Prepare a television public service announcement sponsored by an association of older adults.

CASE STUDY 12: LEASHING IN A CITY'S DOGS

You work as a public relations specialist for your city police department and you are asked to communicate information about an existing city ordinance that is going to start to be enforced more forcefully. City ordinance No. 3134123L is officially labeled the Sanitary Disposal of Animal Feces Required, but most people call it the "pooper-scooper" law, and a lot of people aren't satisfied with the way it is being enforced. It was passed not only because dog feces is a nuisance, but because there is the possibility that it contains worm larvae that enter through human skin and make people very ill with a variety of diseases centered in the intestinal tract that can result in death in serious cases. Although it exempts guide dogs for the blind, the ordinance carries a fine of $25 to $100 for people who don't clean up after their regular, non-guide dogs if they defecate on public property within the city or on private property the offending dog's master doesn't own if it is within the city limits. The ordinance requires dog owners who walk or exercise their dogs to carry a "suitable device" for cleaning up their dog's feces. The pooper-scoopers are available in most pet stores for under $5. The ordinance, which was passed three years ago by a vote of 7–1, with one alderman abstaining, has never been enforced. In those three years since the ordinance passed, not one individual citizen has been cited, let alone tried or convicted, for violating this ordinance. The momentum to finally enforce the governmental decree came from 1st Ward Alderman Manley Alzerhansky. This is the transcript from last week's city council meeting, quoting The Honorable Mr. Alzerhansky: "I'm a city alderman. I introduced the ordinance. And I walked out of my house barefoot last week to get my newspaper in my yard and I step in dog shit. What's the point of passing laws? What's the point of trying to improve the city? What's the point if the police are going to arbitrarily decide that some laws that the city council passes are worth enforcing and other laws are not worth worrying about? Since when do the police have the responsibility to determine what laws are good and what laws aren't? That's my job as a city official. It's not their job. And if I can't walk in my own yard without stepping in this crap that's supposed to be illegal then maybe we ought to think about getting another police chief who gives a shit about shit!" The council then unanimously passed a non-binding resolution that urged the police chief, Karen Ulmer, to vigorously enforce the ordinance. Ulmer, who had been in political hot water from dog owners in another city where she did enforce a pooper-scooper law as assistant police chief, is angry. "They don't understand just how stuck these people are on their dogs," Ulmer said. "They are walking into a minefield if they think these people are going to be happy about cleaning up after their dogs. It's dirty and smelly and that's why people want their dogs to do their business in other people's yards rather than their own." She proposes a one-month educational period during which the city's dog owners would be informed that the ordinance will be enforced. They would be provided with information about what they need to do to adhere to the ordinance's provisions. The ordinance will be enforced six weeks from today.

Management Problems

1. What can Ulmer do to distance herself from what she predicts will be a negative reaction from dog owners?
2. How can Ulmer involve non-dog owners in helping support efforts to enforce the ordinance?
3. Of what sensitivities will you have to be conscious as you prepare your informational materials?

Writing Assignments

4. Compose a short questionnaire to find how dog owners and non-dog owners feel about the need for this ordinance.
5. Write a news release that announces the date when the ordinance will be enforced.
6. Write a direct-mail piece that informs registered dog owners of the new regulations.
7. Write a radio public service announcement urging people to obey the ordinance.
8. Write a script for a humorous video public service announcement intended to be distributed to local television stations.

Index